CONSUMER BEHAVIOR

CONSUMER BEHAVIOR

GILBERT D. HARRELL
MICHIGAN STATE UNIVERSITY

HARCOURT BRACE JOVANOVICH, PUBLISHERS
San Diego New York Chicago Atlanta Washington, D.C.
London Sydney Toronto

TO

Susie,
Rachael, Nicholas, Katherine,
and Mother

Cover Photo: Werner Kalber

Illustrations by Richard Carter

ISBN: 0-15-513451-5
Library of Congress Catalog Card Number: 85-80076
Printed in the United States of America

Copyrights and Acknowledgments and Illustration Credits appear on pages 575–78, which constitute a continuation of the copyright page.

Preface

Students preparing to enter business and related fields should get ready for what might appear to be a paradox. Our knowledge of narrowly defined business functions is deep, complex, and technical. Yet the ability to integrate—to get the big picture—is also important. Business success demands both perspectives at a time when technologies and practices are changing quickly.

The way to deal with and benefit from this paradox is to have an understanding of the basics—those critical areas of knowledge that form the support structure for rapidly emerging areas of thought and action. This book provides a solid understanding of one of those foundation areas, consumer behavior. Business contacts have provided an opportunity for me to see how business is practiced. Now, more than ever, I believe that good practice in business begins with good theory. Every effort has been made to present the relevant theory of consumer behavior and show how it can be applied.

A great deal of conventional wisdom about consumer behavior needs to be preserved, but an emerging view must also be presented. Consequently, part of this book covers the traditional building blocks of consumer behavior, including perception, motivation, learning, attitudes, social class, and reference groups. The emerging view, based on concepts from cognitive psychology (information processing and brain functioning), also occupies a significant part of the book. Chapter 8 on information processing highlights the recent evidence about how information is discovered, perceived, and used to capture our view of the world. A careful attempt has been made to combine both perspectives into a systematic examination of consumer behavior.

Often consumer behavior elicits a picture of individuals and families; but industrial firms, professionals, and governments are also important consumers. Examples from all of these areas are used extensively throughout the book to show how consumer-behavior concepts can be applied in a practical sense. Numerous advertisements are reproduced, which quickly get across points that would otherwise take pages of explanation. An entire chapter is devoted to organizational buying behavior that applies to industrial, professional, and government buying.

Consumer behavior is immensely interesting and fun to study, but it is not simplistic or trivial. The cursory overview of the subject covered in most marketing principles texts is only amusing when contrasted with a more in-depth study. To preserve the revealing nature of the subject, the student must understand numerous concepts both independently and as they relate to each other. One aid in this task are figures and diagrams, which augment the explanations in the text and represent graphically many of the book's main thoughts and ideas. For example, Chapter 1 includes a diagram that helps visualize the major building blocks and knowledge that make up consumer behavior. It is not a model of consumer behavior (several models are presented in the last chapter); rather, it is an educational tool to help the student understand which concepts are related and to present an overview of how the chapters are sequenced in the book.

The field of consumer behavior benefits from the attention it has received from researchers in diverse scientific and business areas. All too frequently, however, each area has tried to understand the big picture with a single clue based on its own investigations. As a result, concepts have not always been well integrated, and there have been some amusing interpretations of reality. Nevertheless, each area has made contributions. In the field of consumer behavior we have been able to borrow from other fields; but in many cases tools and techniques have been created specifically for our use. Both are integrated throughout the book.

Because consumer behavior is still an emerging field, this book should serve as a springboard for more advanced study. For the most part, however, it was written to prepare students to be knowledgably consumer oriented in their future business life, to apply concepts of consumer behavior when appropriate, and to be able to ask specialists the right questions and understand their answers.

Business practitioners cannot be trained in consumer behavior—but they can become educated in the subject. Training requires the presence of well-known problems and their clearly defined solutions. The part of business that involves the understanding of consumer behavior does not work that way. Many of the problems in business are unique, and each solution must have its own character. The theories and principles presented here provide the basis for creating innovative strategies to solve these unique problems.

I would like to thank several of those who contributed to this book. Peter D. Bennett kindled my interest in this subject some time ago, provided support and advice on several occasions, and graciously supplied an outline for Chapter 11 on social class. Special thanks go to Matthew Fors, who, tirelessly and enthusiastically, did library research, checked sources, and developed insightful examples. Margo Bogart and Elizabeth Johnston skillfully edited early drafts, while Karen Machleit researched articles for the bibliographies and Amy Schumacher found examples to illustrate several principles. Glenn Omura, Bixby Cooper, Dale Wilson, and Sevo Eroglu gave important suggestions and material. Richard Lewis and Donald Taylor provided critical support and counsel. For all the help they gave, I am most appreciative. In good spirit, Leslie Denstaedt and Pamela Cook expertly typed the manuscript, sacrificing numerous evenings and weekends to speed turnaround and meet deadlines—thanks so much.

My gratitude extends to the team at Harcourt Brace Jovanovich. Craig Avery immersed himself in the manuscript during final editorial stages, keeping student needs in mind and making sure that the whole fit together with clarity. Don Fujimoto developed original art and graphics, which are a major strength of the book. Ken Rethmeier, whose advice I sought many times, provided important guidance and coordinated the entire project.

I am grateful for the careful attention the following people gave to their reviews of the manuscript for this book, and to the detailed suggestions and helpful criticisms they provided: Harold Kassarjian, University of California, Los Angeles; George Belch, San Diego State University; William Gaidis, Arizona State University; David Gardner, University of Illinois, Urbana/Champaign; Lynn Kahle, University of Oregon; and Delores A. Barsellotti, California State Polytechnic University.

My heartfelt appreciation goes out to my wife, Susie, and to our children, who were so understanding when it counted most.

GILBERT D. HARRELL

Contents

2

Motivation 35

3

Perception 65

4

Learning 101

7

8

PART II SOCIAL ENVIRONMENT

12

Reference Groups 349

13

Opinion Leadership and Diffusion of Innovations 375

CONSUMER BEHAVIOR

1 Understanding Consumer Behavior

Objectives of This Chapter

After you have studied this chapter, you should be able to:

1. Describe the major activities that constitute consumer behavior and identify the types of consumers who are the subjects of study.
2. Trace the origins of the study of consumer behavior.
3. Discuss the types of research and analytical tools used in consumer behavior studies.
4. Distinguish between types of buying situations and their impact on consumers' decision-making processes.

Finding, evaluating, purchasing, using, and discarding goods or services occupies a large part of our daily lives. The study of consumer behavior helps us understand the forces that guide these activities. Consumer behavior also has a direct effect on businesses and our economic system. This textbook is designed to provide overall knowledge about the fundamentals of consumer behavior and the role consumers play in shaping successful business operations. We will stress the main theories and principles of consumer behavior as we know it today. In addition, the questions and the suggestions for further reading at the end of each chapter should provide the foundation for more in-depth exploration by those who are interested.

CONSUMER BEHAVIOR AND MARKETING

consumer behavior

Consumer behavior can be defined as the actions and decision processes of individuals and organizations involved in discovering, evaluating, acquiring, consuming, and disposing of products and services. The study of consumer behavior has been developed by scholars from a broad range of disciplines, including psychology, sociology, anthropology, and marketing. Although the field of consumer behavior is relatively young compared to many other academic disciplines, the study of how buyers think and act is finding considerable application among successful companies. In truly market-oriented organizations, an understanding of consumer behavior is the basis for management decision making. These managers recognize that their success depends on how much they know about potential customers—not just *who* they are, but *how, when, where,* and *why* they consume. Marketers use information about consumer behavior to design new products and services, determine appropriate prices, select methods of distribution, and build effective promotion and advertising. When several companies are competing for the same market, the firm that best anticipates and responds to the customer is likely to reap the greatest reward. All other things being equal, a company's ability to acquire and apply knowledge about consumers often spells the difference between success and failure.

When businesses understand how and why consumers make purchase choices, they are better able to address the needs and wants of consumers and to generate greater customer satisfaction. Administrators of public policy, such as state and federal legislators and local council members, also are interested in consumer behavior so that they can assure adequate protection to both individuals and businesses. Consumers themselves often benefit from a better understanding of how they make purchases. This is particularly true for industrial purchasers, where huge sums may be at stake; but it applies just as well to families and to individuals.

Scholarly interest in consumer behavior has coincided with the development of consumer-oriented thinking in business. Since the end of World War II, the number of consumers and the economy in general have grown rapidly, providing room for more producers in the marketplace and a wider range of product and service options. Technology has provided dramatic changes in the types of goods and services available now and on the horizon. Additionally, increased competition in recent years has placed a premium on consumer orientation. Today, the assumptions a producer makes about buyer preferences are clearly crucial to the firm's success. Reliable forecasts of the needs and wants of the marketplace eliminate costly guesswork. Firms are faced with new and expensive technologies and huge product development costs, as well as increased market size. At the same time, these markets are more fragmented than ever before; further, each firm must deal with highly differentiated and sophisticated competitors who know their customers' needs well. These factors make it difficult for businesses to succeed without the benefit of more reliable information about their markets.

With the advent of consumer behavior research, executives no longer must rely on intuitive decision making based solely on personal experience. During the 1970s and '80s there has been a virtual explosion of knowledge in this field, which continues to hold the attention of businesses, governments, and consumer activists alike. Since the mid-1970s, too, there has been a marked trend toward greater use of consumer-behavior information. Corporations have increased their budgets for consumer research, added qualified personnel to conduct consumer studies, and made greater use of consumer behavior principles and concepts in their business and marketing planning. Excellent corporations must stay very close to the customer.

Thomas Peters and Robert Waterman, Jr., identified the way companies interact with customers as a critical factor that differentiates excellent companies from others:

> What we found most striking was the consistent presence of obsession. This characteristically occurred as a seemingly unjustifiable overcommitment to some form of quality, reliability, or service. Being customer oriented doesn't mean that our excellent companies are slouches when it comes to technological or cost performance. But they do seem to us more driven by their direct orientation to their customers than by technology or by a desire to be the low-cost producer.[1]

Later in their book they indicate that "the excellent companies are better listeners. They get a benefit from market closeness that for us was truly unexpected—unexpected, that is, until you think about it. Most of their real innovation comes from the market."[2]

Most people's lives are a complex interplay of activities that can be understood using consumer-behavior principles. We are all consumers in a consumption-oriented society in which numerous forces influence what and how we buy as well as how businesses respond to and shape our desires. Consider the brief glimpses of daily life described in the following scenarios. Many of the concepts we will be exploring in this text underly the thoughts and actions of these characters. You may want to review them as you study each chapter, to see how many consumer behavior concepts you can discover that apply here. Also, think about your own behavior as a consumer. Whatever your chosen career is, the study of consumer behavior will help you begin to understand how others behave, as well as your own attitudes, desires, and actions.

The remainder of this chapter discusses the major types of activities that comprise consumer behavior. Then, we will briefly trace the origins of the field including the contributions provided by other disciplines. This is followed by a discussion of the tools which help marketers and researchers understand how consumers think and act. Finally, we will present an overall framework which brings together the major concepts of consumer behavior and introduces the principal topics of the text.

THREE SCENARIOS

1. *The Morning Ritual* The first ear-piercing blast of the thin watch-alarm broke the morning silence to begin a new day. A hand fumbled through the designer sheets in search of the timepiece; the fingers quickly hit the button to kill the relentless chime. A new day was awakening.

The morning ritual began when Susie poured a cup of coffee that had been preset to brew the night before in the solid-state pot. The aroma alone was enough to begin clearing the cobwebs from her thoughts; her first sip stirred the mental currents necessary to meet the rush of events about to take place. Nick, her third-grader, was searching for his radio-controlled racer to take to school for show and tell. Rachael, his fifth-grade sister, had only a few minutes to complete her social studies assignment on the family's personal computer, using the new word-processing software. Many of the other children had developed reports printed on personal-computer equipment; but none had been able to use the two-column format with right-justified margins and bold Old English headings that Rachael had mastered, thanks to the self-study program disk she had purchased on the recommendation of a friend. Susie was able to devote full attention to these two kids until Kate, her three-year-old, awoke to demand her fair share of parental nurturing.

The headline in the morning paper announced, STATE INCOME TAX INCREASES—in Susie's view, just another encroachment on personal disposable income so important to meet the needs of a growing family. The paper was not her old standby, the *News,* because during the previous year the *Times* and the *News* had battled for readership and for market share in the suburbs. The *News,* dedicated to strong coverage of local events, had been dropped from delivery by the publisher because it could not hold readers when the *Times* offered introductory subscription rates at half the going rate. The *Times* had recently switched to a new and rather innovative editorial approach that combined local sports with high emphasis on national and international events to reposition the paper in the growing suburban market. Although the *News* launched an aggressive advertising campaign to rekindle loyalty among its longtime readers, the eroding subscriber base soon made it economically impossible to continue home delivery. Susie missed the recognized formats of the *News,* but she was growing accustomed to the splashier, more colorful content of the *Times.*

Nick bounded into the kitchen with one shoe on. "Mom, where's my other Adidas?" he groaned, reaching for a granola bar instead of the Wheaties that Susie had placed on the dining table. When the shoe was located and the screen door slammed behind Nick and Rachael, Susie reached for the paper towels to catch a spill of coffee and restore the original luster of the counter top, which she had carefully selected after visiting four or five local dealers. Although she generally purchased name brands, she had decided to give the generic paper towel a try to see if it was worth the savings. As she turned, she noticed Mary Lou Retton staring at her from the Wheaties box, reminding her of America's proud victories in the 1984 Los Angeles Olympics. A bowl of Wheaties *was* so satisfying! She made a mental note to select a different brand of cereal for the kids next time; one granola bar was hardly an adequate breakfast for an energetic third-grader like Nick.

2. ***The New Venture*** Bill Warren was meeting with Sally Kimbal, product manager for a Fortune 500 electronics firm, to report on a marketing research project his business consulting firm had recently completed. Sally selected Bill's organization for the project because it had a reputation for using sound research techniques and for providing information directed at strategic business decisions. This meeting was preliminary to the presentation to Sally's staff the next week.

Bill began by reviewing the purpose of the research which addressed the decisions Sally's firm was about to make—should they develop and market a new industrial vision system? The answer to the question would be based on whether Sally could develop a solid marketing plan to meet the company's profit requirements while satisfying customers. Bill knew his research addressed only part of the question, but an extremely important part: how and why would companies buy this type of system? The system would electronically look at products during the manufacturing process and through the use of computers compare semifinished products with specifications for quality control purposes.

The first part of the study described the major market segments and indicated which types of companies tend to be early adopters of such products. It went on to describe the buying characteristics and processes of fifteen companies in each of four high-potential segments: automotive manufacturers and suppliers, pharmaceutical manufacturers, electronic component manufacturers, and textile manufacturers.

The report described the buying stages each company would pass through before arriving at a purchase decision about the new system. It included a description of the concerns each type of person in a company might have. The production supervisor would be interested in different elements than those stressed by purchasing agents or maintenance people. And systems design people would look at still other elements. A picture emerged that provided a good idea of how decisions to purchase the new system would be made and how they could be influenced. The report also indicated that it generally takes 12 to 15 months to move ahead with this type of project in some industries, and as little as three months in others.

Another section of the report stressed the importance buying firms place on the seller providing applications engineering to help adjust the systems to each firm's unique manufacturing situation. Also, marketers of such systems would be required before purchase to provide training for users and maintenance people. Further, the report indicated that most firms believe service contracts should be supplied to keep the new system operable and to prevent slowed or shut-down production lines.

Another part of the report discussed the perceptions and attitudes of potential customers regarding Sally's firm's major competitors. The competitor analysis, as this section was called, identified the strengths and weaknesses of each competitor as seen by the potential purchasers. Fortunately for Sally's firm, potential purchasers were dissatisfied with some aspect of each competitor's system and no industry leader had emerged in the minds of the buyers. Some were seen as expensive; others had delivery problems. All were seen as having applications engineers with very limited experience.

At the end of the session, Bill outlined several strategic options Sally could pursue. No single strategy offered a clearly superior approach; there were strengths, weaknesses, opportunities, and threats associated with each. Bill made his final recommendation and for nearly three hours Bill and Sally discussed numerous aspects of it and other approaches before they discussed how to structure next week's presentation to Sally's staff.

Bill wondered what Sally and her team would finally decide. He thought they would accept his recommendation. He knew if they did that, in the next few weeks, Sally's firm would be deciding to commit several million dollars and the talents of over 200 employees to this major marketing thrust.

As Bill was leaving, he recalled a short time ago when these types of decisions were being made with much less knowledge about buying behavior. Bill's study reflected advancements in theories and principles that his firm could apply. From the knowledgeable questions Sally asked, he knew she was also up to date on the latest advances in consumer behavior principles.

3. ***The Campus Consumer*** Fred Hansen had just enough time to stop at Denny's Stereo Shop before his evening study group meeting. The stereo system he had purchased there the year before had provided hours of entertainment, but the stylus of his phono cartridge was showing signs of wear. The sound quality seemed to have diminished over the past few weeks, and there was a possibility that his records could be damaged with further use. Fred did not consider himself a stereo expert but he felt somewhat knowledgeable. He knew that many people purchase a new cartridge when the stylus on theirs becomes worn, to keep current with the latest advances in design. Since buying the system he had found himself reading about stereos more than he did even before his purchase. He was pleased to see that his equipment tended to receive higher than average praise from most stereo equipment reviewers. Fred had read about cartridge specifications in the product comparisons of *Consumer Reports* magazine and felt he knew enough to discuss brands and models. The store was crowded, and while the manager waited on another customer Fred examined the cartridge display. He saw several new models he knew little about. Fortunately, Fred noted that the manager had recognized him from previous visits and would wait on him next. His roommate suggested that he should avoid purchasing from a discount shop unless price was his only concern, because they stock off-brands and offer little advice. When the manager was finally free, Fred only had time for just a few rushed questions.

The manager recommended a cartridge that was nearly $40 more than Fred expected. Fred was uncertain about what to do and delayed his purchase. The extra $40 would seriously diminish discretionary funds that could be used for entertainment or a new pair of running shoes he had seen.

As he headed for the exit, Fred heard a clerk tell another customer that a cartridge was included free with all turntable sales, but that for $30 extra a greatly improved cartridge could be purchased. Fred was beginning to think he may have underestimated the importance of the cartridge in creating sound quality—why do some seemingly unimportant purchases take so much energy? Fred recalled how just that morning his friend Shirley, a graphic arts major, had taken what seemed an eternity to select a mechanical pencil. Fred usually selected pencils casually when he passed a store check-out display. For his friend it was an involving decision to choose a comfortable pencil with an automatic lead feed.

Although it was a short distance to the business school where the study group meeting was being held, Fred jogged most of the way. His light jacket sporting the school colors and logo was no match for the cold November winds. Still, his State jacket was team support worn in anticipation of Saturday's football game against State's traditional rival. The study group had been meeting twice a week since August when they came together to prepare a business case for class. Most of the members were taking several classes together and the interaction helped them get more involved in the course work. When Fred entered the room he noticed that each group member displayed some sign of school spirit: cap, scarf, jacket, notebook, or sweatshirt. He could not help thinking how much more fun it was to have a top-ranked team this year than the losing team they had had the year before.

The group went right to work, reviewing previous assignments, comparing fine points about lecturers, and reviewing material the professor had asked them to study informally. Later Fred found an opening to mention his cartridge purchase dilemma—an apparent turn-off for most, as no one picked up on the subject. Fred was surprised because Beth was often a leader in similar conversations offering numerous opinions and bits of information. He decided then to take time to talk with salespeople at stores on Friday if time permitted.

On his way out of the building Beth caught his arm and pointed to the ski club poster with Robert Redford staring at him. "We're the biggest social club on campus and I want you to join. Forty dollars gets you in, and for that you can select two ski weekends at a great resort a hundred miles north—transportation and lift tickets included." Fred had not skied since junior high school, but his mind flashed an image of a trip he took with his parents and sister in Colorado many years before. He had always seen himself as athletic, and skiing was consistent with his search for adventure. Perhaps he should consider it—at least he decided to engage Beth for the next couple of hours to get her point of view on skiing and maybe stereo systems as well.

Replaying the recent events in his mind, Fred felt it was slightly ironic that principles covered in his consumer behavior class such as motivation, learning, attitudes, reference group theory, and family pertained to the recent events. He wondered if it might help him understand the material and better prepare for next week's exam to relate the material to his own situation. Doing well in that class would be a step toward his goal of graduating next spring and joining a major firm in a marketing position.

CONSUMER BEHAVIOR: MORE THAN SIMPLY BUYING

Consumer behavior is not restricted to the act of buying. It involves three interrelated but distinct activities: prepurchase, purchase, and consumption.[3]

prepurchase

Prepurchase activities entail the discovery of a need or consumption opportunity as well as the information search and processing that lead the prospective buyer to a decision. Prepurchasing may be a relatively active pursuit, such as going to several specialty shops for a wardrobe, or it may be much more passive, such as noticing a billboard or radio advertisement for a certain car. It could involve "letting your fingers do the walking through the Yellow Pages" to compare prices on stereos or to find a specific dealer in Oriental art. Most consumers discuss their purchasing plans with others who may provide general information based on their own experience or even specific product recommendations.

purchase

Purchase activities entail product and brand choice. The buyer must decide what product type to buy (for example, golf clubs or a tennis racquet), then which brand, and finally where to shop and purchase. Depending on the consumer's life-style, environment, individual wants and needs, and the ability to buy, many different choices are available. For example, even after someone decides to buy a Ford, he or she is confronted with 25,000,000 different automobile design combinations, not including the colors available.

consumption

Consumption activities include how consumers use products and services. Consumption is a very important concept in understanding consumer behavior. Yet some firms still fail to recognize its significance. One marketing expert observed that industrial firms actually buy "¼-inch holes rather than ¼-inch drills."[4] In this well-known example, the purchasers (industrial buyers) are more concerned about the *results* of using the product than about the product itself, which is merely a means to an end. Firms that strive to be customer-oriented will do a better job of meeting their customers' needs than will firms that merely attempt to "push" products. If a marketer is to succeed, he must keep in mind the questions industrial consumers expect to have answered: "What will this product or service do for me? How will this product help the public I serve? What benefits will this product offer our company?" The same holds true for consumers. Whether they will purchase the product or service for their own use, for the family, or as a gift influences what product they look for and where they but it.

TYPES OF CONSUMERS

Not all buyers are consumers of the products they purchase. In fact, individuals account for about one quarter of the direct total dollar volume of purchases in the United States. The remaining three quarters comprise purchases by organizational or industrial buyers. One important type of organizational buyer is a purchasing agent in a manufacturing plant. This person weighs input from many sources within the manufacturing firm, such as research-and-development engineers and production engineers. Industrial purchases often involve raw materials for the manufacture of products that may be sold to other industries or to professional buyers or consumers. Some industrial products, such as information systems, computers, tanks, aircraft, and munitions, are also sold to the government.

An example of an organizational purchaser who is *not* an industrial buyer is a professor, who selects textbooks to help students learn a certain subject. Another example is a physician, who prescribes various pharmaceutical products to patients. In both cases, the decision maker advises the purchaser and must consider the particular needs of the individuals being served as well as the consensus of the professional community before selecting a product.

While purchasing situations vary, many of the principles of buyer behavior remain the same in all cases. Therefore, the term *consumer behavior* can be understood to include all types of buyers and buying activities. The theories and methods of analysis used in studying consumer behavior are similar for all types of buyers and consumers, although their application will vary according to the circumstances.[5]

ORIGINS OF THE CONSUMER BEHAVIOR FIELD

Almost everyone is a consumer, and consumers are at the heart of the marketing process. It is not surprising that the past two decades have spawned numerous studies of the complexities of consumer behavior. Additionally, because consumer behavior includes such a broad range of activities and because consumers are influenced by so many interrelated factors, the development of the field has resulted from advances in many scientific and scholarly disciplines. The theories and principles of the behavioral science, and the increasingly sophisticated research and analytical tools at our disposal, have contributed greatly to knowledge of consumer behavior.

Because consumer behavior is one aspect of human behavior, it is only natural that the behavioral sciences have made a substantial contribution. The study of consumer behavior combines information and insights from psychology, sociology, anthropology, and economics. To observe and describe the broad range of consumers and their activities from a single viewpoint—for example, from only the sociological perspective—would severely limit our understanding. Fortunately, researchers have not imposed such restrictions on this field of study as attested to by the interdisciplinary nature of articles in the *Journal of Consumer Research* and other professional publications.

Psychology

The study of the human mind, including mental phenomena, activities of the mind, and human behavior, has made major contributions to the study of consumer behavior. Psychology helps us explore consumers' motivations and the processes consumers use to make decisions. Consumer behavior study is particularly interested in motivation, learning, perception, information processing, and personality. Principles of social and cognitive psychology often find appropriate applications in this field.

social psychology

Social psychology studies the interaction between individuals and groups; as such, it is deeply involved in the study of attitudes, which are a primary area of study in consumer behavior. Social psychology examines the effects of the individual and the community on each other. It helps explain how the social environment (parents, teachers, friends, and institutions) shape behavior and influence the learning process. It analyzes and measures values and attitudes in order to understand the character of these relationships. If we think of groups as market segments, we can see how useful social psychology is to marketers, who must develop market segmentation strategies. Marketing has used attitude measurement and analysis, both tools of the social psychologist, extensively to understand and predict the product and brand choices consumers make.

cognitive psychology

Cognitive psychology is the study of how we process information. It differs from social psychology in that it looks at how mental activities guide learning and behavior. It helps provide insight into the thinking processes of consumers and the ways in which they approach purchase decisions. Cognitive psychology looks at information processing and memory to help explain individual behavior and thought. Knowledge provided by this field influences marketers' decisions about such fundamental issues as how to design and schedule advertising to be memorable and interesting to potential purchasers.

Sociology

sociology

Sociology is the study of social behavior and the formation, structure, and function of human groups. It helps explain how the products a buyer selects relate to the groups to which the buyer belongs. Aspects of sociology most relevent to consumer behavior are the study of families, reference groups, social classes, subcultures, and life-styles.

Anthropology

anthropology

Anthropology is the investigation of human development, including physiological characteristics, geographical distribution, and culture. It is generally carried on through fieldwork and is often more descriptive and historical than theoretical and predictive. Much research in anthropology has centered on other cultures; yet some principles are directly applicable to the United States. With the rising importance of multinational businesses to new markets, cross-cultural consumer behavior research is emerging. The spread of ideas from one person to another was first studied by anthropologists and rural sociologists. Since then, more than 300 marketing studies have described the diffusion of ideas through societies, which has led to insights for product introduction strategies in our own country. Further, many domestic firms export their products, and a great number manufacture them overseas. For these firms, the insights of anthropology into the cultures with which they interact can be extremely valuable.

Economics

economics

Economics is the study of the flow of goods and services, including production, distribution, and consumption. It attempts to understand how society employs its scarce resources. Early consumer behavior studies were developed to answer many of the questions either dismissed in economic theories or stated as assumptions behind elaborate hypotheses. For example, some early economists theorized that the amount of money people spend is primarily a function of their real incomes. However, it is now generally accepted that spending is affected by what people *perceive* their economic situation to be. This principle of consumer behavior is particularly important during times of inflation and economic change, when consumers' perceptions of their economic future shift frequently.

Economists have tended to make assumptions about consumer behavior and marketing in developing their theories. Yet they have done relatively little to test these assumptions. Nevertheless, many of the principles of consumer behavior have direct bearing on economics because they tell us much about why consumption occurs.

While economics might be called the mother discipline to marketing, relatively few popular principles of economics have been directly applied in the marketer's study of consumer behavior.[6]

Much the same is true for microeconomics, a more specialized subdiscipline largely concerned with "the theory of the firm," or the behavior of sellers. It has relevance to consumer behavior, because if consumers are to use their purchasing power most effectively, they must understand and perhaps be able to predict the actions of sellers (firms). Generally, microeconomists address how firms should behave under set conditions and thus provide some insight into how firms actually do behave. In terms of marketing, microeconomic principles serve primarily as a guide for certain types of pricing decisions and some competitive strategies.

RESEARCH AND ANALYTICAL TOOLS OF CONSUMER BEHAVIOR

Through the rapid growth of information technology, particularly the computer, consumer behaviorists have vastly improved their ability to use and test new theories. Research and analytical tools have evolved that help us apply information from the behavioral sciences to consumer behavior. The result is a new technology of marketing, with tools that include measurement techniques, survey methods, experimentation, multivariate analysis, and simulation.

Measurement Techniques

Each day newscasters report on the Dow-Jones average, the current temperature in different areas of the country, and the wind velocity at the nearest weather center. These measures help describe a condition or serve as a reference point. Similarly, an intelligence quotient (IQ) tells how well someone performed on a test and is sometimes used to infer how intelligent that person may be. Although intelligence cannot be directly measured, IQ is a measure that represents it.

Much more so than physical phenomena, behavioral phenomena elude precise measurements. Yet they are critical in testing and applying theories. For example, when marketers talk about satisfying consumers' wants, it helps that they can measure the degree to which consumers perceive their wants as satisfied or not satisfied by a certain product. If an automobile manufacturer seeks to change the public's attitudes toward a particular make and model, it is fundamental to its strategy that those attitudes be measurable.

Behavioral scientists have developed measurements of both physical and psychological behavior. New techniques for measuring consumer behavior have helped marketers understand consumers better. Among them are measures of personality, attitude, brand loyalty, brand awareness, lifestyles, and advertising recall and recognition.

Survey Methods

Before the development of present-day surveying methods, large companies used traveling market surveyors to administer surveys to consumers nationwide. The data, which sometimes took a year to gather, was eventually used by the companies in their merchandising decisions. Today it is unnecessary to talk with every consumer in order to predict what the public's reactions to a product, service, or new advertising campaign will be. Gathering opinions has been streamlined by the development of improved sampling techniques and syndicated survey data used in the United States and much of the rest of the world. Syndicated data is often useful when a firm is initially seeking general information about a particular market. With this data in hand, marketers may then choose to conduct their own survey for more detailed information specific to the firm's product or service.

Current surveying methods include the use of consumer panels, telephone polls, mail surveys, and personal interviews with consumers. These techniques, in combination with behavior theories, yield information which has proven to be quite reliable in assessing the prospects of a new product or an innovative marketing approach.

Experimentation

Marketing is by nature experimental, because even the best marketing research offers no guarantees. As a data collection technique, however, experimentation is more than educated guesswork; it is a means of systematically observing outcomes from selected actions. Experimental designs are generally of two types: market tests (or field experiments) and laboratory experiments. Market tests take place in actual purchasing situations; laboratory tests are conducted in contrived environments. For example, a marketing research firm in Chicago has a method of experimentation that helps them predict what market share a new product will gain. Their method consists of (1) screening shoppers at a leading shopping center to find consumers who could use the test product, (2) showing each consumer subject a series of commercials for the new product and for existing brands, (3) taking the consumer to a simulated store to make a selection (either the new product or a competing brand), (4) giving the consumer a wrapped gift of the test product if it was not the brand selected, and (5) contacting the subjects by mail after several days have elapsed to obtain feedback about the new product.

Statistical Analysis

univariate analysis
bivariate analysis
multivariate analysis

Univariate analysis is used to trace changes in one variable, such as unit sales or brand preference. **Bivariate analysis** shows the movement of two variables—for example, advertising expenditures and sales. It helps determine if the variables are related or if measures of one variable can be predicted by measures of another variable—such as whether sales increase when advertising is increased. **Multivariate analysis** is capable of simultaneously tracking several variables, such as advertising, personal sales visits, and sales volume. Because most marketing problems involve several variables that influence consumer behavior, multivariate statistics are often required for analysis of data. For example, a researcher might try to understand brand preference from variables such as the brands previously purchased, attitudes, and what magazines are read. Until the advent of packaged computer programs, hand calculations were required to perform multivariate analysis. This was too slow and complex to be practical on a regular basis for many researchers. Today computer software is available to do statistical analysis on data collected about such elements as attitudes and psychological traits. These programs form standard research and analysis packages that are used often in consumer behavior studies. Programs for personal computers make this type of analysis convenient and relatively inexpensive.

It is not necessary to understand the mechanics of multivariate analysis to appreciate the impact this technique has had on our knowledge of buyer behavior. We will not discuss statistical analysis, although many of the insights about consumer behavior we do discuss were produced from studies that used elaborate research designs involving multivariate analysis statistical tools.

Simulation

Today buyers on limited budgets can choose from hundreds of simulated products, such as simulated diamonds and pearls, fake furs, imitation leather car seats, and artificial Christmas trees. In these cases, the real thing is rare, expensive to produce, or generally unavailable and, thus, must be simulated. When firms must develop marketing plans for their products, it may be impractical (if not impossible) to try several costly advertising campaigns to pick a winner, to change distribution channels regularly, or to develop elaborate product lines to cover a variety of contingencies. Instead, marketers use far less costly computer-based **simulations** to approximate real world marketing situations. Hundreds of simulations are currently in use for advertising, personal selling, distribution, and new product introductions. Of course, just as a simulated diamond has flaws in its structure, so do behavioral simulations. However, recent advances are producing more complex and realistic behavior simulations that help predict consumer behavior based on various marketing strategies.

simulations

RESEARCH APPLICATION: MARKET SEGMENTATION AND STRATEGY

Before we begin to explore the individual elements of consumer behavior, it is worthwhile to highlight two principal areas of marketing in which consumer behavior plays a decisive role: market segmentation and strategy development. Private industry, nonprofit organizations, and government agencies apply knowledge gained through research about consumers on a daily basis to accomplish these fundamental marketing tasks.

Market Segmentation

Segmentation is a critical element in effective marketing and provides a foundation for business strategy. **Segmentation** is the process of grouping consumers into categories to identify their needs, wants, and responses to marketing programs. By carefully examining current and potential buyers and segmenting them according to important differences, marketing managers can determine which consumers offer the greatest opportunity for the firm. Certain segments can then be selected and marketing pro-

segmentation

target segments grams built to satisfy their unique needs. These groups are called **target segments.**

In the past, many firms approached potential buyers as though they were all similar in their needs and wants. Products were developed and presented to the market with little thought about altering the product to appeal to different types of buyers. This approach may work when the market for a company's product is large and few competitors exist. However, today most industries have several competing firms, giving consumers of their products several alternatives from which to choose. Companies that are market oriented realize the importance of satisfying the unique desires of a target segment in order to compete effectively.

Clearly, a marketing program cannot be designed for each customer; from a time and cost standpoint, this would be impossible for most firms. Through segmentation, firms can identify homogeneous sets of customers and design strategies to appeal to sizable groups in an efficient manner.

Segmentation involves first selecting characteristics by which consumers will be assigned to segments. These characteristics are descriptions or **variables** that show how classes of customers differ from one another. The types of possible variables are almost unlimited: age, sex, location, income, family life cycle are just a few examples of potential variables. Variables are subdivided into *categories,* which are classifications for describing individual customers. For example, the variable *sex* consists of the categories *male* and *female.*

variables

Which variables should be chosen for market segmentation? The correct answer depends on how consumers behave. Segmentation is a creative process that requires an understanding of how customers think and act. To be useful, segments must distinguish between consumers according to variables that are relevant to purchasing behavior. **Demographics** are distinguishing features of populations and markets such as their age, income, and geographic location and distribution. Demographic data, which is usually collected by government agencies, are often useful in segmentation. However, segmentation can also be based on such things as the specific benefits that different users of a product seek (*benefit segmentation*), on where they shop, on how they make purchasing decisions, and so on. The key to effective segmentation is to *select dimensions that are meaningful for a specific marketing strategy.* This requires a sound understanding of consumer behavior—knowledge that can be gained through careful research and analysis.

demographics

Strategy Development

One purpose of segmentation is to give management focal points for decisions about where and how to apply the firm's efforts. **Strategy** was originally a military term that described how a battle would be fought. It involved the deployment of weapons and people to gain an advantage

strategy

over the enemy. Business strategy is similar in the sense that each enterprise tries to do a better job than competitors in satisfying customers in order to accomplish its business goals. Thus business strategies describe how a company will approach its market over a period of time. Strategy development involves plans and operations to use the company's resources most effectively and efficiently.

Using consumer research and analysis, marketers make decisions about which features to include for a new product, how it should be packaged, where it should be located in the store, how and where to advertise, and at what price. Each decision is based on the marketer's beliefs about how consumers are likely to respond. In developing advertising strategies, for example, the marketer would like to know the media habits of intended customers. Do they read magazines, listen to radio, or watch television most often? What magazines do they read and what programs do they attend to? What advertising messages are most likely to influence their purchasing behavior? How frequently must they be exposed to the ad in order to get their attention, stimulate interest, and cause a change in their attitudes toward the product or service?

Advertising is only one aspect of strategy development in which consumer behavior is applied to marketing decisions. Throughout this text, examples illustrate how management also applies consumer behavior research. While we will consider it from the viewpoint of the individual firm, we will also show how the study of consumer behavior applies to public policy issues such as unit pricing and deceptive advertising. In addition, each chapter includes a list of recommended applications-oriented references for further illustrations of consumer behavior in action.

AN OVERVIEW OF TOPICS IN CONSUMER BEHAVIOR STUDIES

The field of consumer behavior brings together a variety of concepts that help explain how and why consumers act the way they do. An understanding of consumer behavior requires knowledge about each topic (such as motivation, perception, learning, and so on) as well as the ability to see the interrelationships among the concepts. This section presents a framework for study that describes the major concepts to be covered in the text. We discuss three major aspects briefly to highlight their importance and provide a flavor for their roles in consumer behavior.

Figure 1-1 represents the key constructs that have been studied as important entities in the field. How the boxes fit together roughly illustrates their immediate relationships to one another. To be sure, all the concepts relate to one another to some extent; but the figure gives an idea of their relative importance based on size and location. There are numerous interactions among the concepts that could be diagrammed more

Figure 1-1
The Components of Consumer Behavior Study

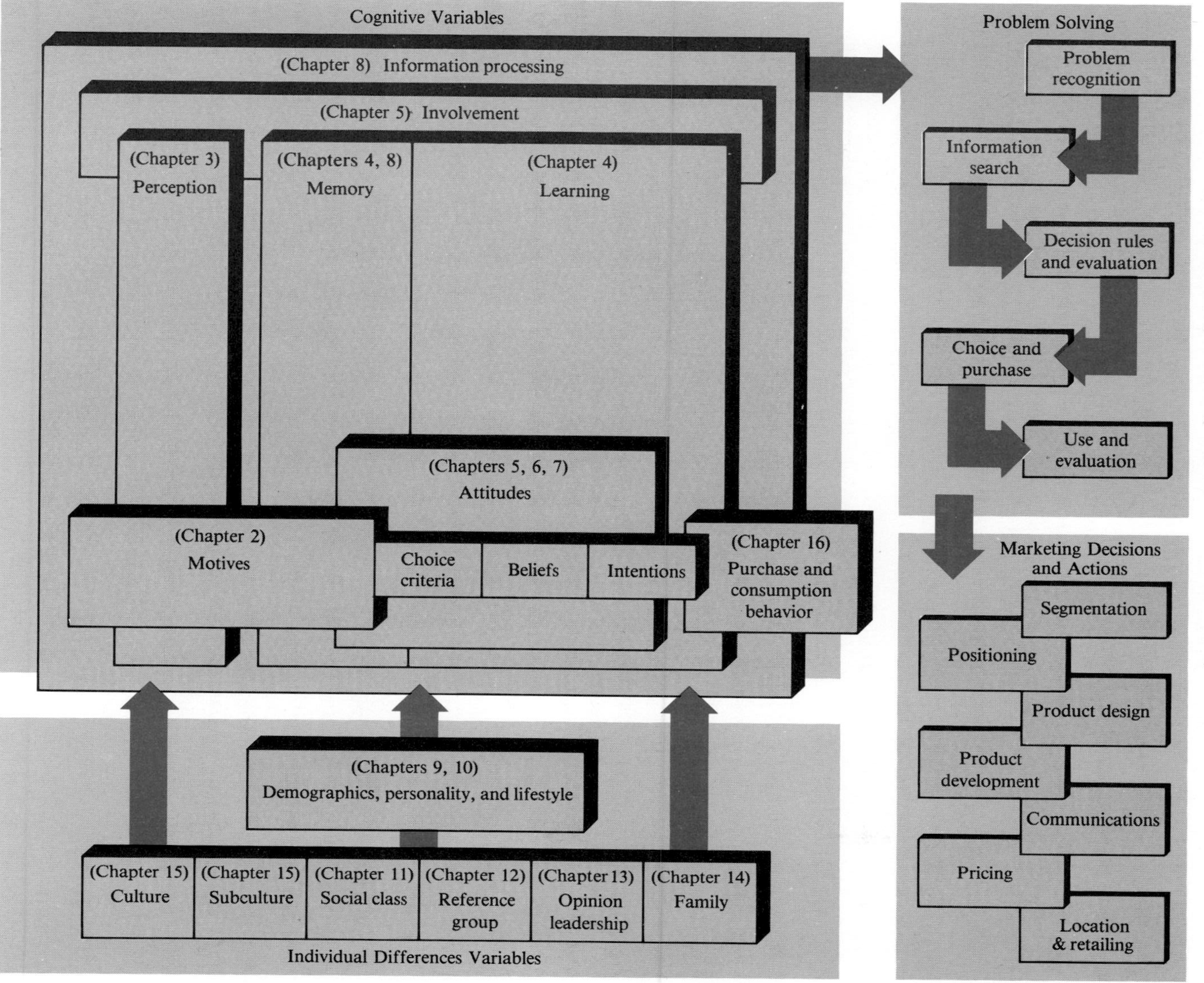

extensively in a very advanced treatment of the subject consumer behavior. For example, one diagram could show how specific motives influence certain attitudes or how previous purchasing might influence trial of new brands.

It is important to remember that Figure 1-1 does *not* describe a model of how consumer decisions are made. (Models of consumer behavior are the focus of Chapter 18.) It simply indicates the concepts that are significant components of consumer behavior and aids visualizing the relationship among the topics. The figure has three major parts: cognitive variables, individual differences, and problem-solving and marketing decisions and actions.

Cognitive Variables

cognitive variables

Consumer behavior involves a complex set of information-processing activities and external environmental influences. Still, most consumer behavior ultimately involves the decisions of individuals. **Cognitive variables** are psychological elements that help us describe how consumers make product and brand choices. Each variable contributes to our understanding of what consumers think and how their thoughts are formed. Each of the variables listed in this area has been extensively studied by psychologists and by researchers of consumer behavior. We have selected these psychological variables from the hundreds that have been written about, because they are the most popular among marketing practitioners and researchers. Also, together they provide a comprehensive picture of thought processes.

Individual Differences

individual differences

At the bottom of Figure 1-1 are five variables that are referred to as **individual differences.** These are not the attributes that make each of us unique, but broad categories into which purchase behavior can be grouped. Examples of these categories are culture, subculture, social class, reference group, and family background. Personality, life-style, and demographics are separate because they relate specifically to the individual; the other components help us describe classes or categories of consumers.

Marketers use individual difference variables for segmentation and other situations where behavior can be more easily understood by looking at relatively homogeneous categories of consumers. Although psychological constructs such as attitude or information processing are likely to operate in a similar fashion for *all* people, the actual attitudes possessed or information processed differs among categories of people. Using individual difference variables, marketers can find categories of people who have, for example, similar attitudes or perception. Many of these variables describe the types of interaction consumers are likely to have with society and other people. Elements such as social class, reference group, and family provide the backdrop for most of the interaction people have with each other.

Once a consumer joins a particular category regarding individual difference variable, he or she remains there for some time. For example, consumers seldom, if ever, change their cultural make-up or social class, just as personality, life-styles, or family condition change only slowly, if at all. By studying categories of people marketers can see main differences in brand choice, as well as attitudes and perceptions leading to choice, among members of different categories.

Problem Solving and Marketing Decisions

problem solving

marketing decisions and actions

The third major section includes the connection between **problem solving,** which is essentially consumers' search for products and brands, and the **marketing decisions and actions** firms take in efforts to generate sales and consumer loyalty.

Purchasing can be seen as a problem-solving behavior. A simple problem-solving process consists of five steps: problem recognition, information search, alternative evaluations (decision rules and evaluation), choice and purchase, and outcomes (or use and evaluation).

problem recognition

Problem recognition occurs when the buyer becomes aware that certain goals he or she might have are not fulfilled and that purchasing some type of product or service might be the solution. This can be a relatively complex series of events, because goals often conflict. For example, the goal of maintaining financial security or having money in the bank might conflict with that of acquiring status by spending money on a prestigious auto.

information and experience search

The second stage, **information and experience search,** consists of thinking through the situation and recalling information learned from previous experiences that has been stored in the memory. Also during this stage, the potential buyer is likely to seek out information from advertisements, friends, salespeople, or other sources.

decision rules and evaluation

The third step, **decision rules and evaluation,** can become quite complex as the consumer evaluates alternatives—that is, attempts to determine which product or service would be most likely to satisfy his or her goals. At this point, complex attitudes often develop as the consumer looks at the pros and cons of each choice.

Once the consumer has made evaluations, he or she is likely to make a purchase choice. At this time, the buyer may decide not to purchase it all but rather to save the money. Alternately, the buyer may decide to purchase only a small trial amount. If a purchase is made, however, it is quite possible the buyer will select the brand a marketer is promoting.

outcomes

The final step, **outcomes,** reveals the amount of satisfaction the buyer receives from the decision. At this point the buyer is likely to seek assurances from other people that the choice made was the correct choice. A positive outcome will reinforce the consumer's decision and make it more likely that such a purchase is made again.

As with the other constructs discussed in this section, this explanation of the buyer's decision-making process is oversimplified. It is important, however, to recognize that buyer behavior is essentially rational, no matter how many emotions are involved. Marketing decisions and actions are generally designed to influence consumer problem solving in favor of the sponsor. Throughout the text examples of marketing actions will be used to illustrate how consumer behavior is influenced by companies. For example, we will see how segmentation and positioning are used to differentiate one brand from another. Numerous examples of communications will show how consumer behavior can be influenced through personal selling, advertising, and other visual and verbal means. We will also indicate how pricing influences perception, and we will discuss the impact of location and retailing in gaining satisfied customers. Other marketing decisions such as product design will also be discussed where consumer behavior is likely to be affected by it.

SUMMARY

The study of consumer behavior involves how individuals and organizations discover, evaluate, consume, and dispose of products and services. It attempts to provide answers to these questions: Who buys? When do they buy? Where do they buy? Why and how do they buy? The field of consumer behavior is relatively new, having grown rapidly due to extensive research during the past two decades.

Three interrelated activities comprise all consumer behavior: prepurchase activities, purchase activities, and consumption activities. These categories are true for individual consumers, industrial consumers, and advisory purchasers. Regardless of the type of consumer, the basic theories and methods of analysis are essentially the same.

Consumer behavior is a interdisciplinary study that has resulted from the advances in several areas of the behavioral sciences. The combined perspectives of psychology, sociology, anthropology, and economics make positive contributions to our understanding of consumer behavior.

A range of research and analytic tools are used by consumer behavior researchers to gather and interpret information about the marketplace. Five major tools are measurement techniques, survey methods, experimentation, multivariate analysis, and simulations.

Market segmentation and strategy development depend upon a good understanding of buyer behavior. As we will see in this text, the principles of consumer behavior are applied on a daily basis by market-oriented firms and organizations.

KEY TERMS

consumer behavior
prepurchase
purchase
consumption
social psychology
cognitive psychology
sociology
anthropology
economics
univariate analysis
bivariate analysis
multivariate analysis
simulations
segmentation
target segments
variables
demographics
strategy
cognitive variables
individual differences
problem solving
marketing decisions and actions
problem recognition
information and experience search
decision rules and evaluation
outcomes

QUESTIONS

1. Define *consumer behavior*. According to your definition, who are consumers?

2. Discuss what is meant by a "consumer orientation." Why is this important to the success of a company or organization?

3. Describe the three major types of activities comprising consumer behavior. Provide an example of each activity to illustrate your explanation.

4. Consumer behavior is considered an interdisciplinary study. What disciplines have had major impact on our understanding of consumer behavior? Explain.

5. What are the primary research tools used to explore consumer behavior? What does multivariate analysis involve?

6. Distinguish between field experimentation and simulation. What factors might determine which research technique to use in a given situation?

7. There are several cognitive variables representing important aspects of consumer behavior. List these variables and provide a brief definition of each.

8. The study of consumer behavior is important from both an academic and applications perspective. Discuss the relevance of consumer behavior to marketers in terms of segmentation and strategy development.

NOTES

1. Thomas J. Peters and Robert H. Waterman, Jr., *In Search of Excellence* (New York: Harper & Row, 1982), 157.
2. Peters and Waterman, 193.
3. Edward M. Tauber described three similar activities—shopping, purchasing, and consuming—in "Why Do People Shop?" *Journal of Marketing* 36 (1972): 46–59.
4. Theodore Levitt, "Marketing When Things Change," *Harvard Business Review* (1977): 108.
5. John A. Howard and Jagdish N. Sheth, *The Theory of Buyer Behavior* (New York: Wiley, 1969), ix.
6. For a classic discussion of how consumer behavior and economics are related, see George Katama, "Rational Behavior and Economic Behavior," *Psychological Review* 60 (1953): 307–18.

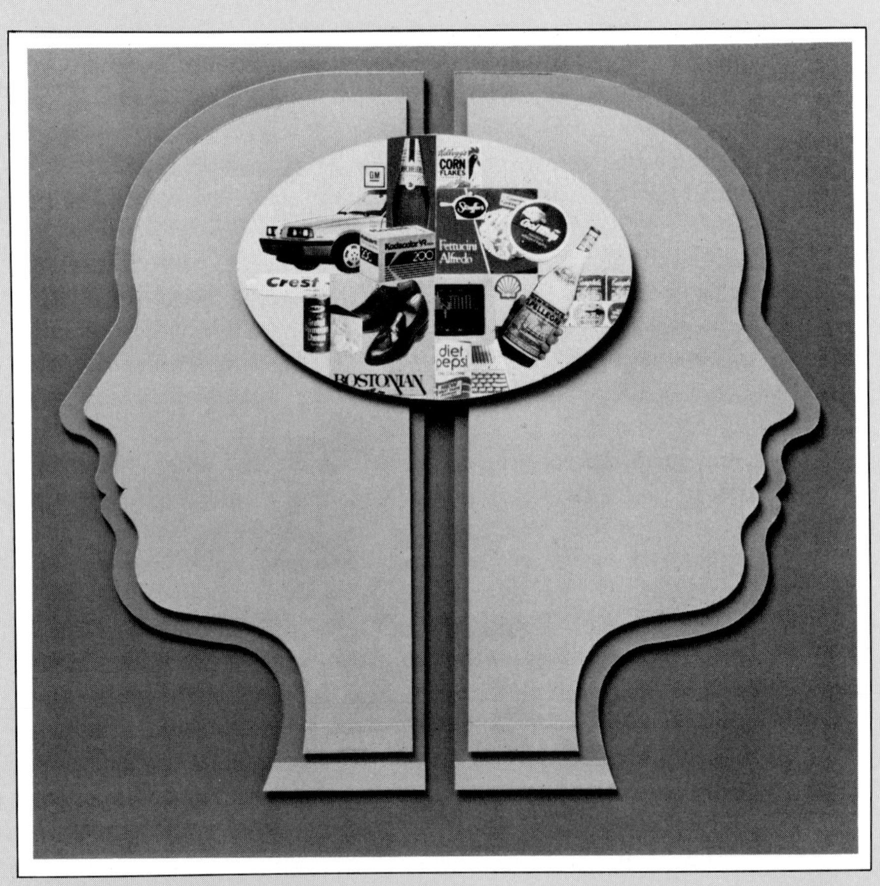
GM
CORN FLAKES
200
Fettucini Alfredo
Crest
diet pepsi
BOSTONIAN

I THE CONSUMER'S DECISION-MAKING PROCESS

Whether the buyer is a consumer, a purchasing agent, a member of an organization's buying committee, or a professional buyer, the purchasing process is ultimately concerned with *individual* decision making. It is safe to say that while all aspects of consumer behavior are important, more studies and attention have been devoted to psychological elements than to other areas. This is because they are so important in understanding how product, service, and brand choice is made. Therefore, concepts about consumers' psychological elements and processes are presented in Part 1 of this book. The chapters follow roughly the cognitive variables portion of Figure 1-1. *Motivation* and *perception* are two of the most fundamental parts of cognitive processing. Memory is an important part of *learning*. The next three chapters are devoted to *attitudes,* which are central to most marketing programs. *Information processing,* in the final chapter in Part 1, is covered last because it integrates much of the topics in earlier chapters. Additionally, the concepts presented in the earlier chapters help lay the groundwork for showing how information processing theory contributes to consumer behavior.

MOTIVES (*Chapter 2*)

Motivation underlies most behavior. It relates to the needs consumers have as well as the amount of effort directed toward satisfying those needs. Motivation helps explain at the most basic level why consumers seek certain types of purchases.

Many motives play a role in the types of products consumers seek. Psychologists believe that human behavior is largely goal directed, and consumer behavior is no exception. Thus, asking why someone buys a certain product is another way of asking what the person expects to gain by purchasing it. That is, people are motivated to buy products and services in order to satisfy their *needs*. These may be basic physiological needs for water, air, food, warmth, sleep, or sex. They may also be social and psychological needs, such as the need for love, friendship, status, self-expression, or a sense of fulfillment.

Maslow's hierarchy needs—physiological, safety, belonging, esteem, and self-actualization—offers insights into the reasons underlying particular types of behaviors. Other well-known social motives are aggression and the need for dominance and for exhibition. Imagine developing a perfume aimed at attracting people with a need for dominance, exhibition, and aggression. It might be called Amazon, Scoundrel, or perhaps Tigress. Because motives also relate to the internal forces that direct consumers to behave in order to fulfill particular needs, a knowledge of motivation is important in identifying how even what people choose to look at is related to the needs they are attempting to satsify. As we will learn in later chapters, motives have much to do with perception, memory, learning, and attitudes as well.

PERCEPTION (*Chapter 3*)

Perception refers to the process consumers use to recognize, select, organize, and interpret stimuli in ways that make sense of the world around them. Perceptions are affected both by the stimuli themselves and by the perceiver. People are very selective about the types of stimuli to which they expose themselves and the amount of attention they give them. They also are selective about the way they comprehend information and what information they retain.

During every waking moment we are surrounded by hundreds of potential stimuli—sights, sounds, textures, aromas, and tastes—in our perceptual field. But since we can only interpret a limited number of stimuli at any given time, we filter out most of these potential stimuli and they never have any impact on our thoughts. If somehow we were able to overcome our natural tendency to focus on only a few in order to fully attend to *all* stimuli, we would experience a chaos of sensations. Fortunately, we are able to attend selectivity to a limited number of stimuli and to organize them into meaningful thoughts.

Even when two people attend to the same stimulus, their interpretations are likely to differ, because each person's interpretation distorts the message according to his or her own needs and attitudes. Selective interpretation is a highly visible factor in controversies over public policy. For example, a loyal Chrysler owner might interpret the federal government's loan guarantees to Chrysler as essential to preserving the auto industry in the United States. By contrast, a loyal Oldsmobile owner might consider federal loans to Chrysler as detrimental to the industry as a whole. In a sense, each human brain constructs an internal representation of the outside world that differs somewhat from every other brain's representation.

Yet there are enough similarities in perceptions to enable people to relate to one another and to the world around them.

Although perception can be treated as an independent concept, it is closely linked to motivation and other constructs. For example, the consumer who has a need for affiliation might perceive a restaurant primarily as a location for social activities. At another time or by another person, the restaurant might be seen as a "food filling station" to satisfy urgent hunger. Marketers often talk about the image of a particular brand. By this they mean the way that brand is perceived in the marketplace. A single brand of perfume can be seen as a way to attract others, to achieve status, or as a purchase to indulge oneself—all different motives.

A great deal of what products, brands, and retail outlets mean to consumers comes to them by way of perception. For example, a particular manufacturer's brand sold in a high-quality department store might be seen as a higher-quality item than if it were sold in a discount shop. The word *Japanese* connotes a certain level of quality that affects the perception of an automobile. At one time, automakers in this country put their own brand names on new models made in Japan, and consumers rated them lower in quality than when the actual foreign manufacturer's name was on the automobile.

MEMORY (*Chapters 4, 8*)

Memory is an important part of learning and refers to the storage of information over time. It also plays a major role in attitude formation. Memory has several components. *Sensory memory* lasts for a split second; *short-term memory* lasts for a few seconds; and *long-term memory* stores information for years. Marketers are interested in what readers remember from an advertisement, what packaging information consumers retain, how much time prospective buyers need to learn particular types of information in communications, and so on. In addition, the amount of repetition required to change attitudes and the optimum timing of messages for placement in memory are important for advertising strategies.

We also know that some information and claims are easier to remember than others. This kind of knowledge helps marketers design more effective messages. In this text a full chapter is not devoted to memory; but the subject is sufficiently important to be included as a major concept in two chapters, on learning and on information processing.

LEARNING (*Chapter 4*)

Learning refers to any change in behavior due to experience. Psychologists have studied in great depth how people learn, but they do not all agree. While there are a number of schools of thought about how learning works, most researchers agree that learning takes place when we adapt our behavior based on experience.

As for *what* we learn, psychologists think that we learn attitudes, likes and dislikes, most of our motives and needs, and beliefs. As consumers, we learn what products satisfy our needs, what stores carry the merchandise we want, what our family and friends expect us to buy, and a host of other purchase and consumption factors.

Learning involves reasoning, classical conditioning, and reinforcement. The cognitive school of learning emphasizes reason and problem solving; it focuses on knowledge, insights, ideas, attitudes, and goals. According to this approach, brand choice is the result of a clearly defined decision processes, involving complex or simple thinking that depends on the circumstances surrounding the purchase. Consumers develop knowledge that helps simplify the process over time.

Classical conditioning (or contiguity learning) was first identified by Ivan Pavlov, whose experiments with a dog, a tuning fork, and meat paste are well known. Conditioning was accomplished by ringing the fork while presenting the meat paste. After conditioning, Pavlov's dog would salivate when only the tuning fork was rung. A similar pattern of association occurs when a brand, such as Mountain Dew soda, is presented along with other stimuli, such as a cool stream on a hot summer day, to elicit a favorable response.

Reinforcement learning emphasizes the consequences of actions. After a purchase is made, consumers find pleasure or pain based on what others say about the brand, or based on their own evaluation. If the consequence is favorable, it is likely that the purchase will be repeated at some future time.

INVOLVEMENT (*Chapter 5*)

Levels of involvement help us understand the importance to the consumer of particular types of purchases. A shopper who is highly involved in a product usually uses a more clearly identified problem-solving process leading up to purchase. High-involvement situations occur when consumers believe their choice of a particular product will yield substantial satisfaction. Low involvement occurs toward items to which consumers attach little importance; they are likely to try these products *before* formulating an attitude about them. When a new chewing gum comes on the market, most people do not spend a great deal of energy and effort to deciding whether to give the brand a try; they simply buy a pack and see how it tastes.

Low-involvement products may require different types of messages than high-involvement products do. For example, someone looking for an automobile will probably attach great importance to the purchase and seek information about it systematically. For low-involvement purchases, the consumer obtains product information much more passively, when and if it is convenient, or even while obtaining information about more important items.

The decision-making process is influenced by these internal factors as well as by the buying situation. In Chapter 5, we will discuss involvement in depth. It is important to remember that the degree to which an individual is involved in a product class has a major impact on the purchase decision process.

Degree of Problem Solving

Three major categories have been identified in consumer behavior literature to describe the extent of problem solving that buyers might engage in for a given situation: extensive problem solving, limited problem solving, and routine response behavior. These categories are related to involvement and are sometimes discussed simultaneously.

In first purchases of high-involvement products, consumers are likely to engage in *extensive problem-solving* activities. For example, a consumer in the market for a new stereo receiver that must meet a number of performance criteria (watts per channel, dynamic headroom, digital tuning) and also convey a personal image (black chassis, not silver) would be considered highly involved with stereo equipment. Accordingly, the prospective buyer would also show extensive problem-solving behavior by gathering and comparing product specifications in order to select the "right" receiver. When prospective buyers are making a purchase decision for the first time, or have limited purchasing experience with an important product category, extensive problem solving generally takes place.

By contrast, *routine response behavior* falls at the other end of the problem-solving spectrum. In these cases, the buyer often has low involvement and makes a purchase decision quickly without much up-front comparison. This type of behavior may also characterize a frequently recurring purchase in which the buyer relies on past experience rather than acquiring new information. For many people, the choice of which brand of soap to buy is a routine response behavior.

Limited problem solving falls between the two extremes. In these purchase situations, the consumer may engage in some information seeking and product comparison, but less effort is devoted to the decision than for extensive problem solving. The selection of which dish to order when dining out in an expensive restaurant is an example of limited problem solving for most people.

It is important to note that the extent of problem solving and level involvement varies from person to person. Those who are highly concerned about dental hygiene, fresh breath, and appearance (such as a television model or celebrity) might be highly involved in buying toothpaste. On the other hand, a purchasing agent for a government agency who needs to add another car to the fleet might have low involvement and show routine response behavior in the buying decision. The study of buyers' decision processes must consider the elements of the buying situation.

ATTITUDES *(Chapters 5, 6, 7)*

Like the words *motive* and *perception, attitude* is used frequently every day. Attitudes convey both feelings and beliefs about an object. Because attitudes provide insight into relatively complex psychological states, they have been important to consumer behavior research. Attitudes are one of the closest links to actual purchase behavior. Because we are interested in *predicting* consumer behavior, as well as understanding it, knowing how to analyze attitudes is essential for marketers.

Attitudes here are consumers' thoughts and feelings about products. They develop through experience and influence the choice of products and brands. There has been so much creative and exciting research on consumer attitudes that three chapters are devoted it. More than any other topic, the study of attitudes has played a major role in current ideas about why and how consumers behave. Chapter 5 will discuss both the structure and function of attitudes. Attitudes are structured sets of beliefs that reflect the person's knowledge of factors such as brands, retail outlets, or suppliers. They also include the like or dislike of certain aspects of these beliefs.

Another important aspect of attitudes is their tendency to direct behavior. We will discuss various attitude components and identify how they influence the selection of products. Three very important aspects of attitudes are (1) *choice criteria,* or the product characteristics used in making judgments about the benefits of each brand; (2) *beliefs,* or the thoughts buyers have about how well particular brands "stack up" according to the criteria; and (3) *intentions,* or the probabilities buyers attach to purchasing particular brands under certain circumstances.

Attitudes help us adjust to other people by expressing values, organizing knowledge, and protecting or enhancing feelings of personal worth. By understanding the function of attitudes, we can develop an appreciation for the pervasive role products and services play in everyday experiences. Chapter 5 will provide useful insights for analyzing the attitudes of most purchasers.

Chapter 6 will explore how attitudes are researched and measured. It is essential for firms to know consumers' attitudes toward competing products and services in order to design more effective marketing programs. Thus, attitude measurement has become a favorite topic of marketing planners and researchers alike.

Perhaps the major reason that attitudes are so important is that many marketing functions—among them, advertising, selling, and product modification—are designed to influence and change attitudes. Chapter 7 will discuss how attitudes can be altered. There are dramatic differences between the effectiveness of promotional campaigns that are designed to meet specific attitude-change objectives and those that are merely aimed at reaching general marketing or business goals.

Marketers spend billions annually on personal selling and advertising to influence and alter customer attitudes. It is not surprising that executives and researchers alike are interested in attitude-change strategies. How important is knowledge or expertise about the source of a message in altering attitudes? How should messages be presented? Should the strongest argument come first, or last? What is the role of a celebrity as a message source? Are some people more resistant to persuasion or attitude change than others? How should each group be handled? What happens if the source is attacked, or a message is distorted? The chapter on attitude change examines all these questions.

INFORMATION PROCESSING (*Chapter 8*)

Information processing involves looking at behavior as one continuous activity of acquiring and analyzing information to arrive at a decision. Researchers who share this view are interested in the types of information buyers receive, the complexity of the information, and the form in which it is communicated (printed, verbal, audiovisual).

Information processing integrates seven other constructs: motives, perception, memory, learning, attitudes, and purchase and consumption behavior. In the past, researchers interested in one of the constructs, such as perception, tended to examine consumer behavior from only that perspective; those interested in attitudes, for example, usually took a different tack than those investigating perception. However, the approach deals with how attention is gained and how information is encoded, remembered, recalled, and used to solve problems. In short, information processing theory helps us interrelate many aspects of purchase behavior.

It is interesting to speculate about how much attention we pay to the different sights, sounds, aromas, tastes, and textures in our environment. Of the thousands of commercial messages from billboards, television, newspapers, and radio we pass every day, how many do we actually notice? How is information transferred from its source to the mind? People encode the environment in different ways, sometimes by visualizing pictures and sometimes by transforming information into words and numbers to be used for analysis. Understanding how these mental pictures are transformed verbally and coded for thinking helps us know how shoppers see their world. We know, for example, that consumers not only receive mental pictures but also develop elaborate interpretations to help them make choices.

Another intriguing aspect of information processing is how memory functions aid decision making. Who are the Doublemint twins? If you begin to think about chewing gum and a particular brand comes to mind, it could be because of advertisements you first saw as a child. How many times did you see the ad before you remembered it? Once, twice, or repeatedly over a number of years? A related question deals with why we remember some communications almost immediately while others slip past us. How do we move information from a memory lasting only a few seconds to a memory that may last a lifetime? Information processing theory leads us to some of the answers, as do earlier studies on basic learning.

Have you ever wondered how you arrive at a particular brand choice? Do other consumers use other ways to make decisions about the same types of products? *Heuristics,* the study of the simple rules of thumb that consumers use to compare alternatives, helps us understand this process. Early work and continuing research on decision making have uncovered some of these decision rules.

Consumers have many decision rules for different purchasing circumstances. While the decision rules may not seem very important to consumers, and may not even be recognized at the time they are used, they can be extremely significant to marketers who are attempting to influence consumer choice.

An important part of information processing is the *scanner interrupt* mechanism, which helps us understand the consumption process as ongoing rather than occurring only at one time. How often do people shop for one item and get sidetracked before returning to their original purpose? Scanner interrupt theory perceives purchasing as taking place over long periods, the process interrupted by new and novel stimuli, time constraints, or opportunities to obtain new and insightful information.

Highlights of Research in Information Processing

The recent work of many researchers has provided important new insights about how information is processed in the human mind. Their findings are at the heart of the current applications of information processing to consumer behavior. Much of the basic theory of information processing for consumer behavior was developed by James Bettman and Peter Wright, and they continue to make significant contributions. Recently, Jerry Olson and his colleagues have added greatly to our theoretical knowledge. From an applications point of view, the work of Jacob Jacoby and others has shown how information-processing principles may be applied to public policy. In 1973, Peter Wright presented a stimulating paper on the many complex decision strategies used by consumers.[1] Since then, work has progressed to the point that James Bettman has developed a model of information processing for consumer behavior.[2]

Although much remains to be learned about how consumers process information, enough is known to merit the application of current concepts to marketing practice. This area will probably be one of the most important and fruitful to be researched by psychologists and consumer behaviorists during the next decade.

Developing the concept of human cognition as information processing has received help from experiential psychologists and researchers using computer simulations to approximate human thought patterns. Laboratories at many universities and corporations are actively pursuing research which uses computer information processing to help us understand human thought. A realistic simulation of consumers' thought processes is probably some time away, because more information is needed on shopping environments as well as methods of problem solving. However, researchers are making progress toward more sophisticated simulation of human thought, and our understanding of the basic elements of information processing is growing.

NOTES

1. Peter Wright, "Consumer Simplification Strategies," paper presented at Doctoral Consortium, Michigan State University, East Lansing, Michigan, 1972.
2. Bettman's information-processing model will be highlighted in Chapter 8 and discussed at length in relation to other models of consumer behavior in Chapter 18.

2 Motivation

Objectives of This Chapter

After you have studied this chapter, you should be able to:

1. Define motivation and explain how it relates to consumer behavior.
2. Contrast current studies of consumer motives with those of early motivation research.
3. Describe a variety of human needs, many of which are satisfied through buying goods and services.
4. Show how wants differ from needs.
5. Explain need hierarchies and how consumers use them in deciding what to buy.
6. Discuss three motives—curiosity, competence, and consistency—and show how they can be activated in the marketplace.
7. Discuss three types of motivational conflicts experienced by consumers and show how marketers seek to help consumers resolve these conflicts.

Motivation does not have a universally accepted definition. However, most definitions have two points in common. First, motivation involves needs that a person seeks to fulfill. Second, motivation can be triggered to drive a person to take action. For our purposes, **motivation** is an internal force that directs behavior toward the fulfillment of needs.

motivation

This chapter will look first at the impact of earlier motivational research on today's marketers. Second, it will examine the categories of motivations by three major researchers—Maslow, Murray, and McGuire. The consumer motives were identified by those researchers as elements that result in drives which stimulate a complex process of consumer problem solving. Three motives will then be considered in detail: curiosity, competence, and consistency. A challenge for the marketer is to help the consumer resolve motivational conflicts that arise when consumers are faced with complex buying situations. The chapter concludes with a look at how firms consider motives and incorporate conflict resolution in their marketing approaches.

Most behavior, including consumer behavior, contributes to the fulfillment of basic needs. However, the complexity of human experience keeps us from being conscious of these needs much of the time. Moreover, motivation seems abstract, because it is not directly observable with the eyes. Therefore, students may find it helpful to consider how the various theories of motivation in this chapter relate to own goal-directed behavior.

Theories of motivation explain little about which brands buyers are likely to choose. But they do explain a great deal about what influences consumer behavior in a general sense. Motivational research allows marketers to make inferences about the types of products and services buyers seek and the amount of energy buyers are willing to exert to obtain them. Knowledge of buyer motivation is also useful in later chapters in the study of perception, learning, and attitudes which relate directly to brand choice.

MOTIVATION RESEARCH, THEN AND NOW

Much of the early research in the field of consumer behavior was directed toward discovering motivational elements in buying. What is now termed motivation research began during the 1950s and early 1960s with qualitative research into buyers' underlying and deep-seated reasons for purchasing various products. Researchers believed that there were strong influences on consumers to purchase a product that they were not even aware of. For example, one consumer may say that he purchased a Mercedes-Benz automobile because it was engineered well, when in fact motivation research may indicate it was purchased to satisfy hidden sexual, social, or other desires.

Although motivation research was the forerunner of much of the excellent consumer behavior research of the 1970s and 1980s, much of it has been discredited for several reasons. First, in its interpretation of buyers' statements, motivation research revealed a strong Freudian bias. Sigmund Freud, the founder of psychoanalysis, suggested in his theories that a large part of human behavior was not determined by conscious thought but by unconscious urges, passions, repressed feelings, and underlying desires. He believed that unconscious wishes were stronger than conscious thoughts. Much of his research discussed the psychosexual aspects of personality development. In their biases toward Freud's theories, motivation researchers suggested, for example, that those who wear suspenders have unresolved castration complexes, convertibles are purchased as substitutes for a mistress, and making cakes is symbolic of giving birth to babies.[1]

Second, motivation research suffered from poor methodology. Relatively small samples were used to generate broad conclusions. Therefore, however interesting it was as reading, its conclusions remained suspect because many of them were not adequately supported by data.

Third, the theories of early motivation research are at odds with those developed by contemporary researchers, who are using sounder methodologies. Today, computer technology allows much larger and more accurate samples to be drawn, and permits researchers to rapidly analyze the data to extract more comprehensive yet precise conclusions.

Finally, most marketing managers find that the conclusions of early motivation research are not very useful in developing sound marketing strategies or intuitively appealing promotions. Although researchers today do not have all the answers to questions about consumers' motives and needs, current theories are on firmer ground and have proven to be much more useful than those of the early motivation researchers.

Motivation research has provided benefits as well as problems for today's marketers. One positive aspect is that it stimulated interest in *why* people buy. It also served as a catalyst for much of today's work, which has been motivated in part by the desire of current researchers to correct the errors of their predecessors. Qualitative research, such as depth-interviewing techniques and focused groups, is still a part of consumer behavior research (see Chapter 6). This approach is an indirect product of earlier motivation research studies. Another by-product is psychographics, which is sometimes known as "life-style analysis" (see Chapter 9). This technique helps the marketer draw profiles of various consumer segments. Marketers use psychographics along with demographics to segment the market based on what people think and how they behave. Psychographics differs from motivation research in that it takes a *quantitative* or numerical approach to studying consumers rather than a qualitative one. Still, motivation research opened the door to this type of consumer profiling.

Unfortunately, however, consumer behavior as a field of study is still suffering from the reputation of the motivation research of the 1950s. In fact, researchers who investigate shoppers' motives today do not generally refer to their work as motivation research because of the images this term evokes. Most researchers would prefer to free their work from its former associations with the id, ego, and superego, and with the stages of psychosexual development theorized by Freud.

MASLOW'S HIERARCHY OF NEEDS

biological needs
psychological needs

Needs are generally divided into two types: biological and psychological. **Biological needs** have been called primary or innate needs because they seem to exist in all people, regardless of their environment. **Psychological needs** are often called secondary or learned needs because they are the result of socialization. For the same reasons, psychological needs are referred to as values by some consumer behavior experts.[2] (A further discussion of values is in Chapter 5.)

Abraham Maslow's classification of needs is often quoted in business literature.[3] According to Maslow, five basic needs encompass most human goals, ranked in a hierarchy, so that higher-level needs arise only after lower-level needs have been satisfied. Figure 2-1 illustrates Maslow's hierarchy.

Physiological Needs

These include nutritious food, clean air and water, warmth, sleep, and sex. Consumer demand for energy-efficient products, "back-to-nature" health foods, pollution control devices, and nutritional information on food packages are all directly related to this class of needs. Until recently, our society seemed to have satisfied the physiological needs of its members; many took for granted these basic requirements for survival. Recently,

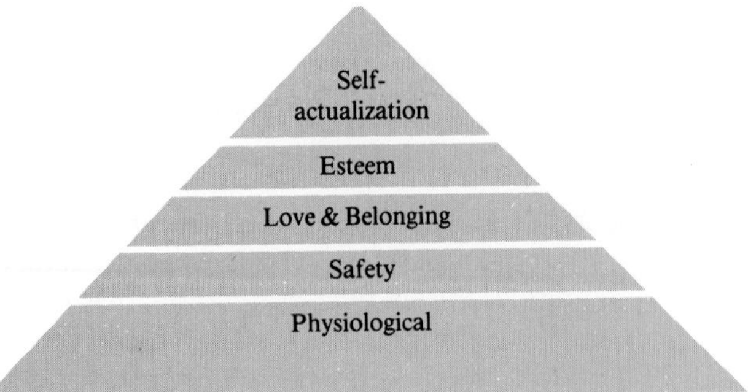

Figure 2-1
Maslow's Hierarchy of Human Needs

Source: Abraham H. Maslow, "A Theory of Human Motivation," *Psychological Review* 50 (1943), 370–96.

however, various threats to our survival (energy crises, polluted air and water, rising food costs) have drastically increased citizen participation in efforts to ensure that our society is not deprived of the essentials.

Physiological needs are continuous; consumers must have a constant supply of various basic products and services. For example, the needs for food and drink arise regularly, and marketers of such products can count on a continuing demand. Direct appeals to physiological needs are commonly made through ads for taste-tempting foods or thirst-quenching drinks.

Often, however, marketers appeal to basic needs by stimulating higher-order needs. In this way, marketers often include a variety of need-satisfying appeals within a particular ad, television commercial, or promotional campaign. For example, a popular Mountain Dew advertisement depicts active, fun-loving teenagers enjoying hot summer activities. While the ad certainly appeals to thirst, other appeals to needs for love and companionship are also present. Another example of combined appeal to different levels of needs is in the Wrangler jeans campaign, "Live it to the limit." Wrangler clothes are promoted as the choice of dynamic, sports-oriented people who are intent on getting the most out of life. In a sense, esteem and self-actualization needs are appealed to as a means of marketing a product that might otherwise be addressing a simple physiological need.

Needs for Safety

Maslow's safety needs refer to needs for security and freedom from physical harm. They are both biological and psychological. Much of the work of the Federal Trade Commission and consumer groups has been to meet these needs by requiring minimum levels of safety in a variety of products. The Occupational Safety and Health Administration (OSHA) requires that employers furnish safe working conditions for employees. Products that have been used traditionally to increase safety and security in the workplace—for example, fire extinguishers, smoke detectors, and burglar alarm systems—are now becoming popular as consumer products for protecting one's home and possessions. Several major industries appeal directly to safety and security. Insurance companies, which represent the largest financial holdings in this country, promote physical and financial security. Institutions such as the Social Security system and employee pension plans have helped younger wage earners obtain financial security sufficient to allow them to spend a portion of their current income to satisfy higher-level needs.

Needs for Love and Belonging

Humans naturally seek out companionship. Affection and a sense of belonging bring joy to even the most introverted people. Family and friends are the most instrumental in satisfying love needs, but clubs and organizations, such as fraternities and sororities, are also important because they provide other means of satisfying these social needs. While many consumer products (such as toothpaste, deodorants, perfumed soaps, and razors) are promoted in relation to our needs for love and belonging, industrial and other technically oriented marketers also emphasize fulfillment of this category of needs by building professional relationships with buying firms.

Needs for Esteem

The desires for prestige, status, and self-respect are all aspects of our need for esteem. Humans fulfill these needs by maintaining their social status—their position in relation to others. Using—and sometimes not using—visible designer labels on clothing is one way that marketers have successfully appealed to esteem needs. Advertising often makes an appeal to these needs by suggesting that those who use a particular product will secure a more favorable status in the eyes of others.

The American Express Gold Card designs its ads to present its credit services as being more prestigious than any other. Although charging purchases, or using this card instead of another, makes little actual differ-

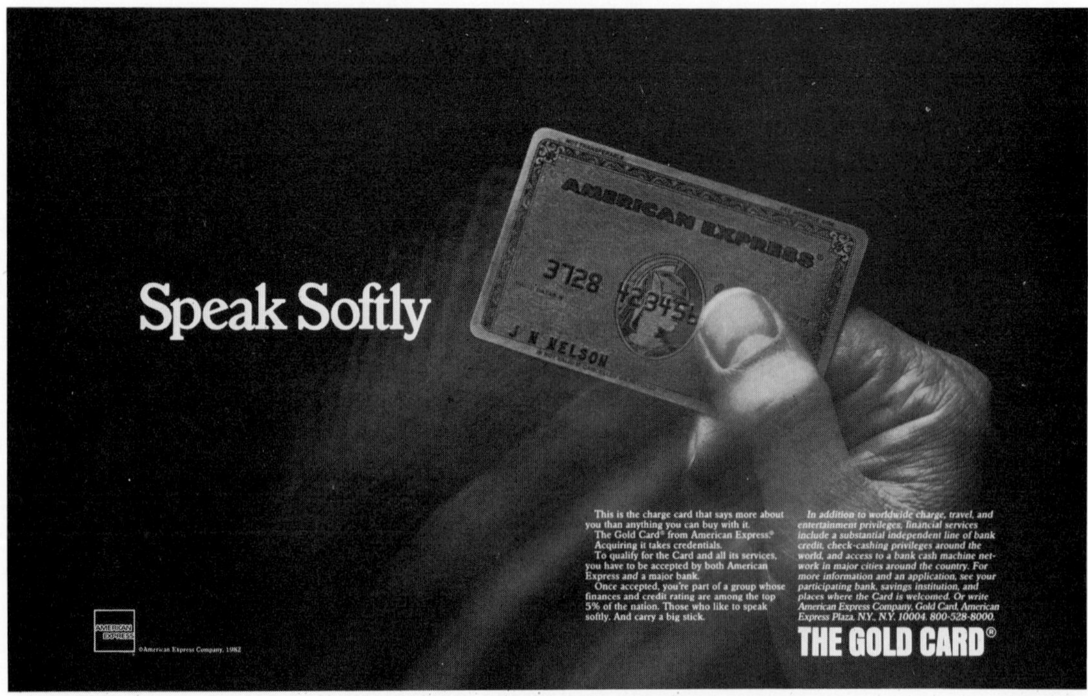

ence in the consumer's net worth, the advertiser suggests that using the Gold Card will cause a rise in the consumer's status and prestige.

Needs for Self-actualization

As people feel increasingly satisfied physically, safe and secure, accepted, loved, and esteemed by others, they become free to pursue a higher level of personal satisfaction in life. People at this level are motivated by a desire to develop themselves, to use their abilities to the fullest degree possible. In many respects, education helps people achieve this goal. Education is directed toward developing the whole person by providing the means for attaining knowledge and experiences that improve the individual's self-worth, sharpen talents, and promote personal growth in many areas. Higher education is one of the most important and expensive purchases people make. Activities such as backpacking, writing, skiing, painting, and composing, which are less expensive, can also fulfill needs for self-actualization.

Advertising Aimed at Needs

Maslow's five levels of needs are all represented in national advertising campaigns for various products and programs. Here are some examples.

- Advertisements for cologne and perfume suggest that use of a certain scent (Brut, Old Spice, Wind Song, among others) will lead to sexual gratification, a physiological need. In one ad, *Playboy* magazine is quite blatant in its appeal to sexual needs by showing a beautiful woman and the words, "Let's Get Involved." This combination makes the ad very suggestive, and to some controversial.
- Using slogans such as "You're in good hands with Allstate," and Prudential's "Get a piece of the rock," insurance companies appeal to the buyer's need for protection and security. By suggesting that having gas siphoned from your car could leave you stranded at night far from help, an ad for locking gas caps would be aimed directly at the buyer's need for safety.
- Beverage advertisements in particular are directed at the buyer's need for belonging. Having fun with friends is the theme of the "Stroh a party" and "Miller time" ads, as well as the "I'm a Pepper" (Dr. Pepper) campaign, which also emphasizes group identification. Bell Telephone has built a long-standing campaign around love needs: "Reach out and touch someone." A typical ad for De Beers diamonds is aimed at the need for love by appealing to those who are considering marriage, or who wish to celebrate their anniversary. Such ads imply that buying a diamond will help guarantee that the love will last.
- Fashion magazines tout Gucci handbags and other designer clothing and accessories as status symbols to appeal to the buyer's need for esteem. One ad for K-Swiss tennis shoes, for example, states almost directly that this shoe is a status symbol. The ad supports its claim by stressing the high quality which made it a status symbol.

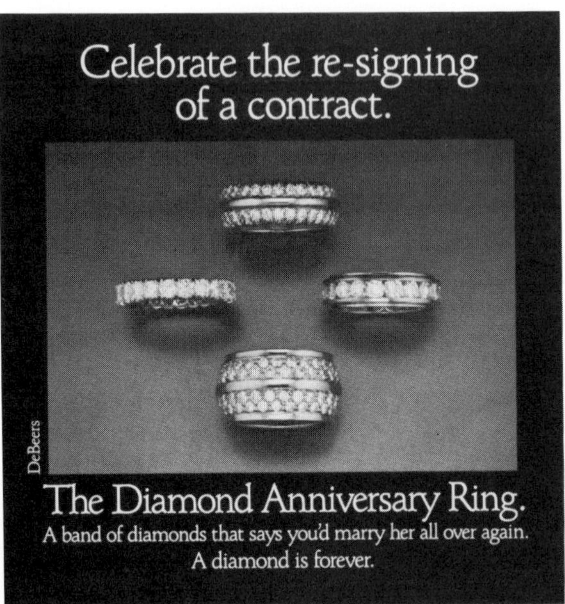

- The slogan ''Be all you can be'' has been used by the United States Army to recruit soldiers. The Peace Corps promotes its overseas work by offering a challenge as well as a reward: ''The toughest job you'll ever love.'' Ads for exotic cruises, skiing in the Alps, and foreign language lessons tend to emphasize the allure of exciting new experiences, expanding horizons, and personal fulfillment. An ad for *Scientific American* magazine appeals to the need for self-actualization through wider knowledge of the latest scientific advances. One advertisement for Johnnie Walker scotch illustrates how marketers may appeal to the need for esteem as well as to those for self-actualization. The ad uses the stairstep effect of office lighting in a dark building to convey an executive's rise to top management, encouraging the reader to view this brand of scotch as a part of the eventual rewards of personal and professional success.

Consumer Needs and Wants

Marketing executives are concerned with satisfying consumer needs and wants. Needs are fundamental requirements—the ultimate goals of behavior. **Wants** are *alternative* means of meeting one's needs or requirements. A person's goal object or want is simply a preference, not a requirement to satisfy a need. For example, if a person is hungry (has a physiological need for food) and prefers to eat lobster (the goal object or

wants

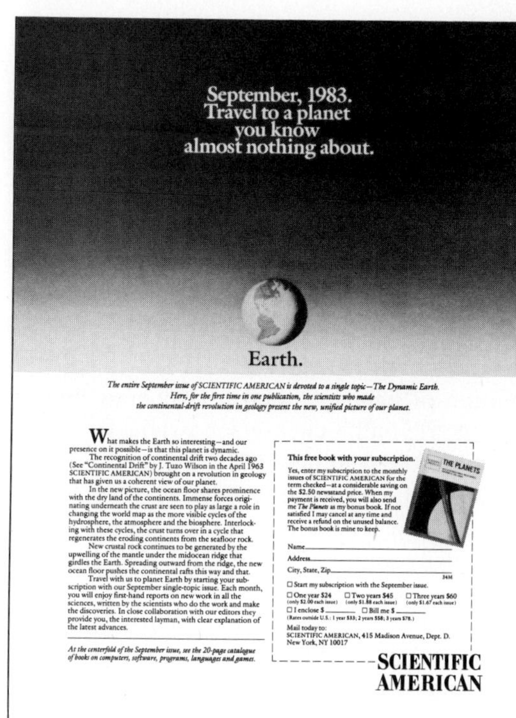

want), lobster is not the only food that will satisfy that need. Or suppose a potential car buyer feels unimportant in his social circle. He feels that owning a high-status sports car will result in more attention from others thus filling his need for esteem. The buyer *wants* to purchase a Jaguar, yet his sense of importance could be boosted just as well with the purchase of another high-status sports car.

Consumers often have more than one need and one want at a time. Product characteristics represent bundles of wants that help satisfy a

Table 2-1 SOME NEEDS AND WANTS ASSOCIATED WITH THE PURCHASE OF A FAMILY CAR

Needs	*Wants*
Physiological	Comfort, basic transportation Economical to run
Safety	Responsive in emergencies Rated better than average in crash tests Equipped with all the usual safety features
Love	Consistent with spouse's choice Favored by all family members
Esteem	High-status make and model, which others notice and aspire to own Customized with extra features
Self-actualization	Integrated with personal goals and social values Aesthetically pleasing design

combination of needs. Suppose a diner is hungry and has a choice between prime rib and a cheese sandwich. Both contribute to nutrition and satisfy a physiological need. If the diner were having lunch with a business associate, the prime rib might increase the need for self-esteem while the cheese sandwich might decrease it. Consumers often choose products to satisfy many wants that, in turn, meet several needs. Table 2-1 lists sample needs and wants for a family car.

In everyday business practice, marketers are not required to know a consumer's every need in order to satisfy his or her corresponding want. However, marketers can develop a better rapport with customers by recognizing the needs behind their particular wants. Consider the real estate agent who is showing a large colonial house to two separate prospective buyers. One prospect likes the house primarily for its location in a safe neighborhood (a safety need). The other prospect is interested in its design and aesthetic qualities (a self-actualization need). Obviously, the agent can relate to each of the prospective buyers better if their needs and wants are understood.

There is a relationship between a person's psychological development and the number, variety, and relative importance of wants corresponding to each need. According to Maslow, as psychological development proceeds, needs at higher and higher levels are taken care of, along with those needs below them in the hierarchy, progressively adding to the number of specific wants. For example, a welfare recipient who is looking for an inexpensive apartment, and is concerned about her own safety is at or near point A on Figure 2-2. Needs that arise between points C and D, such as having an address in the "right" neighborhood, are likely to be of

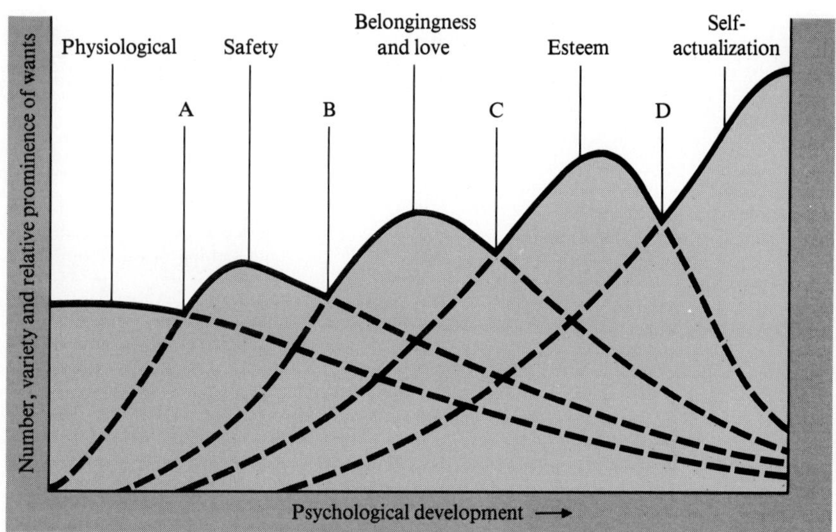

Figure 2-2
The Relative Predominance of Needs and the Number, Variety, and Relative Importance of Wants Recognized for Each Need

Source: adapted from David Krech, Richard S. Crutchfield, and Egerton L. Ballachey, *Individual in Society* (New York: McGraw-Hill, 1962), 77.

less immediate interest to her in making a choice of apartments. This shows that the peak of one class of wants must be passed before wants in the next class can begin to dominate.

Knowledge of the development of needs and wants might be particularly useful to marketers who use cultural buyer behavior studies for their international business. The economics of developing nations tend to center commercial activities on fulfilling the physiological, safety, and love needs, while more advanced, technological societies tend to devote commercial activities to higher-order needs. In any society, the environmental forces affect the psychological development of everyone in the population. As more opportunities become available through growth to satisfy each type of need, the want structures change from concentration on lower-order needs to those of higher orders.

Consumers' Need Hierarchies

We have already examined one hierarchy of human needs—Maslow's, in which needs develop in a simple, step-by-step progression from lower to higher level. However, consumers' need hierarchies are not as simple and straightforward as Maslow's. In fact, buyer behavior involves very complex structures of interrelated goals, all of which contribute to the attainment of larger, more general goals or needs. James Bettman introduced the concept of need hierarchies to the study of consumer behavior to show how consumers move from a need to an eventual choice of prod-

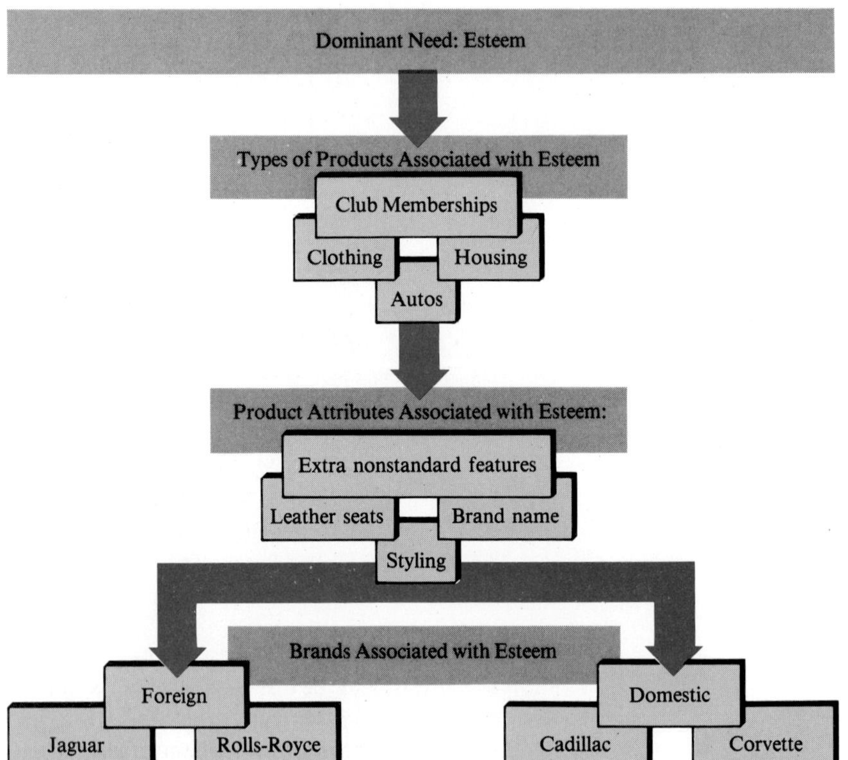

Figure 2-3
Simple Need Hierarchy for a Consumer Seeking Esteem

uct.[4] An example of a simple need hierarchy of a consumer seeking esteem is shown in Figure 2-3. In order to accomplish the general goal of gaining esteem, the buyer must put forth the effort to determine which product class, product attributes, and brand can best meet the need. Only then can a purchase be made. Marketers cannot do much about the need motivating a particular buyer; but they can influence the decision buyers make as they progress from awareness of the need to satisfaction.

Many psychologists have elaborated on the types of basic human needs that motivate behavior. Besides Maslow's work, the work of Henry A. Murray and William J. McGuire have been used by marketers to stimulate ideas for promotional campaigns and other marketing activities. Murray's and McGuire's lists of motives show the types of needs that can be met. Although these two lists are distinct from Maslow's hierarchy of needs, the differences are largely related to each author's degree of detail and focus. The three approaches have more similarities than differences. Each viewpoint can help marketers to understand consumer behavior better. No one list is "right"; each offers a somewhat different perspective worth considering.

MURRAY'S LIST OF SOCIAL MOTIVES

Henry Murray's list of motives differs from Maslow's hierarchy of needs in that Murray's list focuses on human activities as well as goals. Some of the action-oriented items on Murray's list that might not be considered human goals are rejection, aggression, and exhibition. Murray provided the basic concepts for the Edwards Personality Profile, which was used in early marketing studies (see Chapter 9). Table 2-2 summarizes Murray's list of social motives.

Table 2-2 MURRAY'S LIST OF SOCIAL MOTIVES

Social Motive	***Definition***
Abasement	To submit passively to external force; to accept injury, blame, criticism, or punishment; to surrender; to become resigned to fate; to admit inferiority, error, wrongdoing, or defeat; to confess and atone; to blame, belittle, or mutilate oneself; to seek and enjoy pain, punishment, illness, and misfortune.
Achievement	To accomplish something difficult; to master, manipulate, or organize physical objects, human beings, or ideas and to do this as rapidly and as independently as possible; to overcome obstacles and attain a high standard; to excel oneself; to rival and surpass others; to increase self-regard by the successful exercise of talent.
Affiliation	To draw near and enjoyably cooperate or reciprocate with someone who resembles or who likes the subject; to please and win affection or a sexually desirable object; to adhere and remain loyal to a friend.
Aggression	To overcome opposition forcefully; to fight; to revenge an injury; to attack, injure, or kill another; to oppose forcefully or punish another.
Autonomy	To get free, shake off restraint, break out of confinement; to resist coercion and restriction; to avoid or quit activities prescribed by domineering authorities; to be independent and free to act according to impulse; to be unattached or irresponsible; to defy convention.
Counteraction	To make up for a failure by striving again; to obliterate a humiliation by resumed action; to overcome weaknesses; to repress fear; to efface a dishonor by action; to search for obstacles and difficulties to overcome; to maintain self-respect and pride on a high level.
Defendance	To defend oneself against assault, criticism, and blame; to conceal or justify a misdeed, failure, or humiliation; to vindicate the ego.

Table 2-2 MURRAY'S LIST OF SOCIAL MOTIVES, continued

Social Motive	***Definition***
Deference	To admire and support a superior; to praise, honor, or eulogize; to yield eagerly to the influence of someone who resembles or likes the subject; to emulate an exemplar; to conform to custom.
Dominance	To control one's human environment; to influence or direct the behavior of others by suggestion, seduction, persuasion, or command; to dissuade, restrain, or prohibit.
Exhibition	To make an impression; to be seen and heard; to excite, amaze, fascinate, entertain, shock, intrigue, amuse, or entice others.
Harmavoidance*	To avoid pain, physical injury, illness, and death; to escape from a dangerous situation; to take precautionary measures.
Infavoidance*	To avoid humiliation; to quit embarrassing situations; to avoid conditions which may lead to belittlement or the scorn, derision, or indifference of others; to refrain from action because of the fear of failure.
Nurturance	To give sympathy and gratify the needs of an infant or any object that is helpless, weak, disabled, tired, inexperienced, infirm, defeated, humiliated, lonely, dejected, sick, or mentally confused; to assist an object in danger; to feed, help, support, console, protect, comfort, nurse, or heal.
Order	To put things in order; to achieve cleanliness, arrangement, organization, balance, neatness, tidiness, or precision.
Play	To act for "fun" without further purpose; to laugh and make jokes; to seek enjoyable relaxation from stress; to participate in games, sports, dancing, drinking parties, or playing cards.
Rejection	To separate oneself from a sexually undesirable object; to exclude, abandon, expel, or remain indifferent to an inferior object; to snub or jilt.
Sentience	To seek and enjoy sensuous impressions.
Sex	To form and further an erotic relationship; to have sexual intercourse.
Succorance	To have one's needs gratified by the sympathetic aid of an allied object; to be nursed, supported, sustained, surrounded, protected, loved, advised, guided, indulged, forgiven, or consoled; to remain close to a devoted protector; to always have a supporter.
Understanding	To ask or answer general questions; to be interested in theory; to speculate, formulate, analyze, and generalize.

Source: Henry Murray, *An Exploration in Personality: A Clinical Experimental Study of Fifty Men of College Age* (London: Oxford University Press, 1938), 80–83.

* Murray's term.

Another difference between Murray's motives and Maslow's needs is that Murray considers the environment to be an important factor influencing the individual's course of action. Depending on the subject's environmental situation, any one of these twenty motives could be directing his or her behavior. Thus, the motives are listed in alphabetical order rather than in a hierarchy.

Marketers have used Murray's action-oriented list of social motives to make their advertising more effective. Instead of displaying products against a static background, advertisers present their goods within contexts that have meaning to those with particular social motives. As potential buyers perceive models acting out these motives and being satisfied by a certain product or service, their own motives are activated and they may have an urge to purchase the product or service.

An understanding of human motivation does not help determine which brand or product features a buyer will select; it does help identify categories of products and types of activities buyers are likely to pursue. For example, a young man whose aggression, exhibition, defense, and play motives are stimulated might take steps to begin boxing competitively. On the other hand, a young woman motivated by autonomy, understanding, achievement, and order might be driven to pursue a scientific endeavor. An advertisement by Jordache is designed to stimulate the buyer's motives by presenting a product within a certain context. By showing a

sexually attractive couple relaxing in a beautiful outdoor setting, it appeals to the desire for sexual relationships, enjoyment of sensuous surroundings (sentience), play, and affiliation.

McGUIRE'S LIST OF MOTIVES

internal needs
external needs

Another psychologist, William McGuire, identified two categories of needs that affect mass communication: internal, nonsocial needs and external, social needs. **Internal needs** are satisfied by thinking and exploring the world irrespective of social activities. **External needs** center on interactions with other people. Table 2-3 summarizes McGuire's list of motives.

Table 2-3 McGUIRE'S LIST OF MOTIVES

	Internal, Nonsocial Motives or Needs
Consistency	The need for equilibrium or balance in thoughts and attitudes.
Causation	The need to determine who or what causes things to happen to us.
Categorization	The need to establish categories or mental partitions which provide frames of reference.
Cues	The need for observable symbols which enable us to infer what we feel or know.
Independence	The need for feeling of self-governance or self-control.
Curiosity	The need for variety and novelty.
	External, Social Motives or Needs
Self-expression	The need to impress, identify ourselves to others.
Ego-defense	The need to protect our identities.
Assertion	The need to increase self-esteem.
Reinforcement	The need to act in such a way that others will reward us.
Affiliation	The need to develop mutually satisfying relationships with others.
Modeling	The need to base behaviors on those of others.

Source: adapted from W. J. McGuire, "Psychological Motives and Communication Gratification," in *The Uses of Mass Communications: Current Perspectives on Gratification Research*, J. G. Blumler and C. Katz, eds. (Sage Publications, 1974), 167–96.

Table 2-4 THREE WAYS OF LOOKING AT HUMAN MOTIVES

Author, List Name	*Level of Focus*	*Features*
Maslow "Hierarchy of Needs"	Reduces motives to five basic needs encompassing most human goals	The five needs are potentially present in all situations and are common to all individuals. Each level of need must be satisfied before the next level becomes important.
Murray "List of Social Motives"	Lists many human activities (such as aggression and play) as well as goals (such as achievement)	Environment is a very important factor in social motives. In some cases, a combination of motives influences behavior.
McGuire "List of Motives"	Splits needs into two basic categories: internal (nonsocial), such as curiosity, and external (social), such as affiliation	List distinguishes between environmental influences and internal influences. Some motives may be satisfied by the individual alone, while others involve social interaction.

Maslow, Murray, and McGuire present similar concepts in different formats. Each approach can be useful as a means of viewing consumer needs in a particular instance. Table 2-4 points out general similarities and distinctions among the three lists of motives. The needs, wants, and motives reflected in Maslow, Murray, and McGuire are referred to in later chapters; motivation relates to the broad range of consumers' psychological processes.

THREE IMPORTANT MOTIVES

When motives are activated, they result in drives. The term *drive* expresses the action aspect of motivation, because a drive requires a person to act. The resulting actions, or behavior, are directed toward the fulfillment of needs.

In a practical sense, motives are the "fuel" which initiates the human information-processing system. Consumers act on their motives in order to solve a problem or achieve some goal. At one extreme, this goal might be as basic as finding a snack to satisfy a hunger pang between meals. At the other extreme, the goal might be to achieve one's highest potential by attaining an advanced educational degree. Thus, motives set in motion a series of information-gathering and -processing steps as consumers struggle to reach their goals. The process takes them from a point of need in their current situation to a point of satisfaction in the situation or goal they desire. By examining in detail three sample motives—curiosity, competence, and consistency—and the actions which spring from them, we can understand better how consumers' unseen motives and drives influence this problem-solving behavior.

Curiosity

We know from McGuire's list of motives that curiosity[5] motivates humans to seek variety and novelty. Novelty-seeking may take the form of searching out new and possibly conflicting information or products from those known or used in the past. Or it may involve simply varying one's choices of already familiar brands in order to relieve boredom.[6] What is new, unique, and different varies with each person, since each of us has had different experiences. In any case, evidence suggests that all humans seek novelty almost from birth. As is true of other motives, curiosity can be aroused by the impressions taken in by our five senses. Sights, sounds, textures, aromas, and tastes are called **stimuli.** When we perceive stimuli in our environment, our motives are aroused to become drives, which lead to action. One study concluded that the greater the amount of various and new stimuli to which children are exposed, the greater the motivation will be for them to seek out novel and varied stimuli as as adult.[7] Figure 2-4 illustrates a theoretical novelty-seeking process.

stimuli

The four major components of the novelty-seeking process are its antecedents, mechanism, motivational conditions, and behavioral consequents. The following discussion of each should help clarify how the drive for novelty is activated.

Antecedents

Antecedents are characteristics of the situation that precede novelty-seeking. The first antecedent in the novelty-seeking process is the collative properties of the external stimuli. **Collative properties** are the technical features of stimuli. They help us distinguish one stimulus from another. Collative properties include originality, surprise impact, and ambiguity. The second antecedent is the state of the consumer; the desire for variety and change depends in part on how much variety is experienced in a given amount of time. Therefore, the level of the desire for novelty is constantly changing.[8] Consumers who feel adequately stimulated in other aspects of their lives are less likely to seek out new advertisements, spending opportunities, products, and services than those who are generally bored. One study found that, after a new product was introduced, 15% of those who bought the product purchased it not because they needed it, but because it was new.[9] Also, the more similar the new product is to existing items, the less novel and appealing it is to those who are seeking variety.[10] The third antecedent in this process is personal and situational factors. For example, some people have personalities which

collative properties

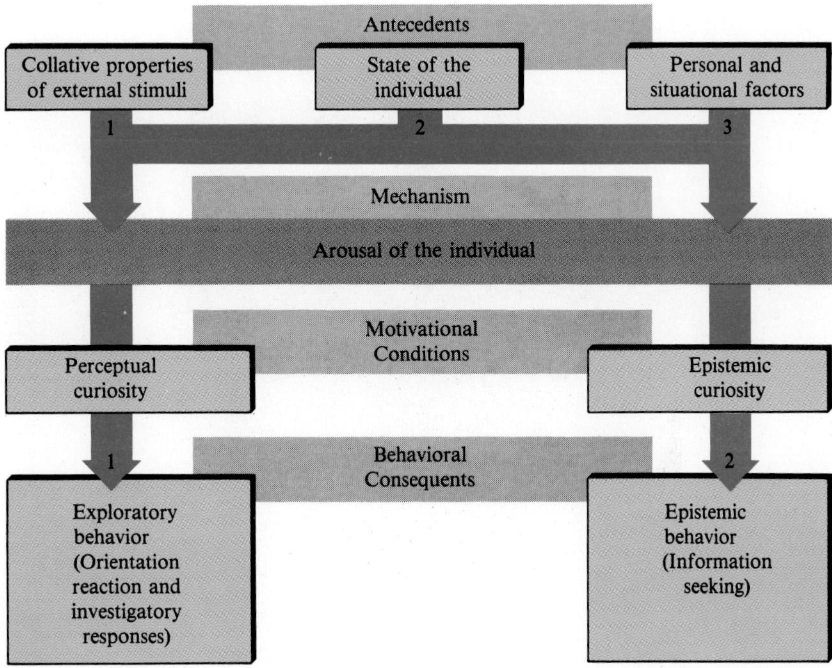

Figure 2-4
A Theoretical Framework to Describe Novelty Seeking

Source: adapted from M. Venkatesan, "Cognitive Consistency and Novelty Seeking," in *Consumer Behavior: Theoretical Issues,* Scott Ward and Thomas S. Robertson, eds. (Prentice Hall, 1973), 378.

are open to new ideas, while others do not; some are more able to afford new products and services than others are; and some can understand new products and their messages better than others can, perhaps due to differences in education.

Mechanism

The three antecedents trigger the individual's novelty-seeking drive, and at this point curiosity is aroused. There are degrees of arousal. On one hand, when a product or message has little novelty, the consumer soon becomes bored. On the other hand, when a product or message is extremely novel, the buyer is likely to panic. For optimal arousal, the product or message should not be too novel.

Much of the genius of the best advertisers is their ability to find the happy medium. One recent New Balance athletic shoe ad prompts curiosity. The unexpected visual impact of a lone runner going in the opposite direction from a parade of uniformed Russians catches the viewer's eye and prompts a search for further information. An interesting headline ("Why runners make lousy communists") helps to build the curiosity that stimulates the consumer to read the ad. Once aroused, the novelty-seeking drive is affected by two motivational conditions.

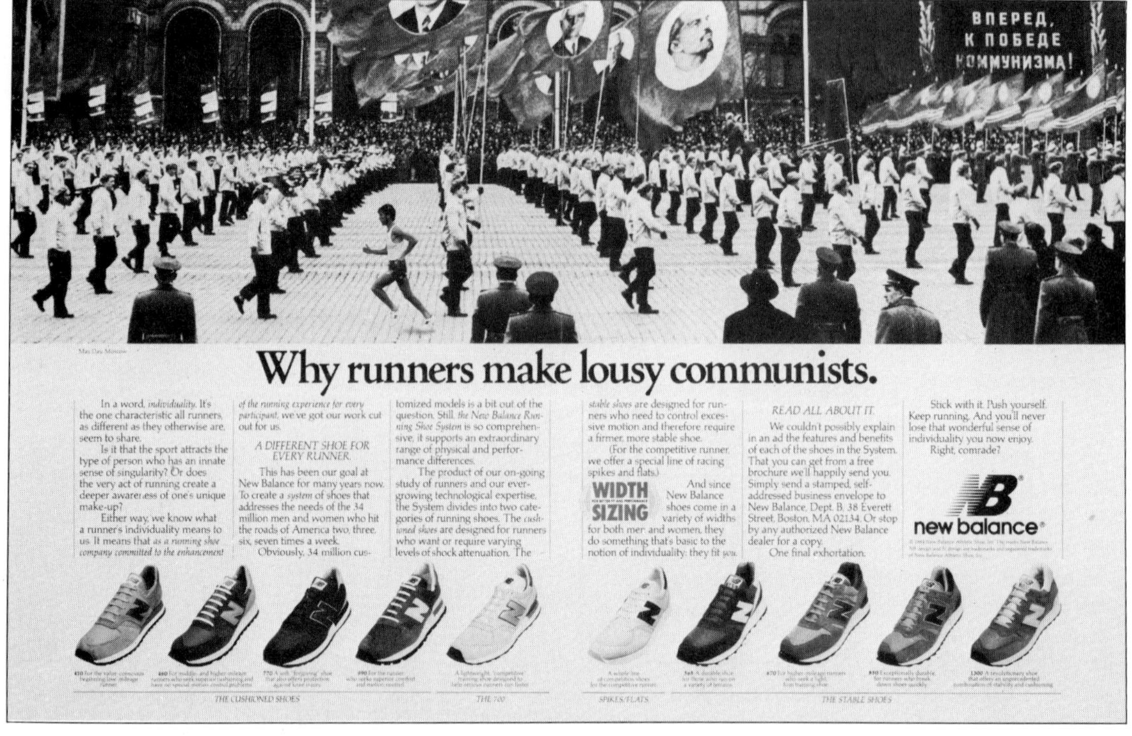

Motivational Conditions

This stage in the novelty-seeking process has been the subject of many articles by the psychologist D. E. Berlyne. His studies of exploratory behavior, which researchers have applied extensively to buyer behavior, have led him to describe two types of curiosity.[11] **Perceptual curiosity** requires a person to *pay attention* to a stimulus in order to make sense of it. Once the person clearly perceives the stimulus, this type of curiosity subsides. **Epistemic curiosity,** on the other hand, requires a person to *seek out knowledge* about what is perceived. A person can only satisfy epistemic curiosity by obtaining information about the object.

perceptual curiosity

epistemic curiosity

The New Balance Shoe ad arouses both perceptual and epistemic curiosity. The viewer may be attracted first by the unusual picture. Once the viewer sees and understands the visual setting, the ad encourages further reading of the ad copy beyond the headline to understand what is being said and learn more about the product.

While these two drives have different goals, each is heightened by novelty in products or messages and lowered by follow-through activities, or behavioral **consequents,** that satisfy curiosity.

consequents

Behavioral Consequents

Two types of behavior—exploratory and epistemic—result from the motivational conditions just described. On one hand, perceptual curiosity

exploratory behavior
orientation reactions
investigatory responses

leads to **exploratory behavior,** which includes **orientation reactions** and **investigatory responses.** For example, if a new household cleaning aid is placed on store shelves, a shopper's perceptual curiosity would be to try to make sense of the item by getting oriented to it (*What is this product? Where is it used? How is it used?*) The shopper would also investigate the item by using physical senses to perceive it (looking closely at the product, touching it, and smelling it). On the other hand, epistemic curiosity leads to **epistemic behavior,** or **information seeking.** This form of curiosity would lead the shopper to gather knowledge about the household cleaner from a variety of sources (asking the opinions of friends who have used the product, questioning store personnel, and reading advertisements). In fact, one study concluded that the probable adoption rate for a new, innovative product could not be determined until prospective buyers had gathered as much information about the innovation as they had about a product they purchased regularly.[12] This stage of the novelty-seeking process is critical to marketers, because at this point the buyer and seller begin to interact in observable ways.

epistemic behavior
information seeking

What conclusions for marketers can be drawn from this theoretical framework? First, shopping can be a rewarding experience for novelty-seeking shoppers if new products or innovative messages are presented in the marketplace. Second, the new product or novel message is only one of three factors that contribute to the arousal of a buyer's curiosity; so unless the other antecedents also favor arousal, advertising may not be effective in stimulating curiosity. Third, some buyers purchase an item for its novelty, without regard for its usefulness or inherent desirability. Fourth, knowing the perceptually curious buyer's need to explore new products, sellers can provide samples to promote this exploration.

Competence

competence

Another human motive that exists almost from birth is competence. While it is not a separate item in the lists of motives we have examined, **competence** is related to independence, achievement, dominance, and counteraction. It involves the individual's constant striving to interact effectively with the environment. A feeling of efficacy occurs when he or she has learned to cope with the demands of the environment.

Robert W. White, a noted researcher of competence, believes that

> there is *competence motivation* as well as competence in its more familiar sense of achieved capacity. The behavior that leads to the building up of effective grasping, handling, and letting go of objects, to take one example, is not random behavior produced by a general overflow of energy. It is directed, selective, and persistent, and it is continued not because it cannot serve until it is almost perfected, but because it satisfies an intrinsic need to deal with the environment.[13]

People seek competence in many ways and in many areas of life. They wish to be competent consumers, as well, for three reasons. First, consumers seek ways to satisfy their needs and wants as fully as possible. For example, upon moving to a new city, shoppers try to become aware of the types of stores there, how prices compare to those elsewhere, and other information related to increasing their shopping opportunities. They know that they can make better shopping choices when they have examined all the alternatives.

Second, consumers seek competence in shopping tasks for the sake of efficiency. The buying task is simpler and requires less effort once the person has become a competent shopper. Those who know that supermarkets advertise their specials in the Wednesday newspaper can shop later in the week to take advantage of currently advertised specials. A shopping list prepared in advance can make the trip to the store a faster and more efficient one.

Third, buyers want to be competent shoppers because of the personal satisfaction they derive from interacting effectively in shopping situations. For example, a buyer on a limited budget who has compared prices on a certain refrigerator-freezer at stores all over town, and then finds the same model available for substantially less at a factory outlet, probably takes a great deal of pride in being able to buy the desired item and still have enough money left over to pay for an unexpected car repair.

The competence motive also has implications for sellers. The degree to which consumers can achieve competence is partially determined by the environment: as more and more types of products, brands, package sizes, prices, and retail outlets become available, shopping becomes more complicated and consumers find competence harder to achieve. Many people prefer to make frequent stops at convenience stores, which often have fewer brands to choose from and higher prices, than to take the time and trouble to comparison shop at several different supermarkets that offer lower prices and many more choices. Furthermore, the extreme popularity of the supermarket can have certain drawbacks as a product showplace. Crowding in supermarkets has been found to lead to customer frustration, changes in shoppers' behavior, and dissatisfaction with the store.[14]

To the degree that marketers can help consumers achieve a higher level of competence by providing such things as product information and an environment conducive to efficient shopping techniques, marketers can begin to influence buyer choices. Understanding consumer drive for competence is important to the seller as well as to the consumer.

Consistency

How can motivation theories reconcile a person's desire for novelty (which complicates things) with a desire for competence (which simplifies things)? These two seemingly contradictory motives are balanced by a

consistency third motive: the desire for consistency. As McGuire defines it, **consistency** is the need for equilibrium (or balance) in thoughts and attitudes. Motivation researchers have developed theories of consistency to explain how a person brings conflicting beliefs into line. These theories are used by researchers in consumer behavior who are interested in how buyers resolve inconsistencies in their opinions about products, commercial messages, retail outlets, and other aspects of buying.

Here are two examples of the consistency motive in typical purchase situations: *The breakfast cereal you like best changes its advertising to feature an athlete you dislike*. Would you stop eating that type of cereal? Would you switch to another brand of the same type of cereal? Or would you start liking the athlete and continue to buy the cereal? In this situation, many people would deal with their mixed feelings by rationalizing that the cereal and the athlete really have nothing to do with each other. Therefore, their preference for the cereal would win out over their dislike of the athlete, and they would continue to buy that brand. Others would change their attitude toward the athlete to be more positive and continue to purchase the cereal. And a third group would change their attitude toward the cereal to be more negative, in line with their feelings about the athlete. The result, in the third group, would be a lower preference for the cereal. Each person's actions depend on which beliefs and opinions are most strongly held.

You must select a suit to wear to campus interviews with employers and to serve as the foundation of a new professional wardrobe to be developed after landing the job. It is important to make a positive first impression on a prospective employer. Yet this suit must also wear well for several years. You go to a prestigious specialty shop and buy an expensive suit. The following week, the same suit is advertised in a discount catalog for much less than what you paid. You feel a tension inside—what psychologists call *cognitive inconsistency,* a form of disequilibrium or instability. You may seek information about the suit that will help you resolve your conflicting feelings thus reducing this cognitive inconsistency. For example, you may ask for an impartial evaluation of the suit's quality and style from a friend. In the end, you may change one or more of your opinions. You may upgrade your opinion of discount catalogs, if you think the suit was a good investment. Or you may lower your opinion of specialty shops, if you feel their fine reputations are not matched by the clothing they sell.

The motives of curiosity, competence, and consistency are three examples among many others that influence consumer behavior. Firms are likely to study these motives in developing effective marketing programs. Most major marketers of consumer products employ in-house research staffs that regularly perform research to explore consumer motives and attitudes. They use their findings as a basis for product development and marketing strategy.

MOTIVATIONAL CONFLICT

Consumers select products and services that they believe will help them achieve particular goals. Because human needs are so numerous and varied, an individual consumer often seeks fulfillment of several goals in a single purchase. These motives may well be in direct conflict. How do consumer behaviorists explain what people do in circumstances of this kind?

Kurt Lewin, in his theory of conflicting motives, states that people move either toward or away from objects.[15] Movement toward an object

approach
avoidance

he calls **approach** and movement away he calls **avoidance.** These two types of movement—these two motives—allow for three forms of motivational conflict.

- Approach-approach conflict
- Avoidance-avoidance conflict
- Approach-avoidance conflict

Approach-Approach Conflict

This conflict occurs when a person desires two objectives but cannot have both. For example, a consumer wants both sports-car styling and family comfort in a new automobile. Perhaps the prospective buyer wants a Porsche *and* a Mercedes, but the family budget prohibits the purchase of both cars. In this case, the buyer would seek more information to refine goals and eliminate the conflict.

Generally, buyers must resolve approach-approach conflicts on their own. But sometimes manufacturers can come to their aid. For example, until a few years ago, toothpaste shoppers were faced with conflicting goals, both of which were desirable. They could use toothpaste with fluoride for dental health *or* brighteners for "sex appeal." Then research and development provided a solution: new brands that contain both fluoride and brighteners.

Avoidance-Avoidance Conflict

Consumers experience this conflict when they must choose between two alternatives, both of which are undesirable. This occurs more often than many people realize. The owner of a car with a bad muffler is an example. If the muffler is not repaired, friends, neighbors, and strangers are likely to make negative remarks or give the driver disapproving looks. However, if it is repaired, it will deplete the owner's savings. The owner wants to avoid both of these unpleasant situations, but must decide which choice of the dilemma will give less pain. People resolve avoidance-avoidance conflicts by selecting the least adverse choice—the lesser of two evils. In the end, the only reward comes from avoiding one of the painful choices. Perhaps the reason there are so many upset customers in automotive service centers is that they feel there is little to be happy about in a lose-lose situation.

Approach-Avoidance Conflict

This conflict involves good and bad aspects of a particular goal. We are drawn to the desirable aspects of something but are repelled by its undesirable aspects. For example, the purchase of a car will give the buyer the pleasure of driving but also the trouble of maintenance. Another example of the approach-avoidance conflict is experienced by the college student seeking an expensive but useful education. Paying for the schooling can be a struggle, but learning new skills is often a joy. Many types of purchases cause approach-avoidance conflict because so many products have drawbacks, side effects, or other undesirable features. In a sense, all purchases can be considered a mixed blessing, because the buyer must forfeit some money sooner or later.

The three types of motivational conflict and sample marketer's response to each are summarized in Table 2-5. Find other examples of each

Table 2-5 TYPES OF MOTIVATIONAL CONFLICT

Conflict Type	*Description*	*Sample Situation*	*Possible Marketing Response*
Approach-Approach	Two objectives are desired, but the shopper cannot have both	Toothpaste → Health with fluoride / Sex appeal with breath freshener	*Provide both benefits:* Toothpaste with fluoride that freshens breath and protects teeth
Avoidance-Avoidance	The purchaser must choose between two unpleasant alternatives	Muffler repair → Depleted savings / Bothersome exhaust noise	*Stress unpleasantness of one alternative to get desired action:* Muffler ads that emphasize how extremely embarrassing it can be to have a defective muffler, or that offer financing or delayed payments
Approach-Avoidance	The buyer's goal has both positive and negative aspects	College education → Hard work and expense / Greater earnings opportunities	*Emphasize positive benefits of desired action:* A college ad campaign that illustrates how long-term earnings compare between a college graduate and a nongraduate

type of conflict and imagine creative ways in which marketers could help consumers solve them.

CONFLICT RESOLUTION

When any type of conflict occurs, buyers are likely to stop and carefully reconsider the impact of the purchase on their various goals. Some people work out a solution by trial and error; others use a cost-versus-benefit analysis. Either way, learning takes place and consumer goals and goal hierarchies are altered. Part of being an effective consumer is knowing how to adjust to new goals, because goals are often subject to change depending on circumstances.

By studying motivational conflicts and how consumers adjust their purchase goals, marketers can begin to identify new products and information strategies (advertising or packaging) that will help minimize these buyer conflicts. The consumer often benefits from better products and services, and the seller may enjoy a larger share of the market.

Consumers are faced with limitations on what they can afford and use. Yet they are forced to make choices from vast numbers of desirable products. The way conflicts of needs are resolved affects patterns of consumption. Marketers can analyze these conflicting situations and choices and try to provide solutions that minimize the conflict and increase sales of the product. Recognizing an approach-approach conflict between one product and another, the marketer develops strategies to make the product appear different from and better than the competition, or better than the alternative uses of the consumer's limited funds.

Seeing an approach-avoidance conflict, the marketer identifies the product's strong and weak points, then either adjusts the product itself to eliminate the unpleasant aspects or employs communication approaches that are designed to accentuate the strong points and lessen the impact of the weak ones.

In an avoidance-avoidance conflict, the marketer must be highly creative to influence the consumer. The consumer with two unpleasant options is likely to postpone making a decision if possible. In these cases, a marketer may seek to emphasize the designed response as the lesser of two evils. An ad by the American Dental Association is a response to a common avoidance-avoidance conflict we all recognize. Many people put off going to the dentist for fear of a painful visit. The ad points out that a visit to the dentist is preferable to gum disease.

Can marketers predict accurately what a consumer will do to resolve conflicts? Using a variety of research techniques, marketing firms study consumer motivations and the underlying concerns of potential buyers in decisions to purchase products and services. Their general findings can help identify likely areas of conflict and potential consumer responses.

"At age 36, I lost 5 teeth.

Not to cavities. But to gum disease."

"I was always told I had such pretty teeth. And it had been years since I'd had any cavities.

"Then the dentist told me I had gum disease and I had to have some teeth pulled."

Gum disease.

It's the major reason adults lose teeth. And it strikes 3 out of every 4 adults.

Because, chances are, they're not visiting the dentist often enough.

So things like pink on the toothbrush and occasional tenderness are ignored.

Things like slight bleeding and receding gums go unchecked.

And that's when gum disease takes hold.

Make an appointment to see your American Dental Association dentist now.

Don't wait till it hurts.

ADA American Dental Association
211 East Chicago Avenue, Chicago, Illinois 60611

However, motivations are specific to each person and each situation; a foolproof prediction of consumer responses to conflict is not realistic.

Studies by James Bettman and others have shed light on the role of conflict in how consumers process information. Bettman describes consumer-choice conflicts in terms of *active* conflict response strategies, rather than some fixed pattern of responses on which a marketer can depend.[16] The dynamics of conflict make it difficult for a marketer to accurately predict exactly how a consumer will respond to changes in price or in packaging, for example. Future research in this area may provide new understanding about whether consumers are likely to ignore conflicts or use certain techniques to resolve them.

SUMMARY

Motivation is an internal force which directs behavior toward the fulfillment of human needs. Although a great deal of marketing involves attempts to motivate buyers, motivation theories are more useful in predicting the types of products buyers will want than the particular brands they will select.

Although the motivation research of the 1950s and early 1960s is now considered antiquated and largely wrong in its conclusions, it focused on why buyers behave as they do. An awareness of early research in motivation helps to appreciate the higher standards used in contemporary studies of consumer motives.

Human needs can be categorized in many ways. Some of the most commonly used classifications are Maslow's hierarchy of needs, Murray's list of social motives, and McGuire's list of motives.

Wants are alternative means of meeting needs. They express preferences rather than requirements. As more product alternatives are made available in a growing economy, buyers' wants increase.

Need hierarchies are constructs that explain how a person's goals interrelate. The purchases made by buyers accomplish specific goals that contribute directly or indirectly to the achievement of the general goals in the buyers' need hierarchies.

The motives of curiosity, competence, and consistency are strongly represented in buyer behavior. Sellers can adjust their marketing strategies to make full use of the buyer's drives to understand, to interact effectively with the environment, and to reconcile conflicting attitudes, beliefs, and opinions.

Consumers are often motivated to satisfy multiple wants related to more than one need. Motivational conflicts are experienced by consumers who (1) must choose between two alternatives, both of which are desirable; (2) are forced to pick between two alternatives, both of which are undesirable; and (3) must accept bad aspects as well as good aspects of a product or service in order to meet a need.

KEY TERMS

motivation
needs
wants
motives
drives
stimuli
antecedents
collative properties
perceptual curiosity
epistemic curiosity
consequents
exploratory behavior
orientation reactions
investigatory responses
epistemic behavior
information seeking
competence
consistency
approach
avoidance

QUESTIONS

1. In what ways has early motivational research contributed to today's study of consumer behavior? What are its major limitations?

2. Develop an outline of Maslow's hierarchy of needs and provide an example that illustrates each type of need.

3. Explain the distinction between consumer needs and wants. To what specific needs and wants might the owner of a fast-food chain appeal in designing a marketing campaign?

4. Motivation theory helps explain what interests people, but it cannot be used to predict exactly what they will buy. Do you agree or disagree with this statement? Why?

5. McGuire divides motives into two categories: internal and external. Describe the difference between these two categories and give an example of each type.

6. What are the marketing implications of the novelty-seeking process? Consider how this drive might be used in marketing (a) a new product and (b) a product already familiar to most consumers.

7. In what ways do buyers develop competence in shopping? Discuss the importance of (a) the consumer's perspective and (b) the seller's perspective.

8. Consider a recent motivational conflict you encountered in a buying situation. Was it approach-approach, approach-avoidance, or avoidance-avoidance? How did you resolve that conflict? What could the marketer have done to help you resolve the conflict?

NOTES

1. Philip Kotler, *Marketing Management: Analysis, Planning, and Control* (Englewood Cliffs, NJ: Prentice-Hall, 1980), 146.
2. John A. Howard, *Consumer Behavior: Application of Theory* (New York: McGraw-Hill, 1977), 137.
3. Abraham H. Maslow, "A Theory of Human Motivation," *Psychological Review* 50 (1943): 370–96.
4. James R. Bettman, *An Information Processing Theory of Consumer Choice* (Reading, MA: Addison-Wesley 1979), 43–72.
5. Material for this section of curiosity is adapted from N. Venkatesan, "Cognitive Consistency and Novelty Seeking," in *Consumer Behavior: Theoretical Issues*, Scott Ward and Thomas S. Robertson, eds. (New York: Prentice-Hall, 1973), 354–84.
6. Elizabeth C. Hirschmann, "Innovativeness, Novelty Seeking, and Consumer Creativity," *Journal of Consumer Research* 7 (1980): 284.
7. Leigh McAlister and Edgar Pessemier, "Variety-Seeking Behavior: An Interdisciplinary Review," *Journal of Consumer Research* 9 (1982): 331–32.
8. Leigh McAlister, "A Dynamic Attribute Satiation Model of Variety-Seeking Behavior," *Journal of Consumer Research* 9 (September 1982): 141–50.
9. George H. Haines, "A Study of Why People Purchase New Products," in *Science, Technology, and Marketing*, 1966 Yale Conference Proceedings, R. M. Hass, ed. (Chicago: American Marketing Association, 1966).
10. Michael R. Hagerty, "Variety Seeking Among Songs Which Vary in Similarity," in *Advances in Consumer Research X*, Richard P. Bagozzi and Alice M. Tybout, eds. (Ann Arbor, MI: Association for Consumer Research, 1983), 75–79.
11. D. E. Berlyne, *Conflict Arousal and Curiosity* (New York: McGraw-Hill, 1960), 283–303. D. E. Berlyne, "Curiosity and Exploration," *Science* 153 (1966): 25–33; D. E. Berlyne, "The Motivational Significance of Collective Variables and Conflict," in *Theories of Cognitive Consistency: A Sourcebook*, R. P. Abelson, et al, eds. (Skokie, IL: Rand-McNally, 1969), 257–66.
12. Peter C. Wilton and Edgar A. Pessemier, "Forecasting the Ultimate Acceptance of an Innovation: The Effects of Information," *Journal of Consumer Research* 8 (1981): 162–71.
13. Robert W. White, "Motivation Reconsidered: The Concept of Competence," *Psychological Review* 66 (1959): 297–333.
14. G. D. Harrell, M. Hutt, and J. Anderson, "Path Analysis of Buyer Behavior under Conditions of Crowding," *Journal of Marketing Research* 17, no. 1: 45–51.
15. Kurt Lewin, *A Dynamic Theory of Personality* (New York: McGraw-Hill, 1935).
16. James R. Bettman, *An Information Processing Theory of Consumer Choice* (Reading, MA: Addison-Wesley Publishing Company, 1979), 62–63.

FURTHER READING

Classics

Atkinson, John W. "Motivational Determinants of Risk-Taking Behavior," *Psychological Review* 64 (1957): 359–72.

Bayton, James A. "Motivation, Cognition, Learning—Basic Factors in Consumer Behavior," *Journal of Marketing* 22 (January 1958): 282–89.

Burnkrant, Robert E., "A Motivational Model of Information Processing Intensity," *Journal of Consumer Research* 3 (June 1976): 21–30.

Deci, Edward L., *Intrinsic Motivation* (New York: Plenum Press, 1975).

Ferber, R., and H. G. Wales, *Motivation and Market Behavior* (Chicago: IL: Richard D. Irwin, 1958).

Haire, Mason, "Projective Techniques in Marketing Research," *Journal of Marketing* (April 1950): 649–56.

Korman, Abraham, *The Psychology of Motivation* (Englewood Cliffs, NJ: Prentice-Hall, 1974).

Markin, Rom J., "Motivation in Buyer Behavior Theory: From Mechanism to Cognition." in *Consumer and Industrial Buying Behavior,* Arch G. Woodside, Jagdish N. Sheth, and Peter D. Bennett, eds. (New York: North-Holland, 1977) 37–48.

Maslow, Abraham H., "A Theory of Human Motivation," *Psychological Review* 50 (1943): 370–96.

Newcomb, Theodore M., Ralph H. Turner, and Philip E. Converse, "The Nature of Motivation." Chap. 2 in *Social Psychology: The Study of Human Interaction* (New York: Holt, Rinehart and Winston Inc., 1965), 20–27.

Weiner, B., *Theories of Motivation: From Mechanism to Cognition* (Chicago: Markham Press; 1972).

Recent Significant Research

Hirschman, Elizabeth C., "Innovativeness, Novelty Seeking, and Consumer Creativity," *Journal of Consumer Research* 7 (December 1980): 283–95.

Hirschman, Elizabeth C., and Morris B. Holbrook, "Hedonic Consumption: Emerging Concepts, Methods, and Propositions," *Journal of Marketing* 46, no. 3 (Summer 1982): 92–101.

McAlister, Leigh, and Edgar Pessemier, "Variety Seeking Behavior: An Interdisciplinary Review," *Journal of Consumer Research* 9 (December 1982): 311–22.

Rogers, Robert D., "Commentary on 'The Neglected Variety Drive'," *Journal of Consumer Research* 6 (June 1979): 88–91.

Applications

Brooker, George, "The Self-Actualizing Socially Conscious Consumer," *Journal of Consumer Research* 3 (September 1976): 107–12.

Cunningham, William H., and William J. E. Crissy, "Market Segmentation by Motivation and Attitude," *Journal of Marketing Research* 9 (February 1972): 100–102.

Domzal, Teresa J., and Jerome B. Kernan, "Television Audience Segmentation According to Need Gratification, *Journal of Advertising Research* 23, no. 5 (October/November 1983): 37–49.

Hamm, B. Curtis, and Edward W. Cundiff, "Self-Actualization and Product Perception," *Journal of Marketing Research* 6 (November 1969): 470–72.

Tauber, Edward M., "Reduce New Product Failures: Measure Needs as Well as Purchase Interest," *Journal of Marketing* 37 (July 1973): 61–70.

3 Perception

Objectives of This Chapter

After you have studied this chapter, you should be able to:

1. Define *perception,* particularly as it relates to buyer behavior.
2. Discuss the internal and external factors that influence perception.
3. Show the selective nature of the perceptual process, including exposure, attention, comprehension, and retention.
4. Indicate how the concept of perceived risk helps understand important aspects of product choice.
5. Describe product positioning as a marketing management tool.
6. Discuss subliminal perception as a controversial issue in the history of marketing.

Perception is the process of recognizing, selecting, organizing, and interpreting stimuli in order to make sense of the world around us. In a way, each of us lives in a different world because we are exposed to different stimuli. We interpret these stimuli in our own ways because each of us has our own set of experiences in the world; each person's history is unique. The different ways in which we recognize, select, organize, and interpret information account for differences in our attitudes (see Chapters 5 through 7). In this chapter we discuss perception as another one of the psychological functions that enter into the buyer's decision-making process.

This chapter begins with an overview of the internal and external factors that determine how people perceive the world around them. Then we look more closely at these factors in terms of the highly selective nature of perception: selective exposure, selective attention, selective comprehension, and selective retention. Discussing perception in this context allows a better understanding of why consumers vary significantly in what they perceive and how they respond to stimuli. Next we discuss product positioning, a technique applying perception to differentiate one product or brand from others in the consumer's mind. Research into brand positioning helps a firm determine how the various market segments perceive its brand in relation to other brands of the same product. We conclude with a review of the current thinking about subliminal perception, which generated intense controversy when it was first used and is still the subject of research.

INTERNAL FACTORS OF PERCEPTION

Physiology

Although many animals have vision, hearing, and other senses far more sensitive than those of humans, we know that the human capacity to recognize elements of the environment is great indeed. Pieces of information taken in through the senses form interactive and overlapping ways of interpreting the environment around us. To the extent that people differ in their perceptual capacities, their interpretations of the world vary as well. The internal factors influencing perception are those that are part of the individual person. (See Figure 3-1.) These factors may be basic ones, such as the person's physical make-up. People with vision or hearing problems do not take in as much visual or auditory information as those with normal vision and hearing. As compensation, such people may emphasize touch, taste, and smell, the other senses through which we gather information about an object. (Often people with normal senses also favor one sense over another.)

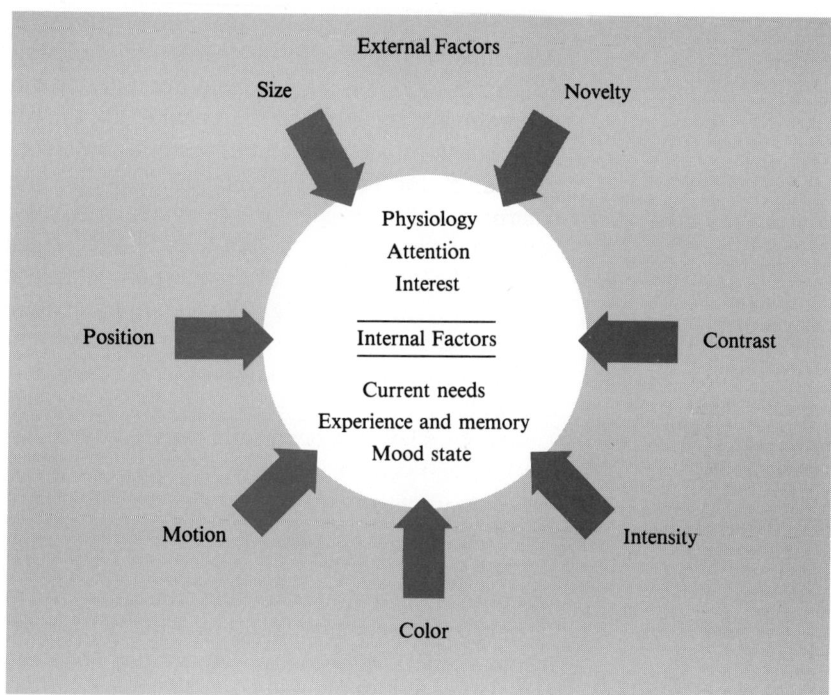

Figure 3-1
Internal and External Factors That Influence Perceptions

Weber's law

Weber's law describes the threshold at which a change in a particular subject tends to be noticed by an individual. The formula that expresses the law is

$$\frac{\Delta I}{I} = K$$

where I is the intensity of the initial object, ΔI is the smallest increase in intensity of the object that is noticeable, and K is a constant that could represent perceptibility (for example, visibility, loudness, taste, or brightness).

Weber's law applies to consumer behavior, since each manufacturer would like its products to be different from those of its competitors.[1] For example, Krylon spray paint has been advertised as being less runny than other brands. Krylon could use Weber's law to find the point at which consumers first notice a difference between brands in terms of paint runniness. Note also that since paint runniness is related in the consumer's mind to the durability of the paint and how rapidly it dries, any change proposed in one attribute in order to satisfy consumer desires would only be acceptable if it did not adversely affect perceptions of the paint's other attributes.

Weber's law has particular implications for the marketer's pricing strategies. The marketer of a gardening tool may wonder, "At what point do buyers notice a significant difference in price that would affect their perception of our product?" Assume that the tool initially sold for $10.00 and is now on sale for $9.00, resulting in an increase of 15% more customers for the tool. Applying the formula, the marketer finds that ΔI, which is $1.00, divided by I, which is $10.00, equals 10%. We could generalize from this that for a $100.00 item a discount of $10.00 would be required to accomplish the same percentage of customers who change their perception. Although there is no published evidence, it appears that price rebates may be more favorable to consumers than discounts on the original price because smaller rebates reach the threshold where they are noticeable.

Weber's law has been reformulated by G. T. Fechner. Now known as the Weber-Fechner law, it states that

$$R = K \, log \, (S + A)$$

where R is the magnitude of response, S is the magnitude of the stimulus, K and A are constants, and *log* is the mathematical exponent. According to the Weber-Fechner law, buyers use lower and upper price thresholds rather than individual prices to judge a product.[2] The significance of this law is that buyers do not judge prices as individual points but instead look at the range of prices. Objects are perceived as being priced realistically if they are within the range. If they are priced too low or too high, buyers perceive a problem in the pricing situation. Thus a price that is too low to be consistent with the image of the product leaves buyers with an uncertain perception of the product's effectiveness or quality. Prices that are too high for the product type leave buyers with the sense that the product was a bad purchase opportunity. Additionally, research has shown that the **price thresholds**—the points at which prices are considered to be too high or too low—vary with buyers' incomes. In one study, as income went down the price thresholds also dropped; moreover, the upper price threshold dropped less than did the lower price threshold. This suggests that, in terms of perceiving the product favorably, a low price is a more potent deterrent to higher-income groups than is a high price to lower-income groups.[3]

price thresholds

Attention

A second internal factor is attention, or the amount of energy a person expends to focus the physical senses and mental facilities on an object. Perception may seem to be automatic; actually, it requires effort. In fact, focusing intently on an object, or concentrating, may be one of the hardest tasks we perform in the course of everyday life. Consumers are constantly bombarded by a vast number of different stimuli. In the shopping environment, marketers struggle to attract attention through point-of-purchase (p.o.p.) displays that often incorporate eye-catching color or motion. A trip to the local grocery store provides a broad variety of tangible examples of these point of purchase merchandising efforts. In their effort to stand out in the shopping aisle, consumer-goods manufacturers spend millions of dollars on signs, displays, and other materials. Advertisers often seek consumer attention by using unusual visual images that raise eyebrows in order to encourage attention to the message.

Interest

Our perception of objects varies according to how much energy or perceptual vigilance we are willing to invest in perceiving them. **Perceptual vigilance** is the tendency to be on the lookout for certain types of stimuli. For example, sports fans watch for sports figures; they have high perceptual vigilance for that type of person in the media and in advertising. Therefore, a third internal factor of perception is interest. Simply put, consumers are more apt to attend to objects or messages that interest them. If marketers wish to capture the perceptual interest of certain customers, they can include visual elements in advertising that are likely to be of high interest to that group. For example, an ad for a product directed at the teenaged male might incorporate athletes or rock stars. By contrast, pictures of babies appeal to young mothers and heighten their perceptual interest in the product. An ad for Jockey underwear in a women's magazine incorporates a baby along with copy directed to the young mother audience.

perceptual vigilance

Current Needs

Another internal factor of perception is the consumer's current needs and how actively he or she is searching for the object or message in question. Hungry shoppers, for example, are more likely to perceive appeals involving food. In one advertising campaign, Burger King chose to broadcast its taste-tempting commercials on late-night television. Ads featuring the question "Aren't you hungry?" are clearly timed to capitalize on the probable need for food among the audience at midnight.

Experience and Memory

Other internal factors of perception involve the consumer's personal experience. Experience depends on memory, the extent to which a person can recall prior events to recognize a stimulus. Advertisers constantly strive to penetrate the consumer's memory and insure that their brand will be recalled when shopping occurs. Given two potential advertisements, a marketing manager may find that both ads communicate the

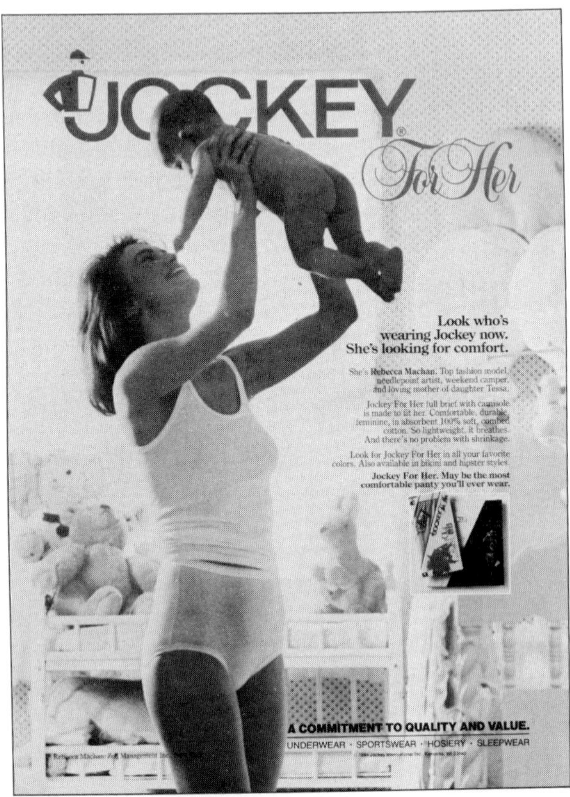

same message to the consumer. In such cases the selection of which ad to use often depends on recall scores. Recall scores reflect the consumer's tendency to quickly think about a brand when situations occur that could involve purchasing or consumption of the brand mentioned in the ad.

In a broader sense, experience encompasses the individual's entire set of prior encounters. Since experience varies from person to person, our ability to perceive and make sense of a stimulus varies also.

Mood States

moods Another internal factor of perception is mood. **Moods** are transitory emotional states which have been shown to influence shopping behavior. How a person feels at any moment influences how he or she will perceive, act, and remember. For example, some people shop when they are lonely or want diversion to cure boredom.[4] For others, shopping relieves temporary depression. Buying ourselves a "reward" can lift spirits and raise our self-esteem. The effect of moods on impulse purchasing behavior is a well-known phenomenon to those who have bought something when they felt depressed or bored, only to discard the product later.

Moods influence perceptions by providing a context in which brands are interpreted. When you are hungry, you are likely to perceive a Burger King ad more positively. A lazy mood influences people to think of brands as items to use for relaxation. A shopper's mood can influence perceptual vigilance toward those brands that could enhance positive moods or alleviate negative ones.

EXTERNAL FACTORS OF PERCEPTION

external factors of perception

External factors of perception are the characteristics of our environment and the objects within it. These elements compose our view of the world that surrounds us and influences how we perceive. From a marketing perspective, external factors incorporate products, pricing, location, and promotion. Managers adjust external factors in order to heighten perception and increase the attractiveness of market offerings. How a product is designed, what features it offers, what price is charged, where it is placed in the store, and how it is advertised all involve decisions about external factors of perception.

Advertising offers many good examples of specific external factors in daily experience. Size and position, color, novelty and contrast, intensity, and motion are the elements advertisers use to influence consumer perceptions favorably for their products.

Size and Placement

The size and placement of an advertisement have a substantial impact on whether the ad is noticed. In print media, readership increases approximately in proportion to the square root of the increase in space. Therefore, doubling the size of an ad does not double the impact. As might be expected, studies have demonstrated a clear relationship between letter height and visibility of copy on signs and outdoor advertising.[5]

Variation in readership of an advertisement is not greatly affected by whether it is placed on the left- or right-hand page in magazines and newspapers. In magazines, the greatest readership is usually for advertisements located on the covers or in the first 10% of the magazine. Beyond that point, readership differences based on size are minor. In newspapers it appears that the position of the ad is not critical, due to the tendency of readers to look at the entire content of most newspapers. However, readership tends to be highest when the message is placed adjacent to compatible news copy.[6]

One Tree Top apple cider ad features a larger than usual picture of a child and prominent product to capture the reader's attention. Although the child catches the eye first, the size of the cider jar ensures that the viewer will not miss seeing the product. Similarly, Tab chose to use a can enlarged to several times normal size to draw attention to its new formula.

Color

The use of color can have a major impact on advertising readership because color can enhance initial attention as well as help hold attention to the ad. Most products look better in color, especially food. Color can also create moods. The use of warm colors (reds, oranges, and yellows) or cooler colors (greens and blues) may affect the consumer's mood. Research also shows that television commercials viewed in color are, on the average, more effective than commercials seen in black and white. Joseph Bellizzi, Ayn Crowley, and Ronald Hasty conducted research which demonstrated that color can have significant drawing power in a retail shopping environment. In their study, warmer colors were more likely to physically attract shoppers than were cooler colors. The researchers suggested, however, that when marketers recognize that customers must deliberate over a purchase, the use of more relaxing greens and blues is appropriate.[7] In its ads for pineapple, Dole uses the three primary colors, with a deep blue, cloud-filtered sky as a background for the bright yellows and reds of a fruit dish and can. In color, the ad is a striking attention-getter that accentuates the fresh, sunny image Dole desires. (Chapter 16 discusses the role of color in establishing consumer mood in retail settings.)

Novelty and Contrast

Ads that rely on novelty and contrast as exterior factors of perception are often attention-getters. Chapter 2 discussed the importance of novelty in products and advertising: one motive of many people is novelty seeking. Perceptually, too, novelty, and contrast are important to marketers because novel stimuli tend to stand out from others. As the advertising environment become increasingly crowded with messages, consumers often may fail to attend to certain ads due to the many conflicting stimuli. The problem of advertising clutter often prompts advertisers to differentiate their message from others through unusual presentation. For example, placing a large border around a single ad may attract more attention than simply blending in the ad with other messages. Novel contrasts are used effectively by Oneida silverware to increase attention. The Bell System yellow pages began offering red type as an option to advertisers who want their listings to stand apart from others. Contrast also involves audio communication. The voice of radio commentator Paul Harvey is anything but dull. His unexpected pauses at unusual points in sentences, his inten-

Pure kid stuff.
CIDER
APPLE CIDER

LET'S TASTE NEW TAB.
New Tab® Taste
Now with NutraSweet® Blend*
Not available in all packages in all areas. Look for the new TAB label.
TAB
TAB

For salad lovers. Act I salad fork in stainless. Complete services and open stock at fine stores.
ONEIDA
The silver cube. Our silversmiths' mark of excellence. Made in America.
For a free brochure write Oneida Silversmiths, P.O. Box 1, Oneida, New York 13421.
For a 22" x 28" poster of this page send $1.00 to: Bunny Poster, Oneida Silversmiths, P.O. Box 1, Oneida, New York 13421.

Without Kitty Litter® Brand, cat box odor can be a crying shame.
If you're unhappy about how the cat box smells, just think how your poor cat feels.
What you both need is moisture-activated Kitty Litter Brand. Because only Kitty Litter Brand eliminates odor instantly. Moisture activates a patented deodorant that works like no other. It eliminates every trace of odor right then and there.
So do something nice for yourself and your cat. Get the one brand that eliminates odor instantly. Kitty Litter Brand.
There's only one Kitty Litter® Brand.
The one that's moisture activated.

tionally different inflections, and the novel cadence of his announcements appeal to many people.

One Kent cigarette advertisement used perceptual novelty and contrast effectively: a carton of cigarettes between two ears of corn elicits initial surprise. The contrast between the two objects is designed to stand out as the casual reader thumbs through the magazine. Similarly, it is difficult to overlook the novelty of a cat that seems to cry at the thought of being denied Kitty Litter brand cat box litter.

Intensity

The intensity of a stimulus also influences perception. Louder sounds and brighter colors are more likely to be noticed. In some communities, the local fire department has changed the color of its fire trucks from the traditional red to bright yellow or yellowish green in order to capture motorists' attention. In packaging, advertising, and point-of-purchase materials, marketers often choose intense colors to heighten perception.

Motion

Motion is a good attention-getter because of the contrast it affords in comparison with more typically presented, stationary scenes. Rotating signs and swinging displays are examples of ways marketers use motion to boost perception. Many roadside billboards feature changing letters or pictures to draw the eye. In department stores, a shopper may be attracted to an appliance display by the glass-front dishwasher in operation, or by a balloon dancing in the breeze of a fan. More obvious uses of motion include such massive displays as the RC Cola billboard that simulates a pouring bottle. More typical are flashing lights and arrows and the traditional spinning barber pole. Even in print, advertisers can add the illusion of motion to stimulate a desired perception. One ad for Fiat X1/9 uses blurred background trees and road to convey a perception of motion and speed.

SELECTIVE PERCEPTION

For many years, researchers have thought of perception as a highly selective process—that is, subject to the choices we make about its content, scope, organization, and duration. The four major stages in perception are selective exposure, selective attention, selective comprehension, and selective retention (see Figure 3-2).

Figure 3-2
The Process of Selective Perception

Selective Exposure

Every day Americans spend $200 million on advertising.[8] Each consumer is exposed to about 1,500 ads per day.[9] One study concluded that of this vast number of exposures, the average person perceives selectively only about 76 ad messages daily.[10]

selective exposure

Selective exposure is based on the fact that consumers actively seek or avoid information sources. They do this by choosing to be absent from the audience when unwanted messages are delivered, or by exposing themselves to desired information.

Consumers select their exposure to stimuli through their behavior. Choosing where and when to shop is one way in which they make this selection. Watching certain television programs or during certain times of the day is another. Reading certain magazines, as well as reading fewer or more magazines, is another example.

Selective Attention

We are constantly bombarded by millions of potential stimuli—far more than we can pay attention to at any given time. Therefore, we must continually choose to focus on certain stimuli and exclude all others. The process of focusing our limited capacity to take in information is called **selective attention.**

selective attention

We tend to pay more attention to stimuli that mean something to us as individuals. Research shows that people attend selectively to messages that support or harmonize with their notions of the world. They use perceptual vigilance (expend energy) to concentrate on information relevant to their past experience or future goals. This screens out irrelevant information, which would prevent them from making the most efficient use of their limited perceptual capacities.

Selective attention has many implications for consumer behavior. First, consumers attend to advertising for products they have already purchased (past experience) or intend to purchase (future goals). They screen out as irrelevant or distracting information that conflicts with their experience or goals. Because consumers want to make efficient use of their perceptual abilities, they attend to two types of information that make the task of shopping easier: general information, which provides a storehouse of knowledge for making future purchases; and specific information that helps to solve current purchase problems. Consumers ignore any messages that tend to make shopping too difficult or complicated.

They also avoid messages that produce fears and anxieties.[14] For example, many cigarette smokers ignore antismoking campaigns or "hazardous to health" warnings on cigarette packages. They may also rationalize their smoking by attributing flaws to studies that link smoking to cancer and heart disease.

Abundant evidence supports the existence of selective attention. Danuta Ehrlich and her colleagues studied recent auto purchasers and found they they preferred advertisements for the car they had purchased.[11] Stuart Surlin and Thomas Gordon indicate that people are more likely to receive exposure to ads for political candidates they already support.[12] And David Paletz and his colleagues, studying the audience for a movie with an antiwar (Vietnam) slant, found that the audience members were opposed to war beforehand.[13] In each case, those favorable to the object or message were more apt to attend to it.

Redundancy causes buyers to tune out an advertising message. Continual repetition of a routine message may defeat the marketer's purpose by causing **habituation,** a form of boredom which occurs when a consumer perceives that unnecessary information is about to be presented. Once a consumer is habituated to a message, he or she screens it out and fails to attend to it any further.

habituation

The following characteristics of stimuli affect habituation:[15]

1. Intensity. The lower the intensity of a stimulus, the more rapidly habituation is likely to occur.
2. Duration. An extremely brief stimulus is less likely to cause habituation.
3. Difficulty of discrimination. The more difficult it is to grasp the details of a stimulus, the less habituation is likely to occur.
4. Time. Habituation occurs more rapidly as time between exposures decreases.
5. Conditioning. A stimulus that has become conditioned so that it is of personal significance to the recipient will not cause habituation even when it is repeated.

Some repetition of advertising messages may help buyers commit the messages to memory. But if marketers intend to repeat an advertising message they should structure it to avoid the characteristics that cause habituation.

Selective Comprehension

comprehension

Comprehension involves how products and messages are interpreted by the consumer. Comprehension varies individually based on learning, attitudes, motivation, and especially on how the mind processes the information. Although message interpretation is highly individual, there are a few rules of thumb that can be used to predict how consumers will comprehend marketing messages selectively. Two approaches to studying comprehension are assimilation/contrast effects (social judgment theory) and perceptual integration.

Assimilation/Contrast

social judgment theory

Muzafer and Carolyn Sherif's **social judgment theory** helps describe how messages are likely to be interpreted. They have shown that for messages and brands that are more highly involving to the consumer, fewer brands are accepted and more brands are rejected. When the consumer is not very involved, more brands are accepted and fewer are rejected. Involvement refers to the degree of importance the product class has to the consumer. Consumers are more involved in product classes that are more important to them; they are less involved in those that matter less to them. Through a series of experiments, Sherif and colleagues were also able to show that consumers distort messages in favor of ideas that are closely related to their strongly held beliefs.[16] In other words, consumers tend to perceive messages about products that they already like as being more supportive of those products than the messages might actually be. Consumers tend to see even neutral messages as supporting their point of view. This process is called **assimilation.**

assimilation

Assimilation is well known in politics. Public figures who cannot afford to alienate their diverse constituencies tend to give middle-of-the-road answers to controversial questions, particularly during campaigns. Such neutral responses allow voters with widely diverging views to perceive by assimilation that the speaker is advocating their particular beliefs.

Television producer Norman Lear exploited assimilation in his highly successful situation comedy, "All in the Family." Each week, highly explosive social issues were discussed by the show's main characters, which contributed to the viewing public's interest in the series. By using a broad range of characters voicing the various positions on each issue, the show represented all views likely to be held by the audience. Although, Archie (the bigot) and Michael (the champion of liberal causes) consistently took extreme positions, their arguments were resolved in relatively neutral outcomes, which viewers on both sides of an issue could accept through assimilation. In fact, while many viewers considered Archie to be laughable for his narrow-mindedness, others who held Archie's opinions took his comments seriously and felt vindicated because, at last, they had found a spokesman for their point of view.

contrast effect

Messages or products that run counter to the consumer's strong beliefs are interpreted as being more negative or further from the buyer's point of view than they really are. This is called the **contrast effect.** For example, some people believe that small cars may be unsafe. Those in this group who own larger automobiles are likely to perceive a compact car as smaller than it actually is. On the other hand, those who own a small car often see it as slightly larger than it actually is, a perception that supports their belief that it is important to have a larger car to ensure safety.

Politicians use the contrast effect to advantage. When the press forces a public figure to take a stand on a controversial issue and the politician expresses an opinion which differs slightly from that of a highly involved voter, the voter is likely to interpret the politician's view as *very* different from his or her own.

Similarly, consumers are likely to reject any information that contradicts their brand attitudes, particularly to brands that they may purchase. This is equally true for consumer activities. A good example is the ineffectiveness of seat-belt use campaigns among nonusers of seat belts. People often play a variety of mental games in order to justify their opinions. When information about the importance of using seat belts is presented, nonusers tend to support their previous activities by distorting the message and then rationalizing that they tend to be luckier than the average person or that the seat-belt safety issue really does not affect them. One tactic consumers use to resist a conflicting message is to reduce the credibility of the source of the ad. For example, the nonuser of seat belts might argue that governmental sources cannot be reliable. They might also cite exceptional cases in which the use of seat belts was to blame for an injury. These issues have been addressed directly in a safety ad by General Motors.

Perceptual Integration

We comprehend messages selectively not only by assimilation and contrast, as the social judgment theory proposes, but also by closure, by our means of grouping perceived objects, and by the context in which we evaluate objects.

According to *gestalt theory,* what the consumer perceives as a whole may be more influential than the component parts. As people attempt to attach meaning to the environment, they group objects together to process the information. A total form is perceived rather than individual aspects. For example, marketers often use stylized symbols that communicate a relevant object, even though the symbol may only vaguely look like the actual object. The NBC peacock was once more detailed in its form. Now it is highly stylized, yet viewers recognize it easily. One implication of gestalt principles is that often marketers must consider the entirety of an image or message in developing communication with the consumer. Symbolic representations that emphasize a total perceptual form can be an effective and creative way to differentiate a product or establish a distinctive brand identification.

closure

Consumers have a strong need for **closure.** That is, they like to perceive an object in its entirety rather than in fragments. The process of closure itself can be reinforcing and thus contribute to the buyer's recall of a particular brand or message. For example, a series of advertisements for beer set the words to music: "For all you do, this Bud's for you." Some ads include the entire slogan. In others, the marketers switch to an incomplete message, dropping the end of the jingle: "For all you do . . ." Listeners are expected to provide their own closure at that point. The commercial's objective is to generate a greater amount of rehearsal and recall by requiring listeners to complete the jingle in their own minds.

One study showed that using an incomplete advertising message and allowing for buyer closure generated 34% more recall than using the completed version of the message.[17]

Although limited use of closure can be very effective, advertisers should be careful to avoid creating complexities that simply frustrate the consumer. If the consumer must exert a great deal of effort to make sense out of a message or a product, he or she may soon decide that the result is not worth the effort and then selectively screen out the advertising message.

Humans interpret information in chunks or *groupings,* according to four principles: proximity, similarity, continuity, and the halo effect. Together, these principles influence how one object is perceived in relation to other objects.

proximity

The principle of **proximity** suggests that objects tend to be perceived according to their nearness to other objects. The nearer an object is to others, the more similar they appear to be. For example, if social status is used to classify an object, nearby objects would be given the same general status. An elite women's shop located next to a K-Mart store will be likely to take on the image of the K-Mart operation in shopper's minds. On the other hand, locate the same store in the high-fashion district of a thriving urban center, and it will probably retain its identity as a select store. Advertisers try to place their product near those people and products whose association with the ad would be most desirable, because the advertised product is perceived in light of what surrounds it.

One ad for Diet Sprite uses proximity with an athletic, attractive woman to associate the product with a desirable appearance. An ad for Sterling cigarettes places the product atop skiwear and suggests that the cigarette is as extraordinary as the elite ski resort of St. Moritz.

Proximity also refers to the human tendency to organize perceived images in a rational sequence. In a familiar study, psychologists showed subjects the configuration of circles depicted in Figure 3-3 and then asked them to describe what they saw. In support of the principle of proximity, the subjects reported that they saw three columns of circles rather than simply twelve individual circles.

similarity

People also group objects according to their **similarities.** In another classic study, researchers positioned squares and circles as in Figure 3-4 and asked study subjects what they saw. Most of the subjects described three sets of objects: a set of squares, a set of circles, and another set of squares.

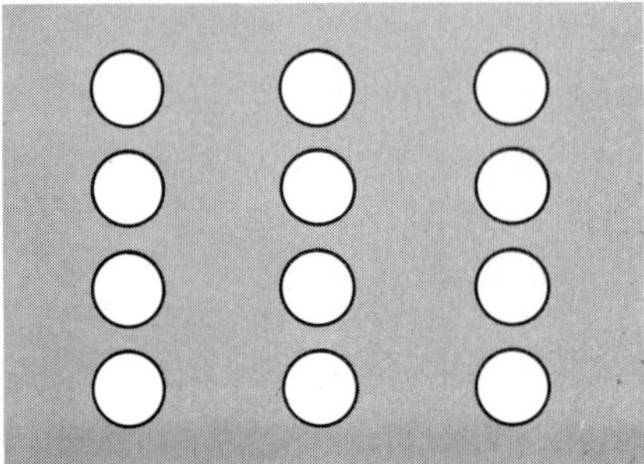

Figure 3-3
An Example of Proximity

There are many examples of how the principle of similarity is applied in consumer behavior. The standardized label design on family items such as Campbell's soup creates an image that embraces all of the flavors and provides a total view of Campbell's soup to shoppers. Sears has often used the labels "good," "better," and "best" to show the quality distinctions among its products. Shoppers see all "good" products as possessing about the same level of quality; "better" a second, higher level; and "best" the top level. Sears has used the Ted Williams label in its sporting goods department in a similar way, to convey an image of quality across a broad range of products from baseball gloves to fishing equipment.

The principle of similarity also applies to personal selling. When a salesperson for paint and accessories for racing sailboats called on owners of sailboat marinas wearing a business suit, she elicited a poor response from her prospects. However, when she dressed in sailing clothes and called on the same prospects, they were much more receptive to the new type of racing paint she was selling. The perceived similarity of her clothing to her customers' environment enhanced her credibility with the owners.

continuity

Continuity is the third way in which people group their perceptions. Images tend to be perceived as interconnected and continuous, as patterns. For example, for most people Figure 3-5 illustrates a sideways V made up of converging circles rather than seven randomly placed circles.

Advertisers can use the principle of continuity to direct buyers to perceive certain aspects of an ad. For example, the word *new* used on many product packages is found in a circle at the end of a line. This

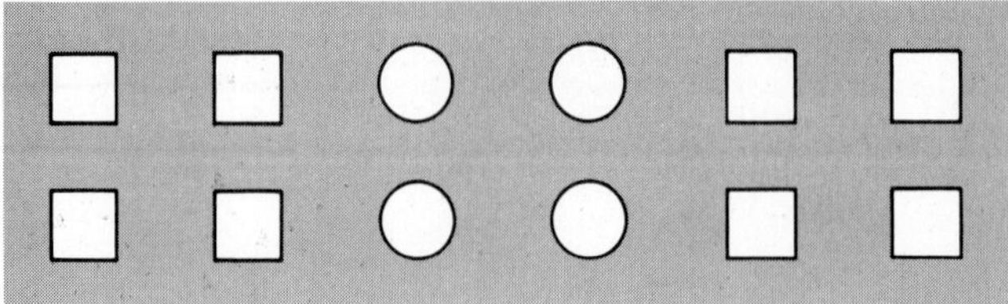

Figure 3-4
An Example of Similarity

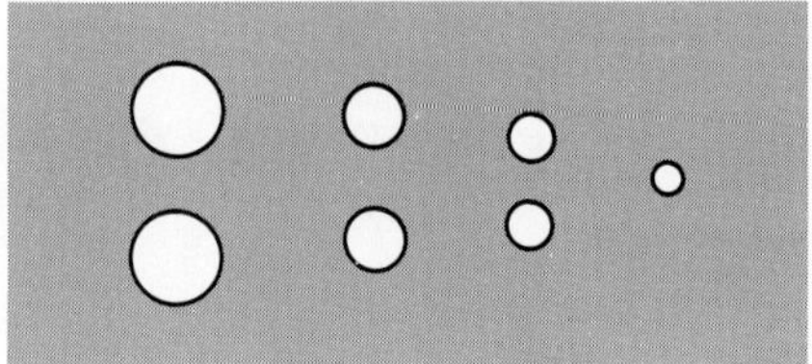

Figure 3-5
An Example of Continuity

arrangement helps to guide the buyer's eyes along the line so they will see the word being emphasized: *new*.

halo effect

The fourth and last way in which people group their perceptions uses the principle of the **halo effect.** Once buyers achieve a favorable overall image of a product, they also have a predisposition for favorable thoughts about specific aspects of the product. For example, for many years, Oldsmobile has focused its advertising on general characteristics of the car, such as quality. Oldsmobile's marketers hope that a favorable *overall* image of their products will lead buyers to have positive thoughts regarding specific characteristics of the cars, such as gas mileage, ease of handling, and smoothness of ride. Research supports the view that a halo effect occurs once consumers form an overall image of a product or idea.[18]

Fisher-Price has worked hard to develop an overall positive perception of its toys that will carry over to specific attributes such as safety, durability, and educational value. In the ad on page 83, the marketers expect the halo of Fisher-Price quality to help convey a positive perception of the characteristics of a new line of products designed for parents.

Because these four grouping principles of perception operate together, there is little wonder that a buyer's first impressions are so important in a sales situation. If a salesperson is wearing attractive clothes of good quality, buyers assume that the salesperson has good taste in other areas as well (*continuity*). Being surrounded by an attractive store, office, or automobile also enhances the salesperson's reputation (*proximity*). Further, a salesperson's pattern of behavior that reflects product knowledge, sales skills, and interpersonal skills conveys an air of overall competency to prospective buyers (*similarity*). And the salesperson's specific statements about the product become acceptable to the prospective buyer because of the buyer's overall first impression (the *halo effect*).

context

A third element of perceptual integration is **context:** Objects are perceived within a setting rather than in isolation. Contexts have three key aspects: frame of reference, constancy, and organization of material.

frame of reference

A **frame of reference** is the particular situation or circumstances against which stimuli are perceived. Consumers never perceive a brand or an advertisement in a vacuum. Therefore, marketers can influence perceptions by helping to establish a frame of reference in which the consumers perceive their product. The Cadillac ad on page 84 illustrates the skillful

CUSTOMER INFORMATION FROM GENERAL MOTORS

HOW TO SAVE YOUR LIFE AND THE ONE NEXT TO YOU.

OVERCOMING YOUR PSYCHOLOGICAL RESISTANCE TO SEAT BELTS MAY BE THE KEY.

The facts are startling. Experts estimate that almost half of all automobile occupant fatalities and many serious injuries might have been avoided if the people had been wearing seat belts. That's because most injuries occur when the car stops abruptly and the occupants are thrown against the car's interior or out of the car. Belts reduce this risk.

Many people say they know the facts, but they still don't wear belts. Their reasons range all over the lot: seat belts are troublesome to put on, they are uncomfortable, or they wrinkle your clothes. Some people even think getting hurt or killed in a car accident is a question of fate; and, therefore, seat belts don't matter.

If you're one of those people who don't use belts for one reason or another, please think carefully about your motivations. Are your objections to seat belts based on the facts or on rationalizations?

Here are a few of the common rationalizations. Many people say they are afraid of being trapped in a car by a seat belt. In fact, in the vast majority of cases, seat belts protect passengers from severe injuries, allowing them to escape more quickly. Another popular rationalization: you'll be saved by being thrown clear of the car. Here again, accident data have proved that to be untrue—you are almost always safer inside the car.

Some people use seat belts for highway driving, but rationalize it's not worth the trouble to buckle up for short trips. The numbers tell a different story: 80% of all automobile accidents causing serious injury or death involve cars traveling under 40 miles per hour. And three quarters of all collisions happen less than 25 miles from the driver's home.

When you're the driver, you have the psychological authority to convince all of the passengers that they should wear seat belts. It has been shown that in a car, the driver is considered to be an authority figure. A simple reminder from you may help save someone's life.

Another common myth: holding a small child in your arms will provide the child with sufficient protection during a crash. The safety experts disagree. They point out that even during a 30 mph collision, a 10-pound child can exert a 300-pound force against the parent's grip. So please make sure Child Restraint Systems are used for children who aren't old enough to use regular seat belts.

If you're an employer, encourage your employees to wear seat belts. At GM, we've made it a matter of policy that everyone riding in company-owned vehicles is expected to wear lap and shoulder belts.

We heartily support the program initiated by the National Highway Traffic Safety Administration to encourage the use of seat belts. So please fasten your own belt, and urge your family and friends to follow your example. Even the best driver in the world can't predict what another driver will do.

This advertisement is part of our continuing effort to give customers useful information about their cars and trucks and the company that builds them.

Chevrolet • Pontiac
Oldsmobile • Buick
Cadillac • GMC Truck

use of frame of reference in advertising. Here, Cadillac tries to create a perception of its automobile as an exciting, dynamic car that appeals to adventurous people. The desired frame of reference is established with the sailboat and the clothing worn by the principal person in the ad. Buyers are expected to perceive the Cadillac in relation to this frame of reference, which suggests *expensive* and *adventurous*. This ad is a clear example of Cadillac's desire to maintain an elegant image while increasing the automobile's appeal among younger, more active consumers.

constancy

The second aspect of context is **constancy,** which characterizes most people's perceptions of objects. Although everyday objects may be placed nearby, farther away, and in varying positions in relation to those who are perceiving them, we see the objects as consistent in their size, shape, color, brightness, and so on. For example, the sailboat in one Cadillac ad is depicted as smaller than the Cadillac. However, most people would visualize the boat as being much larger than the Cadillac. By observing the relationship of several objects in the ad, it becomes apparent that the sailboat is indeed meant to be read as larger. Most people perceive a man as around 5 feet 10 inches tall. A quick comparison of the

same man in the two pictures reveals that the sailboat must be a relatively large object. This ability to perceive *size constancy* across distances allows advertisers to communicate subtle relationships among a broad range of objects.

Shape constancy is also an important contextual factor. Our eyes tend to see rapidly moving objects as somewhat distorted from their normal shape. However, we comprehend them as they really are because we perceive their shape constancy. In advertising, movement can be conveyed simply by altering the dimensions of objects. Perhaps the most common examples of conveying movement through shape alterations are found in cartoon advertisements in which, for example, a car tire in motion is depicted as a slanted oval. The viewer is still aware that the tire is actually round.

Similarly, altering the color and brightness of objects in an ad can highlight certain features the advertiser wishes to enhance without necessarily affecting the viewer's overall perception of the brand. Variations in color and brightness can be used to convey lighting, which associates the object with a particular type of climate or weather. In the Cadillac ad, the shading around the yacht on either side conveys a pleasant sailing envi-

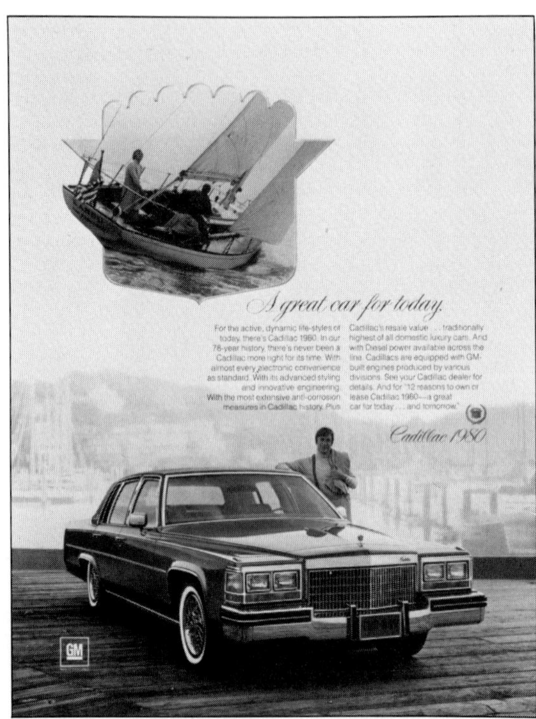

ronment, while the shading around the Cadillac conveys quality and excellence.

organization of material

Third, the **organization of material** has a great deal to do with how objects are perceived. We organize objects on the principle of figure and ground. The *figure,* or the center of concentration of a particular advertisement or presentation, tends to be in the forefront, more focused, or more clearly recognizable. The *ground,* which is used to provide the setting, tends to be less focused. Notice that the most prominent feature of the Cadillac ad—the car itself—is very focused, while the harbor background behind it is out of focus. In the middle is the sailing scene, which is only partially focused. Thus, the ad uses figure and ground so that the buyer's attention is drawn to the Cadillac, yet influenced by perceptions of the context—the harbor and the excitement of a sailing experience. The organization of the ad draws more attention to the brand and less to the setting. Yet the contextual aspects of the setting are preserved enough to obtain the overall effect.

Both outright and implied deception have been used to affect comprehension.[19] Outright deception (such as including false claims in advertising) has been the subject of Federal Trade Commission actions. Corrective advertising is sometimes mandated to marketers who overstep the bounds of "creative license." Implied deception has also raised the concerns of advertising watchdogs, but its use is often quite subtle. For example, an ad that overtly states one message may imply, through the setting pictured, that the product will have a benefit that is not likely to be available to the typical consumer of the product.

However, subtle association may generate the comprehension among consumers desired by advertisers where bold claims or puffery would fail. The phrasing of an ad for psoriasis ointment can convey the impression that the condition will be relieved when it is only the itch that will be helped.

Ivan Preston makes the point that consumers accept overinflated statements of opinion and belief, and that no one takes them so seriously that any harm can be done.[20] He quotes Judge Learned Hand of the Second Circuit Court of Appeals as saying, "There are some kinds of talk which no man takes seriously. . . . Neither party usually believes what the seller says about his opinions, and each knows it. Such statements, like the claims of campaign managers before election, are rather designed to allay the suspicion which would attend their absence than to be understood as having any relationship to objective truth."

Selective Retention

Generally, the way in which someone comprehends information determines how the information will be remembered. Just as consumers attend to and comprehend selectively the various stimuli to which they are exposed, they also retain selectively only those pieces of information they perceive to be important or useful to them. Like attention, retention tends to be highly subjective and based on individual preferences. Each person attends to and retains information in accord with his or her own beliefs, desires, or situation.

Marketers can use certain strategies to help facilitate the retention in memory of their product brands and characteristics. Research has shown that repetition of information often increases retention, even when the information repeated is a message that buyers say they dislike. However, when the same ad is repeated continually, it may reach a point of diminishing retention. It is usually more effective for marketers to carry the central theme of the ad campaign through several different advertisements. This strategy has been used effectively by Polaroid. Their series of camera commercials contain the same theme and format, but they use a variety of situations to minimize boredom and avoid the buyer's tendency to tune out an otherwise repetitious message.

A study by James MacLachlan of the use of time compression in radio commercials found that compressing the spokesperson's speech 25% (from 60 to 48 seconds) caused listeners to perceive the speaker as friendlier, more knowledgeable, enthusiastic, and energetic.[21] Prior studies have shown that time-compressed commercials enhance retention of the product information as well. This seems to indicate that the use of time compression can influence a buyer's perception of the spokesperson positively, which in turn promotes better retention of brand information.

Once a person selectively retains information, it is held until new information either replaces or alters it. Retained information may be removed from the memory (forgotten) when new, conflicting messages are assimilated, or the information already in the memory may be shaped by new information. This is particularly true when the new information is more consistent with the person's beliefs or goals. For example, someone may wish to purchase a Litton microwave oven but is deterred by comments suggesting that they are very expensive. Later, that person sees an ad comparing the prices of top brands of microwave ovens and sees that the preferred brand, Litton, is not the most expensive. The person then *forgets* that Litton microwave ovens are expensive and *retains* the information that other brands cost more.

The marketer must attempt to reach potential buyers at all four stages of the perception process. First, the consumer must be exposed to the product information. Then, the consumer must attend to and comprehend the information favorably. Finally, the consumer must retain the information. Because each person is exposed to a multitude of stimuli almost continuously, the marketer's job of reaching the buyer is an ongoing challenge.

PERCEIVED RISK

While working to determine critical aspects of consumer buying behavior during the 1960s, Donald Cox discovered an important construct for behavior research. He found that consumers perceive a great deal of risk in making product choices.[22] **Perceived risk** is a term used to describe the potential buyer's feelings that the purchase of a particular product could lead to unfavorable consequences.

perceived risk

Types of Perceived Risk

Buyers perceive the risks attached to making a particular purchase in four broad categories: social, functional, physical, and financial. A **social risk** exists when the buyer believes that his or her peers or family may evaluate the purchase negatively. For example, when a husband is worried about what his wife thinks regarding a new suit, he perceives some social risk in the situation. A **functional risk** concerns the buyer's doubts about whether the product will perform as expected. Functional risks include worry that the product may break down, may not have the service life expected, or may have some defect. A perception of **physical risk** exists when the consumer doubts his or her ability to perform adequately in

social risk

functional risk

physical risk

relation to the purchase. For example, the purchase of a week's worth of white-water rafting with an adventure-travel outfitter may hold fright as well as appeal for the buyer. Finally, **financial risk** involves the consumer's worry that a purchased item may carry with it indeterminate further costs. A family buying its first home computer with the intention of buying a printer and other peripherals later may be apprehensive about the shape of the family budget at some future date when accessories are to be added. This concern may cause the family to hesitate about the initial purchase of the computer itself.

financial risk

Elements of Perceived Risk

The following formula is a means of representing perceived risk (*PR*):

$$PR = (\text{the amount at stake} \times \text{the certainty})$$

amount at stake
certainty

The **amount at stake** is the negative consequence that would be experienced should something go wrong. **Certainty** is how confident consumers are that something will not go wrong if they purchase a particular product. Although consumers may not acknowledge it, research shows the importance of perceived risk in brand selection. Buyers do not purchase a brand if the amount at stake is too high and certainty is too low. Therefore, it is important for marketers to strive to overcome any perceived risk in the minds of potential buyers.

Reducing Perceived Risk

Marketers can reduce perceived risk by either reducing the amount at stake or increasing buyers' feelings of certainty about the product. Bringing more people into the purchase situation can reduce social risk. For example, if a life insurance agent suspects that a husband is avoiding the purchase of a particular policy because his wife might not approve, the agent could bring the wife herself into the discussion. Once she approves, the husband will no longer feel that he is doing the wrong thing. Second, a salesperson's obtaining statements from all involved parties regarding the wisdom of a particular purchase can reduce social risk. Joint decision making often reduces the amount of the consumer's social risk, and thereby raises the probability of purchase. (However, the decisions of buying groups usually require more time than do those of individuals.) Third, a price cut or a warranty or service package can reduce functional risk. Many corporations are finding a great demand for service packages today. In fact, service agreements can provide as much profit as the products themselves. This is largely because many buyers see a functional risk of breakdown in making major purchases, and they want to reduce that risk as much as possible by assuring themselves of expert maintenance. Marketers can reduce physical risk for consumers by providing guarantees and showing demonstrated service records for their products. Making price reductions, allowing joint payment, and renting the product rather than selling it are ways marketers can reduce consumers' financial risk.

Certainty can be enhanced primarily by giving the consumer more information, or by allowing the potential buyer to test the product prior to purchase. A recent study showed that omitting a product's attribute in advertising decreased the likelihood of the product being purchased. For example, if an ad does not provide prices the buyer may assume that the price is excessively high, even if it is actually competitive. In the study, the more important the omitted attribute was to buyers, the less likely they were to purchase the product.[23] Failure to provide the information may be interpreted negatively and may even cause potential buyers to avoid purchasing the product due to their uncertainty.

Tylenol's 1982–83 advertising campaign is an example of how providing the consumer with more information can build confidence in a product. Ads were designed to educate buyers about the product's tamperproof packaging, a new feature developed after several Chicago-area consumers died from taking Tylenol laced with cyanide. By providing more information, Johnson & Johnson, Tylenol's maker, overcame widespread shock and fear caused by an incident that no one had anticipated.

PRODUCT POSITIONING

The fact that an object is perceived in relation to other objects is also true of a brand within a product class. Consumer perception of one brand depends on how that brand is evaluated compared with other brands of the same product type. **Product positioning** is a technique marketers use to establish a unique image for their brand. By adjusting the product, price, promotion, and places where products are sold, marketers can differentiate their offerings from those of competitors in order to appeal to certain customers in a unique way. In introductions of new products, marketers carefully consider the product from a positioning standpoint in order to minimize competition or attract an unserved group of potential buyers.

product positioning

Marketers can use a variety of different approaches to build a unique product position in the marketplace. Six of these approaches are shown in Table 3-1 to illustrate the range of marketers' positioning options.

Perceptual mapping is a method marketers use to assess their product's positioning. A perceptual map graphically illustrates buyer perceptions of selected brands in relation to each other. Graphing buyer

Table 3-1 STRATEGIES FOR POSITIONING

Basis for Positioning	***Example***
Specific product features	A coffee positioned as the one that is mountain grown, implying a special taste that is difficult to obtain from other coffees.
Benefits, problem solution, or needs	A trash bag positioned as the toughest, most durable bag on the market and one that will not rip.
Specific use occasions	A restaurant that is positioned as the one to choose when you want to relax and not be hurried through your meal.
User category	A sporty truck that is positioned for off-road enthusiasts and risk takers.
Against another product	A ketchup that is positioned as thicker than the closest competitor.
Product class disassociation	Positioned as apart from a given class, such as orange juice positioned as a drink that is not just for breakfast.

Source: adapted from Yoram J. Wind, *Product Policy: Concepts, Methods and Strategy* (Reading, MA: Addison-Wesley, 1982), 79–81.

perceptions of brands on a two- or three-dimensional map provides a convenient way for marketers to visualize their market. Figure 3-6 is an example of a perceptual map for the beer market in Chicago.

This perceptual map is based on the results of interviews with 500 male beer drinkers conducted in the Chicago area in 1968 by Market Facts' Consumer Mail Panels. The two overriding ranges of characteristics used by participants to evaluate the beers were (1) low price and low quality versus high price and high quality, and (2) lightness versus heaviness. Thus, degrees of price and quality formed the horizontal axis and lightness or heaviness became the vertical axis of the perceptual map. The researchers asked the survey respondents to evaluate eight brands of beer on 35 attributes, some of which are shown on the map. The brands labeled A, B, C, and D were selected from relatively unknown local beers and the other four were easily recognizable national brands. The respondents perceived Budweiser as the highest quality, most full-bodied and thirst-quenching beer, while Miller was seen as a light, mild beer, more popular with women. This kind of study helps marketers determine how buyers perceive their products so that they can either reinforce the image or develop a strategy to change it to one that appeals to a different, perhaps larger target market.

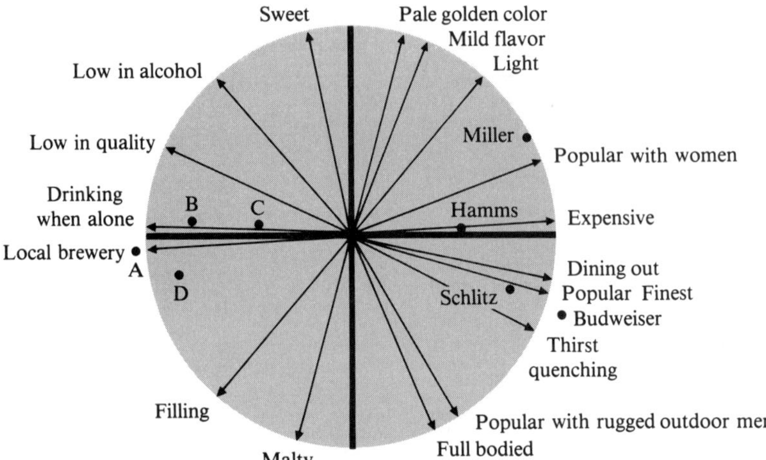

Figure 3-6
A Perceptual Map of the Chicago Beer Market

Source: Richard M. Johnson, "Market Segmentation: A Strategic Management Tool," *Journal of Marketing Research* 8 (1971): 13–18.

Methods of Creating Perceptual Maps

Several methods may be used to construct perceptual maps. However, it is important that the method produce a metric representation of the brands in relation to one another. Distances between the brands on the perceptual map should correspond to the relative differences between brands. Additionally, the method must identify the criteria buyers use to judge the brands. To meet these requirements, researchers use either similarity/dissimilarity data or attribute data.

Using **similarity/dissimilarity** data requires that subjects rate the products according to how similar they are to each other. For example, subjects may be asked to arrange all possible pairs of several products from the most similar pair to the least similar pair. Or respondents are presented with three products and asked to pick the two that are most similar. Computers can quickly sort out which products are most closely related to each other in the subjects' minds and can then translate this rank-order data into metrically scaled brand configurations. Because the products are compared simultaneously with each other, many comparisons are possible from very few brands. The number of possible comparisons is equal to $N \times (N - 1) \div 2$, where N is the number of brands. For example, nine brands compared with each other would provide $9 \times 8 \div 2$, or 36, paired comparisons. Working with this much data, computer programs can provide a relatively accurate perceptual map. This technique is generally used when a researcher does not know at the outset the points of reference buyers use in judging brands.

attribute data

Researchers use **attribute data,** on the other hand, when they know the relevant criteria buyers use when comparing the brands in question. As the beer example showed, characteristics such as price and quality, heaviness and lightness, masculinity and femininity can be used. Attribute data provides a great deal more information about buyer prcferences for each brand and the relative positioning of brands based on those attributes.

Attribute data may be metric or nonmetric, depending on the scaling techniques used. Nonmetric procedures simply require subjects to rank the brands regarding each attribute, whereas metric techniques require the respondents to estimate the *amount* of difference they perceive in the brands. In either case, computer programs provide a scaled output that shows how the brands relate to each other on each characteristic the subjects are asked to use.

Integrating Preference Data

Similarity/dissimilarity and attribute data provide the researcher with a perceptual map that shows buyers' perceptions of brands in a market. Marketers can determine further which types of consumers prefer which brands by gathering preference data. **Preference data** provides ratings or rankings of various brands on a most preferred–least preferred basis. By integrating preference data from various types of consumers (representing market segments) with perceptual maps of the brands, researchers can easily see the product characteristics that would be most preferable to each type of consumer. An **ideal point** is the position on a perceptual map at which the ideal product for a specific market segment tends to fall. The ideal point shows where the brand would be positioned to best meet the perceived desires of consumers in that market segment. The ideal points for eight beer market segments are shown as circles in Figure 3-7. The size of the circles corresponds to the relative size of the market segment.

preference data

ideal point

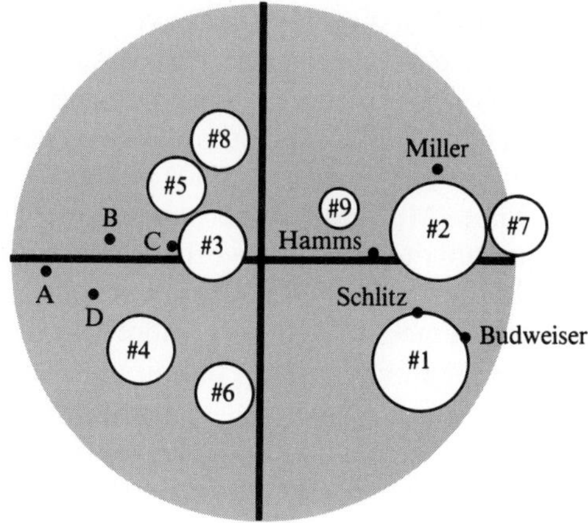

Figure 3-7
Distribution of Ideal Points in Product Size

Source: Richard M. Johnson, "Market Segmentation: A Strategic Management Tool," *Journal of Marketing Research* 8 (1971): 13–18.

Preferences and Context

Although perceptions of a brand are unlikely to change, the buyer's preference for a brand may vary according to how the brand is used. For example, the brand of beer a buyer prefers to serve to guests at a dinner party might be considerably different than the brand the buyer prefers to take on a fishing trip. Marketers often develop a preference map for each context in which their product is likely to be used.

Although many researchers use sophisticated computer programs to create perceptual and preference maps, less elaborate methods can produce adequate maps. For example, Chrysler Corporation has collected data from industry sources on four or five key reasons why various market segments purchase Chrysler models or other car makes. They have simply taken a sample of that data and manually drawn the buyers' perceptions of their cars. In this way, Chrysler management has been able to monitor the public perception of each of its models relative to its competition. Chrysler has also used this method to determine informally the effects of promotional campaigns on the image of their products.

When computer methods are unavailable, researchers can ask buyers to draw their own perceptual maps of selected products. These maps can be aggregated to create a relatively accurate picture of what buyers believe to be their own perceptions of these products.

SUBLIMINAL PERCEPTION

Up to this point, we have considered perception to occur when objects are recognizably apparent to buyers. However, for several years advertisers have attempted to change public perceptions of their products subliminally. **Subliminal stimulation** of perception is generally defined as a condition in which a stimulus may have some effect on a person, but the person is unaware of or denies any knowledge of the stimulus. Implied in this concept is that perception may occur below the threshold of consciousness. Thus a subliminal stimulus is a message designed to be presented to buyers so that they cannot recognize it or its characteristics.

subliminal stimulation

In 1957 James M. Vicary experimented in a New Jersey movie theater using an apparatus to flash the words, "Eat popcorn" and "Drink Coca-Cola" onto a screen for 1/3000th of a second, approximately every five seconds. He claimed to sell 57% more popcorn and 17% more Coke. Although the Federal Trade Commission was interested in Vicary's study, he never made available any scientific data to support his conclusions. Additionally, replication of the study has never produced positive results. This has led researchers to conclude that subliminal messages have little direct effect on consumer behavior.[24] This is not to say that subliminal perception has absolutely no effect on people; there is some evidence that, while subliminal perceptions of stimuli might not directly influence behavior, they can influence *awareness* and therefore indirectly influence behavior.

Sandra Hart and Steven McDaniel recently completed a review of most of the major studies on subliminal stimulation. They conclude that subliminal stimulation can, in fact affect dreams, memory, adaptation, conscious perception, verbal behavior, emotions, and drives. However, most of the studies they reviewed were based on psychology, not on advertising. According to Hart and McDaniel, very few studies have been done on the effects of advertising at the subliminal level. They cite several studies relating to physiological drives. For example, in two separate studies subjects became more hungry when presented with food words at the subliminal level. In another study, researchers were able to stimulate the thirst drive effectively using subliminal stimulation. In yet another study, a subliminal sexual message was embedded in advertisements; after some exposure, respondents were found to have enhanced sexual feelings.[25]

Wilson Bryan Key's book on subliminal messages, *Subliminal Seduction,* stimulated much interest among the general public in this area.[26] Key described subtle images inserted in ads to "sell" the consumer's subconscious on the product. One example he offers is that of a rum ad in which the words *U Buy* were painted into the shadows at the bottom of a glass. Further, the retouch artist painted the words in mirror image, according to Key. He reports that experimental subjects overwhelmingly chose this brand of rum over other brands after seeing ads for each. According to Key, the unconscious mind is capable of reading even upside-down mirror images. He added that some of the subjects were not even rum drinkers. In his chapter, "Sex Is Alive and Embedded in Practically Everything," Key argues that emotionally loaded words and pictures are inserted in most advertising in North America. He adds that *sex* is the most frequently embedded word used as a subliminal trigger to motivate purchasing behavior.

However, many researchers doubt such claims for its effectiveness and widespread impact. Efforts to demonstrate consistently the behavioral effects of subliminal stimulation have not been documented to the satisfaction of most professionals in the field. Some elaborate attempts to change behavior using subliminal advertising produced no results whatsoever. In one study, male subjects were given two perfume advertisements: one using subliminal imagery, the other containing no subliminal clues. The subliminal ad, which showed the brand name of one perfume superimposed over a seductive picture of a woman, had the same effect as the nonsubliminal ad. In another study, J. Steven Kelly selected ads containing subliminal messages from Key's book.[27] Kelly bound the ads in a dummy magazine and allowed subjects to look at the magazine. Then he retested them on their ability to recall the brands or illustrations of the ads. He found that the subliminal aspects of the advertisements had no effect whatsoever on brand recall.

Hart and McDaniel have arrived at several conclusions regarding subliminal advertising:[28]

1. Individuals *do* have the ability to perceive stimuli at a subliminal and unconscious level.
2. Some types of behavior change *might* be influenced by subliminal stimulation.
3. *Physiological drives,* such as hunger, thirst, and sex may be aroused by the use of subliminal stimuli.
4. Brand preference and ad recall appear to be *unaffected* by subliminal inputs or subliminal messages.
5. There is virtually *no* support for the claim that subliminal advertising affects a person's buying behavior.

While subliminal perception is possible, it clearly has little effect on buyer behavior at this point. Because the National Association of Broadcasters in its code for television specifically prohibits subliminal advertising, there is little likelihood that subliminal advertising will find its way into viewers' homes. Further, the Federal Trade Commission and the Federal Communications Commission both have regulations prohibiting the use of subliminal advertising—although the fact that marketers have not been inclined to use this type of promotion means that these agencies have not had to confront any major companies regarding this issue. Certainly, advertisers who are competent in the field of consumer behavior are familiar with many ways of influencing buyers that are supported by much more scholarly evidence than is subliminal advertising.

SUMMARY

Perception is the process of recognizing, selecting, organizing, and interpreting stimuli in order to make sense of the world around us. Perceptions are influenced by our individual experiences and are therefore highly subjective.

Internal factors influencing perception include physiology, attention to stimuli, interests, current needs, experience, memories, and moods. Physiological factors are those of the senses: some consumers see, hear, smell, and think more acutely than others do. Each of the senses influences perception. Attention is the amount of energy the consumer is willing to expend on an object. Concentration increases the detail of a perception. Similarly, consumers tend to use energy on areas that are of interest, such as current needs. Hungry shoppers perceive food ads more positively than do shoppers just coming from a meal. Experience and memory help give more detail to current stimuli, thus influencing how objects are understood. Moods influence how objects are seen as well.

Selective perception is made up of four components: selective exposure, selective attention, selective comprehension, and selective retention. First, buyers expose themselves selectively to various stimuli from among many different ones they encounter every day. They do so by their behavior, from where they shop to what they read. Buyers may have many different motives for shopping, but in every case the result is their exposure to the stimuli within their chosen shopping environment.

Second, buyers attend selectively to the stimuli to which they are exposed. They pay attention only to those items they find relevant to their own circumstances. Marketers facilitate consumers' selective attention through the repetition of messages. However, too much repetition can cause consumers to tune out the message out of habituation. Factors that can affect buyer attention are size and position, color, novelty and contrast, intensity, and motion.

Selective comprehension, the third component of perception, involves the interpretation of products and messages. Assimilation occurs when consumers distort messages in favor of their own point of view. The contrast effect occurs when consumers interpret views opposite than their own as being more divergent than they really are. Perceptual integration brings together perceived objects for comprehension by means of closure, by how we group objects, and by context.

Selective retention refers to the fact that we choose what information will be retained in the memory for future use. Information is retained until new, conflicting information is received which replaces or changes existing information already stored in memory.

Product positioning is a technique marketers use to establish a unique image for their brand in the consumer's mind. Perceptual mapping is one way marketers can determine how consumers perceive their brands in comparison to other brands of the same product. By integrating various types of preference data, marketers can determine those product characteristics most preferred by various market segments.

Another area of perception, perceived risk, is the potential buyer's feeling that a purchase may lead to unfavorable consequences of either a social or a functional nature. The amount of perceived risk for a consumer depends on the amount at stake and the degree of certainty that something will not go wrong.

Subliminal perception occurs when a person is unaware of a stimulus, even though it may have an effect on him or her. Most current research has shown that subliminal advertising is ineffective in changing buyer behavior, although in some cases it produced heightened physiological drives. Most marketers look to other, more accepted practices of influencing consumer behavior.

KEY TERMS

Weber's law
price thresholds
perceptual vigilance
moods
external factors of perception
selective exposure
selective attention
habituation
comprehension
social judgment theory
assimilation
contrast effect
closure
proximity
similarity
continuity
halo effect
context
frame of reference
constancy
organization of material
perceived risk
social risk
functional risk
physical risk
financial risk
amount at stake
certainty
product positioning
attribute data
preference data
ideal point
subliminal stimulation

QUESTIONS

1. Briefly describe the difference between internal and external factors of perception. How are both important to marketers?

2. What is Weber's law? What are its implications for management decision making?

3. Suppose an advertiser would like to maximize the perceptual interest of consumers with a newspaper ad. What external factors would you suggest be considered? Briefly describe your ideal newspaper ad.

4. Discuss the selective nature of perception in terms of exposure, attention, comprehension, and retention.

5. What determines whether habituation will occur with regard to a particular message? Does this mean an advertiser should limit messages? Explain.

6. What is meant by "assimilation"? What is the contrast effect? Give an example of each.

7. How does perceptual integration enhance the interpretation of messages? Include the concepts of closure, grouping, and context in your response.

8. What is product positioning? How does perceptual mapping help marketers better understand their position relative to competition?

9. Develop a hypothetical perceptual map for toothpaste, selecting any dimensions that you believe are relevant. Position some familiar brands on your map. Are there any gaps in the map? What does this suggest?

NOTES

1. Stuart Henderson Britt, "How Weber's Law Can Be Applied to Marketing," *Business Horizons* 13 (February 1975): 21–29.
2. Kent E. Monroe and Susan M. Petroshius, "Buyers' Perceptions of Price: An Update of the Evidence," in *Perspectives in Consumer Behavior,* 3rd ed., Harold H. Kassarjian and Thomas S. Robertson, eds. (Glenview, IL: Scott Foresman and Co., 1981), 48.
3. Kent B. Monroe, "Buyers' Subjective Perceptions of Price," *Journal of Marketing Research* 10 (1973): 70–80.
4. E. A. Tauber, "Why Do People Shop," *Journal of Marketing* (October 1972): 47.
5. Brian D. Copeland, *The Study of Attention Value: A Review of Some Available Advertising Materials* (London: Business Publications, 1958); *Outdoor Advertising Manual,* Foster and Kleiser Outdoor Advertising, 1967; Forest C. Carter, Harvey L. Vredenberg, and C. Robert Patty, *A Historical, Economic, and Statistical Study of the Electrical Sign Industry* (Fort Collins, CO: Colorado State University Press, 1967).
6. "Position in Newspaper Advertising: 2," *Media Scope* (March 1963): 76–82.
7. Joseph A. Bellizzi, Ayn E. Crowley, and Ronald Hasty, "The Effects of Color in Store Design," *Journal of Retailing* 59, no. 1 (Spring 1983): 21–45.
8. Tom Parker, *In One Day: The Things Americans Do in a Day* (Boston: Houghton Mifflin, 1984).
9. Raymond A. Bauer and Stephen Greyser, eds., *Advertising in America: The Consumer View* (Boston: Harvard Business School, 1968).
10. William M. Weilbacher, *The DA's Study on Consumer Judgement of Advertising* (New York: American Association of Advertising Agencies, 1965).
11. Danuta Ehrlich, Isaiah Guttman, Peter Schönbach, and Judson Mills, "Post-Decision Exposure to Relevant Information," *Journal of Abnormal and Social Psychology* 54 (January 1957): 98–102.
12. Stuart H. Surlin and Thomas F. Gordon, "Selective Exposure and Retention of Political Advertising," *Journal of Advertising* 5 (Winter 1976): 32–37.
13. David L. Paletz, Judith Koon, Elizabeth Whitehead, and Richard B. Hagen, "Selective Exposure: The Potential Boomerang Effect," *Journal of Communication* 22 (March 1972): 48–53.
14. J. T. Bertrand, "Selective Avoidance on Health Topics: A Field Test," *Communications Research* 6 (July 1979): 271–94.
15. D. E. Berlyne, *Conflict, Arousal, and Curiosity* (New York: McGraw-Hill, 1980), 345.
16. Muzafer Sherif, Carolyn W. Sherif, and Roger E. Nebergall, *Attitudes and Attitude Change* (Philadelphia: Saunders, 1965).
17. James T. Heimback and Jacob Jacoby, "The Zeigarnik Effect in Advertising," in *Proceedings, 3rd Annual Conference,* M. Venkatesan, ed. (Association for Consumer Research, 1972), 746–58.
18. Richard Nisbett and Timothy DeCamp Wilson, "The Halo Effect: Evidence for Unconscious Alterations of Judgement," *Journal of Personality and Social Psychology* 35 (April 1977): 250–56; Jonathan L. Freedman, David O. Sears, and J. Merrill Carlsmith, *Social Psychology,* 4th ed. (Englewood Cliffs, NJ: Prentice-Hall, 1981).
19. Ivan L. Preston, *The Great American Blow-Up* (Madison: University of Wisconsin Press, 1975), 105.
20. Preston, 105.
21. James MacLachlan, "Listener Perception of Time-Compressed Spokespersons," *Journal of Advertising Research* 22 (1982): 47–51.
22. Donald E. Cox, ed., *Risk Taking and Information Handling in Consumer Behavior* (Boston: Division of Research, Graduate School of Business Administration, Harvard University, 1967).
23. Joel Huber and John McCann, "The Impact of Inferential Beliefs on Product Evaluations," *Journal of Marketing Research* 19(August 1982): 324–33.
24. Timothy Moore, "Subliminal Advertising: What You See Is What You Get," *Journal of Marketing* 46 (1982): 38–47.
25. Sandra H. Hart and Steven W. McDaniel, "Subliminal Stimulation: Marketing Applications," in *Consumers' Behavior: Classical and Contemporary Dimensions,* James U. McNeal and Steven W. McDaniel, eds. (Boston: Little, Brown, 1982), 165–75.
26. Wilson Bryan Key, *Subliminal Seduction* (Englewood Cliffs, NJ: Prentice-Hall, 1973).
27. J. Steven Kelly, "Subliminal Imbeds in Printing Advertising: A Challenge to Advertising Ethics," *Journal of Advertising* 8 (Summer 1979):43–46.
28. Hart and McDaniel, "Subliminal Stimulation."

FURTHER READING

Classics

Allison, Ralph I., and Kenneth P. Uhl, "Brand Identification and Perception," *Journal of Marketing Research* 1 (August 1964): 80–85.

Krugman, Herbert E., "Memory without Recall, Exposure with Perception," *Journal of Advertising Research,* 17 (August 1977): 7–12.

Krugman, Herbert E., and Eugene L. Hartley, "The Learning of Tastes," *The Public Opinion Quarterly,* 24, no. 4 (1960).

Levy, Sidney J., "Symbols for Sale," *Harvard Business Review,* (July–August 1959): 117–24.

McClure, Peter J., and John K. Ryans, Jr. "Differences Between Retailers' and Consumers' Perceptions," *Journal of Marketing Research,* 5 (February 1968): 35–40.

McGuire, W. J., "Selective Exposure: A Summing Up," in *Theories of Cognitive Consistency: A Sourcebook,* R. P. Abelson, E. Aronson, W. J. McGuire, T. N. Newcomb, M. J. Rosenberg, and P. H. Tannenbaum, eds. (Chicago: Rand McNally, 1968).

Monroe, Kent B., "Buyers' Subjective Perceptions of Price," *Journal of Marketing Research* 10 (February 1973): 70–80.

Narayana, Chem L., "The Stability of Perceptions," *Journal of Advertising Research* 16, no. 2 (April 1976): 25–30.

Sears, D. O., and J. L. Freedman, "Selective Exposure to Information: A Critical Review," *Public Opinion Quarterly* 31 (1967): 194–213.

Recent Significant Research

Agarwal, Manoj K., "Using Multidimensional Scaling to Link Physical Attributes and Perceptual Dimensions: A Methodology," in *1984 AMA Educators' Proceedings,* Russell W. Belk, et al., eds. (Chicago: American Marketing Association, 1984), 407–410.

Belk, Russell W., Robert Mayer, and Kenneth D. Bahn, "The Eye of the Beholder: Individual Differences in Perceptions of Consumption Symbolism," *Journal of Consumer Research* 9 (June 1982): 4–17.

Blair, Edward A., and E. Laird Landon, Jr., "The Effects of Reference Prices in Retail Advertisements," *Journal of Marketing* 45 (Spring 1981): 61–69.

Bloch, Peter H., and Marsha L. Richins, "A Theoretical Model for the Study of Product Importance Perceptions," *Journal of Marketing* 47 (Summer 1983): 69–81.

Coughlin, Maureen, and P. J. O'Connor, "Cue Utilization and Person Perception: Evaluation of Models in Print Advertising," in *1984 AMA Educators' Proceedings,* Russell W. Belk, et al., eds., (Chicago: American Marketing Association, 1984) 11–16.

Della Bitta, Albert J., Kent B. Monroe, and John M. McGinnis, "Consumer Perceptions of Comparative Price Advertisements," *Journal of Marketing Research* 18 (November 1981): 416–27.

Holbrook, Morris B., "Using a Structural Model of Halo Effect to Assess Perceptual Distortion Due to Affective Overtones," *Journal of Consumer Research* 10 (September 1983): 247–52.

Moore, Timothy E., "Subliminal Advertising: What You See Is What You Get," *Journal of Marketing* 46 (Spring 1982): 38–47.

Shimp, Terence A., and William O. Bearden, "Warranty and Other Extrinsic Cue Effects on Consumers' Risk Perceptions," *Journal of Consumer Research,* 9 (June 1982): 38–46.

Swartz, Teresa A., "Brand Symbols and Message Differentiation," *Journal of Advertising Research* 23, no. 5 (October/November 1983): 59–64.

Venkataraman, V. K., "The Price-Quality Relationship in an Experimental Setting," *Journal of Advertising Research* 21, no. 4 (August 1981): 49–52.

Applications

Aaker, David A., "Positioning Your Product," *Business Horizons* (May–June 1982): 56–62.

Allison, Ralph I., and Kenneth P. Uhl, "Impact of Beer Brand Identification on Taste Perception," *Journal of Marketing Research* 1 (August 1964): 36–39.

Asam, Edward H., and Louis P. Bucklin, "Nutritional Labelling for Canned Goods: A Study of

Consumer Response,'' *Journal of Marketing* 37 (April 1973): 32–37.

Berkowitz, Eric N., and John R. Walton, ''Contextual Influences on Consumer Price Responses: An Experimental Analysis,'' *Journal of Marketing Research* 17 (August 1980): 349–58.

Della Bitta, Albert, J., and Kent B. Monroe, ''The Influence of Adaptation Levels on Subjective Price Perceptions,'' in *Advances in Consumer Research,* Vol. 1, Scott Ward and Peter Wright, eds. (Urbana, IL: Association for Consumer Research, 1974), 359–69.

Enis, Ben, and James Stafford, ''The Price-Quality Relationship: An Extension,'' *Journal of Marketing Research* 6 (November 1969): 256–58.

Gardner, David M., ''Deception in Advertising: A Conceptual Approach,'' *Journal of Marketing* 39 (January 1975): 40–46.

Green, Paul E., and Yoram Wind, ''New Way to Measure Consumers' Judgments,'' *Harvard Business Review* (July–August 1975): 107–17.

Horowitz, Irwin A., and Russell S. Kaye, ''Perception and Advertising,'' *Journal of Advertising Research* 15, no. 3 (June 1975): 15–21.

Jacoby, Jacob, Jerry C. Olson, and Rafael A. Haddock, ''Price, Brand Name and Product Composition Characteristics as Determinants of Perceived Quality,'' *Journal of Applied Psychology* 55 (December 1971): 570–79.

Kono, Ken, ''Consumer Perception of the U.S.-Built Foreign Cars: Quality Assessment,'' in *1984 AMA Educators' Proceedings,* Russell W. Belk, et al., eds. (Chicago: American Marketing Association, 1984), 52–56.

Monroe, Kent B., and Susan M. Petroshius, ''Buyers' Perceptions of Price: An Update of the Evidence,'' *Journal of Marketing Research* 10 (February 1973): 70–80.

Ray, Michael L., and Peter Webb, ''Experimental Research on the Effects of TV Clutter: Dealing with the Difficult Media Environment,'' Report No. 76–102 (Cambridge, MA: Marketing Science Institute, April 1976), 98.

Scherf, George W. H., and George F. Karvash, ''Husband/Wife Comparisons of Price–Quality Relationships in the Post-Purchase Situation,'' *The Journal of Social Psychology* (October 1976): 99–106.

Turk, Michael A., and Ernest F. Cooke, ''How the U.S. Government Uses Deceptive Advertising to Manipulate the Consumer to Gain an Unfair Advantage over the Private Sector,'' in *1984 AMA Educators' Proceedings,* Russell W. Belk, et al., eds., (Chicago: American Marketing Association, 1984) 319–23.

Wheatley, John J., and John S. Y. Chiu, ''The Effect of Price, Store Image, and Product and Respondent Characteristics on Perceptions of Quality,'' *Journal of Marketing Research* 14 (May 1977): 181–86.

4 Learning

Objectives of This Chapter

After you have studied this chapter, you should be able to:

1. Define *learning* and show how learning techniques relate to consumer behavior.
2. Discuss three schools of thought about learning—cognitive, contiguity, and reinforcement—and compare and contrast their theories.
3. Show how principles of learning theory apply to marketing.

Learning has been defined in many ways, but two popular definitions are provided by experts in learning research. John Hall defines it as "changes in response tendencies due to the effects of experience."[1] Ernest Hilgard and Gordon Bower contend that learning is "the process by which an activity originates or is changed through reacting to an encountered situation."[2] For our purposes, we can define **learning** as any change in behavioral tendencies due to previous encounters. There are three elements in this definition important to the study of buyer behavior: change, behavioral tendencies, and previous encounters. We will examine them in the context of how learning affects behavior.

learning

In this chapter we discuss what learning is and how it relates to consumer behavior. Learning elements such as repetition, elaboration, rehearsal, and the use of evoked sets are ways consumers accumulate the experience necessary to change their behavior. Three schools of learning theory apply particularly to marketers' attempts to change consumer behavior. This chapter concludes with the key marketing principles that are derived from learning theory.

THE REQUIREMENTS OF LEARNING

Change

Inherent in both Hall's and Hilgard and Bower's definitions is that learning is dynamic and can be altered. For example, a shopper who has learned to buy Tide detergent can learn to buy Cheer detergent under different circumstances.

What causes changes in learned behavior? Learning researchers would say that changes occur in response to drives.[3] **Drives** are the result of motivation activated by stimuli. In Chapter 2 we saw that motivation is the force that moves humans to fulfill unmet needs. Stimuli, we saw, are objects of perception that excite the senses. Together, motivation and stimuli create a state of internal imbalance that activates behavior. For example, by 11:30 A.M. a person who has skipped breakfast has a physiological need for food (motivation). If the person walks past a donut shop, looks in the window, and smells the freshly made donuts (stimuli), it is likely that the person will experience a drive in the form of a strong urge to eat donuts. It is important to note that while sellers can do little if anything to affect buyer motivations, they can provide many stimuli to excite buyers to action.

drives

Stimuli can be significative, symbolic, or social. Significative stimuli are the physical characteristics of the brand or item itself. For example, the taste, smell, and texture of a McDonald's hamburger are significative stimuli to millions of consumers each day. Symbolic stimuli are verbal or visual messages given by marketers about their brand. McDonald's ads describing the contents of a Big Mac are an example of this form of stimulus. Social stimuli are messages about a product or brand received through contacts with other consumers. An example of this type of stimulus is the conversation of a group of students who are considering going to McDonald's for a study break. All three types of stimulus serve to direct the buyer toward or away from particular brands.

Note that consumer behaviorists often use the words *stimulus* and *cue* interchangeably. Like stimuli, **cues** are objects in the environment that are perceived by the consumer and guide his or her actions. Creative advertisements, innovative product design, and attractive packaging are some of the cues used by marketers to trigger a drive within buyers to purchase their brands.

cues

Consumer behavior changes because the consumer's needs and motives are constantly shifting and new stimuli are continually being introduced into the marketplace. Actually, without a change in behavior it is very difficult to determine if learning has taken place.

Behavioral Tendencies

Whether we call them *response tendencies* or *activities,* as some learning theorists have, it is the thoughts and actions of the learner that are changed by learning. Learning involves both internal (unobservable) behaviors and external (observable) behaviors. For example, a hungry student might see an ad for Pizza Hut pan pizzas (a symbolic stimulus) or smell a pizza (a significative stimulus) and develop a favorable attitude (an internal behavior) toward pan pizzas and a brand preference (an internal behavior) for Pizza Hut's pan pizzas. As a result, the student might seek more information about them by telephoning (an external behavior) to find out if Pizza Hut delivers its pizzas, or by purchasing one (an external behavior) at the nearest outlet. In this case, the development of an attitude and brand preference would be learning just as much as the telephone inquiry and purchase would be.

Behaviors that result from the presentation of stimuli are called *responses*. Behavioral researchers usually analyze responses according to their amplitude and speed. **Amplitude** refers to the size of the response, such as the amount of product purchased. **Speed** refers to how quickly the response follows presentation of the stimuli. For example, point-of-purchase display stimuli are designed to elicit an immediate purchase response, while some television ads only obtain a response after the consumer has seen them many times.

amplitude
speed

Previous Encounters

Both of the popular definitions of learning suggest that experience is a prerequisite for learning. Hall's phrase "due to the effects of experience" reflects one meaning of experience: something personally encountered, undergone, or lived through. Hilgard and Bower's phrase "reacting to an encountered situation" suggests another: the interaction of an organism with its environment. Although their nuances differ, the definitions imply that learning results from repeated activities or remembered experiences. For example, one study revealed that as children grow older and interact more with others they begin to associate consumption patterns with social class (for example, sports cars and new houses to upper social classes). While preschoolers make few consumption associations, the associative ability of sixth-graders is fully developed, suggesting that children learn associations of this kind through experience.[4] Consequently, this experiential aspect of learning is important to the study of buyer behavior. Buyers learn continually from their experiences, through both encounters and personal interactions. Buyers engage repeatedly in various activities associated with the marketplace, and they generally remember these encounters. In fact, it has been found that a person with more experience and familiarity with a product is often able to remember more new information about that product than a person with less familiarity.[5]

At this point it will be helpful to consider how various techniques contribute to the accumulation of experience necessary for learning.

LEARNING TECHNIQUES: REPETITION, REHEARSAL, AND MNEMONICS

Marketers use a variety of learning techniques to help potential customers understand and remember their brands when they are making purchasing decisions. These techniques include repetition, rehearsal, and other mnemonic devices. Table 4-1 summarizes how each is used by marketers to creating successful advertising campaigns.

Table 4-1 OVERVIEW OF LEARNING TECHNIQUES

Learning Technique	*Description*	*Example*
Repetition	Successive presentations of a slogan phrase or brand name	"Coke is it" phrase used in print and TV ads
Mnemonic devices (jingles and rhymes)	Verbal messages with built-in memory devices	"Let's go Krogering" "Fill it to the rim, with Brim"
Rehearsal	Silent internal speech to maintain in short-term memory	Remembering a telephone number provided by the operator

repetition **Repetition** of a company name or slogan is a method often used for advancing consumer learning processes through advertising. Major advertisers such as Coca-Cola are well known for their use of repetition to boost awareness. However, nearly all advertisers—including those in competition with Coca-Cola—also try to achieve repetitive exposures to establish consumer recall.

The repetition of advertisements or other promotional messages also affects learning. Cacioppo and Petty have examined the effect of repetition on the levels of comprehension and retention and on the persuasiveness of a message. Their findings suggest that repeating a message tends to give more opportunity for the listener to think about it. If the repeated message is convincing, it tends to elicit a more favorable reaction. At higher levels of repetition, however, the message may become tedious and its persuasiveness may decline as listeners tire of it. Figure 4-1 illustrates this relationship.

mnemonic Often marketers rely on **mnemonic** or memory-aiding devices such as jingles and rhymes to facilitate learning. Although consumers may sometimes tire of a campaign jingle, the technique has proven effective for some advertisers who seek to assist consumers in understanding and remembering their product or service. The "Let's Go Krogering" jingle has been used successfully for many years to help consumers remember Kroger supermarkets.

rehearsal Another learning technique is **rehearsal,** a silent inner speech that buyers use when trying to remember things such as telephone numbers. Rehearsal maintains information in memory for a short time. In *Elaborative rehearsal,* additional information is added to information already within the cognitive structure. This information enters memory for the long term.

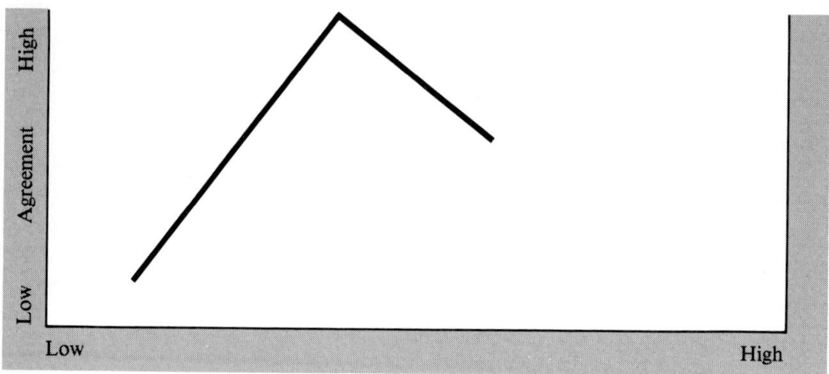

Figure 4-1
Effects of Message Exposure on Agreement

Source: adapted from J. T. Cacioppo and R. E. Petty, *Attitudes and Persuasion: Classic and Contemporary Approaches* (Dubuque, IA: W. C. Brown, 1981), 240–41.

The Learning Curve

Of the mechanisms for accumulating experience, repetition could be considered the more external and observable. It is a basic principle of learning that as a person performs a task again and again, the task becomes easier. This concept is often represented graphically by the **learning curve** (see Figure 4-2). When a task is first performed, much more time is required for its completion. With additional experience (more performances), the time required to complete the task drops sharply. As the learner approaches mastery, the time required to perform the task continues to decrease but at a much slower rate, since most time-saving strategies have already been discovered. Eventually the task may become so easy that the learner performs it almost unconsciously or involuntarily. This common pattern of behavior, developed from repetition, is called **habit.**

learning curve

habit

The same principle holds true for brand choice in consumer behavior. As Figure 4-3 shows, the probability of a shopper choosing the same brand increases dramatically with additional purchases. Notice that the brand choice curve increases the most during the early trials and stabilizes as learning progresses. There is never 100% probability that a given brand will be purchased; but because learning tends to proceed at a predictable rate, marketers have been able to develop mathematical models of brand loyalty. These stochastic or probabilistic models are characteristic of the tendency of consumer behaviorists to blend behavioral theories with statistical procedures.

Stochastic Learning Models

stochastic learning models

One approach to the study of learning is through the use of probabilistic or stochastic models. **Stochastic models** represent consumer responses as *probabilities*. (They are different from deterministic models, which are based on mathematics that lead to a *single* solution given a set of parameters.) Figure 4-4 illustrates the linear learning model (A) developed by two psychologists, Robert Bush and Frederic Mosteller.[6] It was first applied to predicting brand choice by Alfred Kuehn. Two refinements of Kuehn's model (B and C) are also shown.[7] The *linear learning model* assumes that buyers are affected only by their own purchase (and subsequent consumption) of a product—that is, that they get feedback about the product solely from their experience with the product. Any increase in the probability of a purchase is the result of experience derived only from a previous purchase. When this relationship is graphed it looks like a series of steps. The *probability diffusion model* uses a different statistical technique. It assumes that external sources of information, such as word-of-mouth communication and advertising are the only effects on purchasing. This model

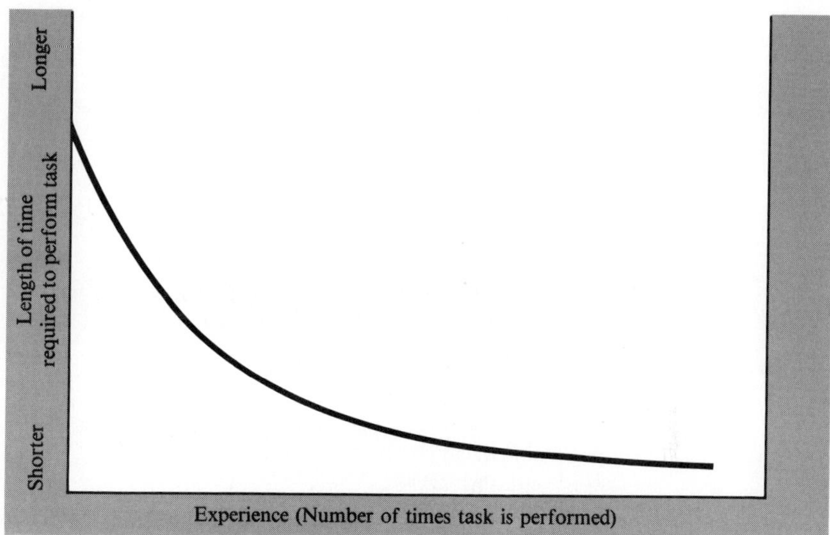

Figure 4-2
The Learning Curve

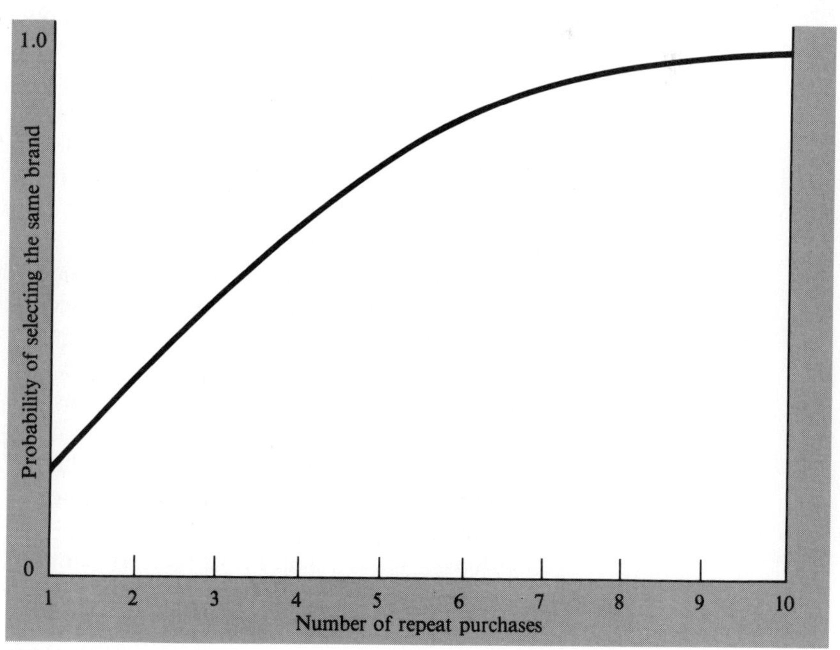

Figure 4-3
The Brand Choice Curve

Source: adapted from J. Morgan Jones, "A Dual-Effects Model of Brand Choice," *Journal of Marketing Research* 7 (1970): 460.

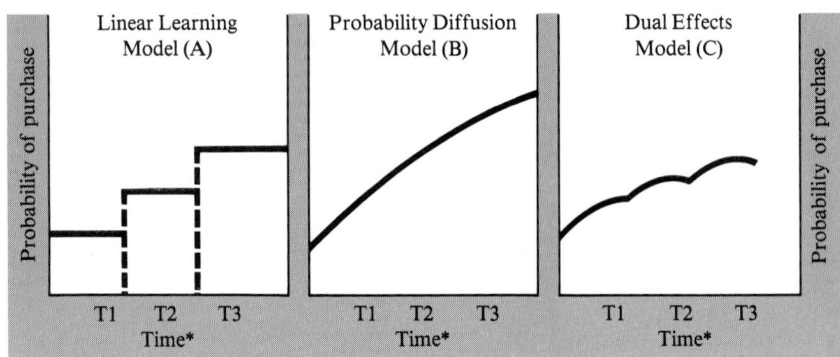

Figure 4-4
Stochastic Models of Brand Choice

Source: adapted from J. Morgan Jones, "A Dual-Effects Model of Brand Choice," *Journal of Marketing Research* 7 (1970): 458–64.

* T1, T2, T3 refer to individual brand purchases whenever they occur; the actual time elapsed between purchases may vary among buyers.

produces a continuous graph, because the external sources of information are a continuous influence on the buyer. The dual effects model uses relatively complex statistical procedures that allow the researcher to make the assumption that both internal information gained from experience and external input gained from communications have predictable effects on brand choice.

These three models largely ignore the amount of time elapsed between purchases in their prediction of brand choice decisions. Yet elapsed time is an important factor in predicting the rate of product adoption and the market share a new product will enjoy. The addition of the time dimension was left to later researchers who used two aspects of time, the new product trial rate and the repeat purchase rate, to predict the success of new products.[8] In the end, their *aggregate market penetration curve* assumed the shape of the basic learning curve.

Other refinements to the stochastic model have increased its usefulness to marketers of new products.[9] For example, recently a model has been developed which explains the probability of repeat purchases of a brand based on relevant explanatory variables such as past purchases, past deals on purchases (that is, sale prices), and consumer characteristics. This represents a significant improvement in our ability to predict brand choice; earlier models did not specifically consider the influence of explanatory variables such as pricing, promotion, or demographic characteristics.[10]

A variety of applications of stochastic models have been discussed in marketing literature. More recently, marketers have begun to apply these probabilistic models to predict how likely an individual consumer is to purchase a brand based on such factors as the number of times he or she has purchased the brand before. From such predictions marketers can estimate the degree of brand loyalty for a product. Morrison developed a model of brand loyalty that relates the probability of purchase to the most recent brand purchase as follows:

$$P\ (At + 1/At) = P$$

where A is the brand preferred by the customer, and $(At + 1)$ is the probability of purchase at time $t + 1$.[11]

Marketers can use probabilistic models when introducing a new product to give them an idea of how successful the introduction will be. By examining panel data which record consumer purchasing patterns, researchers are able to provide mathematical models which can be used to estimate the probability of product purchasing over time given inputs such as distribution, advertising, scheduling, promotional programs, and so on.

For example, a major food products manufacturer used test-market purchase data from consumers to predict success for a new product introduction. By estimating various levels of distribution and altering advertising and couponing schedules, the company was able to obtain a relatively accurate measure of product purchase and market success prior to national launch. The model indicated to management that earlier couponing should be used to boost trial and improve overall sales in the first year of introduction.[12]

While most stochastic models provide for inputs concerning the characteristics of a total population, some researchers have found value in developing different models to represent different market segments.[13] By analyzing panel data for frequently purchased items, marketers in the product introduction above identified nine different market segments according to their degree of brand loyalty:

1. High National Brand Loyal
2. National Brand Loyal
3. Private Label Loyal
4. Cost Purchase Loyal
5. National Brand Switcher
6. Private/National Brand Switcher
7. Private Label Switcher
8. National Brand Switcher (Deal)
9. Deal Oriented

Although the models related to the learning curve are not shown here in their entirety, it is clear that the application of statistical techniques to the theory of learning has yielded tools which can help business executives understand and predict brand loyalty among buyers.

Evoked Sets

The importance of memory is implied in our working definition of learning as "any change in behavioral tendencies due to experience." Without memory, events in our lives would not be recorded. Thus we would not have any accumulated experience upon which to draw in making everyday decisions. Fortunately, we know that memory is a fundamental function of the human mind, although it may not be externally observable.

Memory will be discussed in detail in Chapter 8, which examines the role of information processing in consumer behavior. Here, we look at memory in terms of the evoked set buyers have for brand choices. An

evoked set

evoked set is a group of products a prospective buyer holds in memory and then recalls in order to make a purchasing decision to satisfy a need or solve a problem. For marketers, an evoked set includes the brands a prospective buyer perceives as alternatives in a consumption situation. These brands may come from one product class or several. For example, if you were to ask two people working in the sun on a hot afternoon what they would like to drink, one might answer with Coke, Orange Crush, Pepsi, or Squirt. The other person might be thirsty for 7-Up, Budweiser, Perrier, or Hawaiian Punch. The brands which the first person considers to be substitutes for each other constitutes an evoked set drawn from one product class: carbonated soft drinks. The evoked set of the second person is made up of brands from several product classes. For a brand to be included in a prospective buyer's evoked set, the buyer not only must be aware of it but must also consider buying it. Since consumers tend to buy brands that are in their evoked sets, it is vital that marketers cause *their* brands to be included in those evoked sets. According to Chrysler executives, one problem Chrysler has faced is that its products are not in the evoked sets of a large enough number of consumers.

Brian Campbell, who researched the existence of evoked sets, surveyed 200 housewives regarding the brands of toothpaste and laundry detergent in their evoked sets. He arrived at the following conclusions:

1. . . . The evoked set represents a significant simplification of a complex decision situation and thus enables a buyer to select a preferred brand in at least a pseudo-rational manner.
2. For the two products researched, very few buyers demonstrated an evoked set greater than seven. The evidence strongly suggests that there is a numerical limit to the number of brands in a buyer's evoked set across different products and different buying situations.
3. . . . Respondents who showed a relatively large evoked set for toothpaste has a correspondingly large set for laundry detergent, and vice versa for those with small evoked sets. Consequently, evoked set appears to be an individual phenomenon and not particularly related to the specific product in question.
4. In the two cases of toothpaste and laundry detergent, the size of the buyer's evoked set was not influenced by the number of brands she was

aware of. Therefore, we may say that "relative awareness" was not a determinant of evoked set size.[14]

Since consumers have a limited number of brands in their evoked sets, sellers must be alert to how their products are classified in consumers' memories. That is, marketers who work to make shoppers remember their product would be well advised to present their offering as an alternative to other products and competing brands in various consumption situations. Recent advertisements for orange juice ("It isn't just for breakfast anymore") are examples of this marketing strategy.

The first portion of this chapter provided a working definition of learning and related the components of learning to consumer behavior. The remainder of this chapter will present some theories of learning from the major schools of thought—cognitive, contiguity, and reinforcement—and look at the current integrated approach to the study of learning. While it is beyond the scope of this book to present the various explanations of learning in their entirety, the aspects of each theory that are most relevant to consumer behavior will be highlighted.

LEARNING THEORY

Cognitive Learning

cognitive school of learning

The **cognitive school of learning** emphasizes perception, reason, and problem solving. It focuses on the individual's overall knowledge, insights, ideas, attitudes, and goals. Cognitive learning theory is based on stages in the decision-making process such as those presented in the introduction. It is also closely allied to motivation, in that it deals with goal-directed behavior. (See Figure 4-5). In cognitive learning, a perceived problem causes a person to seek a solution. The *desired goal* is whatever the person perceives to be the solution to the problem. The person directs his or her actions toward achieving this goal, but this behavior is shaped by the person's knowledge, ideas, insights, and attitudes. If the person has adequate problem-solving abilities, he or she will achieve the goal and be

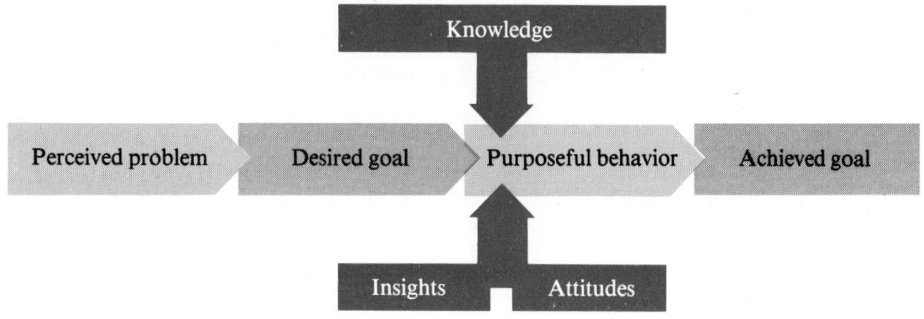

Figure 4-5
The Cognitive Learning Process

satisfied. As Chapter 2 explained, buyers continually engage in goal-directed behavior. For example, assume that one consumer's goal is to own a safe, reliable, and energy-efficient automobile. This prospective buyer's goal-directed behavior might involve discussions with friends and car salespeople, and reading *Consumer Reports*. These prepurchase activities reflect the buyer's problem-solving ability, which draws on knowledge, insights, ideas, and attitudes. Goal-directed behavior might also include the purchase of the selected brand of automobile. To the degree that the buyer achieves safety, reliability, and energy efficiency in his auto purchase, the goal is achieved and the buyer is satisfied.

Simplification and Complication

Some buying problems are complex and challenging while others are quite simple, even routine. Consequently, consumers simplify or make more complex the rules that they use to make their purchase decisions. Sometimes shoppers seek **simplification** in their buying. Increasingly, they rely on previous experience and knowledge of a product's ability to meet their requirements: they purchase that product or brand out of habit. An example is the purchase of toothpaste or soap. For most consumers, such purchases are routine because most people want to simplify the shopping process. By contrast, the repetitive nature of some purchases and consumption situations creates boredom. For many people, buying certain foods becomes monotonous. Eventually, these shoppers may wish to learn more about their routine purchases. A need arises to complicate the buying task to escape boredom. The role of **complication** is related to curiosity and novelty-seeking behavior, described in Chapter 2. Generally, when shopping becomes too routine, buyers explore products that are new to them and the learning process begins again. In one sense, the learning process is a never-ending cycle in which simplification or complication prevails at different times according to the consumer's needs.

simplification

complication

Buyers engage in making a purchase decision in three ways. These are actually three levels of complexity, in which the problem solving becomes less and less complicated the more often an item is purchased:

1. extensive problem solving
2. limited problem solving
3. routinized response behavior

The first approach to a purchase requires the most energy and is the most complex. During *extensive problem solving* the prospective purchaser concentrates on several stimuli, assesses the nature of his or her drive for the product, and analyzes the features available and their comparative benefits. The consumer has no strong preference for any particular brand, but assesses the value of product in general. For example, many freshmen in college are confronted by the question of whether or not to buy a hand calculator. First the student must decide if one is needed. Second, the student decides what functions the calculator should perform (should it only do addition, subtraction, multiplication, and division, or should it be fully programmable?).

The second approach is *limited problem solving*. Stimuli are fairly well known as the buyer compares the rewards anticipated from each brand. The potential buyer is willing to consider several brands. In fact, for low-priced, frequently purchased goods such as beer or gum, the shopper might try many brands. A student selecting a second, perhaps more elaborate, calculator shows limited problem solving. Experience with the first calculator becomes the starting point for the search for a new one.

A third approach, *routinized response behavior,* occurs when a consumer prefers a particular brand. During routine buying, the purchaser pays little attention to stimuli and habit is very strong. Any stimuli that are perceived tend to be distorted to favor purchasing the preferred brand. For example, if the student's second calculator is lost, the student may replace it without considering any additional brands.

The problem-solving approach a buyer uses depends on experience and knowledge about the product or brand. In some situations, purchasers progress through the different approaches, from extensive problem solving through limited problem solving to routinized response behavior, as their experience with the product category or brand grows. For example, certain consumable products, such as health and beauty aids, may have once involved extensive problem solving for a shopper. But when the shopper has found a satisfying product these purchases may become routine. Buyers may seek to simplify purchasing using this progression. In other situations, a purchase may *always* involve extensive problem solving. Prospective auto buyers typically engage in much information search and comparative analysis regardless of their prior experience with a given automobile make or model. Table 4-2 offer examples of each approach and presents typical marketing strategies that respond to consumers' different problem-solving approaches.

As consumers pass through the problem-solving stages toward greater simplification of their purchase decisions, not only do they expend less and less energy but their requirements for product information also decrease. In some experiments, subjects in the extensive problem-solving stage tended to search out information more actively.[15] This was especially true for products the subjects bought infrequently and for high-priced items.[16] As the subjects bought a particular brand repeatedly and their learning became routinized, researchers observed fewer information-seeking behaviors.[17]

However, once buyers achieve routinized response behavior, they do not necessarily remain in the third stage. Innovation in the marketplace provides an unbalancing force which moves customers back to the first or second stage. Marketers are constantly interrupting the buyer's progress

Table 4-2 THREE MAJOR APPROACHES TO PROBLEM SOLVING

Problem-solving Approach	*Product Characteristics*	*Examples of Product/ Situation*	*Typical Consumer Activity*	*Potential Marketing Strategies*	*Sample Situations*
1. Extensive	High priced, purchased infrequently	Automobile, major appliance, personal computer	Much exploration and information gathering to identify choices and criteria	Provide detailed product information in advertisements to educate buyer	Automobile fact sheets
			Much comparative shopping	Help potential customers understand important criteria to evaluate brands	Personal selling by salespeople
				Offer personal assistance and support to guide buyer's decision process	
2. Limited	Moderately priced, purchased occasionally	Clothing, some food items, certain health-care items	Some consideration of alternative brands	Focus on highlighting superiority of brand over competitors	Blue-jeans ads that emphasize proper fit, wearability
			Fair knowledge of choices and potential benefits of each	Clarify product advantages and build buyer loyalty	
3. Routinized response	Lower priced, purchased frequently	Chewing gum, candy, toothpaste	Little or no brand comparison	Introduce new products to stimulate interest and reconsideration of current brand	A new chewing gum with a liquid flavor center
			Habit purchasing of particular brand	Emphasize unique benefits and special capabilities	Striped toothpaste for children

toward routinized buying by introducing new products, making new claims about the benefits of their products, or finding new uses for familiar products.

Simplification and the Product Life Cycle

When the psychology of simplification is teamed with a product's life cycle, many applications for marketing become clear. The **product life cycle** is the sales pattern of a product beginning with market introduction,

product life cycle

moving though a growth stage onto a plateau called maturity, and ending in decline. John Howard has described the relationship between the stages in the psychology of simplification and the phases of the product life cycle.[18]

Early in the product life cycle, most buyers are in the extensive problem-solving stage. Thus, they actively seek out information about the new product. During the growth phase, the greatest number of buyers are experiencing limited problem solving. At this point, buyers are primarily interested in information on how the various brands of the product compare. At the maturity stage of the product life cycle, most buyers are split between limited problem solving and routinized response behavior. Those in the routine category only use information concerning their preferred brand. Figure 4-6 shows this relationship for instant coffee sales. At the time instant coffee was introduced, it was considered a major innovation. During the introduction years of the life cycle many consumers engaged in extensive problem solving while fewer used limited problem solving or routinized response behavior. As the product's use expanded and matured, consumers employed the limited problem solving and routinized response behavior approaches.

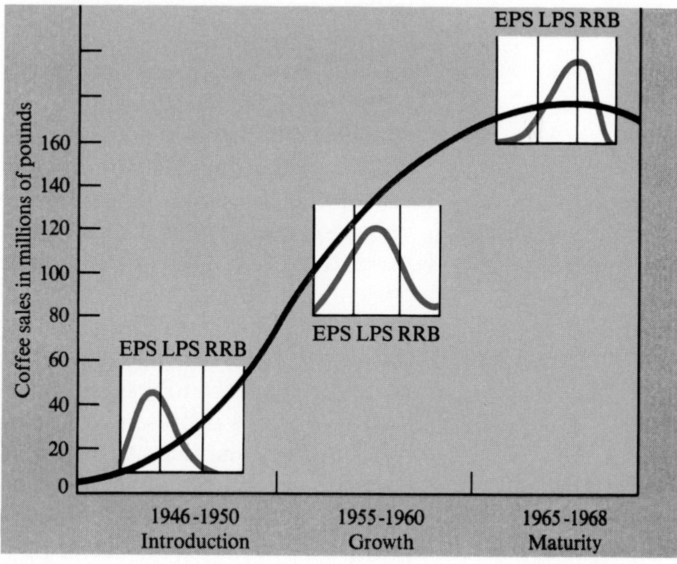

Extensive Problem Solving (EPS)	Many consumers	Few consumers	Few consumers
Limited Problem Solving (LPS)	Few consumers	Many consumers	Many consumers
Routinized Response Behavior (RRB)	Few consumers	Few consumers	Many consumers

Figure 4-6
The Product Life Cycle and Simplification Stages for Purchase of Instant Coffee

Source: adapted from John A. Howard, *Consumer Behavior: Applications of Theory* (New York: McGraw-Hill, 1977), 13.

The implications for the design of marketing messages are clear:

1. Marketers of new products brands must provide adequate information early on in the life cycle, since buyers are more open to it in the first stage of simplification, before buying habits are established.
2. During the product's growth phase when buyers are comparing brands, marketers should use an advertising approach that highlights the superiority of their brand over the other brands.
3. The marketing strategy should allow the brand to gain an early lead over competing brands in order to take advantage of buyer tendency to routinely select the same brand in the third stage of simplification.
4. Firms entering the market late must find ways of disturbing the routinized buyer's equilibrium enough to move the buyer back to the limited or even extensive problem-solving stage.
5. For these recommendations to have the maximum effect, marketers must be aware of the simplification stage each of their market segments is experiencing in regard to a particular product. Then marketers can target appropriate messages to each segment.

Contiguity Learning/Classical Conditioning

In this section we'll examine contiguity learning theory. Contiguity learning is also referred to as classical conditioning in much of the psychology literature, and the terms are interchangeable.

In the 1920s, the Russian physiologist Ivan Pavlov was performing his famous experiments in animal conditioning. When Pavlov presented meat paste to a dog, the dog would salivate. Then, with the simultaneous presentation of a sound from a tuning fork and meat paste, salivation continued. However, when the tuning fork was presented without the meat paste, the dog still salivated.[19] This learned behavior was the result of the presentation of contiguous (or conjoined) stimuli. Thus, behavioral research in the theory of **contiguity learning.** The basic premise of contiguity learning is that when a person responds to one stimulus in a certain way, he or she can learn to respond to another stimulus in the same way if the second stimulus is presented in conjunction with the first one.

contiguity learning

Contiguity learning has been used in marketing to condition buyers to purchase certain brands.[20] A consumer's product preference can be directly influenced by advertising features (stimuli) that are not a part of the product itself. One study found that listening to liked or disliked music in conjunction with viewing a product directly affected the viewer's product preference. This indicates that such elements as color or background music can be as influential in advertising as giving rational product information. In fact, for uninvolved potential buyers who tune out actual product information, "emotionally arousing" background features may be *more* influential.[21]

The cigarette slogan, "You can take Salem out of the country but you can't take the 'country' out of Salem," simultaneously connects two stimuli to a response. Assume that the word *country* elicits a pleasant, clean, fresh feeling in people (an unconditioned response). Through the simultaneous presentation of the unconditioned stimulus, *country,* and the conditioned stimulus, Salem, the conditioned stimulus eventually elicits the response (a pleasant, clean, fresh feeling), which was originally elicited only by the unconditioned stimulus. The pleasant, clean, fresh feeling associated with Salem then becomes a conditioned response. This example of contiguity learning is diagrammed in Figure 4-7.

Generalization and Discrimination

Contiguity learning is closely related to two common learning strategies, generalization and discrimination. Consumers often use these strategies to categorize the countless stimuli presented to them in the marketplace.

generalization
discrimination

Generalization is learning to make the same response to a new similar stimulus as was made to an earlier stimulus. **Discrimination** is learning to make different responses to similar stimuli.[22] For instance, when fast-food restaurants were first introduced, many consumers perceived them to be all alike; they generalized. However, with experience, they begin to find significant differences among restaurants; they began to discriminate one from another.

Marketers take advantage of buyer ability to discriminate among brands. For example, Arby's, Burger Chef, Burger King, McDonald's, and Wendy's spend large sums of money on advertising intended to differentiate their product offerings from those of the competition. Some fast-food chains flame-broil their hamburgers; others fry them. Some use frozen patties; others use fresh meat. Some prepare their sandwiches with standard condiments; others fix theirs "as you like it." Often marketers use taste tests to show the superiority of one brand of beer, peanut butter, or soda over its competitors.

Marketers also capitalize on consumer tendency to generalize by advertising a family brand, thus enhancing the image of the entire product line. Generalization through use of blanket labeling policies can be particularly effective for uncomplicated products, such as food items, to promote brand loyalty.[23] In an effort to create a strong brand identity, Green

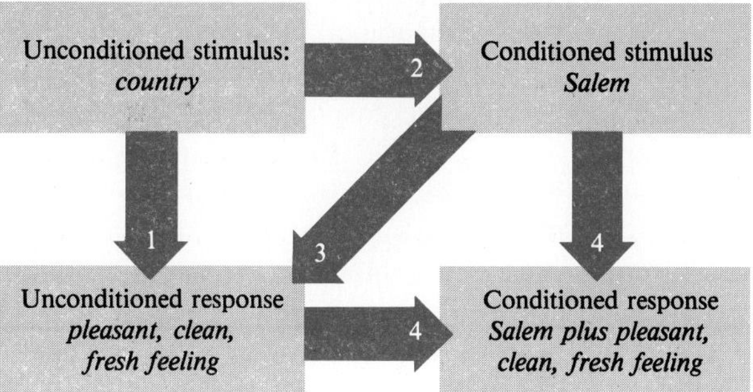

Figure 4-7
Contiguity Learning in Advertising

Giant redesigned the packaging for its frozen food line so that the products appear in similar, easily identifiable containers.[24] Campbell's soups are generally advertised as a group, so that the buyer's reaction to the familiar soups will be extended to other, less familiar soups, or even to soups that may be introduced in the future. Many familiar advertising campaigns have had the goal of creating a positive image "umbrella" over all the products of the firm. General Electric, Gerber, Heinz, and Smucker's are just a few of the companies that have used this approach.

Tactics that affect discrimination and generalization often occur together in the same marketing strategy. For example, the names *Chevrolet, Pontiac, Oldsmobile, Buick,* and *Cadillac* represent General Motors' attempt to differentiate its various brands in order to encourage buyer discrimination. At the same time, however, the designation *General Motors* is used to evoke a positive overall feeling about all of these brands.

Generalization and discrimination can also affect the pricing decisions of new marketing strategies. Research has shown that if shoppers believe that a store's overall pricing structure is higher than that of other stores, they generalize that the prices of individual items in the store are higher also. Furthermore, these generalizations tend to be relatively stable over time and are not subject to rapid changes because of special price promotions.[25] Retail executives should not only plan pricing of individual items but also be aware of the overall price generalizations made about their stores.

The contiguity school of thought has contributed to our understanding of consumer behavior by focusing on two important components of experience: the stimulus and the response. In the next section, we examine the role of motivation in stimulus–response learning.

Reinforcement Learning

Reinforcement learning is a school of thought that originated with the experiments of the psychologist Edward Thorndike. Thorndike investigated the roles of reward and punishment in learning by experimenting with animals.[26] Even before Watson and Pavlov gained notoriety, Thorndike had published the results of his studies, including a fundamental principle of behavior known as the **law of effect.**[27] According to this law, upon presenting an animal with a situation, the responses that are accompanied by or are closely followed by satisfaction to the animal are more likely to recur. The responses that are accompanied by or are closely followed by discomfort to the animal are less likely to recur. Also, the greater the satisfaction to the animal, the stronger the connection becomes between the situation and the rewarded response. The greater the discomfort to the animal, the weaker the connection becomes between the situation and the punished response. In other words, Thorndike was able to use **reinforcement** (rewards) to encourage the repetition of certain

law of effect

reinforcement

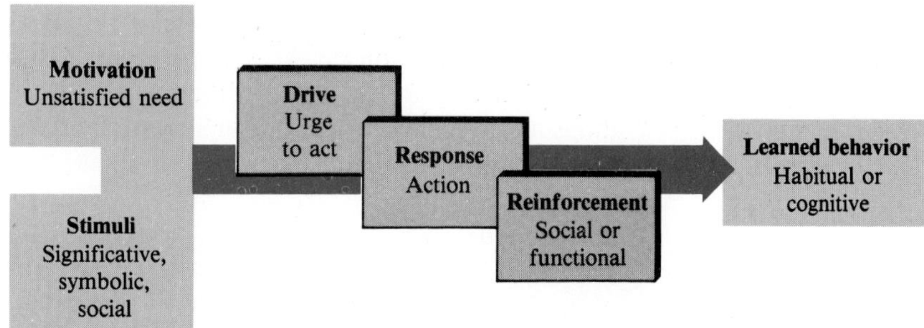

Figure 4-8
The Reinforcement Learning Process

punishments

responses and **punishments** to discourage the repetition of other responses. This type of learning is sometimes known as operant conditioning or instrumental learning as well as reinforcement learning. The reinforcement learning process is represented in Figure 4-8. (Four corollaries to the law of effect—drive reduction, preponent-response, sensory stimulation, and information as reinforcement—are discussed later in the chapter.)

significative stimuli
symbolic stimuli
social stimuli
social reinforcement
functional reinforcement

How reinforcement learning works becomes clearer when it is explained in terms of consumer behavior. The motivation is the underlying need the consumer wants to satisfy. The consumer's motivation is energized by stimuli of different kinds. **Significative stimuli** would be the product's qualities the consumer perceives directly. **Symbolic stimuli** would be advertisements of the brand. **Social stimuli** would be friends' or relatives' recommendation to buy a certain brand. Motivation and stimuli result in a drive, which in this case is a strong desire to buy the item. The response is the purchase of the brand. Reinforcement of two types follows the purchase. **Social reinforcement** occurs when others react favorably to the purchase. **Functional reinforcement** occurs when the brand performs as expected. If reinforcement is sufficiently strong, the consumer learns the behavior of brand loyalty. But if punishment occurs, he or she will probably respond by purchasing other brands. For example, suppose a young woman desires to change her appearance to look more attractive (motive). While looking through a local newspaper she sees an ad for a special on home permanents (stimulus), and as a consequence decides she wants to perm her hair (drive). After she does so, she finds that the product has performed as anticipated (functional reinforcement). Then she turns to friends and family members for their opinions. Her friends, who are younger and more open to change, approve of her new hair style (reinforcement); her family members, who are more traditional, dislike her new look (punishment). Depending on which group is more influential, she will either repeat the purchase or stop giving herself a permanent.

contingency rules

Reinforcement learning works according to **contingency rules** that take the following form. Once a response is made, a consequence occurs. Consequences may be reinforcements, which increase the probability of emitting the response, or punishments, which decrease the probability of emitting the response. As we previously discussed, also, the consequences may be positive (adding something) or negative (taking something away). Therefore, reinforcements and punishments may be either positive or negative, as the following illustrates:

Reinforcement
Positive: "If you buy AIM toothpaste, your breath will be fresh." (Add something good)
Negative: "If you buy AIM toothpaste, you will not have cavities." (Take away something bad)

Punishment
Positive: "If you brush with brand X, you will have more tooth decay." (Add something bad)
Negative: "If you brush with brand X, you will not be kissed." (Take away something good)

cognitive learned behavior

habitual learned behavior

shaping

As a learned behavior, brand loyalty can be categorized in one of two ways. If the buyer continues to purchase the brand and remains fully aware of why it is reinforcing, the brand loyalty is a **cognitive learned behavior.** However, if the buyer continues purchasing the brand without thinking about why it is reinforcing, then brand loyalty has become a **habitual learned behavior.** Marketers take advantage of the consumer's tendency toward habituation by using a process called shaping. **Shaping** is a process of reinforcing only responses that are in the desired direction. Eventually the reinforcement can be withdrawn completely, and the desired responses continues on their own. Shaping builds brand loyalty while gradually diminishing the inducements.[28] For example, a firm introduces a new, low-priced, quickly consumed product and gives out free samples. On the sample the manufacturer includes a coupon for a large discount off the price of the buyer's first purchase. The manufacturer attaches another coupon to the product on the store shelves so that the first purchase leads to a second purchase. However, the second coupon is for a smaller discount. Gradually the manufacture reduces the incentives as the consumer moves from free sample to second purchase, until the buyer is habituated to repeat purchasing at the full price. See Figure 4-9.

Reinforcement is important in learning theory because it provides a rationale for the effort put forth by the learner. In reinforcement learning, the personal value the learner derives from an activity is what justifies the activity. In other words, the *anticipated consequences* of various behaviors determine which behavior the person chooses. Therefore, for marketers to induce, change, or maintain certain consumer behaviors, they must understand these consequences.[29]

Reinforcement plays a major role in marketing. Most commercial messages use positive reinforcement when they promise a reward for purchasing a certain product and a particular brand. Advertisements that warn buyers to avoid the unpleasant consequences of buying the other

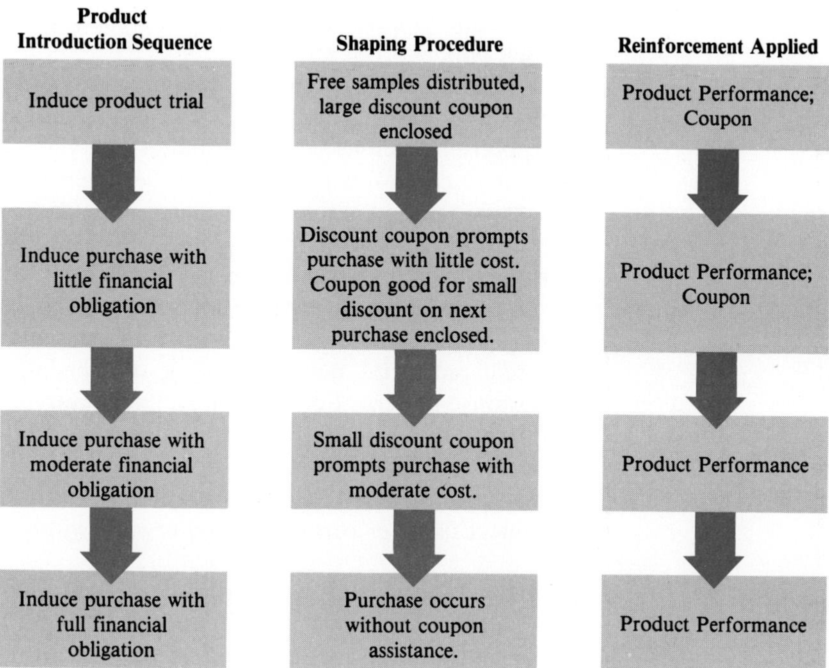
Product Introduction Sequence
Shaping Procedure
Reinforcement Applied
Induce product trial
Free samples distributed, large discount coupon enclosed
Product Performance; Coupon
Induce purchase with little financial obligation
Discount coupon prompts purchase with little cost. Coupon good for small discount on next purchase enclosed.
Product Performance; Coupon
Induce purchase with moderate financial obligation
Small discount coupon prompts purchase with moderate cost.
Product Performance
Induce purchase with full financial obligation
Purchase occurs without coupon assistance.
Product Performance

Figure 4-9
Application of Shaping Procedures to Develop Repeat Purchase Behavior

Source: adapted from Michael L. Rothschild and William C. Gaidis, "Behavioral Learning Theory: Its Relevance to Marketing and Promotions," *Journal of Marketing* 45, no. 2 (Spring 1981): 71.

brands use negative reinforcement. For example, American Express presents scenarios in which vacationers lose their travelers checks and are helpless because they bought another brand.

Reinforcement Schedules

Different rates of reinforcement lead to varying patterns of learning.[30] For example, behavior changes rapidly when there is a reward for every desired response. This is referred to as a *continuous reinforcement schedule*. Behavior changes more slowly but is accompanied by more permanent learning when a reward is received for the desired responses in only some instances. This is known as a *partial reinforcement schedule*. Laboratory experiments with animals confirm that extinction of behavior learned through occasional rewards occurs much more slowly than behavior learned by continuous rewards. This is *partial reinforcement effect*. Consider the different reinforcement schedules presented by a candy vending machine and a Las Vegas slot machine. Vending machines operate according to a continuous reinforcement schedule, if they fail to work, the user will rapidly learn not to insert any more coins. By contrast, slot machines operate on a partial reinforcement schedule. If the slot machine is broken and the user does not know it, the user will continue to insert coins and pull the lever many times, since rewards are not expected with each pull.

There are four types of partial reinforcement schedules. In a *fixed ratio schedule,* a reinforcement is applied after an established number of responses, such as one reward after every 30 responses (or 30 to 1). In a *fixed interval schedule* a reward is given to the first response after a specified period of time (such as ten minutes) from the previous response, regardless of how many responses have occurred in that time. A *variable ratio schedule* is similar to the fixed ratio except that the number of responses between reinforcements is varied. In a *variable interval schedule,* reinforcement occurs at random intervals that vary from one reinforcement to the next. Each type of schedule tends to elicit a different response pattern. For example, a fixed interval schedule causes a drop in the response rate after a reinforcement but an increasing rate of response as the time for the next reinforcement approaches. By contrast, a variable interval schedule will produce a fairly steady rate of response since the subject is never certain when a reward will occur.

Drive Reduction Hypothesis

According to the *drive reduction hypothesis,* when a behavior produces a consequence that reduced a drive, a pleasant feeling (positive reinforcement) occurs. For example, suppose a student who has a drive for excitement and aggressiveness purchases a ticket for a football game that the home team is expected to win. If the student's team does win, the win reduces the drive and rewards the behavior of attending the game. Conversely, if the home team loses, the loss may heighten the drive temporarily. The drive for excitement and aggressiveness may be reduced only when the student attends a game that the home team wins. However, if the team continues to lose, eventually the student must find other behaviors to satisfy the drive; attending the losing football games would be a sort of punishment and an activity to be avoided. Consequently, the student's behavior of purchasing football tickets would change. (In this example drive and motive are somewhat synonymous. See note 3 and the discussion of drives on page 102.)

Prepotent-Response Hypothesis

The *prepotent-response hypothesis*[31] states that if someone wants to engage in a very rewarding activity but can only do so by first performing some other, less appealing task (which the person would otherwise seldom perform), then the normally infrequent behavior will occur more frequently. In this case, the person must believe that the positive reinforcement to be gained in the end is worth the positive punishment to be experienced along the way.[32] This hypothesis might explain the behavior of someone who is not attracted to tobacco, and suspects that smoking cigarettes will lead to poorer health, but still begins smoking to attain the status he or she believes classmates accord to smokers.

Sensory Stimulation Hypothesis

The *sensory stimulation hypothesis* is an exception to the drive reduction hypothesis. It states that some activities are rewarding (reinforcing) even though they do not involve the reduction of drives.[33] For example many people shop to have something to do in environments such as malls and stores that are filled with other shoppers, displays, new products to explore, music and other noises, a range of odors, and numerous other stimuli. Sensory stimulation and novelty-seeking behaviors seem to sustain or even increase a drive level—yet shoppers appear to be rewarded by them. As Chapter 2 explains, this type of motivation explains why consumers are often interested in new products that fulfill few obvious needs.

Information as Reinforcement

Most consumer behavior is directed toward reducing the number of choices until only one—the most desirable alternative—is left. However, the vast array of products available and the many competing brands present the consumer with complex purchasing situations. Occasionally, a consumer may make one purchase in order to gather information useful in making a different purchase later. Thus, the first purchase is merely a means to an end—the anticipated reward of the later purchase. In this case, it would be a mistake to assume that the buyer will continue to purchase the first brand in the future. Such an assumption would not take into account that once the first reward (information) was received, the buyer would use the information to gain other rewards. For example, a shopper might purchase a medium-priced perfume in order to find out how a new friend reacts to perfume in general. Once the user of the perfume assesses the new friend's reaction, she might purchase a more expensive perfume or none at all, depending on the anticipated results of wearing a different brand of perfume.

Learning Theory Applied

Reinforcement learning has contributed to our understanding of consumer behavior by explaining the relationship between a consumer's satisfaction or dissatisfaction with a product and future purchases of the product. In one sense, reinforcement learning occupies a middle ground between the other two schools of learning theory. Like cognitive theory, it acknowledges the importance of problem solving or need satisfaction as the motivator of behavior.

Connectivist Approaches

In 1916, a professor of psychology dared to challenge the traditional approach to psychology pioneered by Sigmund Freud, Carl Jung, and others. In rejecting the study of consciousness by means of introspection,

J. B. Watson expressed the feelings of many scholars that psychology needed a new direction: "Enough of studying what people think and feel; let's begin studying what people do."[34] The publication in 1914 of Watson's book, *Behavior,* marked the beginning of a new school of thought called **behaviorism.** Behavioral psychologists use direct observation and experimentation as the bases of their theories. The most notable features of these theories were the now-familiar terms *stimulus* and *response*. A **stimulus** was defined as an independent variable, and a **response** was the behavior caused or affected by the stimulus.

behaviorism

stimulus

response

Contiguity learning and reinforcement learning are firmly rooted in behaviorism's concept that stimuli and responses are connected. In fact, taken together, contiguity learning and reinforcement learning constitute the **connectivist approach** to learning theory. Figure 4-10 shows the relationship between the three schools of learning theory.

connectivist approach

Marketing communications can be designed to reflect these three approaches to learning. For example, messages intended to promote cognitive learning would present logical explanations in facts to prove that a product solves a particular problem. One ad for Casablanca fans does just this by telling how the fan solves the problem of noise. Additionally, it gives information on the fan's appearance and ease of installation that also promote cognitive learning. Messages aimed at contiguity learning use pleasant stimuli such as attractive settings, nice music, and appealing textures or aromas to surround the product with positive associations. A beautiful meadow, a sensuous but innocent appearance of a woman sleeping on a horse, and soft muted tones in one Jontue ad are aimed at contiguity learning. The sparseness of the copy in the ad helps to promote the viewer's association of Jontue with the features in the picture—there are no distractions from the visual message.

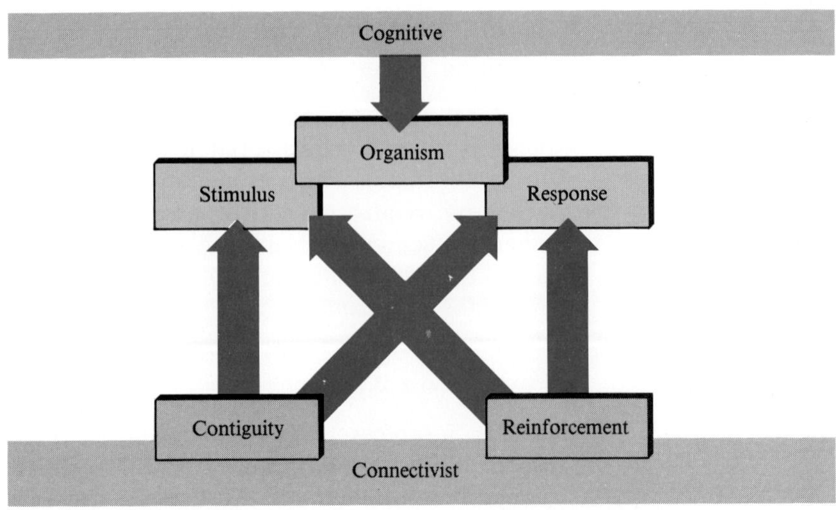

Figure 4-10 *Relationship and Focus of the Schools of Learning Theory*

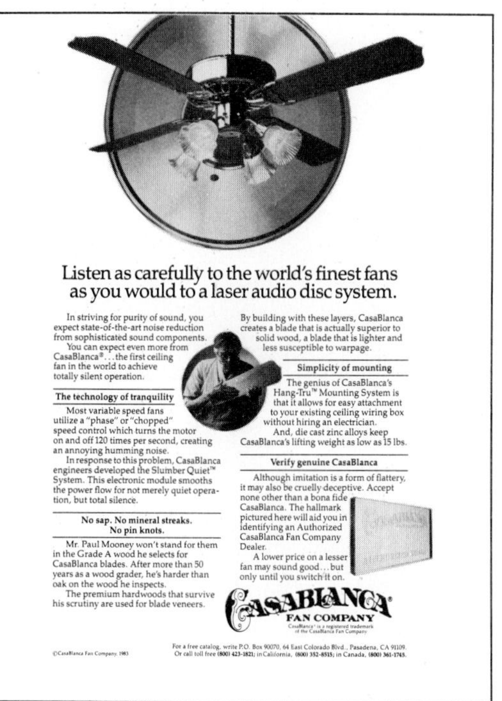

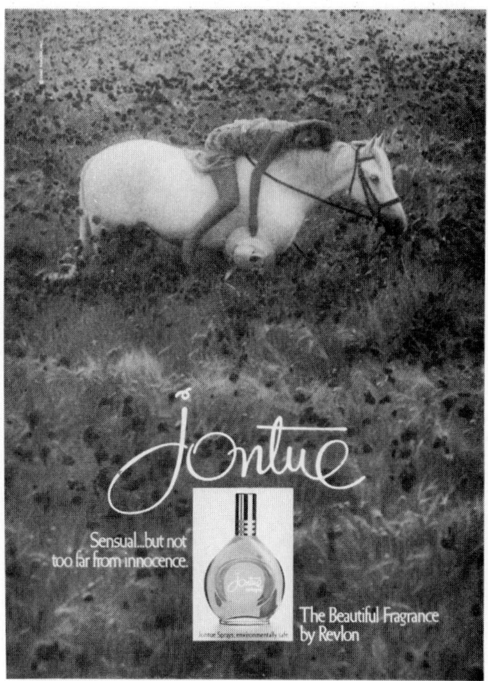

Reinforcement messages would emphasize results with testimonials about the product's performance. An ad for Eureka tents reinforces their use by stating that these tents are used by a million backpackers. It even has a small inset photo of Eureka tents in use on an actual expedition. The copy in the ad lists more expeditions on which the product was used to assure the reader of Eureka's quality and ability to fulfill backpackers' needs.

Integrative Learning Framework

Some researchers have developed mathematical models that integrate the different learning theories. These models provide a relationship between the variables in the buying environment.[35] Marketers can use these models as a guide to calculate the probability of purchases of their brand and to predict brand loyalty.

In the early 1940s, C. L. Hull and K. W. Spence developed a formula for predicting response tendencies that combined the most widely accepted concepts of each of the three major schools of learning theory. The formula was modifed by Donald Campbell in the early 1960s by integrating it with a similar model in cognitive psychology, and thus expanding its use.[36]

The integrative approach to learning is summarized in this equation:

$$R = f(S \times D \times K \times H)$$

where:
f = function
R = response tendency
S = stimulus
D = drive
K = incentive motivation
H = habit

Each of these components is either the same as or similar to concepts already presented in this chapter. Response tendency (R) is the dependent variable which symbolizes action, such as the purchase of a product or the intention to purchase a product.

Stimulus (S) can take the forms of the product itself, advertisements and other commercial messages about the product, or social messages that refer to the product.

> Example: Someone sees a television commercial for Clorox bleach which states that Clorox will make clothes look cleaner.

Drive (D) is a state of tension or imbalance which has its roots in motivation (an unsatisfied need) and is triggered by stimuli.

Example: After viewing the commercial, the person realizes that he or she is out of bleach and has a desire (drive) to buy bleach for cleaner looking clothes.

Incentive motivation (*K*) is the magnitude of the reward of anticipated reward. Changes in the magnitude of the reward produce rapid changes in the level of performance.

Example: The person expects Clorox bleach to remove difficult stains and to make clothes, especially white fabrics, look cleaner and fresher.

Habit strength (*H*) relates to both the practice of a behavior and the amount of information received about the behavior. The more times a person has purchased a brand, the more likely he or she is to purchase it in the future. Habit strength is the tendency to purchase because of previous purchases or uses of the brand.

Example: The person usually buys Clorox bleach if it is available and rarely puts any conscious thought into the purchase.

Although this description of the integrated approach is brief, it shows how parts of the theories which have grown out of the work of early behaviorists such as Watson, Pavlov, and Thorndike function together.

Marketing Principles

Each of the three learning theories complement each other to give a more comprehensive view of consumer behavior. Together the different theories help us understand how consumers are likely to respond to different stimuli and why. Table 4-3 illustrates a number of learning principles marketers might apply to condition consumers to purchase certain brands or otherwise respond favorably to a market offering. Four major categories of learning, here called behavior modification, are respondent conditioning (using conditioned or unconditioned stimuli) operant conditioning (providing rewards), modeling (using instructors, experts, or other models), and ecological modification (providing environments that are conducive to purchase).

Marketers have used learning theory as a tool in developing useful marketing methods. Here are nine basic principles of learning theory that can be used to guide marketing decisions:

- The stronger the stimulus, the stronger the response tendency. The more apparent the stimulus (for example, an advertisement), the more likely it is to generate some response, such as the consumer purchasing the product or saying good or bad things about the product.
- Stimulus strength is relative, not absolute. The intensity of an object as a stimulus depends on other stimuli and the experience of the shopper. (This fact helps explain why a black-and-white ad placed among four color ads can be very effective.)

Table 4-3 SOME APPLICATIONS OF BEHAVIOR MODIFICATION IN MARKETING

I. Respondent Conditioning

A. Conditioning responses to new stimuli

Unconditioned or Previously Conditioned Stimulus	*Conditioned Stimulus*	*Examples*
Exciting event	A product or theme song	Gillette theme song followed by sports event
Patriotic events or music	A product or person	Patriotic music as background in political commercial

B. Use of familiar stimuli to elicit responses

Conditioned Stimulus	*Conditioned Response(s)*	*Examples*
Familar music	Relaxation, excitement, "good will"	Christmas music in retail store
Familiar voices	Excitement, attention	Famous sportscaster narrating a commercial
Sexy voices, bodies	Excitement, attention, relaxation	Noxema television ads and many others
Familiar social cues	Excitement, attention, anxiety	Sirens sounding or telephones ringing in commercials

II. Operant Conditioning

A. Rewards for desired behavior (continuous schedules)

Desired Behavior	*Reward Given Following Behavior*
Product purchase	Trading stamps, cash bonus or rebate, prizes, coupons

B. Rewards for desired behavior (partial schedules)

Desired Behavior	*Reward Given (sometimes)*
Product purchase	Prize for every second or third purchase Prize to some fraction of people who purchase

C. Shaping

Approximation of Desired Response	*Consequence Following Approximation*	*Final Response Desired*
Opening a charge account	Prizes, etc., for opening account	Expenditure of funds
Trip to point-of-purchase location	Loss leaders, entertainment, or event at the shopping center	Purchase of products
Entry into store	Door prize	Purchase of products
Product trial	Free product and/or some bonus for using	Purchase of product

D. Discriminative Stimuli

Desired Behavior	*Reward Signal*	*Examples*
Entry into store	Store signs	50% off sale
	Store logos	K-Mart's big red "K"
Brand purchase	Distinctive brandmarks	Levis tag

III. Modeling

Modeling Employed	*Desired Response*
Instructor, expert, salesperson using product (in ads or at point of purchase)	Use of product in technically competent way
Models in ads asking questions at point-of-purchase	Ask questions of point of purchase which highlight product advantages

Table 4-3 SOME APPLICATIONS OF BEHAVIOR MODIFICATION IN MARKETING, continued

Models in ads receiving positive reinforcement for product purchase or use	Increase product purchase and use
Models in ads receiving no reinforcement or receiving punishment for performing undesired behaviors	Extinction of or decrease in undesired behaviors
Individual or group (similar to target) using product in novel, enjoyable way	Use of product in new ways

IV. Ecological Modification

Environmental Design	*Example*	*Intermediate Behavior*	*Final Desired Behavior*
Store layout	End of escalator, end-aisle, other displays	Bring customer into visual contact with product	Product purchase
Purchase locations	Purchase possible from home, store location	Product or store contact	Product purchase
In-store mobility	In-store product directories, information booths	Bring consumer into visual contract with product	Product purchase
Noises, odors, lights	Flashing lights in store window	Bring consumer into visual or other sensory contact with store or product	Product puchase

Source: adapted from Walter Nord and J. Paul Peter, "A Behavior Modification Perspective on Marketing," *Journal of Marketing* (Spring 1980): 42–43.

- Two stimuli that are perceived similarly tend to evoke the same response. (This relates to generalization.)
- Somewhat similar stimuli tend not to be discriminated as well early in the learning process, as they are later. (This explains why brand-oriented promotion works more effectively after a new product has been introduced in its generic form.)
- Generally, the stronger the drive, the more likely it is to be followed by a response.
- How much satisfaction a customer expects from a product relates directly to whether or not he or she will purchase the product.
- Changes in the magnitude of the reward produce very rapid changes in the level of performance.
- In general, the more times someone has purchased a product, the more likely the person is to purchase it in the future.
- Early experience with a behavior is more important than later experience. Therefore, brands that enter the market early are more likely to build habit than those entering later.

This summary of how learning theory applies to marketing demonstrates that the concepts and theories presented in this chapter are not mere abstractions; they are vital to an understanding of consumer behavior.

SUMMARY

Learning is any change in behavioral tendencies due to experience. When motives are activated by stimuli or cues, drives occur that lead to behaviors, or responses. Responses can be either internal or external. Experience is accumulated through repetition of an activity or through memory. The learning curve illustrates how learning improves with repetition. Memory has three components: sensory memory, short-term memory, and long-term memory. The method of storage in long-term memory (anchor clusters) relates to a buyer's evoked set of brands.

Three major schools of thought about learning have contributed to our present understanding of consumer behavior. The cognitive learning school emphasizes logical problem-solving behavior. Shoppers use simplification and complication in their cognitive learning of purchase behavior. The contiguity learning approach explains how responses can be modified by the connected presentation of stimuli. Generalization and discrimination are learning strategies related to contiguity learning. In reinforcement learning, rewards and punishments are used to condition responses to stimuli. While reinforcement learning acknowledges the role of motivation, it is still classified (along with contiguity learning) as a connectivist approach. Contemporary researchers have combined the leading features of the three learning schools in integrated learning. The combination of a solid theoretical framework and sophisticated analytical tools has contributed much to our current understanding of learning as it relates to consumer behavior.

KEY TERMS

learning
drives
cues
amplitude
speed
repetition
mnemonic
rehearsal
learning curve
habit
stochastic learning models
evoked set
cognitive school of learning
simplification
complication
product life cycle
contiguity learning
generalization
discrimination
law of effect
reinforcement
punishments
significative stimuli
symbolic stimuli
social stimuli
social reinforcement
functional reinforcement
contingency rules
cognitive learned behavior
habitual learned behavior
shaping
behaviorism
stimulus
response
connectivist approach

QUESTIONS

1. After attending the first day of a statistics class, a student decides to drop the course. Using your imagination, what stimuli may have caused this response? Try to include examples of significative and social stimuli in your answer.

2. Briefly define what is meant by the learning curve in terms of consumer behavior. What implications does it have for brand choice?

3. Discuss the implications of probabilistic or stochastic learning models for advertising strategy. Why might a marketer choose to limit the amount of advertising aimed at a particular audience?

4. What is a buyer's evoked set? How does the evoked set differ from brand awareness?

5. How do extensive problem solving, limited problem solving, and routinized response behavior differ in terms of prepurchase activity? Explain why the buyer's experience is important in determining what type of problem solving will occur over time. Consider the product life cycle in your discussion.

6. Discuss the role of generalization and discrimination in contiguity learning. Could both be used as part of one marketing strategy? Explain, using examples.

7. Describe the major steps in the reinforcement learning process. What is meant by shaping?

8. Distinguish between brand loyalty that is cognitively learned versus that which is habitually learned. From a marketer's view, which is more a desirable type of loyalty? Why?

NOTES

1. John F. Hall, *The Psychology of Learning* (Philadelphia: Lippincott, 1966), 3–6.
2. Ernest R. Hilgard and Gordon H. Bower, *Theories of Learning,* 3rd ed. (New York: Appleton-Century-Crofts, 1966), 2.
3. While some writers use the words *need, motive,* and *drive* interchangeably, they are used here to denote three discrete aspects of motivation. Needs are goals, general and common to all human beings. Motives are types of human pursuits or activities; they may or may not be considered goals.
4. Russell W. Belk, Kenneth D. Bahn, and Robert N. Mayer, "Developmental Recognition of Consumer Symbolism," *Journal of Consumer Research* 9 (1982): 4–17.
5. Thomas K. Srull, "The Role of Prior Knowledge in the Acquisition, Retention, and Use of New Information," in *Advances in Consumer Research X,* Richard P. Bagozzi and Alice M. Tybout, eds. (Ann Arbor, MI: Association for Consumer Research, 1983), 572–76.
6. Robert Bush and Frederick Mosteller, *Stochastic Models for Learning* (New York: John Wiley and Sons, 1955).
7. Since Kuehn published his model, many probability models have been produced and refinements made for consumer behavior. For more information, see David B. Montgomery and Adrian B. Ryans, "Stochastic Models of Consumer Choice Behavior," in *Consumer Behavior: Theoretical Sources,* Scott Ward and Thomas S. Robertson, eds. (Englewood Cliffs, NJ: Prentice-Hall, 1973), 531–76.
8. L. A. Fourt and J. W. Woodlock, "Early Prediction of Market Success for New Grocery Products," *Journal of Marketing* 25 (1960): 31–38.
9. For more on the new product trial rate and the repeat purchase rate, see W. F. Massey, D. B. Montgomery,

and D. G. Morrison, *Stochastic Learning Models of Buying Behavior* (Cambridge, MA: Massachusetts Institute of Technology Press, 1970).

10. Morgan Jones and Fred S. Zufryden, "Relating Deal Purchases and Consumer Characteristics to Repeat Purchase Probability," *Journal of Market Research Society* 23 (1981): 84–97.
11. Donald G. Morrison, "Testing Brand Switching Models," *Journal of Market Research* 3 (November 1966): 401–409.
12. Proprietary study by a U.S. food manufacturer.
13. Robert C. Blattberg and Subruta K. Sen, "Market Segments and Stochastic Brand Choice," *Journal of Marketing Research* 13 (February 1976): 34–46.
14. Brian Milton Campbell, "The Existence of Evoked Set and Determinants of Its Magnitude in Brand Choice Behavior," in *Buyer Behavior,* John A. Howard and Lyman E. Ostlund, eds. (New York: Alfred A. Knopf, 1973), 243–44.
15. Jagdish N. Sheth and M. Venkatesan, "Risk Reduction Processes in Repetitive Consumer Behavior," *Journal of Marketing Research* 5 (1968): 307–10.
16. Louis P. Bucklin, "The Informative Role of Advertising," *Journal of Advertising Research* 5 (1965): 11–15.
17. Peter D. Bennett and Robert M. Mandell, "Prepurchase Information-Seeking Behavior of New Car Purchasers: The Learning Hypothesis," *Journal of Marketing Research* 6 (1969): 430–33.
18. John A. Howard, *Consumer Behavior: Application of Theory* (New York: McGraw-Hill, 1977).
19. Ivan Pavlov, *Conditioned Reflexes: An Investigation of the Physiological Activity of the Cerebral Cortex,* trans. G. V. Anrep (London: Oxford University Press, 1927).
20. For further discussions on behaviorism in relation to marketing, see Walter R. Nord and J. Paul Peter, "A Behavior Modification Perspective on Marketing," *Journal of Marketing* 44 (1980): 36–47; and J. Paul Peter and Walter R. Nord, "A Clarification and Extension of Operant Conditioning Principles in Marketing," *Journal of Marketing* 46 (1982): 102–107.
21. Gerald J. Gorn, "The Effects of Music in Advertising on Choice Behavior: A Classical Conditioning Approach," *Journal of Marketing* 46 (1982): 94–101.
22. Winfred F. Hill, *Learning: A Survey of Psychological Interpretations* (San Francisco: Chandler, 1963).
23. Chem L. Narayana and Calvin P. Duncar, "Consumer Generalization Tendencies: An Empirical Study," in *Marketing in the 80s: Educators Conference Proceedings,* series no. 46 (Chicago: American Marketing Association, 1980), 164–67.
24. "Sea of Green Look Adopted in Green Giant Repackaging," *Marketing News,* (March 4, 1983): 3.
25. Harry Nystrom, Hans Tamsons, and Robert Thams, "An Experiment in Price Generalization and Discrimination," *Journal of Marketing Research* 12 (May 1975): 177–81.
26. E. L. Thorndike, *The Fundamentals of Learning* (New York: New York Teachers College, 1932).
27. E. L. Thorndike, *Animal Intelligence: Experimental Studies* (New York: Macmillan, 1911), 244.
28. M. L. Rothschild and W. C. Gaidis, "Behavioral Learning Theory: Its Relevance to Marketing and Promotions," *Journal of Marketing* 45, no. 2 (Spring 1981): 70–78.
29. For more on reinforcement, see Albert Bandura, *Principles of Behavior Modification* (New York: Holt, Rinehart and Winston, 1969), 217–348.
30. Rita L. Atkinson, Richard C. Atkinson, and Ernest R. Hilgard, *Introduction to Psychology,* 8th ed. (New York: Harcourt Brace Jovanovich, 1983), 202–204.
31. D. Premach, "Reinforcement Theory," in D. Levine ed., *Nebraska Symposium on Motivation* (Lincoln: University of Nebraska Press, 1965), 123–180, 219–21.
32. This hypothesis is closely allied to the concept of approach-avoidance motivational conflict discussed in Chapter 2.
33. Premach, "Reinforcement Theory," 219.
34. J. B. Watson, "The Place of the Conditioned Reflex in Psychology," *Psychological Review* 23, no. 2 (1916): 89–116.
35. Michael L. Ray, "Psychological Theories and Interpretations of Learning," in *Consumer Behavior: Theoretical Sources,* Scott Ward and Thomas S. Robertson, eds. (Englewood Cliffs, NJ: Prentice-Hall, 1973), 85–86.
36. Hill, *Learning: A Survey of Psychological Interpretations,* 129–56.

FURTHER READING

Classics

Andreasen, Alan R., and Peter G. Durkson, "Market Learning of New Residents," *Journal of Marketing Research* 5 (May 1968): 166–76.

Hall, John F., *The Psychology of Learning* (Philadelphia: Lippincott, 1966).

Jacoby, Jacob, and David B. Kyner, "Brand Loyalty vs. Repeat Purchasing Behavior," *Journal of Marketing Research* 10 (February 1973).

Kuehn, Alfred A., "Consumer Brand Choice: A Learning Process," in *Classics in Consumer Behavior,* Louis E. Boone (Tulsa: Petroleum Publishing Company, 1977): 185–98.

Newman, Joseph W., and Richard A. Werbel, "Multivariate Analysis of Brand Loyalty for Major Household Appliances." *Journal of Marketing Research* 10 (November 1973): 404–09.

Ray, Michael L., "Psychological Theories and Interpretations of Learning," in *Consumer Behavior: Theoretical Sourcebook,* S. Ward and T. S. Robertson, eds. (Englewood Cliffs, NJ: Prentice-Hall, 1973).

Ray, Michael L., Alan G. Sawyer, and Edward C. Strong, "Frequency Effects Revisited," *Journal of Advertising Research* 11 (February 1971): 14–20.

Ray, Michael L., and Peter H. Webb, "Three Learning Theory Traditions and Their Application in Marketing" in *Combined Proceedings,* Ronald C. Curhan, ed. (Chicago, IL: American Marketing Association, 1974): 101–103.

Sawyer, Alan G., "Repetition and Affect: Recent Empirical and Theoretical Developments," in *Consumer and Industrial Buying Behavior,* Arch Woodside, Jagdish Sheth, and Peter Bennett, eds. (New York: North-Holland, 1977): 229–42.

Sheth, Jagdish N., "How Adults Learn Brand Preference," *Journal of Advertising Research* 8 (September 1968): 25–36.

Zielske, Herbert A., "The Remembering and Forgetting of Advertising," *Journal of Marketing* 23 (January 1959): 239–43.

Recent Significant Research

Chance, Paul, *Learning and Behavior* (Belmont, CA: Wadsworth, 1979).

Gorn, Gerald J., "The Effects of Music in Advertising on Choice Behavior: A Classical Conditioning Approach," *Journal of Marketing,* 46 (Winter 1982): 94–101.

Kass, Klaus Peter, "Consumer Habit Forming, Information Acquisition, and Buying Behavior," *Journal of Business Research* 10 (March 1982): 3–15.

Nord, Walter, and J. Paul Peter, "A Behavior Modification Perspective on Marketing," *Journal of Marketing* (Spring 1980).

Rothschild, Michael L., and William C. Gaidis, "Behavioral Learning Theory: Its Relevance to Marketing and Promotions," *Journal of Marketing* 45 (Spring 1981): 70–78.

Applications

Atkin, Charles K., "Children's Social Learning from Television Advertising: Research Evidence on Observational Modeling of Product Consumption," in *Advances in Consumer Research,* Vol. 3 (1976), Beverlee B. Anderson, ed. 513–19.

Bennett, Peter D., and Robert M. Mandel, "Prepurchase Information Seeking Behavior of New Car Purchasers: The Learning Hypothesis," *Journal of Marketing Research* 6 (November 1969): 430–33.

Deslauriers, B. C., and P. B. Everett, "The Effects of Intermittent and Continuous Token Reinforcement on Bus Ridership," *Journal of Applied Psychology* (August 1977): 369–75.

"How Much Frequency is Enough?" *Media Decisions* 13, no. 11 (November 1978): 74–76, 130, 134.

Krugman, Herbert E., "An Application of Learning Theory to TV Copy Testing," *Public Opinion Quarterly* 26 (1962): 626–34.

Moore, Roy L., and Lowndes F. Stephens, "Some Communication and Demographic Determinants of Adolescent Consumer Learning," *Journal of Consumer Research* (September 1975): 80–92.

Ray, Michael L., and Peter H. Webb, "Three Learning Theory Traditions and Their Application in Marketing," in *Combined Proceedings,* Ronald C. Curhan, ed. (Chicago: American Marketing Association, 1974), 100–103.

Ward, Scott, and Daniel Wackman, "Family and Media Influences on Adolescent Consumer Learning," *American Behavioral Scientist* (January–February 1971), 415–27.

5 Involvement and Attitudes

Objectives of This Chapter

After you have studied this chapter, you should be able to:

1. Discuss involvement theory and its implications for marketing management.
2. Define the term *attitudes*, particularly as it relates to consumer behavior.
3. Discuss the various theoretical models of attitude.
4. Describe some ways in which attitudes are formed, including the attitude–behavior cycle and attribution theory.
5. Explain how attitudes function in consumer behavior.

Theories of involvement and attitudes are popular among consumer behavior researchers and marketing managers because their application has proven valuable in a wide range of consumer, industrial, and professional buying situations. *Involvement* pertains to the perceived importance of a product class to the consumer. *Attitudes* can be thought of for now as consumer opinions and beliefs about brands. Together, they help marketers understand why consumers prefer particular brands over others.

The level of involvement a product class evokes from consumers affects their attitudes about brands in that class. Depending on how highly involved consumers are in a product, they use distinctly different cognitive processes to evaluate the product. How this occurs will in part determine the communication strategies marketers use in their efforts to influence consumer attitudes.

A major objective of most businesses is to understand, respond to, and influence the attitudes of their customers and potential customers. It is not surprising, then, that most of the attitude research has been directed toward three goals: (1) describing attitude components, (2) delineating methods of measuring attitudes, and (3) discovering ways to change the attitudes of potential customers. This chapter defines attitudes and presents an overview of the various theoretical approaches to studying them. We then examine the relationships between attitudes, values, and beliefs. Next we look at the three structural components of attitudes: cognitive, affective, and conative. Attitude formation is discussed in terms of the attitude–behavior cycle and attribution theory. Finally we consider the functions attitudes perform. (Chapter 6 will cover attitude measurement and models. Chapter 7 will deal with attitude change.)

LOW INVOLVEMENT AND HIGH INVOLVEMENT

involvement

Involvement is the perceived importance or concern of a particular aspect of a person's world to that person. For example, someone highly involved with fashion would have stronger opinions about the subject than one who is not involved. On one hand, consumers with a high level of involvement in a product class usually have widely differing views of different brands in the class and increased commitment either for or against them. On the other hand, consumers who have a low level of involvement with a product class do not really care enough about that class to have an opinion about the brands in it; for them, the product is not important enough to warrant concern. For example, some consumers might think that soap, paper towels, razors, floor wax, shoelaces, or film for their cameras are simply not worth devoting much time or effort to their selection. It is much easier for such consumers to walk into the store and select the brand that he or she is familiar with than to evaluate the available brands based on their attributes.

It is important for marketers to recognize that involvement is an individual phenomenon; a particular product category can engender many levels of involvement. For example, to many people the selection of chewing gum is relatively unimportant and may occur on a trial basis or almost at random. For many serious runners the choice of running shoes is the result of hours or days of research and analysis. Yet these points of view are not shared by all people. For some buyers who are concerned about dental health, the selection of a sugarless gum is *very* involving; some weekend joggers are not highly concerned at all about which running shoes they buy. For a particular person a certain product class may or may not be highly involving.

The Development of Involvement Theory

The theory of low involvement is based on four related ideas about how consumers form attitudes and make purchase decisions. First, the level of involvement with any product depends in part on the product's perceived importance to the consumer's self-concept. A high-involvement product may either confirm or conflict with the person's self-image (automobiles, clothing, and jewelry are examples). Low-involvement products tend to be unrelated to self-concept (light bulbs, and shoe polish). Second, the level of involvement depends on *perceived risk*. As a general rule, the higher the consumer's perceived risk, the higher the level of his or her involvement. Buying an expensive personal computer for the first time would be a high-risk, high-involvement situation; selecting a replacement garden hose would be a low-risk, low-involvement situation. Third, the level of involvement depends on the relationship between attitudes and behaviors. With low-involvement products, *behavior tends to precede attitudes*. A consumer may select a given product, try it out, and then form an attitude about it. Experimentation and trial are often the basis for the consumer's choosing the product for the first time. Fourth, information is processed differently in low- and high-involvement situations. For low-involvement products, there may be no active search for information. In fact, consumers may gather information involuntarily, without deliberately paying attention to advertising.

Herbert Krugman was conducting research in the mid-1960s on what consumers learn from their television viewing.[1] He found that while they had a high level of awareness of the brands advertised on television, there was very little attitude change associated with those brands. His interpretation was that while watching television, consumers retain information at random and do not link the incoming information with other product data or with their consumption needs. He called this phenomenon *passive learning,* and designated television as a passive communication medium. Passive learning, then, occurs when a consumer has a low level of involvement with a product. The product is not of much concern to the consumer; therefore he or she does not attempt to learn the product information in the ad. For example, most college students do not have children and have a low level of involvement with disposable diapers. When these students see an ad on television for Pampers, they do not think about the brand and its benefits. Consequently, their attitude toward Pampers does not change. When these students see the ad several more times, they begin to remember randomly some of the aspects of the ad and would probably be able to recognize that Pampers is a brand of disposable diapers.

Low involvement in a product class does not occur only for products which a consumer does not use. Two researchers wanted to identify products for which most college students had either low or high levels of involvement. They found low involvement for light bulbs, facial tissue, blankets, toothbrushes, suntan preparations, and soap—products that most college students buy for themselves. High-involvement products for these students were blue jeans, automobiles, high-fidelity loudspeakers, and beer.[2] Naturally, other population segments, such as grandparents, doctors, and blue-collar workers, would have very different products in their low- and high-involvement categories.

An Example of Involvement

A college student purchasing both a low-involvement and a high-involvement product illustrates the implications of Krugman's theory on the decision-making process. Joe, a student at a large university, has decided that he needs a new pair of blue jeans. For Joe, blue jeans are a high-involvement product. He feels that it is important for him to look his best, and the clothing that he selects reflects that concern. Whenever Joe sees an ad on television for blue jeans, he listens to it and thinks about it; whenever he sees a blue jeans ad in a magazine or newspaper, he pauses to read it. He also notices the brands and styles of jeans his friends and classmates wear. When he goes shopping for the new pair, he compares different brands and styles at different stores and chooses the pair of blue jeans that best meets his criteria. On his way home, Joe decides to pick up a few items at the grocery store. One of the items he needs is a package of frozen corn. Joe believes that the brand he purchases is not important; therefore, he has a low level of involvement with frozen corn. As he walks through the frozen-food section, he sees several different brands of corn. How will he choose among them? He notices a package of Birds-Eye brand frozen corn. The brand name sounds familiar—perhaps he saw an ad for that brand. He picks up the package, puts it in his cart, and gathers the other items he needs from the store. When Joe tries the corn for dinner that evening, he thinks to himself that it tastes good and he made a wise purchase.

Joe's two purchases represent two different types of behavior. In his blue jeans purchase (high involvement) his beliefs were formed through the process of actively seeking information about his anticipated purchase. He evaluated the available brands and then bought, basing his purchase on what information he acquired. In the case of the frozen corn, his beliefs about the brands arose through passive learning. He purchased the product first and *then* evaluated it based on trial. These differences are illustrated in Figure 5-1.

Note that in the low-involvement condition, the consumer might *not* evaluate the brand after purchase. This is shown by the dashed arrow between the decision phase and the evaluation phase. In our example, Joe evaluated the frozen corn purchase by thinking that it tasted good. He could have finished his dinner without giving any thought whatsoever to the corn. This process of belief formation through passive learning and purchase decision without brand evaluation has been called **inertia.**[3]

inertia

A concept that can be interpreted differently in high- and low-involvement situations is **brand loyalty.** If Joe were to buy the same brand of blue jeans or of frozen corn every time, we would say that he was loyal to that brand. However, perhaps he continues to buy the same brand of corn simply because it is familiar and he wants to avoid the process of making a decision. This would be a form of inertia called **spurious loyalty:**[4] The consumer is loyal only to the familiarity of the brand, not to the brand because of the benefits it provides (the traditional view of brand loyalty).

brand loyalty

spurious loyalty

Another form of behavior that low-involvement product classes engender in consumers is **variety-seeking behavior.** If Joe were to purchase a different brand of frozen corn each time he went shopping so that he could experiment or simply because he wanted something different, he would be exhibiting variety-seeking behavior. Variety seeking is seen in low-involvement situations, since low involvement means low risk in experimentation.

variety-seeking behavior

Krugman's theory of involvement has led researchers to look at brand loyalty and, more importantly, the decision-making process from a new

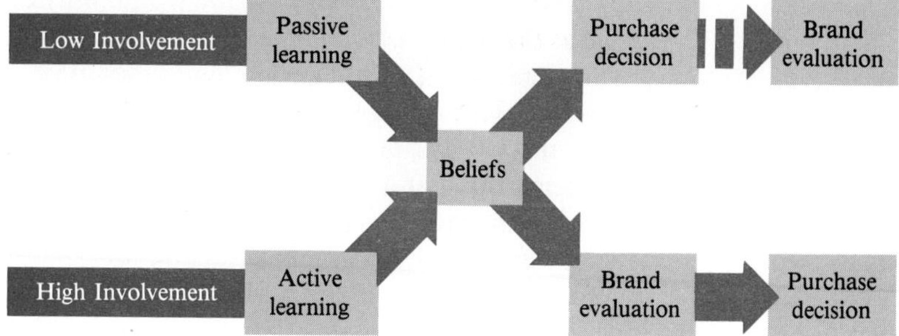

Figure 5-1
Low Involvement and High Involvement in Consumer Decision Making

perspective. Sherif and colleagues have developed a slightly different view of involvement using social judgment theory.[5] They conducted a series of studies on issues such as religion, politics, and race.[6] Their studies refer to the subjects' latitudes of acceptance, rejection, and noncommitment in relation to these issues. In the context of brand loyalty, *latitude of acceptance* means those brands that the consumer would consider adequate for his or her purposes. *Latitude of rejection* means those brands the consumer believes are not suited to his or her needs. *Latitude of noncommitment* means those brands that are neither acceptable nor unacceptable. Those who are highly involved in a product class tend to have narrow latitudes of noncommitment since, by definition, involvement means the level of importance or concern. They would have a definite opinion about an issue or product, and thus it follows they would accept very few positions and reject a large number of them. In other words, such a person would have a narrow latitude of acceptance and a wide latitude of rejection. Those whose involvement in a product class is low would have a wide latitude of acceptance and a narrow latitude of rejection.

The degree to which a person might accept or reject different positions can be equated with how readily he or she will consider an advertising message. For example, Joe is highly involved with blue jeans and he certainly has attitudes, both positive and negative, about different brands. If Joe had a strong positive attitude toward Wrangler, Levis, and Lee jeans, Sherif's theory predicts that Joe would be more attentive to positive advertising messages for those brands and would consider other brands unacceptable. For frozen corn, Joe would have a lack of commitment to any particular brand or brands. The easiest way for him to make a purchase of the corn would be to simply buy the most familiar brand to him.

Researchers have extended Sherif and colleagues' theory to look deeper at the decision-making process in both high- and low-involvement situations. Michael Rothschild and Michael Houston found that while a highly involved person would consider fewer brands within a product category, the person would use a larger number of attributes to make the purchase decision.[7] This finding is summarized in Table 5-1.

According to this theory, Joe would only consider a few brands of blue jeans (Wrangler, Levis, Lee) and evaluate the brands for a large number of attributes (style, fit, price, and amount of shrinkage). A person with a low involvement with jeans would consider almost all brands and use only one or two attributes to make a decision, perhaps using fit to eliminate some of the brands and then selecting among the remaining pairs based on the lowest price. In technical terms, high-involvement decision making is associated with a compensatory model of brand evaluation and low involvement is associated with a noncompensatory model. (We will discuss these models in greater detail in Chapter 6.)

Table 5-1 CONSUMER INVOLVEMENT MATRIX

Level of Involvement	*Number of Attributes Used in Evaluation*	*Latitude of Acceptance*	*Number of Brands Considered*	*Type of Brand Evaluation Model*
Low	Few	Wide	Many	Noncompensatory
High	Many	Narrow	Few	Compensatory

Source: after Michael L. Rothschild and Michael J. Hanston (1977), "The Consumer Involvement Matrix: Some Preliminary Findings," in Barnett A. Greenberg and Danny N. Bellinger, *Proceedings: AMA Educators' Conference,* (Chicago: American Marketing Association), 95–98.

Other Studies of Involvement

Recent significant work on involvement has attempted to clarify the relationship between involvement and attitude change.[8] The researchers tested whether the effectiveness of different methods of persuasion may depend on the amount of thought about the message a consumer develops. The amount of thought or elaboration would vary depending on the situation. In the study, 160 male and female undergraduate students expressed their attitudes about disposable razors after being exposed to magazine ads under conditions of high and low involvement. The ads contained different arguments for the product and students with high and low involvement were studied separately. These ideas were incorporated into the Elaboration Likelihood Model, or ELM. The ELM predicts that increasing involvement leads to a higher probability of elaborating and thinking about the message. The implication of this to marketers is that advertisements directed toward highly involved consumers should include extensive product-related information. The researchers call this the *central* route to persuasion. They believe that attitude changed in this manner will be enduring and that these attitudes will be good predictors of brand choices. Another route to persuasion is the *peripheral* route, according to the researchers. A peripheral persuasion would try to associate the product with positive or negative cues (such as an expert source using the product or an unfavorable situation which will not occur if the consumer uses the product). In theory, the cues shape attitudes without the person's having to interpret the product information.

The peripheral route is associated with low-involvement product decisions. These researchers have found, however, that involvement is not the only moderator of persuasion. They cite as well the importance of situational variables, such as distraction, and of individual differences, such as prior knowledge about the product. This work implies that promoting for varying involvement conditions requires emphasis on the different elements in advertisements.

Investigators have given some attention to the physiological side of attention and learning in an attempt to explain consumers' low-involvement decisions. One researcher explains low involvement as a *right-brain* activity, as is image perception.[9] By contrast, high involvement, and reading and speaking, are *left-brain* activities. The implication is that those with a high exposure to print have a higher level of involvement than do those with a greater exposure to television, an image-perception medium. This nonverbal, right-brain emphasis may point the way to the future paths of low-involvement theory. Right- and left-brain theory is discussed in Chapter 8.

Table 5-2 MARKETING IMPLICATIONS OF INVOLVEMENT LEVEL

Marketing Element	*Strategy*	
	Low Involvement	***High Involvement***
Product positioning	Emphasize overall problem solving, not individual benefit. Stress ability to "get the job done."	Present specific benefits and superiority for evaluation by the consumer.
Product differentiation	Differentiate product to build involvement where possible with advertising. Celebrities could be useful to build brand image.	Use innovation to differentiate or focus on a very important attribute to differentiate product.
Price	Since price is often the key factor in choice, price incentives are useful.	Since price is one of many attributes evaluated, incentives may not be needed.
Place	Since consumer does not search, intensive distribution is needed; shelf space, displays can be important tools.	Intensive distribution is not always necessary, since consumer is more apt to seek out information for purchase.
Promotion	Focus on establishing buying habit through continuing promotion.	Focus on first-time purchase based on consumer's consideration of benefits.
Advertising	Use repetitive advertising to boost awareness and high level of familiarity with brand.	Use advertising less frequently; consumers actively seek to learn about brand.
Media	Broadcast (TV, radio) is effective; awareness and familiarity are vital.	Use broadcast to create initial awareness, but emphasize print to clarify benefits and supply information.
Message content	Limit information to only one or two key points; message is not as important as repetition. Incorporate heavy repetition of brand name to induce trial. Consider the use of a highly credible or trustworthy source to promote product.	Since these consumers seek information, the content of the message is critical. Supply enough information to get consideration of the product and to satisfy the consumer's need for information to evaluate benefits.

Implications of Involvement for Marketing Strategy

Many managerial and strategic implications follow from involvement theory. For example, marketers may use strategies to boost the involvement of consumers in their low-involvement products by differentiating the product from those of competitors. Or marketers may decide to accept the fact that low involvement is a function of their product category and focus instead on building high brand awareness through advertising. Some general marketing implications of high- and low-involvement consumers are summarized in Table 5-2.

ATTITUDES

What Attitudes Are

Much of what we know about attitudes is due to the work of behavioral scientists, particularly those in the field of social psychology. Some authors have gone so far as to define social psychology as the scientific study of attitudes, as the Sherifs have done in their important work dealing with attitudes and involvement.[10]

By 1935, attitude had already become an important construct to behavioral scientists. In that year, Gordon Allport combined several earlier definitions and concluded that **attitude** is a "mental and neural state of readiness, organized through experience, exerting a directive or dynamic influence upon the individual's response to all objects and situations with which it is related."[11] This definition has four parts. First, "a mental and neural state" indicates that attitudes are part of the psychological makeup of the individual and have the potential to be expressed. Thus, we can assess attitudes through measurement techniques (to be discussed in Chapter 7). "Organized through experience" implies that attitudes are learned. This suggests that environmental conditions affect attitude development. "Exerting a directive or dynamic influence upon the individual's response" refers to the link between thoughts and actions. Attitudes are not passive elements of the individual's psychological makeup; rather, they influence what the person thinks as well as what actions he or she takes. Finally, "to all objects and situations with which it [the attitude] is related" reflects the pervasiveness of attitudes; they are instrumental in all facets of the person's life, including buying activities.

attitude

Different aspects of Allport's definition are emphasized by scholars of different behavioral schools. For example, reinforcement learning theorists and perceptual theorists concentrate on the close correspondence between experience, behavior, and attitudes, while cognitive learning theorists emphasize the individual's insight and the organization of attitudes.

To understand attitudes as they relate to consumer behavior, however, we must take an integrated approach, using all of these concepts.

Attitudes and Values

values

Although attitudes and values are similar, for our purposes there are two important differences. First, **values** are broader than attitudes. They pertain to a few very important aspects of a person's life and are a product of the culture (see Chapter 13). An example of a value is the importance of preserving the family. Attitudes toward several subjects can be based on one value. As Figure 5-2 illustrates, the value of preserving the family is represented by multiple attitudes, such as the attitude that open marriages

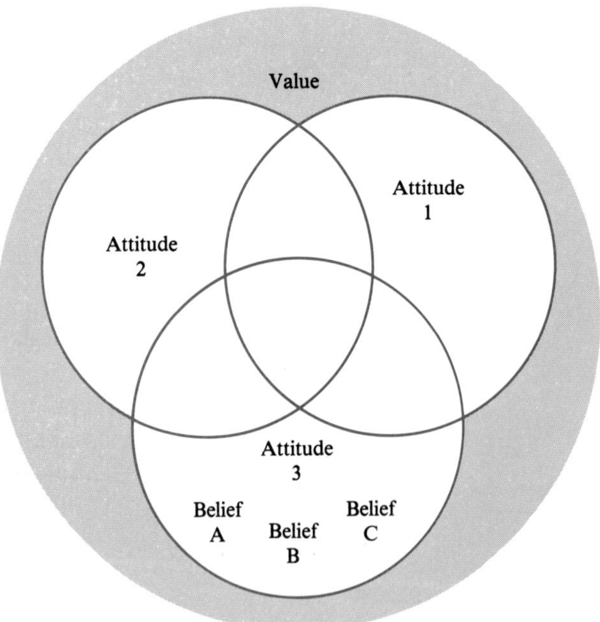

Value: Preservation of the family

Attitude 1: Open marriages, in which spouses date other people, are harmful to family life.

Attitude 2: Mothers should not work when children are young.

Attitude 3: Parents and children should take vacations together.

Belief A: I believe that working mothers often ignore their children. (Descriptive)

Belief B: I believe that a mother's attention to her children is beneficial. (Evaluative)

Belief C: I believe that all mothers should sacrifice work income to care for their children. (Prescriptive)

Figure 5-2
Relationship of Values and Beliefs to Attitudes

are harmful, mothers should not work, and parents and children should take vacations together.

A second distinction between attitudes and values is that values are generally permanent whereas some specific attitudes within one's value system are susceptible to change. If values change at all, they change much more slowly than attitudes do. Although the marketing activities of one firm probably have little impact on consumers' value systems, the firm must understand these values and ensure that its marketing activities do not run counter to them. At the same time, it must try to influence consumers' attitudes toward its products if it is to be successful.

In spite of these distinctions, sometimes values and attitudes are difficult to differentiate. Therefore, the word *attitude* implies here an underlying, if not overt, connection with values.[12]

Attitudes and Beliefs

Whereas values are associated with attitudes, beliefs are related even more directly to them. To a large extent, people are *belief* seekers rather than *fact* seekers. The adage that "beauty is in the eye of the beholder" is consistent with scientific evidence about attitudes[13] in that, for the individual consumer, the most important reality of a product's attributes is what he or she believes the product is or can be. Beliefs are the building blocks of attitudes.

belief

A **belief** is a thought that expresses the perceived relationship between an object or event and an attribute. E. E. Jones and H. D. Gerard express this idea well: "A belief is, or can be transformed into, an assertion with a subject and a predicate: The righteous will enter the Kingdom of Heaven; yogurt leads to slimness. The object and subject are both cognitive concepts and in any particular belief the object is an associated characteristic of the subject."[14]

descriptive belief
evaluative belief
prescriptive belief

Milton Rokeach has defined three types of beliefs: descriptive or existential, evaluative, and prescriptive.[15] A **descriptive belief** reflects a person's knowledge about an object. An **evaluative belief** represents the person's feelings about the goodness or badness of an object or issue. A **prescriptive belief** relates to what action should be taken regarding the object or issue. A descriptive or existential belief might be stated thus: "I believe Crest prevents cavities." A statement reflecting an evaluative belief would be: "I believe cavity prevention is very important (good)." A prescriptive belief is exemplified by this statement: "I believe I should purchase Crest the next time I buy toothpaste." In the next section we will see that each of these types of belief corresponds to one of the three aspects or structural components of an attitude, because attitudes are complexes of beliefs.

THEORETICAL APPROACHES TO THE STUDY OF ATTITUDES

Researchers have used various approaches to understand attitudes and how they influence consumer behavior. Four major approaches are the structural approach, the functional approach, consistency theory, and the multiattribute approach. Each looks at attitudes from a somewhat different perspective. Together they provide an overall understanding of the meaning and function of attitudes.

According to the *structural* approach, attitudes are composed of three major parts: a cognitive (or thinking) component, an affective (or feeling) component, and a conative (or behavioral) component. That is, an attitude is a composite of what a person *thinks* about an object, how he or she *feels* about it, and how the person *behaves* toward it. This approach considers that attitudes toward different objects overlap and are not isolated from one another. For example, a person's favorable attitude toward travel relates to his or her favorable attitudes toward leisure activities and vacations.

The *functional* approach examines attitudes in terms of what purposes they serve for the person. As with motivation, perception, and learning, researchers are concerned with the differences between individuals. This approach assumes that the same attitude may be held by different people for many different reasons. That is, someone may feel a certain way for a variety of reasons. Four major functions that attitudes serve for each person will be discussed later in this chapter. They include the knowledge function, the instrumental-adjustive function, the value-expressive function, and the ego-defensive function.

Consistency theory offers yet another approach to attitude study. This approach incorporates a number of separate but related theories. A principal one is *balance theory,* which states that people seek to maintain consistency between the affective (emotional) and the cognitive (knowledge) parts of each attitude. According to the theory, when a person's affective and cognitive elements are consistent, he or she is in a balanced state and a stable attitude exists. For example, someone knows that seat belts prevent car accident injuries (cognitive) and has a favorable attitude toward seat belts (affective). However, if the attitude components are inconsistent, the person feels psychological tension and must alter the attitude to achieve a balanced state. Markets use the balance theory to influence consumer behavior by purposely creating an unbalanced state for potential buyers: The consumer must alter the attitude—by buying the product, for example—in order to achieve consistency. Advertisements may incorporate this technique in certain instances. For example, the California Avocado Commission used Angie Dickinson, who many consumers believe to be in good shape, in promotions for avocados. Consistency theory would suggest that consumers who did not like avocados because of their high caloric content, but who believed Angie Dickinson to be highly fit, might be encouraged to change their attitude toward avocados.

A fourth approach to attitude theory is the *multiattribute* approach. In some ways, this perspective is similar to the structural approach: it, too, assumes that attitudes are composed of a set of components or beliefs about an object. The Fishbein multiattribute model considers that an overall attitude toward an object is a composite of (a) a person's knowledge about the object's attributes and (b) how he or she evaluates those attributes. An example would be someone's attitude toward Dial soap, which might be composed of *beliefs* about the soap's attributes (ability to clean, deodorize, and moisturize, for example) *plus* an evaluation of how *desirable* each attribute is. Clearly, consumers differ in their beliefs about the characteristics of brands and their relative desirability. These differences explain the overall differences in attitude among people.

STRUCTURAL COMPONENTS OF ATTITUDES

Attitudes are made up of cognitive components, affective components, and behavioral components. *Cognitive* components are thoughts uninfluenced by emotions; *affective* components are feelings, and *behavioral* components are actions. Attitude components are very important aspects of consumer behavior. Taken together, they have a strong effect on buying decisions such as the brand and amount of a product to be purchased. However, to appreciate their significance, we must consider each attitude component in relation to its corresponding belief type. Figure 5-3 shows the relationship between the three types of beliefs and the three components of attitudes.

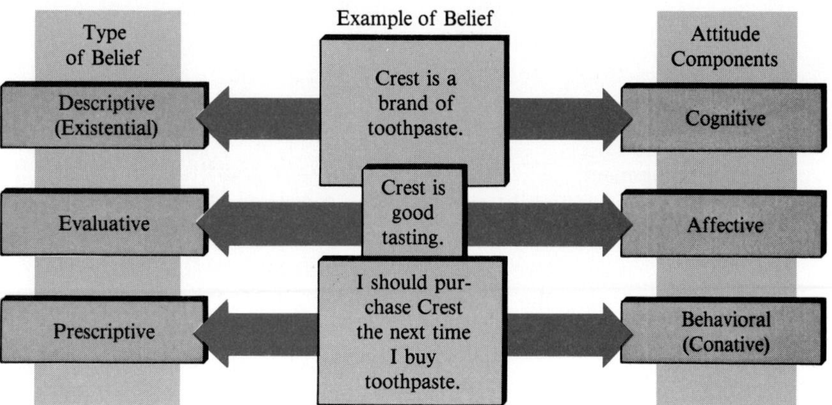

Figure 5-3 *Correspondence between Types of Beliefs and Attitude Components*

The Cognitive Component

cognitive component of attitudes

The **cognitive** component of attitudes, like reasoning, has no emotional content. It deals with neutral information about something rather than its good or bad qualities. Generally, the cognitive component reflects the person's knowledge of a situation: "I believe that Maytag makes dishwashers in addition to washers and dryers."

Descriptive Beliefs

Two types of descriptive beliefs on which the cognitive attitude component is based are particularly important: *cognitions toward objects* and *cognitions toward outcomes*. In terms of consuming behavior, a cognition toward an object could be a belief about a brand: "I believe that Ben Hogan Director golf clubs are often used by professional golfers." A cognition toward an outcome could be a belief about the results that are likely to occur from making a purchase: "I believe using Ben Hogan Director golf clubs will help me improve my golf score"; "If I buy this luxury car it will be comfortable and use a lot of gasoline"; "Having my car rustproofed will probably increase its trade-in value"; "If I purchase a stronger perfume than the one I currently use, I may have more sex appeal."

Cognitions toward outcomes are important to marketers because they relate brands to choice criteria. In this way they are thoughts about what will happen from purchasing a particular brand. Again, the buyer's cognitive attitude component (descriptive beliefs) should be thought of as non-evaluative expressions of his or her subjective estimation of the results of purchasing or using a certain type of product or a specific brand.

Researchers use the words *belief, rating, possession, probability of occurrence,* and *opinion* to describe the cognitive component of attitudes. These terms suggest a few of the approaches investigators use to discover cognitive attitude components. The appropriateness of these terms in a particular study depends on the group under study and the researcher's purposes. (Chapter 6 will discuss research approaches to gathering information on attitudes in detail.)

The Affective Component

affective component of attitudes

The **affective component** of attitudes concerns the desirability or undesirability of an object based on the person's feelings and emotions. In terms of consumer behavior, the affective component involves general evaluative feelings toward brands: "I like Texas Instruments calculators." Thus the affective component is often used as a summary evaluation of one's feelings.

Joel Cohen proposes that as consumers gain more information about products and brands, they tend to recategorize these items in their minds according to the affective components of their attitudes about these products.[16] For example, after a consumer has attended to various messages and experimented with different brands of shampoo, the person may group them according to those he or she likes and would buy. Thus, attitude development is influenced strongly by the affective component of attitudes.

Evaluative Beliefs

We discussed nonemotional, descriptive beliefs in a previous section, the cognitive component of attitudes. *Evaluative beliefs* arise when the consumer attaches emotion to specific product characteristics. As mentioned, beliefs are building blocks of attitudes. All of the consumer's evaluative beliefs combined make up the affective component of attitudes.

When marketers want to assess a consumer's overall affect toward a brand, they may obtain from study subjects evaluative beliefs about the brand's attributes. Evaluative beliefs give a more detailed picture of why a consumer has a particular overall affect concerning a brand. Although each belief is rated on a goodness or badness dimension similar to affect, talking about the affective aspect of attitude is usually reserved for discussions concerning an overall evaluation of the brand. Still, marketers often want to assess the degree of desirability of each attribute. Questionnaires evaluating beliefs ask respondents several distinct things about product attributes: the *importance* and *desirability* of the attributes, *feelings* about them, and whether an attribute is *liked* or *disliked*. They also ask subjects to rate attributes as *good* or *bad*.

Researchers sometimes use sophisticated techniques that analyze

trade-offs

trade-offs, the points at which one attribute ceases to be as valuable or desirable as others. With automobile purchases, for example, as gas mileage increases, comfort decreases. Many types of purchases require prospective buyers to examine the trade-offs and try to find a happy medium for themselves. (Trade-off analysis and other methods of assessing attitudes are discussed in more detail in Chapter 6.) In fact, many researchers assert that cognitive beliefs must precede the development of affective components of attitudes (that is, the feelings and emotions about an object's desirability). However, more recent studies suggest that the affective reaction to a product may often precede cognitive beliefs.[17] This may be particularly true in the case of unfamiliar products.[18]

Although we have discussed the cognitive and affective components of attitudes separately, note that better predictions result when the two are combined in research. For example, if the consumer believes products from large companies are preferable to those from small companies (evaluative belief) and further believes that Westinghouse is a large company (descriptive belief), then for a product type, we could reasonably expect that the consumer would prefer the Westinghouse brand of that product over brands the buyer believes were made by small companies. Such a preference would be an action tendency, the key to behavior prediction.

The Behavioral Component

Descriptive beliefs combined with evaluative beliefs result in prescriptive beliefs: that is, beliefs about what action should be taken. Because actions tend to be guided by attitudes, researchers say that attitudes are "behaviorally charged." In terms of consumer behavior, the action tendency of attitudes is called a *purchase tendency* or an *intention to purchase*.

Researchers study the behavioral component of consumers' attitudes by determining what brands they have bought in the past, and to what degree they are brand loyal or willing to switch brands.

Attitudes may involve objects other than brands. Consumers may have attitudes toward people, companies, and events. For example, most consumers have already developed attitudes toward celebrities featured in advertisements. When people's attitudes are generally in agreement, the object of the attitude is said to have a certain **image.** Companies are particularly concerned about establishing and protecting a positive image for their firm and all its employees, because most marketers consider that a favorable image results in more sales of their product lines.

image

Attitudes toward the action of purchasing a brand are not necessarily similar to attitudes toward the brand itself. For example, a certain university student who is in the market for a personal computer may describe his very favorable attitude toward the IBM PC. However, it soon becomes clear that he has an unfavorable attitude toward purchasing that brand because it does not serve his needs, which center on keeping expenses down. Therefore, attitudes toward the brand, supplier, or store may not be closely related to the purchase action, while attitudes toward *purchasing* a brand are closely related.

Although the importance of focusing on actions rather than simply on intuitive appeal is apparent when it is pointed out, many early studies on attitudes focused on the object rather than on attitudes toward the action they were attempting to predict. It is hardly surprising that the results were less accurate in relating attitudes and purchasing than they could have been. This incorrect emphasis can be found in many of the attitude studies conducted by businesses; when these mistakes occur, erroneous conclusions may be drawn from attitudinal data. Think of the difference in your own responses to the following questions: "What is your attitude toward Mercedes-Benz automobiles?" versus "What is your attitude toward purchasing a Mercedes as your next car?" or, "What is your attitude toward Old Milwaukee beer?" versus "What is your attitude toward buying Old Milwaukee beer for your Friday night date?" In each set of questions the answers might be quite different. A person might express a favorable attitude toward Mercedes-Benz automobiles due to their prestige image but a negative attitude toward purchasing one due to its high cost. Similarly, a person's attitude toward Old Milwaukee beer might be neutral or positive in general but negative regarding its purchase for a date when a foreign brand, a premium beer, wine, or a non-alcoholic drink might seem more appropriate.

ATTITUDE FORMATION

Where do attitudes come from? As Allport's definition suggests, attitudes are learned in at least two ways. First, attitudes, like values, are taught to us as part of our cultural heritage. Second, attitudes are formed directly, through our own experience in the world. In this section we will focus on the second means of attitude formation, the consumer's environment. We discuss the relationship between attitudes and behavior and the self-perception theory.

The Attitude–Behavior Cycle

intervening variables

Does a person first develop an attitude and then behave in a manner consistent with it? Or is it the person's behavior that causes the attitude in the first place? Research shows that behavior and attitudes can give rise to each other through the influence of intervening variables. **Intervening variables** are circumstances which interrupt normal behavior and attitudes, causing changes in both. This process is illustrated in Figure 5-4.

In terms of consumer behavior, we know that people tend to purchase products toward which they have the most favorable attitude. In such cases, their attitudes are causing their behavior. On the other hand, when consumers are given free samples of a brand they have never tried before, the behavior of trying the new brand forces them to form an attitude about the brand. In this instance, the intervening variable is the arrival in the mailbox of the free sample. Since humans need to achieve consistency (in this case, a state of harmony between their thoughts and actions), consumers cannot ignore the experience of sampling something novel. In-

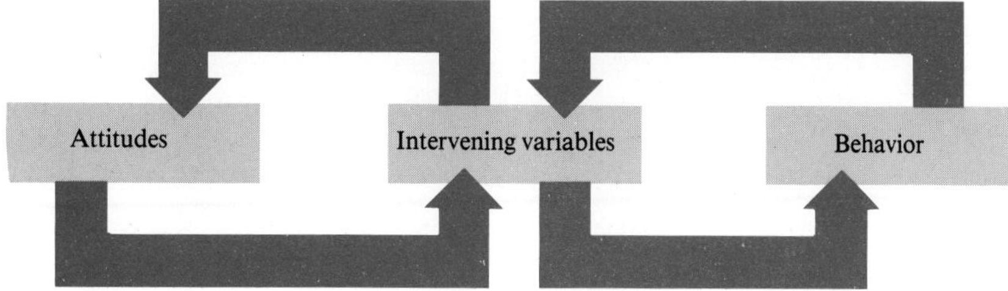

Figure 5-4 *Intervening Variables in the Normal Attitude–Behavior Relationship*

stead, they must fit it into their existing attitude and belief structure. Assuming the product quality is acceptable to those who have tried the samples, they may develop positive attitudes toward the product and perhaps even switch to the new brand. Reception of the free sample was the intervening variable that interrupted the consumers' existing attitudes toward the product type by causing the new behavior: use of the sample.

Conversely, buyers who cannot find the brand they usually buy on a store's shelves may begin examining other brands and end up buying a new one. In this situation, the intervening variable was the preferred brand being out of stock. It resulted in a change of purchasing behavior, which in turn might result in a new attitude toward the brand selected as a substitute.

Intervening variables are common in the environment of the marketplace. They include new promotions, price changes, the recommendations of friends, and the influence of salespeople.

Attitudes and Involvement

Buyers who are highly involved in a product class have stronger views (more feelings about which brands they like and which they dislike) than do persons to whom the product class is unimportant. The strength with which an attitude is held depends in part on confidence. Among marketing researchers, **confidence** usually refers to how much certainty a person has about his or her beliefs regarding a specific brand.[19] George Day concluded that both involvement and confidence relate to the formation and change of the consumer's attitude: "The key feature of the motive properties of involvement and confidence is that, together, they determine the stability of an observed attitude." High involvement plus confidence equals an extremely stable attitude that is unlikely to be altered by marketing efforts.

confidence

> [A consumer's] confidence in brand judgments is likely to mirror the level of involvement in differences among brands, if for no other reason than a person who lacks interest will not likely have the information or experience necessary to make a confident judgment.[20]

The level of a consumer's involvement in product classes is believed to be linked to when and how attitudes toward the product are formed and whether, in fact, the consumer has an attitude toward the product at all. In general, most researchers in consumer behavior believe that attitudes toward high-involvement products are formed *before* purchase, and attitudes toward low-involvement products are formed *after* trying the product. As mentioned, these findings have important implications for product promotion and advertising strategies.

ATTRIBUTION THEORY

attribution theory

Although consumers often form their attitudes by gathering input from outside sources, they sometimes form them by observing their own behavior and the behavior of others. This concept is known as **attribution theory.** Attribution theory describes how people acquire attitudes by considering their behavior, or that of someone else or even an object, after the fact.[21] It is based on the idea that people need to attribute an observed behavior to some cause.

Self-perception theory focuses on the person's attributing these attitudes to his or her own behavior. Self-perception theory postulates that people determine their attitudes toward a product or situation partially by observing their own behavior or the circumstances in which this behavior occurs.[22] If someone lacks sufficient information from external sources to form a distinct opinion, that person acts as an outside observer of his or her own behavior to infer what internal feelings, emotions, and attitudes are being experienced. ("I must have liked that movie; I watched the rerun again.")

Another illustration of self-perception theory sometimes takes place in a sales situation. In order to influence a customer's attitudes positively toward a product or issue, a salesperson might first try to get the customer to engage in some behavior that is consistent with the desired attitude. One example is the "foot-in-the-door" technique. This approach entails gaining the prospective buyer's compliance with a small request in the hope that compliance with a large request will follow. This tactic was illustrated in an experiment conducted by P. Pliner and associates.[23] They asked people first to wear a lapel pin supporting an upcoming cancer drive (a relatively small request). The next day the same representative returned and asked the same people to donate to the cancer fund. The researchers found that people who had been contacted before were more likely to donate to the fund than others who were asked to donate without any prior contact. A more recent study conducted in Sweden revealed similar results when respondents were contacted by telephone prior to receiving a mail survey. Those reached by phone produced a 45% higher response rate than those who received the survey with no prior notice.[24]

The foot-in-the-door technique is a direct application of a self-perception theory. People who agree to a small request come to view themselves as the kind of person who favors that type of behavior: "Since I am willing to wear this pin, I am the type of person who supports the cancer drive." If the person refuses to comply with the larger request, this may cast some doubt on his or her original decision to go along with the first request. Therefore, the person who wants to avoid appearing inconsistent, indecisive, or uncommitted to a worthy cause complies.

The self-perception theory has implications for marketers, especially those using the foot-in-the-door technique. Product samples, particularly ones asking for some form of commitment (trial-size samples for a minimal cost), may be an effective method to generate repeat purchases. Buyers who use such samples are apt to attribute their purchase and use of the samples, at least in part, to their preference for the product. By observing their own behavior, the buyers have inferred that their attitude toward the product is positive, especially as they paid money and made a commitment. To reduce inconsistency, the buyer will probably make repeat purchases of the product.

Valerie Folkes examined consumer reactions when products fail to work using an attributional approach.[25] Her findings indicate that the reasons people give for product failure influence the extent to which they desire a refund, seek to exchange the product, believe they are owed an apology, or want to hurt the firm's business. These reasons are related to whether consumers see the reason for failure as being within their control or beyond it. People who believe the latter are more likely to seek compensation or retribution. However, those who attribute the failure to circumstances within their control are less likely to seek compensation.

HOW ATTITUDES FUNCTION

Research has shown that attitudes serve several purposes. The consumer's attitudes toward brands and purchasing help him or her to cope with the purchasing environment. Daniel Katz has described four important functions of attitudes: (1) the knowledge function, (2) the instrumental-adjustive function, (3) the value-expressive function, and (4) the ego-defensive function.[26] They help us understand how attitudes toward brands and purchasing work for buyers.

knowledge function of attitudes

The **knowledge function** of attitudes order cognitive beliefs to help us organize the millions of aspects of our own world. Attitudes serve as "cognitive anchors,"[27] or reference points for organizing thoughts and understanding new stimuli.[28] Having an attitude toward a brand simplifies product selection. For example, the happy owner of a Hoover vacuum cleaner might be skeptical about the quality of a Eureka vacuum. Consequently, when the Hoover owner must purchase a new vacuum, he or she would probably reject a Eureka and simply buy another Hoover without bothering to compare the two brands beforehand.

instrumental-adjustive function of attitudes

The **instrumental-adjustive function** of attitudes creates a pleasant environment by helping a person steer away from pain and toward pleasant feelings.[29] We see an example of this attitude function in the shopper who refuses to purchase the same kind of washing machine, which previously required excessive repairs, but buys instead a different brand with a reputation for dependability.

value-expressive function of attitudes

The **value-expressive function** of attitudes reflects the link between values and attitudes discussed earlier in this chapter. The attitudes a person forms must be consistent with his or her values or self-concept. Basic values are acquired from the culture and influence attitudes through the affective component. For example, those who value *education* tend to have favorable attitudes toward newspapers and professional journals. As another example, those who value *nature* are likely to have favorable attitudes toward skis, hiking shoes, and camping equipment. The value-expressive function gives the person the chance to express his or her values. Attitudes vary greatly across cultures, largely due to individual differences in values.

ego-defensive function of attitudes

The **ego-defensive function** of attitudes helps protect the person from feelings of inadequacy, depression, or injured ego. Attitudes play an important role in preventing us from feeling inferior. An example is someone who rationalizes that motorcycles are only for the "hoodlum element," but who really avoids motorcycles because of fear of physical injury or concern about an inability to operate them. Often the person is unaware of the emotional purpose such an attitude serves. While the ego-defensive function is widespread, many people are not conscious that it is operating in the formation of their attitudes. Table 5-3 provides examples of attitudes that represent each of the four functions.

The way in which attitudes function for an individual consumer in relation to a particular product can play an important role in the development of purchase criteria for that product. For example, if a potential buyer's attitude toward an automobile performs a value-expressive function, the person might be concerned about such purchase criteria as energy conservation (good mileage) and low smog emissions. Another potential buyer whose attitude toward an automobile functions in an ego-defensive manner may develop purchase criteria such as the image of success the auto projects.

Table 5-3 EXAMPLES OF ATTITUDES AND THEIR FUNCTIONS

Attitude Function	*Example of Attitude*
Knowledge	"Pringles potato chips are different." (Products that are "different" are more expensive.)
Instrumental-adjustive	"Crest whitens teeth." (Whitening teeth is good.)
Value-expressive	"Pepsi drinkers think young." (Thinking young is beneficial to health.)
Ego-defensive	"Marlboro smokers are masculine." (Being masculine makes me a better person.)

Source: Richard J. Lutz. "A Functional Theory Framework for Designing and Pretesting Advertising Themes" in John C. Maloney and Bernard Silverman, eds., *Attitude Research Plays for High Stakes: Proceedings Series* (Chicago: American Marketing Association, 1979), p. 43.

SUMMARY

In consumer behavior, involvement describes the perceived importance or concern a person holds for a given product class. Involvement is an individual phenomenon, yet for most people certain product categories tend to attract lower involvement than others do. The extent to which consumers seek information about a product or brand and how they incorporate that information into their purchase decision depend on the level of involvement.

An attitude may be thought of in many ways, but basically it is a part of a person's psychological makeup which can be expressed in observable ways. Attitudes are learned and, once learned, they influence the person's thoughts and actions toward objects and situations related to these attitudes. Like values, attitudes are influenced by culture and environment. But values are broader and relatively permanent, while attitudes are more specific and susceptible to change.

Beliefs, which express the perceived relationship between objects or events and their attributes, are the building blocks of attitudes. Descriptive, evaluative, and prescriptive beliefs correspond respectively to the cognitive, affective, and behavioral components of attitude. Attitude research questions can be written to elicit information about each of these components of the subjects' attitudes.

Although attitude theorists are far from reaching a consensus on what attitudes are and how they work, much of attitude theory is useful in marketing. The analysis of attitudes helps us understand *why* a particular brand choice occurs and allows us to predict how much will be purchased. Four related approaches to the study of attitudes include the structural approach, the functional approach, consistency theory and the multiattribute approach. These theories provide insights into a broad range of marketing problems and are central to developing marketing programs and strategies.

Although attitudes normally precede behaviors, intervening variables can upset this sequence and cause behaviors to result in attitudes. Attribution theory describes how people make explanations about their behavior, or that of others, after the fact. Attribution theory is not one theory but a collection of research insights that help explain cognition processes.

Attitudes have four functions: the knowledge function, the instrumental-adjustive function, the value-expressive function, and the ego-defensive function. The same attitude may be held by different people for a variety of reasons.

KEY TERMS

involvement
inertia
brand loyalty
spurious loyalty

variety-seeking behavior
attitude
values
belief
descriptive belief
evaluative belief
prescriptive belief
cognitive component of attitude
affective component of attitudes
trade-offs
image
intervening variables
confidence
attribution theory
knowledge function of attitudes
instrumental-adjustive function of attitudes
value-expressive function of attitudes
ego-defensive function of attitudes

QUESTIONS

1. How does the concept of involvement influence attitude formation? Describe how attitude formation differs for a person who has high involvement from one who has low involvement in buying a particular type of product.

2. Explain Sherif's social judgment theory of involvement, using latitudes of acceptance and latitudes of rejection.

3. What are the strategic implications for marketers of products or services that normally exhibit low involvement?

4. How do attitudes and values differ as consumer behaviorists define them? Describe a possible value and related attitudes that a person might have toward (a) career success, (b) personal health, and (c) political activism.

5. Distinguish among the three major types of beliefs that comprise attitudes.

6. According to the structural approach, attitudes are synonymous with feelings. Do you agree or disagree with this statement? Explain.

7. Assume that you have been asked to develop a simple questionnaire to evaluate the three components of attitudes among respondents toward public transportation. What questions might you ask to assess each component? Can you briefly explain why measuring only one component might result in misleading conclusions?

8. What is attribution theory? How does it help explain why samples are sometimes effective for influencing behavior?

9. Bill turns down a friend's offer for an introductory parachuting lesson, saying, "Skydiving seems like a cheap thrill for people who don't value life. I'll stick with more competitive sports." Interpret Bill's comment in light of the four functions of attitudes.

NOTES

1. Herbert E. Krugman, "Low Involvement Theory in the Light of New Brand Research," in *Attitude Research Plays for High Stakes,* John C. Maloney and Bernard Silverman, eds. (Chicago: American Marketing Association, 1979), 16–24.
2. John L. Lastovicka and David M. Gardner, "Compo-

nents of Involvement,'' in *Attitude Research Plays for High Stakes,* John C. Maloney and Bernard Silverman, eds. (Chicago: American Marketing Association, 1979), 65.

3. Henry Assael, *Consumer Behavior and Marketing Action,* 2nd ed. (Boston: Kent Publishing Co., 1984), 83.
4. Assael, 83.
5. Carolyn W. Sherif, Muzafer Sherif, and Roger E. Nebergall, *Attitude and Attitude Change: The Social Judgment-Involvement Approach* (Philadelphia: W. B. Saunders Company, 1965).
6. Muzafer Sherif and Carolyn W. Sherif, *Social Psychology* (New York: Harper and Row, 1969).
7. Michael L. Rothschild and Michael J. Hanston, ''The Consumer Involvement Matrix: Some Preliminary Findings,'' in *Proceedings: AMA Educators' Conference,* Barnett A. Greenberg and Danny N. Bellinger (Chicago: American Marketing Association, 1977), 95–98.
8. Richard E. Petty, John T. Caciappo, and David Schumann, ''Central and Peripheral Routes to Persuasion: The Moderating Role of Involvement,'' *Journal of Consumer Research* 10 (September 1983): 135–146.
9. Herbert E. Krugman, ''Low Involvement Theory in Light of New Brain Research,'' in *Attitude Research Plays for High Stakes,* 16–24.
10. Sherif, Sherif, and Nebergall, *Attitude and Attitude Change,* 1–17.
11. Gordon W. Allport, ''Attitudes,'' in *Handbook of Social Psychology,* C. M. Murchison, ed. (Worcester, MA: Clark University Press, 1935), 810.
12. Boris W. Becker and Patrick E. Connor, ''The Influence of Personal Values on Attitude and Store Choice Behavior,'' in *An Assessment of Marketing Thought and Practice: Educators Conference Proceedings* (Chicago: American Marketing Association, 1982), 21–24.
13. V. Jastrow, ''The Animus of Physical Research,'' in *The Case For and Against Physical Belief,* Carl Churchison, ed. (Worcester, MA: Clark University Press, 1927).
14. E. E. Jones and H. D. Gerard, *Foundations of Social Psychology* (New York: John Wiley & Sons, 1967), 158.
15. Milton Rokeach, ''The Nature of Attitudes,'' in *Behavioral Science Foundations of Consumer Behavior,* Joel B. Cohen ed. (New York: The Free Press, 1972) 205.
16. Joel B. Cohen, ''The Role of Affect in Categorization: Toward a Reconsideration of the Concept of Attitude,'' in *Advances in Consumer Research IX,* Andrew A. Mitchell, ed. (St. Louis, MO: Association for Consumer Research, 1981), 94–100.
17. Robert J. Zajonc and Hazel Markus, ''Affective and Cognitive Factors in Preference,'' *Journal of Consumer Research* 9 (September 1982): 123–31.
18. Meryl Paula Gardner, ''Attribute Determinance: A Function of Past Memory and External Factors,'' in *Advances in Consumer Research IX,* 177–82.
19. Peter D. Bennett and Gilbert D. Harrell, ''The Role of Confidence in Understanding and Predicting Buyers' Attitudes and Purchase Intentions,'' *Journal of Consumer Behavior* (1975), 110–117.
20. George Day, *Buyer Attitudes and Brand Choices* (New York: The Free Press, 1970), 44, 83.
21. Richard W. Mizerski, Linda L. Goldon and Jerome B. Kernan, ''The Attribution Process in Consumer Decision Making,'' *Journal of Consumer Research* (September 1979): 123–40.
22. D. J. Bem, ''Self-Perception Theory,'' in *Advances in Experimental Social Psychology* 6, L. Berkowitz, ed. (New York: Academic Press, 1972), 1–62. For a review of literature of self-concept theory and research in consumer behavior, see M. Joseph Sirgy, ''Self-Concept in Consumer Behavior: A Critical Review,'' *Journal of Consumer Research* 9 (1982): 287–300; and John C. Mowen, ''Attribution, Self-Perception, Salience, and Weird Interactions,'' in *Advances in Consumer Research,* MI 56–58. Chris T. Allen and William R. Dillon, ''Self-Perception Development and Consumer Choice Criteria: Is There a Linkage?'' in *Advances in Consumer Research X,* 45–50.
23. P. Pliner, H. Hart, J. Kohl, and D. Saari, ''Compliance without Pressure: Some Further Data on the Foot-in-the-Door Technique,'' *Journal of Experimental Social Psychology* 10 (1974): 17–22.
24. Chris T. Allen, Charles D. Schewe, and Gösta Wijk, ''More on Self-Perception Theory S Foot Technique in the Re-Call/Mail Survey Setting,'' *Journal of Marketing Research* 17 (1980): 498–502.
25. Valerie Folkes, ''Consumer Reactions to Product Failure: An Attributional Approach,'' *Journal of Consumer Research* 10 (March 1984): 398–409.
26. Daniel Katz, ''The Functional Approach to the Study of Attitudes,'' *Public Opinion Quarterly* 24 (1960): 163–204.
27. Sherif, Sherif, and Nebergall, *Attitude and Attitude Change,* 165.
28. This function of attitudes relates to the concept of *simplification,* presented in Chapter 4.
29. This function of attitudes relates to the concept of *conditioned responses,* presented in Chapter 4.

FURTHER READING

Involvement

Classics

Freedman, J. L., "Involvement, Discrepancy and Change," *Journal of Abnormal and Social Psychology* 69 (September 1964): 290–95.

Houston, M. J., and M. L. Rothschild, "Conceptual and Methodological Perspectives in Involvement," in *Research Frontiers in Marketing: Dialogues and Directions,* S. C. Jain, ed. (Chicago: American Marketing Association, 1978), 184–87.

Krugman, Herbert E., "The Impact of Television Advertising: Learning without Involvement," *Public Opinion Quarterly* 29 (Fall 1965): 349–56.

Krugman, Herbert E., "The Measurement of Advertising Involvement," *Public Opinion Quarterly* 30 (Winter 1966): 584–85.

Robertson, Thomas S., "Low-Commitment Consumer Behavior," *Journal of Advertising Research* 16, No. 2 (April 1976): 19–24.

Rothschild, M. L., and M. J. Houston, "The Consumer Involvement Matrix: Some Preliminary Findings," *Proceedings, Educators' Conference* (Chicago: American Market Association, 1977), 95–98.

Sherif, M., and H. Cantril, *The Psychology of Ego Involvement* (New York: John Wiley Press, 1947).

Recent Significant Research

Arora, Raj, "Validation of an S-O-R Model for Situational, Enduring, and Response Components of Involvement," *Journal of Marketing Research* 19 (November 1983): 505–16.

Calder, Bobby J., "When Attitudes Follow Behavior—A Self-Perception/Dissonance Interpretation of Low Involvement," in *Attitude Research Plays for High Stakes,* J. C. Maloney and Bernard Silverman, eds. (Chicago: American Marketing Association, 1979), 25–37.

Cohen, J. B., "Involvement and You: 1000 Great Ideas," in *Advances in Consumer Research* 10, R. P. Bagozzi and A. M. Tybout, eds. (Ann Arbor, MI: Association for Consumer Research, 1983), 325–28.

DeBruicker, F. S., "An Appraisal of Low Involvement Consumer Information Processing," in *Attitude Research Plays for High Stakes,* J. C. Maloney and Bernard Silverman, eds. (Chicago: American Marketing Association, 1979), 112–30.

Kassarjian, H. H., and W. M. Kassarjian, "Attitudes Under Low Commitment Conditions," in *Attitude Research Plays for High Stakes,* J. C. Maloney and Bernard Silverman, eds. (Chicago: American Marketing Association, 1979), 8–20.

Lastovicka, J. L., and David M. Gardner, "Components of Involvement," in *Attitude Research Plays for High Stakes,* J. C. Maloney and Bernard Silverman, eds. (Chicago: American Marketing Association, 1979), 53–73.

Mitchell, A. A., "Involvement: A Potentially Important Mediator of Consumer Behavior," in *Advances in Consumer Research* 6, William L. Wilkie, ed. (Ann Arbor, MI: Association for Consumer Research, 1979), 191–95.

Muncy, James A., and Shelby D. Hunt, "Consumer Involvement: Definitional Issues and Research Directions," in *Advances in Consumer Research,* Thomas C. Kinnear, ed. (Provo UT: Association for Consumer Research, 1984), 193–96.

Parameswaran, Ravi, and Teri Spinelli, "Involvement: A Revisitation and Confirmation," in *1984 AMA Educators' Proceedings,* Russell W. Belk, et al., eds. (Chicago: American Marketing Association, 1984), 57–61.

Rothschild, Michael L., "Perspectives on Involvement: Current Problems and Future Directions," in *Advances in Consumer Research,* Thomas C. Kinnear, ed. (Provo, UT: Association for Consumer Research, 1984), 216–17.

Applications

Block, Peter H., and Grady D. Bruce, "Product Involvement as Leisure Behavior," in *Advances in Consumer Research,* Thomas C. Kinnear, ed. (Provo, UT: Association for Consumer Research, 1984), 197–202.

Clarke, Keith, and Russell W. Belk, "The Effects of Product Involvement and Task Definition on

Anticipated Consumer Effort," in *Advances in Consumer Research,* William L. Wilkie, ed. (Ann Arbor, MI: Association for Consumer Research, 1979), 313–18.

Hupfer, Nancy, and David Gardner, "Differential Involvement with Products and Issues: An Exploratory Study," in *Proceedings, 2nd Annual Conference of the Association for Consumer Research* (Ann Arbor: Association for Consumer Research, 1971), 262–69.

Petty, Richard E., and John T. Cacioppo, "Issue Involvement as a Moderator of the Effects on Attitude of Advertising Content and Context," in *Advances in Consumer Research* 8, Kent B. Monroe, ed. (Ann Arbor, MI: Association for Consumer Research, 1981), 20–24.

Petty, Richard E., John T. Cacioppo, and David Schumann, "Central and Peripheral Routes to Advertising Effectiveness: The Moderating Role of Involvement," *Journal of Consumer Research* 10 (September 1983): 135–46.

Rothschild, Michael L., "Advertising Strategies for High and Low Involvement Situations," in *Attitude Research Plays for High Stakes,* J. C. Maloney and Bernard Silverman, eds. (Chicago: American Marketing Association, 1979), 74–93.

Sherrel, D. L., and T. A. Shimp, "Consumer Involvement in a Laboratory Setting," *1982 Educators' Conference Proceedings* (Chicago: American Marketing Association, 1981), 104–08.

Shimp, T. A., and Subash Sharma, "The Dimensionality of Involvement: A Test of the Automobile Involvement Scale," *Winter Educators' Conference* (Chicago: American Marketing Association, 1983).

Swinyard, W. R., and K. A. Coney, "Promotional Effects on a High- Versus Low-Involvement Electorate," *Journal of Consumer Research* 5 (June 1978): 41–48.

Tyebjee, T. T., "Refinement of the Involvement Concept: An Advertising Planning Point of View," in *Attitude Research Plays for High Stakes,* J. C. Maloney and Bernard Silverman, eds. (Chicago: American Marketing Association, 1979), 94–111.

Attitudes

Classics

Allport, Gordon, W., "Attitudes," in *A Handbook of Social Psychology,* C. A. Murchinson, ed. (Worcester, MA: Clark University Press, 1935), 798–844.

Bauer, Raymond A., "Attitudes, Verbal Behavior, and Other Behavior," in *Attitude Research at Sea,* Lee Adler and Irving Crespi, eds. (Chicago: American Marketing Association, 1966), 3–14.

Clawson, C. Joseph, and Donald E. Vinson, "Human Values: A Historical and Interdisciplinary Analysis," in *Advances in Consumer Research* 5, H. Keith Hunt, ed. (Provo, UT: Association for Consumer Research, 1978), 396–402.

Katz, Daniel, "The Functional Approach to the Study of Attitudes," *Public Opinion Quarterly* 24 (Summer 1960): 163–91.

Mueller, E., "Effects of Consumer Attitudes on Purchases," *The American Economic Review* 47 (1957): 946–65.

Myers, James H., and Mark I. Alpert, "Determinant Buying Attitudes: Meaning and Measurement," *Journal of Marketing* 32 (October 1968): 13–20.

Olshavsky, Richard W., and John O. Summers, "A Study of the Role of Beliefs and Intentions in Consistency Restoration," *Journal of Consumer Research* 1 (June 1974): 63–70.

Olson, Jerry C., and Andrew A. Mitchell, "The Process of Attitude Acquisition: The Value of A Developmental Approach to Consumer Attitude Research," *Advances in Consumer Research* 2 (1975): 249–64.

Recent Significant Research

Belch, George E., "The Effects of Television Commercial Repetition on Cognitive Response and Message Acceptance," *Journal of Consumer Research* 9 (June 1982): 56–65.

Cacioppo, John T., Stephen G. Harkins, and Richard E. Petty, "The Nature of Attitudes and Cognitive Responses and Their Relationships to Behavior," in *Cognitive Responses in Persuasion,* Richard E. Petty, T. M. Ostrom, and Timothy C. Brock, eds. (Hillsdale, NJ: Lawrence Erlbaum Associates 1981), 31–54.

Lutz, Richard J., "A Functional Theory Framework for Designing and Pretesting Advertising Themes," *Attitude Research Plays for High Stakes,* (Chicago: American Marketing Association, 1979), 37–49.

Lutz, Richard J., "The Role of Attitude Theory in Marketing," in *Perspectives in Consumer Behavior,* Harold H. Kassarjian and Thomas S. Robertson, eds. (Glenview, IL: Scott, Foresman and Company 1981) 233–50.

Miniard, Paul W., and Joel B. Cohen, "Modeling Personal and Normative Influences on Behavior," *Journal of Consumer Research* 10 (September 1983): 169–80.

Morrison, Donald G., "Purchase Intentions and Purchase Behavior," *Journal of Marketing* 43 (Spring 1979): 65–74.

Applications

Assael, H., and Day, George, "Attitudes and Awareness as Predictors of Market Share," *Journal of Advertising Research* 8, No. 4 (1968): 3–10.

Boote, Alfred S., "Market Segmentation by Personal Values and Salient Product Attributes," *Journal of Advertising Research* 21, No. 1 (February 1981): 29–35.

Boyd, Jr., Harper W., Michael L. Ray, and Edward C. Strong, "An Attitudinal Framework for Advertising Strategy," *Journal of Marketing* 36 (April 1972): 27–33.

Johnson, Richard M., "Trade-off Analysis of Consumer Values," *Journal of Marketing Research* (May 1974).

King, Charles W., and John O. Summers, "Attitudes and Media Exposure," *Journal of Advertising Research* 11 (February 1971): 26–32.

Lutz, Richard L., "An Experimental Investigation of Causal Relations Among Cognition, Affect, and Behavioral Intentions," *Journal of Consumer Research* 3 (1977): 194–207.

Magidson, Jay, "Estimating the Impact of Advertising on Consumer Attitudes and Purchase Behavior: A Maximum Likelihood Approach," in *Proceedings of the Division of Consumer Psychology,* James C. Anderson, ed. (San Antonio, TX: American Psychology Association, 1983), 33–36.

Reibstein, David J., Christopher H. Lovelock, and Ricardo de P. Dobson, "The Direction of Causality Between Perceptions, Affect, and Behavior: An Application to Travel Behavior," *Journal of Consumer Research* 6 (March 1980): 370–76.

Schlinger, Mary Jane Rawlins, Linda F. Alwitt, Kathleen E. McCarthy, and Leila Green, "Effects of Time Compression on Attitudes and Information Processing," *Journal of Marketing* 47 (Winter 1983): 79–85.

Woodside, Arch G., James D. Clokey, and Joan M. Combes, "Similarities and Differences on Generalized Brand Attitudes, Behavioral Intentions, and Reported Behavior," in *Advances in Consumer Research,* M. J. Schlinger, ed. 2 (Ann Arbor, MI: Association for Consumer Research, 1975), 335–44.

6 Attitude Measurement and Models

Objectives of This Chapter

After you have studied this chapter, you should be able to:

1. Discuss the four multiattribute (compensatory) attitude models and show how they relate to consumer purchase decisions.

2. Explore the role of purchase criteria in attitude measurement for consumer and industrial buying situations.

3. Explain the major qualitative and quantitative techniques used to assess buyer attitudes.

4. Understand four noncompensatory attitude models that are used to describe consumer analyses of available brands and eventual brand choice.

In recent years, the research in marketing and consumer behavior has spawned many articles about various attitude models. Yet only a few, very similar models have received extensive discussion. The attention these models have received is due to their excellent applicability to actual marketing problems. The models help clarify and summarize many of the concepts discussed in Chapter 5.

First we discuss the four major multiattribute attitude models. Next we explore the role of purchase criteria and their applications to attitude measurement. Following this, we outline techniques for qualitative assessment of attitudes, including such research techniques as the depth interview and the focused group. Then we turn to techniques for the quantitative assessment of attitudes, including the Thurstone and Likert scales, and conclude with an overview of noncompensatory attitude models. (Chapter 7 describes how attitudes can be changed or influenced once their nature and strength are understood).

MULTIATTRIBUTE MODELS OF ATTITUDE

Much of the recent work in consumer behavior and attitudes has been on the development, testing, and application of a class of formulas we call **multiattribute models of attitude.**[1] The most notable of these (in the order in which they were developed) are *Rosenberg's Attitude toward an Object Model, Fishbein's Attitude toward an Object Model, Fishbein's Attitude toward an Action Model* and the *Adequacy-Importance Model.*[2]

multiattribute models of attitude

A number of different multiattribute models have been developed as research and knowledge in the area of attitude measurement has grown. While certain models have similarities, each is different in how it attempts to measure attitudes. In some instances, a researcher will want to use a particular model depending on whether the goal is to measure attitudes toward an object itself (such as a particular brand) or to measure a person's attitude toward *behavior* with respect to an object (such as the act of purchasing a particular brand). Note that these are different issues, because though a person may have a highly favorable attitude toward a diamond necklace, she may have a less favorable attitude toward its purchase given the financial cost, the possible security risk of owning the necklace, and so on. Researchers must be keenly aware of what they really wish to measure and select the appropriate model for that purpose. We will examine each model and show how it might be used in actual practice.

Rosenberg's Attitude toward an Object Model

In the 1950's, Milton Rosenberg formulated the first attitude model to receive a great deal of attention in the field of buyer behavior, his **Attitude toward an Object (A_o) Model.** His work was influenced by Helen Peak, a psychologist who held that overall affect (liking or disliking) toward an

Rosenberg's A_o Model

object is a function of "(1) the judged probability that the object leads to good or bad consequences, and (2) the intensity of the affect expected from those consequences."[3] Simply stated, to Rosenberg the attitude toward an object is equal to the sum of the person's beliefs about the potential of the object to attain or block a valued state multiplied by the importance of that valued state, where a specified number of valued states are being evaluated and summed. We define a **valued state** as a goal one wishes to attain, such as status or personal safety. Rosenberg first used his formula to measure attitudes about two relatively important social issues: abolishment of segregated housing for blacks and free speech for communists in the United States. He first selected 35 related goals or value states, such as the prestige of the United States in other countries. Rosenberg then obtained (1) a measure of the subject's judgment about the probability that abolishment of segregated housing for blacks or free speech for communists would lead to or block attainment of each goal, multiplied by (2) a measure of the satisfaction to be derived from each goal. These indexes were added to form composite scores, which were related, in turn, to the subject's overall affect[4] for (like or dislike of) the issue of segregation or free speech.

valued state

Meanwhile, marketers were looking for a model to help them understand consumer attitudes. If valued states could be replaced with purchase criteria, the model could be used to represent attitudes toward products, rather than attitudes toward social issues. The values used in measuring attitudes toward a mouthwash with Rosenberg's A_o model are:[5]

Keeping in good health
Associating with the opposite sex
Being recognized as a leader
Socializing
Presenting a young, dynamic image
Protection against physical harm
Thriftiness
Meeting new people
Care in personal cleanliness

Fishbein's Attitude toward an Object Model

Fishbein's A_o Model

Martin Fishbein's **Attitude toward an Object (A_o) Model** was the first of two well-known models bearing his name. The more general of the two, Fishbein's A_o Model, was similar to Rosenberg's. Fishbein's A_o Model was expressed in the following formula:[6]

$$A_o = \sum_{i=1}^{n} B_i a_i$$

where:

A_o = attitude toward an object, o;
B_i = the individual's belief about the probability that the object is related to an outcome, i;
a_i = the person's evaluation of or affect for outcome i; and
n = the number of beliefs.

This formula states that a person's attitude toward an object is equal to the sum of a specified number of beliefs that the object is related to an outcome multiplied by the person's evaluation of the outcome.

Fishbein's A_o Model is used in consumer behavior when the marketer wishes to assess attitudes toward a brand or a supplier. In this case, B_i is a cognitive measure of the probability that the brand possesses a particular characteristic, and a_i is an affective measure of the desirability of that characteristic.

Fishbein's Attitude toward an Action Model

Fishbein's second model is based on a verbal learning theory[7] and states that a person's "intention to perform a behavior is a function of (1) his attitude toward performing the behavior in a given situation; and (2) the norms governing that behavior in that situation and his motivation to comply with these norms."[8]

Fishbein's Attitude toward an Action Model

Fishbein's **Attitude toward an Action (A_{act}) Model** may be represented with the following formula:

$$B \cong BI = \sum_{i=1}^{n} B_i a_i \, w_1 + NB \cdot Mc \, w_2$$

where:

B = behavior regarding a specific brand;
BI = behavioral intention regarding a specific brand in a specific situation;
B_i = beliefs about the consequences or outcomes from performing the behavior;
a_i = the evaluative aspects of the consequences;
NB = the normative beliefs;
Mc = the motivation to comply with norms;
w_1 = a statistically derived weight
n = the number of relevant consequences of the behavioral act.

Beta weights are the output of statistical analysis that give some idea of how much each part of the equation helps understand behavioral intentions. In contrast to Fishbein's first model, this model concerns the consumer's attitude toward an *act* and not simply an *object*. Also, the A_{act}

model accounts for an attitude toward a highly specific situation. Further, the attitude toward the particular action is a function of beliefs about the outcomes of taking that action and the desirability of those outcomes. Finally, this model includes two specific components that reflect the influence of other people on behavior: normative beliefs (*NB*) weighted by the motivation to comply with norms (*Mc*). This model has been used and tested in many different situations including—for example, attitudes toward religion and donating blood.[9] We can relate each of these features of the A_{act} Model to consumer behavior.

First, an important aspect of this model is its focus on attitudes toward actions (in this case, purchasing) rather than on attitudes toward objects (brands). As mentioned, attention to attitudes toward actions is often appropriate. For example, a prospective buyer's attitude toward a certain ranch house might be favorable, while his or her attitude toward *purchasing* it might be negative due to high interest rates, rising property taxes, the buyer's uncertainty about future employment, and other, more pressing demands on the buyer's income. It is far more important for the owners of the house and the agent selling it to find out the prospective buyer's attitude toward purchasing the home, than merely to ascertain the prospect's attitude toward the house itself.

Second, the A_{act} Model accounts for a prospective buyer's attitude toward a very specific buying situation. A study of physicians' attitudes toward prescribing various pharmaceuticals required the author and Peter Bennett to use the A_{act} model to obtain precision. To determine the physicians' attitudes toward prescribing antidiabetic drugs, it was necessary also to study the context of the prescribing situation: the physicians' perception of patients diagnosed as diabetic. In this study, specific patient conditions were described to the physician and his or her attitudes toward the use of that particular drug were noted.[10] The study found strong relationships between attitudes, what doctors intended to prescribe, and actual prescribing behavior.

Third, A_{act} is a function of beliefs about the outcomes of taking an action (purchasing a product) and the desirability of those outcomes. When negative outcomes are associated with a product, consumers' attitudes toward purchasing the product are likely to become more negative. In recent years the trend away from products containing fluorocarbons (which are believed to harm the earth's ozone layer), saturated fats, saccharine, excessive salt, sugar, or preservatives, and the move away from cigarette smoking—all linked to human diseases or health threats—reflect the public's association of bad outcomes with these products. Clearly, changes in attitudes toward actions change behavior.

Fourth, the last part of the equation accounts for how other people's opinions affect choice. Normative beliefs (*NB*) reflect the consumers' assessment of the extent to which people from whom they accept opinions would recommend a brand. Motivation to comply (*Mc*) is the degree to which the buyer likes to accept others' product recommendations. Because these two factors usually add little to the prediction of purchase behavior, many marketing practitioners have neglected these parts of the model. Some marketers consider *NB* and *Mc* to be a measure of social compliance—a personality variable—and therefore separate from attitudes.[11] However, Chapter 9, which discusses personality, and Chapter 12, which discusses group influences on consumer behavior, emphasize the importance of these factors.

The Adequacy-Importance Attitude Model

Adequacy-Importance Model

Although it differs in some significant ways, the **Adequacy-Importance Model** is similar to the three previous models. It combines the affective and cognitive components of attitude in one construct, A_i, to form satisfaction scores for each specified criterion (i). The formula representing this model is:

$$A_o = \sum_{i=1}^{n} A_i IM_i$$

where:

A_o = attitude toward an object;
A_i = the adequacy of the object regarding the ith criterion—that is, the amount of satisfaction with the object regarding criterion i;
IM_i = the subjective evaluation of the importance of the ith characteristic in evaluating the object; and
n = the number of attributes.

The Adequacy-Importance Model also adds a variable not found in the other models: IM_i. This variable weighs each purchase criterion according to a subjective measure of its importance.

determinance

Although it is not part of the Adequacy-Importance Model per se, the concept of determinance, introduced by James Myers and Mark Alpert, is closely allied to the IM_i element in this formula. In terms of consumer behavior, **determinance** is a characteristic of those purchase criteria which are most closely related to actual purchase behavior. In the words of Myers and Alpert, "Attitudes toward features [purchase criteria] which are most closely related to preference or to actual purchase decisions are said to be determinant; the remaining features or attitudes—no matter how favorable—are not determinant.[12] For example, consider a hypothetical buying situation involving various makes of automobiles. Suppose we select two choice criteria at random: *four wheels* and *styling*.

Table 6-1 COMPARISON OF FOUR MULTIATTRIBUTE ATTITUDE MODELS

Model	***Behavioral Component***	***Unidimensional Affective Component***	***Purchase Criteria Affective Component***	***Cognitive Component***	***Importance of Each Criterion***
Rosenberg's A_o Model	(Not measured) Inferred from A_o	A_o (Attitude toward a brand)	V_i (Value importance)	I_i (Perceived instrumentality)	(Not measured) Inferred from V_i
Fishbein's A_o Model	(Not measured) Inferred from A_o	A_o (Attitude toward a brand)	a_i (Desirability)	B_i (Belief about an outcome)	(Not measured) Inferred from a_i
Fishbein's A_{act} Model	B (Actual behavior) and BI (Behavioral intention)	A_{act} (Attitude toward purchasing a brand)	a_i (Desirability)	B_i (Belief about an outcome)	Measured with weights from statistical programs
Adequacy-Importance Model	BI (Behavioral intention) or inferred from A_o	A_o (Attitude toward a brand)	A_i (Adequacy) The affective element is not measured independently from the cognitive element	A_i (Adequacy) The cognitive element is not measured independently from the affective element	I_m (Attribute importance)

Are they determinant criteria? Most buyers would consider the wheels a very important aspect of their cars, and they would say so if asked on a questionnaire. However, car buyers would not choose among brands based on this criterion, since almost all cars have four wheels. On the other hand, styling, which is less crucial to the car's functioning, might have a major effect on which brand is purchased. In this example, styling would be a determinant choice criterion, while four wheels would not.

Thus, the IM_i (importance) scale of the Adequacy-Importance Model is a direct measure of determinance. However, for Rosenberg's and Fishbein's models, correlations between an attitude measure of a criterion and a measure of purchase intention, preference, or actual purchase behavior can be used in assessing determinance.

Table 6-1 summarizes the similarities and differences among the four major attitude models. All three aspects of attitude are included: the behavioral, the affective (both overall and by criteria), and the cognitive components. The construct *importance of each criterion* from the Adequacy-Importance Model is also added.

THE ROLE OF PURCHASE CRITERIA

choice criteria

John Howard and Jagdish Sheth define **choice criteria** or purchase criteria as "those attributes of the brands in a product class that are salient in the buyer's evaluation of the brand. These attributes are ultimately related to the buyer's motives that are relevant to this product class in the sense that the product class has the potential for satisfying them."[13] In other words, the consumer uses choice criteria when evaluating the pros and cons of brands in a product class and when developing attitudes toward the brands. Sheth used this concept in an investigation of instant breakfast drinks and determined that "delicious taste, good buy, meal substitute, snack, protein source, filling, and nutritious" are relevant choice criteria.[14] For ready-to-eat cereals, the criteria often mentioned are protein, minerals, vitamins, and absence of sugar.[15]

Table 6-2 gives examples of the choice or purchase criteria consumers use for six consumer product categories.

Ads for two of these items show how advertisers address some of the selected criteria. Bali bras emphasizes fit, comfort, and even style in its ads by showing three different bras. Aqua-fresh toothpaste appeals to the criteria of cavity prevention, breath freshening, and cleaning power. When marketers know what purchase criteria are important to most buyers of a product they can design their messages to emphasize those factors.

Firms that have access to information about the buyer's purchase criteria can adjust the product, packaging, price, advertising messages, and other marketing mix factors to fit the characteristics sought by the target market or markets.

Table 6-2 PURCHASE CRITERIA FOR SELECTED CONSUMER PRODUCTS

Brassieres	***Lipstick***	***Mouthwash***
Comfort	Color	Color
Fit	Container	Effectiveness
Lifespan	Creaminess	Kills germs
Price	Prestige factor	Price
Style	Taste/flavor	Taste/flavor
Frozen Orange Juice	***Toilet Tissue***	***Toothpaste***
Nutritional value	Color	Decay prevention
Packaging	Package size	Freshens breath
Price	Price	Price
Taste/flavor	Strength	Taste/flavor
Texture	Texture	Whitens teeth

Source: Frank M. Bass and William L. Wilkie, "A Comparative Analysis of Attitude Predictions of Brand Preference," *Journal of Marketing Research* 10 (1973): 263.

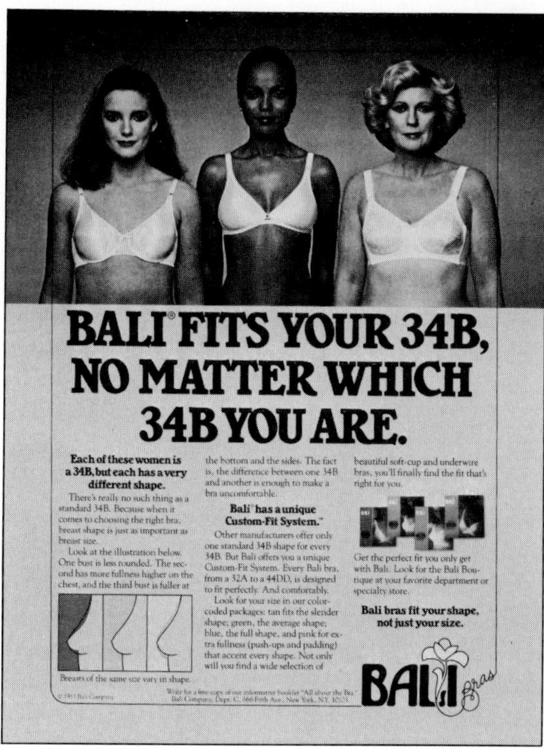

For example, research conducted in the retail food industry revealed that the key determinants of store patronage are convenience of the store's location and low prices.[16] Knowing this, food retailers can concentrate more heavily on these factors when developing marketing strategies.

This type of information is valuable not only for consumer buying, but for other types of purchasing as well. In a study of industrial purchasing criteria conducted in the United States and England, Donald Lehmann and John O'Shaughnessy found that the ranking of the seventeen purchase criteria listed in Table 6-3 varied according to the type of product.[17] (The study also revealed some variations according to whether buyers were from England or the United States. These results were combined with the others in the table.)

We discussed the attitude–behavior cycle in Chapter 5: Whether an attitude or a behavior occurs first, they are consistent with one another. That is, once a behavior occurs, attitudes are formed to support the behavior; once an attitude is formed first, subsequent behavior is usually in line with that attitude. Yet many sources contribute to the formation of purchase criteria, and there are three components of attitude that lead to

Table 6-3 SEVENTEEN PURCHASE CRITERIA RATED BY PURCHASING AGENTS

Purchase Criterion	Rank: Product 1	Rank: Product 2
Overall reputation of the supplier	4	7
Financing terms	9	16
Supplier's flexibility in adjusting to your company's needs	3	5
Experience with the supplier in analogous situations	6	13
Technical service offered	12	1
Confidence in the salesperson	14	15
Convenience of placing the order	15	17
Data on reliability of the product	11	11
Price	2	8
Technical specifications	5	9
Ease of operation in use	10	2
Preference of principal user of the product	13	14
Training offered by the supplier	16	3
Training time required	17	12
Reliability of delivery date promised	1	4
Ease of maintenance	8	10
Sales service expected after date of purchase	7	6

Source: adapted from Donald R. Lehmann and John O'Shaughnessy, "Differences in Attribute Importance for Different Industrial Products," *Journal of Marketing* 38 (1974): 38.

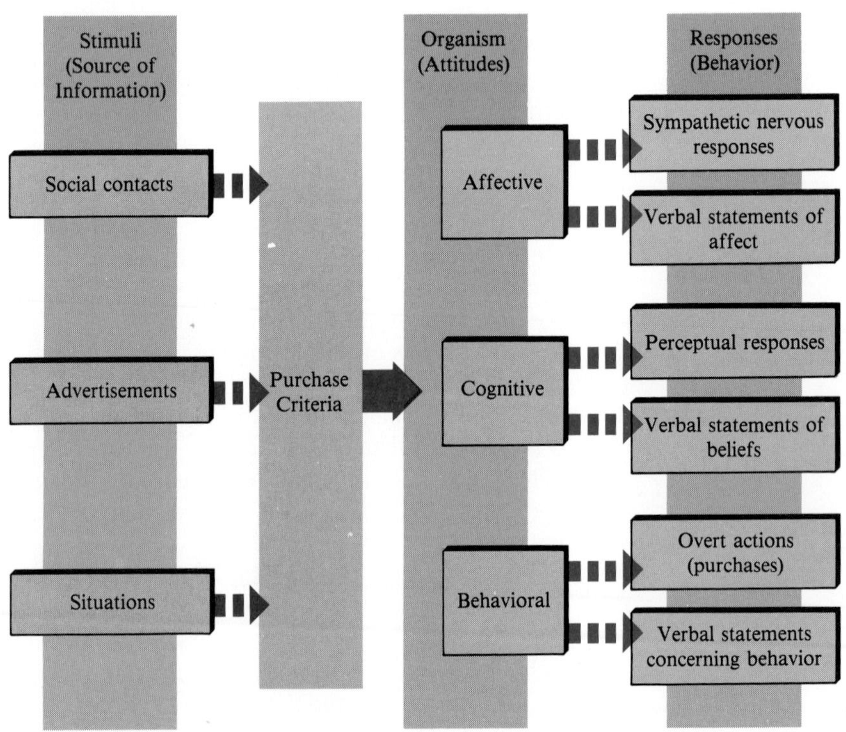

Figure 6-1 *Relationship of Purchase Criteria to Source of Information, Attitudes, and Behavior*

Source: adapted from Milton J. Rosenberg, Carl J. Havland, et al, *Attitude Organization and Change* (New Haven, CT: Yale University Press, 1960), 3.

purchase behavior: cognitive, affective, and behavioral. The process of attitude formation is not as simple as Chapter 5 outlined. By expanding the stimulus–organism–response model, discussed in Chapter 4, we can represent in full the relationship between the various elements, as shown in Figure 6-1.

Stimuli from many sources affect the choice criteria. In turn, these criteria affect the development of beliefs and attitudes. For each purchase criterion, the consumer develops both affective and cognitive beliefs by which he or she evaluates brands and forms behavioral tendencies such as intention to buy. These action tendencies lead to behaviors such as trial use of the brand, repeated purchases, and brand loyalty. In any case, the relationship between attitudes and behaviors is apparent. However, some researchers have questioned whether attitudes actually lead to some form of expected behavior in all circumstances.

ATTITUDE ASSESSMENT

Qualitative Techniques

qualitative techniques

Marketing researchers assess attitude using qualitative techniques, quantitative techniques, or a combination of the two. **Qualitative** research techniques generally allow for an in-depth probing of consumers' attitudes but not a sufficient quantification of the findings to determine the percentages of the population experiencing the specific attitudes uncovered. Qualitative methods are often used as a preliminary step in designing surveys and questionnaires that are used in turn to ascertain quantitative measures. Many researchers believe that the two techniques go hand in hand.[18]

Qualitative techniques can be used for research into areas other than attitude assessment—for example, in new product screening and ad testing where consumers are asked their opinion of a new product or ad. However, our purpose here is to briefly explain qualitative techniques as they are used in attitude studies. The two major qualitative techniques are the depth interview and the focused group.

The Depth Interview

depth interview

Investigators often use the **depth interview** to enumerate purchase criteria and to gain an understanding of the possible features on which brands are evaluated. Generally it employs a sampling technique that is not appropriate for quantification of the data gathered. The interviewer does not ask specific, predetermined questions; the interview seems to flow in an unstructured manner from one area of inquiry to another according to the interaction of the interviewer and the particular respondent.

Although the depth interview *seems* unstructured, the skilled interviewer can exert control over the general topics discussed and the flow of the interview. For example, an interview might begin with a general discussion of a broad range of similar products and end with in-depth probing about a particular brand and that brand's competitors. Often the flow of the interview is designed to get participants to discuss all of the aspects of each component of the respondent's attitudes. The marketer uses the compiled results of many depth interviews to help develop a marketing program.

The Focused Group Interview

focused group

When the depth interview is adapted to a group, it becomes the **focused group** technique. This popular type of depth interview involves interviewing several buyers at the same time.[19] The focused group is generally used in research projects that also involve attitude surveys later. Unlike the attitude survey, the focused group does not use predetermined questions. Therefore, focused groups minimize researchers' preconceived notions about buyer attitudes. Indeed, the researcher looks for unexpected attitudes that may suggest innovative marketing strategies and focuses much of the group's attention on questions raised by the group members themselves. In a sense, the group members interview themselves with the help of a skilled group moderator, or facilitator. As the moderator guides the group discussion, the respondents are encouraged, by verbal and nonverbal cues, to probe each other's feelings about brands. The social interaction of group members exploring common purchasing problems often results in insights into attitudes—and at times even motives—that exceed those achievable through one-on-one interviews.

There are several basic rules of focused group interviewing. A group of eight people generates more ideas than a group of four,[20] but one much larger than eight becomes cumbersome and difficult to moderate. Most groups should consist of about eight people. Further, it is generally preferable to use people who are similar to each other, because with a homogeneous group the common behavioral experiences of its members provide the basis for more in-depth analysis. Homogeneous groups are less likely to form role structures that inhibit individuals from speaking. The presence of just one exception to the members' norm can greatly hinder the effectiveness of this technique. For example, one researcher was interested in the attitudes of college students toward the sale of life insurance on campus. The researcher included seven freshmen and one senior in the focused group. Although the senior was outnumbered by the freshmen, he was clearly more knowledgeable about insurance and intimidated the others without realizing it. The focused group interview failed because the freshmen refused to express their true feelings and knowledge about the subject. However, in another group, consisting of all freshmen, the conversation led to interesting and useful insights into their attitudes regarding the sale of life insurance on campus. Although heterogeneous groups are likely to have more lively interviews covering a broader range of topics, homogeneous groups generally produce more in-depth analysis because role structures are minimized.

Finally, the researcher should use several groups to investigate each target market to ensure that the findings are accurate. One focused group is certainly not enough; findings for a single group could easily be at variance with the population under study. By using several groups, the researcher can better judge if the findings are *typical* of the feelings in the particular market segment.

snowball interview

One variation on the focused group technique is the **snowball interview.** It is used most often to determine attitudes toward new products or new product concepts. As its name suggests, the snowball interview allows for the accumulation of input during the interview process. The researcher analyzes each group interview after it is concluded; and often the researcher, the marketer, and the research and development department use the results to redesign the product concept before the next interview. In this way, the suggestions of each group help guide the revision of the concept for the following group.[21] This allows a gradual refinement and improvement of the product concept over the series of interviews.

Quantitative Techniques

quantitative techniques

attitude scales

psychophysical scales

While qualitative research methods are useful in assessing buyers' attitudes, quantitative methods also play an important role. Marketers use **quantitative** research techniques to put in statistical form the responses from a group of buyers or to infer to what degree certain attitudes exist in a population by measuring a sample. The most common means of measuring attitudes is with **attitude scales.** Attitudes cannot be observed through physical means, as temperature can. **Psychophysical scales,** requiring both mental and physical input, approximate the observation and measurement of attitudes. The physical input involves the recording of respondents' answers to questions on some observable form such as a questionnaire. Psychophysical attitude scales are discussed later in this chapter. As background, first we must review the classifications of all scales in general (see Table 6-4).

Types of Attitude Scales

Nominal and ordinal scales are nonmetric. That is, they are not metered or marked off into equal divisions. Therefore, the actual amount of distance between the points on such scales is unknown. However, metric scales are metered; it is easy to judge precisely how far one point on the scale is from any other point.[22]

Table 6-4 SCALE CLASSIFICATIONS

Class	*Type*	*Characteristic of Number System*	*Common Examples*	*Marketing Examples*
Nonmetric	Nominal	Unique identification by number	Telephone number Street address Sex	Brand choice Store type Market segment
	Ordinal	Describes relative position (greater than or less than)	School grade National college football standings	Social class Attitudes (ranked) Brand preference rank
Metric	Interval	Describes the distances between points	Temperature	Attitudes (distanced)
	Ratio	Has a zero point; thus, we can multiply and divide distances	Miles Feet Pounds	Number of buyers Sales volume

nominal scales

ordinal scales

Nominal scales are used only for identification or classification—for example, to place people in market segments. **Ordinal scales** provide more information because they indicate the direction one point is from another: *greater than/less than; stronger than/weaker than; more preferable than/less preferable than; more satisfying than/less satisfying than;* and so forth.

interval scales

Interval scales provide more information than do ordinal scales because the investigator can assess the relationship between the points on the scale using the distance between them as a basis. For example, an interval attitude scale could show that one person's attitude toward a certain product feature is two points stronger than another's attitude toward that feature. The familiar Fahrenheit temperature scale is an interval scale: the distance between two points can be clearly measured but it cannot be divided or multiplied. For example, if it were 30°F outside yesterday and 60°F today, we would not say that it is *twice* as warm today as it was yesterday, but rather that the difference was an *increase* of 30°. Again, if tomorrow it will be 90°F, the interval or difference between today and tomorrow will be the same: a positive 30°. While the measurement of distance on an interval scale for attitudes is useful, researchers using this scale should recognize that the measurement may contain a fair amount of error, since attitudes are subjective and difficult to measure in this way.

Most marketers would agree that attitude scales lack the precision of the interval scales used in the physical sciences. However, the measurement errors associated with attitude scales generally are not great enough to force us to classify all these scales as merely ordinal. The benefits of treating these attitude scales as we would other interval scales may outweigh the problems, because more powerful and complex statistical procedures are available for application with interval data.

ratio scale

The most precise scale is the **ratio scale,** because it has a zero point. Therefore, all mathematical processes (addition, subtraction, multiplication, and division) can be performed on its data. For example, a person 6 feet tall is twice as tall as a person who is 3 feet tall. Also, the 6-foot-tall person is three feet taller than the 3-foot-tall person. Attitude data is seldom attributed the quality of a ratio scale, because of the data's imprecise nature.

Figure 6-2 shows some of the overlapping use of scales in the physical sciences and the social sciences. As the figure suggests, the types of scales can be thought of as occurring on a continuum.

The Thurstone Scale

The four most popular psychophysical attitude scales are the Thurstone scale, the Likert scales, the Bipolar adjective scales, and the semantic differential scales.

Thurstone scale

The **Thurstone scale** is closer to a true interval scale than most other scales used in attitude assessment. However, the process required to develop this scale is elaborate and time consuming:[23]

1. Researchers develop approximately 100 to 150 statements about the topic under study.
2. Several judges sort the statements into eleven categories ranging from "most favorable" to "least favorable." The sixth category represents the neutral point.
3. Scale values are computed for each of these statements. The number of times the statement falls in each category is multiplied by the value assigned to the category. (The first category is given a value of 1, the second 2, and so on.) The mean score for each statement is then computed to provide its scale value.
4. About 20 to 25 items are chosen for the final scale. The items selected should provide a continuum of scores from low to high. Also, each item selected should be one that was categorized very similarly by all of the judges.

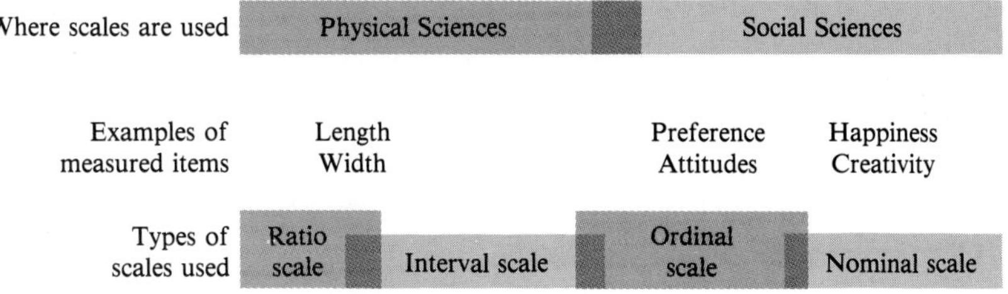

Figure 6-2 *Measurement Scales and Their Overlapping Uses*

Source: adapted from Thomas C. Kinnear and James R. Taylor, *Marketing Research: An Applied Approach* (New York: McGraw-Hill, 1979), 287.

5. In the final questionnaire, these 20 to 25 statements are presented to the subject, who is asked to select those with which he or she agrees or disagrees.
6. The subject's attitude score is an average of those items selected.

Despite the elaborate process used to develop a Thurstone scale, its use with multiattribute attitude models is limited. Over a hundred statements are often required to explore attitudes using this measure; this makes it cumbersome to use with multiattribute models. For this reason, researchers choose the Thurstone scale when they seek to know the unidimensional affect or overall attitude, undissected by component. In other words, the Thurstone scale is very useful when little information is required regarding *why* the person's attitudes are what they are.

One researcher altered the principles set forth by Thurstone to develop a scale more applicable to the measurement of consumer's attitudes. This researcher used the revised scale to determine the best methods for improving nurses' attitudes toward their job so that the hospital could attract and maintain a quality nursing staff. Rather than using numbered points on the Thurstone scale, the researcher asked respondents to determine the monetary value of a range of offerings.

Rather than rank priorities on a scale of one to eleven, the nurses were asked to put a dollar value on each priority that reflected its importance to them in evaluating job benefits. These were later ranked after the dollar values were added to arrive at a summary score for the group. The responses were then translated into an annual budget for the hospital administrators to use in their financial planning. Table 6-5 shows the results of that study.[24]

Table 6-5 ANNUALIZED BUDGET VALUE OF ADDITIONAL JOB BENEFITS FOR NURSES

Job Benefit	***Annualized Perceived Value***
Feeling that I am part of a patient care team	$224,800
Working the shift of my choice	194,400
Assignments consistent with my training	194,400
Nurse preceptors at the clinical unit level	158,400
Knowing my work schedule a month in advance	147,600
Improved cleanliness	133,200
Better equipment	122,400
Better parking facilities	104,400
Better supervision of my work	82,800
Better lounge/conference facilities for nurses	82,800
A minibus that picks me up at my home and returns me after work	10,800
Day-care services for my children at no cost to me	10,800
Better social life	0

The Likert Scales

Likert scale

Likert scales tend to provide ordinal information about a person's attitude. Many scales used in consumer behavior are referred to as Likert scales, because variations on the theme abound. In its simplest form, it is essentially a two-step procedure used to classify subjects according to five degrees of approval regarding a particular statement. It allows for an expression of intensity of feelings. After the list of statements is developed, subjects are asked to indicate their degree of agreement or disagreement with each statement in a series by checking the appropriate cell.[25] It is important to recognize that Likert scales are ordinal, not interval scales; a researcher cannot conclude, for example, the exact degree of approval. Unskilled researchers may mistakenly assume that Likert scales can be interpreted as interval scales.

Here is an example of a Likert scale:

	Strongly Disapprove	*Disapprove*	*Undecided*	*Approve*	*Strongly Approve*
Mouthwash with coloring	_______	_______	_______	_______	_______
Use of mouthwash to enhance attractiveness	_______	_______	_______	_______	_______

These are the most common steps in developing Likert scales:

1. Researchers create many statements to cover "favorable" as well as "unfavorable" aspects of the topic under study.
2. A pretest is conducted in which subjects indicate whether they (a) strongly approve, (b) approve, (c) are undecided, (d) disapprove, or (e) strongly disapprove of each statement.
3. Each statement receives a weight or numerical value −2, −1, 0, +1, +2, and each person's score is computed by summing the values. (While it is not strictly appropriate to sum ordinal information, many researchers feel it helps in selecting items.)
4. The researcher selects only those items that best discriminate between high and low total scores, based on either judgment or computer routines.
5. The researcher uses these items to create a questionnaire that is administered to a sample of people from the market segments being studied.

The proper procedure for developing a Likert scale is often shortcut. These alterations in procedure could weaken the results. For example, the researcher may ignore the pretest, so that the scale is based almost entirely on the researcher's judgment. Often the response category "approval" is often replaced with "likelihood," or other words that seem practical from the researcher's point of view. One strength of the Likert scale is that respondents usually find it easy to understand their part in the procedure.

The Bipolar Adjective and Semantic Differential Scales

bipolar adjective scales

Bipolar adjective scales are perhaps the most often used scales in marketing. *Bipolar adjective* is a literal description of the scale. Respondents are asked to evaluate a brand according to where they visualize it between two poles representing two extreme, opposite qualities (for example, extremely expensive and extremely cheap, or beautiful and ugly). Generally three, five, or seven points are placed between the two poles and the respondent is asked to place the brand somewhere on the scale.

semantic differential scale

The **semantic differential scale** is the most notable bipolar adjective scale and was a forerunner to many of the bipolar adjective scales used today. The two are so closely associated that many times the terms are (incorrectly) used interchangeably. The semantic differential scale, developed by Charles Osgood,[26] has certain specific requirements that are unduly restrictive in a consumer behavior context, since it necessitates measuring three dimensions: (1) evaluative (*good/bad*), (2) activity (*active/passive*), and (3) potency (*strong/weak*). Therefore, our discussion focuses on the more general bipolar adjective scale.

Here is an example of the bipolar adjective scale:

Inexpensive	____ :	____ :	____ :	____ :	____ :	____ :	X :	Expensive
Strong	____ :	X :	____ :	____ :	____ :	____ :	____ :	Weak
Good	____ :	____ :	____ :	X :	____ :	____ :	____ :	Bad

The bipolar adjective scale is generally treated as an interval scale; when properly constructed, interval statistics (such as means and standard deviations) are legitimately used with it. This scale is relatively easy to construct and many dimensions can be included in a relatively short questionnaire. It is the appropriate choice for a broad range of attitude scaling problems.

A HYPOTHETICAL ATTITUDE ASSESSMENT

Figure 6-3 illustrates how qualitative and quantitative measurement procedures can be combined. In this hypothetical example, a marketer of health products is planning to introduce a new brand of mouthwash. Although the firm has a long history of success with soaps and shampoo, management has no prior experience in the mouthwash category. The market for mouthwash is growing but it is also highly competitive. To better understand how the net product should be designed and marketed,

Qualitative Measurement Technique	*Sample of Output*
Focused groups with consumers aged 21–39 including users and nonusers of mouthwash to explore attitudes toward these products and selecting among brands. Individual depth interviews with heavy users of the best-selling brands to identify the important features of these products.	Results suggest that mouthwash use is related to the following: • concern over good health • desire for sex appeal • desire to be sociable • concern over personal cleanliness • desire for personal success Heaviest users tend to be young and socially active and have high career aspirations. Several attributes seem to be the basis for choice, including: • flavorful taste • cleaning effectiveness • breath freshening capability • economy

Quantitative Measurement Technique	*Sample of Output*
Attitude scaling survey of young, socially active men and women at major universities to quantify responses and attitude brands based on the key features identified in the qualitative phase.	Among the sample, 90% strongly agree that "freshening capability" is the most important attribute in choosing a mouthwash. Only 26% agree that economy is important in choosing a brand of mouthwash. Compared to other brands, the top-selling "Clean 'n' Fresh" brand mouthwash was rated more favorably on breath freshening power but less favorably on economy by those who use mouthwash regularly.

Figure 6-3
An Example of Combining Qualitative and Quantitative Attitude Measurement Techniques

the marketer uses qualitative and quantitative measurement of potential purchasers attitudes.

In the example, focused groups and depth interviews are used to identify the attributes which seem to be the basis for choice in selecting a mouthwash. Notice that the output of this qualitative state is used to guide the quantitative attitude measurement in the next phase. Figure 6-4 gives examples of the Thurstone, Likert, and bipolar adjective scales using the mouthwash marketing problem to highlight the relative merits of each approach.

Both qualitative and quantitative measurement techniques are used to some extent in the formulation and use of attitude models. In the following section, we explore some of the models researchers use to assess

Figure 6-4
Comparison of Selected Quantitative Measurement Techniques

Scaling Procedure	Sample Scale	Merits of Each Approach
Thurston scale	Agree / Disagree 1. Clean 'n' Fresh tastes great ____ ____ 2. Clean 'n' Fresh is powerful in freshening breath ____ ____	Gives overall view of attitude toward object or issue Provides little information about attitude components Cumbersome to develop
Likert scale	Clean 'n' Fresh mouthwash is especially good tasting Strongly disagree ☐ Disagree ☐ Neither agree or disagree ☐ Agree ☐ Strongly agree ☐	Relatively easy to develop Can be used to measure components of overall attitude Does not allow interval comparison of attitude intensity
Bipolar adjective scale	Clean 'n' Fresh mouthwash is: Bad tasting :____: ____: ____: ____: ____: ____: ____: Good tasting Weak breath freshener :____: ____: ____: ____: ____: ____: ____: Strong breath freshener	Offers a means to measure intervals of attitude intensity Many dimensions can be included in a short questionnaire

consumer attitudes and the types of information derived from these models.

NONCOMPENSATORY ATTITUDE MODELS

Models that are meant to show how buyers arrive at decisions based on their attitudes are beginning to receive widespread attention.[27] While many of these assumptions have yet to be clearly supported by empirical research, they make good theoretical sense and can offer insights into creative marketing strategy. Attitude models can be classified as compensatory or noncompensatory according to how buyers deal with the advantages and disadvantages associated with each brand under consideration. **Compensatory models** allow buyers to select the brand that scores highest overall on their purchase criteria. Thus compensatory models assume that low ratings for a brand on some choice criteria can be offset by high ratings on others and that buyers will consider the trade-offs involved in each brand. The multiattribute models discussed earlier in the chapter are compensatory models. **Noncompensatory models,** on the other hand, assume that buyers make decisions in a more simplified way and, to a large extent, do not take trade-offs into consideration.

compensatory attitude models

noncompensatory attitude models

Noncompensatory models fall into four categories: lexicographic, se-

lexicographic model

quential elimination, conjunctive, and disjunctive. In the **lexicographic model,** a consumer ranks the choice criteria from most important to least important and then uses these criteria (now in descending order) to evaluate each brand. The consumer selects the first brand that ranks highest on the most important choice criterion. If two or more brands tie on that criterion, the consumer looks to the next most important criterion. For example, if a prospective automobile buyer ranks comfort and gas mileage as criteria one and two, respectively, and makes A and B have similar comfort ratings but B rates better on gas mileage, the car buyers will prefer B.

A typical ad for Carlton cigarettes lends itself to lexicographic decision making by comparing Carlton's tar and nicotine levels to those of other leading brands. If low tar and nicotine are the most important criteria a buyer has for choosing a brand of cigarettes, Carlton ranks as the best of all those brands presented and would likely be selected.

sequential elimination model

In the **sequential elimination model,** the consumer establishes minimum criteria for product acceptability, looking to the most important criterion first and eliminating all brands that do not meet the minimum standard. If several brands pass the test, the consumer uses the second most important criterion to further eliminate brands that do not meet the second criterion, and so on. For example, a prospective new-car buyer selects gas mileage as the first criterion on which to judge those on his list of makes to examine. The buyer eliminates makes that do not meet a certain level of acceptability: say, at least 35 miles per gallon. Then the buyer chooses a second criterion, perhaps passenger capacity, and evaluates the remaining makes on the basis of the maximum number of passengers they can accommodate. The buyer eliminates those cars that cannot carry at least five adults, the minimum acceptable number of passengers. Eventually, the buyer should find one make that has an important quality or feature that no other make has. An ad for Ford's Country Squire station wagon might appeal to a buyer using sequential elimination decision making. Assuming that room for several people is one of the most important criteria for selecting a car, Ford claims room in the Country Squire for six people and their luggage. However, the ad also states that the car offers luxury. This may be the one unique quality some prospective buyers desire that distinguishes the Country Squire from the rest, especially if they perceive other brands as having equally roomy interiors.

conjunctive model

The **conjunctive model** assumes that buyers establish a minimum level of acceptance for a brand regarding each important choice criterion. Any brands that do not meet *all* the minimum standards are rejected. For example, assume a prospective car buyer's minimum standards for purchase are: (1) it gets 25 miles per gallon, (2) it seats four comfortably, and (3) it costs no more than $8,000. Suppose that make A gets only 20 miles per gallon, seats four, and costs $7,500. Make B gets 28 miles per gallon, seats only two, and costs $8,200. Make C gets 25 miles per gallon, seats five, and costs $7,800. How many of these makes would be chosen? Low

gas mileage eliminates A. While B gets the necessary gas mileage, it is eliminated due to its small capacity and high cost. Therefore, make C is the only choice. Note that if more than one make meets all the conjunctive criteria, the consumer must either add more criteria or apply another decision-making model in order to make a purchase choice.

In its ad, Wilderness hiking boots addresses six separate criteria for hiking boots, making the ad relevant to the conjunctive decision-making model. Someone looking for hiking boots could see whether or not Wilderness boots fit the minimum level of acceptance that has been set for each or any of these criteria.

The Wilderness boots ad might also appeal to a buyer using a disjunctive process. In the **disjunctive model,** as in the conjunctive model, the buyer establishes minimum levels of acceptability for a few criteria considered crucial in the decision. In this model, however, any brands that meet the (usually rather high) standards for *any* of the criteria are acceptable. Thus, if Brand A has generally good scores on all criteria, but its scores on the really important criteria are not outstanding, and Brand B scores poorly on some criteria but very high on one of the crucial criteria, the consumer chooses Brand B. If more than one brand meets or exceeds the consumer's high standards for one or more crucial criteria, he or she

disjunctive model

can either select the first acceptable brand or apply another decision model.

Different people use these different strategies for processing attitude information under varying circumstances. However, research suggests that some models are used more than others. In one exploratory study, consumers were asked to evaluate automobiles using seven choice criteria and then to describe which method of evaluation they used. From their descriptions of the four methods used (lexicographic, sequential elimination, conjunctive, and disjunctive), the study concluded that most of the consumers used the lexicographic approach. The sequential elimination approach was the second most used, and a few consumers used the disjunctive and conjunctive approaches.[28]

Engel and colleagues make an interesting point concerning how knowledge of decision models can be used in formulating a marketing strategy. At least for big-ticket items such as cars, consumers tend to think first about choice criteria, which are the benefits they seek, and then look at brands afterward. Marketers of these products would be wiser to specify the benefits to buyers than to dwell on brand.

SUMMARY

Four popular multiattribute models are found in much of the buyer behavior literature and are employed by marketing researchers and planners. The Rosenberg A_o Model, the Fishbein A_o Model, the Fishbein A_{act} Model, and the Adequacy-Importance Model are similar in two ways: (1) they describe attitudes in the context of the consumer's feelings about choice criteria, and (2) they reflect the consumer's estimates of how well particular brands rate on each criterion. The first two models focus on the buyer's attitudes toward the brands themselves while the second two models emphasize the buyer's purchase of (or intention to purchase) the brands. The action focus of the latter two models has enabled researchers to better predict purchase intention and ultimate brand choice.

Marketers generally use both qualitative and quantitative tools in assessing attitudes. The depth interview and the focused group interview are designed to provide qualitative assessments of buyers' attitudes. Once the qualitative attitude information is gathered, scales are used to yield quantitative measures of attitudes. In general, each of the four kinds of scales can be classified as either nonmetric or metric. These categories reflect the types of statistical tests which can be used. Four specific attitude scales are commonly used to measure consumers behavior. Thurstone scales, bipolar adjective scales, and semantic differential scales approximate interval (metric) scales; Likert scales are closer to rank-order (nonmetric) scales.

Consumers use two methods of evaluating brands based on their existing attitudes. Compensatory models (such as the four multiattribute models) quantify the trade-offs among many evaluative criteria, allowing buyers to choose the ''best overall'' brand. Noncompensatory models allow for independent analysis of criteria among brands. They may use fewer decision criteria, but these criteria tend to be those of greatest significance to the consumer. Noncompensatory models include the lexicographic model, the sequential elimination model, the conjunctive model, and the disjunctive model.

KEY TERMS

multiattribute models
Rosenberg's Attitude toward an Object Model
valued state
Fishbein's Attitude toward an Object Model
Fishbein's Attitude toward an Action Model
Adequacy-Importance Model
determinance
choice criteria
qualitative techniques
depth interview
focused group
snowball interview
quantitative techniques
attitude scales
psychophysical scales
nominal scales
ordinal scales
interval scales
ratio scale
Thurstone scale
Likert scales
bipolar adjective scales
semantic differential scale
compensatory attitude models
noncompensatory models
lexicographic model
sequential elimination model
conjunctive model
disjunctive model

QUESTIONS

1. What are the basic similarities among the Rosenberg and Fishbein attitude models? What are some important differences? Can you think of a situation in which one or the other might be a preferable measure?

2. What is meant by *determinance* in regard to attitudes? Briefly explain its importance in measuring attitudes.

3. Make a list of ten possible choice criteria for selecting a job after graduation. Which are most salient to you?

4. Focused group interviews are a major technique in qualitative research. What design considerations are important in using this research tool?

5. When is the Thurstone scale most appropriate? What are its inherent limitations?

6. How do compensatory and noncompensatory attitude models differ? Distinguish between the four types of noncompensatory models using a hypothetical example of each.

NOTES

1. Other authors have referred to these models as *valence expectancy models, expectancy × value models,* and *summated* and *disaggregated attitude models.* We prefer to use their more popular names.
2. Much of this material is derived from the excellent review of these models in Michael B. Mazis, O'lli T. Ahtola, and R. Eugene Klippel, "A Comparison of Four Multiattribute Models in the Prediction of Consumer Attitudes," *Journal of Consumer Research* 2 no. 1 (1975): 38–52.
3. Helen Peak, "Attitude and Motivation," in *Nebraska Symposium on Motivation,* Marshall R. Jones, ed. (Lincoln, NE: University of Nebraska Press, 1955), 149–89.
4. We discussed the cognitive and affective components of attitude in Chapter 5.
5. Adapted from Milton J. Rosenberg, Carl I. Hovland, et al., *Attitude Organization and Change* (New Haven, CT: Yale University Press, 1960), 42.
6. Martin Fishbein, "An Investigation of the Relationships between Belief about an Object and the Attitude toward That Object," *Human Relations* 16 (1963): 233–40.
7. Don E. Dulany, "Awareness, Rules, and Propositional Control: A Confrontation with S-R Behavior Therapy," in *Verbal Behavior and S-R Behavior Theory,* D. Horton and T. Dixon, eds. (New York: Prentice-Hall, 1967).
8. Martin Fishbein, "Attitude and the Prediction of Behavior," in *Attitude Theory and Measurement,* Martin Fishbein, ed. (New York: Wiley, 1967), 477–92.
9. For use of Fishbein's second model to measure attitudes toward religion, see Richard P. Bagozzi, "The Construct Validity of the Affective, Behavioral, and Cognitive Components of Attitude by Analysis of Covariance Structures," *Multivariate Behavior Research* 13 (1978): 9–31. For its use with attitudes on donating blood, see Robert E. Burnkrant and Thomas J. Page, Jr., "An Examination of the Convergent, Discriminant, and Predictive Validity of Fishbein's Behavioral Intention Model," *Journal of Marketing Research* 19 (1982): 550–61.
10. Gilbert D. Harrell and Peter Bennett, "An Evaluation of the Expectancy/Value Model of Attitude Measurement for Physician Prescribing Behavior," *Journal of Marketing Research* 11 (1974): 269–78.
11. Michael J. Ryan and E. H. Bonfield, "The Fishbein Extended Model and Consumer Behavior," *Journal of Consumer Research* 2 (1975): 118–35.
12. James H. Myers and Mark I. Alpert, "Determinant Buying Attitudes: Meaning and Measurement," *Journal of Marketing* 32 (1968): 13–20.
13. John Howard and Jagdish N. Sheth, *The Theory of Buyer Behavior* (New York: Wiley, 1969), 118.
14. Jagdish N. Sheth, "A Field Study of Attitude Structure and the Attitude Behavior Relationship," in *Models of Buyer Behavior* (New York: Harper & Row, 1974), 242–68.
15. Harper W. Boyd, Michael LeRoy, and Edward C. Strong, "An Attitudinal Framework for Advertising Strategy," *Journal of Marketing* 36 (1972): 27–33.
16. Stephen J. Arnold, Tae H. Oum, and Douglas J. Tigert, "Determinant Attributes in Retail Patronage: Seasonal, Temporal, Regional, and International Comparisons," *Journal of Marketing Research* 20 (1983): 149–57.
17. Donald R. Lehmann and John O'Shaughnessy, "Differences in Attribute Importance for Different Industrial Products," *Journal of Marketing* 38 (1974): 36–42.
18. Larry Percy, "Using Qualitative Focus Groups in Generating Hypothesis for Subsequent Quantitative Validation and Strategy Development," in *Advances in Consumer Research,* Andrew Mitchell, ed. (St. Louis: Association for Consumer Research, 1981), 57–61.
19. For a review of both theory and methodology of focused groups, see Martin E. Lautman, "Focus Groups: Theory and Method," 52–56, and William A. Cook, "Turning Focus Groups inside Out," 62–71, both in *Advances in Consumer Research,* Andrew Mitchell, ed. (St. Louis: Association for Consumer Research, 1981).
20. Edward F. Fern, "The Use of Focus Groups for Idea Generation: The Effects of Group Size, Acquaintanceship, and Moderator on Response Quantity and Quality," *Journal of Marketing Research,* 19 (1982): 1–13.
21. An excellent review of the focused group interview is in Alfred E. Goldman, "The Group Depth Interview," *Journal of Marketing* 26 (1962): 61–68.
22. For an excellent review of scale classifications, see Thomas C. Kinnear and James R. Taylor, *Marketing Research: An Applied Approach* (New York: McGraw-Hill, 1979), 280–86.
23. For a review of the properties of each scale, see Paul E. Green and Donald S. Tull, *Research for Marketing Decisions,* 3rd ed. (Englewood Cliffs, NJ: Prentice-Hall, 1975). Much of the material in this discussion is adapted from that book.
24. G. David Hughes, "Monetized Utilities for Product

and Service Benefits," in *Consumer and Industrial Buying Behavior,* Arch G. Woodside, Jagdish N. Sheth, and Peter D. Bennett, eds. (New York: North-Holland, 1977), 179–89.

25. For a more detailed discussion of scale construction, see Gilbert A. Churchill, Jr., *Marketing Research* (Hinsdale, IL: The Dryden Press, 1979), 225–28.
26. Charles Edgerton Osgood, G. C. Suci, and P. H. Tannenbaum, *The Measurement of Meaning* (Urbana, IL: University of Illinois Press, 1957).
27. Material for this section is abstracted from James F. Engel, Roger D. Blackwell, and David T. Kollat, *Consumer Behavior,* 3rd ed. (Hinsdale, IL: The Dryden Press, 1978), 391–92.
28. Michael D. Reilly, Rebecca H. Holman, and Roger Evered, "Individual Differences in Information Processing: An Exploratory Report," Working Paper No. 50, College of Business Administration, Pennsylvania State University, November 1976.

FURTHER READING

Classics

Bettman, James R., Noel Capon, and Richard J. Lutz, "Cognitive Algebra in Multi-Attribute Models," *Journal of Marketing Research* 9 (February 1975): 93–97.

Bruno, Albert, V., and Albert R. Wildt, "Toward Understanding Attitude Structure: A Study of the Complementarity of Multi-Attribute Attitude Models," *Journal of Consumer Research* 2 (September 1975): 137–145.

Fishbein, Martin, "The Relationship Between Beliefs, Attitudes, and Behavior, in *Cognitive Consistency,* Shel Feldman, ed. (New York: Academic Press, 1966), 199–223.

Fishbein, Martin, "A Behavior Theory Approach to the Relations between Beliefs about an Object and the Attitude toward the Object," in *Readings in Attitude Theory and Measurement,* M. Fishbein, ed. (New York: Wiley, 1967), 389–399.

Lavidge, Robert J., and Gary A. Steiner, "A Model For Predictive Measurements of Advertising Effectiveness," *Journal of Marketing* (October 1961): 59–62.

Locander, William B., and W. Austin Spivey, "A Functional Approach to Attitude Measurement," *Journal of Marketing Research* 15 (November 1978): 576–587.

Lutz, R. J., and J. R. Bettman, "Multiattribute Models in Marketing: A Bicentennial Review," in *Consumer and Individual Buying Behavior,* Arch G. Woodside, Jagdish N. Sheth, and Peter D. Bennett, eds. (New York: North-Holland, 1977).

Osgood, C. E., G. J. Suci, and P. H. Tannenbaum, *The Measurement of Meaning* (Urbana, IL: University of Illinois Press, 1957).

Roper, Burns, "The Importance of Attitudes, the Difficulty of Measurement," in *New Ideas for Successful Marketing,* J. S. Wright and J. Goldstucker, eds. (Chicago: American Marketing Association, 1966).

Rosenberg, Milton J., "Cognitive Structure and Attitudinal Affect," *Journal of Abnormal and Social Psychology* 53, (November 1956): 367–372.

Sampson, Peter and Paul Harris, "A User's Guide to Fishbein," *Journal of the Market Research Society* 12 (July 1970): 145–166.

Thurstone, L. L., "The Measurement of Social Attitudes," *Journal of Abnormal and Social Psychology,* 26 (1931): 249–269.

Wilkie, William L., and Edgar A. Pessemier, "Issues in Marketing's Use of Multi-Attribute Models," *Journal of Marketing* 10, (November 1973): 428–441.

Recent Significant Research

Cacioppo, J. T., and R. E. Petty, "Attitudes and Cognitive Responses: An Electrophysiological Approach," *Journal of Personality and Social Psychology* 37 (1979): 2181–2199.

Hartwick, Jon, "Intentions to Purchase Tylenol: Headaches for Fishbein and Ajzen?," in *Proceedings of the Division of Consumer Psychology,* James C. Anderson, ed. (American Psychological Association, 1983), 100–103.

Levine, Phil, "Attitude Research in the Eighties: A Maturing Discipline Faces a Difficult Decade," in *Attitude Research Enters the 80's,* Richard W. Olshavsky, ed. (Chicago: American Marketing Association, 1980), 129–137.

Miniard, Paul W., and Thomas J. Page, Jr., "Causal Relationships in the Fishbein Behavioral Intention Model," in *Advances in Consumer Research,* Thomas C. Kinnear, ed. (Provo, UT: Association for Consumer Research, 1984) 137–142.

Oliver, Richard L., and Philip K. Berger, "A Path Analysis of Preventive Health Care Decision Models," *Journal of Consumer Research* 6 (September 1979): 113–122.

Applications

Alpert, Mark I., "Identification of Determinant Attitudes: A Comparison of Methods," *Journal of Marketing Research* 8, (May 1971): 184–191.

Assael, Henry, and George S. Day, "Attitudes and Awareness as Predictors of Market Share," *Journal of Advertising Research* 8 (December 1968): 3–10.

Axelrod, Joel N., "Attitude Measures that Predict Purchase," *Journal of Advertising Research* 8 (March 1968): 3–18.

Bass, Frank M., and William L. Wilkie, "A Comparative Analysis of Attitudinal Predictions of Brand Preference," *Journal of Marketing Research* 10 (August 1973): 262–269.

Bruno, Albert V., and Albert R. Wildt, "Toward Understanding Attitude Structure: A Study of the Complimentarity of Multi-Attribute Attitude Models," *Journal of Consumer Research* 2 (September 1975): 137–145.

Fishbein, Martin, "Some Comments on the Use of 'Models' in Advertising Research," in *Proceedings: Seminar on Translating Advanced Advertising Theories Into Research Reality* (Amsterdam, The Netherlands: European Society of Marketing Research, 1971).

Hunt, H. Keith, "The Use of Attitude Research—What's Happening at the FTC?" in *Attitude Research Enters the 80's,* Richard W. Olshavsky, ed. (Chicago, American Marketing Association, 1980), 157–167.

Kirkman, Walter B., "Attitude Research Enters the Financial World," in *Attitude Research Enters the 80's,* Richard W. Olshavsky, ed. (Chicago: American Marketing Association, 1980), 180–184.

Mazis, Michael B., and Olli T. Ahtola, "A Comparison of Four Multi-Attribute Models in the Prediction of Consumer Attitudes," *Journal of Consumer Research* 2 (June 1975): 38–52.

Robinson, Patrick J., "Applications of Conjoint Analysis to Pricing Problems," in *Market Measurement and Analysis,* David B. Montgomery and Dick R. Wittink, eds. (Cambridge, MA: Marketing Science Institute, 1980).

Sheth, Jagdish N., "A Field Study of Attitude Structure and the Attitude–Behavior Relationship," in *Models of Buyer Behavior,* Jagdish N. Sheth, ed. (New York: Harper and Row 1974), 242–268.

Wilson, David T., H. Lee Matthews, and James W. Harvey, "An Empirical Test of the Fishbein Behavioral Intention Model," *Journal of Consumer Research* 1 (March 1975): 39–48.

7 Attitude Change

Objectives of This Chapter

After you have studied this chapter, you should be able to:

1. Explain how attitudes can be changed by altering several aspects of the buyer's cognitive structure.

2. Describe how the source of a message, its characteristics, and the characteristics of message receivers influence attitude change.

3. Provide examples which illustrate the attitude change strategies used by companies and other organizations.

Advertisers spend billions annually to influence and change consumer attitudes. Personal selling, used to market products to buyers of all types, is directed largely toward the same goals. Advertising used by political campaigns and nonprofit organizations is often aimed at changing public attitudes about an issue. Chapters 5 and 6 focused on the structure and measurement of attitude. This chapter discusses influences on attitudes and, specifically, how they can be altered.

The impact of communication on attitude change has been studied for many years, because it underlies so many aspects of everyday life in society. Much of the research has led to important findings concerning how the sources of the message, the characteristics of buyers, and the method of presentation influence the effectiveness of persuasive messages. A more recent area of investigation has provided insights on psychological aspects of persuasion that influence cognitive processing.

In this chapter we discuss the general concepts that facilitate or restrict the impact of communications on attitude change. Then we look at strategies that influence how people think in order to see how their attitudes may be altered. The chapter also highlights what some companies do to influence attitudes and how their actions influence consumers' attitudes and subsequent purchase behavior. We will first look at the routes to modifications of cognitive structure. Then we will consider the modifications themselves, including changing cognitions or beliefs, changing the goodness or badness of product attributes, altering the importance of product characteristics, the addition of attributes, and the use of direct action.

Next we will consider how communication sources affect attitude change, giving attention to source credibility and to celebrities as sources. How important is the source's credibility to consumer acceptance of a message? Does it matter whether messages come from reference groups or from celebrities? How do people resist persuasion?

Then we will give attention to the characteristics of messages to answer questions such as these: When communicating in order to persuade, is it better to use one-sided or two-sided messages? Does it help to present arguments in a certain order or to draw conclusions for the receiver? What is the impact of humor on susceptibility to persuasion? What aspects of a person's attitude can be changed most readily? To what do people attribute their attitudes, and what role do these attributions have in the process of changing attitudes?

Following this, we turn to resistance to persuasion, refuting arguments, attacking the source, distorting the message, rationalization, and blanket rejection. The final section focuses on other factors that affect persuadability, including level of involvement, intelligence, and self-esteem.

ROUTES TO ATTITUDE CHANGE

To understand the processes of attitude change, it helps to discuss them in the context of a model. Petty and Cacioppo's Elaboration Likelihood Model, shown in Figure 7-1, provides an overview of the process involved in attitude change.[1] According to their view, the extent to which a persuasive communication will result in attitude change depends on two crucial

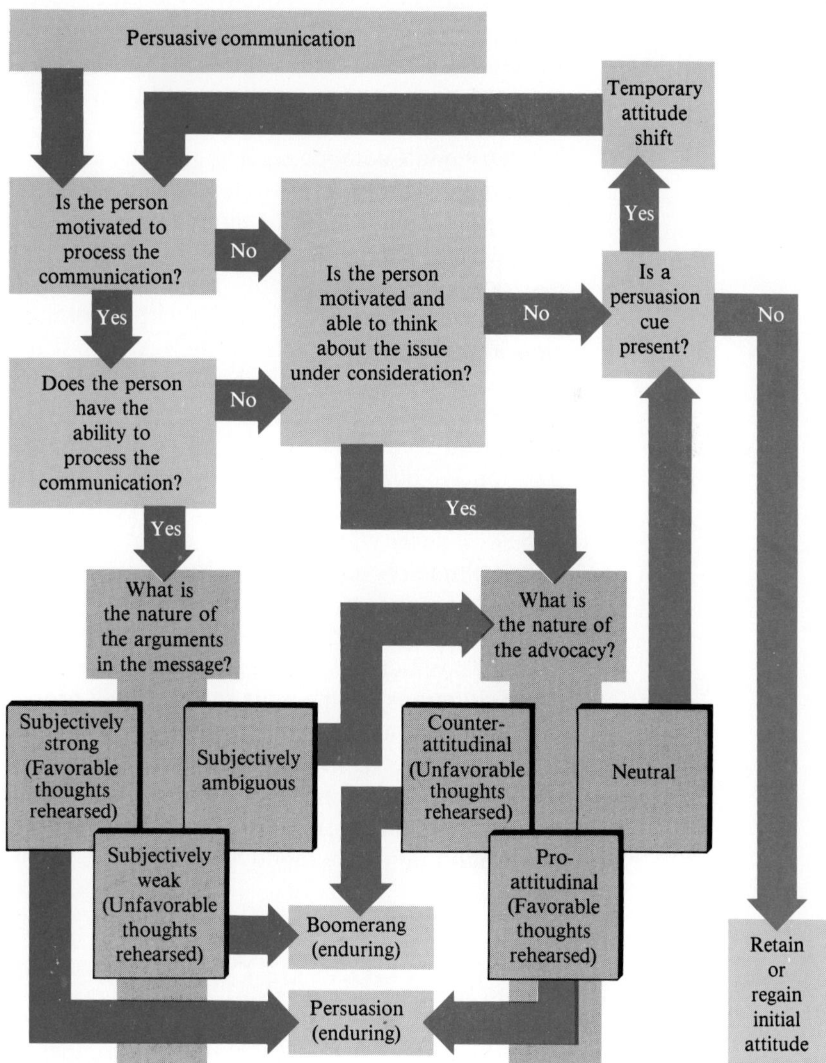

Figure 7-1
The Elaboration-Likelihood Model of Attitude Change

Source: Richard E. Petty and John T. Cacioppo, *Attitudes and Persuasion: Classic and Contemporary Approaches* (Dubuque, IA: William C. Brown Co., 1981), 264.

questions. First, is the person *motivated to think about* (elaborate on) the issue? Second, does the person have the *ability to process* the communication? If the answer to both questions is yes, then the nature of the arguments in the message become important. If the answer to either question is no, then attitude change is less likely, since no message processing, or elaboration, occurs.

central route

Petty and Cacioppo go a step further to define two different routes to attitude change: the central route and the peripheral route. The **central route** to attitude change occurs when the message recipient has both the motivation and the ability to process the information. In these cases, the person thinks about the arguments in the message, determines whether they are strong and compelling, and then develops favorable or unfavorable thoughts about the issue.

Petty and Cacioppo suggest that the central route can produce a lasting change in attitudes. But this change may be difficult to accomplish: the message recipient must be motivated to consider the arguments, be able to understand the arguments, and find them convincing. Attitude change can occur if the arguments result in strong favorable or unfavorable thoughts. If the person responds with favorable thoughts, persuasion occurs and an enduring attitude will result. If unfavorable, the ''boomerang'' effect occurs, in which the person develops an attitude counter to the message.

peripheral route

Attitudes can also be changed by the **peripheral route.** In this way, the position advocated in the message is associated with some preexisting positive attitude. For example, an advertiser might choose to associate a popular celebrity or recognized expert with a product to favorably influence attitude change. Thus, recipients are not asked to think a great deal about issues and arguments. The peripheral approach can be successful in changing attitudes, but not when consumers are highly involved in the issue or product and have a great deal of prior information about them. In these situations the message recipient will probably consider the pros and cons of the arguments and not give much weight to the peripheral aspects.

As we proceed in the discussion of attitude change, it may be helpful to look back at Figure 7-1 and consider how such elements as the source of the communication, message characteristics, and so on would fit into the Elaboration Likelihood Model.

MODIFICATIONS OF COGNITIVE STRUCTURE

Chapter 5 discussed the affective, cognitive, and behavioral components of attitudes. In Chapter 6, these basic components were used to describe specific aspects of Fishbein's popular multiattribute attitude model. When consumers alter one or more of these components of attitude, they may

modification of cognitive structure

influence their own attitudes. This alteration is referred to as a **modification of cognitive structure.** One of the major appeals of multiattribute models (such as the Fishbein model) is that their use in marketing studies readily reveals aspects of the buyer's cognitive structure. Marketers can develop strategies of attitude change for each component of the consumer's attitude structure.

Using a multiattribute model to describe cognitive structure, Richard Lutz suggested five strategies for changing attitudes:[2]

1. Change an existing cognition or belief (B), such as the buyer's belief about a brand and one or more of its attributes ("Payday candy bars are a nutritious snack").
2. Change an existing affective element (A) such as the goodness or badness of an attribute ("High-calorie snacks are nutritious").
3. Alter the importance or determinance of characteristics—that is, the criteria that carry the most weight in decision making ("Although cars differ in safety and price, safety is more important in selecting a brand").
4. Add attributes (B_1 or A_1) so that the buyer considers the product in light of characteristics never thought of before ("When buying a car, it is important to consider where the car was manufactured").
5. Change the attitude toward an entire brand or a particular product by direct action ("After riding in this Oldsmobile, I like it").

To develop these five attitude-change strategies, Lutz used a Fishbein-type model, which is generally recognized for its diagnostic power. We discuss each of these approaches in more detail in following sections.

Changing Cognitions or Beliefs

One of the most popular ways of changing attitudes is to use advertising or personal selling to influence the cognitive component of attitudes. The following example illustrates how this particular component of attitude was first formed and later changed to improve attitudes toward Ford Motor Company. During 1980 and 1981, Ford had record losses, largely due to inroads made by competitors who were seen, among other things, as building higher-quality cars. At that time, many consumers had the cognition (belief) that if they purchased a Ford they would not be getting the quality they desired. This cognition led to a negative attitude toward Ford overall, and to unexpectedly low sales. In 1982 and 1983, Ford engaged in a company-wide strategy to alter the public's belief about the quality of its products. The goal was to improve overall attitudes toward Ford and thereby increase sales. First, Ford made significant design and production modifications to enhance product quality. Second, Ford's management enlisted the support of key parts suppliers and established employee work programs to improve quality. Third, it developed a strong

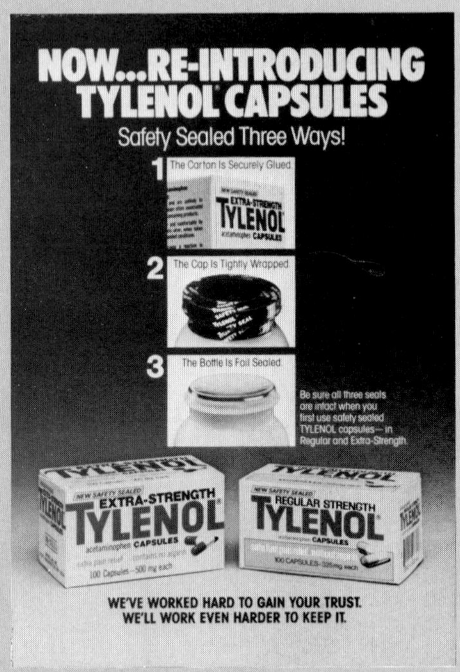
NOW...RE-INTRODUCING
TYLENOL® CAPSULES
Safety Sealed Three Ways!
1 The Carton Is Securely Glued.
2 The Cap Is Tightly Wrapped.
3 The Bottle Is Foil Sealed.
Be sure all three seals are intact when you first use safety sealed TYLENOL capsules— in Regular and Extra-Strength.
EXTRA-STRENGTH
TYLENOL
CAPSULES
REGULAR STRENGTH
TYLENOL
CAPSULES
WE'VE WORKED HARD TO GAIN YOUR TRUST.
WE'LL WORK EVEN HARDER TO KEEP IT.

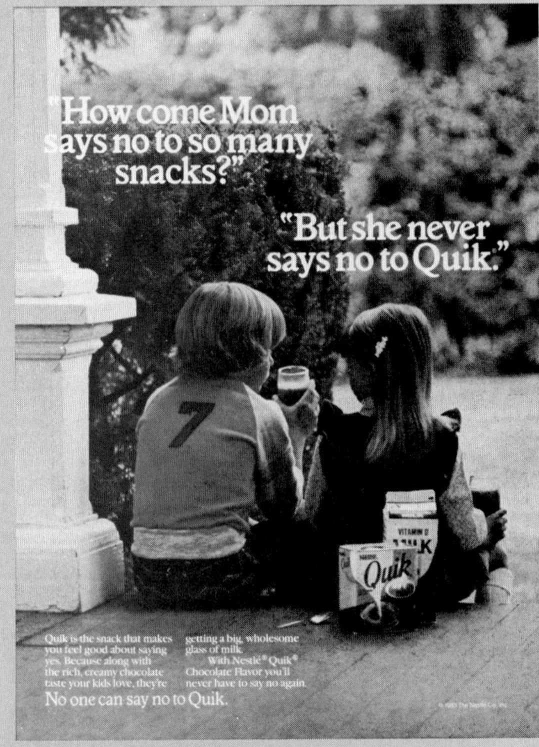
"How come Mom says no to so many snacks?"
"But she never says no to Quik."
Quik is the snack that makes you feel good about saying yes. Because along with the rich, creamy chocolate taste your kids love, they're getting a big, wholesome glass of milk.
With Nestlé® Quik® Chocolate Flavor you'll never have to say no again.
No one can say no to Quik.

advertising campaign with the theme of quality: "At Ford, Quality Is Job One!" News stories were given to mass media. At dealerships, salespeople stressed the quality of Ford's products. The results were a significant increase in the company's sales volume and higher corporate profits. Ford's experience exemplifies the importance of understanding buyers' beliefs and of designing products and communication strategies that contribute positively to consumers' overall attitudes toward the product and the brand.[3]

Many firms have succeeded in changing the cognitive component of attitudes. When Wendy's added a salad bar to its fast-food restaurants, the chain was using a product extension strategy to alter the prevalent belief that fast-food restaurants serve only high-calorie offerings. The product extension strategy included an advertising theme that enhanced the reputation of the entire Wendy's chain at the time. Tylenol has made an effort to change consumer beliefs about the safety of the product seal following the poisoning of several bottles of Tylenol in 1982. Nestle's Quik stresses the product's nutritional value to counter any beliefs to the contrary.

Changing the Goodness or Badness of Attributes

A second way to modify cognitive structure is to enhance the desirability of particular brands' attributes. For example, when choosing some types of pharmaceutical products, physicians look at potency as an important purchase criterion. For other pharmaceutical products, physicians associate potency with undesirable side effects. In the latter cases, physicians conclude that high-potency drugs are undesirable. Therefore, for these products, pharmaceutical salespeople and advertising sponsored by pharmaceutical companies stress that potency results in the drug's entering the bloodstream faster to attack specific symptoms. Communication campaigns are designed to alter the way physicians evaluate potency in drugs. Clearly, those drugs that are seen as most potent have the most to gain from such a campaign.

Altering the Importance or Determinance of Characteristics

determinant characteristics

Determinant characteristics are those brand attributes that buyers use to differentiate one brand from another. In many cases, rather than enhancing the goodness or badness of a particular characteristic, marketers influence cognitive structure by suggesting which criteria should be used in making decisions. Here advertising is aimed at changing the relative importance of attributes used in making brand selections.

The way consumers analyze and compare products depends on the attributes on which they choose to focus. Without the marketer's persuasive communication of all the product's attributes, consumers often fail to evaluate brands based on some important criterion. Promotion or personal selling that uses this strategy is directed at persuading buyers that they should use a certain criterion for making brand-choice decisions. For example, advertising campaigns for Kodak and Polaroid cameras were designed to direct the public's attention to different criteria. Polaroid stressed the ease and speed of instant photography and provided immediate reinforcement by showing instant snapshots of the stars who had their picture taken at the beginning of the commercial. Kodak emphasized the lasting value of family pictures taken with their cameras. Polaroid focused on picture-taking as part of the entertainment; Kodak stressed the quality of its snapshots.

In addition to enhancing the importance of a single attribute, such strategies often center on looking at trade-offs between attributes. For example, while heavy automobiles are safer, they are likely to be lower in gas mileage than are lighter cars. In that case, marketers might sacrifice emphasizing the importance of gas mileage to stress the importance of safety, or vice versa.[4]

Adding Attributes

Closely related to the previous approach is the strategy of adding product attributes or purchase outcomes to consumers' thought processes. Recently Seven-Up successfully in enhancing its own reputation at the expense of Coca-Cola, Pepsi-Cola, and other soft drinks that contain caffeine. Through advertising, Seven-Up implied strongly that soft drinks containing caffeine should not be consumed. Seven-Up's no-caffeine theme ("Never had it—never will") created such a shake-up in market shares of the soft drink business that giants such as Coca-Cola and Pepsi were forced to modify their product lines to include caffeine-free products. When the cola companies had recovered from Seven-Up's no-caffeine advertising campaign, it was poised with another aggressive campaign: "No artificial color." Although this new approach may not be as effective as the first one in creating change, it is more difficult for the colas to attack with product formulation changes, because altering cola's color significantly changes the appearance of the product. For highly innovative products, the strategy of adding criteria can be particularly useful because buyers are more open to information that helps them understand and assess these items.

Using Direct Action

Many advertisers influence consumers' attitudes by persuading them to try their products. Often advertisers invite consumers to compare the product to their favorite brand, sometimes facilitating trial by distributing free or low-cost product samples. By using the product, consumers may develop favorable attitudes toward it and perhaps dispel any negative attitudes they held previously.

When advertisers invite potential buyers to test and compare their products, it can indicate that these firms have confidence in their products' superiority. For example, in one ad campaign Lee Iacocca, as a spokesman for Chrysler, asked prospective car buyers to test drive its cars and offered a $50 check to each buyer if after testing the car he or she bought a different brand. This implied that Chrysler had a great deal of confidence in its products; such a campaign was likely to incite potential buyers to at least try the brand and, Chrysler hoped, form a positive attitude toward it.

COMMUNICATION SOURCES

Credibility

Consumers do not receive messages in a perceptual vacuum. In fact, even when several people communicate precisely the same message, it is received differently depending on who is doing the communicating. Generally, the more highly regarded the source of a message, the stronger and more rapid is its impact on attitude change. That is why advertisers try to select exactly the right type of person to carry their messages. For example, due to his stature in the automobile industry, Lee Iacocca, president of Chrysler Corporation, has been used in advertisements for his company's products. Because the public generally credits Iacocca with the rescue of Chrysler Corporation from near-collapse, many consumers believe him when he communicates Chrysler's dedication to improving the quality and reliability of its cars and trucks. Therefore, Iacocca is considered a *credible source* of information about Chrysler.

One source does not usually have high credibility among all segments of the population, different people respect, admire, trust, or identify with different qualities in other people. For example, Jhirmack selected actress Victoria Principal to represent its hair-care products because she has more credibility among younger professional women (Jhirmack's target audience) than, for example, announcer Ed McMahon. Generally, what makes a source credible is what people perceive as the source's expertise and trustworthiness or attractiveness.

Expertise

Consumers attribute expertise to a communicator for many reasons. First, the listener may believe that the communicator has had specialized training (or a great deal of experience) that gives him or her a thorough knowledge of the topic of the message. Second, it is usually important that the source have a reputation of reliability, either personally or as a member of a profession. This is one reason why some companies hire engineers for certain industrial sales positions. The employers believe that engineering degrees will lend their salespeople more credibility than would other types of degrees. Similarly, some companies have elaborate training programs to build the expertise of their salespeople in all of the technical aspects of their field. Dentists serve as sources in advertising messages about the benefits of fluoride in toothpaste. Doctors—or people in hospital clothing—are highly credible spokespersons in advertisements for pain relievers. A recent ad for Anacin-3 pictures three medical professionals. Marketers have even used actors who have built strong images in fictional roles to convey their messages with authority. The parts they have played in popular television series have caused them to be seen as experts in those fields. A good example of this is the well-known series of commercials featuring actor Robert Young to promote Sanka, a low-caffeine coffee. Young starred in the television series, "Marcus Welby, M.D." (It should be noted that the Federal Trade Commission objected to Young's wardrobe—a white lab coat often associated with doctors—in the initial ads because he is not a physician. As a result, he wore regular clothing in later ads.) Third, consumers attribute expertise to a source because they can identify with the person. Therefore, the use of an expert can backfire if he or she is seen as extremely distant and a person with whom it is difficult for consumers to identify. In such cases, the audience may feel that their own experiences and desires are so removed from those of the expert that the expert's technical knowledge of the product is of little value. In order to achieve credibility, the advertiser may be forced to emphasize another of the expert's attributes, such as trustworthiness or attractiveness. Most likely, the advertiser must find another spokesperson.

Timothy Brock conducted an important study to show the influence of experience on establishing expertise.[5] In the study, salespeople in paint stores ascertained where and how their customers were using paint. In some cases, the salespeople indicated that they had painting experiences similar to those anticipated by the customer; in other cases, the salespeople indicated that they had dissimilar painting experiences. After each customer selected a particular paint, the salesperson would suggest a higher- or lower-priced paint. In cases where the buyer perceived that the salesperson had a similar set of experiences—and, therefore, similar attitudes—the customer was more likely to follow the salesperson's suggestion. This was true regardless of whether the salesperson recommended the higher- or the lower-priced paint. A recent ad for Cutex nail polish remover applies this strategy by featuring a hand model who has extensive experience with this type of product.

Clearly, consumers judge expertise not only by the spokesperson's understanding of the subject, but also on the relevance of that understanding to the receiver. One reason for the success of advertising featuring "average people" is that the audience attributes relevant expertise to people who are in life situations similar to their own. "Madge the manicurist" was created to promote Palmolive dishwashing liquid in a series of commercials on television. Her role as an average person working in a beauty shop was designed to give credibility to Palmolive's claims about how mild its dishwashing liquid is. In the commercials, Madge indirectly persuades the audience that using Palmolive will soften their hands by telling various women who come for a manicure to soak their fingers in the dishwashing liquid. In this case, Madge is similar enough to members of the target audience that her expertise is assumed.

One of the youngest assumed experts ever used in television commercials was Mikey ("He hates *everything!*"), the three-year-old who convinced the other children in the commercial that Life cereal tastes good—simply by eating it ("Mikey likes it!"). The assumption is that a demanding young child is the best judge of what tastes good; therefore, other children will trust his judgment and persuade their parents to buy the cereal. In the 1970s, Quaker Oats introduced Mikey to stimulate sales of the cereal which had grown very slowly for many years. Other ele-

ments of the Life cereal campaign remained unchanged. However, with the introduction of Mikey, sales increased substantially.[6]

A recent ad for Silver Reed typewriters uses expertise with a celebrity connection. Professional tennis player Martina Navratilova is fixed in many people's minds as a performance-oriented person. Silver Reed hopes that many people assume that Navratilova is just as demanding of the typewriter for her business affairs as she is of her tennis racket on the court.

There are many other examples of expertise used in the context of an advertising message; among the most well known are those featuring famous tennis players. Arthur Ashe endorses a Head tennis racket, and Bjorn Borg (who spent a lot of time on sunny tennis courts) promotes PreSun, a sunscreen lotion.

Expertise can be conveyed in a number of ways: through the symbols associated with a profession, such as clothing, through the muscular physique of an athlete, or through the degrees and honors earned by scholars and scientists.

Trustworthiness

Organizations such as Underwriters Laboratory, the American Medical Association, the American Dental Association, the Good Housekeeping Institute, and Consumers Union have gained a great deal of credibility because of their trustworthiness. Not only do these organizations employ people who possess a great deal of technical knowledge, but consumers perceive their knowledge as relatively unbiased.

People tend to trust the messages they receive from such "objective" sources. Receivers of communications typically challenge the source's message by trying to understand how acting upon the communicator's message might help the communicator. When their heeding the message results in a clear-cut benefit to the source, the credibility of the source falls. In fact, consumers tend to discount or openly distrust messages (communicated by experts or others) that obviously will benefit the source in some way. For example, arguments about the value of service contracts for home appliances by a salesperson who is paid a commission are more likely to be discounted than the same arguments by a salesperson who does not stand to gain from the transaction. In general, the greatest degree of objectivity and trustworthiness accrue to those who are disinterested observers. Receivers of messages tend to believe that disinterested sources provide unbiased evaluations of products.

It is difficult for salespeople to appear trustworthy; many prospective buyers believe that salespeople have something to gain from making a sale. Studies indicate that attitude change is greater when people believe that the communicator has nothing to gain or, in fact, has something to lose by the position that they have taken. In one study, a convicted criminal who argued for more personal freedom and against increased police powers produced no attitude change. However, when the same criminal argued in favor of stronger tools for law enforcement, a substantial attitude change took place.[7] Salespeople who use this strategy may be building credibility with prospective buyers in the long run. (Studies have not tested the proposition that a source can gain long-term credibility by taking a position apparently contrary to his or her self-interest; nevertheless, many salespeople use this strategy.) For example, when a real estate agent tells a family that the particular house they are considering is not suited to their needs, the agent may sacrifice a possible sale in order to develop a reputation for objectivity. This apparent objectivity enhances the agent's credibility later when he or she shows additional houses to the family.

Another principle of source trustworthiness involves the intent of the communicator. When people believe that the communicator does not know others are listening, they are more persuaded by the spokesperson's arguments. In such cases, the audience believes that the communicator is not trying to influence their behavior. However, when it appears that the source is consciously trying to influence the consumers' opinions, the audience members are likely to resist.

Hidden-camera commercials involving taste tests can enhance credibility in two ways. For these types of commercials, shoppers are selected to compare brands by sampling each competitor's product with the brand names concealed. The shopper, who in the commercial becomes the message source, is asked to judge impartially which product he or she prefers. First, the experience of trying the product makes the shopper, as the source, an expert of sorts. Second, the hidden camera establishes that the source is trustworthy because persuasion was not his or her intent. The "Pepsi challenge" series of commercials was designed to enhance credibility in these ways. A number of beer companies have also used the taste-test approach to increase trial use of their products. Generally, these commercials are effective because consumers usually believe those who have nothing to gain or lose from stating their product preference.

However, there is an exception to this rule. Where the communicator is extremely well liked and is considered to be an expert, some researchers have found that attitude change is more probable when the communicator's motives (whether or not he benefits from the sale) are overt rather than disguised.[8] In these cases, buyers find the communicator to be highly credible; and because they also like that person, they want to benefit the source.

Attractiveness

People who are pleasant, energetic, and positive are persuasive. It is not surprising that attractive, pleasant, likable spokespersons have more influence than those who are unpleasant or difficult to enjoy or admire. Receivers of messages tend to listen to and identify with people they like more than people they dislike. Further, when receivers feel that the communicator has attitudes similar to their own, they are usually attracted to the source. People want to be accepted by those they like; in an effort to fit into groups of people they admire, they assume attitudes similar to those of the respected group. If members of their own groups present arguments or endorse products, these are likely to be accepted. On the other hand, arguments and endorsements from members of groups that are considerably different from the audience are less likely to be persuasive. Thus, the overall likability or attractiveness of the source may play an influential role in the marketer's message.

Celebrities are often excellent sources of advertising messages because they are attractive, articulate, and possess a public image. Advertisers must be sure that the characteristics associated with the celebrities used in their ads match the product characteristics they are attempting to portray, or with the personal characteristics they believe the target audience finds appealing. The competition between two leading camera companies led both to use celebrities to present their messages. Eastman Kodak, wishing to appeal to families, selected Michael Landon as its star presenter. He is well known for his roles as a wise and loving father in "Little House on the Prairie" and as an "angel" in "Highway to Heaven," both family-oriented television series. Landon's name became a household word when he starred in another very popular series, "Bonanza." The message Landon delivered and the music used in the Kodak ads were nostalgic and sentimental. Polaroid, on the other hand, employed James Garner and Mariette Hartley to present its products. Polaroid used humorous banter between Hartley and Garner to draw attention to the ease of use and technical innovations of its cameras. This appealing couple was so convincing that Mariette Hartley was often asked about being married to James Garner. She finally had a t-shirt made declaring "I am not Jim Garner's wife," and one for her child saying, "I am not Jim Garner's baby." Both campaigns were extremely well designed and millions of dollars were paid to these celebrities.

Stars are attention getters. Their persuasive impact, due to their attractive image, is enhanced by the high probability that consumers will see the advertisement in the first place. Several years ago, a panty hose commercial featured an unusual celebrity spokesperson: professional football player Joe Namath. The commercial, in which Namath was shown modeling the product, had novelty, as it would have had with any other man. Moreover, the panty hose commercial used Namath's famous and very valuable legs to create an association in the viewer's mind between the product and the celebrity. One ad for Cie perfume pictured actress Candice Bergen in various situations to show the product's ability to fit in with the many moods and activities of the target audience. Advertisements are more effective when celebrities have characteristics that buyers associate with the product. Water Pik has relied on comedian Jonathan Winters (and his smile) to "sell" its product with almost no copy. However, in some cases some of the advertiser's message may be lost if the audience pays more attention to the source than to the message. To reduce the chances that buyers will pay more attention to the star than to the ad's message, advertisers should choose their celebrity spokespersons carefully and should limit their range of choices to celebrities with images compatible to the market. The reputations and public recognition of celebrities make their services extremely valuable in advertising. In fact, the advertising trade magazine *Ad Age* even rates stars on their effectiveness in ads.

Often celebrity status allows these famous personalities to gain credibility in areas outside their expertise. For example, some movie stars have influenced political campaigns, despite their limited political savvy. When informed celebrities endorse or make a personal commitment to a particular event, their power can be substantial. For example, actor Robert Redford has sponsored activities to protect the environment that have contributed significantly to that cause. In his case, credibility based on expertise, trust, attractiveness, and celebrity status are all combined in one source.

Recently, close to 100 major vocal artists joined forces to sing "We Are the World" as a benefit for famine relief efforts in Ethiopia. This campaign also featured the first broadcasting of a message on hundreds of major radio stations all over the world, all at once. The campaign brought in millions of dollars in relief funds and drew attention to poverty worldwide.

MESSAGE CHARACTERISTICS

There are countless ways to communicate any given message. Marketers must know the best ways to get their points across. Extensive research has been conducted on the characteristics of messages that influence or change attitudes effectively. Communication can take place when messages are one-sided or two-sided. Such messages may or may not include recommendations or a conclusion. The order of presentation also affects how easily the message is taken in and recalled. Humor can call attention to the message, or can obscure it in consumers' minds. Similarly, fear appeals can gain rapid attention or elicit denial from consumers. And messages that compare the product to other products or brands can build consumer awareness for the marketer's brand—or for those of competitors.

One-sided and Two-sided Messages

Messages can be presented from one point of view or from two, depending on whether or not the receiver agrees with the position of the communicating organization. **One-sided messages** present only arguments that are favorable to the communicator. **Two-sided messages** present arguments that are unfavorable as well as favorable to the communicator's position. An example of a one-sided message for a fast-food chain is an ad that mentions only positive aspects of the ingredients or cooking methods of the sponsor's brand. An example of a two-sided message is an ad that both presents and responds to a competitor's charge of inferior ingredients or cooking methods.

one-sided messages
two-sided messages

In situations where the source and the receiver take relatively similar positions, one-sided messages are most appropriate. On the other hand, in situations where disagreements exist, two-sided messages have been found to be most useful. Sales or marketing managers are wise to vary their tactics according to whether the target of their communication initially agrees with or disagrees with their position.

Another consideration is the newness of the brand (and, therefore, the amount of information the consumer is likely to have about it). In one study related to a new brand, two-sided messages were found to be more effective in developing positive attitudes and intention to buy among consumers who had not previously developed beliefs about the brand.[9]

A great deal of research has been done on one-sided and two-sided messages. It has been shown that in some instances a two-sided message may have a more positive effect on the perceived credibility of the source.[10] One study involved appeals introducing a new brand where prior beliefs did not exist. It was found that two-sided messages yield significantly more positive attitudes toward the brand than does a one-sided appeal.[11] However, researchers disagree on the true impact of each approach. George Belch investigated the effects of one- and two-sided messages presented through print and television.[12] His findings do *not* support the conclusion that a two-sided message is significantly better at strengthening source credibility. Research conflicts regarding the value of two-sided messages in creating favorable attitude changes. Additional investigation is certainly warranted in this area.

Recommendations or Conclusions

The communicator can provide recommendations or conclusions or these can be left to the receiver. On one hand, messages with conclusions are more easily understood. On the other hand, researchers believe that when the audience is allowed to draw its own conclusions, and the desired conclusion is reached, there is a stronger likelihood of acceptance.

Some evidence suggests that more highly educated people are likely to respond better when they are given the opportunity to draw their own conclusions. For example, salespeople in pharmaceutical firms who call on physicians often clearly lay out evidence regarding their products. But they allow the physician to draw his or her own conclusions about the efficacy of the product for their particular patients or practice. When consumers draw their own conclusions, there is a good chance that the process of reasoning will reinforce (that is, contribute to their learning of) the message. (The principle of closure, which was discussed in Chapter 3, also supports this argument.)

If an advertising message will be repeated, the absence of any stated conclusions probably makes the ad more effective. Here the assumption is that repeated exposures over a period of time allow the target audience many opportunities to draw conclusions. On the other hand, if the marketer wants the message to have immediate impact, the ad should probably be direct and draw conclusions. For example, one mental health board concluded that open-ended ads were more likely to be remembered and the board's services used.[13]

Order of Presentation

The order in which a message is presented affects which parts of the message are taken in and later recalled by buyers. More is remembered from the beginning and the end of a message than from the middle. Therefore, effective sales presentations generally open and close with strong statements and arguments, sandwiching weaker arguments in the middle. The same approach is useful in television advertising.[14] Many messages aimed at teaching consumers or changing their attitudes are hampered by low involvement on the part of the audience. Consumers do not actively seek information about products that are not involving; they take in such messages passively, often while watching television. Under these conditions in particular, sellers should structure their messages to reflect the fact that information presented early in the ad or at the end of the ad tends to be retained and recalled better than information in the middle. The careful use of humor, or other devices for maintaining the audience's attention throughout the message, may stimulate some involvement, increasing the value of content in the middle of the message. However, it appears that information is processed more easily at the beginning and end of a communication for both high-involvement and low-involvement situations.

Humor

Impressionist Rich Little, the acting team of Stiller and Meara, and comedienne Joan Rivers gain the attention and interest of their audiences with humor. Viewers attend selectively to humorous ads because they are novel and enjoyable. Qantas Airlines uses humor in the form of its koala, which hates people (and Qantas for bringing them to Australia). However, advertisers who use humor must be careful to avoid obscuring the message with the novelty of the humor itself. Harold Ross, Jr. offers several suggestions for using humor to increase the effectiveness of messages.[15]

1. If the brand name is not mentioned within the first ten seconds, the advertiser runs the risk of inhibiting recall of key selling points.
2. Subtle humor is more effective than the bizarre in advertising.
3. The humor must be relevant to the brand or key selling point (see the Vivitar ad). Without this linkage, recall and persuasion are diminished.
4. It is best not to use humor which belittles or otherwise makes fun of the potential user. Making light of the brand, the situation, or the subject matter is usually a much more effective strategy in the use of humor.

Point four is addressed by an ad for Pioneer speakers, which used humor effectively to gain the attention of potential buyers. The brand name appeared boldly at the top of the ad in the headline, "Pioneer Speaker Owners: Please Keep Your Windows Rolled Up," and at the end. The humorous situation—a photo of urban destruction—was directly related to the product, linking the power of the speakers to the demolished buildings. Another example of humor based on the product itself comes from Sunsweet prunes and Stan Freeberg, the developer of one of its advertising campaigns; "Today the Pits. Tomorrow the Wrinkles. Sunsweet Marches On!!!" Through the use of humor, a seemingly negative and unattractive aspect of the product was used to tremendous advantage. By poking fun at the aging process, the advertising was able to change the public's attitude toward trying prunes and to increase sales significantly. According to Sun Diamond Growers, when the prune advertising campaign was introduced in 1967, shipments of prunes increased from 4,900 tons to 7,700 tons in the first year. When the campaign ended in 1972, Sunsweet had increased its annual volume to 9,700 tons of prunes.[16]

However, evidence does not indicate that a humorous approach is necessarily more effective than a serious one. Researchers have questioned the true effectiveness of humor in marketing communications. The results suggest that while it increases attention to the ad it may also decrease acceptance of the message.[17] Marketers must be careful when they consider using humor, because the humor itself might be attended to at the expense of the primary message. Humor can compete with the other parts of the ad for the consumer's attention. Despite this, the use of humor in advertising seems to be on the rise.[18]

Fear Appeals

fear appeals

Advertisers sometimes turn to **fear appeals** to gain the attention and interest of their audience. Two familiar examples of fear appeals used by nonprofit firms include antismoking campaigns by the American Cancer Society, which indicate that cigarette smoking is linked to lung cancer, and the toothbrushing campaigns by the American Dental Association, which indicate that poor dental hygiene can result in tooth decay, gum disease, and loss of teeth. Another example is that ad against drunk driving by the Commercial Union Assurance Companies, which shows a smashed-up car above the headline, ''The Party's Over.''

In some instances, advertisers appeal to fears for one's loved ones. An advertisement for child restraints by the Michigan Association for Traffic Safety that pictures a wheel chair—''It's your choice''—is designed to strike fear into parents and prompt action to ''buckle up'' their children.

PIONEER MAXXIAL™ SPEAKER OWNERS:
PLEASE KEEP YOUR CAR WINDOWS ROLLED UP.
SUPPLY
NATIONAL SHOES
Kablowee. Blam. Bam. Boom. Bam.
It's not World War III, ladies and gentlemen. Merely our *Maxxial*™ car speakers, the most awesome sounding speakers yet. With greater power handling capacity.
Great enough, in fact, to handle up to 100 watts of Max Music Power.
Our newly designed voice coil uses a slightly thicker wire. It won't break down because of overheating. And it can withstand (you guessed it) greater power.
But sorry, all you power-hungry people. The story isn't power alone.
Pure and accurate tonal quality. High efficiency and wide frequency response. These are qualities you've come to expect from a speaker made by Pioneer.
And *Maxxials* are a complete line of the most popular sizes. With our compact, yet powerful Strontium Magnet, *Maxxials* enable big power handling to fit into tight spaces.
Now for the most thunderous announcement yet. All this improvement at a price that's designed to get you to gravitate toward power. Not away from it.
PIONEER®
Because the music matters.

Commercial marketers also use fear appeals in advertising products and services. One Liberty Mutual insurance ad, an obvious example of the use of fear, depicts a frightened couple in bedclothes. In this case, the fear is of fire and of financial loss due to fire. An Os-Cal calcium supplement ad shows a bent-over elderly woman, her condition the result of long-term calcium loss. It is a somewhat more subtle use of the fear appeal; yet the fear of aging in poor health no doubt presents a real concern to many young people.

Is fear effective in advertising? In many instances fear appeals are indeed very effective. They are believed to create higher attention and interest in the message and may encourage the viewer to seek a solution to the problem represented in the ad. However, fear appeals may also cause inhibitions if they are too strong. That is, the viewer may engage in selective perception and tune out the message, or respond with denial, in order to deal with extremely fearful ad presentations. A fear appeal that is too strong can have negative results. Rather than acting on the message, the consumer screens it out in order to avoid discomfort. Figure 7-2, discussed next, illustrates these two countereffects.

Michael Ray and William Wilkie proposed that marketers should consider using a market segmentation approach to decide when to use fear

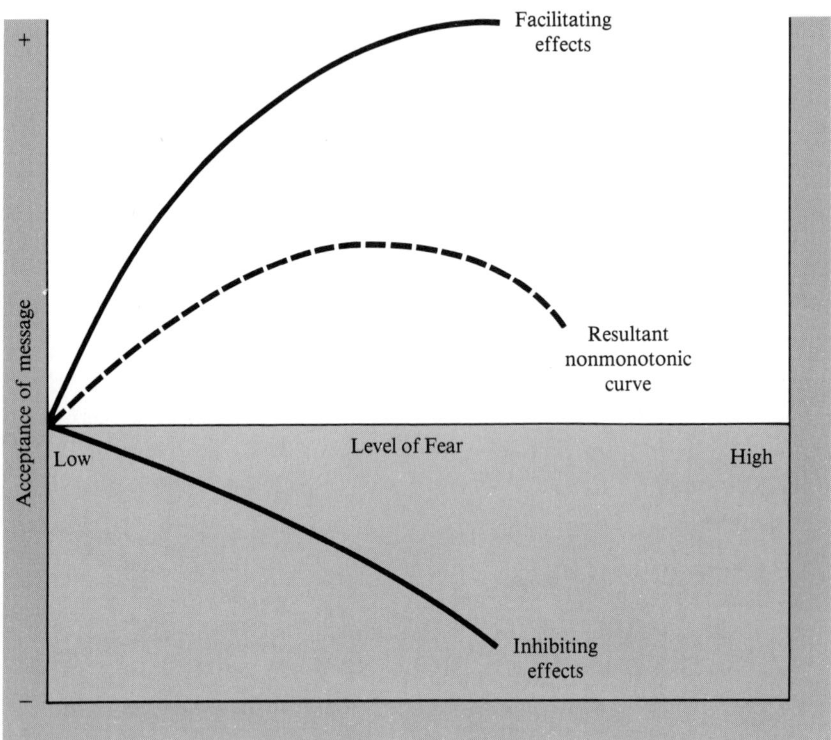

Source: Michael L. Ray and William L. Wilkie, "Fear: The Potential of an Appeal Neglected by Marketing," *Journal of Marketing* 34 (January 1970): 54–62.

Figure 7-2
Facilitating and Inhibiting Effects Leading to Nonmonotonic Curve

appeals.[19] As an example they point out that fear is likely to be most effective for those who have low anxiety to begin with, high esteem, and who generally respond to dangers rather than avoid them. Thus, anti-smoking campaigns may be more effective with younger smokers who do not consider themselves as vulnerable to cancer as older smokers. Figure 7-2 shows the overall effects of fear appeals. The bottom curve suggests that as the appeal to fear is increased, a segment of consumers will tend to reject the message. The top curve shows that as the fear appeal increases, acceptance of the message increases for another segment, but at a declining rate. The dashed curve represents the overall impact on all segments of the market. It is *nonmonotonic,* indicating that the impact of fear influences acceptance in *two* directions; up at first as fear increases, then down.

Comparative Advertising

The area of comparative advertising has grown in recent years. Since television networks began allowing advertisers to name their competitors

in ads, a host of companies have chosen to compare their products with those of the competition and emphasize their own superiority on specific features. Familiar comparative advertising campaigns include those for headache remedies, food products, and durable goods such as electric shavers and televisions. In the early 1980s, the major fast-food hamburger chains became engaged in the so-called burger wars, as McDonald's, Burger King, and Wendy's directly confronted each other on television.

THE PARTY'S OVER
Last year, 49,500 Americans lost their lives in 43,500 auto accidents. In over half of the accidents, alcohol was a factor.
When you think about it, 49,500 is a pretty big number, but it seems even bigger when you consider that it's also the approximate population of a city the size of White Plains, New York or Elkhart, Indiana. The entire population.
But as big as this number is, it takes on even more importance and has even more impact when someone close to you is added to it. There's the suffering of friends and families left behind.
And when you realize that drinking was a factor in at least half of these needless traffic fatalities, it's enough to make you mad. Get mad. Then do something that will make that number smaller.
Don't drink and drive. Don't let friends drink and drive. And, finally, let's work together to get the drunks off the road. Write your legislators and urge them to sponsor tough new laws. Tell them you're concerned.
Because now that we've raised your consciousness by giving you the facts about drunk driving, we'd like to ask you to raise your conscience and do something to change them.
CU
Commercial Union Assurance Companies
Box 417
Cathedral Station
Boston, Mass. 02118
Drunk driving is a crime...take action against crime.

The research findings concerning the true effectiveness of comparative advertising are inconsistent.[20] Comparative ads that receive more attention from users of competitive brands will obtain results if they appear to be objective to viewers in their claims. However, while comparative ads allow marketers to present clear, seemingly objective reasons for adopting their product over others, many companies hesitate to use the technique. On one hand, they fear that by showing a competitor's product or mentioning a competing brand name, they may inadvertently cause the consumer to recall the competitor's product at the time of purchase. Since most television commercials are slightly less than thirty seconds long, advertisers are concerned about accidentally building brand awareness

for competitors. On the other hand, advertisers may be reluctant to use comparative advertising if the competitor is likely to legally challenge the claims for superiority or to initiate a comparative ad campaign of its own in retaliation. Such responses can prove to be costly and offset potential advantages of a short-term increase in sales. As a result of possible legal challenges, major firms take care to conduct well-documented, independent consumer research to support their comparative claims.

When should the comparative technique be used? There is no clear-cut answer. Advertisers must consider the potential advantages of higher attention versus the possible pitfalls of confusing viewers or prompting aggressive retaliation by competitors. Comparative advertising may be most useful for lower-share brands that have little to lose by taking on the leader. For these companies, the potential gain in consumer awareness and consideration of their brand outweighs the likelihood that the large competitor will launch a major countercampaign. In practice, advertisers aim to measure carefully the impact of any comparative claims and monitor market response closely to insure that the desired results are in fact achieved. Consumers tend to notice selectively the names of brands they purchase in order to attend to messages about those brands. Therefore, they often selectively attend to a comparative ad in which their brand is noted. Once they pay attention to the ad consumers are also likely to notice the sponsor's brand. The consumer may continue the cognitive processing to make the comparison and influence attitudes toward both brands accordingly.

CHARACTERISTICS OF MESSAGE RECEIVERS

Despite the persuasive power of credible sources, particularly celebrities, buyers are not easily influenced. They do not absorb advertiser's messages passively, without thinking. They resist persuasion by refuting arguments, attacking the source, distorting the message, rationalization, and blanket refutation.[21]

Refuting Arguments

Points of view that are contrary to the consumer's own position often create stress. To reduce this stress, the recipient of such a message is likely to engage in counterarguments, maintaining the current position and even growing to hold it more strongly. Social scientists have long known that we mentally debate or argue against positions or statements that are contrary to our own beliefs. When we are sufficiently committed to a particular position in a controversy, and understand the issue well enough, we develop strong counterarguments with which to refute opponents. In a sense, we inoculate ourselves against the effects of contradictory messages.

inoculation theory

Some researchers have shown how counterarguments can be used to strengthen a position. Stewart Bither provided evidence of the usefulness of this technique, called **inoculation theory,** in marketing.[22] Interfering with the process of internal debate can enhance the marketer's chances of changing the consumer's attitudes. One way sellers interfere with counterarguments is by distracting the person while giving the argument. The receiver generally fails to muster enough attention or concentration to develop strong counterarguments and become inoculated. Various distractions can be used. Background noise or a video display requires some energy from the receiver, leaving less energy to think about counterarguments. However, marketers should use this technique carefully. There is some evidence that using a distraction mechanism can actually work *against* the communicator. In some cases, the distraction can be so great that not only does the audience fail to create counterarguments, it also fails to perceive or understand the message in the first place. Thus distraction to overcome counterarguments can backfire.

The use of distraction to achieve attitude change can actually make an ad appear more detailed and perhaps of higher quality. However, weak arguments on the part of the seller, covered over by distractions, are not likely to change strongly held beliefs. In fact, through inoculation these weak arguments can solidify attitudes that already exist. But allowing the audience to focus its complete and absolute attention on the message might be detrimental because the message receivers will be able to refute the seller's arguments more effectively. In a personal selling situation, many of the prospective buyer's arguments are spoken and come out as objections. Sales training programs often include tips on how to overcome objections. One of the well-known techniques is the "boomerang" method, in which the argument used by a potential buyer to refuse the salesperson's offerings is thrown back at the customer as a benefit. For example, if the potential purchaser of an automobile says, "I don't believe I can afford a service contract at this time," the salesman responds, "You can't afford *not* to have the service contract at this time."

Attacking the Source

Consumers sometimes resist persuasion by attacking the source directly. For example, they may discount claims for the comfort, prestige, or gas mileage of an automobile because they do not trust the company that sells the auto. When the source is attacked, all messages are automatically rejected. Anything that the source says is considered invalid.

Attacking the source of a communication rather than the ideas being communicated is common in politics. Republicans sometimes imply that a claim could not possibly be true if the claim was made by a Democrat, and vice versa. In personal selling, prospects have been known to attack the source by saying that the salesperson is simply "out to make a fast buck" and, therefore, that the salesperson's claims are not to be believed. By derogating the source, the prospective buyer feels superior to the salesperson and resists any arguments he or she presents.

Distorting the Message

In Chapter 3 we saw that most messages are perceived in the manner most agreeable to the receiver. The processes of assimilation and contrast, described in relation to perception, are relevant to attitude change as well. Recall that when people perceive a message that is *similar* to their own, they are likely to assimilate it—that is, they consider it to be even closer to their own position. Conversely, messages that are somewhat *different* from their position are likely to be seen as even more different than they actually are. In some cases, receivers drastically distort messages, to the extent of suggesting that the messages are ridiculous or out of the question. For example, smokers may reject the surgeon general's warning that cigarette smoking may be hazardous to health by distorting the message to mean that smoking may only be hazardous to "one in a million," even though objective reasoning would suggest that the health risk is much more widespread.

Rationalization

Chapter 4 explained that people exhibit ego-defensive behaviors. In order to support their own positions on an issue,[23] they rationalize situations which might otherwise point up weaknesses. An example of rationalization is this poor reasoning on the part of an obese consumer: "Although Coca-Cola has high sugar content and therefore could be fattening, it also has the potential to provide a great deal of energy to motivate me to exercise more and therefore lose weight." Marketers sometimes provide consumers with many less-than-logical reasons for purchasing their products. In recent years labor unions have produced bumper stickers to boost sales of American-made cars and save American jobs. The bumper stickers imply that purchasing a foreign automobile endangers the economic well-being of the nation. Nevertheless, some consumers in the United States might rationalize their purchase of a European or Japanese car by saying that it will help stimulate firms in this country to be more competitive in the future; therefore, U.S. automakers will be stronger in world automotive markets in the long run.

Blanket Rejection

Jonathan L. Freedman and colleagues have concluded that one of the most common ways of resisting attitude change is a simple blanket rejection of the message.[24] Consumers who use blanket rejection do not think about why they reject the message, nor do they go to the trouble of coming up with counterarguments, rationalizations, or attacks on the source. They simply indicate that they do not want to hear the message or deal with it, and they reject it. Blanket rejection is easy, and it helps buyers simplify their lives, at least temporarily.

Blanket rejection is one of the major obstacles faced by life insurance salespeople. Often consumers reject the idea that they need life insurance outright because they do not wish to deal with the concept of death—particularly their own. They resist purchasing insurance policies by simply rejecting the whole notion of death.

OTHER FACTORS AFFECTING RESISTANCE TO PERSUASION

Some consumers simply cannot be persuaded as easily as others. Persuasion does little to influence people who are uninvolved in the product type or who cannot comprehend the communicator's messages. Many factors affect the degree to which a person can be persuaded and point to the most effective methods for accomplishing this persuasion. Among these factors are (1) the level of involvement a consumer feels toward a product, (2) the intellectual capacity of the consumer, and (3) his or her self-esteem.

Level of Involvement

In Chapter 5 we discussed how high and low involvement affects attitude formation. Involvement is also a factor in attitude change. Recall that the level of involvement depends on how much effort consumers expend to gather information prior to purchase. In low-involvement situations, consumers view the purchase as relatively unimportant; consequently, they seek little or no information about the product before purchasing it. By contrast, high-involvement situations are likely to prompt extensive information searches before purchase. Given these two extremes, how does the level of involvement affect attitude change? Early models of attitude theory took the view that people respond to information (through advertising, for example) by changing their level of awareness, which results in a change in attitudes and finally alters their behavior (see Figure 7-3). This hierarchy may apply to high-involvement situations; but researchers now have a different view about attitude change where low involvement exists.

Strategies to change attitudes in low-involvement situations must take into account that the consumer is a passive recipient of information, not an active information seeker. The key is to build awareness and prompt behavioral response without extensive explanation and without any reasoning on the part of the consumer. Long, complicated communications are not useful. Instead, strategies should include short, highly repetitive messages that stress a few important points.[25] Television may be more

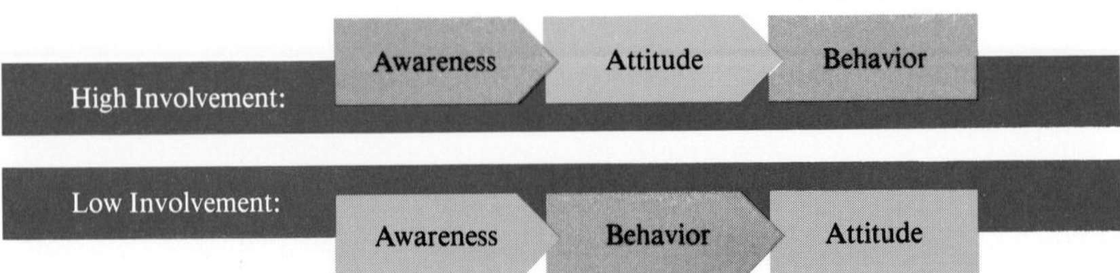

Figure 7-3
High- and Low-Involvement Hierarchies

appropriate for such messages than print media, since it requires less active participation from the recipient.[26]

For high-involvement situations, ads with extensive informational content may be required to produce an attitude change. Therefore, longer advertising messages are in order. Since highly involved consumers are interested in obtaining and processing information, many repetitions of ads are not needed to obtain awareness. Print media are appropriate because print lends itself to information-rich messages and calls for active involvement by the message recipient.

Intelligence and Susceptibility to Persuasion

Many researchers have questioned whether there is a relationship between intelligence and the ease with which an individual may be persuaded. On the surface, it appears that more intelligent people might form their attitudes independently and might be better equipped to refute arguments and thereby resist persuasion. In fact, highly intelligent people are persuaded about as often as are individuals of low intelligence. On the other hand, there is a difference between the persuasive approaches that are effective for these types of individuals. Highly intelligent people are more likely to be influenced by logical, precise, and complex arguments. People of lower intelligence are more responsive to persuasion when they are carefully led through an argument. Therefore, it is better for marketers to allow highly intelligent people to formulate their own conclusions and to provide clear-cut conclusions for people of lesser intelligence.

Self-esteem and Susceptibility to Persuasion

Self-esteem relates to persuasion in opposite ways, depending on the type of arguments used. In simple situations people with low self-esteem tend to be more gullible or persuadable. People who do not have positive feelings about themselves doubt their ability to make judgments or properly solve complex problems. Thus they often rely on others in developing attitudes and making subsequent choices. They are followers. In highly complex situations their low self-esteem prevents them from clearly analyzing the information presented to influence them. Therefore, sales messages designed for people with low self-esteem should not use complex arguments because they make these people less subject to persuasion and do not produce the desired results.[27]

SUMMARY

Changing consumer attitudes toward products and brands is a major focus for many advertising campaigns. In order to be effective, most ads that intend to alter attitudes must be persuasive.

When attitudes are altered it is referred to as modification of cognitive structure. Five strategies for changing attitudes are: (1) changing an existing cognition or belief, (2) changing an existing affective element, (3) altering the importance or determinance of characteristics, and (4) adding other attributes, and (5) direct action.

Marketers are careful to choose the right type of person to carry their messages. They try to find someone who will have a great deal of credibility among their target market. Expertise, trustworthiness, and how well the spokesperson is liked are all factors that contribute to the source's credibility.

Often celebrities are used as spokespeople for a product due to their attractiveness and public image. Celebrities can be particularly effective if there is some link between the product they are endorsing and a personal trait, such as an athlete promoting a health spa.

In order to be effective in their efforts to change attitudes, marketers must know the message characteristics which best communicate their product and brand information. One-sided messages are best used when the source and the receiver hold similar views. Two-sided messages are more effective when opposing views are held or a new brand is being introduced. Messages which draw conclusions for the viewer are generally more effective for viewers of lower intelligence, and those which allow viewers to draw their own conclusions are more effective with more intelligent viewers. Finally, humor can be an effective means of drawing attention and bringing about a positive attitude, if it is not too bizarre and does not ridicule the potential buyer.

Consumers are not always easily influenced and often resist persuasion by refuting arguments, attacking the source, distorting the message, rationalization, and blanket refutation. Other factors which may effect the persuadability of buyers are the level of involvement the buyer has with the product, the level of intelligence of the buyer, and the buyer's self-esteem.

Changing attitudes can be vital to many marketing situations. The elaboration likelihood model indicates that the central route to attitude change requires both the motivation to think about the issue and the ability to process the communication. Using the peripheral route, consumers simply associate the object with some existing attitude. Because attitudes are an integral part of the buyer's makeup, they come into play in many other facets of consumer behavior, including motivation (Chapter 2) and learning (Chapter 4).

KEY TERMS

central route
peripheral route
modification of cognitive structure

determinant characteristics
one-sided messages
two-sided messages
fear appeals
inoculation theory

QUESTIONS

1. Five principal strategies may be used to alter attitudes. Briefly describe each approach.

2. Using the aspects of communication sources we've discussed, why might an "average" car driver be a more (or less) credible spokesperson for Ford than auto racing champion Jackie Stewart?

3. In what situations are two-sided messages likely to be more effective than one-side messages? Explain your answer.

4. Fear appeals can be powerful advertising weapons but they may also backfire. Explain why.

5. Comparative advertising has become an increasingly popular approach for number-two brands. Discuss the pros and cons of comparative advertising for such brands.

6. Describe several ways in which a message receiver may resist persuasion, apart from blanket rejection.

7. What factors determine the degree to which a person may be persuaded? Design a brief message intended to change someone's attitude (either favorable or unfavorable) about joining the Peace Corps.

NOTES

1. Richard E. Petty and John T. Cacioppo, *Attitudes and Persuasion: Classic and Contemporary Approaches* (Dubuque, IA, W. C. Brown Company Publishers, 1981), 262–69.
2. Richard J. Lutz, "Changing Brand Attitudes Through Modification of a Cognitive Structure," *Journal of Consumer Research* 1 (1975): 45–58. Also by Lutz: "An Experimental Investigation of Causal Relations Among Cognition, Affect, and Behavior Intention," *Journal of Consumer Research* 3 197–207. For additional comments, see Carnegie-Mellon University Marketing Seminar, "Attitude Change or Attitude Formation? An Unanswered Question," *Journal of Consumer Research* 4 (1978): 271–76. A rejoinder by Richard J. Lutz follows on pp. 276–78.
3. For ways of changing intentions by changing beliefs, see Jeffrey E. Danes and John E. Hunters, "Designing Persuasive Communication Campaigns: A Multimessage Communication Model," *Journal of Consumer Research* 7 (1980): 66–77.
4. A marketing research technique called conjoint analysis allows marketers to obtain data on this sort of attribute trade-off. Although it is not within the scope of this book to describe the technique, conjoint analysis has become extremely important to researchers looking at the trade-offs buyers are forced to make between brand attributes.
5. T. Brock, "Communication Recipient Similarity and Decision Change," *Journal of Personality and Social Psychology* 1 (1965): 650–54.
6. Brian Sternthal and C. Samuel Craig, *Consumer Behavior and Information Processing Perspective* (Englewood Cliffs, NJ: Prentice-Hall, Inc., 1982), 293.
7. E. Walster, E. Aronson, and D. Abrahams, "On Increasing the Persuasiveness of a Low Prestige Communicator," *Journal of Experimental Social Psychology* 2 (1966): 325–42.
8. J. Mills and E. Aronson, "Opinion Change as a Function of Communicators' Attractiveness and Desire to

Influence," *Journal of Personality and Social Psychology* 1 (1965): 173–77.

9. Michael Etgar and Steven A. Goodwin, "One-sided versus Two-sided Comparative Message Appeals for New Brand Introductions," *Journal of Consumer Research* 8 (1982): 460–65.
10. E. Walster, E. Aronson, and D. Abrahams, "On Increasing the Persuasiveness of a Low Prestige Communicator," *Journal of Experimental Social Psychology* 2 (1966): 325–42.
11. Etgar and Goodwin, 460.
12. George Belch, "The Effects of Message Modality on One- and Two-sided Advertising Messages," *Advances in Consumer Research* (1982): 21–26.
13. Paul Chance, "Ads Without Answers Make the Brain Itch," *Psychology Today* 9 (1975): 78.
14. H. E. Krugman, "Memory Without Recall, Exposure Without Perception," *Journal of Advertising Research* 17 (1977): 7–12.
15. Harold L. Ross, Jr. "How to Create Effective Humorous Commercials Yielding Above Average Brand Preference Change," *Marketing News* (March 26, 1976), 4.
16. Robert Garfield, "Stan Freeberg Writes Ads With a Wrinkle," *U.S.A. Today* (Sept. 21, 1983), 3B.
17. Brian Sternthal and C. Samuel Craig, "Humor in Advertising," *Journal of Marketing* 37 (October 1973): 12–18.
18. J. Kelly and P. Soleman, "Humor in TV Advertising," *Journal of Advertising* (1975): 31–35.
19. Michael L. Ray and William L. Wilkie, "Fear: The Potential of an Appeal Neglected by Marketing," *Journal of Marketing* 34 (January 1970): 54–62.
20. William L. Wilkie and Paul Farris, "Comparison Advertising: Problems and Potential," *Journal of Marketing* 39 (October 1975): 7–15.
21. Jonathan L. Freedman, David O. Sears, and J. Merrill Carlsmith, *Social Psychology* (Englewoods Cliffs, NJ: Prentice-Hall, 1978), 309–12.
22. Stewart W. Bither, "Resistance to Persuasion: Inoculation and Distraction," in *Consumer and Industrial Buying Behavior,* Arch G. Woodside, Jagdish N. Sheth, and Peter D. Bennett, eds. (New York: North-Holland, 1977), 243–50.
23. R. P. Abelson, "Modes of Resolution of Belief Dilemmas," *Conflict Resolution* 3 (1959), 343–52.
24. Freedman, Sears, and Carlsmith, *Social Psychology*.
25. Rothschild, Michael L. "Advertising Strategies for High and Low Involvement Situations," in *Attitude Research Plays for High Stakes,* J. C. Maloney and B. Silverman, eds. (Chicago: American Marketing Association, 1979), 74–93.
26. Krugman, H. E. "The Measurement of Advertising Involvement," *Public Opinion Quarterly* 30 (Winter 1966): 583–96.
27. M. Zellner, "Self Esteem, Perception, and Influenceability," *Journal of Personality and Social Psychology* 25 (1973): 87–93.

FURTHER READING

Classics

Bither, Stewart W., "Resistance to Persuasion: Inoculation and Distraction," in *Consumer and Industrial Buying Behavior,* Woodside, Sheth, and Bennett, eds. (New York: North-Holland, 1977), 243–50.

Calder, Bobby J., M. Ross, and Insko C., "Attitude Change and Attitude Attribution: Effects of Incentive, Choice, and Consequence," *Journal of Personality and Social Psychology* 25 (1973): 84–99.

Cannell, Charles F., and James C. MacDonald, "The Impact of Health News on Attitudes and Behavior," *Journalism Quarterly* 33 (1956): 315–23.

Day, G. S., "Theories of Attitude Structure and Change," in *Consumer Behavior: Theoretical Sources,* S. Ward and T. S. Robertson, eds. (Englewood Cliffs, NJ: Prentice-Hall, 1973), 303–53.

Lutz, Richard J., "Changing Brand Attitudes Through Modification of Cognitive Structures," *Journal of Consumer Research* 1 (March 1975): 49–59.

McGuire, W. J., "The Nature of Attitudes and Attitude Change," in *Handbook of Social Psychology,* Vol. 3, G. Lindzey and E. Aronson, eds. (Reading, MA: Addison-Wesley, 1969), 136–314.

Olson, Jerry C., and Philip Dover, "Effects of Expectation Creation and Disconfirmation on Belief Elements of Cognitive Structure," in *Advances in Consumer Research,* Vol. III, B. B. Anderson, ed., (Cincinnati: Association for Consumer Research, 1976), 168–75.

Osgood, E. C., and P. H. Tannenbaum, "The Principle of Congruity in the Prediction of Attitude

Change," *Psychological Review* 62 (1955): 42–55.

Pinson, Christian, and Eduardo L. Roberto, "Do Attitude Changes Precede Behavior Change?" *Journal of Advertising Research* 4 (August 1973): 33–38.

Rokeach, M., "Attitude Change and Behavioral Change," *Public Opinion Quarterly* 30 (1967): 529–50.

Rosenberg, Milton J., "Inconsistency Arousal and Reduction in Attitude Change," in *Current Studies in Social Psychology,* Ivan D. Steiner and Martin Fishbein, eds. Holt, Rinehart and Winston, Inc., (New York: 1965), 121–33.

Sherif, E. W., M. Sherif, and R. E. Nebergall, *Attitude and Attitude Change* (Philadelphia: W. B. Saunders Company, 1965).

Recent Significant Research

McCullough, James, Douglas MacLachlan, and Reza Moinpour, "Impact of Information on Preference and Perception," in *Advances in Consumer Research,* Vol. 9, Andrew Mitchell, ed. (Ann Arbor, MI: Association for Consumer Research, 1982), 402–05.

Miller, Norman, and Debbra E. Colman, "Methodological Issues in Analyzing the Cognitive Mediation of Persuasion," in *Cognitive Responses in Persuasion,* Petty, Ostrom, and Brock, eds. (Hillsdale, NJ: Lawrence Erlbaum Associates, 1981), 105–25.

Petty, Richard E. and Timothy C. Brock, "Thought Disruption and Persuasion: Assessing the Validity of Attitude Change Experiments," in *Cognitive Responses in Persuasion,* Petty, Ostrom and Brock, eds.

Petty, Richard E., Thomas M. Ostrom, and Timothy C. Brock, "Historical Foundations of the Cognitive Response Approach to Attitudes and Persuasion," in *Cognitive Responses in Persuasion,* Petty, Ostrom, and Brock, eds., 5–29.

Raj, S. P., "The Effects of Advertising on High and Low Loyalty Consumer Segments," *Journal of Consumer Research* 9 (June 1982): 77–89.

Sawyer, Alan G., "The Effects of Repetition of Refutational and Supportive Advertising Appeal," *Journal of Marketing Research* 10 (February 1973): 23–33.

Stuteville, John R., "Psychic Defenses Against High Fear Appeals: A Key Marketing Variable," *Journal of Marketing* 34 (April 1970): 39–45.

William L. Wilkie and Paul Farris, "Comparison Advertising: Problems and Potential," *Journal of Marketing* 39 (October 1975): 7–15.

Wilson, R. Dale, and Aydin Muderrisoglu, "An Analysis of Cognitive Response to Comparative Advertising," in *Advances in Consumer Research,* 7, Jerry C. Olson, ed. (Ann Arbor, MI: Association for Consumer Research, 1980), 566–71.

Applications

Appel, Valentine, "Attitude Change: Another Dubious Method for Measuring Advertising Effectiveness," in *Attitude Research at Sea,* Lee Adler and Irving Crespi, eds. (Chicago: American Marketing Association, 1966), 141–52.

Czepiel, John A., "Word-of-Mouth Processes in the Diffusion of a Major Technological Innovation," *Journal of Marketing Research* 11 (May 1974): 172–80.

Davis, H. L., and A. J. Silk, "Interaction and Influence Process in Personal Selling," *Sloan Management Review* 13 (Winter 1972): 54–56.

Day, George S., "Attitude Change and the Relative Influence of Media and Word-of-Mouth Sources," in *Models of Buyer Behavior,* Jagdish N. Sheth, ed. (New York: Harper and Row, 1974), 199–217.

Gitner, James L., "An Experimental Investigation of Attitude Change and Choice of a New Brand," *Journal of Marketing Research* 11 (February 1974): 30–40.

Lutz, Richard J., "Changing Brand Attitudes Through Modification of Cognitive Structure," *Journal of Consumer Research* 1 (March 1975): 49–59.

Olson, Jerry C., Daniel R. Toy, and Philip A. Dover, "Mediating Effects of Cognitive Responses to Advertising on Cognitive Structure," in *Advances in Consumer Research,* Vol. 5, H. Keith Hunt, eds. (Provo, UT: Association for Consumer Research, 1978), 72–78.

Robertson, Thomas S., and John R. Rossiter, "Children and Commercial Persuasion: An Attribution Theory Analysis," *Journal of Consumer Research,* 1 (June 1974): 13–20.

Wright, Peter, "Cognitive Responses to Mass Media Advocacy," in *Cognitive Responses in Persuasion,* Petty, Ostrom and Brock, eds., 263–82.

8 Information Processing

Objectives of This Chapter

After you have studied this chapter, you should be able to:

1. Provide highlights of information-processing research.
2. Define *information processing* and show how it relates to consumer behavior.
3. Explain the five functions of the information-processing system: attention, encoding, memory, information acquisition, and problem solving.
4. Suggest ways in which marketers can structure product messages to make them simpler for buyers to use in the decision-making process.
5. Show how information processing encompasses all the topics presented in prior chapters: motivation, learning, attitudes and beliefs, and perception.

Up to now, the various components of the decision-making process have been described individually. Earlier chapters discussed the roles of motivation, learning, attitudes and beliefs, and perception in the selection of a product type and a certain brand. But these discussions have presented human behavior from a fixed or static viewpoint, almost like still pictures of a moving subject taken from various angles.

Lately, psychologists have proposed a more comprehensive approach: a way of viewing human behavior as one continuous activity. This larger perspective is called *information processing,* and it is as different from the study of individual components of behavior as a movie is from a series of snapshots. This new area of psychological research enables marketers to answer two all-important questions: Why do consumers choose some brands over others? How do they make these decisions?

This chapter begins with a brief review of some of the highlights of information-processing research. Next we develop a working definition of information processing and look at several models for an overview of the concept. Succeeding sections examine the five aspects of information processing, attention, encoding, memory, problem solving, and information acquisition, and discuss the stored rules consumers use in making purchase decisions. Finally a list of practical suggestions is included to guide marketers in structuring messages based on information-processing principles.

WHAT IS INFORMATION PROCESSING?

The following questions, posed by Morton Hunt, help show how the human mind processes information. It is easy to see that the processes you use to answer these questions are related to the ways consumers sort out and use information to make purchase decisions.

1. *Consider this word—the word "word" that you just read. What happened in your mind when you read it?* . . . first you saw the variously shaped letters, then compared those images to your stored memories of printed letters. . . , thereby recognized the ones you had seen, recognized at the same time the word they stood for when assembled, understood its meaning, and fitted that meaning into the context of the sentence. And you did all this in a fraction of a second.
2. *In the place where you lived two residences ago, did your front door open at the left side or the right?* . . . To answer that question, you somehow sent a signal through the unseen branching network of your mind to exactly the right storage place, plucked out a reel of filed imagery, and projected an image upon some inner screen, all in a moment.
3. *What is George Washington's phone number?* . . . Most likely you recognized that the question was absurd. But how did you know it was without even considering the matter? Did you consult the encyclopedia

of history in your head? Look up the dates of Washington and of the telephone and do some logical reasoning based on them? Or none of these?

4. *If four days before tomorrow is Thursday, what is three days after yesterday?* . . . To arrive at the answer (Tuesday), you consciously went through a series of steps of naming, counting, and reasoning. Though the content of the problem is insignificant, the mental processes you used in solving it are highly consequential; they're comparable to the processes we all employ in solving everyday problems . . . and even in tackling problems of great moment.[1]

The human mind has a remarkable ability to comprehend and apply the information it has been fed. Although the field of information processing is so new that a precise definition is difficult, research indicates that **information processing** involves cognitive activities for the acquisition and analysis of data to arrive at goal-directed behaviors. It integrates functions such as perception, memory, and judgment into a system of human thought. Thus, information processing focuses on the *process* of thinking rather than on types of thoughts.

information processing

Because information processing takes such a comprehensive view of human mental processes, its complexities exceed the limits of the basic mathematical formulas and simple statistics used in more traditional psychological studies. In fact, the study of information processing in humans requires a great deal of information processing on the part of computers (as well as cleverly designed psychological experiments). As investigators learn to build computer systems that have increasingly sophisticated logic systems, they will be better able to understand the brain's cognitive complexity.

Our definition of information processing can be diagrammed in simple form. Figure 8-1 illustrates the three stages of information processing. Whether the decision is made by a computer selecting the best site to drill for oil, or by a person choosing an outfit to wear to a concert, the three elements of input, processing, and output are always present in some form. **Input** is the information needed to make a decision. The act of gathering information is part of this stage. **Processing** is the sorting out of this information in light of established general criteria and according to the organism's problem-solving abilities, thinking capacity, or intelligence. **Output** is the conclusion, answer, or decision resulting from the processing of the input. In the case of the oil company's computer, it might be the statement of which of the alternative drilling sites would be most likely to yield oil; for the person going to a concert, it would be the choice of an outfit that best meets the criteria for dress at such an event.

input
processing
output

Figure 8-1
A Basic Representation of a Process

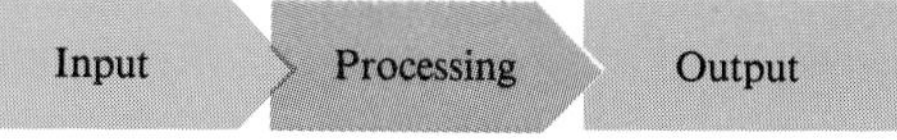

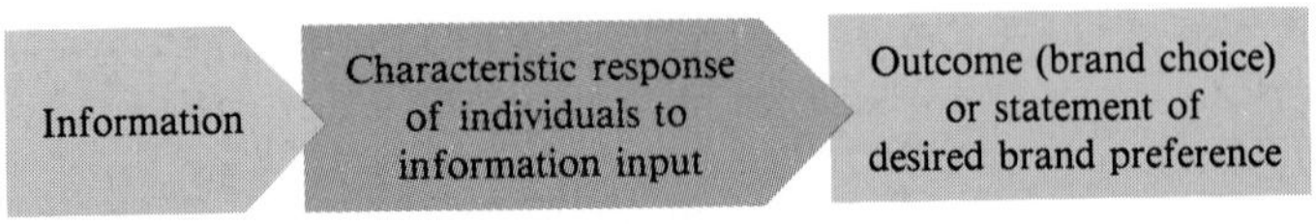

Figure 8-2
Simplified Diagram of Consumer Information Processing

Source: adapted from Stewart W. Bither and G. Ungson, "Consumer Information Processing Research: An Evaluative Review," Working Paper, Pennsylvania State University, 1975.

For all humans, output comes in the form of goal-directed behavior. For consumers, the goal is to purchase a product or service. A simplified diagram of information processing as performed by consumers would resemble the one in Figure 8-2, which is a variation on the simple stimulus-organism-response model discussed in Chapter 4. At the bottom of the figure are examples of questions marketing researchers ask that pertain to information processing. Answers to these questions can help marketers understand how to use promotion more efficiently and effectively to inform consumers. To understand the many aspects of information processing, however, a more detailed description of the information-processing system is needed.

THE INFORMATION-PROCESSING SYSTEM

The human brain has five information-processing functions: attention, encoding, remembering (memory), information acquisition, and problem solving. Bettman's model of information processing, Figure 8-3, shows the interrelationships of these functions.

The discussion in this chapter follows this model by considering the major functions of the information processing system: attention, encoding, memory, information acquisition, and problem-solving decision processes. Bettman uses the terms *scanner and interrupt* to describe mechanisms consumers use to examine their environment and stop their current behavior to interpret new situations and make decisions about how to handle conflict. This model will be discussed in more detail, and compared to other models, in Chapter 18.

Each of the major information processing functions will be described and related to buyer behavior in the following five sections. Since information acquisition often encompasses all four of these brain functions, this topic will be presented last.

ATTENTION

attention

Attention is the focusing of the thoughts and physical senses on stimuli in order to receive information. Attention requires mental effort—we call this *concentration*—but insofar as attending to sights, sounds, aromas,

Figure 8-3
Bettman's Model of Information Processing

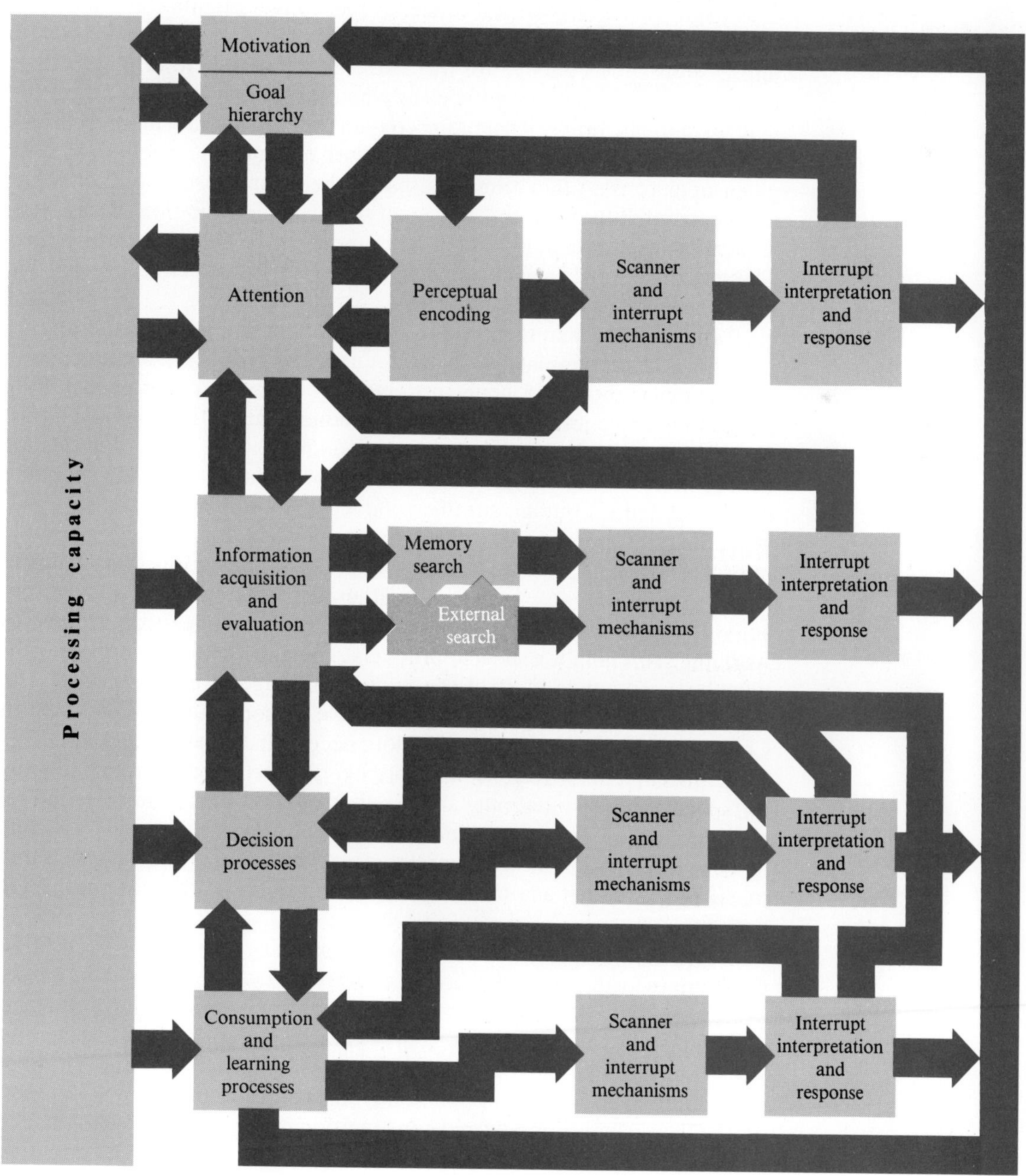

Source: James R. Bettman, *An Information Processing Theory of Consumer Choice* (Reading, MA: Addison-Wesley, 1979), 17.

tastes, and textures in our environment will help us achieve our goals, we are willing to expend the necessary energy.

Chapter 2 introduced the concept of selective attention in relation to human goals. Most of the stimuli which surround us do not make mental impressions strong enough for us to be conscious of them. The reason so many stimuli are filtered out is clear when we look at the capacity of the average human brain. The brain contains a great many more cells for processing visual data than for auditory data, and the number of cells given over to the other three senses fall between these two. Yet it has been estimated that just to analyze all the visual information we are constantly exposed to would require a brain one cubic light year in volume.[2] The brain's limited capacity explains why we are selective in what we attend to.

As humans, consumers are selective in their attention to the myriad stimuli in the marketplace such as products and product messages. However, because they have goals (unsolved problems or unmet needs), they invest time and energy thinking about products, advertisements, and purchasing situations that will lead to satisfaction of those needs. Purchasers devote their mental energies to gathering information about (1) shopping in general and (2) buying specific product types and brands.

General shopping knowledge—about price and quality, where reliable information about products can be found, and which stores carry particular types of products—is usually gathered passively. During everyday activities such as reading newspapers, watching television, riding to work, or searching for specific products, consumers have many opportunities to accumulate general shopping knowledge in a casual way. The tendency to do so is related to the motive of competency (discussed in Chapter 2). The desire to become more accomplished at activities such as shopping explains why consumers are likely to be diverted from shopping for specific items to learning about new stores or merchandise. The motive of competency also explains why consumers are ready to take in new information that is unrelated to immediate problems but that might be recalled at a later time to help them solve a different purchasing problem.

When consumers devote attention to gathering information on specific products in order to make brand choices, they actively and intensely pursue particulars such as comparative features, price, warranty, and quality. Whatever information source they attend to is often affected by two other motives: novelty seeking and consistency. New and different promotions attract the attention of buyers seeking to break up the monotony of their usual shopping and consumption routines. Those who receive contradictory information or who have conflicting goals become attentive to advertisements or other stimuli that help them resolve the contradictions or settle the conflicts.

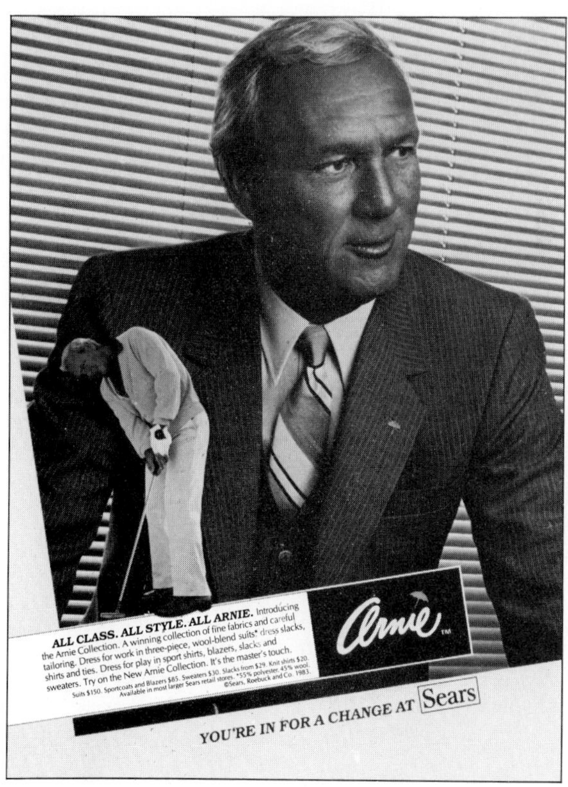

One way in which marketers try to attract attention is through the use of celebrities in their advertising campaigns. Also, when a well-known figure who has high credibility endorses a product, such as Arnold Palmer for Sears, this may help buyers resolve such conflicts or contradictions. (For more on the use of celebrities in advertising, see Chapter 7.) At any rate, once a person has chosen to pay attention to a subject, information about the subject must be encoded to be understood.

ENCODING

encoding

Encoding is the process of taking information in the environment and converting it to knowledge.[3] How are stimuli encoded? Research has led to three different theories about the symbolic codes we assign to sensory information.[4] One theory holds that encoding is *pictorial*—in other words, information is stored in our minds as pictures or images. Another theory suggests that mental encoding is *verbal*—that is, words and other symbols are used. However, there is growing evidence that encoding is actually both verbal *and* pictorial.[5]

Mental Imagery

The mental-imagery approach to encoding is based on some researchers' contention that thoughts are held in picture form. Although the imagery theorists have failed to specifically define what these images are, they describe them as **episodes** or pictorial representations. These images are probably not like the pictures we take with a camera; but somehow they can be felt and visualized without words. Certainly dreams are often episodic. In sleep, our mental images tend to involve sensations such as light, color, sound, and so on. Aesthetics, taste, symbolic meaning, and other subjective phenomena are probably represented in our mental imagery as well.[6] The ad for Budweiser beer showing cans of beer falling from the sky is one example of an ad with high-impact imagery. In fact, it contains no ad copy at all. The image of this ad may be stored in picture form, since no written information is given.

episodes

It is not difficult to conceive of some commercials as pictorially represented in the mind. For example, the television commercial for Stroh's beer that pictured players in a sandlot baseball game used actions, more than words, to communicate its message. In the advertisement, the catcher shouted, "Stroh it in here!" Then a can of Stroh's beer hit the catcher's mitt. Ads that are high on emotion with little verbal content are likely to be retained as episodes. Commercials such as these may be

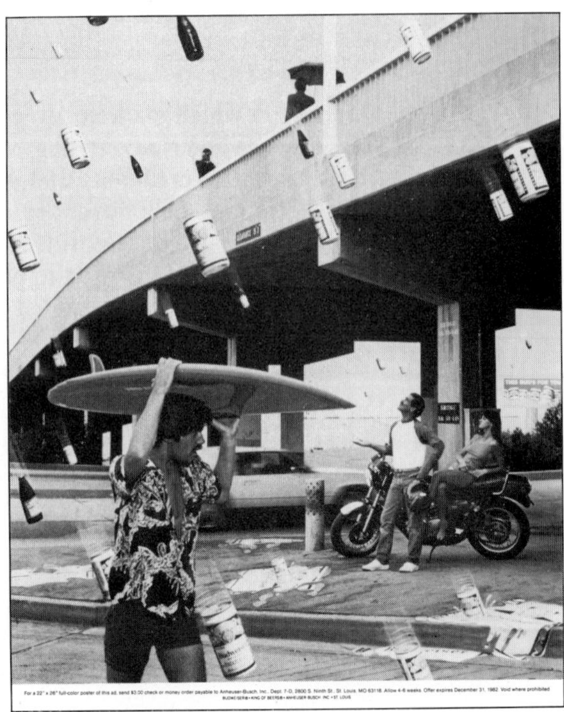
For a 22" x 26" full-color poster of this ad, send $3.00 check or money order payable to Anheuser-Busch, Inc., Dept. 7-D, 2800 S. Ninth St., St. Louis, MO 63118. Allow 4-6 weeks. Offer expires December 31, 1982. Void where prohibited
BUDWEISER® • KING OF BEERS® • ANHEUSER-BUSCH, INC • ST. LOUIS

particularly effective for low-involvement purchases, such as gum or soft drinks, which do not require prospective buyers to seek a great deal of information before making a choice. Marketers of these products are likely to be more concerned that buyers remember their brand by associating it with a distinctive image than that they actually receive information about the product.

Verbal Encoding

Many researchers assume that content, whether perceived as words and symbols or as pictures, is stored basically as words and symbols—that is, in **semantic memory.** This view holds that general knowledge, facts, and principles gleaned from experience are held verbally in memory. John Howard has suggested that the meaning of a brand is its "semantic structure."[7] Figure 8-4 shows a hypothetical semantic structure for some brands of beer. In this example, a certain brand such as Michelob Lite is placed in relation to other brands in the category of light beers. These are grouped opposite the category of regular beers, but both groups are classified as domestic beers. On the other hand, imported beers might have different subclassifications than those shown for domestic beers. However, all of these would be types of beer; therefore, they are linked in memory to beer as a type of alcoholic beverage. Much more complex semantic structures could be constructed for other products. These could involve product characteristics such as package size, package material, cost, and manufacturer, as well as what brands one's family or friends use, and so on.

semantic memory

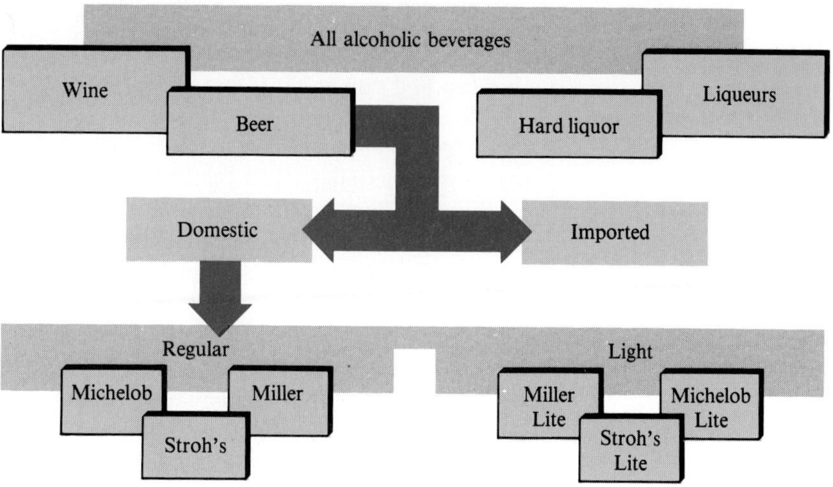

Figure 8-4 *Hypothetical Semantic Structure of Selected Beers*

Source: adapted from John A. Howard, *Consumer Behavior: Application of Theory* (New York: McGraw-Hill, 1977), 41.

Marketers often evaluate consumer responses to products or packaging using similar semantic scales. The multiattribute attitude models and attitude scales, discussed in Chapter 6, collect this type of information from respondents. Much of the research on information processing for consumer-behavior studies assumes that storage is basically semantic.

Combined Verbal and Pictorial Representations

dual-coding hypothesis

There is a strong possibility that consumers use both verbal and pictorial representations of information about the world. The **dual-coding hypothesis** holds that pictures are processed in one memory system at the same time that words are received, handled, and filed in another memory system.[8] Research suggests that there is a good deal of feedback and "cooperation" between the two systems, so that the information stored as words is consistent with the information stored as pictures and sensations. For example, the Stroh's beer advertisement using sandlot baseball would be stored pictorially, in images—the surprising action of a Stroh's beer landing in the catcher's mitt—and verbally, with words and other symbols that represent Stroh's as a fun, social, good-time beer.

The dual-coding hypothesis has been further refined and tested by psychologists. For example, Kosslyn and Schwartz have developed a computer model that can account for both pictorial and verbal inputs in problem solving.[9] They use arrays of dots of various colors and intensities to represent pictures, and strings of words for verbal storage in the computer. The computer can then be programmed to use these two forms of coded information to solve problems.

There are two explanations of how dual coding is likely to occur. One involves the knowledge schemata framework and the other is the left and right brain hemispheres framework. Although they are different explanations of encoding, they are not necessarily in conflict. Both are useful in understanding consumer behavior.

Knowledge Schemata

Jerry Olson has suggested that consumers encode stimuli according to their existing knowledge structures.[10] Some of those structures operate primarily on episodic (pictorial) events and other structures lend themselves to semantic (verbal) input. According to Olson, both encoding processes are likely to exist within a single framework. Over a lifetime, buyers learn many **schemata** to help them perceive the world. For the Stroh's ad example, at first some buyers might perceive only the novelty, color, and social activities displayed by the actors in the ad, an *episodic encoding frame*. If they did not already know that Stroh's is a brand of beer, they could hardly be expected to compare its characteristics with those of another brand, as is done in semantic memory. On the other

schemata

hand, for important problems consumers are likely to develop semantic structures to store their perceptions for more in-depth analysis.

Left and Right Brain Hemispheres

According to a popular theory, the human brain has two relatively distinct halves, or hemispheres.[11] Each hemisphere has a specific function in thought. The left side is responsible for verbal, symbolic, and analytical thinking. The right side processes pictorial, geometric, and nonverbal information. (An exception to this is that for many left-handed people the locations are reversed.) An anatomical bridge between the two hemispheres allows them to communicate with each other, resulting in integrated perceptions of sights, sounds, and sensations.[12]

The explanation of attention put forward by proponents of the left- and right-brain theory has been particularly enlightening. Early in the attention process, it appears that right-hemisphere function is predominant. Later, when verification and more analytical thoughts are required, the left side dominates. However, the left side has a limited attention span, whereas the right side can stay fixed on one subject longer.[13] Therefore, visual, musical, creative, and pictorial elements of ads catch the consumer attention first, because they are largely processed on the right side. Facts, reasoning, data, and details of product messages are likely to be picked up later, because analysis is performed on the left side.

Additionally, the left- and right-brain theory can explain why consumers often recognize the general idea of an ad but fail to remember such important elements as the products being advertised and the name of the manufacturer or brand. **Recognition** is a right-brain process involving pictorial or episodic representation; **recall** requires the involvement of the left brain, which is content-oriented (verbal).[14]

recognition
recall

Encoding is probably both episodic and semantic. Encoding processes, because they prepare information for storage, are intimately connected with memory. Encoding and memory are so interrelated that it is probably impossible to separate them. However, they are discussed as separate entities to make them easier to grasp.

MEMORY

According to James Bettman, the following important questions about consumer behavior can be addressed by looking at memory functions:[15]

1. What is remembered from an advertisement or a product-related conversation?
2. Under what conditions do consumers tend to emphasize information on packages or stored in memory when they are in the store?

3. How much time is necessary for consumers to learn some piece of information from an ad?
4. How many repetitions are needed before a consumer can remember a piece of information?
5. What can be done to facilitate in-store recognition of a brand by consumers?
6. What types of new information, claims, and so on are easier for consumers to remember, given their current knowledge about the product?[16]

The study of memory involves exploring how coded information (knowledge) is stored and recalled. To understand the link between memory and these six issues, we must first consider the three stages.

Multiple Memory

Most researchers think that there are three parts or stages to human memory: sensory memory, short-term memory, and long-term memory. They interact, as Figure 8-5 shows.

Sensory Memory (SM)

sensory memory

The first and most basic stage of memory is **sensory memory.** It retains an almost unlimited amount of uncoded information as sense impressions, but only for a fraction of a second. Most of the countless impressions it

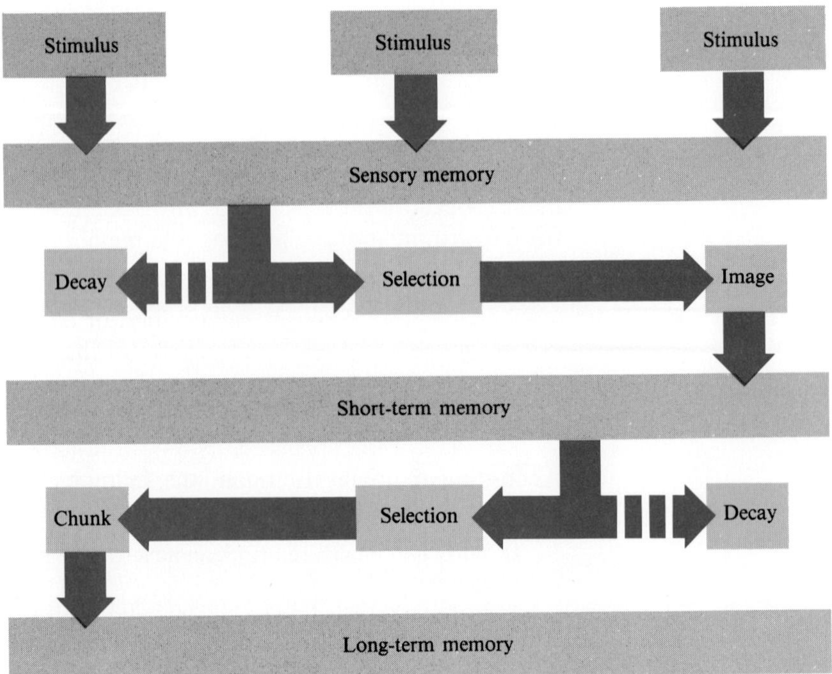

Figure 8-5
Components and Characteristics of Memory

holds never even reach the level of our conscious awareness, because we are selectively attending to other perceptions.[17] Thus, much of what sen-

decay

sory memory contains at any given time **decays,** or is forgotten, almost immediately. However, when attention is focused on a few selected stimuli, sensory information about these stimuli is transferred in an uncoded form to short-term memory, where it can be interpreted.

What is most significant to buyer behaviorists about sensory memory is the control that it exerts over which information is passed to short-term memory. Clearly, marketers want consumers to attend to their products and messages so that these images will be transmitted and do not simply decay.

Short-term Memory (STM)

short-term memory

This second stage of memory, **short-term memory,** interprets the uncoded information sent from sensory memory. Although short-term memory can usually hold information for about eighteen seconds before it decays, its capacity is much smaller than that of sensory memory. Only about four to

chunk

seven chunks of information can be held there at one time.[18] A **chunk** is an organization of information which is recalled for use in solving specific problems of short duration, such as remembering rules for playing a game. The content of a chunk may vary greatly among persons focusing on the same object. For example, when most chess players look at a chessboard, they are likely to see twenty-five separate chess pieces. These players can only hold seven pieces in thought while they plan the next move. On the other hand, grand master chess champions have learned how to see the entire game as consisting of about seven configurations of several chess pieces each. This strategy allows them to hold more information in short-term memory. Therefore, they are more likely to spot and avoid the bad moves less accomplished chess players fail to see.

Short-term memory uses chunks to associate new information with what is already known and therefore to interpret it. Chunks can grow larger as relevant new information is integrated into them.[19]

Short-term memory is responsible for determining what newly interpreted information, now integrated into the existing chunks, will be sent to long-term memory. But first this information must be rehearsed before

rehearsal

transfer

it can be stored. **Rehearsal** is silent, inner speech that helps to maintain information in short-term memory. The amount of time required to **transfer** the selected information to long-term memory varies according to its future uses. If the information is to be fully recalled later, about five to ten seconds are required. If it is only to be recognized but not recalled in detail, transfer takes one to five seconds. Perhaps this is because recognition is a right-hemisphere function, whereas recall requires verbal, analytical, left-hemisphere activity. Rehearsal for recall may be more extensive, requiring a longer time to pass into long-term memory.

Short-term memory has many implications for consumer behaviorists and marketers alike. First, product labels and advertising messages should contain no more than seven chunks of information. (Of course, marketers must learn how consumers organize information about their product in order to determine what these chunks should contain.) Second, marketers should design messages in ways that facilitate rehearsal so they will be moved to long-term memory.[20] Some repetition of key points in advertising is likely to encourage rehearsal and therefore aid message retention. However, research has shown that too much repetition of a pattern on television commercials causes reduction in the effectiveness of the commercials and less favorable viewer evaluations of the products advertised. This phenomenon is known as **wearout.**[21] Finally, intervals between message repetitions should be geared to the type of information presented and whether it is to be stored in long-term memory for recall in detail, or merely recognized.

wearout

Long-term Memory (LTM)

long-term memory

interference

The last stage, **long-term memory,** may be capable of retaining an unlimited amount of information for years, even indefinitely. Information in long-term memory remains until it is replaced by contradictory information. This replacement, called **interference,** is exemplified by diners who go to their favorite restaurant, receive a poor meal or poor service, and then reclassify the restaurant to a lower status.

anchor clusters
cluster
anchor

An important element of long-term memory is its organization, because the way information is organized determines how it is recalled or retrieved. Information in long-term memory is organized in **anchor clusters.** A **cluster** is composed of several chunks of information related to a product classification. An **anchor** is a concept or image of a product within a cluster. For example, *carbonated soft drinks* could be a cluster and the anchors it contains could be *cola/noncola* or *regular/diet*. Recently, marketers have emphasized an aspect of soft drinks that previously went unnoticed: the addition of caffeine to certain brands. The shift in anchors to *caffeine/no caffeine* is due largely to the advertising campaign of one brand: Seven-Up. In the past Seven-Up attempted to differentiate itself from colas, which have long held the greatest share of the carbonated soft-drink market, by advertising itself as "The Uncola." This served to remind consumers that there is an alternative to colas, but it did not convey any differential *advantage* of Seven-Up over the cola drinks. Then a breakthrough came with a change in Seven-Up's advertising approach. The fact that Seven-Up has no caffeine became the focus of its advertising messages on television, radio, and billboards nationwide. The slogans "Crisp and clean, no caffeine" and "Never had it, never will" caused consumers to see it as superior to the drinks containing caffeine. In fact, several competing brands with caffeine were actually displayed in some ads to undercut their image in the consumer's mind. The result was

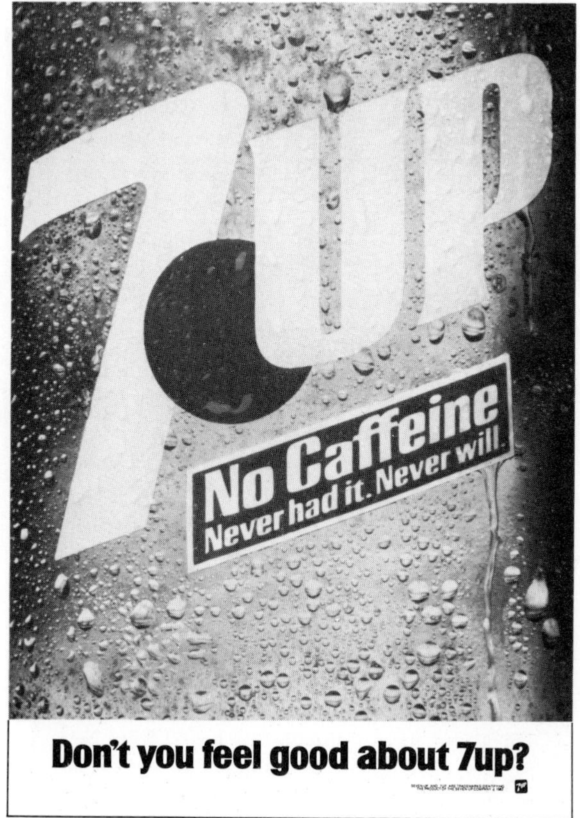

that Seven-Up's competitors hurried to produce new caffeine-free versions of their cola products in order to hold on to their market share. Now we have RC 100, Decaffeinated Pepsi Free—and Seven-Up's own Like cola. (Like is not a competitor of Seven-Up's anchor but of the other non-caffeine colas.) With the success of the advertising campaign, we can be sure that some consumers' anchor clusters for the Seven-Up brand have changed, as shown in Figure 8-6.

The research findings about long-term memory have three major implications for marketers:

1. *The more anchors a brand has, the more likely it is to be remembered.* Therefore, the brand should be presented to create more than one image.
2. *The more basic the cluster to which a brand belongs, the easier it is to retrieve from memory.* Therefore, the brand should be portrayed as belonging to or directly related to a familiar product classification.
3. *Once a brand is stored in long-term memory,* (becomes a part of the consumer's evoked set[22]), *it will stay until some contradictory information about the brand or a negative experience causes interference.* Therefore,

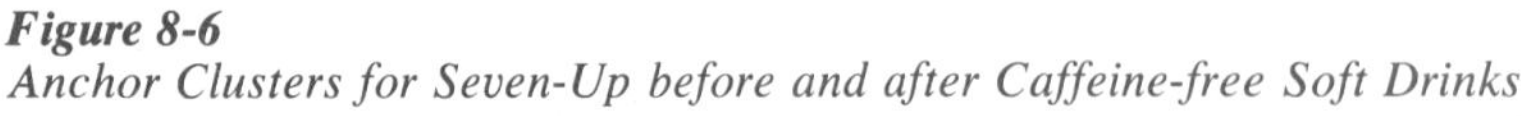

Figure 8-6
Anchor Clusters for Seven-Up before and after Caffeine-free Soft Drinks

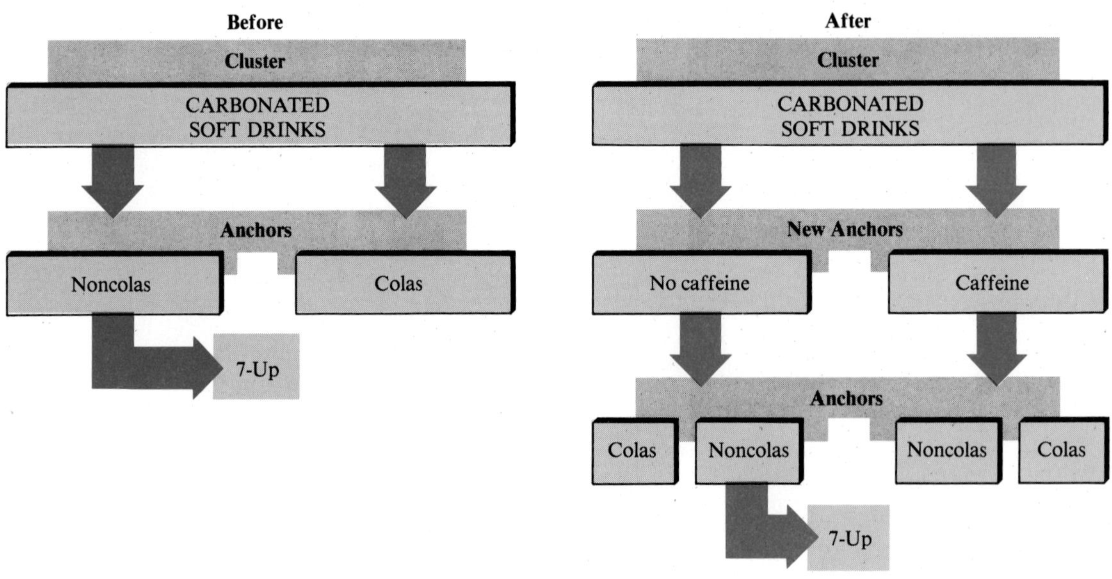

to prevent the brand from being replaced in the evoked set, sellers should protect the image of the brand and ensure that the brand performs according to customer expectations.

An interesting study by Alice Tybout, Bobby Calder, and Brian Sternthal put these concepts into practice. They used the elements of information storage and retrieval to find a more effective way to combat negative rumors about a product.[23] Participants were exposed to the rumor that McDonald's restaurants uses worm meat in its hamburgers. Then they were asked to evaluate McDonald's. Results showed that simple refutation of the rumor had little effect on combating it. However, when participants were asked questions about such things as the location of the nearest McDonald's, how frequently they ate there, and whether or not it had indoor seating, they tended to give a better rating than those exposed to a straight refutation. This intermediate step of the questions seemed to cause a retrieval of thoughts about McDonald's aside from the worm rumor and make the rumor less prominent in participants' minds. Another strategy was to expose participants to a positive statement about worm meat in connection with its use as a specialty item in a gourmet restaurant. The purpose was to minimize the chance that the worm rumor would be stored with McDonald's, or to assure that the association of worm meat with a positive statement would minimize the rumor's negative effects. This strategy also resulted in a higher evaluation of McDonald's.

Levels of Processing Theory

levels of processing theory

Another view of how information is stored in memory is the **levels of processing theory,** originally adapted to consumer behavior by Jerry Olson.[24] In recent years there have been several updates and enhancements of the original explanation from Fergus Craik and Robert Lockhart.[25] These researchers claimed that memory functions in a series of steps. The greater the analysis a consumer makes about a brand, the longer the series of steps the information must pass through. Thus, one reader might glance at an advertisement and quickly forget it; another might study the ad and recall it later.

The original levels of processing theory assumed that sensory and pictorial coding is done during earlier, shallow levels of analysis, and verbal, semantic coding takes place at later, deeper levels. Recent revisions of the theory suggest that either type and either level of processing can occur first, and that they can both take place simultaneously.

Activation Theory

memory activation
short-term store
long-term store

The theory of **memory activation** suggests that there is one memory, not three. However, it recognizes two parts, called **short-term store** and **long-term store.** According to this theory, short-term store "is a temporary activation of information permanently stored in long-term store. . . ."[26] It also holds that only one of these parts can be activated and used at a time. If the part is not activated, it cannot be used. Finally, any activation is temporary and will stop unless attention is devoted to maintaining it.

All three views of memory structure and functions have research support.[27] Fortunately, all three views lead to similar conclusions regarding consumer behavior. Each suggests that information is processed in ways that help categorize and integrate new information with information stored in memory. Table 8-1 summarizes and compares the three theories.

Most marketing researchers use the multiple-memory approach. Although there are probably not three (or even two) separate memories, it is conceptually acceptable to discuss them as distinct from one another. In any case, theorists agree that short-term memory *relates* concepts (it is the working memory) and long-term memory *stores* concepts.

PROBLEM SOLVING

heuristics
stored rules

Attention, encoding, and memory all provide inputs for problem solving, the fourth major aspect of information processing. The rules consumers use to arrive at decisions are called **heuristics.** In some cases, consumers have **stored rules** that are used in several similar buying situations. Otherwise, a *constructive mechanism* formulates decision rules at the time of purchase.[28]

Table 8-1 THEORIES OF MEMORY OF USE TO MARKETERS

Theory	***Concept***	***Description***
Multiple memory	Memory has three parts:	
	Sensory	Uncoded sense impressions that last for a fraction of a second
	Short-term	Coded information that is held for short duration (18 seconds)
	Long-term	Unlimited amount of information that can be held indefinitely and later retrieved
Levels of processing	Memory functions in steps: Sensory and pictorial Verbal and semantic coding	May occur in either order, or simultaneously
Activation	There is one memory with two parts:	
	Short-term store	Temporary activation of long-term memory
	Long-term store	Permanent memory storage

The stored rules can be fairly simple: for example, *when buying canned vegetables, always select the cheapest brand,* or *always buy the store's own brand,* or *always buy Del Monte brand.* They can also be more complex: for example, *buy the store's brand or Del Monte brand, depending on whichever is cheaper.* In many cases, consumers have little actual experience with particular brands, and the rules are more general: for example, *when making major purchases, compare at least three brands.* Additionally, consumers have problem-solving approaches that determine how their attitudes toward particular purchases are structured. More complex rules involve the development and change of attitude structure (refer to Chapter 7).

Heuristics are involved in the four stages of consumer decision making: (1) defining the pool of alternative brands, (2) reviewing information about the alternatives, (3) selecting or constructing the decision rule, and (4) applying the decision rule. Figure 8-7 illustrates these four stages.

Defining the Pool of Alternative Brands

An *evoked set* is composed of those brands the consumer would consider purchasing to solve some consumption problem. Those brands represent the pool of alternatives from which the consumer chooses. The evoked set can only include the brands the consumer has heard about. The larger the pool is, the greater the potential becomes for expending large amounts

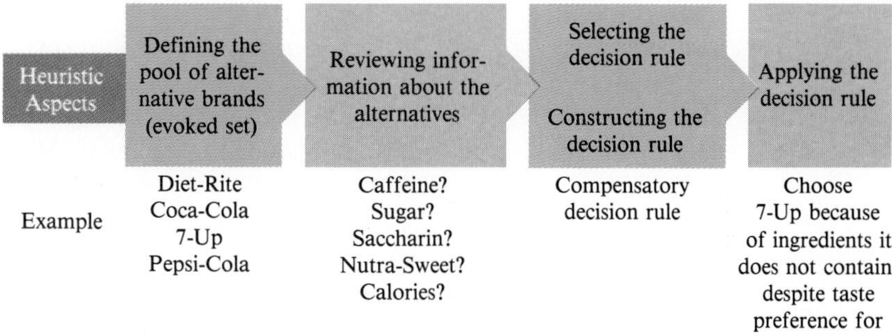

Figure 8-7
Consumer Problem-Solving Structure

of energy arriving at a purchase decision. In the interest of simplicity, once the consumer makes a choice the evoked set might shrink to one or two favorite brands. It is important to marketers that *their* brand be included in the pool when decisions are made. A brand promoted in the context of its purchase environment (such as a store) will more likely be included in the evoked set when the decision is made.

Advertising geared toward increasing awareness plays an important part in this stage of the problem-solving process. Those ads with high potential to stimulate awareness during the decision process are more likely to result in the desired sales.

Reviewing Information about the Alternatives

Once the pool of alternative brands is determined, consumers review the information they have about each brand. Beliefs about the brands are the most important information the consumer has, and these beliefs are reviewed in light of the particular decision process used. Global, or general, impressions and estimates of the importance of attributes under consideration are also reviewed. This information review is not a closed process; at times additional information is sought. (The last section of this chapter will deal with how information is acquired.) When needed information is unavailable, the decision is postponed or a new rule is used.

Selecting the Decision Rule

Consumers use many decision rules. However, there are five basic approaches that represent most decision procedures: (1) affect-referral, (2) compensatory (trade-off), (3) lexicographic (dominant), (4) conjunctive (sequential elimination), and (5) risk models.[29] (Chapter 6 introduced compensatory, lexicographic, and conjunctive attitude models.)

Affect-Referral

affect-referral decision process

In the **affect-referral** decision-rule process, decisions are made based on very little analysis of the product's characteristics at the time of purchase.

The amount of *liking* for the brand is the only criterion used. A good example is a customer ordering beer at a restaurant:

Waitress: "Would you like anything to drink?"
Customer: "I would like a Heinekin."
Waitress: "We have Budweiser, Miller, and Miller Lite."
Customer: "I'll have a Bud."

As the customer ordered, no review of any specific information about the brands was made other than an overall preference ranking. Of course, a good deal of thought on the buyer's part might have been required before arriving at the affective rating. By this time, however, many of the details of the original analysis might be long forgotten. Consumers who use the affect-referral method of decision making are simply sparing themselves the mental effort required to recall *why* they prefer certain brands over others. They use unidimensional, global indices that represent their feelings toward a brand. Appeals to such global indices—for example *the best* or *the greatest*—are often used in advertising and other marketing communications.

Compensatory (Trade-off)

compensatory or trade-off decision process

The **compensatory** or **trade-off** approach to decision rules involves looking at the pros and cons of buying one or more brands, comparing the relative value of each brand. This differs from the affect-referral decision process in that consumers think about several trade-offs in their choices. For example, someone who is in the market for a power boat is considering two brands. One is larger, more expensive, and gives poorer gas mileage, but affords more comfort and safety. The other boat is smaller, and thus provides good gas mileage and speed, but it appears to be too unstable for rough water. Eventually the prospective buyer may decide that the cost savings justifies buying the smaller boat. However, he may also have to restrict his boating to inland bodies of water. Trade-offs in relation to brand attributes is often used.

Lexicographic (Dominant)

lexicographic decision process

In the **lexicographic** decision-rule process, the consumer selects one or two aspects of the product class that are most important and compares only those aspects. That is, the decision is made on the most dominant aspects of the product. When two or more brands have the same most important aspect, the second most important aspect of the product becomes the basis for comparison. This process of eliminating matching aspects continues until one brand possesses an aspect of importance that no other brand does. Suppose you are trying to choose a cola from a vending machine and must decide between one with caffeine but without sugar and one without caffeine but with sugar. If controlling your weight is a major issue, you will choose the one without sugar even though you would mildly prefer to avoid caffeine. Your decision is made on the most dominant aspect of the product—sugar and nonsugar. The caffeine factor is of less importance.

When the most dominant characteristics of several brands are similar, the shopper continues to compare the brands on less important characteristics. Thus the lexicographic decision format is fairly complex because the buyer must evaluate many product attributes and brands almost simultaneously. However, using the sequential process of determining the major criteria (discussed below) before evaluating different brands helps to minimize the effort. In the lexicographic method, the brand finally purchased is likely to be the first one that demonstrates a clear advantage in a significant characteristic.

Conjunctive (Sequential Elimination)

conjunctive decision process

The **conjunctive** or **sequential elimination** method involves establishing minimum standards of acceptability for the product type, based on anticipated performance. Brands are evaluated sequentially, and the first brand to meet all the minimum standards is selected. If no brand meets all the minimum standards, or if *all* brands meet minimum standards, the standards must be changed or a different decision rule used. Conjunctive processing often limits the number of brands under consideration. Here is an example of this form of processing. A motorist wishes to stop for a quick lunch. Criteria for choosing where to stop might be a fast-food drive-through restaurant that is near the expressway and is not crowded. The first restaurant is bypassed because it has no drive-through window and looks busy. The second restaurant is not selected because it is also busy even though it does have drive-up service. Finally, the motorist notices a restaurant that meets all the criteria and quickly selects it—regardless of what other restaurants meeting the criteria may be available just down the road.

The conjunctive process differs from the lexicographic approach in two ways. First, conjunctive buyers usually establish more purchase criteria; second, they tend to compare a few brands on many criteria rather than comparing all available brands on a few criteria.

Risk Models

risk models

The final category of heuristics used by consumers consists of risk models. **Risk models** consider the negative aspects of purchasing a product or brand. (See the discussion of perceived risk in Chapter 3.) Using this approach, consumers focus attention on what could go wrong with the purchase. They are concerned about how friends will view the purchase (social risk) and whether the product will perform as expected (functional risk). Consumers using risk models look for information about how others feel about the options and what product failures are possible.

An example of this is a purchasing agent who does not select the most advanced, state-of-the-art equipment but chooses the tried and tested "sure bet" that is least likely to fail based on past performance.

Constructing the Decision Rule

When consumers are making a first-time purchase for which they do not have a stored rule, they must develop a new heuristic for the new purchase situation. The newly constructed rule is generally a hybrid of the five decision approaches just described. When a buyer combines more than one decision rule to make a purchase decision, he or she is said to be using a **constructive mechanism** to develop the new rule. For example, a shopper might begin with affect-referral processing but change to another approach when the favorite brands are out of stock. Thus, the heuristic that evolves is probably constructed from bits and pieces of stored rules.[30]

constructive mechanism

When a shopper is facing a first-time purchase, he or she may not even know what purchase criteria, are important for that product category. In these situations certain types of promotional messages can be very influ-

ential. For example, an ad comparing one brand to another on a few selected attributes suggests which factors should be considered important and how they should be compared. Such ads guide the first-time buyer through problem-solving process, to the benefit of the advocated brand.[31] Sanyo does this for its video recorders by stressing picture clarity and price as major choice criteria. A first-time buyer might be influenced by these and view Sanyo favorably.

An exploratory study of the grocery shopping trips two consumers took over several months showed that they used many different heuristics. Researchers performed protocol analysis on over one hundred decisions made. The two shoppers taped their thoughts while making purchases; in the protocol technique, the respondent thinks aloud to describe his or her thought processes during the shopping trip. Judges listened to the tapes and evaluated the types of decision rules the shoppers had applied. About one-fourth of the decisions involved a preprocessed choice much like the affect-referral method. Another fourth involved recognizable decision rules similar to the other rules just described. The third fourth used a constructive mechanism to build a hybrid heuristic. The remaining decisions were difficult to interpret or involved interaction with the researcher.[32]

Applying a Decision Rule

The final step of the problem-solving process is making the decision. The decision rule has been selected and only needs to be applied. This systematic analysis is called the "mental calculus," which connotes a logical method or process of reasoning using computations. A shopper finds the optimal solution to a consumption problem: the best value. The brand that best meets the criteria, according to whatever decision-making rule the shopper uses), is the brand eventually selected.

Application of the decision rule requires mental work to integrate the first three stages. For example, each application is likely to be influenced by the number of brands evaluated as well as what is already known about each brand. When the affect-referral decision rule is used, a consumer must have more than awareness of the brand for it to be in the pool; the brand must also be desired from the outset. When the compensatory model is used, the brands in the pool are clearly defined. Because a lot of work is required to make decisions this way, the pool is kept small. On the other hand, when the lexicographic decision rule is applied, several brands can easily be evaluated on a single characteristic. Thus, the evoked set may be quite large. When the conjunctive approach is used, marketers should seek to have their brands included first in the choice process because buyers may decide without looking at alternatives. Thus, variables such as distribution, the location of brands in the store, and point-of-purchase displays would be extremely important so that the sponsor's brand is evaluated before the other brands. Since different people may use different decision rules to select the same products, marketers may find it beneficial to try to gear their marketing approach to the rule or rules most often used to select their product.

Brand or Attribute Processing Strategies

For most of the decision rules discussed before, consumers must evaluate both attributes and brands to arrive at a choice. They may focus on each attribute one at a time and evaluate each one across several brands, or they may focus on a single brand and complete analysis of all its attributes before moving to the next brand. This analysis does not occur simultaneously.

choice by processing brands

choice by processing attributes

Thus consumers use two major ways to apply decision rules in making brand choices: **choice by processing brands** (CPB) and **choice by processing attributes** (CPA).[33] Using CPB strategies, consumers look at a single brand and its attributes, then go to the second brand and its attributes (which may be different from the first), and so on. In CPA strategies consumers first take an attribute and evaluate all the brands on it. Then they move to the next attribute and evaluate the brands based on it, and so on. Unit pricing practices in supermarkets aid CPA strategies by providing a common denominator, price, for judging across brands. Whereas some studies have shown that consumers prefer using the CPB strategies, most have found that the majority of buyers use the CPA approach.[34]

Consumers who use a choice strategy that involves attributes (CPA) seek to acquire information about the products somewhat differently than consumers who choose by brand (CPB). The method used to gather and process information is strongly influenced by how the information is presented.[35] When data is presented by attribute, it is stored and used by attribute. When it is presented by brand, it is stored and used in that manner. Marketers may choose to ignore consumer preferences for one of the two types of strategies because of the tendency to adapt use and storage of information to the form in which the information is presented. However, if marketers want to make the entire information-processing function easier, they should present marketing messages in ways that are the easiest to remember and use.

Few researchers have examined whether marketers structure messages to conform to particular decision rules. However, in one study which did address the appeal to various types of decision rules in television and magazine advertising, the researchers found that CPB was most often used. In most cases in the study, the ad content could be adjusted in various ways for use with compensatory, lexicographic, or conjunctive decision rules. CPA was used in less than one-third of the ads in either medium, and those ads tended to emphasize the lexicographic process. Table 8-2 reports the results of this study.

Table 8-2 AN ANALYSIS OF THE DECISION PROCESS USED FOR VARIOUS TYPES OF TELEVISION AND MAGAZINE ADVERTISEMENTS

Choice by Processing Brands (CPB)		***Television***	***Magazine***
Affect-referral	Ads describing overall value of the product (*McDonald's meal value*)	14%	12%
Compensatory or Lexicographic	Ads asserting the product has certain attributes, causes, outcomes (*weight-loss pills make you thinner*)	80%	94%
	Ads asserting the product causes outcomes which in turn causes outcomes (*mouth freshener gives sex appeal*)	45%	72%
Conjunctive	Ads asserting the product has several features, and any without these should be disqualified (*Seven-Up has no caffeine*)	4%	1%
Choice by Processing Attributes (CPA)			
Lexicographic	Ads making a comparative assertion about the brand or a particular attribute (*Burger King broiled hamburgers vs. McDonald's fried hamburgers*)	18%	24%
	Ads positioning the brand against identified competitors regarding an attribute, and asserting that this dimension should be most important (*Wendy's uses more beef than other hamburger chains*)	7%	5%
	Ads asserting that a particular attribute is most important in buying this type of product (*luxury cars have a smooth, comfortable ride*)	3%	9%
Compensatory	Ads asserting that when all attributes are weighed and balanced, the advocated brand will win (*Ford truck ads showing cab room, twin I-beam suspension, horsepower and weight capacity*)	1%	4%
Risk models	Ads citing negative consequences of not adopting the brand (*Home Fire Alarm ads showing loss of home without fire warning*)	4%	2%

Source: adapted from Peter Wright and Fredric Barbour, "The Relevance of Decision Process Models in Structuring Persuasive Messages." *Communication Research* 2 (1975); 246–59.

INFORMATION ACQUISITION

The functions of paying attention, encoding, memory, and problem solving all depend on the *availability* of information. Bettman's model of information processing (Figure 8-3, shown previously) illustrates the interaction of external and internal information acquisition with each of the other four aspects of information processing. The broad scope of this fifth and last aspect is not surprising when we realize that **information acquisition** refers to all the ways in which we obtain information. **External information** comes from the environment while **internal information** is recalled from storage in memory. External information in the marketplace includes advertisements, personal sales messages, the comments of other shoppers, free sample promotions, data on package labels, displays in

information acquisition
external information
internal information

stores, brochures, and other types of communications. Internal information is the consumer's own insights developed from experience and stored for use when needed.

Marketers can use different strategies to influence the external information buyers receive, and therefore the types of internal information they store for future use. They should be aware of the effects of various marketing strategies on information processing. For example, research conducted on two new-product commercials—one run for viewers at normal speed and one run 20% faster than normal—showed a difference in how the viewers processed the information. Although viewers of the speeded up commercial were seldom aware of the time compression, apparently "time compression can interfere with the way a viewer attends to, encodes, or recalls information from a commercial so that fewer ideas are played back." The investigators found that time compression can inhibit both positive and negative attitudes toward a brand, and that the effects of time compression tend to vary according to the product and the commercial format. For example, cartoons and more familiar advertising campaigns are probably less affected by the use of time compression.[36] Another study concluded that the structure and content of pictorial print

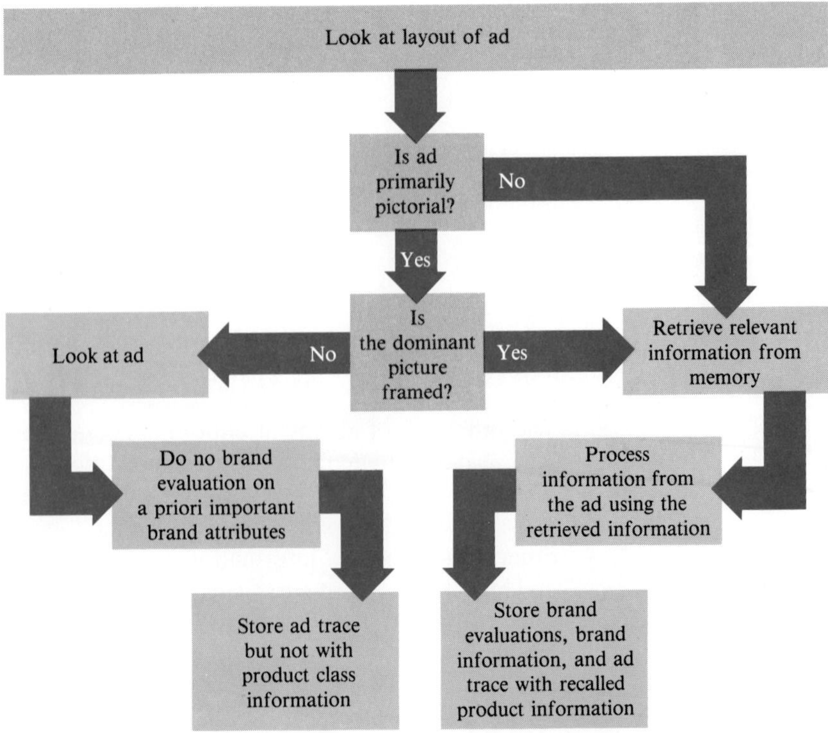

Source: Julie A. Edell and Richard Staelin, "The Information Processing of Pictures in Print Advertisements," *Journal of Consumer Research* 10 (1983), 48.

Figure 8-8
Process Model of How People View a Print Ad

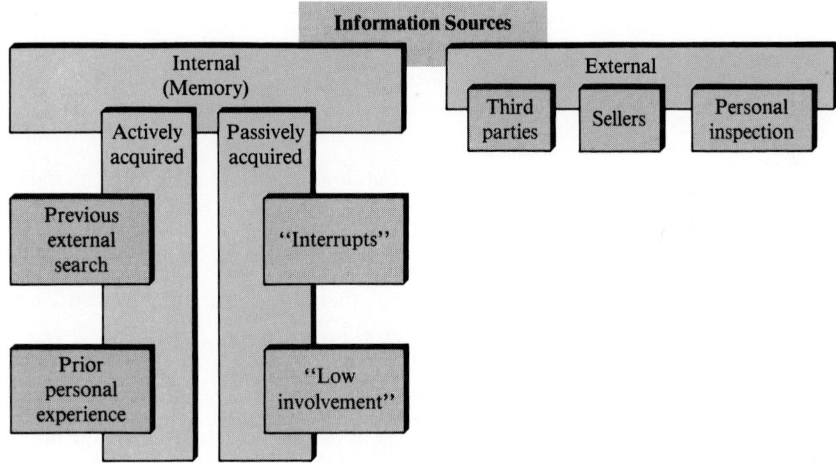

Figure 8-9
Sources of Consumer Information

Source: adapted from Howard Beales, Michael B. Mazis, Steven C. Salop, and Richard Staelin, "Consumer Search and Public Policy," *Journal of Consumer Research* 8 (June 1981), 12.

advertisements had a noticeable effect on how readers process such ads.[37] Figure 8-8 shows a model of this process.

Since strategies such as time compression and pictorial content can affect the type and amount of information retained, marketers should be careful in their use of such techniques. However, it is not always necessary to remember all the attributes of a product. In fact, consumers use their memories economically. Rather than memorizing all the details about products they may want to buy, shoppers tend to rely on information stored externally. Data which is readily available on packages, in *Consumer Reports* magazine, or from other information sources need not clutter up their minds. Memory can be reserved for strategies for certain *types* of purchases and for other generalized rules.

Figure 8-9 provides an overview of the sources of information.[38] Sources may be internal or external. Internal (memory) sources may be of two kinds: that which was actively acquired in the past (such as by shopping, trial, experience) and that which was passively absorbed (such as an ad casually noticed while thumbing through an unfamiliar magazine in a doctor's office). External sources may include third parties (friends, relatives, and neighbors), sellers (a car dealer), or personal inspection (a test drive).

THE MARKETING APPLICATION: RULES FOR STRUCTURING MESSAGES

Here are a few of the general rules for structuring messages based on information processing concepts:

1. Gain consumer attention by using new and novel ideas in messages, and use them early in the message.
2. Encoding is both pictorial (episodic) and verbal (semantic). Messages with both pictorial and verbal content are more easily understood and remembered.
3. Messages containing pictorial elements enhance recognition; those with verbal content aid recall and analysis.
4. Make the amount of information presented proportionate to the amount of time buyers have to process it. Repeat key content so that rehearsal takes place and the amount of information put in long-term memory increases.
5. Present content information in chunks that are consistent with the consumer's previous experiences.
6. Because consumers rely on external storage for much of the information they use, repeat claims presented in ads at the point of purchase.
7. To facilitate brand comparisons, present information by attribute.
8. If consumers are considering only one brand (or to make brand comparisons difficult), present information by brand.

SUMMARY

Information processing explains how the human brain uses information and decision rules to make brand choices. Five aspects of information processing are important: (1) attention, (2) encoding, (3) memory, (4) problem solving, and (5) information acquisition.

Before any information is processed, the consumer must be ready to work on it. Attention is the allocation of limited perceptual capacity to one of many purchase situations with which they could be involved. Once attention is gained, marketing messages are encoded. Both pictorial, or episodic, codes and verbal, or symbolic, codes achieve an optimal representation of reality in the mind. The encoded information can then be stored in memory. Although there are several interpretations of how memory functions, the most important aspects are short-term and long-term memory. Short-term memory takes newly coded information and interprets it in light of existing information recalled from storage. Long-term memory stores information indefinitely for recall and use at appropriate times. The fourth area of information processing, problem solving, concerns how brand choices are made. Five types of stored rules, or heuristics, allow consumers to arrive at choices: affect-referral, compensatory, lexicographic, conjunctive, and risk models.

All aspects of the information processing concept involve the internal and external acquisition of information. Information stored on packages, published in brochures, announced in ads, and presented at the point of purchase are often needed because buyers do not memorize everything about the products they buy. This external information is combined with stored (internal) information during the decision-making process. When marketers present information in easy-to-use formats, they aid consumers in the difficult task of sorting and sifting all the information necessary to make their purchase decisions.

KEY TERMS

information processing
input
processing
output
attention
encoding
episodes
semantic memory
dual-coding hypothesis
schemata
recognition
recall
sensory memory
decay
short-term memory
chunk
rehearsal
transfer
wearout
long-term memory
interference
anchor clusters
cluster
anchor
levels of processing theory
memory activation
short-term store
long-term store
heuristics
stored rules
affect-referral decision process
compensatory or trade-off decision process
lexicographic decision process
conjunctive (sequential elimination) decision process
risk models
constructive mechanism
protocol analysis
choice by processing brands (CPB)
choice by processing attributes (CPA)
information acquisition
external information
internal information

QUESTIONS

1. Information processing brings together what five major functions? What is meant by *scanner-interrupt*?
2. Briefly explain the dual-coding hypothesis. How does this relate to left/right brain theory and what are the potential implications for advertisers?
3. Describe the three states of memory: sensory, short-term, and long-term. Why is long-term memory so important to marketers? Include the concepts of anchors and clusters in your response.
4. What are heuristics? Give an example of a stored rule for choosing what brand of coffee to buy.
5. Distinguish between CPA and CPB strategies for brand choice. Which type of strat-

egy do you believe is used most often by new-car purchasers? Explain.

6. Information acquisition includes both internal and external sources of information. Briefly describe three ways in which marketers can manipulate external information.

NOTES

1. Morton Hunt, *The Universe Within* (New York: Simon and Schuster, 1982), 18–19.
2. Wilbert J. McKeachie and Charlotte L. Doyle, *Psychology* (Reading, MA: Addison-Wesley, 1966), 171.
3. James P. Forkan, "Houseman Named '82 Star Presenter," *Advertising Age* (August 16, 1982): 3, 67.
4. J. Edward Russo, "Comments on Behavioral and Economic Approaches to Studying Market Behavior," in *The Effects of Information on Consumer and Market Behavior,* A. A. Mitchell, ed. (Chicago: American Marketing Association, 1978), 65–74.
5. For a complete review of the theoretical underpinning of encoding processes in buyer behavior, see Morris B. Holbrook and William L. Moore, "Cue Configurality in Esthetic Responses," in *Symbolic Consumer Behavior,* Elizabeth C. Herschman and Morris B. Holbrook, eds. (Ann Arbor: Association for Consumer Research, 1981).
6. Morris B. Holbrook and William L. Moore, "Feature Interactions in Consumer Judgments of Verbal Versus Pictorial Presentations," *Journal of Consumer Research* 8 (1981): 103–13.
7. John A. Howard, *Consumer Behavior: Application of Theory* (New York: McGraw-Hill, 1977), 41.
8. Allan Paivo, *Imagery and Verbal Processes* (New York: Holt, Rinehart and Winston, 1971), and Paivo, "A Dual Coding Approach to Perception and Cognition," in Herbert L. Pick, Jr. and Elliot Saltzma *Modes of Perceiving and Processing Information* (Hillsdale, NJ: Lawrence Erlbaum, 1978) 16–25.
9. S. M. Kosslyn and S. P. Schwartz, "A Data-Driven Simulation of Visual Imagery," *Cognitive Science* 1 (1977): 265–96.
10. The knowledge schemata approach is summarized from Jerry C. Olson, "Encoding Processes: Levels of Processing and Existing Knowledge," in *Advances in Consumer Research* VII, Jerry C. Olson, ed. (Chicago: Association for Consumer Research, 1979), 154–60.
11. Much of this material has been summarized from Flemming Hansen, "Hemispherical Lateralization: Implications for Understanding Consumer Behavior," *Journal of Consumer Research* 8 (June 1981): 23–36.
12. For further discussion of brain hemisphere research, see Sidney Weinstein, "A Review of Brain Hemisphere Research," *Journal of Advertising Research* 22 (1982): 59–63; and William A. Katz, "Point of View: A Critique of Split Brain Theory," *Journal of Advertising Research* 23 (1983): 63–64.
13. Doreen Kirmura, "The Asymmetry of the Human Brain: Recent Progress in Perception," *Scientific American* 232 (1973): 232, 246–54, as reported in Flemming Hansen, "Hemispherical Lateralization," 23–36.
14. Herbert E. Krugman, "Memory Without Recall, Exposure Without Recognition," *Journal of Advertising* 17 (1977): 7–12.
15. Material for this section is adapted from James R. Bettman, "Memory Factors in Consumer Choice: A Review," *Journal of Marketing* 43, No. 2 (1979): 37–53.
16. Adapted from James R. Bettman, "Memory Factors," *Journal of Marketing* p. 37.
17. Selective attention is briefly explained in Chapter 2 on motivation and discussed in detail in Chapter 3 on perception.
18. Herbert A. Simon, "How Big Is a Chunk?" *Science* 183 (February 8, 1974): 369, citing E. A. Feigenbaum, "The Stimulation of Verbal Learning Behavior," in *Proceedings of Western Joint Computer Conference,* (1961): 121–32.
19. James R. Bettman, "Issues in Designing Consumer Information Environments," *Journal of Consumer Research* 2 (1975):171.
20. Consumer groups and the Federal Trade Commission are exploring how rehearsal can be used to help consumers shop more wisely.
21. Bobby J. Calder and Brian Sternthal, "Television Commercial Wearout: An Information Processing View," *Journal of Marketing Research* 17 (1980): 173–86.
22. For more on evoked sets, refer to Chapter 4.
23. Alice M. Tybout, Bobby J. Calder, and Brian Sternthal, "Using Information Processing Theory to Design Marketing Strategies," *Journal of Marketing Research* 18 (1981):73–79.
24. Olson, "Encoding Processes," 154–60.
25. Fergus I. M. Craik and Robert S. Lockhart, "Levels of Processing: A Framework for Memory Research,"

Journal of Verbal Learning and Verbal Behavior (1972): 671–84.

26. Richard M. Schiffrin and R. C. Atkinson, "Storage and Retrieval Processes in Long-Term Memory," *Psychological Review* 76 (1970): 179–83, as quoted by Bettman, "Memory Factors in Consumer Choice: A Review," *Journal of Marketing* 43 (Spring 1979): 39.
27. James R. Bettman and Michael A. Zins, "Constructive Processes in Consumer Choice," *Journal of Consumer Research* 4 (1977): 75–85.
28. Peter Wright and Fredric Barbour, "The Relevance of Decision Process Models in Structuring and Persuasive Messages," *Communication Research* 2 (1975): 246–59.
29. Wright and Barbour, "Relevance," 246–59.
30. Bettman and Zins, "Constructive Processes," 75–85.
31. Peter Wright and Peter D. Rip, "Product Class Advertising Effects on First-Time Buyers' Decision Strategies," *Journal of Consumer Research* 7 (1980): 176–88.
32. Bettman and Zins, "Constructive Processes," 75–85.
33. These are merely broader groupings of the five decision rules presented in the previous section.
34. Jacob Jacoby, Robert W. Chestnut, Karl C. Weigl and William Fisher, "Prepurchase Information Acquisition: Description of a Process Methodology, Research Paradigm, and Pilot Investigation," in *Advances in Consumer Research* III, Beverlee B. Anderson, ed. (Chicago: Association for Consumer Research, 1976), 306–404; Edward Russo and Larry D. Rosen, "An Eye Fixation Analysis of Multi-Alternative Choice," *Memory and Cognition* 3 (1975): 267–76.
35. James R. Bettman and Pradeep Kakkar, "Effects of Information Presentation Format on Consumer Information Acquisition Strategies," *Journal of Consumer Research* 3, No. 4 (1977): 233–40; Eric J. Johnson and J. Edward Russo, "The Organization of Product Information in Memory Identified by Recall Times," *Advances in Consumer Research* V, in H. Keith Hunt, ed. (Chicago: Association for Consumer Research, 1978), 79–86.
36. M. J. Rawlings Schlinger, L. F. Alivett, K. E. McCarthy, and Leila Green, "Effects of Time Compression on Attitudes and Information Processing," *Journal of Marketing* 47 (1983): 79–85.
37. Julie A. Edell and Richard Staelin, "The Information Processing of Pictures in Print Advertisements," *Journal of Consumer Research* 10 (1983): 45–60.
38. Howard Beales, Michael B. Mazis, Steven C. Salop, and Richard Staelin, "Consumer Search and Public Policy," *Journal of Consumer Research* 8 (June 1981): 11–22.

FURTHER READING

Classics

Bettman, James R., "Information Processing Models of Consumer Behavior," *Journal of Marketing Research* 7 (August 1970): 370–76.

Bettman, James R., "Issues in Designing Consumer Information Environments," *Journal of Consumer Research* 2 (December 1975): 169–77.

Bettman, James R., and Jacob Jacoby, "Patterns of Processing in Consumer Information Acquisition," in *Advances in Consumer Research,* Vol. III, B. B. Anderson, ed. (Chicago: Association for Consumer Research, 1975).

Chestnut, Robert W., and Jacob Jacoby, "Consumer Information Processing: Emerging Theory and Findings," in *Consumer and Industrial Buying Behavior,* Woodside, Sheth, and Bennett, eds. (New York: North-Holland, 1977), 119–33.

Edell, Julie A., and Andrew A. Mitchell, "An Information Processing Approach to Cognitive Response," in *Research Frontiers in Marketing: Dialogues and Directions,* Subhash C. Jain, ed. (Chicago: American Marketing Association, 1978), 178–83.

Hansen, Flemming, "Psychological Theories of Consumer Choice," *Journal of Consumer Research* 3 (December 1976); 117–42.

Jacoby, Jacob, Donald E. Speller, and Carol A. Kohn, "Brand Choice Behavior as a Function of Information Load: Replication and Extension," *Journal of Consumer Research* 1 (1974): 33–42.

Jacoby, Jacob, George J. Szybillo, and J. Busato-Schach, "Information–Acquisition Behavior in Brand Choice Situations," *Journal of Consumer Research* 3 (March 1977): 209–16.

Miller, George A., "The Magical Number Seven, Plus or Minus Two: Some Limits on Our Capacity for Processing Information," *Psychological Review* 63 (1956): 81–97.

Russo, J. Edward, "More Information is Better: A

Reevaluation of Jacoby, Speller, and Kohn," *Journal of Consumer Research* 1 (December 1974): 68–72.

Scammon, Debra L., " 'Information Load' and Consumers," *Journal of Consumer Research* 2 (December 1975): 148–55.

Simon, Herbert A., "How Big Is a Chunk?" *Science* 183 (February 8, 1974): 482–88.

Wilkie, William L., "Analysis of Effects of Information Load," *Journal of Marketing Research* 11 (November 1974): 462–66.

Recent Significant Research

Bettman, James R., "Memory Factors in Consumer Choice: A Review," *Journal of Marketing* 43 (Spring 1979): 37–53.

Capon, Noel, and Marian Burke, "Individual, Product Class, and Task-Related Factors in Consumer Information Processing," *Journal of Consumer Research* 7 (December 1980): 314–26.

Furse, David H., Girish N. Punj, and David W. Stewart, "A Typology of Individual Search Strategies Among Purchasers of New Automobiles," *Journal of Consumer Research* 10 (March 1984): 417–31.

Gardner, Meryl Paula, "Advertising Effects on Attributes Recalled and Criteria Used for Brand Evaluations," *Journal of Consumer Research* 10, No. 3 (December 1983): 310–18.

Jacoby, Jacob, "Perspectives on Information Overload," *Journal of Consumer Research* 10 (March 1984): 432–35.

Jacoby, Jacob, and Wayne D. Hoyer, "Viewer Miscomprehension of Televised Communication: Selected Findings," *Journal of Marketing* 46, No. 4, (Fall 1982): 12–26.

Lynch, John G., Jr., and Thomas K. Srull, "Memory and Attentional Factors in Consumer Choice: Concepts and Research Methods," *Journal of Consumer Research* 9 (June 1982): 18–37.

Malhotra, Naresh K., Arun K. Jain, and Stephen W. Lagakos, "The Information Overload Controversy: An Alternative Viewpoint," *Journal of Marketing* 46 (Spring 1982): 27–37.

Punj, Girish N., and David W. Stewart, "An Interaction Framework of Consumer Decision Making," *Journal of Consumer Research* 10 (September 1983): 181–96.

Applications

Beales, Howard, Michael B. Mazis, Steven C. Salop, and Richard Staelin, "Consumer Search and Public Policy," *Journal of Consumer Research* 8 (June 1981): 11–22.

Biehal, Gabriel, and Dipankar Chakravarti, "Information Accessibility as a Moderator of Consumer Choice," *Journal of Consumer Research* 10 (June 1983): 1–14.

Dommeyer, Curt J., and Stephen D. Calvert, "An Empirical Investigation of the Effects of Information Load," in *Proceedings of the Division of Consumer Psychology,* James C. Anderson, ed. (San Antonio, TX: American Psychological Association, 1983), 17–20.

Edell, Julie A., and Richard Staelin, "The Information Processing of Pictures in Print Advertising," *Journal of Consumer Research* 10 (June 1983): 45–61.

Firstenberg, Iris R., and Robert A. Bjork, "Memory Dynamics and Marketing," in *Proceedings of the Division of Consumer Psychology,* James C. Anderson, ed. (Washington, D.C.: American Psychological Association, 1983), 4–6.

Goodwin, Stephen, and Michael Etgal, "An Experimental Investigation of Comparative Advertising: Impact of Message Appeal, Information Load, and Utility of Product Class," *Journal of Marketing Research* 17, No. 2 (May 1980): 187–202.

Holbrook, Morris B., and William L. Moore, "Feature Interactions in Consumer Judgments of Verbal Versus Pictorial Presentations," *Journal of Consumer Research* 8 (June 1981): 103–13.

Jacoby, Jacob, "Consumer Reaction to Information Displays: Packaging and Advertising," in *Advertising and Public Interest,* Salvatore F. Divita, ed. (Chicago: American Marketing Association, 1974), 101–18.

Kelley, Craig A., and Teresa A. Swartz, "An Empirical Test of Warranty Label and Duration Effects on Consumer Decision Making: An Information Processing Perspective," in *1984 AMA Educators' Proceedings,* Russell W. Belk, et al., eds. (Chicago: American Marketing Association, 1984), 309–13.

Punj, Girish N., and David W. Stewart, "An Interaction Framework of Consumer Decision Making," *Journal of Consumer Research* 10 (September 1983): 181–96.

Ross, Ivan, "Applications of Consumer Information to Public Policy Decisions," in *Marketing Analysis of Societal Problems,* Jagdish N. Sheth and Peter L. Wright, eds. (Urbana, IL: University of Illinois, 1974).

Russo, J. Edward, Gene Krieser, and Sally Miyashita, "An Effective Display of Unit Price Information," *Journal of Marketing* 39 (April 1975): 11–19.

Webb, Peter H., "Consumer Initial Processing in a Difficult Media Environment," *Journal of Consumer Research* 6, No. 3 (December 1979): 225–36.

Zeithaml, Valarie A., "Consumer Response to In-Store Price Information Environments," *Journal of Consumer Research* 8, No. 4 (March 1982): 357–69.

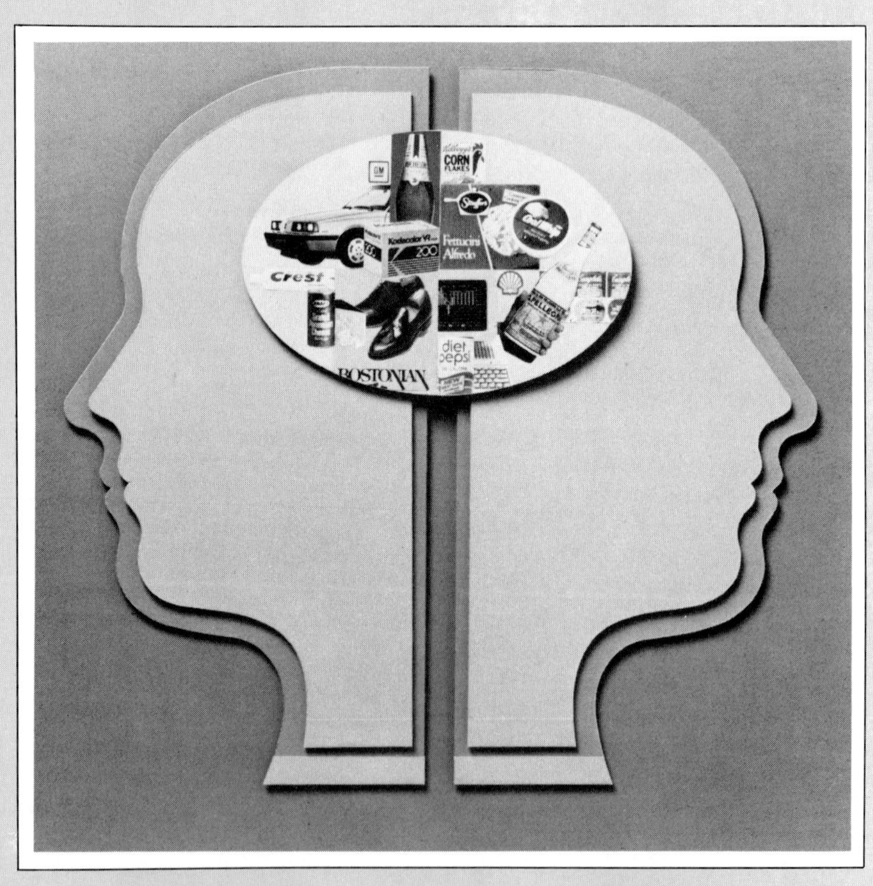
GM
CORN FLAKES
Kodacolor VR
200
Fettucini
Alfredo
Crest
diet
pepsi
BOSTONIAN

II SOCIAL ENVIRONMENT

As Part I has shown, the decision-making processes of consumers are affected by characteristics of consumers themselves. Consumers are also influenced by other people, as Part II demonstrates. This influence, which affects all of us, operates directly or indirectly at a variety of levels. People we see every day as well as those we never see, people who are living now as well as those who went before and helped to shape the culture in which we live—all have an influence on our thought processes. These are social influences that, together with individual characteristics of motivation, perception, learning, attitude, and information processing, affect the consumer's decision-making process:

- Personality and life-style (Chapter 9)
- Demographics (Chapter 10)
- Social class (Chapter 11)
- Reference groups (Chapter 12)
- Opinion leadership (Chapter 13)
- Families and households (Chapter 14)
- Culture and subculture (Chapter 15)

As Chapter 1 points out, the study of consumer behavior draws on a number of disciplines. Psychology deals with human behavior at the individual level. Sociology and cultural anthropology deal with the behavior of humans in groups, at various levels of aggregation, from the household, which might consist of only one person, to the culture as a whole. In Part II we will explore some of the individual characteristics and sociological influences on consumer behavior. Figure 1 shows that the level of aggregation diminishes and the strength of its influence intensifies as the social sphere approaches the individual at the center of his or her own "social universe." The sum of these social influences shape how an individual might consistently interact with the environment.

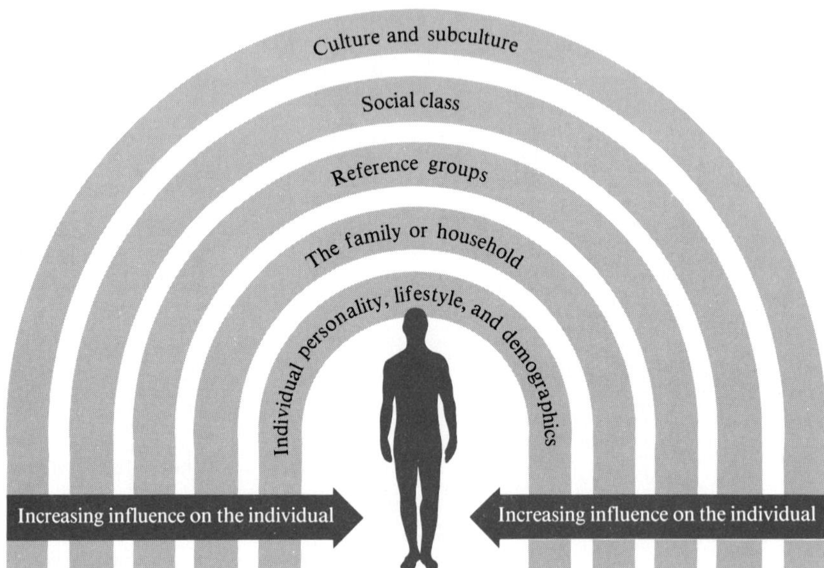

Figure 1
Spheres of Social Influence

In this introduction, we will take a brief look at the individual elements of personality, life-style, and demographics. Following this we will present an overview of each sphere of social influence beginning with broad cultural influences and proceeding to the most immediate influence, the family.

PERSONALITY *(Chapter 9)*

Psychologists disagree on what the concept of *personality,* is; but we know from experience that individuals exhibit a consistent pattern of responses to the world. We frequently categorize or ''type'' people as having personalities that are aggressive, shy, authoritarian, creative, and so on. Personality is the unique conglomeration of traits that influence how an individual behaves or responds to nearly all situations. Personality traits are unlike opinions and attitudes in that they are more enduring (they tend to stay the same, or to change ever so slowly) and more pervasive (they affect how the person responds to a broad range of objects, whereas attitudes are specific to a particular object). Furthermore, while personality is very specific to the individual, it is not a direct part of the consumer's decision-making process. Therefore, personality must be viewed as an *influence* on consumer behavior.

Because *personality* is a set of consistent responses which consumers make in relation to their environment, people have sought ways to show how it influences consumer behavior. Ever since Freud hypothesized that personality traits which develop during childhood could explain adult behavior, researchers have been intrigued with the concept. Marketers have used personality to show how consumers are likely to select particular brands. Personality is not part of information processing because it is not likely to change with regard to a particular purchase. The individual's personality will probably remain constant; and although it may influence specific thoughts, it should not be considered part of the thought process. However, personality can give us important insight into another behavioral element: life-style.

For decades there has been an ongoing controversy over how personality affects the behavior of buyers. Recent evidence shows that although many questions remain unanswered, our current knowledge of consumers' personalities is useful in the development of product features, the selection of appeals in promotional campaigns, and other marketing decisions.

LIFE-STYLE *(Chapter 9)*

Life-style refers to a consumer's distinctive mode of living, including how money and time are spent on activities that occupy important portions of a person's life. For example, some consumers are particularly interested in cooking or politics, while others focus on physical fitness and nutrition. Life-style has become a catch-all word for how people live, particularly in terms of their interests, activities, and opinions regarding a broad range of subjects. Whereas demographic data (discussed in Chapter 10) tends to describe people in quantitative terms, psychographic data adds a qualitative dimension by describing consumers according to how they function in society and particularly the situations in which they use various products.

Recently, consumer behavior researchers have begun to study the influence of life-style on purchasing decisions. This type of research is called *psychographics*. Psychographic research involves the study of consumer activities, interests, and opinions. Thus life-style data on consumers reflects their work, use of leisure time for recreation or travel, their interests, such as job, family, sports, the opposite sex, or public affairs, and their opinions about family, politics, environmental quality, and a host of other issues.

Life-style or psychographic studies paint a more meaningful picture of groups of buyers than demographics alone do. For example, in an early study of women who use eye makeup (Wells and Tigert, 1971), it was found that heavy users could be typified by several life-style characteristics.[1] The typical user is interested in being attractive to all men; she takes meticulous care of her body; and she likes travel, parties, art, ballet, splashy colors, and "things that are bright and exciting." She does not like housework or grocery shopping and does not think of herself as a homebody. She would prefer a color television to a refrigerator, prefers furniture to appliances, and furnishes her home for style rather than comfort. She describes herself as a bit of a swinger, who believes that blondes really do have more fun. She rejects traditional ideas such as these: "Women should not smoke in public," "What was good for my mother is good enough for me," and "There is too much emphasis on sex today." Do you see any differences between the characterizations in this early study and typical users of eye makeup today? Times have certainly changed; differences in life-style between then and now point up the marketer's need for the latest studies of the life-style characteristics of the target market.

It is easy to see how such good psychographic information, coupled with information on the consumer's media habits and demographics, can help marketers select the most appropriate target markets, develop product features, establish advertising appeals, and select advertising media.

DEMOGRAPHICS *(Chapter 10)*

In order to better understand their behavior, researchers classify consumers according to the characteristic or behaviors they exhibit. The oldest approach to this classification is based on demographic data. Demographics include age, sex, income, stage in the life cycle, and geographic location. These characteristics of the individual or household influence purchase behavior. Although they are not subject to influence or change by marketers, it is useful for marketers to have demographic information when developing marketing programs. This valuable data is readily available from federal, state, and local government agencies.

Age influences how consumers dress, the types of cars they prefer, and the amount of cosmetics or toiletries they use. Age can also affect the buyer's attitude rigidity, personality, and loyalty to particular brands. A person's sex is obviously a factor in which products are used. Some products are specifically designed for one gender or the other. In the case of shared-use products, marketers are interested in whether wives or husbands exert the stronger influence in the decision to buy. The social roles of men and women, and how they are changing, are also of interest to marketers.

Economists have studied the influence of income on behavior for decades. While it is not the only influence on buying decisions, or even the major one in many cases, income does play a part in determining consumer behavior.

Demographics are particularly interesting because they are continually changing. Consider the implication for marketing of the following demographic shifts of families from 1970 to 1980: unmarried couples living together rose 158%; persons living alone increased approximately 60%;

and the traditional families (married couple with children) decreased about 4%. The average household size went from 3.3 persons in 1970 to 2.8 persons in 1980 (down 15.2%).[2] Naturally, these characteristics influence the consumption of fast foods, use of convenience stores, the demand for housing of various types, and the market for different kinds of entertainment.

In short, demographic data is very important in the development of products for different market segments, the choice of channels of distribution, the selection of advertising media, and other aspects of marketing.

SOCIAL CLASS *(Chapter 11)*

Social class encompasses the distinction between groups within a culture based on such aspects as occupation, income, and education. The concept of class implies that there are homogeneous groups that are relatively permanent. While a person's occupation may change, that person will probably remain in or near the social class associated with his or her former occupation, parents' occupation, type of education (for example, Ivy League college as opposed to trade school), and so on. A clear understanding of the values and motivations within a particular class is, of course, useful to a marketer hoping to target that class effectively. Within every culture, the society is stratified into a number of levels, or *classes*. The fact that all societies are stratified in some way stems from two general truths: (1) individuals perform different roles in society, and (2) society places different values on those roles.

Whether the society is primitive (with roles such as hunter, warrior, and soothsayer) or modern (with roles such as physician, professor, merchant, and garbage collector), the *members* of the society itself create and occasionally review the system of social classes. (The fact that we have begun to call garbage collectors "sanitary engineers" indicates that society is conferring the higher status of engineer on a role that traditionally has been looked down on by many people.)

The phrase *socioeconomic status* suggests that there is some relationship between a family's social stratum (high, middle, or low) and its income level (high, middle, or low). However, the two are not the same. More important than the amount of wealth is the *source* of that income—that is, whether it is inherited, earned as professional fees, salary, or wages, or is received as welfare payments. To illustrate the difference between wealth and social class, there are many unionized factory workers who have larger incomes than most college professors, but society generally assigns the professor a higher social status.

Apart from income, there are several other determinants of social class. Sociologists are not in full agreement on which characteristics are most important, but some of the ones most often mentioned are occupation, source of income, neighborhood of residence, education, and social interactions. These characteristics are used to classify the population into four to six social strata.

Marketers have found social class data to be useful in segmenting markets, developing product features, and selecting media in which to advertise those features in order to position products for specific social classes.

REFERENCE GROUPS *(Chapter 12)*

In addition to being influenced by large aggregates of other persons (a culture, subculture, or social class), individuals are influenced by smaller groups to which they belong or aspire to belong. These are called *reference groups,* because the person refers to them for guidelines on how to behave. If these groups are large enough to include those with whom the individual does not come into personal contact, they are called secondary reference groups. Examples of secondary reference groups are a political party (such as the Republican party), the student body of a university, (Associated Students of Michigan State University), and an entire religious denomination (all Presbyterians). These large reference groups influence the individual indirectly in various ways, among them their positions on public issues, the style of dress they consider acceptable, and their personal stands on certain moral issues.

While large or secondary groups do exert an influence on the behavior of their members, the influence of smaller, primary groups is considerably stronger and is much more significant in understanding consumer behavior. Primary groups are characterized by personal interaction. By way of comparison with the three examples of secondary groups, primary groups for the same person might include the local Young Republicans organization, a college fraternity or sorority, and a specific Presbyterian congregation. Work groups and loosely organized groups of people who spend their leisure time together are also primary groups.

These smaller groups are of particular interest to marketing because they are highly important and highly credible sources of information to buyers. Chapter 12 will refer to word-of-mouth communication as an extremely important source of consumer information. Consumers discuss the brands of products they like or dislike with their friends; physicians discuss their successes and failures in prescribing brands of drugs with their colleagues; and industrial buyers such as plant engineers discuss with each other experiences they have had using various materials. In short, although sellers communicate with buyers in many ways, marketers must understand that buyers also communicate with each other. Communication among primary-group peers can be an extremely important influence on purchase decisions. Chapter 12 will examine the ways in which groups influence buyers and the implications of these influences for marketers.

OPINION LEADERSHIP *(Chapter 13)*

Communication from one person to another is one of the most important ways new product information is diffused throughout groups. Some people are given special roles in the communication process—they are *opinion leaders*. They search out and screen information from numerous sources, forming opinions that are listened to by other members of their group. In this way opinion leaders have a great deal to say about which products, styles, and brands other group members prefer. Additionally, they are important links in getting new ideas and brands accepted—they are *gatekeepers* for their social groups, moving information from outside the group to each group member.

Opinion leaders have different media habits than nonleaders do. They exhibit more product knowledge and interest in certain products. Also, they have distinctive life-style characteristics. Some people are opinion leaders in one group and followers in another. Therefore, they also provide the means for connecting one group with another and help spread new ideas throughout a community.

Aside from identifying opinion leaders and targeting messages to them, marketers can speed acceptance of their communications and products in several ways by understanding the *diffusion* process. Consumers can be categorized based on their use of information and the speed with which they adopt new products. In the chapter, we will explain some of the values, personal characteristics, communication behavior, and social relationships of each of these types of consumers.

FAMILIES AND HOUSEHOLDS *(Chapter 14)*

In consumer markets, the buying unit is generally the *household*. Within the household are a number of individual family members (or in some cases, cohabitants). Family members usually make purchases from a common family budget. They also generally share in making decisions about what products and services, as well as what brands, will be purchased. Marketers are interested in answers to questions such as these: which family member has the greatest influence over what is purchased, when it is purchased, what brands are purchased, and what features the product is to have? How do households consisting of a single person differ from traditional family households? How do single-parent homes differ from two-parent homes?

In any purchase situation, there may be (1) the buyer (that is, the one who actually makes the purchase), (2) the user (who may not be the same as the buyer), and (3) influencers (others who neither use nor buy, but have a strong voice in the buying decision). For example, in the purchase of toothpaste for children in a traditional household, the children themselves are the users; the mother or father may be the buyer, since one or the other usually makes the weekly trip to the supermarket; and the family dentist is an influencer because he or she insists on the family's using a brand that contains fluoride and is recommended by the American Dental Association.

Family refers not just to a household but to one within which there is long-term interaction. The concept is not limited to the traditional nuclear family of two parents and their children. Changing patterns within American society have resulted in a variety of family patterns of which the nuclear family has become one component. There are various categories of divorced, remarried, and recombined families both with and without children. There are also families comprised of unmarried adults. One challenge to the marketer is understanding decision making within different types of families. It is important to know, for example, whether mouthwash is generally purchased by the wife, the husband, or the children in a nuclear family. If it is a joint decision, who has the greatest influence on brand choice, and how is it exercised? Answers to such questions help the marketer target the product to the right audience.

CULTURE AND SUBCULTURE *(Chapter 15)*

A culture includes more than just the aggregation of people in a social system. It encompasses the values, mores, customs, folkways, and norms that are shared by those making up the social system. In addition, these shared values and norms are transmitted from generation to generation, within the social system, so there is a strong link between culture and learning. All of us are products of our culture to some extent. The process by which we learn the patterns of a certain culture is called *socialization* when we are reared in that culture, and *acculturation* when we enter that culture later in life. Whereas the family unit is the principal instrument by which culture is transmitted, socialization is really a responsibility of the entire social system, including the educational, political, and legal subsystems called institutions.

At a very broad level, we can refer to our values as common to "the Western world," meaning most of Europe, Australia, and North and South America. Because people in these continents are descendants of Europeans who treasured their Greco-Roman and Judeo-Christian heritages, they share many values, mores, customs, folkways, and norms which differentiate them from the cultures of the East. These two worlds were traditionally called the Occident and the Orient.

At another level, most of North America, Australia, and Northern Europe comprise a separate culture from that of Southern Europe and Latin America. We can continue the refinement by speaking of American culture or French culture or German culture, because in each of these countries the citizens have a unique history as a nation, an official national language, and their own federal laws, political structure, and other institutions to transmit their cultural norms in unique ways.

Cultural norms may be as simple as how people hold eating utensils—a point on which the English and American cultures differ for instance. They can also be as important as how one behaves toward another person's property (''Thou shalt not steal'' is a generally accepted standard in most cultures throughout the world.) Those pervasive norms which influence consumer behavior must also influence how marketers behave.

Within a culture such as that of the United States, there are a number of subcultures. Among them are blacks, Latinos, American Indians, American Jews, the Amish, and others. Regardless of which level of aggregation we are considering, the individuals within that social system generally share a set of values, folkways, and customs. Therefore, the person's culture and subculture influence the way in which the individual behaves, including prepurchase, purchase, and consumption activities.

Within the culture of the United States, it is important for marketers to recognize differences between the value systems of America's subcultures. This is even more important in international marketing: much of the fabric of everyday life may differ from one country to the next. Naturally, consumers expect sellers to understand and appreciate their culture—or at least to respect it—as the sellers interact with them.

ORGANIZATIONAL BUYING BEHAVIOR *(Chapter 17)*

We have discussed the dimensions of consumer behavior primarily in terms of individual consumers. Yet, a tremendous portion of purchase transactions are made not for individual consumption but for organizations. For most students, the industrial buying environment is unfamiliar territory; however, it clearly represents an important part of understanding buyer behavior. In Chapter 17, we will examine organizational buying from a number of different perspectives.

Organization buying and consumer buying can both be understood as problem solving in a social context. That is, rational thoughts and emotions affect decisions for both consumer and organizational buying processes. While many parallels exist with consumer purchasing, the introduction of new concepts and terminology help explain the unique aspects of organizational buying.

Researchers have identified three categories of organizational buying tasks: (1) the *straight rebuy* situation, in which the organization is purchasing the same product it has used before; (2) the *modified rebuy* situation, in which the organization is purchasing a product it has used before but now faces changes in the available alternatives; and (3) the *new task* situation, which is the purchase of a product or service that the organization has not purchased before. Various members of the buying organization may play a role in the industrial purchase decision. For example, in the purchase of a new typewriter for a business office, the buyer is likely to be a purchasing agent, the user will probably be a secretary, and the decision about the brand, type style, and features may be influenced by the secretary's superior, who acts as an influencer. The social environment—in this case, co-workers—can be an important influence on the purchase decision.

Two other topics will be discussed in Part II: situational factors and consumer behavior models. In Chapter 16, we will examine the environmental influences that effect retail patronage and shopping behavior, including the impact of colors, music, and space. Chapter 18 will review the most widely used models of consumer behavior in order to show how they are useful in solving marketing problems.

NOTES

1. William D. Wells and Douglas J. Tigert, "Activities, Interests, and Opinions," *Journal of Advertising Research* 11 (August 1971): 27–35.
2. "Special Section on Families," *U.S. News and World Report* (June 16, 1980): 50.

9 Personality and Life-style

Objectives of This Chapter

After you have studied this chapter, you should be able to:

1. Define *personality* and briefly summarize major theories of personality.
2. Describe trait theories in consumer behavior.
3. Discuss the relationship between life-style and consumer behavior.
4. Explain how psychographic measures can help quantify life-style characteristics.

Marketers have taken advantage of the important research psychologists were completing in the late 1950s and the 1960s on personality development and measurement. These findings in hand, marketers were able to gain a better understanding of purchase behavior. Today, important research on personality and its application to consumer behavior continues. Recently marketers have begun to use data on consumer life-styles in predicting behavior. Measures called *psychographics* have been developed to quantify this research.

This chapter outlines the individual differences among consumers: their varied personality and life-style factors that influence purchase behavior. First it begins with a discussion of how personality has been defined and researched. We will look at different methods used to measure personality and how the study of personality contributes to our understanding of consumer behavior. In the second half of the chapter life-style and psychographics will be examined. Several life-style segmentation approaches will be discussed.

We tend to describe strangers according to their *physical characteristics*. However, once a stranger becomes an acquaintance, we begin to recognize and appreciate the person's unique *individuality,* in addition to his or her appearance. After we have accepted someone as a friend, we usually describe the person in terms of *behavioral characteristics*. Some people are impulsive, and others are cautious; some are very detail oriented, while others tend to look at the "big picture." Some people enjoy solitude, and others prefer social interactions. Such characteristics are components of human personality. They describe how the individual tends to respond to the surrounding world.

personality

For our purposes, **personality** is the set of consistent responses the individual makes to the environment in which he or she lives and works. Because individuals do tend to respond with relatively consistent patterns of behavior to a very broad range of behavioral circumstances, we are able to identify personality "types." For example, those who tend to compare their performance to others' and consistently try to surpass the performance of others would be described as highly competitive. Because their competitiveness is a consistent response, we are not surprised when they show competitive behaviors while playing golf or tennis, taking exams, or pursuing their career goals. There are many other personality types with a wide variety of characteristics, or **traits,** such as aggressiveness, independence, affiliation, and compliance.

traits

HISTORY OF PERSONALITY RESEARCH

From its inception with Freud, through the neo-Freudians with their emphasis on the social factors affecting the personality, to the more recent quantitative trait and factor theories, personality theory has long influ-

Table 9-1 HISTORICAL REVIEW OF THEORIES OF PERSONALITY

Theory	*Emphasis*
Freud	Instinctive human drives and urges as the strongest force in personality development
Neo-Freudians	Social influences as the most important force in personality development
Adler	Drive to overcome feelings of inferiority
Fromm	Love and companionship
Horney	Interpersonal orientation
Trait and Factor Theories	Quantification of personality according to scaled descriptions
Gordon	Personal profile
Edward	Personal preference
Thurstone	Temperament
Rokeach	Dogmatism
Inventory	Personality measures

enced the study of consumer behavior.[1] This short history of personality research provides the background for the discussion, later in the chapter, of how personality theories have been applied to consumer behavior research. Table 9-1 summarizes the efforts of the most influential personality theorists for consumer behavior.

The Freudian Foundation

Sigmund Freud and his colleagues were the first to make major contributions to our understanding of personality. Although many of his specific findings are no longer widely accepted, Freud, the founder of psychoanalysis, did provide an important starting point for personality research. He was the first to postulate the existence of the unconscious. He also theorized that personality traits develop during stages of childhood. Freud introduced the concepts of the id, the ego, and the superego—three divisions of the psyche that are expressed in human personality.

id According to Freud's theory of psychoanalysis, the **id** represents the basic source of inner strengths and energies the person draws upon in efforts to avoid pain and achieve pleasure. Freud related many human drives and urges to sex, death, and other deep-seated impulses of the id. He believed that most of the impulses would be socially unacceptable unless they were moderated by the ego, the second basic division of the **ego** psyche in Freud's psychoanalytic theory. The **ego** helps the id relate to the real world in socially acceptable ways; it is the conscious mediator between the individual and reality. Generally, the ego allows the id's basic drives to emerge only when it is possible to achieve their gratifica- **superego** tion in a form acceptable to society. The **superego** is the third division of personality Freud postulated. It represents the moral aspect of the psyche; the superego embodies societal ideals. In essence, the superego is a moral force causing the ego to consider ethical objectives. Freud believed that much of personality is the result of the ego and the superego interacting with the id to shape the behavior of the individual. He was the first to popularize the concept that motivational forces comprise personality.

Freud's second contribution was his study of the development of human personality during the childhood years. He believed that children pass through several stages of development—oral, anal, phallic, and genital—and that these stages have a great deal to do with the development of human personality. Freud considered the feelings and emotions experienced between parents and their children (frustration, tension, love, and so on) to have much to do with the personality characteristics of the children in later years. As Chapter 2 showed, the motivation research work done by marketers in the 1950s often related to developmental phases Freud had hypothesized.

During the late 1940s, the 1950s, and the early 1960s *motivation research* emerged as a significant force in marketing. Psychoanalytically based interviews and projective techniques were used in attempts to uncover the deeper motives and needs behind consumer behavior. The interviews involved depth probing of consumers to encourage them to explore the forces that shaped their behavior. Additionally, the projective techniques involved the use of cartoons, sets of words and pictures rather than direct questioning, to provide data for researchers to make inferences about why consumers behave as they do.

Perhaps the most notable research was conducted by Mason Haire.[2] He investigated the purchase of instant coffee when it was first introduced. Respondents were given two identical shopping lists, except that one specified a brand of instant coffee and the other a brand of ground coffee. The respondents were then asked to describe the shoppers who had made up the lists. Those who had made up the instant-coffee list were portrayed as poor planners and lazy, while those who had made up the list with ground coffee were not. This research led to more research attention paid to consumer motivation.

Ernest Dichter was recognized as a major author of motivation research.[3] Studies were completed for numerous corporations and associations during this period. Examples of some of the conclusions reached by motivation researchers were that a convertible is purchased as a substitute for a mistress; power tools enhance manliness; baking a cake is a symbolic of giving birth; and prunes are a symbol of parental authority.

Today most of the conclusions drawn by the earlier motivation research have been discounted by scholars. Much of this research involved very small samples of consumers, and often the measurement techniques used were designed for clinical purposes rather than to study consumer behavior. Additionally, conclusions drawn by those interpreting the data were often very speculative. A number of critics thought some of the findings were more useful in drawing attention to motivation research rather than for objective scientific purposes. Yet motivation research did generate a great deal of interest in consumer purchase motivation that stimulated marketers to take a closer look at consumer behavior in general.

Although the contributions of Freud find very little direct application in marketing today, this does not mean that Freudian theory has not had an impact on marketing. Many forms of motivation research reflect a desire to get below the surface of conscious motivation and understand the hidden reasons for product purchases.

Neo-Freudian Theories

Whereas Freud considered instinctive, inborn needs and wishes to be the strongest forces in personality development, later researchers believed that *social* influences on the individual were more important. Three psychologists who developed social theories of personality are Alfred Adler, Erich Fromm, and Karen Horney.

Adler published over a hundred books and articles on personality. He stressed the human drive to overcome feelings of inferiority imposed during childhood and expressed by constantly striving to better oneself. Adler emphasized the conscious processes people use to create a unique personality within a social context: people gain fulfillment by developing a unique life-style. This theory could be related to the tremendous appeal of high-prestige products in any status-conscious society. Chivas Regal scotch whiskey, Brooks Brothers suits, and Rolls-Royce automobiles are all promoted in ways that convey superiority—not only of the product, but also of the owners of the product. Designer jeans became popular because they provided instant status in some social circles. Fur coats, diamonds, and prestigious housing also appeal to the urge to be better than others. Some women purchase handwoven Nantucket lighthouse basket purses at prices that range from $300 to $1,000. These are recognized status symbols in some social circles. The demand for these items illustrates Adler's theories of personality. Adler also perceived altruism and cooperation as part of the development of a **creative self.** Thus those seeking a simplified, creative life-style emphasize feelings of uniqueness, value, and dignity—and gain status by their *lack* of luxury consumption.

creative self

Erich Fromm believed that love and companionship are the primary forces that develop personalities. Fromm held that people are inherently lonely because they have been separated from nature and from each other. He saw the desire for satisfying human relationships as a critical element in personality development. The fraternity and sorority systems in colleges and universities, as well as the student's choice of roommates and living environments, serve as illustrations of Fromm's theory of personality development. These types of associations and situations often result in close personal relationships of the kind Fromm described and may thus influence an individual's personality development.

Karen Horney, in her *social personality theory,*[4] emphasized the *interpersonal orientations* of the individual that develop from parent–child relationships. Her theory was that personalities could be divided into three types: compliant, aggressive, and detached (CAD). She described compliant people as those who move toward others. Horney believed that these people like to behave according to the wishes of others and tend to avoid social conflict. According to Horney, because compliant people want to be accepted, well liked, and helpful to the group, they would even be likely to subjugate their own desires to those of the group. People with this type of personality tend to have a high degree of social awareness. The Dial soap slogan is aimed at the compliant personality: "Aren't you glad you use Dial? Don't you wish everybody did?"

Horney's second type was aggressive people, who desire power and stress achievement. The self-image of people with aggressive personalities depends on their competitiveness and their status relative to others.

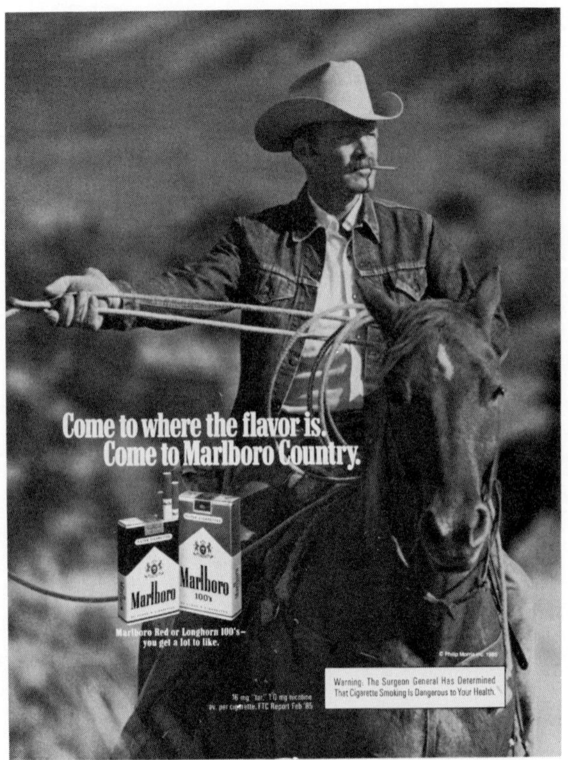

While compliant people move toward others, aggressive people tend to move against others.

The detached personality was Horney's third type. Such people tend to be highly independent and seek to avoid close relationships because they find them encumbering. Film star John Wayne symbolized rugged individualism in America. Likewise, many products are advertised in ways that would appeal to a detached personality. For example, the "Marlboro Man," perceived as a symbol of masculinity and individuality, has been credited with much of that cigarette brand's success.

Quantitative Trait and Factor Theories

The third important influence on consumer behavior theory derives from trait and factor theories, which attempt to quantify the individual personality based on a series of scaled descriptions. Thus personality traits are the names given to describe the tendencies to behave in particular ways. Gordon Allport claims that there are over 17,000 names available to label personality traits.[5]

quantitative trait theories

To apply **quantitative trait theories,** the researcher selects an individual characteristic, such as aggressiveness, and creates scales to measure that trait. To test whether a scale is appropriate, the researcher finds people who have been characterized by other researchers as aggressive, for example. The researcher then applies the scale to the aggressive group and to a group selected at random from the population and compares the scores of the two groups. If the scale is accurate, the scores should differ in the expected way, making the aggressive people stand out. Scales for many different traits and characteristics have been developed in this manner.

factor theories

Factor theories also result in scales to measure traits, but the scales are achieved differently. First researchers ask large groups of people a wide variety of questions; then the responses are analyzed. Tabulating the responses by hand, or using computerized tabulation techniques, they find questions that tend to separate the individuals according to key behavioral characteristics. Finally, using a computer, the researchers group the most significant questions into a few categories that represent the underlying personality traits. The result is a questionnaire that has a scale for each personality that is measured.

In 1967, Joel Cohen measured compliant, aggressive, and detached personalities as described in Horney's social personality theory.[6] Cohen believed that *compliant* personality types would more often favor products designed to enhance social relationships; *aggressive* types would probably choose products symbolizing high status; and *detached* individuals would respond most favorably to products that offer independence. He gathered a great deal of data and found some support for his contentions.

Most notably, Cohen found that compliant people tend to use more mouthwash, Dial soap, and wine than noncompliant people do. Aggressive people use Old Spice cologne and after shave, Right Guard deodorant, and electric razors more frequently than those who are less aggressive. Detached people tend to serve tea several times a week, apparently because coffee is the norm.

Although the study found correlations with personality for the products just mentioned, several other products that were also tested showed no apparent relationship to personality. Those products included cigarettes, men's dress shirts, men's hair dressing, toothpaste, beer, diet products, brands of gasoline, and brands of headache remedy. Therefore, the results of the study were mixed. Cohen found a number of relationships between personality and brand choice or product choice; but none of the relationships was extremely strong and most were discovered only after a large number of products and brands were tested.

The trait and factor theorists contributed two elements to the study of consumer behavior. First, they identified hundreds of traits or factors which have since been included in buyer behavior studies. Second, in attempting to learn more about personality, they refined many of the techniques used in quantitative data analysis. For example, many of these researchers improved computerized techniques, factor analysis, and other multiple-variable techniques for analyzing quantitative data. For consumer behavior applications, the most important trait and factor scales have been Gordon's Personal Profile, the Edwards Personal Preference Schedule, the Thurstone Temperament Schedule, the California Personality Inventory, and Rokeach's Dogmatism. Table 9-2 briefly lists the traits these tests measure.

Marketing Studies Using Personality

In their excellent review Harold Kassarjian and Mary Jane Sheffett listed over 200 studies concerning personality and consumer behavior which have been undertaken by marketers.[7] However, the usefulness of personality theories in predicting purchase behavior has not yet been proven. Clearly, there are some relationships between the two fields of study; but no conclusions can be drawn regarding the relationship between various traits and the broad range of marketing situations. Nevertheless, it is interesting to look at some of the major research findings based on the application of personality theories. The most notable marketing studies are based on trait theories and Horney's social personality theory, which are discussed next.

Trait Theories in Marketing

The Edwards Personal Preference Schedule (EPPS) is similar to Henry Murray's list of social needs, shown in Chapter 2. The EPPS was first

Table 9-2 PERSONALITY TRAITS MEASURED BY DIFFERENT TESTS

Gordon's Personal Profile	***Edwards Personal Preference Schedule (EPPS)***	
ascendancy	achievement	change
responsibility	deference	aggression
emotional stability	exhibition	heterosexuality
sociability	autonomy	order
cautiousness	affiliation	succorance
original thinking	intraception	nurturance
personal relationships	dominance	endurance
vigor	abasement	

Thurstone Temperament Schedule		***Rokeach's Dogmatism***
activeness	stability	open-mindedness vs. closed-mindedness
vigor	sociability	
impulsiveness	reflectiveness	
dominance		

California Personality Inventory

I. Measures of poise, ascendancy and self-assurance:

dominance	social presence
capacity for status	self-acceptance
sociability	self–well-being

II. Measures of socialization, maturity, and responsibility

responsibility	tolerance
socialization	good expression
self-control	communality

III. Measures of achievement potential and intellectual efficiency
- achievement via conformance
- achievement via independence
- intellectual efficiency

IV. Measures of intellectual and interest modes
- psychological mindedness
- flexibility
- femininity/masculinity

used by Franklin Evans in what has become a classic study of consumer behavior.[8] Evans attempted to discover the differences between the personalities of Ford and Chevrolet owners. He concluded that the differences could be better accounted for using demographic studies (see Chapter 10) than with the EPPS, although he did find that there were some weak relationships between brand and personality. Approximately two dozen related studies or articles grew out of this interesting and controversial original work.

Ralph Westfall used the Thurstone Temperament Schedule in another attempt to find differences between Ford and Chevrolet owners' personalities. In an extension of that study, Westfall researched the personalities of owners of compact and standard-sized cars. While he found no significant differences in the personalities of the two types of car owners, he did discover personality differences between owners of convertible and standard automobiles.[9] In another study, William Tucker and John Painter found that aspects of Gordon's Personal Profile could be related to the use of headache remedies, vitamins, mouthwash, alcoholic beverages, automobiles, chewing gum, and the acceptance of new fashions. Tucker and Painter were able to explain about 10% of the variance in the purchase of those items with personality measures.[10] Additional marketing studies using Gordon's Personality Profile have also discovered a correlation between personality and purchase behavior of approximately 10%.

In the late 1950s the J. Walter Thompson advertising agency collected data on nearly 9,000 persons using the EPPS scale. It found that the needs expressed in this personality test could be related to cigarette smoking and the purchase of coffee, tea, beer, and other products. That study provided a great deal of data for a number of research projects. One researcher found that cigarette smoking was related to aggressiveness, sex dominance, and achievement needs, and that it was inversely related to compliance needs. Personality differences were found between those who smoked filter cigarettes and those who smoked nonfilters. These differences were most pronounced for heavy smokers.[11] Using the same data, other researchers found that personality had little to do with the purchase of coffee, tea, or beer.

Several researchers have been interested in opinion leadership as it relates to purchase behavior. The California Personal Inventory has been used to show that gregariousness and venturousness are related to opinion leadership. Additionally, the studies have shown a relationship between innovation and social participation, cosmopolitan, and perceived risk.[12]

In another study of innovation, Jacob Jacoby found that dogmatism was related to innovation. People who tend to be less dogmatic appear to be more willing to take risks and to innovate in their purchases of products.[13]

These pioneer studies of personality and consumer behavior indicate that while there are relationships between personality and the products or brands purchased, the relationships tend to be relatively weak. This is not surprising when one considers that personality is only one of many factors influencing purchase behavior.

After extensively analyzing studies of personality and consumer behavior, Harold Kassarjian concluded,

> What is amazing is not that there are many studies that show no correlation between consumer behavior and personality, but rather that there are any studies at all with positive results. That 5% or 10% or any portion of the

> variance can be accounted for by personality variables (taken out of context and studied independently of other cognitive or physical variables) . . . is most remarkable, indeed![14]

There are several reasons why personality does not relate more strongly to consumer behavior, including the following:

1. Many of the personality measures were designed with activities other than buying in mind. Many of these instruments were designed to measure abnormal behavior rather than normal behavior. There is little reason to believe that consumer behavior would generally coincide with deviant behavior.

2. Even recent studies designed to measure and identify personalities that deal only with purchasing are not specific enough to relate to many single-brand-choice situations. There are simply too many choice situations to be covered by the few scales developed to date that relate directly to consumer behavior.

3. Often marketers have adapted the instruments used to measure personalities in their efforts to make measurement easier, quicker, and more convenient for the respondents. In some cases, they have shortened the questionnaires. In other cases, they have asked people to respond to paper-and-pencil tests in a distracting environment in their homes, in shopping centers, or elsewhere. Given the situation in which they were administered, much of the accuracy of the personality measures may have been lost.

4. Behavior is probably determined by a broad range of personality characteristics that combine to form certain specific actions. The marketing research studies to date have generally looked at one personality trait in relation to a single type of behavior. Studies that examined more generalized types of behavior, such as innovativeness, detected stronger relationships between personality and behavior.

5. In the past, the concept of personality has often been taken out of the context of a total consumer-behavior model. Because of this, personality has not been related to other psychological constructs and to systematic action. (This may account in part for the lack of findings in earlier studies.) In recent models of consumer behavior, however, personality is related to other constructs—but as yet has still not been directly related to *purchase* behavior. To understand the true relationship more clearly, the researcher might wish to add other constructs to the research approaches. For example, perception and attitude may be important. Someone with a highly aggressive personality may perceive a Cutlass as an aggressive auto and may purchase it; on the other hand, the same person may see the brand as relatively low on the aggressiveness scale. While the aggressiveness trait might relate to the type of auto chosen, it would not predict the brand, simply because the same brands can be perceived in numerous ways even by purchasers who have similar personalities.

Although, in general, the research findings correlating personality to behavior have been less than spectacular, they have received a great deal of attention. Personality research does help describe some aspects of consumer behavior and shows how our rich traditions in psychology have helped us to better understand buyer behavior.

LIFE-STYLE AND PSYCHOGRAPHICS

After much research during the 1950s and 1960s regarding demographics and personality, it became clear that these two measures alone could not adequately account for differences in purchasing behavior. Marketers needed more information to develop effective advertising campaigns and marketing strategies. Consequently, during the 1970s life-style research became popular.

life-style

A person's **life-style** is his or her distinctive mode of living. As used in this chapter, it relates to how the individual spends time and money and the emphasis and importance he or she gives to certain aspects of life. It refers to intrinsic characteristics that help predict the person's actions.

The relationship between personality and life-style is complex, and the line separating the two is not an easy one to draw. One way of approaching the matter is to think of life-style as an improvement on theorists' early attempts to relate personality to consumption. Since life-style is to some extent a result of an individual's personality but is a more wide-ranging description of that individual's life situation and in some cases it offers a better prediction of consumer behavior.

Life-style trends are constantly evolving—a fact that affects what and how marketers sell. For example, in one recently conducted focused group, the women interviewed announced that they hated cooking. This major change in attitude may have an impact on how ads are aimed at women as well as on the types of new products developed for them.[15]

Recently Americans have been experiencing other life-style changes as well. The presence of more women in the work force (due in part to the rising number of divorced women with dependents) means that there are more "latchkey children" coming home from school to an empty house.[16] This trend may have implications for the snack-food and toy industries, insofar as parents try to keep these items on hand to compensate for their absence. A far more visible trend is the increased interest in health through physical fitness and nutrition. This major change in life-style is reflected in popular activities such as jogging and aerobics, and in record numbers of women lifting weights to get into shape.[17] Furthermore, 70 million Americans are on diets[18] and are changing their eating patterns to include fewer animal products and more grain and crop products.[19] Vegetarian and health-food diets are becoming acceptable alternatives to the traditional "meat and potatoes" meals many Americans still cherish.

One example of how marketers use these changing trends is the opening of the D'Lites chain of fast-food restaurants. These restaurants cater to weight- and health-conscious people who desire fast food but are concerned about the high calories and low nutritional value of most fast foods available from other chain restaurants. The founder of D'Lites considered the changing life-styles of Americans and developed this new food-service concept. The firm's mission is to satisfy customers' desire for healthful

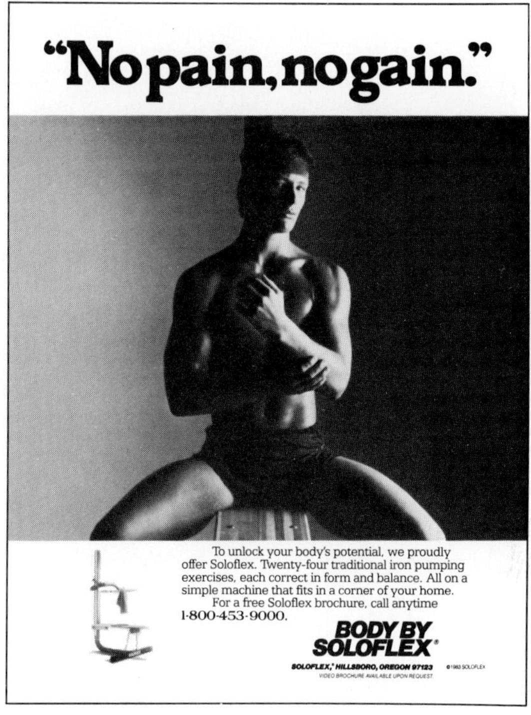

food while recognizing that the time constraints faced by many customers necessitate quick service.[20]

The new health consciousness encompasses only a few of today's changing life-styles. Recent surges in unemployment, as well as increasing concern over environmental issues, have caused more people to seek a simplified style of living. More people are interested in making rather than buying items,[21] demonstrating a higher level of self-sufficiency. Also, many people are choosing less costly camping and outdoor vacations.[22] The results of these and other trends are reflected in the products being developed and the ads used to promote them. Ads for Soloflex body-building equipment appeal to the desire to be physically fit. An ad for Stresstabs is designed to attract the attention of dieters in order to create a larger market for this brand of vitamins. One ad for the American Express Card suggests that users of its credit card lead interesting lives, by showing a woman in executive clothes leaving a sporting-goods store with a lacrosse stick over her shoulder.

"No pain, no gain."
To unlock your body's potential, we proudly offer Soloflex. Twenty-four traditional iron pumping exercises, each correct in form and balance. All on a simple machine that fits in a corner of your home.
For a free Soloflex brochure, call anytime 1-800-453-9000.
BODY BY SOLOFLEX®
SOLOFLEX,® HILLSBORO, OREGON 97123
©1983 SOLOFLEX
VIDEO BROCHURE AVAILABLE UPON REQUEST

Because life-styles are so relevant to marketing,[23] it is not surprising that marketers want to measure what life-style changes are taking place and among how many people. To do this, life-style research has combined the best aspects of demographics and personality research with several

The American Express Card.
It's part of a lot of interesting lives.

additional measures of individual differences. The resulting measures are called **psychographics,** because they are used to describe the individual's mental characteristics and their development. Psychographic measures of life-style have enabled researchers to identify groups of consumers who have their own behavior patterns.

psychographics

Psychographic researchers have added the concept of AIO (activities, interests, and opinions) to demographics and personality. This has resulted in a quantification of behavior which can be used in segmenting markets. The following lists describe some of the key aspects of the AIO concept:[24]

Activities	***Interests***	***Opinions***
work	family	themselves
hobbies	home	social issues
social events	job	politics
vacations	community	business
entertainment	recreation	economics
club memberships	fashion	education
community events	food	products
shopping	media	future
sports	achievements	culture

In much the same way that psychologists have developed trait and factor theories of personality, marketing researchers have developed psychographic scales. For example, in the early 1970s William Wells and Douglas Tigert asked consumers to indicate their degree of agreement with 300 activity, interest, and opinion statements. Following is a list of the 22 life-style dimensions Wells and Tigert discovered through factor analysis, with examples of statements that relate to each one of the dimensions.

1. ***Price conscious***
   "I shop a lot for specials."
   "I usually watch the advertisements for announcements of sales."
2. ***Credit user***
   "I don't like to pay cash for everything I buy."
   "It is good to have charge accounts."
3. ***Satisfied with finances***
   "Our family income is high enough to satisfy nearly all of our important desires."
   "I don't wish we had a lot more money."
4. ***Financial optimist***
   "I will probably have more money to spend next year than I have now."
   "Five years from now the family income will probably be a lot higher than it is now."
5. ***Fashion conscious***
   "I often try the latest hair-styles when they change."
   "An important part of my life and activities is dressing smartly."
6. ***Child-oriented***
   "When my children are all ill in bed I drop almost everything else in order to see to their comfort."
   "I try to arrange my home for my children's convenience."
7. ***Compulsive housekeeper***
   "I don't like to see my children's toys lying about."
   "I usually keep my house very neat and clean."
8. ***Dislikes housekeeping***
   "I find cleaning my house an unpleasant task."
   "My idea of housekeeping is once over lightly."
9. ***Seamstress***
   "I like to sew and frequently do."
   "I often make my own or my children's clothes."
10. ***Homebody***
    "I like parties where there is lots of music and talk."
    "I spend most of my leisure time in my home."
11. ***Community-minded***
    "I do volunteer work for a hospital or service organization on a fairly regular basis."
    "I like to work on community projects."

12. ***Sports spectator***
"I usually read the sports section in the daily paper."
"I thoroughly enjoy conversations about sports."

13. ***Cook***
"I love to cook."
"I am a good cook."

14. ***Self-confident***
"I am more independent than most people."
"I like to be considered a leader."

15. ***Self-designated opinion leader***
"I sometimes influence what my friends buy."
"People come to me more often than I go to them for information about brands."

16. ***Information seeker***
"I often seek out the advice of my friends regarding which brand to buy."
"My neighbors or friends usually give me good advice on what brands to buy in the grocery store."

17. ***New brand trier***
"I often try new brands before my friends and neighbors do."
"I like to try new and different things."

18. ***Canned food user***
"I couldn't get along without canned foods."
"Things just don't taste right unless they come out of a can."

19. ***Dieter***
"During warm weather I drink low-calorie soft drinks several times a week."
"I buy more low-calorie foods than the average housewife."

20. ***The wrapper***
"Food should never be left in the refrigerator uncovered."
"Leftovers should be wrapped before putting them into the refrigerator."

21. ***Wide horizons***
"I'd like to spend a year in London or in Paris."
"I would like to take a trip around the world."

22. ***Art enthusiast***
"I like the ballet."
"I enjoy going to concerts and attend at least one a month."[25]

Another general life-style segmentation study provided examples of male psychographic segments. In this study, conducted by the Newspaper Advertising Bureau, 4,000 respondents completed questionnaires comprised of approximately 300 questions. As in the previous study, factor analysis was used to reduce the responses to these questions to a few highly significant categories. The men in this study were grouped into eight different categories described in Table 9-3.[26]

Table 9-3 EIGHT MALE PSYCHOGRAPHIC SEGMENTS

Type	*% of All Males*	*Description*
Quiet family man	8	He is a self-sufficient man who wants to be left alone and is basically shy. He tries to be as little involved with community life as possible. His life revolves around the family, simple work, and television viewing. He has a marked fantasy life. As a shopper he is practical, less drawn to consumer goods and pleasures than other men. He is of low education and of low economic status, and he tends to be older than the average.
Traditionalist	16	The traditionalist feels secure, has self-esteem, and follows conventional rules. He is proper and respectable and regards himself as altruistic. As a shopper he is conservative, likes popular brands and well-known manufacturers. He has low education, low or middle socioeconomic status, and is in the oldest age group.
Discontented man	13	He is a man who is likely to be dissatisfied with his work. He feels bypassed by life, dreams of better jobs, and more security. He tends to be distrustful and socially aloof. As a buyer he is quite price-conscious. He has the lowest education and is in the lowest socioeconomic group. He is mostly older than average.
Ethical highbrow	14	This is a very concerned man, sensitive to others' needs. He is basically a puritan, content with family life, friends, and work. He is interested in culture, religion, and social reform. As a consumer he is interested in quality, which may at times justify greater expenditures. He is well educated, of middle or upper socioeconomic status, and is primarily middle-aged or older.
Pleasure-oriented man	9	He tends to emphasize his masculinity and rejects whatever he perceives as soft or feminine. He views himself as a leader among men. He is self-centered, and dislikes his work or job. He seeks immediate gratification for his needs. He is an impulsive buyer, likely to buy products with a masculine image. He has generally low education, is of a lower socioeconomic class, and is middle-aged or younger.
Achiever	11	He is likely to be a hardworking man, dedicated to success and all that it implies, including social prestige, power, and money. He is in favor of diversity and is adventurous about leisure-time pursuits. He is stylish, likes good music and food. As a consumer he is status conscious, thoughtful, and a discriminating buyer. He has a good education, is of a high socioeconomic status, and is generally young.
He-man	19	He is gregarious, likes action, and seeks an exciting and dramatic life. He thinks of himself as capable and dominant. He tends to be more of a bachelor than a family man—even after marriage. The products he buys and the brands he prefers are likely to have self-expressive value, especially a "man of action" dimension. He is well educated, is primarily of middle socioeconomic status, and is the youngest of the male groups.
Sophisticated man	10	He is likely to be an intellectual, concerned about social issues, and admires men with artistic and intellectual achievements. He is socially cosmopolitan with broad interests. He wants to be dominant and a leader. As a consumer he is attracted to the unique and the fashionable. He is the best educated and has the highest economic status of all groups. He is younger than the average.

Source: adapted from William D. Wells, "Psychographics: A Critical Review," *Journal of Marketing Research* 12 (May 1975): 196–213.

Table 9-4 VALS LIFE-STYLE GROUPS

Type	*Percent of Adult Population*	*Description*
Need-Driven Groups		
Survivors	4	Old, poverty-stricken, poorly educated, fearful. High purchasers of used cars and meatless meals.
Sustainers	7	Resentful, living on the edge of poverty, youngish, feisty.
Outer-Directed Groups		
Belongers	35	Aging, conventional, content, patriotic, traditional Middle American. High purchasers of both large and compact American cars, freezers, cold cereal, and gelatin desserts.
Emulators	9	Young, ambitious, flashy, urbanized, average household incomes, spenders, socially inclined. Heavy purchasers of high-sugar and high-carbohydrate products, stereo sets, and prerecorded tapes or cassettes.
Achievers	22	Middle-aged, prosperous, self-confident, conventional. Heavy readers of newspapers and business magazines; enjoy playing golf and drinking cocktails before dinner. Heavy purchasers of luxury and mid-size cars, appliances, photographic equipment, and home electronic products.
Inner-Directed Groups		
I Am Me	5	Very young, impulsive, narcissistic, enjoy recreational activities. High purchasers of exercise equipment, motorcycles, and racing bicycles.
Experiential	7	Youthful, artistic, oriented to inner growth, permissive in personal living, highly educated. High purchasers of foreign cars, video games, sugar-free soft drinks.
Societally Conscious	9	Affluent, highly educated, politically liberal, self-confident, high degree of interest in consumer issues, enjoy healthful outdoor sports such as jogging. Above-average readers of newspapers, magazines, and books. Heavy purchasers of subcompact cars, alcoholic beverages, coffee, and fresh, frozen, or canned seafood.
Combined Inner- and Outer-Directed Group		
Integrated	2	Psychologically mature, flexible, tolerant. Have not yet been identified on the basis of demographic and attitudinal items.

Source: from Arnold Mitchell, *The Nine American Lifestyles* (New York: Macmillan, 1983), 61–145.

The most recent extension of general life-style, psychographic research is provided by Stanford Research Institute's Values and Lifestyle Program (VALS). The findings of this research program rest on data obtained in a 1980 mail survey conducted by VALS. The survey asked over 1,600 respondents more than 800 questions. Again, statistical analysis was used to produce a minimum number of items for classification purposes. The VALS typology consists of four groups that are subdivided into nine lifestyles. Each group is characterized by distinct values, drives, beliefs, needs, activities and consumption patterns. Table 9-4 describes the nine VALS life-style groups and the percentages of the population in the United States.

Studies that describe general psychographic segments are useful as a basis for visualizing overall marketing opportunities. However, they are limited because they generally do not contain statements about specific products or types of advertising campaigns. Often marketers must follow up with specific psychographic studies covering particular types of products. For example, many psychographic studies have been done of beer drinkers. The results of two of these studies show the usefulness of (1) a demographic and personality study and (2) a psychographic study.

The following studies concerning beer drinkers exemplify two types of psychographic studies: those dealing with general market segments and those specific to certain types of products and brands. Psychographics have been most useful in providing a creative basis for market segmentation. The quantitative nature of psychographic research allows marketers to determine the size of the segment as well as its major characteristics. In this way they can judge the relative success a marketing campaign might have. For example, a study by Alfred Boote used psychographic segmentation to determine whether standardized marketing across European countries would gain sufficient results, or if these efforts should be tailored from country to country. His results suggested that, due to the similarity in underlying value structures between countries, a standardized marketing approach would be appropriate for some products. He concluded that only slight variations in theme among countries would be necessary in order for the standardized approach to be effective.[27]

In the first study, the personality types and demographics of beer drinkers were of primary interest to the researchers. First they described the market segments, as shown in Table 9-5. Then the researchers developed beer commercials with actors that were stereotypes of the four personality types identified as beer drinkers. Each commercial had a fictitious brand of beer associated with it. After the subjects viewed the commercials and sampled the four brands, they tended to choose the brand that corresponded to their own personality type. Furthermore, the subjects believed that the brands were different and that they could detect differences among the brands, although the four brands of beer were actually identical. In subsequent studies, the researchers found that Michelob, Budweiser, and Busch appealed to different personality segments. The parent company, Anheuser-Busch, was thus able to adjust its advertising and promotional campaigns to more efficiently and effectively target the market segments that preferred each of their brands.[28]

In the other study, a researcher identified the psychographic characteristics of male heavy beer drinkers. He was able to learn a great deal

Table 9-5 DEMOGRAPHIC, PERSONALITY, AND BEHAVIOR PATTERNS OF BEER DRINKERS

Type of Drinker	*Demographics*	*Personality Type*	*Drinking Patterns*
Reparative drinker	Middle-aged	Sensitive and responsive to needs of others; adapts to those needs by sacrificing own aspirations; well adjusted to this situation.	Drinks at the end of day, usually with a few close friends; controlled drinker, seldom drunk; drinking is self-reward for sacrifices made to others.
Social drinker	Younger adult	Driven by own ambitions; attempts to manipulate others to get what he or she wants; has not yet attained level of aspirations but expects to.	Drinks heaviest on weekends; in larger groups in social settings; drinks as a means of acceptance of and by others; controlled drinker.
Indulgent drinker	Various ages	Considers self a failure, blames environment and others.	Heavy drinker; drinks in isolation as a form of escape.
Oceanic drinker	Various ages	Considers self a failure but blames own shortcomings.	Also heavy drinker and drinks to escape recognition of shortcomings; does not drink alone.

Source: based on Russell L. Ackoff and James R. Emshoff, "Advertising Research at Anheuser-Busch (1963–1968)," *Sloan Management Review* 16 (Winter 1975), 1–15.

about this segment of the population. Table 9-6 highlights the main findings of that study.

The changing life-styles and roles of women were explored in a study by Alladi Venkatesh.[29] Three groups of women were identified in the research based on their responses to a questionnaire dealing with feminism, life-style statements, magazine readership, and demographics. The three groups identified were *traditionalists, moderates,* and *feminists*. So-called feminists were found to be younger, better educated, and more independent than the others. They were more opposed to sexual stereotyping, showed a greater willingness to take risks and enjoy physically demanding leisure activities. Clear distinctions in magazine readership habits were noted among the three groups. Feminists read *Time, Newsweek,* and *Ms*. magazines most frequently; *Readers Digest, Family Circle,* and similar magazines scored higher among moderates and tradi-

Table 9-6 PSYCHOGRAPHIC CHARACTERISTICS OF HEAVY BEER DRINKERS

- He is self-indulgent, enjoys himself, and likes risks.
  "I like to play poker."
  "I like to take chances."
  "I would rather *not* spend a quiet evening at home than go out to a party."
  "If I had it my way, I would own a convertible."
  "I smoke too much."
  "If I had to choose, I would rather have a color TV than a new refrigerator."
- He rejects responsibility and is a bit impulsive.
  "I like to work on community projects." (inverse relationship)
  "I'm not very good at saving money."
  "I find myself checking prices even for small items." (inverse relationship)
- He likes sports and a physical orientation.
  "I would like to be a pro football player."
  "I like bowling."
  "I usually read the sports section."
  "I would do better than average in a fistfight."
  "I like war stories."
- He rejects old-fashioned institutions and moral guidelines.
  "I go to church regularly." (inverse relationship)
  "Movies should be censored." (inverse relationship)
  "I have old-fashioned tastes and habits." (inverse relationship)
  "There is too much emphasis on sex today." (inverse relationship)
- He has a very masculine view.
  "Beer is a real man's drink."
  "*Playboy* is one of my favorite magazines."
  "I am a girl watcher."
  "Men should not do the dishes."
  "Men are smarter than women."

Source: Joseph T. Plumber, "Lifestyles and Advertising: Case Studies," in Fred C. Allvine, ed., *Combined Proceedings, 1971 Spring and Fall Conferences,* (Chicago: American Marketing Association, 1972), 294.

tionalists. The findings suggest that advertisers consider different media depending on the audience they want to reach and adjust ads to appeal to different women's segments.

Another example of the application of psychographics to marketing strategy is a study conducted among blood donors and nondonors.[30] Significant differences exist between those who donate blood and those who do not in terms of demographics but also psychographic variables. According to the study, blood donors tend to have low self-esteem and are unwilling to take risks. The researchers suggest that donating blood may be an individual effort to raise self-esteem or, on the other hand, a result of peer pressure to which those with low self-esteem are more susceptible. In any case, the findings that promotional programs geared to increasing blood donorship would focus on reinforcement and testimonials to address the psychographic aspects of potential donors.

Although psychographic research is quantitative in nature, it provides many qualitative by-products, because the statements used in psychographic analysis tend to be highly descriptive. Therefore, they stimulate artistic and creative people in the marketer's company to develop new ideas for specific advertising and marketing campaigns. At the same time, the quantitative psychographic data can be matched with information on media alternatives to place advertisements and messages appropriately. When researchers are able to determine the psychographic segments most likely to view certain television programs, listen to certain radio programs, and so forth, then they can communicate their messages efficiently and effectively to these segments.

In his excellent review of psychographics, William Wells indicates that psychographic profiles have contributed to our understanding of opinion leadership, innovativeness, retail shopping behavior, private brand buying, social class, catalog buying behavior, store loyalty, differences between Canada and the United States, differences between French-speaking and English-speaking Canadians, and concern for the environment.[31] In many cases, psychographic analyses of activities, interests, and opinions have contributed significantly more to the explanation of consumer behavior than has either demographics or personality alone. In other cases, psychographic profiles have tended to be redundant with these approaches, contributing little to the explanation of consumer behavior. Clearly, psychographics can provide a richer understanding of the market segments marketers are attempting to attract. Therefore, they can be useful in developing competitive business and marketing strategies.

SUMMARY

Personality and life-style are two important influences on individual behavior. Marketers have found that personality and life-style information is useful in segmenting and targeting markets.

Personality is defined as the set of consistent responses the individual makes to the environment in which he or she lives and works. Consumer behavior research has been influenced over the years by Freudian and neo-Freudian theories of personality. Many of these theorists developed lists of personality "types." Some researchers used trait and factor theories to try to quantify personalities according to scaled descriptions. Marketers have used personality traits in many studies of consumer behavior; but personality alone does not always relate strongly to buyer behavior.

Life-style and psychographics are more reliable in predicting buyer behavior. Trends in our style of living have a great influence on the types of items we purchase. Marketers have used various methods of gathering information on personality and lifestyle in order to gain insights into these aspects of buyer behavior.

KEY TERMS

personality
traits
id
ego
superego
creative self
quantitative trait theories
factor theories
factor analysis
life-style
psychographics

QUESTIONS

1. Briefly discuss the contributions and shortcomings of Freudian theory in explaining consumer behavior. What implications might neo-Freudian theorists offer for marketing of (a) a Club Med vacation and (b) public television.

2. Research into the impact of personality on consumer behavior has often shown little correlation. Cite several reasons why this is so.

3. What do consumer behaviorists mean by *life-style?* Describe how psychographics differs from demographics using a list of characteristics that could be used to describe yourself with each measurement approach.

4. What benefits does life-style have over personality for explaining behavior.

5. Refer to Table 9-5 to develop a hypothetical advertising message aimed at each of the segments of beer drinkers. Consider what other promotional approaches might be used to target each group. Are there any segments you might try to avoid?

6. Neither psychographics nor demographics nor personality stands alone as a thorough explanation of consumer behavior. Explain.

NOTES

1. For a review of personality and psychology, see Calvin S. Hall and Lindzey Gardiner, *Theories of Personality* (New York: Wiley, 1969). For a thorough review of personality and consumer behavior, see Harold H. Kassarjian and Mary Jane Sheffett, "Personality and Consumer Behavior: An Update," in Harold H. Kassarjian and Thomas S. Robertson, eds., *Perspectives in Consumer Behavior* (Glenview, IL: Scott, Foresman and Co., 1981), 160–80. The latter work is the basis for much of the section on Freud.
2. Mason Haire, "Projective Techniques in Marketing Research," *Journal of Marketing* 14 (April 1950): 649–56.
3. Ernest Dichter, *The Strategy of Desire* (Garden City, NJ: Doubleday and Co., Inc., 1960), 35–47.
4. Karen Horney, *Our Inner Conflicts,* (New York: Norton, 1945).
5. Gordon Allport, "Traits Revisited," *American Psychologist* 21 no.1 (1966): 1–10.
6. Joel B. Cohen, "An Interpersonal Orientation to the Study of Consumer Behavior," *Journal of Marketing Research* 4 (August 1967): 270–78.
7. Kassarjian and Sheffett, "Personality and Consumer Behavior."
8. F. B. Evans, "Psychological and Objective Factors in the Prediction of Brand Choice," *Journal of Business* 25 (1959): 340–69.
9. Ralph Westfall "Psychological Factors and Predicting Product Choice," *Journal of Marketing* 26, no. 2 (April 1962): 34–40.

10. William T. Tucker and John Painter, "Personality and Product Use," *Journal of Applied Psychology* 45, No. 5 (October 1961): 325–29.
11. Kopenen, Arthur, "Personality Characteristics of Purchasers," *Journal of Advertising Research* 1 (1960): 6–12.
12. Thomas S. Robertson, *Innovation and the Consumer* (New York: Holt, Rinehart & Winston, 1971).
13. Jacob Jacoby, "Personality and Innovation Proneness," *Journal of Marketing Research* 8 (May 1971), 244–47.
14. Harold H. Kassarjian, "Personality and Consumer Behavior: A Review," *Journal of Marketing Research* 8 (November 1971): 409–18.
15. "Lifestyle Research Can Benefit Parity Products," *Marketing News* (April 29, 1983): 7.
16. Lynn Langway and Pamela Abramson, "The Latchkey Children," *Newsweek* (February 16, 1981): 96.
17. "Pumping Iron, Chapter II," *Time* (November 12, 1979): 131.
18. "As 70 Million Americans Try to Shed Weight," *U.S. News and World Report* (December 22, 1980): 61.
19. "What Americans Eat—And How Their Diet Is Changing," *U.S. News and World Report* (December 8, 1980): 64–65.
20. "D'Lites Goes After Calorie Watchers Eating on Run," *Marketing News* (April 29, 1981): 5.
21. "Whole Earth Revisited," *Newsweek* (November 17, 1980): 100.
22. "Why More Vacationers Are Roughing It," *U.S. News and World Report* (July 21, 1980): 71–72.
23. For a review of literature on life style traits, see John L. Lastovicka, "On the Validation of Lifestyle Traits: A Review and Illustration," *Journal of Marketing Research* 19 (February 1982): 126–38.
24. Joseph Plumber, "Applications of Lifestyle Research to the Creation of Advertising Campaigns," W. Wells, ed., *Lifestyle and Psychographics* (Chicago: American Marketing Association, 1974).
25. William D. Wells and Douglas J. Tigert, "Activities, Interests and Opinions," *Journal of Advertising Research* 11 (1971): 35.
26. William D. Wells, "Psychographics: A Critical Review," *Journal of Marketing Research* 12 (May 1975): 196–213.
27. Alfred S. Boote, "Psychographic Segmentation in Europe," *Journal of Advertising Research* 22 (December 1982/January 1983): 19–25.
28. Russell L. Ackoff and James R. Emshoff, "Advertising Research at Anheuser-Busch, Inc. (1968–1974)," *Sloan Management Review* 16, No. 2 (Winter 1975): 1–15.
29. Alladi Venkatesh, "Changing Roles of Women: A Lifestyle Analysis," *Journal of Consumer Research* 7, No. 2 (September 1980): 189–97.
30. John J. Burnett, "Psychographic and Demographic Characteristics of Blood Donors," *Journal of Consumer Research* 8 (June 1981): 62–66.
31. William D. Wells, "Psychographics: A Critical Review," *Journal of Marketing Research* 12 (May 1975): 196–213.

FURTHER READING

Classics

Allport, Gordon W. "The Open System in Personality Theory," *Journal of Abnormal and Social Psychology* 16 (1960): 301–11.

Brody, Robert P., and Scott M. Cunningham, "Personality Variables and the Consumer Decision Process," *Journal of Marketing Research* 5 (February 1968): 50–57.

Kassarjian, Harold H., "Personality and Consumer Behavior: A Review," *Journal of Marketing Research* 8 (November 1971): 409–18.

Kassarjian, Harold H., and Mary Jane Sheffet, "Personality and Consumer Behavior: One More Time," *AMA 1975 Combined Proceedings,* Series No. 37 (1975), 197–201.

Lazer, William, "Life Style Concepts and Marketing," *Proceedings,* Winter Conference, American Marketing Association (1963), 130–39.

Peterson, R. A., "Moderating the Personality-Product Usage Relationship," in *Proceedings of the American Marketing Association,* R. C. Curhan, ed. (1975).

Wells, William D., *Life Style and Psychographics* (Chicago: American Marketing Association, 1974).

Wells, William D., "Psychographics: A Critical Review," *Journal of Marketing Research* 12 (May 1975): 196–213.

Wells, William D., and Douglas J. Tigert, "Activities, Interests, and Opinions," *Journal of Advertising Research* 11 (August 1971): 27–35.

Recent Significant Research

Cosmas, Stephen C., "Life Styles and Consumption Patterns," *Journal of Consumer Research* 8 No. 4 (March 1982): 453–55.

Hirschman, Elizabeth C., "Innovativeness, Novelty Seeking, and Consumer Creativity," *Journal of Consumer Research* 7 (December 1980): 283–95.

Hirschman, Elizabeth C., and Morris B. Holbrook, "Hedonic Consumption: Emerging Concepts, Methods and Propositions," *Journal of Marketing* 46, No. 3 (Summer 1982): 92–101.

Roberts, Mary Lou, and Lawrence H. Wortzel, "New Life-Style Determinants of Women's Food Shopping Behavior," *Journal of Marketing* 43 (Summer 1979): 28–39.

Robertson, Thomas S., and Yoram Wind, "Organizational Psychographics and Innovativeness," *Journal of Consumer Research* 7 (June 1980): 24–31.

Sirgy, M. Joseph, "Self-Concept in Consumer Behavior: A Critical Review," *Journal of Consumer Research* 9 (December 1982): 287–300.

Applications

Bernay, Elayn K., "Life Style Analysis as a Basis for Media Selection," in *Attitude Research Reaches New Heights,* Charles King and Douglas Tigert, eds. (Chicago: American Marketing Association, 1971), 198–95.

Burger, Philip C., and Barbara Schott, "Can Private Brand Buyers Be Identified?" *Journal of Marketing Research* 9 (May 1972) 219–222.

Burnett, John J., "Psychographic and Demographic Characteristics of Blood Donors," *Journal of Consumer Research* 8 (June 1981): 62–67.

Engel, James F., David T. Kollat, and Roger D. Blackwell, "Personality Measures and Market Segmentation," *Business Horizons* 12 (June 1969): 377–391.

Fry, Joseph N., "Personality Variables and Cigarette Brand Choice," *Journal of Marketing Research* 8 (August 1971): 298–304.

Good, Walter S., and Otto Suchsland, *Consumer Life Styles and Their Relationship to Market Behavior Regarding Household Furniture* (East Lansing, MI: Michigan State University Research Bulletin, No. 26, 1970).

Hornick, Jacob, and Mary Jane Schlinger, "Allocation of Time to the Mass Media," *Journal of Consumer Research* 7 (March 1981): 343–355.

"How Nestle Uses Psychographics," *Media Decisions* (July 1973): 68–71.

Kinnear, Thomas C., James R. Taylor, and Sadrudin A. Ahmed, "Ecologically Concerned Consumers: Who Are They?" *Journal of Marketing Research* 38 (April 1974): 20–24.

Kono, Ken, "Psychographic Profile of Generics Buyers," in *AMA Educators' Proceedings,* Patrick E. Murphy, et al., eds. (1983): 11–15.

Peterson, Robert A. (1972), "Psychographics and Media Exposure," *Journal of Advertising Research* 12 (June) 17–20.

Plummer, Joseph T., "Life Style Patterns and Commercial Bank Credit Card Usage," *Journal of Marketing* 35 (April 1971): 35–41.

Plummer, Joseph T., "The Concept and Application of Life Style Segmentation," *Journal of Marketing* (January 1974): 33–37.

10 Demographics

Objectives of This Chapter

After you have studied this chapter, you should be able to:

1. Define *demographics* and discuss the various categories of demographic statistics.

2. Show how demographic characteristics are changing in the United States.

3. Explain the importance of demographic information to marketers.

Each shopper is somewhat different from others in terms of age, income, geographic location, personality, and general mode of living. For years, marketers have been interested in analyzing individual differences among consumers. Their purpose has been to developed useful generalizations about which products and brands are purchased by which of the various types of buyers, and why.

demographics

In the 1950s, great emphasis was placed on the use of demographics in predicting behavior. **Demographics** is the study of populations with reference to their size, density, distribution, and vital statistics such as age, income, occupation, and education.

Demographics involves grouping individuals into a limited number of categories based on relevant characteristics. For example, using the demographic characteristic of "annual income," a given population might be divided into four categories: Under $10,000; $10,000 to $19,999; $20,000 to $39,999; and over $40,000 per year. Based on this simple classification, one might predict behavioral differences from each group. Those with high incomes might be more likely to be homeowners, travel more frequently, and purchase more luxury items than those with lower incomes. By using a *combination* of demographic characteristics, a more specific picture of an individual can be obtained. For instance, one could use the demographics of sex, age, income, and location in order to specify a young high-income woman who lives in the western United States. Thus, demographics are a useful means of defining differences among people for marketing purposes. As Chapter 9 showed, another method of classification is *psychographics,* or life-style characteristics. Psychographics differs from demographics in that it focuses on how people think and act. An example of using psychographics would be to classify people by their level of self-confidence (are they adventuresome or reclusive, have active or sedentary lives, tend to spend money or are frugal?). Together, demographics and psychographics help provide a useful profile of the many differences among consumers.

A variety of government publications of demographic statistics, published by the United States Bureau of the Census, are available through the Department of Commerce. Every ten years a complete census of the population is conducted to gather characteristics about U.S. households. These figures are updated on a regular basis by the Bureau of the Census through its series of *Current Population Reports,* using estimates and projections for the intervening years. This data is organized into numerous sourcebooks available for sale directly from the Government Printing Office or through local libraries.[1]

DEMOGRAPHIC CHARACTERISTICS

Because many demographic characteristics are readily available, marketers frequently use them to segment markets. For any given product type, marketers need only look at the types of demographic statistics that are likely to affect consumer behavior for that product. A closer examination of each of the major demographic units is in order, beginning with those on the national level.

The Size of the Population

population size The population of the United States as a whole grew by 11.3 million between 1980 and 1984, an increase of 5%, or roughly 1% per year.[2] A growing population can mean greater opportunities for marketers of nearly every kind of product because, in most cases, the number of potential buyers is thereby increased. For products purchased by a declining percentage of the population, a growing population may help to stabilize sales. For example, total sales of cigarettes in the United States have fallen off due to a growing awareness of the health risks of smoking and an increase in legislation restricting smoking in public places. As per capita use declines, cigarette manufacturers may look to a larger population for more potential smokers.[3] Figure 10-1 shows the growth of the population in the United States over the past 200 years. Since the women born during the post–World War II baby boom are now reaching their prime child-bearing years, the population is expected to continue growing in the near future, despite the fact that women are having fewer children.

Figure 10-1
Total Population and Percent Change from the Preceding Census for the United States, 1790 to 1984

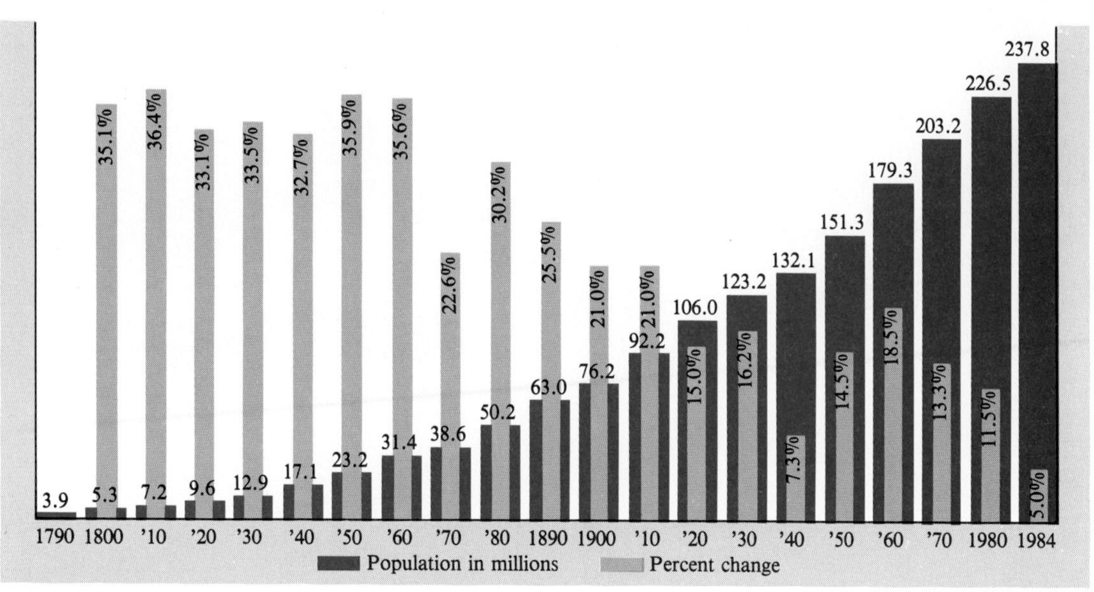

Source: U.S. Bureau of the Census, *1980 Census of the Current Population,* Vol. 1, Part 1, Series PC 80-1-B1 (May 1983), 11; Current Population Reports, Series P-25, No. 966 (March 1985).

Although statistics on the size of the population as a whole are important to marketers, they are much more useful in predicting consumer behavior when they are used in conjunction with geographic data.

Geographic Location

geographic location

Where individuals or populations live is especially significant in predicting their purchase patterns. For example, people in the northern states buy more snow skis, down clothing, and snowmobiles than those in the South, who purchase more summer-weight clothing, air conditioners, and exterminating services. Skateboards and surfboards were first popularized on the West Coast, while "preppy" clothing originated on the East Coast.

Since World War II there has been a continual shift in the population to the Southwest.[4] Figure 10-2 shows the projected growth and decline in population of the various states between 1980 and 2000. Growth in Pa-

Figure 10-2
Projected Growth for Areas of the United States, 1980–2000

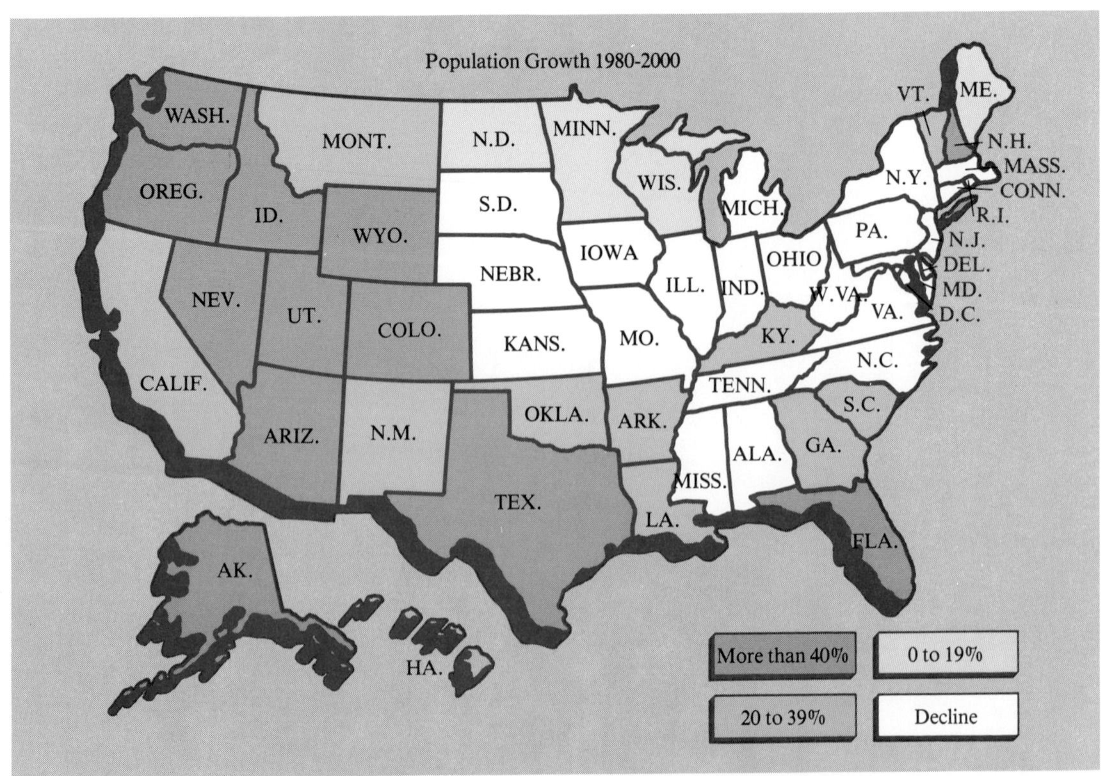

Source: U.S. News and World Report (September 19, 1983):58, and U.S. Department of Commerce data.

cific, Mountain, and Southern states can be attributed in part to an exodus from the snowbelt and the growing influx of immigrants to those areas. Each year the United States receives over 430,000 newcomers, many of whom are from Cuba or Mexico, and these people tend to settle in the South or Southwest.[5]

But the demographic *unit* of geographic location, such as urban or rural, tells more about populations than the larger regions in which they live. This characteristic accounts for additional differences in the products which appeal to various people. For example, herbicides formulated to kill quack grass in cornfields would be best marketed in the country, while commuter passes for a mass transit system would appeal mainly to city dwellers living in and around metropolitan centers.

Geographic data can tell marketers which cities are growing or declining in size, and, therefore, where to concentrate their efforts to reach city dwellers. Table 10-1 lists the fifty largest metropolitan markets in the United States for 1982 and projected for 1987, and the projected percent change in population during this period. These estimates clearly parallel those for regional growth and give sunbelt cities, as populous markets, the advantage over cities elsewhere in the country that are losing population or only holding their own.

These changes and growth patterns will continue to affect where, how, and what marketers sell. For example, the influx of Spanish-speaking people may require marketers to translate advertisements into Spanish or, better yet, to depict Hispanic people in their ads as well, if they hope to reach this growing market. Also, the population shift to the sunbelt may mean a decline in sales of products used in winter, along with an increase in the popularity of warm-weather items. In light of the trend away from northern and eastern addresses, marketers may need to relocate sales personnel to the South and Southwest in order to market more heavily in these growing areas.

A useful source of demographic information about geographic markets is *Sales and Marketing Management Survey of Buying Power*. This annual publication contains market data for counties and cities, metropolitan areas, states, and regions for the United States and Canada.

Age

age The **age** of the buyer is an important characteristic for a great many products. For example, toys are aimed at children; designer fashions appeal to teens and young adults; skin creams and hair coloring products are often geared toward middle-aged consumers, and arthritis medicine is targeted toward senior citizens.

Age can be a determining factor when marketers select media and promotional strategies for products. For example, toy manufacturers would probably use television as their major advertising medium, and

Table 10-1 THE FIFTY LARGEST METROPOLITAN MARKETS IN THE UNITED STATES, 1982 AND 1987

Rank 1982	*Rank* 1987	*Metropolitan Market*	*Projected 1987 Pop. (Thous.)*	*Projected % Change 1982–87*
2	**1**	Los Angeles–Long Beach	8,005.2	+ 4.74%
1	**2**	New York	7,907.2	− 2.60
3	**3**	Chicago	5,978.1	− 0.85
4	**4**	Philadelphia	4,713.1	+ 0.58
5	**5**	Detroit	4,371.0	− 1.10
6	**6**	Boston	3,647.6	− 0.24
8	**7**	Houston	3,638.0	+20.15
7	**8**	Washington, DC	3,465.1	+ 4.49
9	**9**	Nassau–Suffolk, NY	2,679.8	+ 1.61
10	**10**	Atlanta	2,501.7	+10.58
14	**11**	Dallas	2,383.3	+13.99
12	**12**	Minneapolis–St. Paul	2,334.8	+ 6.44
15	**13**	Anaheim–Santa Ana, CA	2,312.7	+10.68
11	**14**	Baltimore	2,254.2	+ 1.37
16	**15**	San Diego	2,232.8	+11.84
13	**16**	Pittsburgh	2,137.1	− 2.05
23	**17**	Riverside–San Bernardino, CA	2,020.9	+18.49
22	**18**	Tampa–St. Petersburg–Clearwater, FL	1,976.6	+13.41
25	**19**	Phoenix	1,950.5	+18.01
21	**20**	Miami–Hialeah	1,923.6	+ 8.80
19	**21**	Oakland, CA	1,915.4	+ 5.62
24	**22**	Seattle	1,862.3	+12.45
20	**23**	St. Louis	1,849.7	+ 2.22
17	**24**	Newark, NJ	1,836.2	− 1.52
18	**25**	Cleveland	1,796.8	− 3.01
26	**26**	Denver	1,719.3	+11.96
27	**27**	San Francisco	1,518.3	+ 1.25
30	**28**	San Jose, CA	1,474.4	+ 7.52
28	**29**	Cincinnati	1,430.9	+ 1.73
29	**30**	Milwaukee	1,421.5	+ 1.41
31	**31**	New Orleans	1,399.2	+ 7.23
35	**32**	Sacramento, CA	1,343.0	+13.25
33	**33**	Columbus, OH	1,291.2	+ 1.69
39	**34**	Fort Lauderdale–Hollywood–Pompano Beach, FL	1,267.1	+14.40
32	**35**	Bergen–Passaic, NJ	1,257.8	− 1.57
37	**36**	Portland, OR	1,253.5	+10.39
34	**37**	Norfolk–Virginia Beach–Newport News, VA	1,242.4	+ 3.89
38	**38**	San Antonio, TX	1,229.6	+ 8.80
41	**39**	Fort Worth–Arlington, TX	1,211.4	+16.50
36	**40**	Indianapolis	1,211.0	+ 2.70
45	**41**	Salt Lake City–Ogden	1,124.3	+15.38
42	**42**	Charlotte–Gastonia–Rock Hill, NC-SC	1,095.3	+ 9.07
40	**43**	Hartford–New Britain–Middletown–Bristol, CT	1,074.2	+ 1.65
50	**44**	Oklahoma City	1,010.9	+11.63
44	**45**	Rochester, NY	991.3	+ 0.93
48	**46**	Memphis	986.5	+ 5.87
46	**47**	Louisville, KY	978.5	+ 1.59
52	**58**	Monmouth–Ocean, NJ	971.4	+ 8.17
54	**49**	Nashville	965.4	+ 8.50
43	**50**	Buffalo	938.9	− 5.61

Source: "Sales & Marketing Management's 1983 Survey of Buying Power, Part 2," *Sales and Marketing Management* 13(October 31, 1983):11.

they would be likely to sponsor children's programs to reach their market. On the other hand, the makers of youthful designer fashions might choose to advertise in magazines such as *Seventeen* and *Teen,* and on cable television networks such as MTV, which shows rock videos. Often marketers use different strategies for the same product to appeal to more than one age group.

For many products, however, age is becoming less important due to social trends. Older adults are taking on the attitude of "thinking young," and young people are moving into positions of responsibility (such as corporate presidents, elected officials), which were traditionally held by older people.[6] The breaking down of age barriers may mean that distinctions between the products purchased by these two groups will become less clear. For example, ads for Lightdays PantiLiners are designed to reach two different age groups. One ad, which appeared in *Seventeen* magazine, depicts a high-school girl and tells why she uses the product. Another, which appeared in *Mademoiselle,* shows a somewhat older career woman and explains how the product fits into her life-style. Here Kimberly-Clark, the product's maker, uses differing approaches to advertise its product to two different age groups, each with its own concerns.

Examples of the breakdown of age as a barrier to product purchase abound. In the future, athletic equipment may become more popular

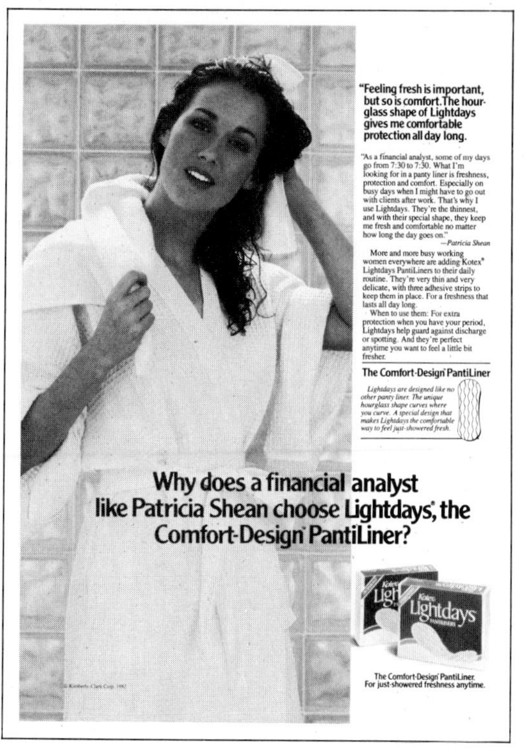

among senior citizens while prestigious cars may be selected more and more by young executives. Wilson Sporting Goods has tested a line of golf clubs called Squire. With weighted bottoms and large grips, the line is especially good for arthritic seniors.[7] In 1984 Sears, Roebuck and Company formed Mature Outlook, a club offering discounts to people over 55. Selchow & Righter Company brought out a version of the game Scrabble with letter tiles 50% larger than normal, for those whose vision has deteriorated with age. And General Foods Corporation won the first commendation given out by *50 Plus* magazine for its use of realistic and cheerful older couples in its Jell-O ads.[8] Meanwhile, Johnson and Johnson is taking a gamble with a special new shampoo formulated for people over 40. Promotions bluntly state that Affinity is for "brittle, hollowed out" older hair, and the spokeswoman for the product is 51.

As with all demographic characteristics, marketers need to be aware not only of the current age statistics on individuals in their target markets, but also of the future trends. The median age in the United States is expected to increase from 28 years in 1970 to 37 years by 2020.[9]

Figure 10-3 summarizes the changes that have taken place in the percentages of Americans in each age group between 1980 and 1983. These changes have important implications for marketers. Products appealing to older individuals (recreational and leisure items) are likely to enjoy increasing popularity, especially since today's senior citizens are generally

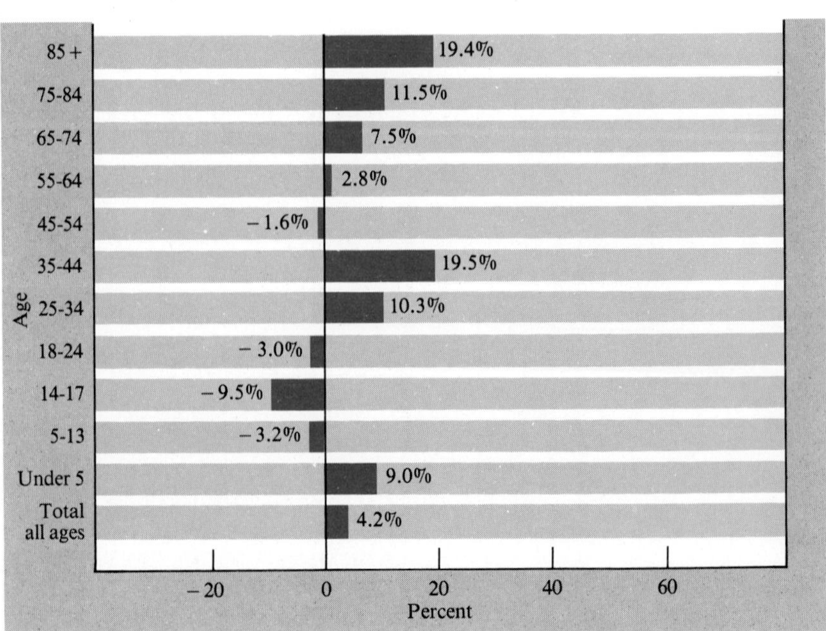

Figure 10-3
Percent Change in Age, 1980–1984

Source: U.S. Bureau of the Census, Current Population Reports, *Estimates of the Population of the United States by Age, Sex, and Race:* 1980 to 1984, Series P-25, No. 965 (March 1985), 2.

better off financially than were their predecessors.[10] Conversely, decreases in the number of children under 15 years of age could affect the volume of toys, children's games, children's books, records, snack foods, and soft drinks sold in the years to come. The fact that members of the post–World War II baby boom generation are now at the ages when people establish households could create opportunities for marketers of housing, furniture, appliances, and other consumer durables.

An older market is getting increased attention in recent years as they increase in financial strength and numbers. The trend toward early retirement and growth in private pension funds is producing a newly revitalized market.[11] Also, improved health care has resulted in a population that is living longer and participating more actively in the marketplace. Thus, marketers of products other than health-related items are growing more interested in appealing to this older market. Use of older spokespersons in television commercials is obvious evidence of this trend. Advertisers are also using models who reflect a more mature, yet vigorous look than did models in the past. The use of actresses Joan Collins and Linda Evans is typical of this trend.

Gender

gender Obviously, many products are marketed according to **gender.** This is true not only for products which are specifically designed for males or females, such as clothing and cosmetics, but also for those items which tend to be used more often by one gender than the other, such as auto parts by men and household products by women. However, as more women enter the workforce and as both sexes break out of stereotypical roles, marketers are beginning to change their strategies for items traditionally used by one sex or the other. Marketing messages are being broadened to appeal to both men and women. An ad for Johnson's Baby Shampoo depicts the father bathing the baby, a function traditionally performed by mothers. Such ads reflect the recent trend toward young fathers taking a more active part in child care. They are likely to appeal to many young parents, of either gender.

While some traditionalists fear the unisex trend (on the basis that the blending of men's and women's roles will result in a disservice to both), the strategy of addressing both sexes may help firms tap new markets for some products. For example, ads for alcoholic beverages, traditionally found only in men's magazines such as *Playboy* and *Esquire,* are now being placed in many women's magazines such as *Working Woman* and *Mademoiselle.* Aside from the crossover in roles between men and women, marketers may be paying more attention to women consumers in part because there are more women than men in the population. Figure 10-4 shows the continual decrease in the proportion of men to women in the United States over the past 90 years. Since the 1950s, women have

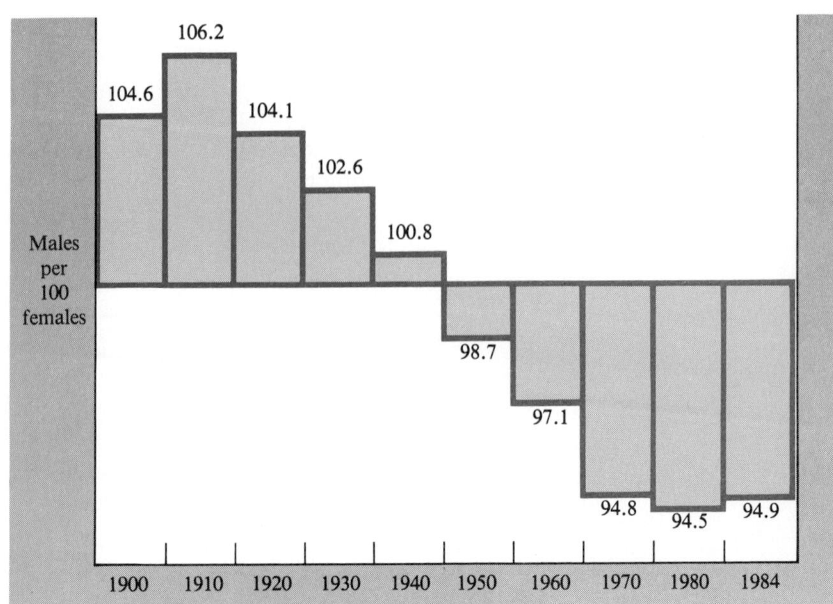

Figure 10-4
Ratio of Males to Females, 1900 to 1983

Source: Bureau of the Census, *1980 Census of the Population,* Vol. 1, Part 1, Series PC 80-1-B1 (May 1983); Current Population Reports, Series P-25, No. 965 (March 1985), 9.

outnumbered men by an increasing margin. With the increased buying power they are gaining from entering the workforce in greater numbers and attaining higher-paying positions than ever before, women represent a growing market segment for many products.

Income

income How much money a person makes has a major impact on what products he or she is able to buy. Not surprisingly, marketers of luxury items such as diamonds and other jewelry, furs, and sports cars focus their advertising on those who can afford these expensive products through selected magazines and other media. However, as an item decreases in price and becomes affordable (and attractive) to a larger percentage of the entire population, the advertising media marketers select become more diversified to reach a more diverse market.

For example, when personal computers were first introduced, prices were relatively high. These computers were marketed primarily through business journals to which prosperous executives subscribe. As the prices of personal computers began to decline, ads began to appear in popular magazines, widely read by people with average incomes. Ads for home computers appear on television and radio, in newspapers, and in many magazines, because they are now affordable to most people. Nevertheless, certain top-of-the-line models with expensive extra features are still pitched to the higher income levels through ads appearing primarily in the more elite business magazines such as *Harvard Business Review* and *Forbes*.

Media planners look for audience demographics of television shows and magazines, matching them to the demographic composition of the market they wish to reach. Segmenting the market by income is important not only for more expensive products, but also for low-priced, low-quality goods. Marketers of these items may choose to sponsor television programs—perhaps wrestling or certain situation comedies—which appeal to those at lower income levels. This advertising approach is often used by marketers of lower priced "gadgets" or products made of synthetic materials that are only available through television offers.

Occupation

occupation Although it is related to income, sometimes **occupation** is an important segmenting characteristic in its own right. Consider the typical factory worker and the average middle manager. While they may have similar incomes, the product they buy may differ considerably. The clothes they wear to work, the vehicles they drive, and even the types of vacations they choose are likely to be completely different. Therefore, marketers of apparel, cars and trucks, and travel packages must differentiate between these two types of consumers on the basis of occupation—and advertise accordingly. In a Levi Strauss commercial, for example, a construction worker wore Levi's blue jeans to appeal to that part of the labor force. On the other hand, a suit manufacturer would likely direct its ads toward a completely different market. For example, in its ads Cricketeer suits would most likely appeal to men and women in business or the professions where suits are the standard work uniform.

Education

education As with income and occupation, the level of **education** an individual has attained can be a major determinant of the products the person uses. This is especially true for many of the new, high-technology products on the market. For example, some computer software programs are so complex that those who lack the necessary knowledge and abilities cannot operate them. Also, data on education level can often help marketers identify prospects for some investment plans or insurance policies which might be difficult for those with little education to understand. Conversely, schools

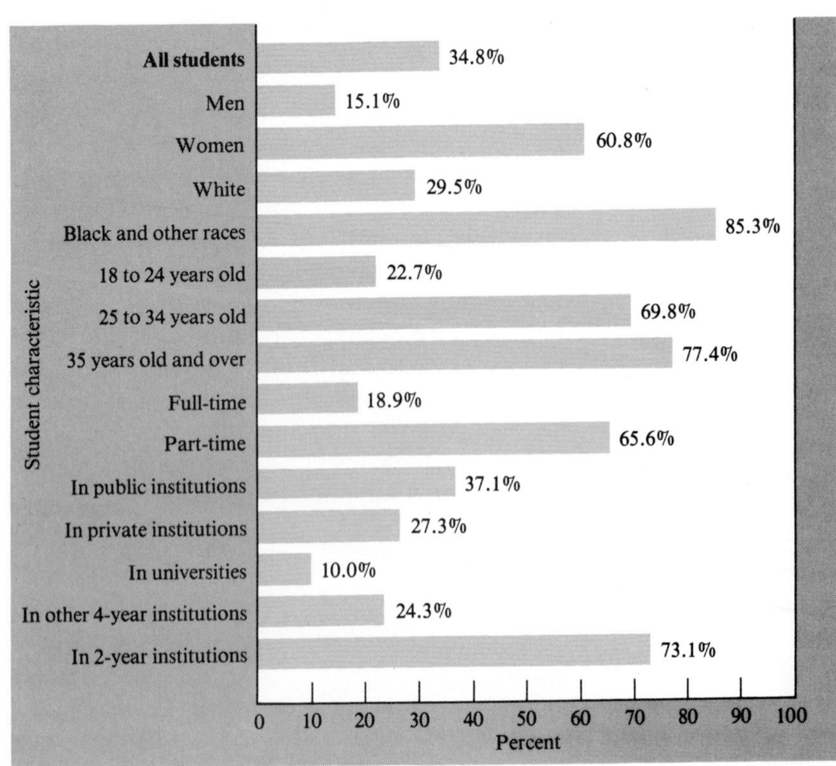

Figure 10-5
Percentage Increases in the Enrollment of College Students with Selected Characteristics, Fall 1972 to Fall 1982

Source: National Center for Education Statistics, *Digest of Educational Statistics 1983–1984* (Washington, D.C.: U.S. Government Printing Office, 1984), 98.

Table 10-2 YEARS OF SCHOOL COMPLETED, 1980

	Elementary	*High School*		*College*	
Region	***8 Years or Less***	***1–3 Years***	***4 Years***	***1–3 Years***	***4 Years or More***
Total U.S.	100.0	81.7	66.5	31.9	16.2
Northeast	100.0	82.4	67.1	30.8	17.2
North Central	100.0	82.9	68.0	29.4	14.7
South	100.0	77.4	60.2	29.4	15.0
West	100.0	86.8	74.5	40.9	19.4
Pacific	100.0	86.5	74.3	41.4	19.4

Source: U.S. Bureau of the Census, *Statistical Abstract of the United States,* 105th ed. (1985), 135.

promoting continuing education would probably want to target people who have had less education as likely prospects for their programs.

Higher education is becoming increasingly a part of American society. Between 1972 and 1982, the number of students enrolled in college increased by 34.8%. Figure 10-5 reflects other significant trends in college enrollments over this period, such as a 60.8% increase in the number of female enrollees and a 77.4% increase in the number of students over the age of 35.[12] Table 10-2 shows education differences by region of the country.

ZIP CODE DEMOGRAPHICS

Income, occupation, and education are the three demographic factors generally used to determine a buyer's social class. (The determinants of social class and its role in consumer behavior will be discussed in detail in Chapter 10.) Although each demographic characteristic can be very revealing by itself, most marketers try to predict consumer behavior and segment their markets by using a *combination* of those factors most likely to affect the purchase of their product. For example, the manufacturer of hang gliders might use age, income, and geographic location to categorize potential buyers, while a clothing designer would more likely consider the sex, occupation, age, and income of those who would be attracted to a certain line of clothing.

ZIP code demographics

One marketing support company has developed what it terms **ZIP code demographics.**[13] The firm has divided the country's ZIP codes into forty clusters which help marketers determine where their products are most likely to sell. Every ZIP code in the United States is placed in a particular cluster according to the type of neighborhood found in that ZIP code area. The type of neighborhood is evaluated based on statistical averages for family size, income, average age, and when the homes were built. Additionally, this company has developed a "ZIP Quality (ZQ)" scale which ranks ZIP codes by how much money residents in that ZIP code tend to have and to spend. Here is an example of a description for a ZIP code in Grosse Pointe, Michigan, in which the cluster "Young Influentials" predominate:

> 48236 (Grosse Pointe, Michigan)—"Young Influentials"
> Up-and-coming young professionals living in townhouses and apartments. Residents like to sail, ski, and play tennis. Lots of joggers and airline travelers. A good place to sell yogurt and mutual funds but not wall paneling, motorcycles, or guns and ammunition. Residents buy 3.8 times the average number of Rolls-Royces. ZQ is seventh [out of forty].[14]

From this description we can infer that demographics alone does not tell marketers everything they need to know about their target markets. Other important factors, interrelated with demographics, are personality and life-style, covered in Chapter 11.

SUMMARY

Demographics involves grouping individuals into a number of categories based on relevant characteristics that describe a population in terms of its size, structure, and distribution. Such categories as geographic location, age, sex, income, occupation and education are demographic measures often used by marketers to segment markets.

The size of the population of the United States has been growing since its inception. Between 1980 and 1984, the population has grown about 1% per year. A growing population means larger potential markets. For products purchased by fewer and fewer people, an expanding population can help stabilize sales.

Where members of the population live helps to determine purchase patterns. There has been a continual shift of the population to states in the South and Southwest, and this shift is projected to continue at least through the end of the century. In turn, metropolitan markets in these areas are projected to increase in population, while those in other parts of the country should decrease or remain stable.

Age is still an important demographic characteristic by which marketers target many products. Yet age has become less and less a factor in the products purchased as age barriers for young and old alike are falling in the areas of health, employment, and life-style. The average age of the population is increasing as members of the baby-boom generation are maturing. Similarly, sex is a primary characteristic by which certain markets are segmented. However, recent trends toward unisex products, and the strategy of addressing both sexes for a product, minimize sex as a segmentation variable. Women are becoming a larger and larger share of the total marketplace, and their income has been rising steadily, making them a growing segment for many products.

Income has a major affect on the products a person is able to buy, and marketers use income as a way of segmenting markets for luxury items and for low-cost, low-quality items as well. Occupation and education also have a major impact on what products are purchased. Those with similar incomes but who make their living in different ways often make different choices of what products to buy; middle managers may buy different kinds of clothes and automobiles than factory workers, for example. Further, those with similar incomes yet different levels of education are the targets of different types of products that often demand different levels of knowledge and abilities to use. The trend toward increasing numbers of the population with education beyond high school continues.

Most marketers combine income, occupation, and education characteristics, as well as other demographic characteristics, to determine the social class of members of their market. One such attempt is ZIP code demographics, which combines ZIP code clusters with the "ZIP quality" characteristics of those who live in that cluster.

KEY TERMS

demographics
population size
geographic location
age
gender
income
occupation
education
ZIP code demographics

QUESTIONS

1. Today's trends in age, income, and education suggest important changes for society in coming years. Select a particular product category (such as health care) and briefly describe the potential implications of these demographic shifts.

2. In what cases might demographics be somewhat misleading for marketers? Given these potential shortcomings, why do you think demographics are often relied on so heavily?

3. Occupation, education, and income are all similar measures and information about one tends to make looking at the other unnecessary. Do you agree or disagree? Explain.

4. Identify three market segments based on demographics which you might choose to target in marketing a new brand of breakfast cereal. What does your choice of segments imply for how and where you will advertise your new cereal?

5. As geographic shifts continue to occur in the United States, what product categories are likely to be most affected? For each category, will the impact be positive or negative? Why?

6. Consider five popular magazines: *Car and Driver, Good Housekeeping, People, The New Yorker,* and *Time*. Quickly describe your estimate of the demographic profile for a "typical reader" of each publication. Which do you feel most confident about? Why?

NOTES

1. For a comprehensive guide to the statistical publications of the federal government, see the *American Statistics Index,* 1985 and Supplements (Bethesda, MD: Congressional Information Services).
2. U.S. Bureau of the Census, Current Population Reports, *Estimates of the Population of the United States 1980–1984,* Series P-25, No. 966 (March 1985), 1.
3. *Progressive Grocer* 63 (September 1984): 122–24.
4. "Who's Gaining, Losing in Population Race," *U.S. News and World Report* (February 16, 1981): 57–59.
5. "The Wave of New Americans," *U.S. News and World Report* (June 23, 1980): 58.
6. "When Age Doesn't Matter," *Newsweek* (August 11, 1980): 74.
7. Charles D. Schewe, "Research Dispels Myths about Elderly; Suggest Marketing Opportunities," *Marketing News* (May 25, 1984): 12.
8. Ronald Alsop, "Firms Try New Ways to Tap Growing Over-50 Population," *The Wall Street Journal* (August 23, 1984): 19.
9. "Life Begins at 55," *U.S. News and World Report* (September 1, 1980): 51.
10. "Life Begins at 55," 50.
11. Hillary DeVries, "The Growing Clout of the Older Generation," *Christian Science Monitor* (Thursday, July 19, 1984): 29.
12. The National Center for Education Statistics, *Digest of Educational Statistics,* 1983–1984 (Washington, D.C.: U.S. Government Printing Office, 1984), 98.
13. Bob Minzesheimer, "You Are What Your ZIP Is," *Michigan: The Magazine of the Detroit News* (May 15, 1983): 22–26.
14. Minzesheimer, 24–26.

FURTHER READING

Classics

Bogue, D. J., *Principles of Demography* (New York: Wiley, 1969).

Ellis, R. B., "Composite Population Descriptors: The Socioeconomic/Life Cycle Grid," in *Advances in Consumer Research,* Vol. II, J. J. Schlinger, ed. (Chicago: Association for Consumer Research, 1975).

Enis, Ben M., and Keith K. Cox, "Demographic Analysis of Store Patronage Patterns: Uses and Pitfalls," in *Marketing and the New Science of Planning,* Robert L. King, ed. (Chicago: American Marketing Association, 1968), 381–85.

Gelb, Betsy D., "Exploring the Gray Market Segment," *MSU Business Topics* (Spring 1978): 41–46.

Wasson, C. R., "Is It Time to Quit Thinking of Income Classes?" *Journal of Marketing* 33, No. 2 (1969): 54–57.

Recent Significant Research

Barabba, Vincent P., "Demographics That Will Shape the Next Decade," in *Attitude Research Enters the 80's,* Richard W. Olshavsky, ed. (Chicago: American Marketing Association, 1980), 69–77.

Burnett, John J., "Psychographic and Demographic Characteristics of Blood Donors," *Journal of Consumer Research* 8, No. 1 (June 1981): 62–66.

"Dual-Earner Families: Doubling Marketers' Pleasures," *Sales and Marketing Management* (October 26, 1981): 43.

Jones, J. Morgan, and Fred S. Zufryden, "An Approach for Assessing Demographic and Price Influences on Brand Purchase Behavior," *Journal of Marketing* 46 (Winter 1982): 36–46.

Schaninger, Charles M., and Chris T. Allen, "Wife's Occupational Status as a Consumer Behavior Construct," *Journal of Consumer Research* 8 (September 1981): 189–96.

Schaninger, Charles M., and Donald Sciglimpaglia, "The Influence of Cognitive Personality Traits and Demographics on Consumer Information Acquisition," *Journal of Consumer Research* 8, No. 2 (September 1981): 208–16.

"Societal Shift," *The Wall Street Journal* (June 29, 1982): 1.

"The Newest Mass Market—Women Go-Getters," *Advertising Age* (November 9, 1981): 56.

"Urban Centers' Population Drift Creating a Countryside Harvest," *The New York Times* (March 23, 1980): 1, 50.

"Working Women Now More Attractive—Y&R," *Advertising Age* (January 11, 1982): 76.

Applications

Alexis, Marcus, "Food Shopping Behavior of Low-Income Households," in *Models of Buyer Behavior,* Jagdish N. Sheth, ed. (New York: Harper & Row, 1974), 218–41.

"Americans Change," *Business Week* (February 20, 1978).

Assael, Henry, "Segmenting Markets by Group Purchasing Behavior," *Journal of Marketing Research* (May 1970): 153–58.

Keon, John W., and Judy Bayer, "Analyzing Scanner Panel Households to Determine the Demographic Characteristics of Brand Loyal and Variety Seeking Households Using a New Brand Switching Measure," in *1984 AMA Educators' Proceedings,* Russell W. Belk, et al., eds. (Chicago: American Marketing Association, 1984), 416–20.

"Large Numbers of Husbands Buy Household Products, Do Housework," *Marketing News* (October 3, 1981): 1, 3.

Roscoe, A. Marvin, Arthur LeClaire, and Leon G. Schiffman, "Theory and Management Applications of Demographics in Buyer Behavior," in *Consumer and Industrial Buying Behavior,* Woodside, Sheth, and Bennett, eds. (New York: North-Holland 1977), 67–76.

Roscoe, A. Marvin, and Jagdish N. Sheth, "Demographic Segmentation of Long Distance Behavior: Data Analysis and Inductive Model Building," in *Proceedings of the 3rd Annual Conference,* M. Venkatesan, ed. (Chicago: Association for Consumer Research, 1972).

Slocum, J. W., Jr., and H. L. Mathews, "Social Class and Income as Indicators of Consumer Credit Behavior," *Journal of Marketing* 34, (1970): 69–74.

"The Graying of the Soft-Drink Industry," *Business Week* (May 23, 1977).

Tigert, Douglas J., Richard Lathrope, and Michael Bleeg, "The Fast Food Franchise: Psychographic and Demographic Segmentation Analysis," *Journal of Retailing* 47 (Spring 1971): 81–90.

11 Social Class

Objectives of This Chapter

After you have studied this chapter, you should be able to:

1. Define *social class* and the purpose it serves in human societies.
2. Describe the six classes in the social structure of the United States and trends affecting this structure.
3. Describe the various measures of social class for marketing purposes.
4. Explain how social class affects consumer behavior.
5. Give examples of how social class findings can be applied by marketing management.

Who has the highest status in your mind: a physician, a professor, or a lawyer? How would you rank the following occupations by status: salesperson, high school teacher, accountant? Your views agree with research findings if you rated each group from highest to lowest in the order they were presented.[1] The feelings you have about the relative status of these occupations are indicative of the human tendency to make social class distinctions.

Status distinctions exist in the animal kingdom as well. Beehives, ant colonies, monkey troops, and deer herds are just a few of the stratified societies found in nature. The pecking order of chickens is a familiar example of how highly structured social systems work. Each hen is given a specific rank which determines the order in which it is allowed to eat, drink, and so on.[2] Deviations in the pecking order cause skirmishes which can interfere with egg production. One enterprising agriculturist developed a novel but fruitful solution to the problem. He put contact lenses on the disgruntled chickens to blur their vision. The hens then stopped bickering and got down to the business of laying eggs.

Just as egg processors need to understand the chickens' class-related behaviors to improve production, marketers need to understand human behavior related to social class in order to operate more effectively in the marketplace. This chapter offers a conceptual definition of social class, then discusses how social class affects consumer behavior. We will then discuss the hierarchical order of social classes in the United States and some alternative ways of measuring social class.

SOCIAL CLASS DEFINED

social class

While most people have an idea of what the term social class means, few could offer a precise definition. For the purposes of this book, **social class** is "a relatively permanent and homogeneous division in a society in which individuals or families sharing similar values, life-styles, interests, and behavior can be [hierarchically] categorized."[3] To make this definition more useful, each of its major elements will be discussed in detail.

First, a social class is a *relatively permanent* categorization of individuals. That is, class distinctions persist even when a person changes his or her behavior to conform to that of another class. Those who know the background of the person attempting to "move up" socially often continue to perceive the person as a member of the same social class, in spite of obvious behavioral changes. For most people a sudden move to a different social class is unlikely. Although the characteristics of a social class might change over a long period of time, the entire class adopts these changes while membership in the class remains static.

Second, a social class is a *homogeneous division*. Although everyone in a free society has a different combination of mental, financial, and experiential resources at his or her disposal, each can aspire to almost any level of education, income bracket, occupation, and life-style. Insofar as people can overcome their background limitations, they can choose the role that they wish to perform in society. To some extent, people make career choices based on the value they think society places on the various roles for which they may be qualified. Once they choose a particular role, such as a professional or skilled worker, they tend to interact with others who perform the same or a similar role. This interaction tends to reinforce set values and behavior in their social class. Thus, they have similar attitudes, engage in similar activities, watch similar television programs, and buy similar kinds of products. Their purchases send out signals that they are members of a particular class: for example, the location and type of houses they live in, the clothes they wear, and the cars they drive.

Since there can only be a limited number of purchases at any given time, it is not surprising that selections made by members of a social class tend to reflect their homogeneity. Of course, the ability to afford a product is a factor in the decision to buy it, but certainly not the only factor. Given the same amount of money to spend on a vehicle, members of different classes may arrive at very different purchases: a van, a luxury car, a jeep, a family-sized compact sedan, a pickup truck, and so on. We can say the members of a social class *share similar values, life-styles, interests, and behavior.*

Third, *individuals or families* may be categorized into classes. The basic social class unit has been the nuclear family, although this is changing. Traditionally, all family members have been considered to belong to the same social class as the husband, who has most often been the wage earner. Now, however, there are so many working mothers and young people with part-time jobs that we can say that the entire family may now contribute to the family's social class.

Finally, social classes are *hierarchical* categorizations. They are structures so that one class is at the top and another is at the bottom with various strata in between. From this hierarchy status judgments are made, perhaps because the need for esteem is one of the basic needs motivating human behavior.[4] By categorizing people within a hierarchy, almost everyone is able to feel superior to someone farther down in the social structure. However, those at the lowest level desire a higher status and all that comes with it.

To a great extent, people are categorized according to the work they do or the role they perform in society. Research suggests that children learn at an early age to perceive clearly the occupational prestige and inequality of opportunity in the social class system. In one study, elementary school children were asked to rate fifteen occupations based on prestige. Their ratings were almost identical to the ratings of the parents and of older high school students.[5] However, occupation is not the only determinant of social status, as we shall see in the next section. **Socioeconomic**

socioeconomic status

status is another term sometimes used to identify social status. Because social status is clearly related to a consumer's economic well-being, the two terms are often used interchangeably.

SOCIAL STRATIFICATION IN THE UNITED STATES

Descriptions of the social stratification of our society generally use a structure of six familiar categories: upper-upper, lower-upper, upper-middle, lower-middle, upper-lower, and lower-lower. This six-class structure is depicted in Figure 11-1.

The Upper-Upper Class

Sociologists and economists have long agreed that the higher social classes (upper-upper and lower-upper) have also been the higher economic classes. However, distinctions can be made between the upper-upper class and the lower-upper class using several other criteria.

First, the upper-upper class includes families who have been wealthy for generations and belong to the "social register." Some sociologists call this class the **old rich.**[6] Only about one percent of the population belongs to this class, and they were born into it.

old rich

Second, members of the upper-upper class do not have to work for a living, so they may enter public service—as did Nelson Rockefeller, Franklin Roosevelt, and John, Robert, and Edward Kennedy. Their positions of leadership in government made them politically as well as socially influential. On the other hand, some of the old rich may choose to carry on the family business that created their fortunes. For example, William Clay Ford took over his grandfather Henry's multimillion-dollar corporation, Thomas Watson, Jr., relieved his father as president of IBM, and Laurance Rockefeller assumed the duties of chief executive officer of the family's Chase Manhattan Bank. In these cases, too, the reputation and influence of the family name were perpetuated and extended.

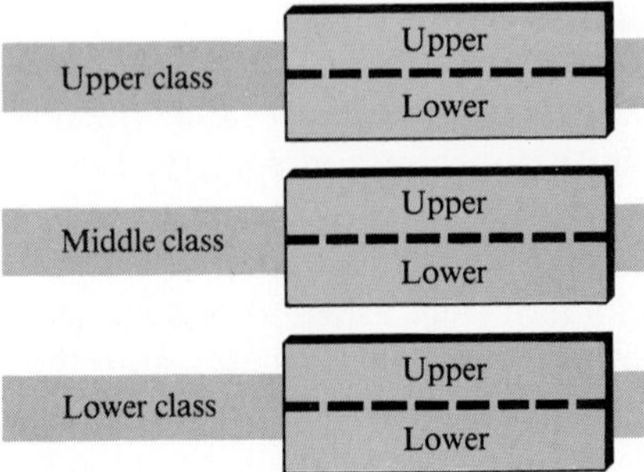

Figure 11-1
Social Stratification in the United States

Third, because the old rich are frequently in the public eye as leaders in government, business, and the cultural world, they are expected to behave in an exemplary manner. Their family name must be protected from scandal at all costs. Although they do not always succeed in maintaining the highest personal reputations, they are also subject to more scrutiny than other classes. For example, Nelson Rockefeller's divorce and remarriage received widespread news coverage, whereas similar personal events among members of lower social classes would be of far less interest or concern to the public.

Finally, the old rich generally send their sons and daughters to the "best" schools: perhaps Wellesley, Radcliffe, Swarthmore, or Smith for women, and Harvard, Yale, Dartmouth, or Princeton for men. Traditionally, these Ivy League schools were expensive and, therefore, exclusive; only the children of the intellectual and social elite were able to gain admission.

The Lower-Upper Class

Members of the lower-upper class differ from the upper-upper class in several ways. First, they are often referred to as the *nouveaux riches* or **new rich** because their fortunes were recently made rather than inherited. The first-generation wealthy of yesteryear, such as John D. Rockefeller, Joseph P. Kennedy, and Henry Ford, are familiar as the parents or grandparents of today's old rich. Often the new rich have acquired their fortunes by timely financial investments, which have resulted in their cornering an important market (J. Paul Getty, H. L. Hunt, and a number of Texas oil barons). Others have become rich quickly because they have helped to create new industries (Howard Hughes, Thomas Watson, Sr., Harvey Firestone). As our natural and human resources became increasingly exploited by its early entrepreneurs, it became popular to refer to them as "self-made men." Today's self-made millionaires—men and women—tend to be executives, physicians, consultants, movie stars, and high-technology entrepreneurs who have earned distinction in their fields. Another occupation represented among the nouveaux riches is the superstar entertainer. Barbara Streisand, Barry Manilow, Cher, and Michael Jackson are examples of performers in the lower-upper class.

new rich

Another difference between the two levels of the upper class is that even though the new rich are often celebrities, they are not usually accorded the respect and status which society gives to the old rich. Thus, they are more concerned with *establishing* the family name than with defending it. Furthermore, their acceptance among the upper-upper class is tenuous at best. Many members of the lower-upper class hope that their children or grandchildren will someday win the respectability of members of the upper-upper class.

In the meantime, the new rich have a strong desire to demonstrate their newly attained status. They turn to conspicuous consumption of very high quality products to validate their membership in the upper class. Their money-is-no-object consumption patterns include having the "in" design, or particular brand considered chic by the tastemakers.[7] Such compensatory behaviors may reflect a certain insecurity on the part of the new rich, due in part to their background in the middle or lower classes.

Finally, the lower-upper class is less likely to have had the benefit of the schools considered proper for members of the old rich. Consequently, they lack "old school ties" that traditionally have bound graduates of these schools to each other. Therefore they must earn respect on the basis of their talents and what they have accomplished with them, rather than whom they know.

JOY
DE
JEAN PATOU
PARIS
JOY® de JEAN PATOU
THE COSTLIEST PERFUME IN THE WORLD
One ounce in Baccarat crystal . . . Limited quantity available . . . Imported from Paris

However, for upcoming generations these traditional distinctions between the old rich and the new rich within the upper class may become less meaningful. First, as time passes, there will be relatively more family fortunes held by second, third, and later generations. (Even most of the Texas oil fortunes were made by members of the new-rich who are now dead.) And although fortunes are still being made today, they are not being accumulated at the rapid rate of several generations ago. Second, even the best colleges and universities have admissions policies and scholarship programs to benefit young people of modest means. Also, many more universities and colleges are providing high-quality education

and research programs once offered by only a few schools. Finally, and most importantly, America's social values are more egalitarian than they once were. For example, business people are less inclined to base their social acceptance of their peers on the university they attended; actual job performance is much more important now.

Therefore, we may eventually see a virtual blending of the new rich and the old rich into a unified upper class. The upper class is a relatively small percentage of the population of the United States—probably less than 3% (about 1% is upper-upper class).[8] Yet in actual numbers this group represents nearly two million families with huge discretionary income. Theirs is a sizable market segment to which exclusive jewelry designers, furriers, beauty salons, automotive outlets, architectural firms, and investment firms gladly cater. For example, Joy perfume is aimed at the upper class. One ad states that it is the "costliest perfume in the world" and there is a limited quantity available. Its presentation in Baccarat crystal flacons is further indication of its exclusivity. The ad appears in black and white, denoting a simple elegance which might appeal to the upper-class market.

The Upper-Middle Class

Doctors, professors, lawyers, veterinarians, state politicians, architects, and business executives typically comprise the upper-middle class. Their income range begins at about $30,000 per year and may approach several hundred thousand dollars per year. Their occupations typically require college degrees (many of them advanced) and a definite career path. Members of the upper-middle class are upwardly mobile, committed to their profession, and success oriented. To the extent income permits, they are likely to copy the upper class.

Like the upper classes, they would prefer that their children go to excellent schools; but in any case they are especially concerned that the children go to college. Education is a key to membership in this class, and those children who fail to follow in their parents' footsteps are educationally likely to face a step down.

This social class includes what Thorstein Veblen, a noted economist, and others referred to as the "technocrats." Their specialized knowledge and education places the technocrats in increasingly influential roles as society becomes more and more complex. The upper-middle class also includes the "new elite." The knowledge explosion, along with the increasingly rapid rates of social, economic, and technological change in our advanced society will likely foster continued growth in the upper-middle class. The number and variety of occupational specialties of the members of this class are also growing and, because of the higher incomes of its members, this class represents an increasingly lucrative market segment.

From a life-style point of view, the upper-middle class appears to indulge in simple pleasures—jogging, photography, and art shows, for example—and expensive fringe benefits such as condominiums, skiing, travel, and elegant dining. With annual family incomes in excess of $50,000, discretionary income is abundant.

Because their incomes are well above national averages, and because they are striving for upper-class status, it has been suggested that the upper-middle class can be linked with the upper class to form a group of "upper status people" for most marketing and advertising purposes.[9] This suggestion, however, is probably a dangerous one; for while it may be useful for marketers of some products and services, it is not valid for others. It tends to overemphasize the importance of social class at the expense of income as a determinant of buying behavior. True, there have been and still are dramatic differences in income levels within the middle class itself, but the income differences between it and the upper class are more significant. Since the bulk of the income of upper-middle-class people comes from salaries and professional fees, tax laws often have a more dire effect on their incomes than on the incomes of those in the upper classes, where tax loopholes are easier to find. Thus, the marketer should be aware that large differences in disposable income may exist among households in these higher classes.

The upper-middle class is substantially larger than the combined upper class. Though current figures are imprecise, this class probably comprises about 10% of the population—perhaps as much as 20%, an estimate that differs dramatically from the approximately 10% reported by Warner in the 1940s.[10]

The Lower-Middle Class

white collar

The lower rung of the middle class is best described as the "**white-collar** working class." The lower-middle class is made up of occupations too numerous to list here, though among them are clerks, some salespeople and bank tellers, public school teachers and owners of small businesses (mostly merchants). The lower-middle class includes nearly all nonmanagerial office workers and a large percentage of the women who have recently joined the labor force. Many of the occupations require some education or specialized training beyond high school, and a variety of college and specialist degrees are earned by members of this class.

Respectability is important to members of this class. Members tend to live in reputable neighborhoods, attend religious organizations, value education for their children, and to a certain extent are more motivated to retain their middle-class status than to achieve the higher status sought by the upper-middle class. This may be because there is a greater income disparity between the lower-middle class and the upper class than there is for the upper-middle class. Traditionally, those in this class have not been union members, although this tradition is changing rapidly. Incomes are typically below those of the upper-middle class and comparable to those of the upper-lower class. In contrast, however, values tend to be comparable to those of the upper-middle class and different from those of the upper-lower class.

This white-collar working class is of particular importance to marketers for two reasons. First, it is a huge market; as one of the two largest classes (the other is the upper-lower class) it comprises 25% to 30% of the population. Second, these two large classes are *not* distinguishable on the basis of income. They form a single economic marketplace for many goods and services, which will be discussed in more detail later in the chapter.

The Nissan Pulsar NX is a car that is apt to appeal to those in the upper-middle and lower-middle classes. One ad stresses that the car is less expensive than it appears, inferring that the owner will appear wealthier, and thus of a higher social class than the one to which he or she may actually belong. The ad also emphasizes mileage and price, two factors that are more important to those in the middle classes than to those with more to spend for transportation.

The Upper-Lower Class

blue collar

The second of the two largest social classes is composed of skilled and semiskilled "**blue-collar** workers." Incomes in this class are comparable to those in the white-collar working class, but they come from wages rather than salaries. A large portion of this class (30% to 40% of the class population) are union members. Their work tends to be more routine, so their jobs may be threatened by automation more than most. As a percentage of the total population, this class has declined and will continue to do so as automation becomes more prevalent. Yet, due largely to strong unions, the incomes of its members were on the rise until 1980, when economic conditions forced unions to make concessions to protect jobs. Even so, the number of union members is declining,[11] and this may affect many members of this social class.

Upper-lower class values differ somewhat from those of the lower-middle class; there is noticeably less concern on the part of blue collar workers for education. Although their work is fairly routine—not only from day to day but from year to year—the rest of their lifestyle has become more varied and interesting as their relative affluence has grown. For example, recreational vehicles are a popular purchase.

The "industrial slave" image of the blue-collar worker presented in the popular literature of the early decades of this century is largely outdated. Workdays have shortened and working conditions have improved. In plants where robotics have not replaced the factory workers, automation has been introduced to serve them. The worker in a modern automobile assembly plant rarely lifts anything heavier than a wrench and has 5 to 20 days vacation each year (which he often adds onto the end of a paid holiday, of which there are 11 each year). This example may not be typical of the work life of all blue-collar workers. But it points to trends which may affect the upper-lower class in the future. Like most other classes, this group watches specific television programs, likes specific kinds of ads, and represents a major market in the United States.

The Lower-Lower Class

At the bottom of the social class system are those members of society who are often either unemployed or underemployed and have typically achieved lower educational and income levels. Many are on some form of public welfare, and those who are employed are usually in unskilled occupations such as farm worker or day laborer. Many families in this class are second- and third-generation welfare recipients. Although government aid and training programs have attempted to lift individuals from lower-lower-class status, this class still comprises 10% to 15% of the population. While its discretionary purchasing power is low (many are below the official poverty level), it still remains a large market segment for producers of basics such as food and clothing. Additionally, governments and private organizations sponsor programs to address this consumer segment. In some cases these programs are communicated to members of this social class with marketing programs.

The four- to six-class social stratification system has been used for over 30 years to describe relative status. But shifts in income, education, and values are continually occurring, however gradually.

MEASURES OF SOCIAL CLASS

For social stratification concepts to be of use to marketers, they must have a way of measuring social class. There are several approaches to measurement depending on the marketer's specific purpose. First, however, let us briefly review the factors which determine social class. Occupation is the most important factor, because it tends to affect the others. Performance within the occupation also counts heavily. Levels of income and education are also important and help round out the picture. Another factor is possessions, particularly the home and its location. Finally, because social class deals with the interactions of people, associations with clubs, organizations, and groups of friends also play a part in determining social class.

Each of these variables has been a part of one or more social class measurement instruments. The measures have been divided according to the amount of depth and accuracy required, the size of samples used, and whether personal interviews, telephone surveys, or mail surveys are generally appropriate. The three major classifications of these measurement methods are: (1) intensive social-class studies, (2) complex large-population studies, and (3) large-sample surveys. Examples of each of these approaches to measurement are included in the following sections.

Intensive Study Methods

intensive study methods

When measuring many facets of social class are important, marketers use **intensive** study methods. These generally involve personal interviews by skilled researchers. Because of their depth, they are appropriate for limited geographical areas such as a town or community. This approach was developed for sociological research, but it can be adapted for marketing research studies in certain settings. One research situation in which such methods would be useful is the retail organization that is interested in studying store patronage or location. Intensive social class study methods may also be appropriate in conjunction with market tests in which the number and size of the test marketing locations are quite limited. The two types of intensive social class study methods are the reputational method and the sociometrical method.

Reputational Method

reputational method

Using the **reputational method,** researchers ask consumers to rate or rank the social status or prestige of other persons. This technique requires highly trained interviewers to collect and interpret the qualitative data, and to collaborate social ratings of the individuals interviewed. With careful administration, this method provides a rich and valid measurement of social class. Used improperly, however, its results are meaningless. The reputational method is used widely by sociologists in their basic research and rarely for applied research in marketing where its cost is high due to the need for highly paid interviewer specialists.

Sociometric Method

sociometric method

sociograms

The **sociometric** method also requires highly skilled researchers to collect and interpret the data. In essence, the researcher measures the social and professional interactions among study subjects. Computerized techniques manipulate the data collected to create **sociograms.** Figure 11-2 is a hypo-

Figure 11-2
A Hypothetical Sociogram for Physicians

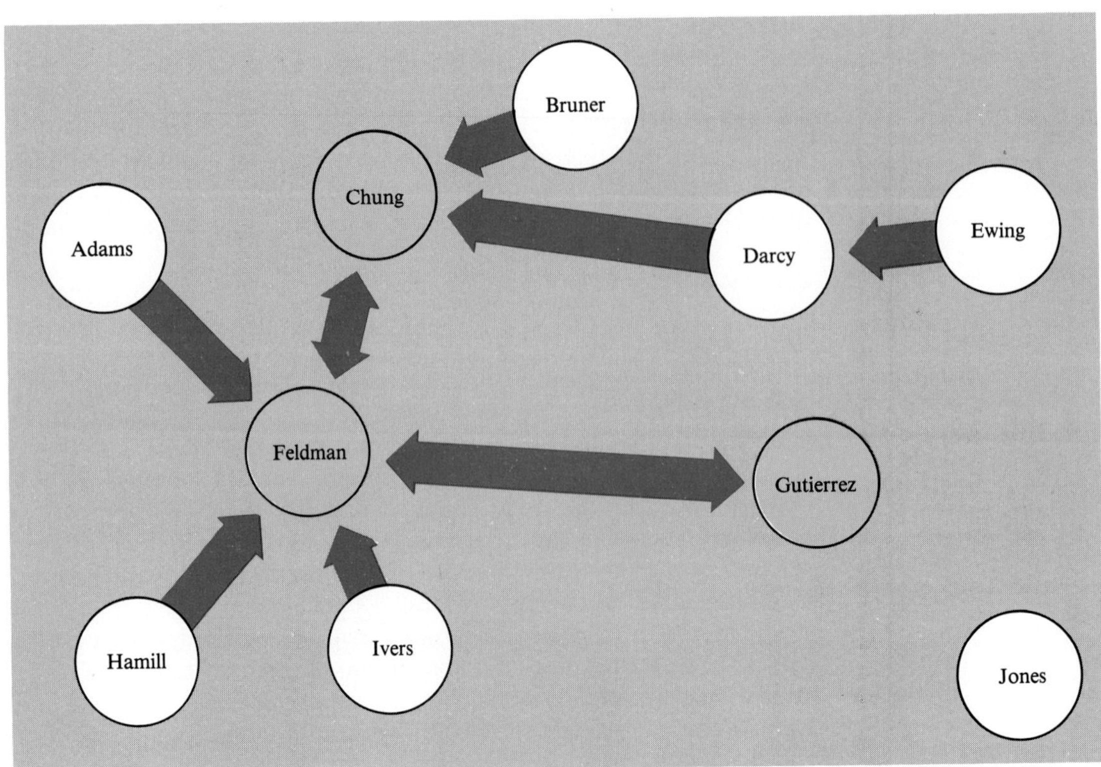

thetical sociogram indicating the professional contacts among physicians in a community. A market research study by a pharmaceutical company might very well contain such a sociogram.

The direction of the arrows indicates which doctor asks the other doctors' advice about medical issues such as what drug to prescribe. It is clear that Dr. Feldman is asked for advice by several others, and that she seeks advice from only Drs. Chung and Gutierrez. These two also seek advice from Dr. Feldman. Note that although Drs. Adams, Bruner, Ewing, Hamill, and Ivers go to others for advice, they are not sought out by others. Dr. Jones is an isolate, neither asking for medical advice from nor giving advice to the other doctors. Such sociograms could also be developed for social situations by asking subjects with whom they had lunch, played golf, went to dinner, and so on. (Sociograms are also discussed in regard to opinion leadership in Chapter 13.)

When the market segments to be measured are relatively small and geographically limited in size, these methods of intensive measurement can be very useful in helping marketers better visualize the types of buyers in a market and how they interrelate with one another. However, because these methods of measurement require intensive interviews, the scope of the population being studied is necessarily limited.

Complex Large-Population Studies

complex large-population studies

The second major classification of social class measures is **complex large-population studies.** When the market research study requires a large sample from a geographically dispersed population, intensive techniques are not practical. Indeed, many varied research problems require some measure of social class as a part of a more comprehensive study. Thus, several somewhat more objective techniques have been developed. Some complex large-population study techniques are suitable for mail questionnaires; others require personal interviews. Three techniques of the second type are described below.

Warner's Index of Status Characteristics

Index of Status Characteristics

Lloyd Warner, a sociologist deeply involved with the measurement of social class, contributed much to the development of the reputational method. However, he recognized that the technique was not suitable for a large number of research settings. So, he developed the **Index of Status Characteristics** (ISC) as an objective measure of the underlying construct: social class. Although it is only one of a number of multiple-item index measures, it is by far the most frequently used in marketing research. Consumer researchers have pointed to three main advantages of the ISC: (1) its solid theoretical support, (2) its validation by reputational methods and other scales, and (3) its applicability to a variety of research settings.[12]

The ISC includes the respondent's occupation, source of income (inherited, professional fees, salary, wages, and so on), house type, and dwelling area. The latter two parts of the index depend on the subjective judgment of the interviewer but are constructed so as to minimize bias. For each of the four categories, a numerical rating is made and then multiplied by a predetermined weight. The weights are as follows:

Occupation	(Rating) × 4
Source of income	(Rating) × 3
House type	(Rating) × 3
Dwelling area	(Rating) × 2

The result is a quantitative measure of social class that can be used, with adjustment for location, on a regional or national basis.

Coleman's Index of Urban Status

Index of Urban Status

Richard Coleman, working with the Social Research Institute, expanded Warner's ISC. Coleman's **Index of Urban Status** (IUS) includes all four of Warner's measures and adds educational attainment of both husband and wife as well as informal and formal associational variables[13] such as clubs, religious memberships, and civic organizations.

The Index of Urban Status has been used for a significant number of market-related studies conducted by the Social Research Institute. In fact, the market researcher might find the IUS more useful than Warner's ISC when the researcher suspects that education may influence the subject's buying behavior (such as purchases and media habits) in regard to the marketer's product. Also, the IUS may be more appropriate when word-of-mouth communication or opinion leadership is of particular interest, as is often the case in studying the adoption of innovations or new product brands.

Hollingshead's Index of Social Position

Index of Social Position

Another well-conceived and frequently used measure of social class is the **Index of Social Position** (ISP) developed by A. B. Hollingshead.[14] It differs from Warner's ISC in that it does not include *source of income,* because *Occupation* presumably includes this information. It also leaves out the category *house type* found in the ISC, but it retains a category which measures area of residence or neighborhood. Finally, it retains *occupation* and adds *education.* The result is an index constructed as follows:

Residence	(Rating) × 6
Occupation	(Rating) × 9
Education	(Rating) × 5

As with Coleman's IUS, Hollingshead's streamlined three-item method may be desirable when education may be expected to explain or predict the dependent variable in question. Used extensively in sociological studies, the three-item ISP has not been used widely in marketing studies. However, a two-item version of Hollingshead's method has been used, as the next section points out.

Large-Sample Surveys

Many large marketing research projects do not require or cannot afford the luxury of personal interviewing to measure social class, so a shorter, less complex approach is called for using telephone interviews, mail interviews, or short retail-intercept interviews. These large-sample survey methods are popular among marketers because they are practical to administer.

Hollingshead's Two-Item Index

Two-Item Index

A simplified version of Hollingshead's ISP, the **Two-Item Index,** omits the *area of residence* category. It consists of the categories *occupation* and *education*. This version of the Hollingshead index has been used in researching a variety of marketing issues from the use of bank credit cards[15] to consumers' awareness of brands and advertising slogans.[16]

Carman's Index of Cultural Classes

Index of Cultural Classes

James Carman's **Index of Cultural Classes** (ICC) is the only social class measurement method created *by* a marketing researcher *for* marketing researchers.[17] Carman developed this scale after realizing that some of the readily available Census Bureau data were more than cold statistics and that, if confirmed, they could be used to present a picture of social class. For example, census statistics were used to show that social class is a significant variable in predicting housewives' loyalty to certain chain food stores. Carman selected *occupation, education of the total household,* and *expenditures for housing* as the categories of his scale.

As with the measures developed by sociologists, Carman's ICC emphasizes occupation and education. Additionally, *expenditures for housing* may be compared to *house type* and *neighborhood* in some scales.

National Opinion Research Center (NORC) Occupation Index

As should be clear by now, occupation shows up consistently as an important (usually *the* most important) item in multiple-item indexes. Remember that this is because occupation really includes much of the other information. To some extent it comprises the amount of income. To a greater extent it includes education, because people are educated for their careers. Finally, occupation includes the source of income (professional fees, profits, salaries, wages). For this reason the National Opinion Research Center (NORC), an organization involved in public opinion polling as well as marketing research, developed the NORC **Occupation Index** scale as a measure of the status or prestige of a long list of occupations. The index was developed using a rating scale approach; respondents indicate the standing of each listed occupation in relation to the others.

Occupational Index

Self-Rating Scales

self-rating scales

Finally, the market researcher may wish to use a technique which directly asks the respondent to state his or her own social class standing. There can be problems with this technique. First, when put on the spot, many people tend to rate themselves higher while others see their class as lower than the more objective techniques reviewed above would indicate. Second, some people's desire to avoid appearing out of the ordinary may cause them to say that they are middle class. Finally, a small proportion of the population is simply not aware of social classes.

Yet for some purposes a person's perception of his or her own class may be as important as an objective measure. Some people behave like those in the class to which they *think* they belong. Their self-rating relates strongly to their buying practices. For example, those who perceive themselves as belonging to the upper-middle class might purchase a car or home beyond their means in an attempt to live up to that status. An objective observer might classify that person as lower-middle class due to income, occupation, or education. Consequently, the type of car or house such people purchase is a function more of self-perceived social class than of the class to which they more likely belong. Self-rated measurement of social class may be useful in some studies as a supplement to more objective measures. It might also be useful when accurate measures are not required, such as for some initial market investigations.

HOW SOCIAL CLASS AFFECTS CONSUMER BEHAVIOR

To be of use to marketers, the concept of social class must classify buyers in ways that help interpret their behavior. That is, social class data is available insofar as it can be used to segment consumers into distinct groups requiring different marketing approaches. For example, if consumers in different social classes tend to have different wants, then marketers can target products and services to satisfy the specific desires of each group. Promotion is also more effective when advertising messages are designed and media are selected that are likely to appeal to members of a specific class.

Several aspects of consumer behavior have been explored using social class measures. In particular, social class research has contributed to an understanding of: (1) retail shopping behavior, (2) the use of certain products and services, (3) consumer perception of quality versus price, and (4) media habits and responses to advertising.

Retail Shopping Behavior

Social class explains several aspects of consumer shopping patterns. The upper classes and lower classes differ in terms of the types of retail stores they frequent, the extent of their information search, the frequency of their shopping, and their attitudes toward shopping in general.

Consumers are keenly aware of the status of particular stores and typically choose to shop where they feel most comfortable. Traditionally, consumers classified in the lower strata have avoided shopping in high-status stores because they would feel out of place. They perceive that they would be treated differently than upper-class shoppers.[18] Similarly, upper-class consumers have been less likely to frequent discount stores than their lower-class counterparts. Many ads are intended to appeal to buyers in the higher social classes. Such ads often state that the product is available at "fine stores," indicating a certain amount of prestige connected with the product.

Recent studies, however, have taken a closer look at differences in store selection by social class and have found some additional factors that complicate the situation. Members of different social classes who shop at the same stores seek different types of products.[19] A consumer classified as lower class might patronize a high-status store for a gift but would be unlikely to purchase personal items there. Conversely, an upper-class consumer might visit a discount store for appliances but never purchase clothing there.

Second, there are differences in the number of stores higher- and lower-class buyers usually visit before purchasing. One study revealed that in shopping for furniture, consumers in lower-class neighborhoods were aware of fewer stores and exhibited less prepurchase shopping behavior than did higher-class consumers.[20] Other research supports the findings of restricted shopping among those in lower strata, suggesting that it may be due to restricted means of travel among the lower classes.[21] Researchers found that subjects of mid- to high-socioeconomic status seemed to be more accomplished information processors than those of low-socioeconomic status. They sought more information in general, especially under high perceived risk conditions. These findings are similar to those of prior research, which showed subjects with low education levels to be less able to complete successfully a simple proportional reasoning task (calculation of unit prices for grocery products) than were highly educated subjects.[22]

Upper and lower classes also differ in their shopping frequency and attitudes towards shopping. According to one study, middle- and upper-class females shop more often than do females in the lower classes.[23] However, this finding may reflect more fundamental differences in general attitudes to shopping among various social classes. For example, the same research revealed that although women in all social classes enjoyed shopping, lower-class consumers usually attributed their enjoyment to acquiring new items, whereas middle- and upper-class shoppers were more likely to identify the "entertainment" aspects of shopping such as store atmosphere and aisle displays. Therefore, because lower-class shoppers usually have less disposable income and do not usually shop just for the pleasure of shopping, they tend to shop less frequently than do those in the upper classes.

Products and Services Used

Some researchers have identified a relationship between membership in a social class and the use of certain products or services. Television ownership, commercial air travel, and possession of a United States passport were found to correlate more closely with the social class of buyers than with their income level.[24] However, the same study suggests that the ability to buy (based on income) is as good as or better than social class in segmenting the market for a variety of home furnishings, appliances, and ready-to-wear products.

Other studies have explored the value of social class in explaining the use of some convenience-type products. These studies suggest some basis for using social class to predict purchases of instant and frozen products. They also show that social class can explain the use of some diet foods, such as cottage cheese, and diet soft drinks.[25]

Social class is also a factor in the use of consumer credit services. Lower social class members tend to rely on credit cards primarily for credit purchases to stretch their budgets; higher social classes use credit cards primarily for convenience. According to one study, the types of products purchased on credit also differed. Upper-class credit users bought luxury items while lower-class consumers used credit cards for essentials and durable goods. Further, in choosing where to shop, members of the lower class were more likely to seek out stores that would honor their credit cards.[26]

Does social class influence children's buying? There may be a relationship between adolescents' social class and the strength of their brand preferences.[27] Even at an early age, brand name appears to be an important consideration in buying decisions. However, children from higher social classes tend to be more aware of their environment, and the availability of products in the marketplace, than do children from lower classes. Thus, they have a greater awareness of brands.

Perceptions of Price and Quality

Only a limited amount of research has been done on how different social classes perceive price and quality. However, the available evidence suggests that lower-class consumers are more likely to associate price with quality. In one study, when faced with a choice among brands, lower-class consumers were more likely to use price in judging quality because they felt incapable of evaluating the alternatives on other criteria.[28] Such products as Preference hair coloring, by L'Oreal, make a direct effort in their messages to associate price with quality. The slogan for Preference is, "It costs more, but I'm worth it." One ad for Tabasco pepper sauce also equates higher price with higher quality; its copy states: "A few nickels extra buys extra flavor and strength." For both of these products, however, *reasons* for the higher price are given; this approach appeals to all classes of buyers regardless of how they judge quality. Although it is likely that there are differences in the price-related behavior of various classes, additional research must be conducted before reliable generalizations can be made.

Media Habits and Responses to Promotions

Media habits vary by social class. Consumers in lower class strata tend to be frequent viewers of television, while consumers in higher-classes are more likely to subscribe to magazine and newspapers. Further, social classes seem to differ in terms of which television networks they prefer to watch. For example, in 1973 lower-class members typically enjoyed watching CBS television stations, while middle- and upper-class viewers preferred NBC channels.[29]

Similar research indicates that specific magazines attract readers of different social classes. For example, *The New Yorker* and *Vogue* magazines have greater upper- and middle-class readership than do *Reader's Digest* or *Ladies Home Journal,* which appeal more to lower-class readers.

Social class seems to have an impact on the reaction of consumers to promotional techniques as well. Members of the lower classes respond better to advertising that features coupons and special offers. They also tend to be less critical of advertising in general and prefer advertisements that are more active and visual in character. Middle-class buyers, on the other hand, are less likely to take advantage of premiums and money-saving inducements and tend to be more suspicious of advertising. They also react more positively to advertising that features a sophisticated and stylish approach.[30]

Two ads for separate brands of panty hose help to demonstrate how marketers use different methods to appeal to the various social classes.

No Nonsense Comfort Stride panty hose uses a coupon to attract buyers and stresses the more practical aspects of this brand of hose, thus probably reaching those from the lower social classes. Round the Clock panty hose uses a more sensual photograph in one of its ads and calls its line the "Luxury Leg Collection," creating a more sophisticated and stylish appeal aimed at the higher classes.

In a relatively complex study, three researchers investigated the amount of status consciousness in the various social classes. They then related those findings to advertising and promotional approaches. They found that status consciousness was lower for higher-class consumers but higher for those in lower classes. Higher-class consumers were less status conscious but essentially more rational, cosmopolitan, and achievement oriented. Thus, promotion directed at those in higher classes are better received if snob appeal is avoided in favor of facts regarding product functions, features, and benefits.[31]

The measures used in most class studies deal only with part of the complexity of social class distinctions. In some ways, therefore, it is surprising that researchers have been able to find so many differences in buying behavior between the classes. Nevertheless, additional research is needed to explain more fully how behavior varies by social class. Some authors have reviewed the field and pointed out that social class can be a very important concept in understanding market segmentation and promotion.[32] They recommend looking at more than single measures of social

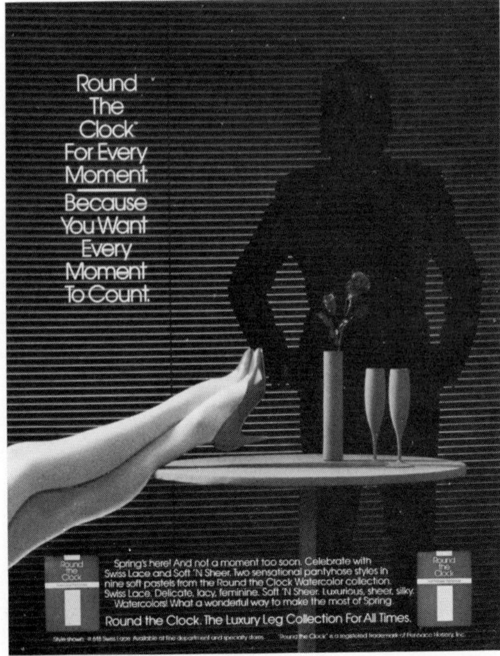

class. For example, income variations within social classes are likely to be important, and social class may be combined with other segmentation variables, such as occupation and education, to effectively divide buyers into meaningful groups.

As a final illustration of the usefulness of social class in explaining buyer behavior, the last section of this chapter shows how class data can be used to distinguish the working classes when income alone fails to do so.

DETERMINANTS OF SOCIAL CLASS

The five major factors most often used to identify social class are income, occupation, education, possessions and ownership, and affiliations. Each of these factors reflect an aspect which differentiates members of one class from another.

Income

In the early decades of this century, social status was clearly determined by the amount of income. Because managers and professionals earned more than white-collar office workers, they were in a higher class. Similarly, office workers earned more than blue-collar factory workers, so they were accorded higher status than the factory workers. In fact, income was so useful an indicator of buying behavior that marketers tended to rely on income data exclusively. This tendency was reinforced by the fact that income data were usually readily available. It is understandable that pragmatic marketers found economists' measure of income more important than sociologists' measure of social class.

However, a number of economic factors eventually began to change this picture. Unionization, graduated tax systems, greater affluence nationwide, and other factors began to blur the income distinctions among social classes. For example, with union representation the incomes of blue-collar worker rose much faster than did those of white-collar employees. At the same time, the values and cultural influences transmitted by families and reference groups continued to affect how the working classes spent their take-home pay. Thus income alone no longer explained the consumption patterns or life-style of these buyers. Marketers were forced to gather other types of data in addition to income. Today, although income is an important class indicator, as it is related to the ability to buy (and, therefore, to one's possessions and ownership), income data is more meaningful in combination with occupation data. The advantage of income as a measure of social class is that it can be stratified easily. The disadvantage is that there has been some blurring of this factor in recent decades. For example, a professor in the liberal arts, someone who by vocation is considered in the upper-middle class, may well have an income significantly lower than that of an auto worker, traditionally a member of the lower-middle class.

Another problem with income as a measure of social class arises due to the fact that in every class there are some individuals and families whose incomes are significantly above or below the average for their class. Richard P. Coleman has referred to these groups as the "overprivileged" and the "underprivileged" groups. Because of their income, the purchasing patterns of these groups may be somewhat different than the purchasing patterns of other members of their social class.[33]

Occupation

Occupation has a great deal to do with social class; but while occupation correlates with income, the two are far from synonymous. Today income varies considerably within occupations. For example, marketing executives' salaries range from about $50,000 to well into six figures. It is safe to say the physician who is a hospital chief of staff making $400,000 annually has more status than the physician in a health maintenance organization who earns $40,000 a year. Therefore, occupation alone is insufficient to determine class. Nevertheless, occupational data is useful when determining the classes of workers in different occupations. For example, we would probably consider a flight attendant to have more status than a taxi driver. While both occupations are necessary and important to travelers, *flight attendant* has a set of associations that are quite different from those of *taxi driver*. The fact that a taxi driver might earn more than a flight attendant does not change the relative prestige of the two occupations.

Table 11-1 gives the results of a study that reflects respondents' perception of the prestige of several occupations. In a similar study, conducted first in 1947 and again in 1963, the rankings of these occupations were much the same as in this 1977 study. Thus, the occupational status has shifted little over time.[34]

Some occupations, such as the professions in higher education, medicine, law, accounting, and the clergy, owe their prestige partly to the fact that they require advanced educational degrees. The advantage of measuring social class through use of occupational data is that prestige in terms of an individual's job is easily ranked. The disadvantage is that the results do not necessarily relate to purchasing power.

Education

Obviously, the type of occupation and the earning power a person is eligible for depends on the education he or she has received. For many of the occupations listed in Table 11-1, no more than a high school education is required, if that. Some occupations, such as barber, beautician, ma-

Table 11-1 FIFTY SCORES SELECTED FROM TREIMAN'S STANDARD INTERNATIONAL OCCUPATIONAL PRESTIGE SCALE*

Occupation	*Rank*	*Occupation*	*Rank*
University professor	78	Soldier	39
Physician	78	Post office clerk	39
Lawyer	71	Receptionist	38
Dentist	70	Telephone operator	38
Head of large firm	70	Machine operator	38
Accountant	68	Car salesperson	36
Executive	67	Model	36
High school teacher	64	Beautician	35
Veterinarian	61	Firefighter	35
Clergy	60	Plumber	34
Lives off property	57	Undertaker	34
Journalist	55	Sales clerk	34
Nurse	54	Truck driver	33
Secretary	53	Cashier	31
Flight attendant	50	Assembly-line worker	30
Real estate agent	49	On Social Security	30
Bank teller	48	Barber	30
Farmer	47	Factory worker	29
Construction worker	46	Taxi driver	28
Keypunch operator	45	Doorman	27
Office clerk	43	Gas station attendant	25
TV repairer	42	Janitor	21
Proofreader	41	Laborer	19
Police officer	40	Migrant worker	18
Cabinetmaker	40	On welfare	16

Source: Donald Treiman, "Occupational Prestige," *Human Behavior* 6, No. 11 (November 1977): 25.

* *Scale: 0 to 100.*

chine operator, and police officer, might require completion of a trade school program.

As the degree of occupational prestige increases, the level of required education generally rises as well. The college degree is a standard requirement more often than it was forty or fifty years ago, when most college students were children of the wealthy. Despite recent cutbacks in federal financial aid programs, many more students from low- or average-income families are earning college degrees. In 1940, 4.6% of adults over 25 had college degrees, while in 1978 the percentage reached 15.7%. Fifteen percent of those in college in 1940 obtained advanced degrees; today the figure is approaching 40%.[35]

Of course, as our technological society becomes more complex and occupations become more specialized, more education will be needed. Already *U.S. News and World Report* has announced the advent of a new elite in society.[36] This rising group consists of professionals who are highly educated in areas of specialized knowledge required in an advanced economy. Their power comes from use of words, symbols, and ideas in complex fields. The article cites examples of "college trained experts on problems ranging from air safety to marketing and youth crime." Their elite status comes from education and the ability to contribute to growth in specialized fields. Many of these experts have advanced degrees.

The new elite is likely to be a permanent aspect of our society, because technical expertise based on the knowledge explosion and an information-oriented economy will continue to demand it. Because the roles these new professionals will play are valuable to society, higher status will be conferred on them than on those with less education. While education alone does not determine class, a combination of income, occupation, and education is very indicative of class.

Income, Occupation, and Education as a Combined Indicator of Class

Richard Coleman and Lee Rainwater developed a scale using occupation, education, and income to provide a more complete indication of social status. Table 11-2 summarizes their index, which is based on a study of respondents who were asked to evaluate the status associated with 129 hypothetical profiles. Three major dimensions and their relative weights were extracted from the responses: occupation, education, and income. In turn, these were applied to come up with status estimates. Since the scale uses a combination of these three factors, a factory manager with a master's degree is ranked higher than a board chairman who has a bache-

Table 11-2 RANKING OF SOCIAL STATUS BY OCCUPATION, EDUCATION, AND INCOME

The Three Factors in Profile Specification			
Occupation, Title, and Description	***Level of Education***	***Annual Income***	***Status Estimates (Index Numbers)***
Shoeshiner	06	$ 1,600	23
Ditchdigger	03	8,500	52
Janitor	03	8,700	53
Grocery clerk	12	4,800	53
Hardware clerk	14	5,400	73
Gardener	11	8,100	73
*Airplane mechanic	12	9,700	83
*Restaurant cook	04	9,600	84
*Airplane mechanic	07	6,000	86
Gas station attendant	12	8,400	86

Table 11-2 Continued

The Three Factors in Profile Specification			
Occupation, Title, and Description	***Level of Education***	***Annual Income***	***Status Estimates (Index Numbers)***
*Loom operator	09	9,200	90
Machine operator in bag company	07	9,500	92
*Loom operator	11	11,100	92
*Owner of drycleaning store	14	7,100	93
Shoe repairman	04	9,700	93
Assembly line worker	10	10,600	93
Stock clerk	13	10,700	93
Dockworker	10	13,200	94
Fireman	09	9,100	96
Manager of a small store	12	8,000	97
Government accounting clerk	B.A.	8,500	98
Shipping clerk	09	10,500	98
Carpenter	12	9,800	99
Printing press operator	12	10,200	99
Barber	07	11,200	99
Plasterer	09	12,700	100
Machinist	14	9,500	103
Electrician	08	10,800	103
*Chemist	13	9,500	103
*Restaurant cook	13	11,700	108
Bookkeeper	B.A.	11,100	109
Government accounting clerk	13	12,000	112
Construction foreman	12	14,300	120
Assistant manager, office supply company	M.A.	11,700	121
Tool and die maker	12	14,700	125
Factory foreman	14	18,200	130
Accountant	12	19,200	130
New-car salesman	10	20,500	132
High school teacher	M.A.	13,300	138
Office manager, moving company	B.A.	23,400	144
*Owner of drycleaning store	12	22,600	150
Salesman, electrical manufacturing company	B.A.	23,400	162
Civil engineer	13	29,400	173
*Chemist	B.A.	21,000	174
Department head, state government	M.A.	22,800	203
Owner of factory	10	60,000	225
Traveling salesman	12	90,000	233
College professor	Ph.D.	30,000	238
Physician	M.D. but no B.A.	40,000	276
Board chairman	B.A.	200,000	370
Manager of large factory	M.A.	200,000	425
President of billion-dollar corporation	Ph.D.	2,000,000	537

Source: adapted from Richard P. Coleman and Lee Rainwater, *Social Standing in America: New Dimensions of Class* (New York: Basic Books, 1978), 213–15.

* This occupation is listed more than once. Note difference in education and income levels.

lor's degree, although they have comparable incomes. The study underscores that social status is the product of several dimensions.

Possessions and Ownership

Housing type and dwelling area are important social status indicators.[37] In many communities classes are divided according to the type and location of their housing: central city, newly developed areas of row houses, apartment complexes, older neighborhoods with starter and smaller homes, suburban ranch-style tracts, and exclusive neighborhoods. These classifications differ for each city. For example, in New York City exclusive brownstone condominiums are emerging from renovated apartments in the center of each borough. Marketers can obtain data on housing costs by looking at census tract datas published by the Census Bureau, or state, county, and municipal tax records, to determine where the most expensive houses are located. Marketers may also question homeowners or realtors directly about property value and size. Many possessions besides real property are related to status. Consumers often purchase items that are overt expressions of their status; these are called *status symbols*. A status symbol can be the *type* of purchase as well as the brand. Most people become aware of these status symbols at an early age, but research shows that males and children of the higher social classes tend to draw more social class inferences from these items because they are more achievement oriented than are most females or children of the lower classes.[38] Table 11-3 lists some types of purchases that reflect high status in five American cities as of 1977. Note that some items which were "in" in some cities were "out" in other cities.

status symbols

The advantage of using possessions and ownership to measure social class is that major purchases such as automobiles, houses, and furnishings usually correlate to income and family class. The disadvantage is that differences among individuals' ownership priorities can blur distinctions related only to social class.

Affiliations

People tend to associate and feel most comfortable with others who hold values and exhibit behavior similar to their own. Consequently, people most often interact with others in their own social class. In fact, it is important to the maintenance of one's social status to have frequent and close association with others in that class.

Some sociologists place a heavy emphasis on affiliations in determining social class. The types of people a person spends leisure time with, the specific clubs in which they enjoy membership, or the church to which they belong can all be determinants of one's social class. For example, a person who associates primarily with professionals, belongs to the local

Table 11-3 STATUS SYMBOLS IN AND OUT OF FAVOR, 1977

	"In"	*"Out"*
New York		
	Ownership of horses	Pedigreed dogs
	Season opera tickets	Color television
	Private-club membership	European trip
	Persian rugs	Wall-to-wall carpeting
	Ivy League degree	Winter suntan
	Corner office (executives)	Seashore cottage
	Penthouse (the rich)	Suburban split-level
	Rolls-Royce (the rich)	Swimming pool
	Bathroom telephone	Famous-designer labels
	Customized van (the young)	Gas-guzzling car
Atlanta		
	Indoor plants	Unisex clothes
	BMW car	Patched-elbow tweeds
	European trip	Trail biking
	Discos (the young)	Motor boat
	Citizen's band radio (working class)	Swimming pool
	Backgammon	Formal furniture
	Cheap original paintings	Mink coat
	Adidas sneakers	Men's pony-tail hairdos
	Small farm	Suburban split-level
	Transcendental meditation	Chagall posters
Houston		
	Custom pickup trucks	Personalized, low-number auto tags
	Pool and tennis court	Men's polyester leisure suits
	Personal wine cellar	Nightclubs
	High-rise condominium	Cheap original paintings
	Sable coat	Fake fur
	Trimmed beard	Prefaded Levis
	Halston and Gucci apparel	Landscaped yard
	Season opera tickets	Bridge
	Pair of hounds	Men's pony-tail hairdos
	Women's jumpsuits	Unisex clothes
Chicago		
	Indoor plants	U.S. Indian jewelry
	Owned or rented sculpture	Astrology
	Cabin cruiser (the rich)	Citizens' band radio
	Renovated brownstone	Art posters
	Mixed china and crystal	Initialed accessories
	Membership in private disco	Necklaces for men
	Whirlpool bath	Home sauna
	Harbor condominium (the rich)	Transcendental meditation, yoga
	Personal backgammon table	Frosted hair
	Limousine with bar, color TV (the rich)	Owning a Playboy Club key
San Francisco		
	Indoor plants	Pedigreed cats and dogs
	Recreation vehicle	Swimming pool
	Discos	Nightclubs
	Jogging	St. Bernard dogs
	Personal wine cellar	Long hair (men and women)
	Own winery (the rich)	Double-knit suits
	Faded jeans, imported (the young)	Mink coat
	Season opera tickets	Initialed accessories
	Transcendental meditation and est	Costly French red wines
	Pottery making	Chauffeur (the rich)

Source: U.S. News and World Report (February 15, 1977): 39.

Table 11-4 RELATIVE MERITS OF VARIOUS DETERMINANTS OF SOCIAL CLASS

Advantage	*Measurement Method*	*Disadvantage*
Data is easily stratified.	*Income*	There has been some blurring as social patterns change (professors earn less, auto workers earn more).
Prestige by job is easily ranked.	*Occupation*	Can be deceptive (physicians' income can be $40,000 or $400,000, depending on specialty).
Usually a good predictor of earning power.	*Education*	There are "soft" degrees and "hard" degrees (so education may not directly translate into social class).
Major purchases such as cars, houses, and so on usually correlate to income, family class.	*Possessions and ownership*	Differences among individual priorities can blur distinctions related only to social class.
May indicate individuals' priorities.	*Affiliations*	Individual may hold particular affiliation out of habit, not strong priority.

country club, and is a member of a book club would be considered by most people to belong to a higher social class than one who affiliates most often with factory workers, belongs to a bowling league, and is a member of the Moose Lodge.

The advantage of using affiliations as a measure of social class is that such ties may well indicate an individual's priorities. The disadvantage is that in some cases, an individual may hold a particular affiliation out of habit, and not because of a strong priority. The advantages and disadvantages of all five of these measurement criteria are summarized in Table 11-4.

DIFFERENTIATING THE WORKING CLASSES

The debates continue over the relative effectiveness of explaining consumer behavior according to only income or social class. On one hand, it is argued that homogenization of pay scales has made income lose its value as a separator of class and that social class, as measured by other factors besides income, has become all-important.[39] However, more recent research maintains just the opposite: that income is *more* meaningful to marketers than is social class.[40] To some extent both positions are valid, as Figure 11-3 illustrates. If we compare the income levels and the

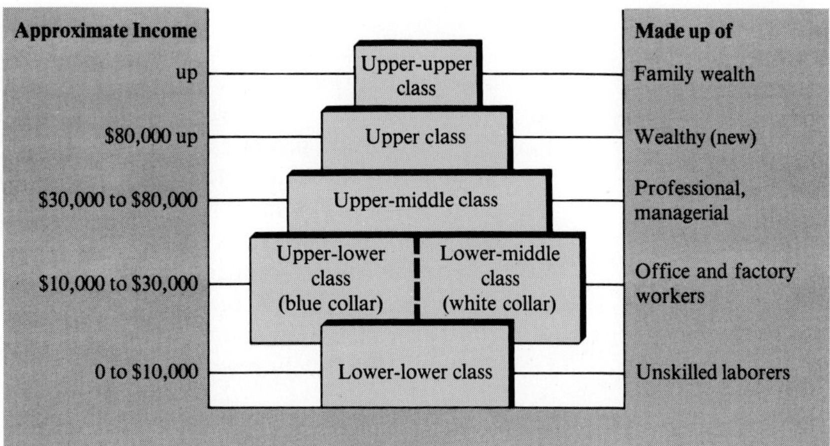

Figure 11-3 Income and Social Structure in the United States

social class structure of the United States, we can see that the upper class, the upper-middle class, and the lower-lower class stand alone and are as easily identified by income level as by social stratum. However, the incomes of upper-lower class and lower-middle class workers are comparable. In this case, social class can be helpful in explaining the differences in buying behavior of the blue-collar and white-collar workers.

In 1958, Pierre Martineau introduced social class as a major marketing variable. His research examined the major psychological differences between middle-class and lower-class consumers. Table 11-5 presents his

Table 11-5 PSYCHOLOGICAL ASPECTS OF MIDDLE- AND LOWER-CLASS CONSUMERS

Middle Class	*Lower Class*
1. Pointed to the future.	1. Pointed to the present and past.
2. His viewpoint embraces a long expanse of time.	2. Lives and thinks in a short expanse of time.
3. More urban identification.	3. More rural identification.
4. Stresses rationality.	4. Nonrational, essentially.
5. Has a well-structured sense of the universe.	5. Vague and unclear structuring of the world.
6. Horizons vastly extended or not limited.	6. Horizons sharply defined or limited.
7. Greater sense of choice making.	7. Limited sense of choice making.
8. Self-confident and willing to take risks.	8. Very concerned with security and insecurity.
9. Immaterial and abstract in his thinking.	9. Concrete and perceptive in his thinking.
10. Sees himself tied to national happenings.	10. World revolves around his family and body.

Source: Pierre Martineau, "Social Classes and Spending Behavior," *Journal of Marketing* 23 (1958): 129.

findings. The research shows major differences between the middle and lower social classes. For example, members of the middle class are generally more future oriented, stress rationality, and are self-confident. Therefore, as consumers they would be more likely to make their own judgments about the products and brands to buy.

It is apparent that differences in social class affect buyer behavior and may be an important element in marketing strategy for particular products and services. The differences in social class and buying behavior extend beyond income alone, especially in the case of blue-collar and white-collar workers. Although their incomes are comparable, the different ways in which they view the world create a need for different marketing techniques to effectively reach these two social classes.

APPEALING TO A SPECIFIC SOCIAL CLASS: A MARKETING PROBLEM

To see how social class might be of use to marketing management, consider a hypothetical problem of marketing to different social classes. For many years, Midwest Hospital has maintained an alcoholism treatment program at its downtown facility. Due to location and its historical service area, most of the patients admitted for treatment of alcoholism are blue-collar workers from the local manufacturing plants.

In recent years, greater public concern over drunk driving and alcoholism has prompted an increase in the number of persons entering alcoholism treatment nationally. In Midwest's area, several other hospitals have begun similar alcoholism treatment services, and local psychologists have also been attracted to alcoholism counseling as a means of building a larger treatment practice. Many of these groups have developed contacts with the local manufacturing companies to serve their employees at low rates. This increased competition has resulted in a decline in patients entering the Midwest alcoholism program.

While blue-collar workers are a highly competitive market segment for alcohol treatment, Midwest Hospital sees a major opportunity in serving a largely untreated white-collar market. At the same time, the hospital is uncertain exactly why very few white-collar employees have entered their program in the past. To understand the reasons for apparent white-collar resistance to entering their program, Midwest's management begins a research study.

The study includes a series of focused group interviews with former white-collar alcoholism patients from other treatment programs. An analysis of the focused groups suggests several reasons why local white-collar workers are unlikely to enter the Midwest program. One key finding is that while white-collar managers have a high incidence of alcoholism, they do not perceive the aging, local downtown facility as appropriate for their treatment. They also want a more executive-oriented program that addresses their job stress problems. Because they are more apt to see alcoholism as a "weakness" in their ability to handle on-the-job executive stress, white-collar individuals are less likely to admit to alcoholism than are blue-collar employees. In addition, they do not feel comfortable going to the company personnel office due to concerns about confidentiality. Thus no referral support network exists for them. As a result, those few who do enter treatment go to clinics in other communities rather than to the local Midwest program. This desire for "geographic escape" means that local managers were unlikely to see Midwest as a potential treatment option.

Midwest's management took several bold steps as a result of these research insights. First, a new suburban facility was opened and positioned as an "executive stress reduction center" to communicate a special emphasis on white-collar alcoholism problems. Second, the hospital launched a promotional campaign in *other* communities to attract executives there who want to protect the confidentiality of their treatment. Next, a white-collar oriented referral support system was developed with specific emphasis on getting cooperation from physicians who treat patients in executive residential areas. Finally, certain amenities were added to cater to these white-collar patients. For example, copies of the *Wall Street Journal* were available to patients and special discussion groups were conducted regarding executive stress in the office. The knowledge gained about social class differences prompted Midwest Hospital to consider new ways to appeal to the largely untreated white-collar alcoholic.

SUMMARY

Class structures seem to exist in human societies because the various roles performed by individuals have different values to society. While some people attempt to move into a higher class, the characteristics of the social strata are relatively permanent and change only very slowly. A new elite segment is emerging from the upper-middle class as college-educated specialists with healthy family incomes become more important to our technical society. However, the United States can still be described quite accurately in terms of a six-category social stratification: the upper-upper class ("old rich"); the lower-upper class ("new rich"); the upper-middle class (professionals); the lower-middle class (white-collar skilled employees); the upper-lower class (blue-collar skilled and semiskilled employees); and lower-lower class (chronically dependent on welfare).

Social class can generally be measured using income, occupation, education, ownership and possessions (particularly housing), and affiliations. These variables reflect the available lifestyles which differentiate the social strata.

Because people tend to interact with those in their own social class, they are likely to hold similar values, watch the same television shows, and purchase similar products from the same retail outlets. All of these characteristics are useful to marketers in tailoring their marketing efforts.

KEY TERMS

social class
socioeconomic status
old rich
new rich
white collar
blue collar
intensive study methods
reputational method
sociometric method
sociograms
complex large-population studies
Index of Status Characteristics
Index of Urban Status
Index of Social Position
Two-Item Index
Index of Cultural Classes
Occupational Index
self-rating scales
status symbols

QUESTIONS

1. Define social class as we have discussed it in this chapter. Can an individual easily change social classes? Explain.

2. In terms of general shopping behavior, do lower social classes differ from higher social classes? What underlying explanations might you offer for these differences?

3. Some research has suggested that consumers from higher social classes may be less status conscious than those from lower social classes. If so, what reasons can you suggest for this?

4. Who are the so-called old rich? In what respects do these people differ from the new rich?

5. "From a marketer's perspective, there really is no middle class." Do you agree or disagree? Explain.

6. Compare and contrast the reputational method and the sociometric method of intensive social class study.

7. List the elements which make up the Index of Status Characteristics (ISC), Index of Urban Status (IUS), and Index of Social Position (ISP), all indices of social class. Briefly discuss when one might be more appropriate than another for a market research study.

8. Briefly discuss the advantages and disadvantages in using each of the five determinants of social class by itself.

NOTES

1. Richard P. Coleman and Lee Rainwater, *Social Standing in America: New Dimensions of Class* (New York: Basic Books, 1978), 213–15.
2. T. Schjelderup-Ebbe, "Social Behavior of Birds," in *A Handbook of Social Psychology*, C. Murchison, ed. (Worcester, MA: Clark University Press, 1935).

3. James F. Engle and Roger D. Blackwell, *Consumer Behavior,* 4th ed. (Chicago: The Dryden Press, 1982), 111. (*Hierarchically* was added to the definition of social class by the author.)
4. See Chapter 2 on motivation for a discussion of esteem.
5. Robert G. Simmons and Morris Rosenberg, "Functions of Children's Perceptions of the Stratification System," *American Sociological Review* 36 (1971): 235–49.
6. W. Lloyd Warner, Marcia Meeker, and Kenneth Eels, *Social Class in America: A Manual of Procedure for the Measurement of Social Status* (Chicago: Social Research Associates, 1949).
7. Edward O. Laumann and James S. House, "Living Room Styles and Social Attributes: The Patterning of Material Artifacts in a Modern Urban Community," *Sociology and Social Research* 54 (1970), 321–42.
8. See Richard P. Coleman, "The Significance of Social Satisfaction in Selling," in *Marketing: A Maturing Discipline,* Martin Bell, ed. AMA Proceedings, Winter Conference (1960), pp. 171–84.
9. Richard P. Coleman, "The Significance of Social Stratification in Selling," in *Marketing: A Maturing Discipline,* Martin L. Bell, ed. (Chicago: American Marketing Association, 1960), 171–184.
10. W. Lloyd Warner and Paul S. Lunt, *The Social Life of a Modern Community,* Yankee City Series 1 (New Haven: Yale University Press, 1941).
11. David T. Cook, "Reeling U.S. Labor Movement Grapples with Adversity," *The Christian Science Monitor* (September 6, 1983): 12.
12. For a review of research on the Warner Index, see James F. Engel, Roger D. Blackwell, and David T. Kollat, *Consumer Behavior,* 3rd ed. (New York: Holt, Rinehart and Winston, 1978), 119–20.
13. Lee Rainwater, Richard P. Coleman, and Gerald Handel, *Workingman's Wife* (New York: Oceana, 1959): 224–25.
14. A. B. Hollingshead, *Elmstown's Youth: The Impact of Social Class on Adolescents* (New York: Wiley, 1949).
15. H. Lee Mathews and John W. Slocum, Jr., "Social Class and Commercial Bank Credit Card Usage," *Journal of Marketing* 33 (1969): 71–78.
16. Stephen K. Keiser, "Awareness of Brands and Slogans," *Journal of Advertising Research* 15, no. 4 (August 1975): 37–43.
17. James M. Carman, "Correlates of Brand Loyalty: Some Positive Results," *Journal of Marketing Research* 7 (1970): 67–76.
18. Pierre Martineau, "Social Classes and Spending Behavior," *Journal of Marketing* 23 (1958): 129.
19. Kanti V. Prasad, "Socioeconomic Product Risk and Patronage Preferences in Retail Shopping," *Journal of Marketing* 39 (1975): 42–47.
20. Arieh Goldman, "Do Lower-Income Consumers Have a More Restricted Shopping Scope?" *Journal of Marketing* 40 (1976): 46–54.
21. Raymond Hubbard, "A Review of Selected Factors Conditioning Consumer Travel Behavior," *Journal of Consumer Research* 5, no. 1 (1978): 9.
22. Noel Capon and Marian Burke, "Individual, Product Class, and Task-Related Factors in Consumer Information Processing," *Journal of Consumer Research* 7 (1980): 314–26.
23. Stuart Rich and Subhash Jain, "Social Class and Life Cycle as Predictors of Shopping Behavior," *Journal of Marketing Research* 5, no. 1 (February 1968): 41–49.
24. James H. Myers and John F. Mount, "More on Social Class vs. Income as Correlates of Buying Behavior," *Journal of Marketing* 37 (1973): 71–73.
25. James H. Myers, Roger R. Stanton and Anne F. Haug, "Correlates of Buying Behavior: Social Class vs. Income," *Journal of Marketing* 35 (1971): 8–15.
26. Matthews and Slocum, "Social Class and Commercial Bank Credit Card Usage," 71–81.
27. George P. Moschis and Roy L. Moore, "Decision Making Among the Youth: A Socialization Perspective," *Journal of Consumer Research* 6, no. 2 (1979): 101–12.
28. Joseph N. Fry and Frederick H. Siller, "A Comparison of Housewife Decision-Making in Two Social Classes," *Journal of Marketing Research* 7 (1970): 333–37.
29. Sidney J. Levy, "Social Class and Consumer Behavior," in *On Knowing the Consumer,* Joseph Newman, ed. (New York: Wiley, 1973), 153.
30. Levy, "Social Class," 153.
31. William Cunningham, W. Thomas Anderson Jr., and John H. Murphy, "Status Consciousness vs. Status Position: Marketing Implications," *Journal of Business Research* 2 (1974): 147–56.
32. Ronald E. Frank, William F. Massy, and Yoram Wind, *Market Segmentation* (Englewood Cliffs, NJ: Prentice-Hall, 1972), 47–49.
33. R. P. Coleman, "The Significance of Social Stratification in Selling," in *Proceedings of the 43rd National American Marketing Conference of the American Marketing Association,* Martin Bell, ed. (December 1960) 171–84.
34. Robert W. Hodge, Paul M. Siegel, and Peter H. Rossi, "Occupational Prestige in the United States, 1925–1963," in *Class, Status, and Power,* 2nd ed., Reinhard Bendix and Seymour Martin Lipset, eds. (New York: Free Press, 1966), 322–34.
35. "Our New Elite: For Better or For Worse," *U.S. News and World Report* (February 25, 1980): 66.
36. "Our New Elite," *U.S. News and World Report,* 65–68.
37. Warner, Meeker, and Eels, *Social Class in America.*

38. Russell W. Belk, Kenneth D. Bahn, and Robert N. Mayer, "Developmental Recognition of Consumption Symbolism," *Journal of Consumer Research* 9 (1982): 4–17.
39. Chester R. Wasson, "Is It Time to Quit Thinking of Income Classes?" *Journal of Marketing* 33 (April 1969), 54–57.
40. Myers and Mount, "More on Social Class vs. Income," 37 (1973): 71–73.

FURTHER READING

Classics

Coleman, Richard P., "The Significance of Social Stratification in Selling," in *Marketing: A Maturing Discipline,* Martin L. Bell, ed. (Chicago: American Marketing Association, 1960), 171–84.

Foxall, Gordon R., "Social Factors in Consumer Choice: Replication and Extension," *Journal of Consumer Research* 2 (June 1975): 60–64.

Jain, Arun K., "A Method for Investigating and Representing Implicit Social Class Theory," *Journal of Consumer Research* 2 (June 1975): 53–59.

Levy, Sidney J., "Social Class and Consumer Behavior." in *On Knowing the Consumer,* Joseph W. Newman, ed. (New York: Wiley 1966), 146–60.

Martineau, Pierre, "Social Classes and Spending Behavior," *Journal of Marketing* (October 1958): 121–30.

Martineau, Pierre, "Social Class and Its Very Close Relationship to the Individual's Buying Behavior," in *Marketing: A Maturing Discipline,* Martin L. Bell, ed. (Chicago: American Marketing Association, 1960).

Myers, J. H. and J. F. Mount, "More on Social Class vs. Income as Correlates of Buying Behavior," *Journal of Marketing* 37 (1973): 71–73.

Myers, J. H., R. R. Stanton, and A. F. Haug, "Correlates of Buying Behavior: Social Class vs. Income," *Journal of Marketing* 35 (1971): 8–15.

Rotzoll, Kim B., "The Effect of Social Stratification on Market Behavior," *Journal of Advertising Research* 7, no. 1 (March 1967): 22–27.

Warner, W. Lloyd, Marchia Meeker, and Kenneth Eells, *Social Class in America: Manual of Procedure for the Measurement of Social Status* (New York: Harper & Brothers, 1960).

Warner, W. Lloyd, "Social Class in America," in *Perspectives in Consumer Behavior,* Kassarjian and Robertson, eds. (Glenview, IL: Scott, Foresman and Company, 1981), 443–49.

Wind, Yoram, "Incongruency of Socioeconomic Variables and Buying Behavior," in *American Marketing Association Fall Conference Proceedings,* Philip R. McDonald, ed. (Chicago: 1969), 362–67.

Recent Significant Research

Coleman, Richard P., "The Continuing Significance of Social Class to Marketing," *Journal of Consumer Research* 10, no. 3 (December 1983): 265–80.

Munson, J. Michael, and W. Austin Spivey, "Product and Brand User Stereotypes Among Social Classes," in *Advances in Consumer Research,* Kent B. Monroe, ed. (Ann Arbor MI: Association for Consumer Research, 1981), 696–701.

Schaninger, Charles M., "Social Class versus Income Revisited: An Empirical Investigation," *Journal of Marketing Research* 18 (May 1981): 192–208.

Shimp, Terence A., and J. Thomas Yokum, "Extensions of the Basic Social Class Model Employed in Consumer Research," in *Advances in Consumer Research,* Vol. 8, Kent B. Monroe, ed. (Ann Arbor MI: Association for Consumer Research, 1981), 702–07.

Applications

Fry, Joseph N., and Frederick H. Siller, "A Comparison of Housewife Decision Making in Two Social Classes," *Journal of Marketing Research* 8 (August 1970): 32–35.

Hollingshead, August B., *Elmtown's Youth: The Impact of Social Class on Adolescents* (New York: Wiley, 1949).

Hisrich, Robert D. and Michael P. Peters, "Selecting the Superior Segmentation Correlate," *Journal of Marketing* 38 (July 1974): 60–63.

Levy, Sidney J., "Social Class and Consumer Behavior," in *On Knowing the Consumer,* Joseph W. Newman, ed. (New York: Wiley, 1966), 146–60.

Mathews, H. Lee, and John W. Slocum, Jr., "Social Class and Commercial Bank Credit Card Usage," *Journal of Marketing* 33 (January 1969): 71–78.

Peters, William H., "Relative Occupational Class Income: A Significant Variable in the Marketing of Automobiles," *Journal of Marketing* 34 (April 1970): 74–77.

Prasad, V. Kanti, "Socioeconomic Product Risk and Patronage Preferences of Retail Shoppers," *Journal of Marketing* 39 (July 1975): 42–47.

Rich, Stuart U., and Subhash C. Jain, "Social Class and Life Cycle as Predictors of Shopping Behavior," *Journal of Marketing Research* 5 (February 1968): 41–49.

12 Reference Groups

Objectives of This Chapter

After you have studied this chapter, you should be able to:

1. Name and discuss the types of groups to which individuals belong.
2. Explain how the developmental and enduring functions of groups serve the individual.
3. Show how groups influence consumer behavior.
4. Briefly discuss roles played by group members, and the importance of these roles to marketing.

Although motivation, perception, learning, and attitudes are processes that take place within the individual mind, they do not develop in a vacuum. John Donne wrote that "no man is an island, entire of itself; every man is a piece of the continent, a part of the main." We all live with, depend on, and are nurtured by other people. We influence and are influenced by those with whom we have frequent contacts, such as friends, associates, and family members. Further, we are influenced by people we know only indirectly, through the mass media. The fields of sociology and social psychology provide a growing body of knowledge about how groups affect the individual. Research shows that groups have an immense influence over their members' purchasing behavior, their search for and use of information, their response to advertisements, and their brand choices.

We look first at the distinguishing characteristics of the types of reference groups. Next we will consider how groups function to influence consumer perceptions, attitudes, and behavior. Selected research highlights how these functions have been measured in practice. We will also note the different roles group members may play and discuss marketing implications of group influences.

DEFINITION OF A GROUP

It is important to distinguish between a mere aggregation of people and a **group**. People in groups have a common purpose—an interdependency—and they generally share similar values. Further, most groups have a structure that allows members to perform specific roles, as well as mechanisms for internal communication. By contrast, people in aggregations have no unifying factor other than their physical proximity.

group

Circumstances can cause an aggregation to become a group. For example, large numbers of travelers were scheduled to fly from Los Angeles to Chicago on a jumbo jet. When they boarded the plane they were merely an aggregation of travelers, each with his or her own purpose for traveling. After all were on board, the plane was unable to take off on schedule due to technical difficulties. The passengers were forced to wait in the jet for two hours while the repairs were made. As the delay grew longer than estimated, strangers began to converse. Most of the passengers had begun to develop a mild concern about their inconvenience and delay; some began to worry about their safety. Sensing the growing concern, the flight attendants offered complimentary drinks to the passengers. Several business people on their way to a convention began leading the other passengers in songs. During their five hours on the jet, the aggregation became a group with a common purpose. Some passengers assumed leadership roles while others were followers, and a great deal of communication took place. When the jet landed in Chicago, the group again became an aggregation, and the passengers went their separate ways. (Because of the social interaction caused by the delay, one passenger said it was one of the most enjoyable flights he had experienced in years!)

In the consumer behavior field, groups that "provide norms and values which become the perspectives that influence behavior"[1] are called

reference groups

reference groups. Members of these groups *refer* to other members and the norms and values established by the group for information, comparisons of purchases, and rules about what is correct or incorrect behavior. The major difference between a reference group and other groups or aggregates of people is that a reference group *influences the behavior* of an individual. Groups also influence the beliefs, attitudes, and values of their members. (Henceforward in this chapter, reference groups will be referred to simply as *groups*.)

Advertisers capitalize on the human tendency to rely on groups. Consider the many ads for laundry detergents and fabric softeners, which show friends comparing these products as they do their laundry. A Kraft mayonnaise commercial depicts two elderly women making a list of friends they want to tell about the product's superiority. Many ads go so far as to assert that using a particular brand is accepted social behavior. For example, the Virginia Slims campaign, "You've come a long way, baby!" has used this approach to increase cigarette sales among women. The slogan was intended to make the product a symbol for the liberation and independence of today's woman; at one time, society frowned on women smoking in public.

In one form or another, groups are a part of almost all mass media advertisements and are used in many personal selling presentations. Perhaps this is because the sheer number of groups to which the average person belongs suggests that sales messages using reference groups are likely to be successful.

Social psychologists and consumer behaviorists have developed ways of classifying the many types of groups that affect an individual's beliefs, attitudes, values, and behavior. These categories distinguish between groups on three levels: (1) associative versus disassociative groups, (2) formal versus informal groups, and (3) primary versus secondary groups. We can belong to many groups in any of these categories at once. Each classification enhances our understanding of the role of reference groups in consumer behavior.

Associative and Disassociative Groups

associative groups

Associative groups are groups with which people enjoy being associated. Besides those in which the individual already enjoys membership, there are groups the person aspires to join, such as a higher social class. The desired membership in such an aspirational group may be prohibited by reason of income, occupation, or educational constraints. Another example is that of the young managers who aspire to membership in clubs dominated by senior executives. To gain acceptance, they are likely to pattern their behavior after these executives by purchasing Brooks Brothers suits, drinking Beefeaters gin, and frequenting the same restaurants as their bosses when their budgets permit.

Promotions appealing to aspirational motives command a good deal of attention. Ads in youth-oriented magazines often depict people in aspirational poses because the readers are full of hopes and dreams for the future. For example, *Seventeen* magazine presents pictures of professional models because modeling is a professional aspiration of many teenage girls. Typical ads for *Playboy* magazine appeal to the assumed aspirations of many men. One ad states that *Playboy*'s readers represent a quarter of this country's professionals and managers, appealing to work and status aspirations, as well as to the desire to be with a beautiful woman.

disassociative groups

In contrast to associative groups, **disassociative groups** are comprised of people one does *not* enjoy being associated with. For example, the Hell's Angels motorcycle gang is one group many people would like to avoid being associated with. In marketing communications, disassociative groups are seldom depicted in isolation, but rather in contrast with associative groups. For example, a deodorant ad could depict nonusers of

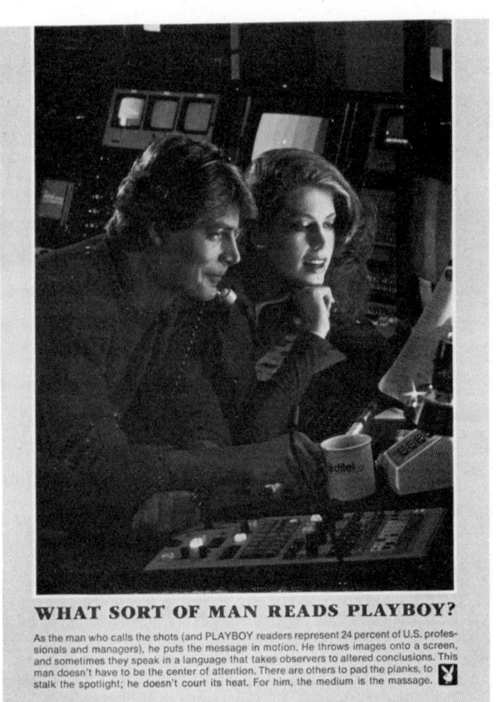

WHAT SORT OF MAN READS PLAYBOY?
As the man who calls the shots (and PLAYBOY readers represent 24 percent of U.S. professionals and managers), he puts the message in motion. He throws images onto a screen, and sometimes they speak in a language that takes observers to altered conclusions. This man doesn't have to be the center of attention. There are others to pad the planks, to stalk the spotlight; he doesn't court its heat. For him, the medium is the massage.

Table 12-1 CLASSIFICATION OF GROUPS

	Informal ***(No membership required)***	***Formal*** ***(Membership required)***
Primary (Frequent face-to-face interaction)	Families Friends Work groups Purchasing groups	Fraternities Sororities Teams Clubs Churches
Secondary (Little or no face-to-face interaction)	Sports heroes Entertainment personalities Admired occupations Representatives of specific life-styles	Professional associations Political parties Religious affiliations

its product as sitting alone while others dance at a party. Users of the product would be shown as attractive to the opposite sex. The wallflowers, of course, are the disassociative group.

Generally, associative groups can be classified as primary or secondary, based on the frequency of the member's interaction with the group. Another common classification is formal or informal, depending on how the group obtains members. Table 12-1 combines these two classifications into one system and provides examples of each combination.

Formal and Informal Groups

formal groups

Formal groups require membership through established procedures for joining. Country clubs, fraternities, sororities, student clubs, Boy Scout and Girl Scout troops, professional clubs, political parties, churches and religious affiliations are formal groups because they have clearly stated membership policies, standards, and expectations.

Because so many people are involved in these formal groups, a good deal of commercial activity is directed toward their members. For example, the manufacture and distribution of scout uniforms and equipment is a multimillion-dollar business. On a national level, the fraternity and sorority systems have substantial land holdings supported by rentals, dues, and contributions, and several religious organizations own or control vast amounts of real estate around the world.

informal groups

On the other hand, **informal groups** have no membership requirements as such. People belong to these groups because of birth, marriage, or their day-to-day activities. Participation in informal groups ranges from a few close friends to associating with large groups, such as relatives, circles of friends and acquaintances, and contacts at work. Informal groups tend to be more conducive to general discussion of products and brands, and thus have more influence on consumer behavior, than do formal groups. (This is particularly true of primary informal groups, discussed next.)

Promotions aimed at formal groups emphasize coercive elements. Such promotions are likely to stress behavior required to maintain membership by conforming to group expectations. Promotions emphasizing informal groups tend to be much more indirect, and they rely on people's desires to join these groups.

Primary and Secondary Groups

primary groups
secondary groups

Primary groups are those with which the members have frequent face-to-face contact; **secondary groups** have little or no face-to-face interaction with their members. Primary groups are very important to marketers; the bulk of the members' everyday conversations, many of which relate to economic topics, are held with other group members. Because of the frequency of members' purchases, expressions of taste, and indications of preference, a member of a primary group can easily gather and interpret information about these consumer-related topics.

For most people the family is an extremely important informal primary group—because the impact of the family is so great, Chapter 15 will cover this group in detail. Friends are an equally important informal primary group. Advertisers often show groups of friends in ads. For example, many Coca-Cola ads have groups of friends together playing frisbee or football and quenching their thirst with Coke. Lowenbrau beer ads use the theme "Here's to good friends." American Express uses groups of friends in one of its ads, suggesting not only camaraderie but also approval and congratulations from peers on getting an American Express card.

Work groups are informal primary groups which are also depicted in ads. Beer companies in particular tend to set good examples of ads using work groups. One such ad showed several business associates celebrating with Pabst Blue Ribbon beer after completing a successful design. Another ad, for Miller beer, depicts a group of young executives going off after work to play softball and relax ("Now—it's Miller Time").

Formal primary groups are comprised of clubs, teams, churches, and other groups that require membership and meet often. To earn and keep the rights and privileges of membership in formal primary groups, certain behavior is required. For example, boating clubs require their members to pay dues, attend meetings, and sail certain types and brands of boats. In exchange, members gain interaction with other members and perhaps a certain amount of social status. Ads appealing to status motives often show the product being used by members of a socially elite group. The

status-conscious person may want to buy the product in order to gain or maintain high social status.

Secondary groups are generally large groups which can be either formal or informal. Because members of secondary groups do not have frequent face-to-face interaction, the influence of the group on individual members is achieved more impersonally through the mass media, public relations, and publications.

Formal secondary groups influence their members by published standards and recommendations. For example, religious denominations have doctrines and political parties have platforms. Formal secondary groups represent a significant segment of the population, as the following three examples show. First, the conference and publishing business serving professional associations is a billion-dollar business in the United States alone. Most associations have journals and newsletters by which they communicate with their members. These often contain ads for products and services available to members. The American Marketing Association, for example, sponsors the *Journal of Marketing* and the *Journal of Marketing Research;* both contain advertising for marketing research and planning firms. Second, a large percentage of voters in this country are affiliated with either the Democratic or Republican party, which hire research firms and advertising agencies who use many of the principles of consumer behavior to better influence and understand voters. Third, religious organizations could be considered the largest single category of formal secondary group. Despite the fact that professional associations, political parties, and religious organizations wield a great deal of power, they are seldom depicted in advertisements. This is because, generally, their purposes are to move people to actions other than the purchase of certain products. Thus their impact on their members' consumption practices is so low that they are of little help to advertisers.

significant other

In contrast to formal secondary groups, informal secondary groups are widely used in marketing communications. This is because informal secondary groups are made up of people we admire from a distance and hope to emulate. They are typified by the **significant other**—usually a well-known celebrity that symbolizes the (often ideal) qualities many people aspire to possess. For example, Bruce Jenner, gold medalist in the Olympic decathlon, endorses Wheaties cereal in ads aimed at people who want to be strong and healthy; so does Olympic gymnast Mary Lou Retton. O. J. Simpson, racing to the Hertz counter, appeals to the business person's sense of professionalism, efficiency, and excellence. Ads for the Cheryl Tiegs fashion collection use her name and glamorous image as a fashion model and fashion designer to appeal to potential buyers who desire to be fashionable and up-to-date.

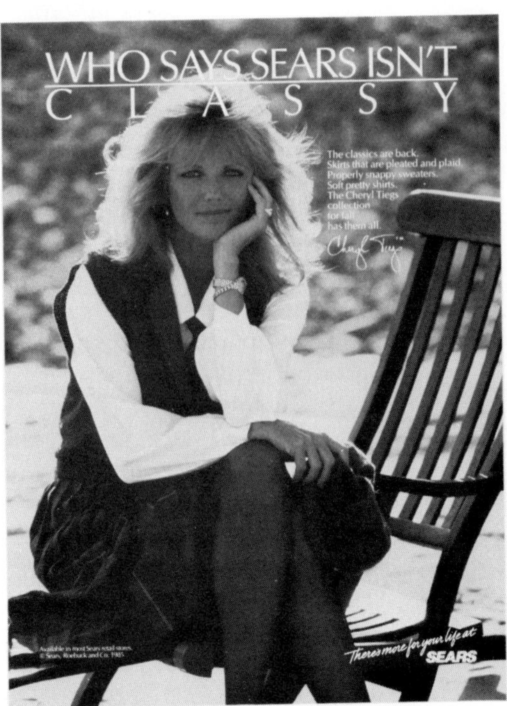

stereotypes More general personality types, or **stereotypes,** are also used in advertising. For example, ads depicting rugged adventurers who love the great outdoors, such as mountain climbers and soaring pilots, are used to sell Old Milwaukee beer. Diet soft drink ads often show a shapely female in a swimsuit attracting the attention of men as she sips her favorite thirst quencher. Ads for Marlboro cigarettes depict a "macho" cowboy type as an image for the Marlboro brand. The general personality type or stereotype can be very effective in influencing people toward certain brands because the audience can quickly identify with the stereotypes.

In the 1960s and 1970s, a preponderance of the ads featured celebrities; but in the 1980s a new style of ad began featuring less familiar actors and actresses playing average, everyday people. This addition may be related to a trend in which people are more concerned with themselves and people very much like them than they were in the past. Celebrity ads, of course, continue to be a dominant type.

Since informal secondary groups are made up of celebrities and abstract types, they allow for little, if any, two-way communication with the group member. However, they do provide one-way communication in the form of role models, and these can have a powerful impact on the consumer's opinions.

THE FUNCTIONS OF GROUPS

It is no accident that the relatively few hermits there are in the world are considered deviant rather than normal. Normal behavior for humans includes living in groups. This stems not just from the economic necessity of living with others in order to survive and thrive; human contact is a basic psychological and personal need. Because we are much less instinctive than are other animals in much of their behavior, we cannot develop in isolation. The complex and advanced nature of human mental processes and human society demands that we learn through interaction with other people. Further, our sense of personal fulfillment is related to interacting with others.

Developmental Functions

family Groups help the individual develop from the time of birth. The first group the child is aware of belonging to is the **family.** Then the child learns to interact with relatives, neighbors, classmates, and teachers in school, and other social groups with which he or she associates. The key to the developmental process for most children is the family. Without the years of care the family provides from birth, the child would find it more difficult to interact with other groups.

Children begin at a very early age to take on the values of their parents. During their preteen and teenage years, many children are socialized right into the same large secondary groups to which their parents belong or aspire to join. During socialization, the child's peers also have a large impact on value development. This is particularly true when the parents are absent from the child much of the day. However, to the extent that the child tends to play with children from families with similar values, the family "stamp" still comes through.

In addition to introducing children to many values, the family also supports or discourages values introduced by others. For example, most school systems teach the value of education. When education is reinforced in the family (perhaps by requiring homework to be completed before play or watching television), it usually becomes rooted in the child. When the value of education is not reinforced by the family, the child may lose interest in school altogether. In the same way, families can reinforce moral standards, nutritional practices, and participation in sports.

Personality development is also affected by group influences. Some traits, such as aggressiveness or a strong need for achievement, are partially learned from parents, peers, and role models in other groups.

Enduring Functions

In addition to influencing young people during socialization and development, groups have lasting influences on the behavior of members throughout their lives. First, they shape perceptions and attitudes. Second, they reward conformity with group norms. Third, they punish deviations from their standards.

Shaping Perceptions and Attitudes

What do you believe is the proper weight for a person of your height? In answering this question, do you take cues from primary groups such as family members and friends, or from secondary groups such as professional athletes, actors, and the American Medical Association? The answer most people would give to this question would be influenced by their perceptions of and attitudes towards slimness and obesity. Studies have indicated that the trait of obesity is passed down from parents to children partially through heredity and partially through environmental and social channels. Some people who eat obsessively simply do not perceive that they are becoming overweight until their condition is extremely difficult to alter. Others might have positive attitudes or only slightly negative attitudes toward obesity, reflecting the values of their primary groups. These tendencies to perceive, misperceive, or distort are related to the individual's overall psychological structure, which is strongly affected by the group.

One of the reasons advertisers depict buyers in groups is to introduce and reinforce implied common perceptions they want consumers to have. Some companies chose to promote products primarily by depicting group consensus on the subject rather than by presenting any concrete facts about their products' characteristics. Examples of this include automobile advertisements that emphasize the car's popularity among certain age groups or promise that the buyer will join an elite class of car owners.

The influence of groups on attitude is so important that some attitude models have an explicit component representing reference group influences. The Fishbein model of attitude measurement (see Chapter 6) has its limitations, but it does provide a conceptual formula for measuring this type of social influence: *normative beliefs times motivation to comply.* The normative beliefs component reflects what brands the consumer thinks others would recommend. The motivation to comply component indicates how strongly the person wishes to comply with the others' choices.

Rewarding Behavioral Conformity

norms
normative behavior

All groups, regardless of their size or degree of formality, have norms. **Norms** define the behavioral patterns expected of members of the group. **Normative behavior** is action that conforms to group values. Some norms are obvious; others are so subtle that they are not recognized by those outside the group. For example, unwritten norms have developed among sailboaters that help to identify members of this group to each other. They wear khaki-colored shorts of a design that closely resembles safari shorts. Boat owners wear them even on nonboating days, to maintain their identification with the sporty set. In this case, the implied reward for their normative behavior is the status they will maintain by continuing to be an accepted member of the boat club. As Chapter 2 on motivation made clear, affiliation and status are important human needs. Groups use rewards to reinforce their members' conformity. Members' desire to belong gives groups a great deal of power to perpetuate themselves. Thus, group values and identity are maintained over time.

In a classic consumer behavior study, James Stafford found that brand choice could be traced to group membership, but that group cohesiveness was not always the cause. Stafford conducted research with "natural groups" (groups already formed spontaneously). He studied informal friendship groups of homemakers who frequently met for coffee. He asked them to taste and then to select bread from one of four loaves labeled H, L, M, and P. Each week for eight weeks he allowed each person to select a brand. He found that women within each friendship group tended to select the same brand, although the favorite brand selected varied from group to group. Members of these groups demonstrated a tendency toward conformity. However, Stafford concluded that their conformity was due not to group cohesiveness but to the brand loyalty of the group leaders.[2]

A more recent study produced findings contrary to those developed by Stafford. Jeffrey Ford and Elwood A. Ellis replicated Stafford's research with regard to group influence.[3] Their findings support those of Robertson, that susceptibility to group influence is limited for products (such as bread) that are low in visibility, complexity, and perceived risk and that can be tested by the consumer.[4] Future research should provide insight into how group influence varies by product category and buying situation.

Asch phenomenon

This tendency toward conformity is called the **Asch phenomenon,** after Solomon E. Asch, the psychologist who originally experimented in this area of human behavior. In Asch's classic study of conformity, test participants were asked to indicate which of three lines was closest in length to a fourth line. Among the sample of eight participants, seven were actually working with the experimenter and made incorrect choices on purpose. By design, the naive participant announced his or her choice last. Results showed that when this participant heard the incorrect responses of the others before making a choice, he or she was much more likely to choose incorrectly and in agreement with the group.

Personal selling in group settings can be enhanced by using the Asch phenomenon to advantage, as this example shows:

> A group of potential customers—owners and salesmen of small firms—are brought together in a central location for a sales presentation. As each design is presented, the salesman scans the expressions of the people in the group, looking for the one who shows approval (e.g., head nodding) of the design. He then asks that person for an opinion, since the opinion is certain to be favorable. The person is asked to elaborate. As he does so, the salesman scans the faces of the other people looking for more support. He then asks for an opinion of the next person now showing most approval. He continues until he reaches the person who initially showed most disapproval (who initially might have reacted negatively). In this way, by using the first person as a model, and by social group pressure on the last person, the salesman gets all or most of the people in the group to make a positive public statement about the design.
>
> If the group includes a highly authoritarian owner accompanied by submissive subordinates, there will be a tendency for the subordinates to look to the boss before expressing an opinion. This is solved by seating the boss so that the subordinates cannot see his expression. The ensuing social pressure works on the boss even though it comes from subordinates, because often such a boss has a great need for social approval.[5]

The *multiple-step communication flow* also applies when buyers are in the process of adopting an innovative product. A closely related concept called the *diffusion process,* covered in Chapter 13, describes how new ideas are passed from consumer to consumer.

Another classic study of conformity examined how group behavior influences the selection of the "best" men's suit.[6] Students were asked to select the suit that they believed was the best of three identically styled suits, labeled A, B, and C. Four students were brought into a room and were asked to examine the suits for two minutes, after which they would be asked for their decision. The first three students asked were actually confederates and were part of the experiment. Each replied that suit B was the best. It was found that under this condition the true subjects tended to conform to the group norm and select suit B also. However, if the first confederate selected suit B and the next two confederates selected suit B "just to go along with" the first, the true subject tended to resist the group pressure. This study provides an interesting conclusion that individuals are more likely to conform to the group norm when they are not overtly pressured to do so.

Punishing Behavioral Deviation

deviant behavior

Groups also exercise power to prevent members from engaging in **deviant behavior,** or action that violates group values or standards. For example, the boating club referred to earlier might take steps to reprimand a member who wore "unacceptable" clothing, such as a black leather motorcycle jacket. Implicit in such a reprimand would be the threat of loss of membership (and the status associated with it) if the deviant behavior were to continue.

While formal groups often set down norms and the punishments for violating them in writing, informal groups may develop unwritten standards enforced by the mutual consent of their members. For example, a group of male students in a dormitory, fraternity, co-op, or apartment might develop dating norms such as "Leave other members' dates alone." If one group member deviates from this norm by dating another member's serious girlfriend, it may result in the deviant's ostracism by the group. The next time the group makes plans for a round of beer at the local pub, they would probably not invite the offender. While this may appear trivial, to the one ostracized it is a serious form of social punishment of which he is keenly aware. If the deviant values membership in the group more than continuing to date the off-limits girlfriend, he takes this punishment seriously and reverses his behavior in order to bring it into conformity with the group's expectations. Even then, the member may have already lost much of his former status as a group member.

Sororities can also use rewards and punishments to enforce a certain level of status. If applicants for membership do not have a particular style of dress, they might be rejected. Izod has exploited this type of elitism by attaching alligator labels to its clothing lines and charging higher-than-average prices for them. Consequently, not everyone can have these status symbols. Those who do are more likely to win acceptance in a status-conscious sorority.

Groups exert an enduring influence on their members' perceptions, attitudes, and behavior. These functions help to prevent the group from disintegrating into an aggregation of independent individuals. The group's

cohesiveness

influence over the individual is proportional to its **cohesiveness**—that is, the degree to which members are attracted to each other and to the group as a whole. Clearly, cohesiveness reflects the value placed on group membership.

Another factor which affects the group's influence is the size of the group. That is, the smaller the group, the more completely members can observe each other's behavior. That is why groups such as families, small friendship coteries, and other face-to-face groups have the strongest control over the individual. Even when the goals of several groups to which a person belongs are in conflict, there is a tendency to resolve the conflict in favor of the smallest group.

Several studies have been made to classify products according to their susceptibility to group influence. These studies have considered the relative amount of group influence on choices of product category and brand for a limited number of products. Table 12-2 illustrates the results of an update of these earlier studies.

The matrix is divided into four quadrants. Selected products have been placed in the quadrants based on how study respondents felt their product and brand choices were influenced by others. The findings suggest that socially conspicuous products—those most likely to be seen by

Table 12-2 GROUP INFLUENCE ON PRODUCT AND BRAND CHOICES

Reference Group Influence on Brand or Type	*Reference Group Influence on Product Category*	
	***Weak* (−)**	***Strong* (+)**
Strong (+)	Magazines Furniture Clothing Instant coffee Aspirin Air conditioners Stereos Laundry detergent Microwave ovens	Automobiles Color TV
Weak (−)	Canned peaches Toilet soap Beer Cigarettes Small cigars	

Source: Donald W. Hendon, "A New and Empirical Look at the Influence of Reference Groups on Generic Product Category and Brand Choice: Evidence from Two Nations," in *Proceedings of the Academy of International Business: Asia-Pacific Dimensions of International Business* (Honolulu: College of Business Administration, University of Hawaii, 1979), 757.

or discussed with other people—tend to have higher group influence than do less conspicuous product types. Consequently, choices of products such as canned peaches and soap were found to have little susceptibility to group influence, whereas choices of automobiles and color televisions (both very socially conspicuous products) showed high group influence for both product and brand selection. Purchases of other products in the study (magazines, furniture, clothing, instant coffee, and so on) were strongly influenced by others in terms of brand choice only. The study did not include any products that were weak in both product and brand choice influence.

A later examination of group influence distinguished between luxuries and necessities as well as whether the products were consumed privately or publicly. The researchers also differentiated between buyer choice of which *product* to buy and, secondly, which *brand* to buy. Table 12-3 summarizes the findings of that study. Products that are considered necessities and seen publicly by others appear to have weak reference group influence for *product* choice but strong group influence for *brand* choice. An automobile is an example of a public necessity. Since nearly everyone

Table 12-3 COMBINING PUBLIC–PRIVATE AND LUXURY–NECESSITY DIMENSIONS WITH PRODUCT AND BRAND PURCHASE DECISIONS

Public

	Brand \ Product	Weak reference group influence (−)	Strong reference group influence (+)	
Necessity	Strong reference group influence (+)	*Public necessities* Influence: Weak product and strong brand Examples: Wristwatch, automobile, man's suit	*Public luxuries* Influence: Strong product and brand Examples: Golf clubs, snow skis, sailboat	***Luxury***
	Weak reference group influence (−)	*Private necessities* Influence: Weak product and brand Examples: Mattress, floor lamp, refrigerator	*Private luxuries* Influence: Strong product and weak brand Examples: TV game, trash compactor, icemaker	

Private

Source: William O. Bearden and Michael J. Etzel, "Reference Group Influence on Product and Brand Purchase Decisions," *Journal of Consumer Research* 9 (1982): 183–94.

must use a car, groups do not strongly influence the decision to buy one. However, groups *do* strongly influence which *brand* of auto is selected.

At the other extreme are so-called private luxuries. These items are more likely to have group influence in terms of whether the product is purchased at all and less influence on which *brand* is selected. An icemaker is an example of a private luxury. The decision to buy an icemaker may be strongly influenced by reference groups. But the choice of which brand to buy is not, because few people will probably ever see it. As the figure shows, public luxuries such as a sailboat will have high group influence for both product and brand choice. Conversely, private necessities (such as mattresses) have *low* group influence for both product and brand choices.

HOW GROUPS INFLUENCE CONSUMER BEHAVIOR

Previous sections have shown that groups influence their members in several ways. In this section three of these ways will be explored in more detail as they apply to consumer behavior: Groups (1) provide prepurchase information to members, (2) facilitate value expressiveness and comparisons of purchases, and (3) encourage conformity with established norms for purchasing behavior.

Groups Provide Information to Members

One of the most important determinants of consumer choice is knowledge of available products and suppliers. One role of groups is supplying vast amounts of these types of information to consumers. A study by William Bearden and Michael Etzel revealed that although value-expressive and normative influences of reference groups varied among product and brand categories, the use of these groups as information sources was fairly consistent among all products and brands.[7] More importantly, group members tend to believe the information provided by the reference group.

A study by David Midgley revealed that for symbolic products that are not necessarily utilitarian, such as clothing, dominant sources of information come primarily from interpersonal sources.[8] The intention to buy a product the primary purpose of which is social may invoke a search for information from others in the purchaser's reference groups, rather than from objective or impersonal sources.

Robert Burnkrant and Alain Cousineau found that consumers agree with reference group evaluations of products because the consumers believe that the groups do indeed know what they are talking about.[9] Members refer to and use these group recommendations because they believe that the group *knows* that some products are better. In such cases, the strongest factor motivating a member to buy what the reference group recommends is the desire to obtain the best possible purchase. To put it another way, reference groups often have a good deal of **source credibility**—that is, reference groups are trusted by their members. Consequently, they are often considered to be good information sources.[10] The prospective buyer tends to believe that group members know how the product under consideration is likely to be used due to their common values, life-styles, and so on. Moreover, group members are seen as having a perspective that includes most of the concerns of each other group member; hence they are believed and trusted by the other members. Thus, consumers often seek information from other group members not simply to demonstrate compliance with group norms but to benefit from the other groups members' identification with and knowledge about a product.[11] As an example, a record promoter once exclaimed, "100 million fans can't be wrong!" on the cover of an Elvis Presley album. This was an appeal to potential buyers through group identification and knowledge, represented by the growing popularity of Elvis and his fan club.

source credibility

Groups Facilitate Value Expressiveness and Comparisons

Consumers try to maintain their identification with certain groups by comparing their preferences and purchases with those of other group members. Thus a second function of groups is to promote the expression of their own values, at least in part, by influencing members' purchase behavior. Additionally, comparing a member's purchase choices, and associated attitudes and beliefs, with those of other members reveals the member's status in the group. The greater the similarity is between a member's beliefs, attitudes, and interests and those of the group, the greater the group's **referent power** is over the member.[12] The greater the referent power, the more likely it is that the group will influence purchase behavior.

referent power

Advertisers use referent power to communicate changes in products to consumers by means of a "typical consumer" in their ads. This makes it easy for those with similar needs and wants to identify with this consumer and the product he or she is promoting. One ad for Dove soap, in which typical women from across the country are shown endorsing the product, is an example of an advertiser's use of referent power to influence product purchase.

Groups Encourage Conformity with Purchasing Norms

The third major way groups influence their members' purchasing behavior is through enforcement of the groups' established norms. Although outsiders might be totally unaware of a particular group's normative behaviors, they are very apparent to members and have an effect on their purchases. The effect varies indirectly with the size of the group. That is,

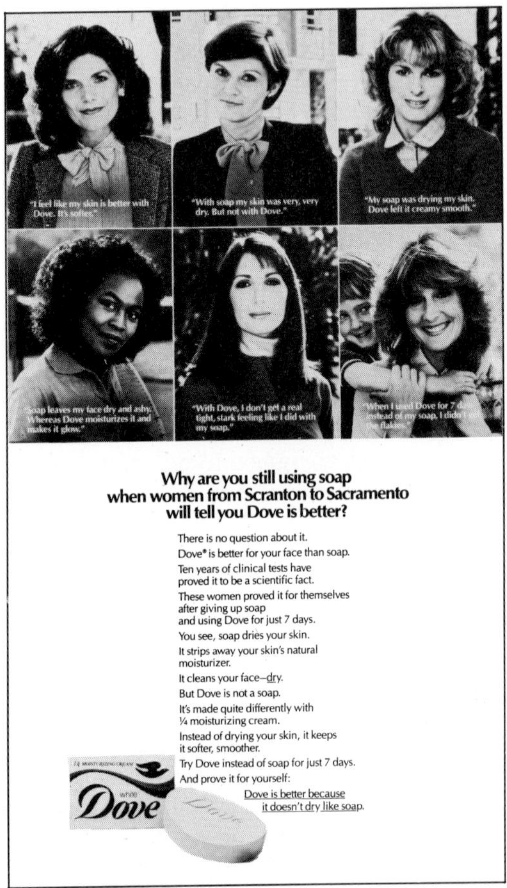

the smaller the group, the more obvious is each member's behavior. Thus, the individual consumer is more motivated to follow the recommendations of a small group than a large one. Small groups are often used in advertisements based on this principle of group dynamics. Apart from the fact that smaller groups mean fewer actors to pay, advertisers select smaller groups because they connote conformity and agreement.

As we have seen, the pressure to conform is particularly noticeable among cohesive groups. Highly cohesive groups tend to operate as a unit and they exert much influence over individual group members' actions, including purchasing. A study was conducted among upper-level corporate planning staffs and lower-level or operational managers who had to agree on details of strategic planning. Investigators found that the cohesiveness within each group was so strong that the two groups were unable to come to an agreement. In fact, cohesiveness strengthened the opposing attitudes of members of each group.[13] Due to their strong attraction to the group, members of highly cohesive groups are motivated to relinquish self-control in order to remain members. One example of cohesiveness would be in a close-knit group of high school students who have made it socially acceptable among themselves to smoke cigarettes (perhaps even a particular brand). Although several members may not want to smoke, peer pressure forces them to conform to the norm if they desire to remain in the group.

Three principles of cohesiveness relate directly to consumers.[14] As cohesiveness increases, (1) the amount of communication among group members increases, (2) the interactions among group members become more positive (less conflict oriented), and (3) the degree of influence the group has on members' choices increases. Members of highly cohesive groups frequently discuss the products they like, and they have a significant impact on the brands purchased by others in the group. For example, groups of motorcyclists can be considered cohesive. The next time you are driving along a highway toward resort and camping areas, notice the makes and models of motorcycles driven by each group of cyclists. While it is not always the case, within each group you will probably find that the cycles are all of an identical make, similar size, and perhaps even the same models.

Group size and cohesiveness are not always the measures of an individual's conformity with the group; the relative strength of an opinion leader within the group can sometimes determine the conformity of other members regarding brand choices.

reward power

We have seen how groups maintain their norms by rewarding members who uphold them and punishing those who deviate from them. **Reward power,** as this is called, is often used in advertisements. For example, in an ad for Cascade automatic dishwasher detergent, a woman is expecting guests for dinner when her mother notices spots on the glasses. The mother quickly wipes them clean and mentions the sponsor's brand of dishwasher detergent as a solution to the water-spotting problem. In the next scene (after several days), the daughter has begun using Cascade and is enjoying spot-free glasses. Joy uses a similar ad for "dishes so clean you can see yourself." Perhaps the most famous normative slogan, recently revived by Dial soap, is the one that says, "Aren't you glad you use Dial? Don't you wish everybody did?" The implications for nonusers are obvious.

Groups may influence the purchase behavior of their members simultaneously in one, two, or all three of the ways just described. Table 12-4 summarizes the three ways in which groups work to influence their members' consumer behavior. Table 12-5 compares the influences of groups on members as consumers. First, groups provide information, which meets the consumer's need for knowledge from a credible source. The expertise of the group leads to the consumer's acceptance of a brand. Second, groups influence consumer behavior in a value-expressive, comparative

Table 12-4 THE THREE MAJOR WAYS REFERENCE GROUPS INFLUENCE CONSUMERS

Informational Influence	1. Consumers seek information about brands from a professional association or group of experts. 2. Consumers seek information from those who work with the product as a profession. 3. Consumers seek brand-related knowledge and experience from friends, neighbors, relatives, or work associates. 4. The brand consumers select is influenced by observing a seal of approval of an independent testing agency (such as Good Housekeeping Institute and Underwriters Laboratories). In this case, the consumer gets information from a group to which she or he does not actually belong but with which the consumer feels comfortable. 5. Consumer observations of what experts do influence their choice of a brand (observing the brand of television which repairmen buy).
Value-Expressive (Comparative) Influence	1. Consumers feel the purchase or use of a particular brand will enhance the image others have of them. 2. Consumers feel that those who purchase or use a particular brand possess the characteristics they would like to have. 3. Consumers sometimes feel that it would be nice to be like the type of person advertisements show using a particular brand. 4. Consumers feel that the people who purchase a particular brand are admired or respected by others. 5. Consumers feel that the purchase of a particular brand helps them show others what they are, or would like to be (an athlete, a successful business person, a good mother).
Normative Influence	1. To satisfy the expectations of fellow workers, consumers allow coworkers' preferences to influence their brand decisions. 2. Consumer decisions conform to the preferences of people with whom they interact socially. 3. Family members' preferences influence consumer choices. 4. The desire to satisfy others' expectations has an impact on the brand consumers choose.

Source: adapted from C. Whan Park and V. Parker Lessig, "Students and Housewives: Differences in Susceptibility to Reference Group Influence," *Journal of Consumer Research* 4:2(1977): 105.

Table 12-5 HOW GROUP INFLUENCES WORK

Type of Influence	*Consumer's Goal*	*Characteristics of the Group as a Source*	*Implications for Consumer*
Informational	Gain knowledge	Group is highly credible	Acceptance of brand due to expertise of the group
Value Expressive (Comparative)	Maintain status	Group is similar to consumer	Identification with the group
Normative	Obtain external reward	It is desirable to be a member of the group	Conformity with the group

Source: adapted from Robert E. Burnkrant and Alain Cousineau, "Informational and Normative Social Influence in Buyer Behavior," *Journal of Consumer Research* 2 (1975): 207.

manner that meets the consumer's need for self-maintenance and status within a group that is seen as made up of people similar to the consumer. This referent power leads to identification with the group's buying choices. Third, groups influence consumer behavior by supplying a normative interest that meets the consumer's need for rewards from a desirable affiliation. The group's power to reward leads the consumer to conform in his or her behavior.

Although groups tend to reward conformity, encouraging institutionalization and stifling creativity, changes do take place in consumption patterns. The marketplace always teems with innovations, and Chapter 13 will explain how new ideas, tastes, preferences, and brand choices are spread through society.

Roles within Reference Groups

We have just seen how reference groups can influence members' attitudes and behavior. Yet members of a group do not all behave identically; each **roles** fulfills a role that differs from those of others in the group. **Roles** are patterns of behavior expected of people who occupy a position in the group. Members of a family, for example, play different roles as a result of their position in the group. Shopping for groceries has been the traditional role of women within the family structure. Clearly, roles may change over time, but some are quite enduring. As we will see in Chapter 14, family members may assume different roles in purchasing decisions for different products.

In studying a broad range of reference groups, including the family, social groups, and work groups, researchers have identified several roles that may be present among members of any group. One common role is **gatekeeper** that of "gatekeeper." The **gatekeeper** filters information and selects what information will be passed on to other members of the group for decision making. In a family, the mother may decide what choices are offered to a child in selecting a toy. While the child may have a say in the final choice, the parent performs a gatekeeper role by limiting the external information given to the child. As we will see in Chapter 17, the gatekeeper role is an important function within the organizational buying process as well. Purchasing agents within companies often act as gatekeepers by deciding which suppliers will be allowed to present proposals to the company's decision makers.

influencer
decision maker
purchaser
user

A variety of other roles have also been identified, among them **influencer, decision maker, purchaser,** and **user.** In a toy purchase, the child will probably be an important influencer and the user of the product. On the other hand, the mother or father (or both) may assume the roles of decision maker and purchaser. One role that has received a great deal of attention is that of opinion leader. In the next chapter we will look closely at opinion leadership and how it relates to innovation and the diffusion process. By identifying various role structures within groups, marketers are able to develop appeals that address those who are important in purchase decisions.

MARKETING IMPLICATIONS OF GROUP INFLUENCE

The research findings regarding groups suggests that marketers may benefit from understanding group influences and the roles members play within groups. Indeed, it is easy to see how companies have incorporated reference group appeals in their advertising and promotion strategies. Certain products are more likely to lend themselves to group influence. Research indicates that group effects tend to be most common for products that are highly visible or that reinforce members' attachment through conformity. However, groups also serve as important information sources and thus can be used to assure consumers that a product is worthwhile where they cannot (or do not care to) test it themselves. To lend support to promotions, referent power can be used in ads by showing typical consumers with whom the potential buyer identifies. This may be useful for products that are low in visibility, such as soap and medicine. In either case, advertising communications that convey a sense of belonging through membership in a reference group can be highly effective.

SUMMARY

Generally there are four types of groups: (1) informal primary groups (such as family and friends), (2) formal primary groups (such as fraternities and sororities), (3) informal secondary groups (such as aspirational groups), and (4) formal secondary groups (such as professional associations).

Associative groups are those the person enjoys belonging to, while disassociative groups are those the person has no desire to associate with. Aspirational groups, those a person would like to belong to, are often linked to the products the aspiring individual buys.

Group size and cohesiveness have some impact on consumer behavior. In general, smaller groups afford better interaction and, therefore, have greater impact. However, cohesiveness also influences the behavior of group members. The more attracted members are to the group, the greater their tendency is to comply with group choices. All groups affect consumer choice to some extent, but family and friends usually have the greatest impact. Their closeness is conducive to frequent communication and mutual observation. Nevertheless, secondary groups have an impact, often through mass communications.

Because group influences on consumer behavior are immense, appeals to groups are used frequently in marketing communications, particularly in advertising and personal selling. Groups influence their members by defining the tastes and preferences that lead to brand choice. Moreover, groups help diffuse new products through the market. Groups provide information to their members, establish bases for comparing products and brands, and set some norms for brand selection.

Groups benefit the consumer by providing useful information for brand selections. Groups also facilitate value expressiveness by providing consumers with a means for comparing their purchases with others'. In addition, groups suggest norms for product purchases, which allow buyers to conform to group tastes and preferences.

KEY TERMS

group
reference groups
associative groups
disassociative groups
formal groups
informal groups
primary groups
secondary groups
significant other
stereotypes
family
norms
normative behavior
Asch phenomenon
deviant behavior
cohesiveness
source credibility
referent power
reward power
roles
gatekeeper
influencer
decision maker
purchaser
user

QUESTIONS

1. How does a true reference group differ from a simple aggregation of people? Give an example of each in your explanation.

2. Distinguish between associative and disassociative reference groups. Which is most likely to find its place in advertising and why?

3. Compared to informal groups, formal groups are more likely to have clearly defined membership requirements and procedures. Yet often informal groups exert more influence on an individual's behavior. Is this a contradiction? Explain.

4. Make a list of the reference groups to which you belong. Classify them as primary or secondary and formal or informal. Which do you believe have the most impact on your attitudes and behavior? Why?

5. Briefly describe the two principal functions of reference groups. Discuss several

ways in which reference groups shape, reward, or punish behavior.

6. How does social visibility and perceived risk affect group influence? Provide illustrations to help clarify your description.

7. In practice, can marketers really use reference groups to influence the behavior of potential buyers? If so, discuss how this might be accomplished.

8. Discuss the concept of roles within reference groups. What implications does this have for advertising and personal selling strategies?

NOTES

1. James F. Engel and Roger D. Blackwell, *Consumer Behavior,* 4th ed. (Chicago: The Dryden Press, 1982), 144.
2. James E. Stafford, "Effects of Group Influence on Consumer Brand Preferences," *Journal of Marketing Research* 3 (November 1966): 68–75.
3. Jeffrey Ford and Elwood A. Ellis, "A Reexamination of Group Influence on Member Brand Preference," *Journal of Marketing Research* 17 (February 1980): 125–32.
4. Thomas S. Robertson, *Innovative Behavior and Communication* (New York: Holt, Rinehart and Winston, 1971), 191, 192.
5. P. Zimbrado and E. Ebbesen, *Influencing Attitudes and Changing Behavior* (Reading, MA: Addison-Wesley, 1970), 119.
6. M. Venkatesan, "Experimental Study of Consumer Behavior Conformity and Independence," *Journal of Marketing Research* 3 (November 1966): 384–87.
7. William O. Bearden and Michael J. Etzel, "Reference Group Influence on Product and Brand Purchase Decisions," *Journal of Consumer Research* 9 (1982): 183–94.
8. David F. Midgley, "Patterns of Interpersonal Information Seeking for the Purchase of a Symbolic Product," *Journal of Marketing Research* (1983): 74–83.
9. Robert E. Burnkrant and Alain Cousineau, "Information and Normative Social Influence in Buyer Behavior," *Journal of Consumer Research* 2 (1975): 206–15.
10. John R. French and Bertram Raven, "The Bases of Social Power," in D. Cartwright, ed., *Studies in Social Power* (Ann Arbor: Institute for Social Research, 1959), 150–67.
11. George P. Maschis, "Social Comparisons and Informal Group Influence," *Journal of Marketing Research* 13 (1976): 237–44.
12. French and Raven, "The Bases of Social Power," 150–67.
13. John C. Whitney and Ruth A. Smith, "Effects of Group Cohesiveness on Attitude Polarization and the Acquisition of Knowledge in a Strategic Planning Context," *Journal of Marketing Research* 20 (1983): 167–76.
14. The three aspects are summarized from propositions found in Gerald Zaltman and Melanie Wallendorf, *Consumer Behavior: Basic Findings and Management Implications* (New York: John Wiley & Sons, 1983), 113.

FURTHER READING

Classics

Bourne, Francis S., "Different Kinds of Decisions and Reference Group Influence," in *The Great Writings in Marketing,* Howard A. Thompson, ed. (Tulsa, Oklahoma: PenWell Publishing Co. 1981), 302–10.

Burnkrant, Robert E., and Alain Cousineau, "Informational and Normative Social Influence in Buyer Behavior," *Journal of Consumer Research* 2 (December 1975): 206–15.

Foundation for Research on Human Behavior, "Group Influence in Marketing," in *Marketing Classics,* Ben M. Enis and Keith K. Cox, eds. (Boston, MA: Allyn and Bacon, Inc., 1981), 206–19.

Ostlund, L. E., "Role Theory and Group Dynamics," in *Consumer Behavior: Theoretical Sources,* S. Ward and T. S. Robertson, eds. (Englewood Cliffs, NJ: Prentice-Hall, 1973).

Park, C. Whan, and V. Parker Lessig, "Students and Housewives: Differences in Susceptibility to Reference Group Influence," *Journal of Consumer Research* 4 (September 1977): 102–10.

Stafford, James E., "Effects of Group Influence on Consumer Brand Preferences," *Journal of Marketing* (February 1966): 68–75.

Stafford, James E., and A. Benton Cocanougher, "Reference Group Theory," in *Selected Aspects of Consumer Behavior,* Robert Ferber, ed. (Washington, D.C.: Government Printing Office, 1977), chapter 16.

Thornton, Russell, and Peter M. Nardi, "The Dynamics of Role Acquisition," *American Journal of Sociology* 80 (January 1975): 870–85.

Venkatesan, M., "Experimental Study of Consumer Behavior Conformity and Independence," *Journal of Marketing Research* 3 (November 1966): 384–87.

Recent Significant Research

Bearden, William O., and Michael J. Etzel, "Reference Group Influence on Product and Brand Purchase Decisions," *Journal of Consumer Research* 9, No. 2 (September 1982): 183–94.

Churchill, Gilbert A., Jr., and George P. Moschis, "Television and Interpersonal Influences on Adolescent Consumer Learning," *Journal of Consumer Research* 6 (June 1979): 23–35.

Richins, Marsha L., "An Analysis of Consumer Interaction Styles in the Marketplace," *Journal of Consumer Research* 10 (June 1983): 73–82.

Venkatesh, Alladi, "Changing Roles of Women—A Life-Style Analysis," *Journal of Consumer Research* (September 1980): 189–97.

Applications

Asch, Solomon E., "Effects of Group Pressure upon the Modification and Distortion of Judgments," in *Perspectives in Consumer Behavior,* Kassarjian and Robertson, eds. (Glenview, IL: Scott, Foresman and Company, 1981), 343–50.

Bartos, Rena, "What Every Marketer Should Know About Women," *Harvard Business Review* (May–June 1978): 73–85.

Busch, Paul, and David T. Wilson, "An Experimental Analysis of A Salesman's Expert and Referent Bases of Social Power in the Buyer–Seller Dyad," *Journal of Marketing Research* 13 (February 1976): 3–11.

Calder, Bobby J., and Robert E. Burnkrant, "Interpersonal Influence on Consumer Behavior: An Attribution Theory Approach," *Journal of Consumer Research* 4, No. 1 (June 1977): 29–38.

Stafford, James E., "Effects of Group Influence on Consumer Brand Preferences," *Journal of Marketing Research* 3 (February 1966): 68–75.

Stanley, Thomas J., "Are Highly Credible Sources Persuasive?" *Journal of Consumer Research* 5 (June 1978): 66–67.

Sternthal, Brian, Ruby Roy Dholakia, and Clark Leavitt, "The Persuasive Effect of Source Credibility: Tests of Cognitive Response," *Journal of Consumer Research* 4 (March 1978): 252–60.

13 Opinion Leadership and Diffusion of Innovations

Objectives of This Chapter

After you have studied this chapter, you should be able to:

1. Explain how the opinion leader in groups contributes to behavioral conformity among group members.
2. Describe the general characteristics of opinion leaders and how opinion leadership is measured.
3. Discuss the three major categories of innovation.
4. Discuss how innovations are diffused among buyers.
5. Identify people's characteristics according to their patterns of product adoption.

In order for purchasing patterns to change, new ideas, tastes, preferences, and brand choices must be communicated from one group member to another and from group to group. Members may follow opinion leaders in their purchasing behavior. But to what degree do opinion leaders play a part in sifting and sorting information to set buying trends, and how do purchases of innovative products gradually spread to various groups within the social structure? These questions, addressed in this chapter, are extremely important to marketers of innovative products.

OPINION LEADERSHIP[1]

Marketing communications reach consumers both directly and indirectly. In **one-step communication,** all group members are simultaneously exposed to the same marketing messages, but much of the time these messages are first screened by key group members called **opinion leaders.** In **multiple-step communication,** opinion leaders can filter advertising messages before they reach most of the group members, modifying their impact on most of the group. Figure 13-1 illustrates the two ways in which marketing messages can reach consumers.

one-step communication

opinion leaders

multiple-step communication

There is strong evidence that communications about products, tastes, preferences, and brands are bidirectional, between opinion leaders and other members. That is, opinion leaders seek advice from others as well as give it.[2] This is called **feedback** and is indicated by the two-way arrows in Figure 13-1. Opinion leaders have been called *gatekeepers* to connote the control they exert over what ideas flow into the group through multiple-step communication.

feedback

In one-step communication, consumers may arrive at their preferences somewhat independently based on advertisements to which they have been exposed. In multiple-step communications, opinion leaders are likely to feed information to other group members in ways that foster value expressiveness (comparisons) and convey group norms regarding brands.

In another approach to understanding how opinion leadership functions in a group setting,[3] the two-way flow of communication between leaders and group members is represented by a matrix, as in Table 13-1. On one axis, opinion leadership is classified as either high or low, depending on how much or little information the leader gives out. The other axis considers the amount of information sought by the opinion leader. According to this view, there are four categories of communication between group members and their opinion leaders. **Socially integrated** people seek a great deal of information from others; they also supply others with a great deal of information as feedback. **Socially dependent** people must rely on others for much of their information but do not give out much information in return. **Socially independent** people are opinion leaders

socially integrated

socially dependent

socially independent

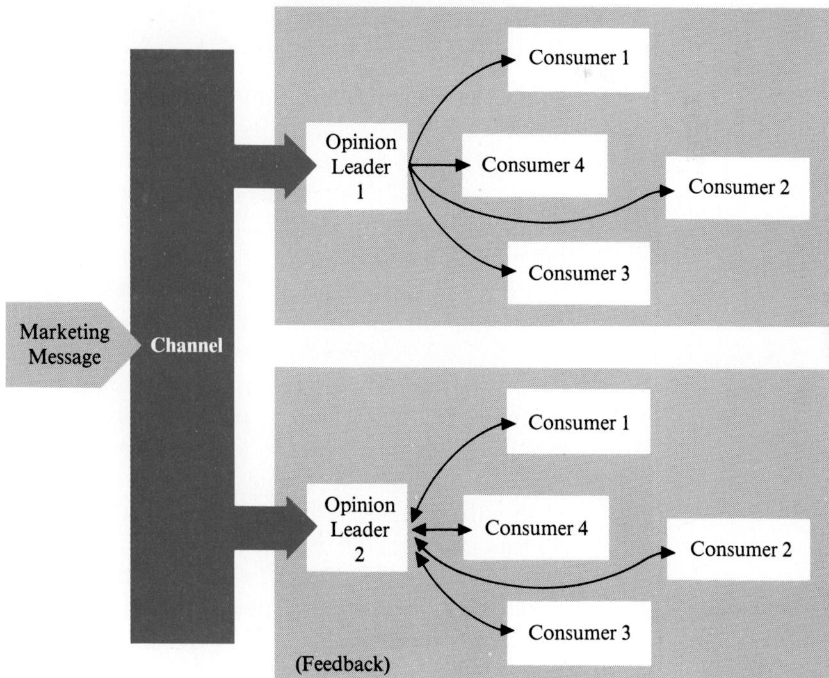

Figure 13-1
One-Step and Multiple-Step Communications

socially isolated

who do not seek information from others very frequently. **Socially isolated** people are neither opinion leaders nor information seekers. The table reflects an either-or view of the information-seeking and information-providing activities of communication. In reality, each activity can occur on a continuum from low to high, as each person gives and receives information based on his or her own abilities, temperament, and interests in particular products.

Table 13-1 MATRIX OF OPINION LEADERSHIP AND INFORMATION SEEKING

		Amount of Information Sought	
		High	*Low*
Opinion Leadership	*High*	Socially Integrated	Socially Independent
	Low	Socially Dependent	Socially Isolated

Source: adapted from Fred D. Reynolds and William R. Darden, "Mutually Adaptive Effects of Interpersonal Communication," *Journal of Marketing Research* 8 (November 1971): 451.

Who Are Opinion Leaders?

Extensive research has been devoted to studying opinion leadership and innovation. Many studies have focused on trying to identify certain characteristics that opinion leaders might have in common. If marketers can identify the opinion leaders for their brands or products, they can target communications to them. This can be highly useful in helping accelerate the adoption of new products among others in the population. Eliha Katz and Paul F. Lazarsfeld were the first researchers to investigate the characteristics of opinion leadership.[4] Their research provided profiles of opinion leaders in several product categories. In the study, personal influence was found to be more powerful than other sources of information (such as print ads, radio, or personal selling). This and several other studies confirmed the important role that word-of-mouth communications can have in influencing consumer purchases and brand selection.[5] Word-of-mouth influence can be both positive and negative, however. Johan Arndt conducted an experiment involving residents of an apartment complex for married students to evaluate the impact of word-of-mouth influence on adoption of a new food product. He found that favorable comments increase the probability of purchase, while unfavorable comments decrease the probability.[6]

Unfortunately, no clear evidence of *generalized* opinion leadership has been found.[7] That is, opinion leadership tends to vary by the type of product and situation. Myers and Robertson conducted a study of opinion leadership among households and the potential for overlap across product categories. Their findings suggest that opinion leaders do not differ from nonleaders on demographic characteristics. However, there is some evidence that opinion leaders in certain areas are also opinion leaders in similar products. For example, a woman who is among the more fashion conscious in her group and tends to influence the opinions of others about clothing may also be an opinion leader in cosmetics.

Table 13-2 CHARACTERISTICS OF OPINION LEADERS IN COMPARISON WITH OTHER GROUP MEMBERS

Related Characteristics	***Illustrative Research***
Media Habits	
Greater overall exposure to media	King and Summers (1970)
More well read in their special area of leadership	Robertson and Myers (1969)
Product Knowledge and Interest	
More interested in product category	Myers and Robertson (1972)
More knowledgeable about product area	Myers and Robertson (1972)
More innovative in trying new products	Myers and Robertson (1972)
Life-style	
More involved with community affairs and organizations	Tigert and Arnold (1971)
More price and style conscious	
Unrelated Characteristics	
Demographics	Myers and Robertson (1972)
Personality (although may be related for certain products)	Robertson and Myers (1969)

Although no specific characteristics can be identified that apply in every situation, researchers have found some overall characteristics of opinion leaders. (For the sources of this research, see the Further Reading section at the end of this chapter.) These are summarized in Table 13-2.

Measuring Opinion Leadership

sociometric technique

Four techniques have been used to measure opinion leadership: the sociometric technique, the key informant method, the self-designating technique, and the observation methods. The **sociometric technique** involves asking members of a group whom they are likely to seek out for advice about various decisions, such as which physician to choose, places to shop, and so on. Based on the recurrence of names among the answers, it would be possible to determine which group members are opinion leaders. A model can be devised to illustrate the communication network, or *sociogram,* and identify which members function as opinion leaders and which are followers. The process can be useful with consumers in a specified population group or within defined groups of industrial purchasers. Figure 13-2 shows a sociogram developed in a study of several firms concerning the adoption of a new method for industrial casting. The lines represent contacts among key people in the various firms. Certain firms stand out as being sought out by others for advice more frequently (Firms 28, 27, and 25). (This sociogram also shows that the opinion lead-

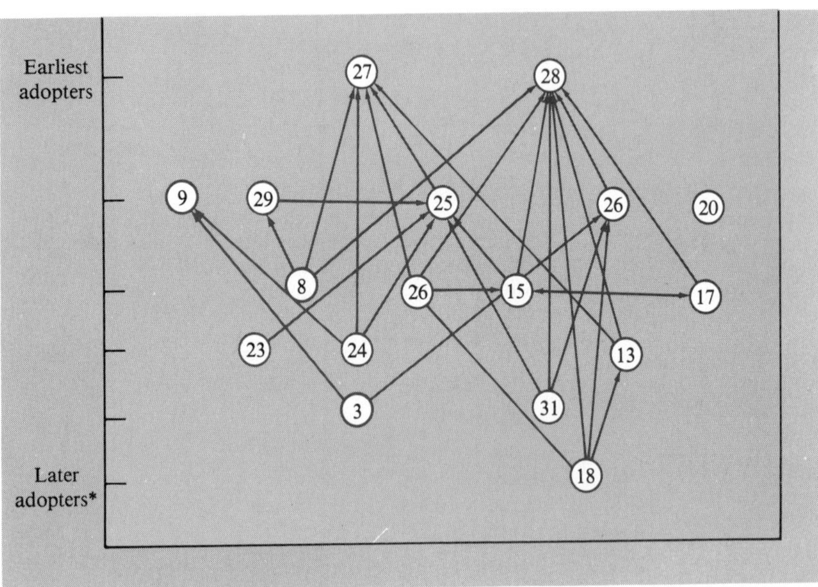

Figure 13-2
An Example of a Sociogram for Adoption of a New Industrial Process

Source: John A. Czepiel, "Word-of-Mouth Processes in the Diffusion of a Major Technological Innovation," *Journal of Marketing Research* 11 (May 1974): 172–80.

ers were earlier adopters, a point we will discuss in the next section of this chapter).

key informant technique

The **key informant technique** involves simply asking certain members of a defined group to identify those whom they believe are opinion leaders. Clearly this approach is practical only for relatively small groups.

self-designation technique

A third approach involves asking group members to describe the extent to which they influence others. This technique, called **self-designation,** usually consists of a survey with questions relating to the amount of communication between the respondents and their friends, how often they are asked for advice and so on. Figure 13-3 illustrates an opinion leadership scale using the self-designation technique. The answers to the various questions are combined to arrive at a summary score of opinion leadership for the person who answered the survey. This technique is the most commonly used approach in research studies.

observation approach

Finally, opinion leadership can be determined through direct observation. That is, a researcher records how often a group member performs a leadership role in a given setting. The **observation approach** is sometimes used in small group sessions in which teams must work together to complete a task. In these cases, a leader may emerge to which others will defer. However, this person may not necessarily represent a true opinion leader in circles outside the limited group session.

1. In general, do you like to talk about ________ with your friends?
   Yes____ —1 No____ —2
2. Would you say you give *very little information, an average amount of information,* or *a great deal of information* about ________ to your friends?
   You give very little information . . . . ____ —1
   You give an average amount of information . . . . ____ —2
   You give a great deal of information . . . . ____ —3
3. During the *past six months,* have you *told anyone* about some ________ ?
   Yes____ —1 No____ —2
4. Compared with your circle of friends, are you *less likely, about as likely,* or *more likely* to be asked for advice about ________ ?
   Less likely to be asked . . . . ____ —1
   About as likely to be asked . . . . ____ —2
   More likely to be asked . . . . ____ —3
5. If you and your friends were to discuss ________ , what part would you be most likely to play? Would you *mainly listen* to your friends' ideas or would you *try to convince them* of your ideas?
   You mainly listen to your friends' ideas . . . . ____ —1
   You try to convince them of your ideas . . . . ____ —2
6. Which of these happens most often? Do you *tell your friends* about some ________ , or do *they tell you* about some ________ ?
   You tell them about some ________ ____ —1
   They tell you about some ________ ____ —2
7. Do you have the feeling that you are generally regarded by your friends and neighbors as a good source of advice about ________ ?
   Yes____ —1 No____ —2

Source: adapted from Everett M. Rogers and F. Floyd Shoemaker, *Communication of Innovations* (New York: Free Press, 1971).

Figure 13-3
An Example of an Opinion Leadership Scale

THE DIFFUSION PROCESS

diffusion process
innovation

The **diffusion process** is the spread of innovations throughout a social system.[8] An **innovation** is something new, or a rearrangement of something old. It can be an idea, a service, or a product. Marketers of new products are keenly aware of the impact the diffusion process has on the success of product introductions. To enhance the diffusion process, marketers want to understand who is likely to adopt the product first and "spread the word" to others about the product's uses and benefits. They also are anxious to learn how best to reach these "innovators" and how the process of diffusion might be accelerated through media exposure. Since no organization has an unlimited supply of resources, marketers of innovations must make informed judgments about how long diffusion will take in order to determine the financial feasibility of their new introductions.

There are thousands of published studies that document how communications regarding ideas move from person to person and throughout groups of people.[9] These studies indicate the characteristics of people who tend to adopt an innovation quickly as well as the characteristics of those who adopt the innovation more slowly.

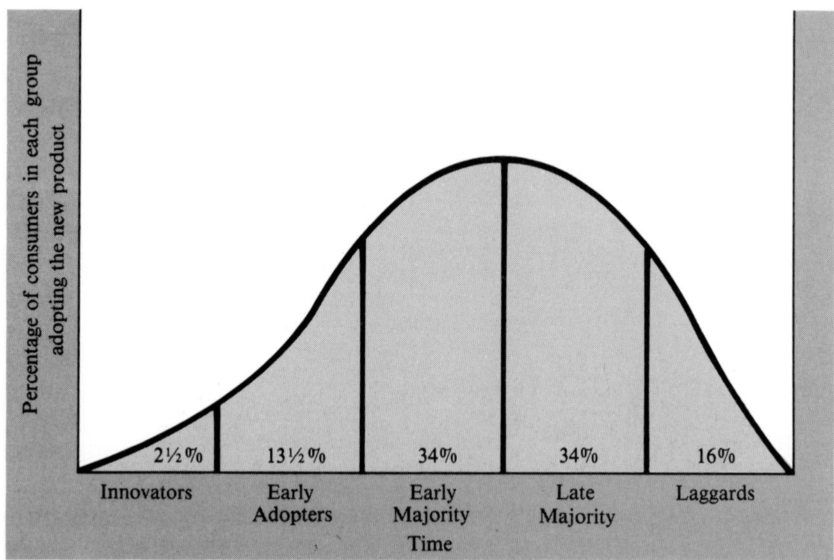

Source: adapted from Everett M. Rogers, *Diffusion of Innovations* (New York: Free Press, 1962), 162.

Figure 13-4
The Diffusion Process: Percentage of Consumers in Each Group Adopting the New Product

innovators
laggards

The diffusion of a new product can be traced from the first adopters, called **innovators,** to the last adopters, called **laggards.** Each group of consumers has its own definite characteristics. Over time, the product is gradually accepted by more and more consumers. Figure 13-4 illustrates each of the five types of people who are expected to eventually adopt the new product innovation. Estimates of the proportion of the population in each category results in a *normal distribution* with approximately 2.5% classified as innovators, 13% early adopters, 34% early majority, 34% late majority, and 16% laggards.

A related way of looking at the diffusion process is illustrated in Figure 13-5, a typical S-shaped diffusion pattern that shows the cumulative proportion of adopters over time. In most instances, marketers of new products want to increase the speed of adoption; as a result of changing such factors as distribution, promotion, pricing, and so on to favor early adoption, the result can be a steeper curve that climbs more quickly in the early stages. This is dependent on many factors including distribution, promotion, pricing, and so on.

While the S-shaped pattern of adoption is typical for many new products, different patterns result when the new product is a fad or a fashion item. Robertson suggests that there are actually three different adoption curves (see Figure 13-6). A fashion, such as the reintroduction of miniskirts, rises and drops off more rapidly than the typical new product; a fad (such as Cabbage Patch dolls) rises quickly and then may disappear.

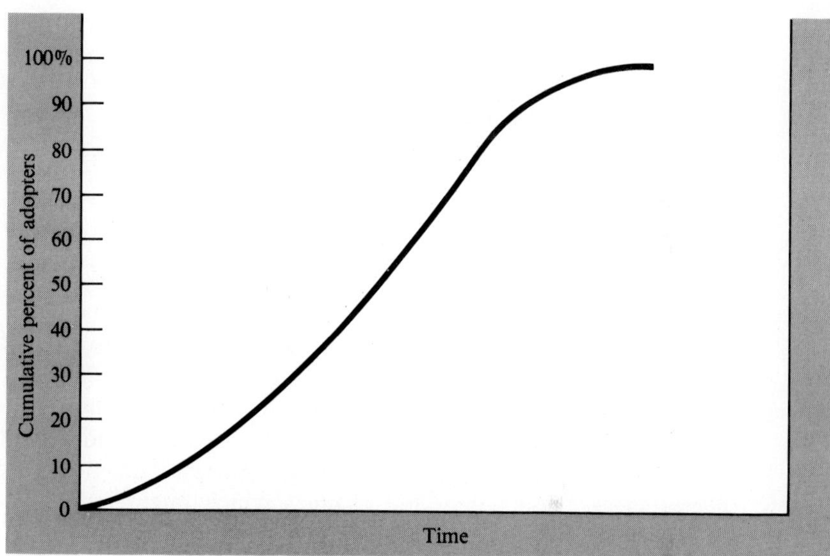

Figure 13-5
Cumulative S-shaped Diffusion Pattern

Source: Thomas S. Robertson, *Innovative Behavior and Communication* (New York: Holt, Rinehart and Winston, 1971), 50.

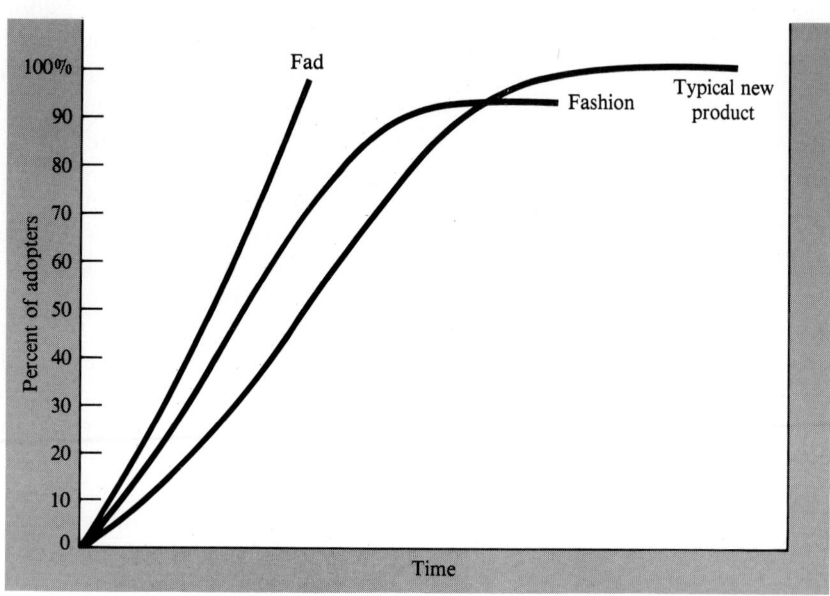

Figure 13-6
Generalized Diffusion Patterns for a New Product, a Fashion, and a Fad

Source: adapted from Thomas S. Robertson, *Innovative Behavior and Communication* (New York: Holt, Rinehart and Winston, 1971), 50.

Before we look at the characteristics of these groups, it will help to examine first what innovations are and what contributes to their diffusion. Essentially, three elements are important in the diffusion process: (1) the type of innovation, (2) the characteristics of innovators versus early adopters, and (3) the communications about the product which take place over them.[10]

Types of Innovations

continuous innovation

dynamically continuous innovation

discontinuous innovation

Marketers use three categories to classify innovations. A **continuous innovation** is an extension of a product line by way of a minor modification to an existing product. Continuous innovations require few behavioral changes and are easily adopted. A **dynamically continuous innovation** is an existing product with new features and benefits. Dynamically continuous products offer more newness and, therefore, require some learning and behavioral changes which might inhibit adoption. A **discontinuous innovation** is an entirely new product with new functions. Discontinuous innovations are extremely high in novelty and require consumers to make major behavioral adjustments which are likely to impede their adoption. For example, in the 1940s television was a discontinuous innovation. In the 1950s color television was a dynamically continuous innovation. The introduction of wide-screen projection television in the 1970s could be considered a continuous innovation. The type of new product has a great deal to do with how easily and rapidly it is adopted.

Innovations have certain characteristics that may facilitate their adoption. Five key factors have been identified which contribute to the success of an innovation: relative advantage, compatibility, complexity, trialability, and observability (see Table 13-3).[11] First, successful innovations possess high *relative advantage* over existing products and allow consumers to easily recognize these advantages. Consider the automatic shut-off iron, a recent innovation. This iron is designed to address a perceived need and offers distinct advantages to forgetful consumers. Second, successful innovations are *compatible* with current use systems and customer's current thinking. That is, they are easy to understand and incorporate into present patterns of behavior. One ad for Colgate's new pump packaging for toothpaste illustrates ease of use by children, thus minimizing concerns about whether the pump is difficult to operate. Similarly, an ad for Norelco's innovative digital thermometer pictures the product in use to stress its simplicity and show that it is used in the same manner as a traditional mercury thermometer.

Third, innovative products are adopted more readily if they are *not highly complex*. Products that require extensive learning and are confusing at first often discourage rapid adoption. The growth of personal computers might have progressed even more rapidly if software documentation were easier for nonexperts to understand. Recognizing

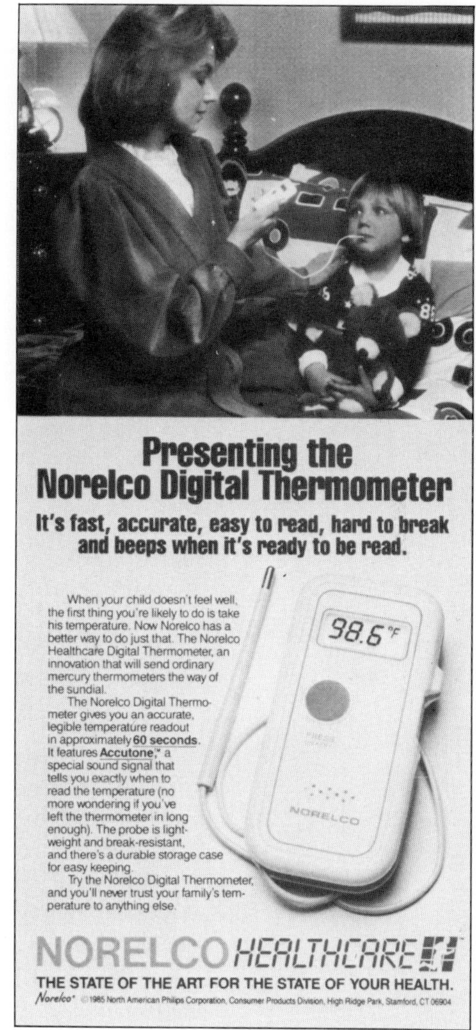

this, many manufacturers now stress the effortlessness of learning how to use their products. Apple computer corporation recently introduced the new Macintosh computer by calling it "the computer for the *rest* of us" to emphasize its lack of complexity. *Trialability,* the fourth factor, is the ease with which a potential buyer can gain first-hand experience with the innovative product before purchasing it. Marketers routinely use free samples, taste tests, demonstrations, and free home trial periods to encourage the adoption of their innovations. Each of these is designed to increase the trialability of the new product or service. When an innovation offers a high relative advantage but may be perceived as too complex by first-time buyers, trialability can be a key element in getting buyers to

Table 13-3 CHARACTERISTICS OF SUCCESSFUL INNOVATIONS

Factor	***Description***	***Example***
Relative Advantage	Innovation is perceived to offer unique benefits that make it superior to existing products	Microwave ovens offer obvious time savings over conventional ovens for busy consumer lifestyles
Compatibility	The innovation fits in with the current attitudes, behaviors, and use patterns, or target customers	Home video cassette recorder machines, conform neatly to existing TV-watching patterns of most Americans
Complexity	The innovation is not so complex as to make it difficult to understand or use	A digital thermometer is used just as a normal one but simply is read differently
Trialability	The innovation can be easily tried and tested before purchase (through samples, trial period, product demonstrations or loaners)	Sampling of "Wash and Dry" disposable towelettes for cleaning hands after meals
Observability	The innovation is conspicuous to others, thereby encouraging awareness and interest among other potential buyers	Post-it office message pad has adhesive on one side for notes.

Source: adapted from Everett M. Rogers and F. Floyd Shoemaker, *Communication of Innovations,* 2nd ed. (New York: Free Press, 1971).

consider an innovation and thus stimulate purchase. Trialability helps reduce the perceived risk in making an initial purchase by limiting the up-front financial commitment.

Finally, *observability* is a highly important attribute of successful innovators. This is the extent to which others can easily see product benefits. Such social visibility is especially needed in the adoption of fashion items. The hula-hoop was successful as an innovative form of recreation partly because other children in the neighborhood could see the fun that their friends were having.

Rogers and Shoemaker developed a diagram that illustrates these five innovation characteristics in a broader context of consumer decisions and communication. Figure 13-7 shows this decision process over time, beginning with "receiver variables," which describe the personality, needs, and attitudinal aspects of the consumer with respect to the innovation. These variables, together with the characteristics of the social system, affect the amount of knowledge the consumer has about the product (stage 1). In stage 2, persuasion, the five characteristics of the innovation itself further influence the consumer's disposition toward purchase. In stage 3, the potential buyer chooses either to adopt or reject the product. In stage 4, the consumer continues to evaluate his or her decision to

Figure 13-7
The Innovation Decision Process

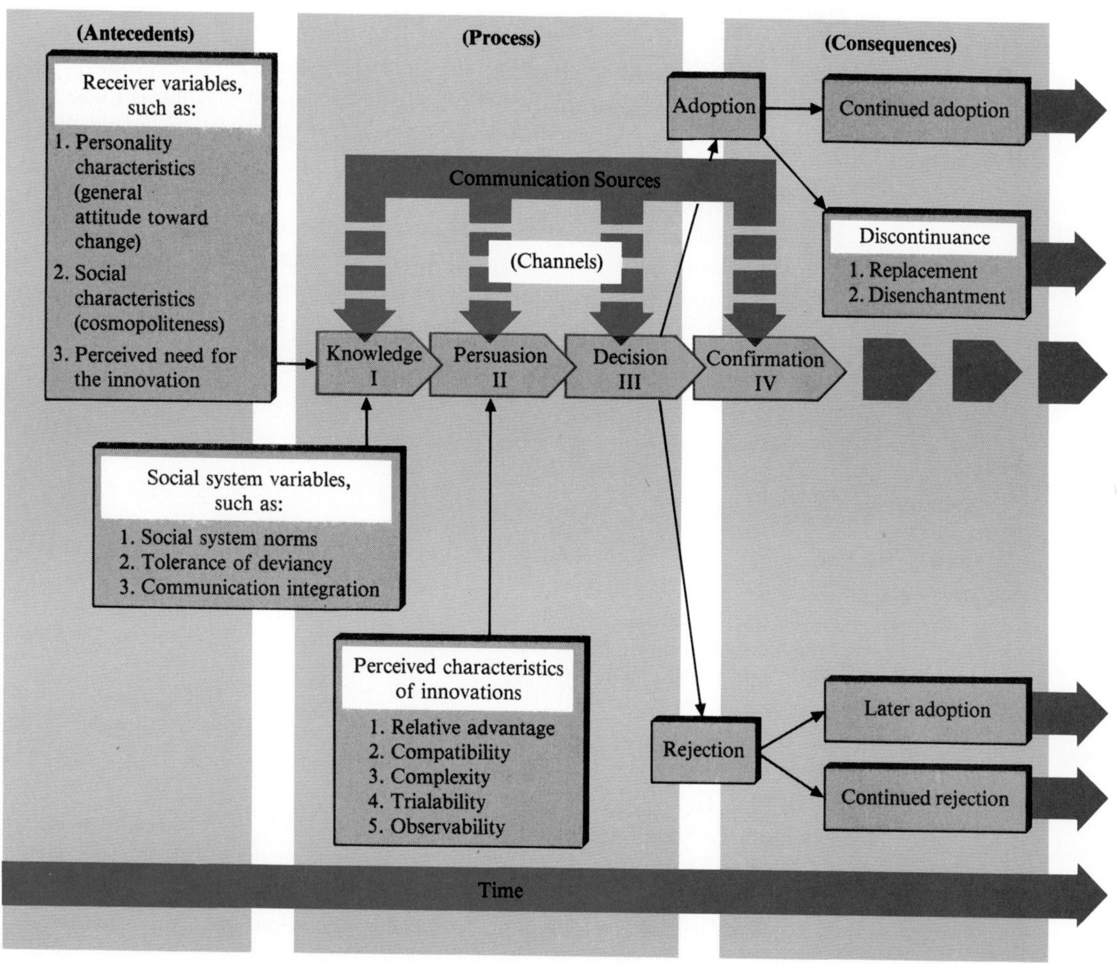

Source: adapted from Everett M. Rogers and F. Floyd Shoemaker, *Communication of Innovations*, 2nd ed. (New York: Free Press, 1971), 102.

confirm whether the right choice was made and whether the product should be reconsidered in the future.

It is the marketers themselves who should consider the characteristics of innovations and the innovation decision process when evaluating potential new products; those in research and development, who invent the new products, generally lack the marketer's customer orientation. Engineers, who tend to be technically oriented, sometimes "overengineer" their products. That is, the innovation may be too complex and difficult to explain to the average buyer. Overengineered products may require complex technical support and new use systems, and they may be expensive for the company should they fail. Knowing this can help marketers avoid launching an overengineered product that will not fit easily into the users' environment. Also, by carefully checking prospective buyers' attitudes about the new product in advance, marketers can develop a more effective communication program for the product—one designed, for example to boost trial, communicate low complexity, or promote observability.

Characteristics of Potential Buyers

Which of the five categories of buyers is most important in stimulating product acceptance: innovators or early adopters? Although innovators act sooner, early adopters are probably more important because of their interpersonal characteristics. Looking at Table 13-4, it is easy to see how differences among the groups affect both the communication of new ideas

Table 13-4 A COMPOSITE PICTURE OF ADOPTER CATEGORIES

Adopter Category	*Salient Values*	*Personal Characteristics*	*Communication Behavior*	*Social Relationships*
Innovators	"Venturesome"; willing to accept risks	Youngest age; highest social status; largest and most specialized operations; wealthy	Closest contact with scientific information sources; interaction with other innovators; relatively greatest use of impersonal sources	Some opinion leadership; very cosmopolitan
Early adopters	"Respect"; regarded by many others in the social system as a role model	High social status; large and specialized operations	Greatest contact with local change agents	Greatest opinion leadership of any category in most social systems; very localist
Early majority	"Deliberate"; willing to consider innovations only after peers have adopted	Above-average social status; average-sized operation	Considerable contact with change agents and early adopters	Some opinion leadership
Late majority	"Skeptical"; overwhelming pressure from peers needed before adoption occurs	Below-average social status; small operation; little specialization; small income	Secure ideas from peers who are mainly late majority or early majority; less use of mass media	Little opinion leadership
Laggards	"Tradition"; oriented to the past	Little specialization; lowest social status; smallest operation; lowest income; oldest	Neighbors, friends, and relatives with similar values are main information source	Very little opinion leadership; semi-isolates

Source: Everett M. Rogers, *Diffusion of Innovations* (New York: Free Press, 1962), 185.

and their adoption. While innovators are technologically competent, they tend to be very independent. Thus they have only a slight effect on other people by providing demonstrations of the product in use. As the first to use new products, they provide marketers with proof of how the product functions. In turn, marketers may point to the experience of innovators in their attempts to educate other prospective buyers. For example, the marketer of a new computerized vision system designed to find flaws in manufacturing products first applied its system with a small, very innovative manufacturer of electronic parts. Later the marketer pointed to successful use with this company in efforts to sell the innovation to larger manufacturers who were looked to as leaders in their industry. The marketer was then able to build its reputation industry-wide by pointing to the success with the larger buyer. The second buyer was the early adopter, a critical link in the diffusion process.

While innovators play a small role in diffusion, early adopters are vital to the marketing of innovations. They are the key to good word-of-mouth publicity and acceptance of new products by almost all buyers. The strong social position of early adopters makes their purchase of new products an important catalyst for future sales. Once *they* accept a new product, buyers in the other adopter categories follow almost automatically, like a chain reaction.

Understandably, much research attention has been devoted to innovators and early adopters, since they are of primary concern to marketers of innovations in the critical stages of product success. However, the laggard segment poses interesting problems for marketers as well. Why do some people wait so long to adopt a product, service, or idea? What characteristics do laggards have in common that distinguish them from others? These questions are important for marketers who wish to penetrate a complete market. Kenneth Uhl, Roman Andrus, and Lance Poulsen examined a sample of households to measure the variables that might differentiate laggards, intermediate adopters, and innovators.[12] Their findings suggest that laggards differ from the others primarily in terms of income and brand loyalty: they tend to cling to proven products and see new products as too risky and unproven. To reach the laggard segment, marketers must be able to provide sufficient risk-reducing incentives. Trialability becomes more important and *incentives* (coupons, specials, and so on) may be needed to draw laggards into purchasing the new product. In efforts to make trialability very easy, a major soap manufacturer offered free bars to certain motel chains who would place them in guest rooms. Although the soap had been on the market for fifteen years, the free soap gained trial by many potential consumers who stayed in the motel. Placement of brochures in the bathrooms highlighted the brand, drew attention to the product, and reinforced the trial.

Although the discussion of diffusion has centered on consumer product innovations, the same adopter categories can be used to describe industrial and professional buyers. We will cover industrial innovations in Chapter 17 with organizational buying. Developing marketing strategies based on diffusion for professional product innovations as well as consumer and industrial innovations is discussed next.

Developing Marketing Strategies Based on Diffusion

Clearly, marketers should be sensitive to the diffusion categories of individuals and firms buying their products. A pharmaceutical firm introduced a new product developed to relieve pain from sprains and strains. Their salespeople were asked to identify physicians that fit their early-adopter profile (that is, younger, heavy prescribers, on hospital boards, with modern-looking offices and equipment, and so on). Then a company task force gave these physicians special attention through direct mail, sampling, and sales calls. The targeted physicians were also asked to test and evaluate the new product. These early-adopter physicians quickly tried and supported it. For the marketer, the result was an efficient use of resources to target those physicians who in turn would tell others about the new drug. Not surprisingly, diffusion of new product acceptance from early adopters to other physicians was rapid.

For consumer marketing, advertisers are careful to depict early adopters and early majority adopters in advertisements for new products.

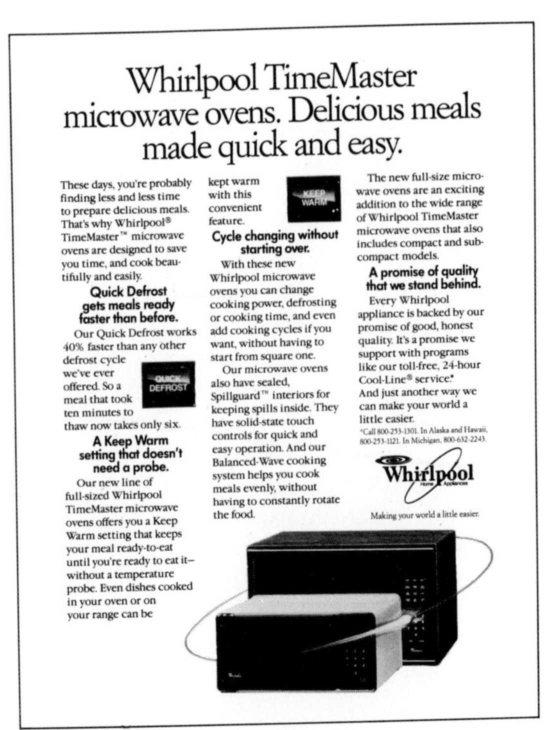

Later, as the product moves from one diffusion state to another, the actors and messages can be altered to conform to that particular target audience. For example, when microwave ovens were first introduced, the ads tended to stress their novel aspects such as high-speed cooking. As more people began to purchase microwaves, the ads began stressing each oven brand's unique features, such as quick defrost, solid-state controls, programmability, size, and price. Marketers used feedback from early adopters to ascertain those features that were most desirable to buyers and adjusted their product and promotional messages accordingly.

Peter Wilton and Edgar Pessemier examined the acceptance of innovations and information effects.[13] In a study of electric vehicles, they found that marketers can exert strong influence over adoption through product design and communication methods. As a practical guide, they recommend that an introduction be preceded by a careful analysis of potential buyers' cognitive and affective reactions to the innovation and its eventual competitors. They also stress the importance of effective marketing communication to address these concerns.

During the diffusion process, the innovating firm must be aware of how consumers who try the new product react to its characteristics. Successful marketers seek to achieve a two-way flow of information with all segments of the marketplace. Figure 13-8 depicts the flow of information between marketers and the various types of adopters. The marketer's

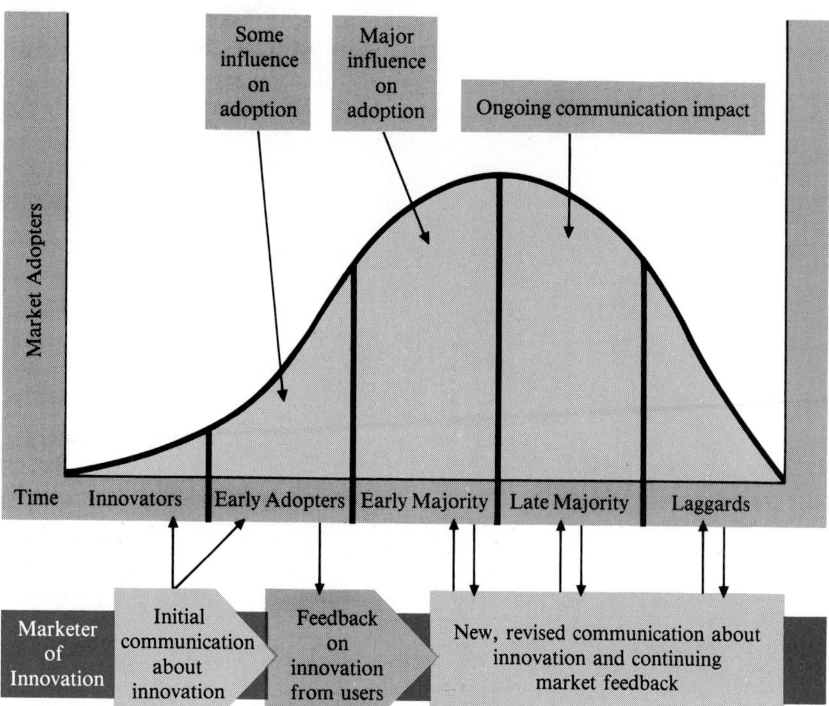

Figure 13-8
Two-Way Flow of Information Between Marketer and Innovation Adopters

initial messages about the new product are directed at innovators and early adopters. Innovators are influenced to some degree by these messages. However, some members of this group might normally purchase the product anyway, regardless of the message. It is the early adopters who receive the full impact of the marketer's message. They continue the information flow to the early majority, as well as present feedback about the product to the marketer. The marketer uses this information to alter the promotional campaign to better influence the early majority, late majority, and laggards. Those who adopt the product at later stages are influenced both by adopters earlier than themselves and by the marketer's messages. Clearly, the diffusion process is *not* inevitable—as evidenced by the failure of many new product introductions. However, the process does typify the stages through which many successful launches pass.

The Accelerating Rate of Innovation Adoption

Research has shown that the rate of adoption of innovations in consumer markets is increasing over time. Richard Olshavsky[14] examined the growth rate of twenty-five selected innovations based on the year of introduction (see Table 13-10). The results, shown in Figure 13-9, suggest that adoption rates for innovations have accelerated over time. More rapid adoption rates reflect changes in how consumers obtain information and respond to innovations. The trend toward more rapid adoption of innovation coincides with evidence that the average product life cycle is shortening.[15] This shortening would be a natural result of an increasing rate of adoption for innovations that replace existing products.

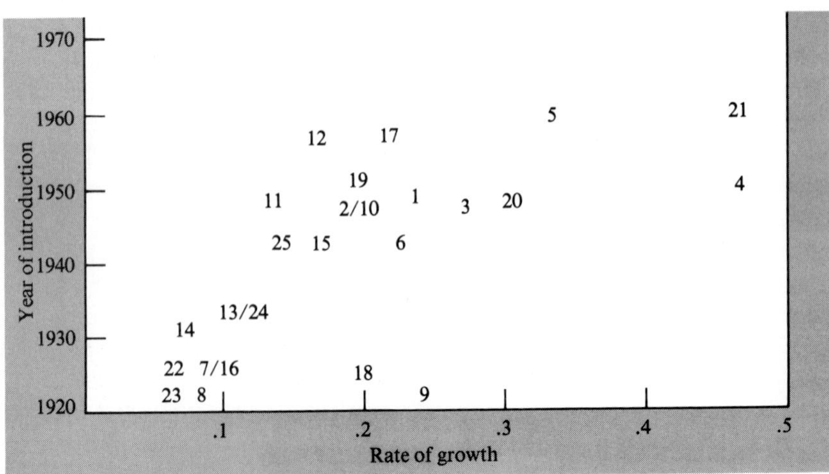

Figure 13-9
Rates of Adoption versus Year of Introduction for 25 Innovations

Source: Richard W. Olshavsky, "Time and Rate of Adoption of Innovations," *Journal of Consumer Research* 6 (1980): 425–28.

Table 13-10 OLSHAVSKY'S LIST OF 25 SELECTED INNOVATIONS

1. Air conditioners	14. Hotplates
2. Bed coverings	15. Mixers
3. Blenders	16. Ranges, standard
4. Broilers	17. Ranges, built-in
5. Can openers	18. Refrigerators
6. Clothes dryers	19. Steam irons
7. Clothes washers	20. Televisions, black-and-white
8. Coffee makers	21. Televisions, color
9. Dishwashers	22. Toasters
10. Disposals	23. Vacuum cleaners
11. Freezers	24. Waffle irons
12. Frypans	25. Water heaters
13. Heating pads	

Source: Richard W. Olshavsky, "Time and Rate of Adoption of Innovations," *Journal of Consumer Research* 6 (1980): 425–28.

SUMMARY

Opinion leadership and the diffusion of innovations are key concepts of importance to marketers. The success of new-product introductions depends on the extent of favorable word of mouth among those who introduce others. Opinion leaders are group members who filter messages and guide the attitudes and purchasing decisions of other members. Evidence suggests that opinion leaders also seek information; therefore, communication between leaders and other members is bidirectional. There are four major categories of people in the interpersonal communication process based on opinion leadership and information seeking: the *socially integrated,* the *socially dependent,* the *socially independent* and the *socially isolated.* Certain characteristics of opinion leaders have also been identified by researchers. However, opinion leadership is largely product- and situation-specific. To measure opinion leadership in a given situation, researchers use four methods: sociometric, key informant, self-designation, and observation.

Diffusion is the process by which innovations are spread through society. The dynamics of this process are of critical concern to marketers of new products. Five categories are used to describe the propensity of individuals to adopt an innovation: innovators, early adopters, early majority, late majority, and laggards. The diffusion of innovations has accelerated over time as the average product life cycle has shortened.

An understanding of the diffusion process helps marketers recognize the needs to adjust product designs and tailor communications to maximize the influence of innovators and early adopters.

KEY TERMS

one-step communication
opinion leaders
multiple-step communication
feedback
socially integrated
socially dependent
socially independent
socially isolated
sociometric technique
key informant technique
self-designation technique
observation approach
diffusion process
innovation
innovators
laggards
continuous innovation
dynamically continuous innovation
discontinuous innovation

QUESTIONS

1. How do opinion leaders function to influence group behavior? What does this have to do with consumer behavior?

2. Think of opinion leaders you know. What are some of the roles they play in gaining support for their ideas?

3. How do the characteristics of successful innovations influence their adoption and diffusion?

4. Give an example of a recent innovation that has been diffused in society. Discuss which types of people adopted it first and later on.

5. It helps successful adoption to be able to observe a product prior to purchase. List as many ways as you can think of about how consumers could observe a new auto before purchasing the brand.

6. If you were working with a design group who was creating a new high tech industrial product, what cautions would you raise to them based on the material in the chapter?

7. Where do you fit in the diffusion cycle for stereo equipment, sports clothing and other products purchased by college students? Explain.

8. Is it more important to be a leader in product introduction or can a firm succeed as an early follower? Justify your answer.

NOTES

1. Thomas S. Robertson's excellent book addresses the topics in this section. See *Innovative Behavior and Communication* (New York: Holt, Rinehart and Winston, 1971).
2. Jagdish N. Sheth, "Word-of-Mouth in Low Risk Innovations," *Journal of Advertising Research* 11 (1971): 15–8.
3. Fred D. Reynolds and William R. Darden, "Mutually Adaptive Effects of Interpersonal Communication," *Journal of Marketing Research* 8 (November 1971): 449–54.
4. Eliha Katz and Paul F. Lazarsfeld, *Personal Influence* (Glencoe, IL: The Free Press, 1955).
5. William H. Whyte, Jr. "The Web of Word of Mouth" *Fortune* 50 (November 1954).
6. Johan Arndt, "Role of Product-Related Conversations in the Diffusion of a New Product," *Journal of Marketing Research* 9 (August 1967): 291–95.

7. James H. Myers and Thomas S. Robertson, "Dimensions of Opinion Leadership," *Journal of Marketing Research* 9 (February 1972): 41–46.
8. For a detailed review of the use of the diffusion process in marketing, see Thomas S. Robertson, *Innovative Behavior and Communication* (New York Holt, Rinehart and Winston, 1971).
9. For a review of current work on diffusion, see Everett M. Rogers, "New Product Adoption and Diffusion," *Journal of Consumer Research* 2 (March 1976): 290–301.
10. Everett Rogers, *Diffusion of Innovations* (New York: Free Press, 1962), 12–20.
11. Everett M. Rogers and F. Floyd Shoemaker, *Communication of Innovations,* 2nd ed. (New York: Free Press 1971).
12. Kenneth Uhl, Roman Andrus, and Lance Poulsen, "How Are Laggards Different? An Empirical Inquiry," *Journal of Marketing Research* 7 (February 1970): 51–54.
13. Peter C. Wilton and Edgar A. Pessemier, "Forecasting the Ultimate Acceptance of an Innovation: The Effects of Information," *Journal of Consumer Research* 8 (September 1981): 162.
14. Richard W. Olshavsky, "Time and Rate of Adoption of Innovations," *Journal of Consumer Research* 6 (1980): 425–28.
15. The product life cycle concept has been used in most introductory marketing texts to explain the periods of growth, stabilization, and decline in sales of a product. It is a key tool businesses use to develop marketing strategies.

FURTHER READING

Classics

Arndt, Johan, "New Product Diffusion: The Interplay of Innovativeness, Opinion Leadership, Learning, Perceived Risk, and Product Attributes," in *Models of Buyer Behavior,* Jagdish N. Sheth, ed. (New York: Harper and Row, 1977), 327–35.

Cunningham, Scott M., "Perceived Risk as a Factor in the Diffusion of New Product Information," in *Proceedings of the American Marketing Association Fall Conference,* Raymond M. Haas, ed. (Chicago: American Marketing Association, 1966), 698–721.

Engel, James F., Robert J. Kergerreis, and Roger D. Blackwell, "Word-of-mouth Communication by the Innovator," *Journal of Marketing* 33 (July 1969): 15–19.

Kegerreis, Robert J., James F. Engel, and Roger D. Blackwell, "Innovativeness and Diffusiveness: A Marketing View of the Characteristics of Earliest Adopters," in *Research in Consumer Behavior,* D. T. Kollat, R. D. Blackwell, and J. F. Engel, eds., (New York: Holt, Rinehart and Winston, Inc., 1970), 671–89.

Midgley, D. F., and G. R. Dowling, "Innovativeness: The Concept and Its Measurement," *Journal of Consumer Research* 4 (March 1978): 229–41.

Myers, James H., and Thomas S. Robertson, "Dimensions of Opinion Leadership," *Journal of Marketing Research* (February 1972): 41–46.

Robertson, Thomas S., "The Process of Innovation and the Diffusion of Innovation," *Journal of Marketing* 31 (January 1967): 14–19.

Robertson, T. S., "A Critical Examination of 'Adoption Process' Models of Consumer Behavior," in *Models of Buyer Behavior,* Jagdish N. Sheth, ed. (New York: Harper and Row, 1974), 271–95.

Robertson, Thomas S., and James H. Myers, "Personality Correlates of Opinion Leadership and Innovative Buying Behavior," *Journal of Marketing Research,* 6 (May 1969): 164–168.

Rogers, Everett M., "New Product Adoption and Diffusion," *Journal of Consumer Research* 2 (March 1976): 290–301.

Rogers, Everett M., "A Personal History of Research on the Diffusion of Innovations," in *Public Policy, and Marketing Thought,* A. R. Andreason and S. Sudman, eds. (Chicago, IL: American Marketing Association, 1976), 43–63.

Rogers, E. M., and P. C. Thomas, *Bibliography on the Diffusion of Innovations* (Ann Arbor, MI: Department of Population Planning, University of Michigan, 1975).

Tigert, Douglas J., and Stephen J. Arnold, *Profiling Self-Designated Opinion Leaders and Self-Des-*

ignated Innovators through Life Style Research (Toronto: School of Business, University of Toronto, June 1971).

Recent Significant Research

Carlson, Lee, and Sanford L. Grossbart, "Toward a Better Understanding of Inherent Innovativeness," in *1984 AMA Educators' Proceedings,* Russell W. Belk, et al., eds. (Chicago: American Marketing Association, 1984), 88–91.

Dickerson, Mary Dee, and James W. Gentry, "Characteristics of Adopters and Non-Adopters of Home Computers," *Journal of Consumer Research* 10 (September 1983): 225–35.

LaBay, Duncan G., and Thomas C. Kinnear, "Exploring the Consumer Decision Process in the Adoption of Solar Energy Systems," *Journal of Consumer Research* 8 (December 1981): 271–78.

Mahajan, Vijay, Jerry Wind, and Subhash Sharma, "An Approach to Repeat-Purchase Diffusion Analysis," in *AMA Educators' Proceedings,* Patrick E. Murphy, et al., eds. (Chicago: American Marketing Association, 1983), 442–46.

Midgley, David F., and Grahame R. Dowling, "Innovativeness: The Concept and Its Measurement," *Journal of Consumer Research* 4 (March 1978): 229–42.

Mittelstaedt, R. A., S. L. Grossbart, W. W. Curtis, and S. P. DeVere, "Optimal Stimulation Level and the Adoption Decision Process," 3 (September 1976): 84–94.

Olshavsky, Richard W., "Time and the Rate of Adoption of Innovations," *Journal of Consumer Research* 6 (March 1980): 425–28.

Settle, Robert B., Michael A. Belch, and Pamela L. Alreck, "Temporic Effects on Opinion Leadership, Brand Loyalty and Perceived Risk," in *Proceedings of the AMA Educators' Conference,* Kenneth Bernhardt et al., eds. (Chicago: American Marketing Association, 1981), 221–24.

Wilton, Peter C., and Edgar A. Pessemier, "Forecasting the Ultimate Acceptance of an Innovation: The Effects of Information," *Journal of Consumer Research* 8 (September 1981): 162–71.

Applications

Arndt, Johan, "Role of Product-Related Conversations in the Diffusion of a New Product," *Journal of Marketing Research* 4 (August 1967): 291–95.

Atkin, Charles, and Martin Block, "Effectiveness of Celebrity Endorsers," *Journal of Advertising Research* 23, no. 1 (February/March 1983): 57–61.

Baumgarten, Steven A., "The Innovative Communicator in the Diffusion Process," *Journal of Marketing Research* 12 (February 1975): 12–18.

Darden, William R., and Fred D. Reynolds, "Predicting Opinion Leadership for Men's Apparel Fashions," *Journal of Marketing Research* 9 (August 1972): 324–28.

Donnelly Jr., James H., and John M. Ivancevich, "A Methodology for Identifying Innovator Characteristics of New Brand Purchasers," *Journal of Marketing Research* 11 (August 1974): 331–34.

King, Charles W., and John O. Summers, "Overlap of Opinion Leadership Across Consumer Product Categories," *Journal of Marketing Research* 7 (February 1970): 43–50.

Mancuso, Joseph R., "Why not Create Opinion Leaders for New Product Introductions?" *Journal of Marketing* 33 (July 1969): 20–25.

Ostlund, Luman E., "Perceived Innovation Attributes as Predictors of Innovativeness," *Journal of Consumer Research* 1 (September 1974): 23–29.

Reynolds, Fred D., William R. Darden, and Warren S. Martin, "Developing an Image of the Store-Loyal Customer," *Journal of Retailing* 50 (Winter 1974–1975): 73–84.

Sheth, Jagdish N., "Word-of-Mouth in Low-Risk Innovations," *Journal of Advertising Research* 11 (June 1971): 15–18.

Summers, John O., "The Identity of Women's Clothing Fashion Opinion Leaders," *Journal of Marketing Research* 7 (May 1970): 178–85.

Summers, John O., "Media Exposure Patterns of Consumer Innovators," *Journal of Marketing* 36 (January 1972): 43–49.

14 Families and Households

Objectives of This Chapter

After you have studied this chapter, you should be able to:

1. Discuss the family life cycle concept and the major types of family units.

2. Examine the composition of households in the United States and show how the family structure is changing.

3. Explain how family decision making occurs and discuss the relative importance of family members in purchase decisions.

4. Describe the implications of family decision making for marketing strategy development.

Consumers are strongly influenced by the values, attitudes, and tastes learned from a powerful primary reference group: the family. But this group is even more important to marketers as a purchasing and consumption unit. The **households** in the United States consist of both family units (relatives sharing living quarters) and nonfamily units (single persons and those living with nonrelatives). These households account for the majority (in number, not dollar value) of all products consumed in the United States, including professional and industrial products. With the increasing number of households and of family units has come greater emphasis on the study of family decision making.

households

Family members interact with each other to select a broad range of products: *durables,* such as television sets and automobiles; *nondurables,* such as cleaning agents, food, and cosmetics; *financial services,* such as savings plans and insurance programs; and a host of other categories of products and services. Until recently much of the consumer research related to these types of products investigated only individual consumers. Now, however, there is a growing recognition that entire families should be studied to determine precisely why a given consumer product is purchased and consumed. Marketing research firms employed by consumer goods manufacturers have long been aware of joint decisions made by husbands and wives regarding certain types of purchases. They have also recognized the influence of children on the selection and purchase of breakfast cereals and toys. More recently, however, academic researchers have improved these types of research by studying the interactions of family members that result in product class and brand choice decisions.

This chapter will discuss four key areas: (1) the major characteristics of families, (2) changes in the family life cycle in the United States, (3) the characteristics of households, and (4) family decision making. In the section on major characteristics of families we will introduce the concept of the family life cycle and show how purchasing behavior varies at each stage. Advertising directed at different family stages will help highlight how marketers use the life cycle concept to target potential buying households.

Is the structure of the American family truly changing? We will explore what elements have changed and how they impact company marketing strategies. Next, we consider household characteristics and how the decision-making process among household members has been studied. This will include a discussion of alternative decision-making strategies used by families. Finally we will explore how these subjects are applied to develop marketing strategy.

MAJOR CHARACTERISTICS OF FAMILY HOUSEHOLDS

There are approximately 83.4 million households (family and nonfamily dwellings) in the United States, of which 61.4 million are traditional fami-

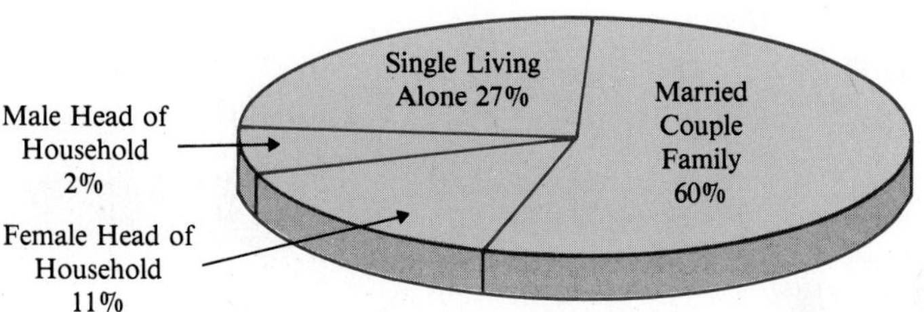

Figure 14-1 *Household Composition in the United States*

Source: U.S. Bureau of the Census, Current Population Reports, *Household and Family Characteristics, March 1983,* Series P-20, No. 388 (May 1984), 2, 101.

lies (two or more related persons). Thus, about 73% of the total population lives in family households consisting of a husband, a wife, and possibly children. Figure 14-1 shows the makeup of all households. Slightly more than half of these families have two or more breadwinners.[1]

The Family Life Cycle

family life cycle

Since the early 1930s authors have used the concept of the family life cycle to show the stages of family development. The **family life cycle** is the classification of the family into stages over a period of time. It is based on a number of demographic variables including age, marital status, the number of children at home, and the working status of the head of household. Traditionally, researchers defined the following nine stages of the family life cycle:

1. *Bachelor stage:* young single people not living at home.
2. *Newly married couples:* young, no children.
3. *Full nest I:* young married couples with youngest child under six.
4. *Full nest II:* younger married couples with youngest child age six or over.
5. *Full nest III:* older married couples with dependent children.
6. *Empty nest I:* older married couples with no children living at home, household head in labor force.
7. *Empty nest II:* older married couples, no children living at home, head of household retired.
8. *Solitary survivor in labor force.*
9. *Solitary survivor, retired.*[2]

Today's family structure is considerably different than it was when earlier researchers were working. There are more single-head-of-household families comprised of divorced people and their children. Additionally, young people are choosing to marry later and are postponing childbearing, for at least two reasons. First, the financial pressures of a troubled economy force young workers to save up for marriage and children. Second, the high cost of living and the creation of new work oppor-

Figure 14-2
Family Life Cycle Flows

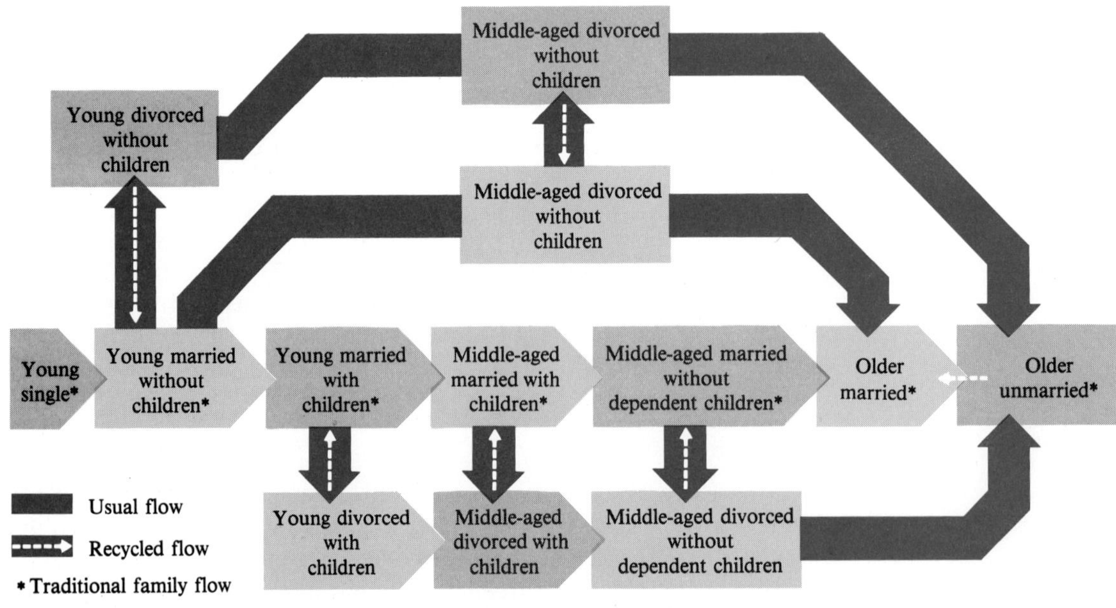

Source: Patrick E. Murphy and William A. Staples, "A Modernized Family Life Cycle," *Journal of Consumer Research* 6 (1) (June 1979): 17.

tunities for women has resulted in more wives working. Although the media has paid a good deal of attention to unmarried cohabitants, there is evidence that less than 1% of American households are of this form.[3]

In light of these recent changes, an up-to-date classification of families was needed. Patrick Murphy and William Staples investigated the history of the family life cycle concept and, in 1979, provided their own *Modernized Family Life Cycle* for use by marketers.[4] Figure 14-2 is a flow diagram of the Modernized Family Life Cycle.

Young Single

Young singles are generally from eighteen to their mid-twenties in age. Most will eventually marry. Approximately 8.2 percent of the population in 1970 and 12.5 percent in 1982 were in this class.[5] Recently, larger numbers of individuals have remained single until after college graduation, and often a few years beyond. In addition, because more women are electing to attend college, the trend toward later marriages is steadily growing. Further, more and more students are attending graduate school, which tends to extend their time as single students. When they finish their advanced degrees, they emerge with salaries of $20,000 to $30,000, so they have a great deal of spending power. Here is one description of this "bachelor" stage in the family life cycle:

> Although earnings are relatively low, they are subject to few rigid demands, so consumers in this stage typically have substantial discretionary income. Part of this income is used to purchase a car and have equipment and furnishings for their first residence away from home—usually an apartment. They tend to be more fashion and recreation oriented, spending a substantial portion of their income on clothing, alcoholic beverages, food away from home, vacations, leisure time pursuits, and other products and services involved in the mating game.[6]

Ads for Salem cigarettes, which often show an uneven number of young people all enjoying themselves in the water, are typical of those targeted to appeal to the young-singles group. The fact that Salem does not feature couples gives the impression that they are probably single; therefore, others in this stage of the life cycle can more easily identify with the ad and the product.

Young Married without Children

Young marrieds without children are usually in the under-35 age category and represent 3.5% of the population. Since husbands and wives in these families tend to be alike in education, age, and religion, their tastes and preferences are relatively similar. Generally, they have two incomes in the family and, because they are without children, many reward themselves for centering their daily lives on their careers by heavy spending for lavish vacations, expensive automobiles, and recreation. One extreme type within this group is the childless professional couple whose combined income are generally over $50,000, and sometimes as much as $100,000. One profile, presented in *U.S. News and World Report,* suggests that young marrieds without children are particularly geared toward expensive consumption:

> Steve, 29 years old, is a marketing representative for IBM and his wife, Nancy, 28 years old, is a specialist in international hiring for General Electric. Their two careers bring in $90,000 to support a suburban home, frequent dinners at restaurants, two automobiles and regular skiing and hiking weekends away from home. They work approximately 50 hours/week and spend another 10 hours/week commuting to their jobs in New York City. They are currently saving for a weekend house or boat. On children, says Steve: "We don't feel that our lifestyles and our commitments to our jobs allow us to devote the proper amount of attention to children. We've decided to put it off for a few years until we would be better able to spend more time with them."[7]

Of course, most working couples have combined incomes that do not approach the $90,000 Steve and Nancy enjoy. Nevertheless, these typical working couples also use their nonworking hours in pursuit of recreation outside the home. Couples at this stage tend to set aside earnings for a house or, in some cases, a mobile home; but wherever they are living, most are in the process of buying durable goods, such as furniture and appliances, to furnish and equip their new household.

Young marrieds with no children might be attracted to ads for Jacuzzi whirlpool baths, which depict a young couple in a luxurious bathroom. Since couples in this stage are usually interested in improving their homes, and couples with children would not be as likely to purchase a costly whirlpool, young marrieds with no children are a logical group for such marketers to reach.

Young Divorced without Children

Some young marrieds end in divorce prior to child-rearing. Only about 1% of the population of the United States is in this stage of the life cycle. Many of these people behave similarly to those in the young-single category because they are seeking another marriage partner. Their life-styles are considerably less affluent than those of young marrieds because the spouse's income is lost. Most young divorced people without children could be termed "not yet remarried" because many eventually marry again and reenter the "young married without children" stage.

Young Married with Children

A little over 17% of the population of the United States is in this life-cycle category. Parents are under 35 years old and children in these families are generally under 12 years of age, though a few may be adolescents. (Because most families have children in more than one age category, no breakdown of child ages is made.) Children often cause major life-style changes. Usually there is considerably less discretionary income and leisure time because children are time consuming and expensive. During a baby's first year, disposable diapers alone can cost the parents about $400. Dental and doctor bills may siphon off what the family saved before they had children. Additionally, many women decide to quit their jobs to devote more time to the children's development, so the family's income drops. Young married with children derive enjoyment from family-oriented activities. They also eat out less and take family vacations nearer home.

Teresa and Mike, a young working couple with children, were also profiled by *U.S. News and World Report*. Their total income of $19,000 covers rent for a modest three-bedroom house, food, car payments, and child-care costs for their four-year-old, Daniel, and eighteen-month-old Christopher. Buying a home is impossible now because they lack the money for a down payment, and vacations are out of the question. They have little time for relaxation because working, cleaning, and running errands demand most of their time. They spend a few hours a day with the children; their sources of recreation are television and an occasional dinner with friends.[8]

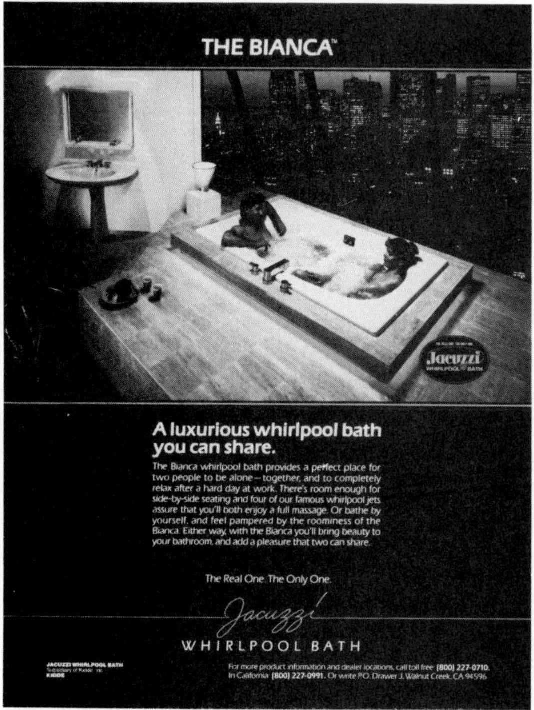

Couples at this stage are the target for many types of products, including durable goods, children's products, and many food items. Ads for Ethan Allen furniture are aimed directly at this market by addressing the fact that most couples at this stage are not wealthy. Such ads stress the advantages of investing in quality furniture, further appealing to this group by showing the family playing together next to some of their furnishings.

Young Divorced with Children

Households of young divorced people with children comprise about 2% of the population of the United States. After divorce, life-style and income changes are dramatic, particularly for women. Mothers head 90% of all one-parent families; they usually maintain custody of the children while receiving support payments from the fathers. It should be noted, however, that more and more fathers are obtaining child custody in divorce cases which may result in somewhat fewer single mothers heading households. Divorced mothers who seek employment may have been out of the labor force for many years; in any case, their incomes are usually lower than those of their male counterparts when they find employment. Single parents can experience severe time constraints as they attempt to raise their families and develop their careers simultaneously. Without the support of a spouse, the emotional strain on both single mothers and single fathers can also be high. Paul Glick and Arthur Norton reported that about 60% of all divorces involved women under age 30 and that two-thirds of these women had children.[9] Although the ability to purchase durables declines after divorce, the needs for easy-to-prepare foods and household items on sale remain strong.

Middle-aged Married with Children

The largest percentage of the population—about one in three—is made up of families of middle-aged married couples with children. The head of the household is 35 to 64 years old. While this group is the sequel to the "young married with children" category, it is likely to grow in relation to its predecessor, for two reasons. First, more couples are postponing having children due to tight finances and the need or desire for both husband and wife to work. Second, there will be more middle-aged adults overall as the "baby boom" generation matures, causing a major shift in the population.

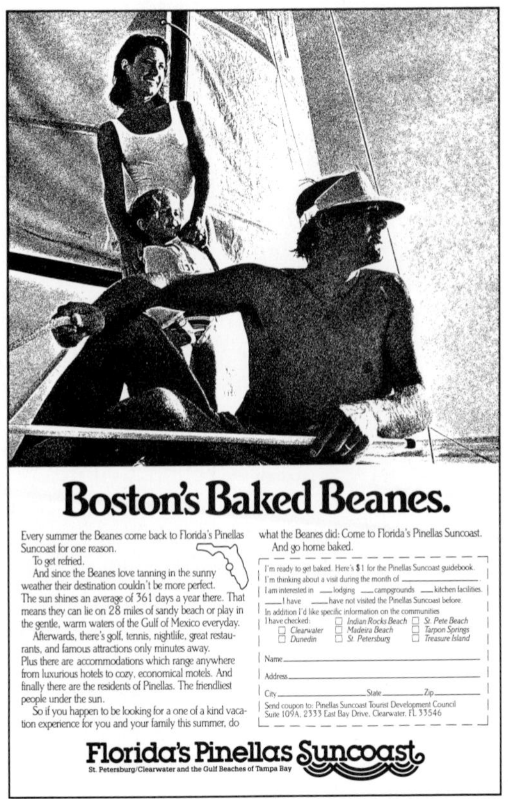

Earning power and incomes are strongest for middle-aged married couples because they tend to be well established in their career cycles. At this stage the parents are apt to be family oriented, politically active, and disinclined to move from their current residence.[10] Many families in this category spend money on replacing old furniture and other durable goods purchased earlier. They are also investment and savings oriented, so they contribute significantly to the investment base of the community.

Because these couples tend to have higher incomes than do younger couples with children, they are able to spend more on vacations and recreational items. Travel ads often direct their messages toward these couples by showing families in this age range enjoying themselves together in the advertised location. Couples shown, however, are often around their middle thirties, to appeal to a broader range of both younger and older couples with children.

*Middle-aged Divorced with Children**

Nearly 2% of the population of the United States lives in households of middle-aged divorced parents with children. Generally, when a middle-aged couple divorces, the mother and children live together, while the father sets up his own household. However, children are staying with their fathers in increasing numbers as the courts change their attitudes toward paternal custody of children. Often both parents are financially strapped by trying to maintain their former life-style on one income. The behavior of people in this category is similar to that of the young divorced with children.

Middle-aged Married without Children

About 4.7% of the population consists of middle-aged married couples without children. These are people who have never had children. Although this group has been small in the past, Murphy and Staples predict that it will grow because more couples are making a conscious decision not to reproduce.[11] Highly educated couples are selecting this style of family living in increasing numbers. Alan Kerckhoff used 1973 Census Bureau reports to support that highly educated women choose to remain childless more often than do women who have less education. According to Kerckhoff, 6.2% of college-educated married women opted for this life-style, compared to only 2.7 percent of those married women who had no high-school diploma.[12]

Middle-aged Married without Dependent Children

Sometimes people in this stage are said to be in the "empty nest" because their children have left home. They represent 5.5% of the population in the United States. Couples in this category often exercise their freedom to

* Only about .3% of households are middle-aged divorced without children. Therefore, this category is not discussed in the text.

travel, spend evenings away from the house (more than couples with children at home do), and explore new life-style options. At this stage incomes are generally still increasing and are used to purchase luxury items, home improvements, and short-range investment interests. Also, many of these people begin making long-range investments to ensure their financial security during retirement.

One travel ad for the tourism board of Missouri would probably appeal to both middle-aged couples who never had children and to those whose children are no longer dependent. In the ad, "Missouri Is for Kids," the most prominent picture is of a middle-aged couple backpacking, and the accompanying series of smaller photos of Missouri's tourist areas depicts only one child. The ad appeals to couples in this age bracket who like to think of themselves as young and active, by associating the term kids with the middle-aged couple shown.

Older Married

The older married stage begins at retirement: between ages 60 and 65 for most couples. Retirement changes older people's life-styles considerably. Although they have more time to enjoy life, they often have reduced incomes and, unfortunately, more health problems. For these reasons, many older married people move south (or at least spend winters in the Sunbelt) and carefully budget their discretionary income. The number of people in this stage is likely to grow unless federal laws are changed to raise the minimum age at which retirees are eligible for Social Security benefits. This change would decrease or stabilize the number of people in this group.

Older Unmarried

About 2% of the population is made up of solitary survivors. Because women tend to live longer than men do, more than half of the older people in this category are women. Often the expenditures of older unmarried people are travel- and health-related. Many of these people sell their homes and move into condominiums or retirement centers. Whereas in other cultures solitary survivors move in with their married children, this practice is not as prevalent in the United States, perhaps because American families tend to be extremely mobile.

Senior citizens, including older married and older unmarried people, now account for about 22% of the population of the United States. In 1970, they were only 19% of the population, but they will have grown to 28% in 2020 when today's college students reach retirement age.[13]

The median disposable income has risen more than 50% since 1965 for senior citizens. About 70% own their own homes and of those, 85% have

Table 14-1 FAMILY LIFE CYCLE STAGES AND PURCHASE BEHAVIOR AT EACH STAGE

Stage	***Income Characteristics***	***Examples of Purchase Behavior***
Young singles	Low income but also low demands on income	Buying record albums on a regular basis
Young married without children	Possible dual income and relatively low demands on income	Jacuzzi whirlpool purchased as a "necessary" luxury
Young married with children	Increased demands on income and time	Durable goods such as furniture bought to meet long-term family needs
Young divorced with children	Decreased income and higher demands on income and time	Inexpensive household items purchased on sale
Middle-aged married with children	Significant demands on income	Family recreation such as trips to Disneyland
Middle-aged divorced with children	Similar to young divorced with perhaps slightly higher income	Easy to prepare foods purchased to ease time constraints
Middle-aged married without dependent children	Lessened demands on income	Luxury items purchased and investments made for future
Older married	Income decreases with retirement but demand on it is relatively low	Purchases health-related items with an eye to buying on sale
Older unmarried	Income is stable or, in case of widows, greatly decreased	Purchases highly controlled, very price conscious
Middle-aged divorced without dependent children	Low demands on income, much of which is discretionary	Purchases center on self-interest products and travel

paid off their mortgages.[14] With improved health care and increasing life expectancy, senior citizens are enjoying life more. Yet inflation has hit these people heavily and they must be careful about spending their decreasing nest egg.

Table 14-1 summarizes the various stages of the family life cycle and provides a brief example of typical purchasing behavior at each stage.

Changes in the Family Life Cycle

There has been a good deal of speculation that the American family structure is changing. Some researchers claim that there is more communal living and that more unmarried couples are cohabiting. While slight shifts such as these are likely to occur in a modern society, there is evidence to suggest that some shifts away from the traditional family will occur in the foreseeable future. Still, although divorce rates are up, most divorced people remarry and live in traditional family structures.

Figure 14-3
Number of Births, by Year, 1910–1983

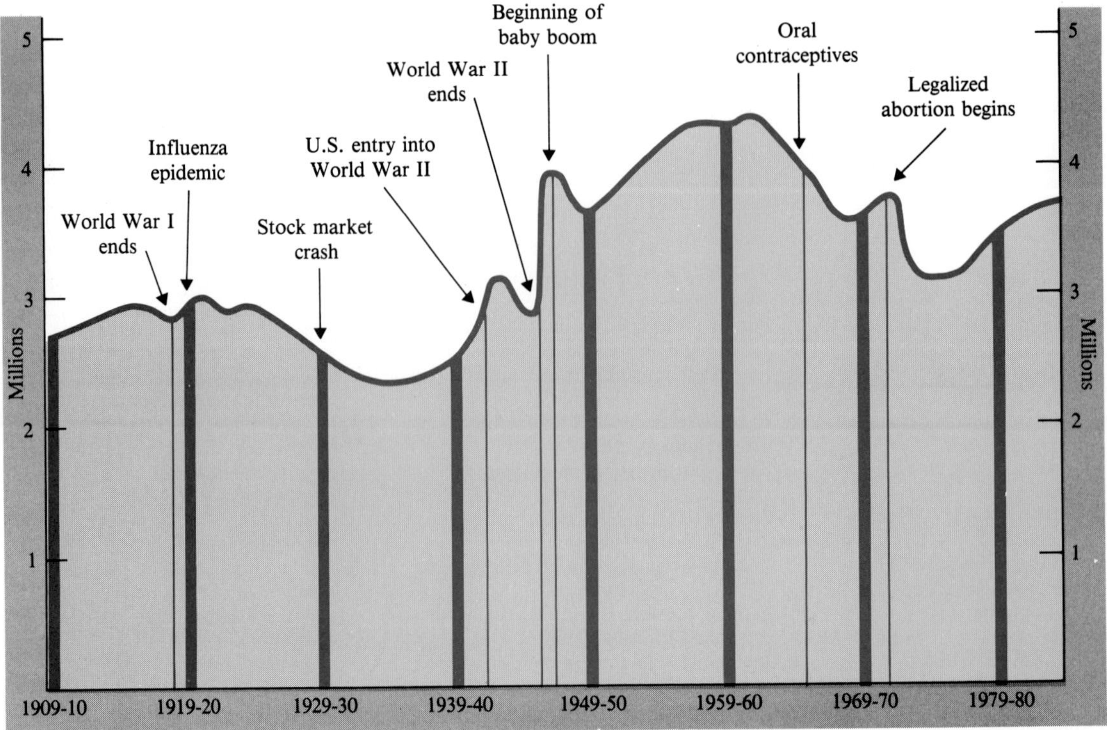

Source: U.S. Department of Commerce, Bureau of the Census, Current Population Reports, Series P-25, No. 949, May 1984, 3.

The changes taking place in the family structure can be attributed not only to changes in society's values, but also to the post-war baby boom. From 1946 to 1961, 64 million children were born. Today, the baby-boom generation is between 25 and 40 years old. Because of its sheer size, the tendencies of this group to marry later and have fewer children significantly affect the national average for age at marriage and for number of children.

Today many young people are delaying marriage. The average age of women marrying has risen from 20.8 years old in 1970 to 22.1 years old in 1980. A similar pattern exists for men: from 23.2 years old in 1970 to 24.7 years old in 1980. Higher levels of education, fear of divorce, desire for autonomy, women's pursuit of careers, and the general attitude that marriage at an early age is not necessary for fulfillment have been cited as reasons for delaying marriage.

The fertility rate reached its peak of 3.8 children per woman in 1957, dropping to a low of 1.9 children in 1980. The resulting decrease in the number of school-aged children (6.5 million fewer in 23 years) has had the effect of closing 9,000 elementary schools in recent years. However, the fertility rate is likely to increase as more members of the baby boom generation reach ages at which they are forced to decide between having children before they are too old and forgoing children altogether. Figure 14-3 shows the rise and fall in the number of births that preceded and followed the peak years of the baby boom.

Changes in Children's Living Arrangements

Because the family life cycle starts with young adults, there is no category for children. Yet children are present in many households. One could argue that it would be more appropriate to include children in the family life cycle by describing their various living arrangements as well. Table 14-2 and Figure 14-4 compare the types of households in which white, black, and Hispanic American children live. Notice that most white and Hispanic children live in traditional households with a mother and a father. From 1970 to 1981, the percentages of children living with one parent has increased from 8.0 to 16.9 for white children, and from 33.8 to 53.6 for black children. Today about 28.6 percent of Hispanic children live with only one parent.

Table 14-3 summarizes the family classifications as set forth by both Murphy and Staples (the classifications used in this text), and the earlier categories of Wells and Gubar. Although the members are derived from earlier data, the table gives some idea as to how these different categories compare. Figures 14-5 and 14-6 show some of the same data graphically.

Record High Divorce Rate

Americans have the highest divorce rate in the world. Between 32 and 42% of all people in the United States are expected to divorce eventually,

Table 14-2 LIVING ARRANGEMENTS OF CHILDREN UNDER 18, BY RACE

	White	***Black***	***Hispanic***	***All Races***
Living with:				
Two parents	81.0%	40.7%	68.5%	74.9%
One parent	16.9	53.6	28.6	22.5
Mother only	15.0	51.1	26.8	20.5
Father only	2.0	2.5	1.8	2.0
Other relatives only	1.6	5.1	2.4	2.2
Non relatives only	0.4	0.6	0.6	0.5
Total	100%	100%	100%	100%

Source: U.S. Bureau of the Census, Current Population Reports, Series P-20, March, 1983, No. 389, 4.

Figure 14-4
Living Arrangements of Children under 18, by Race

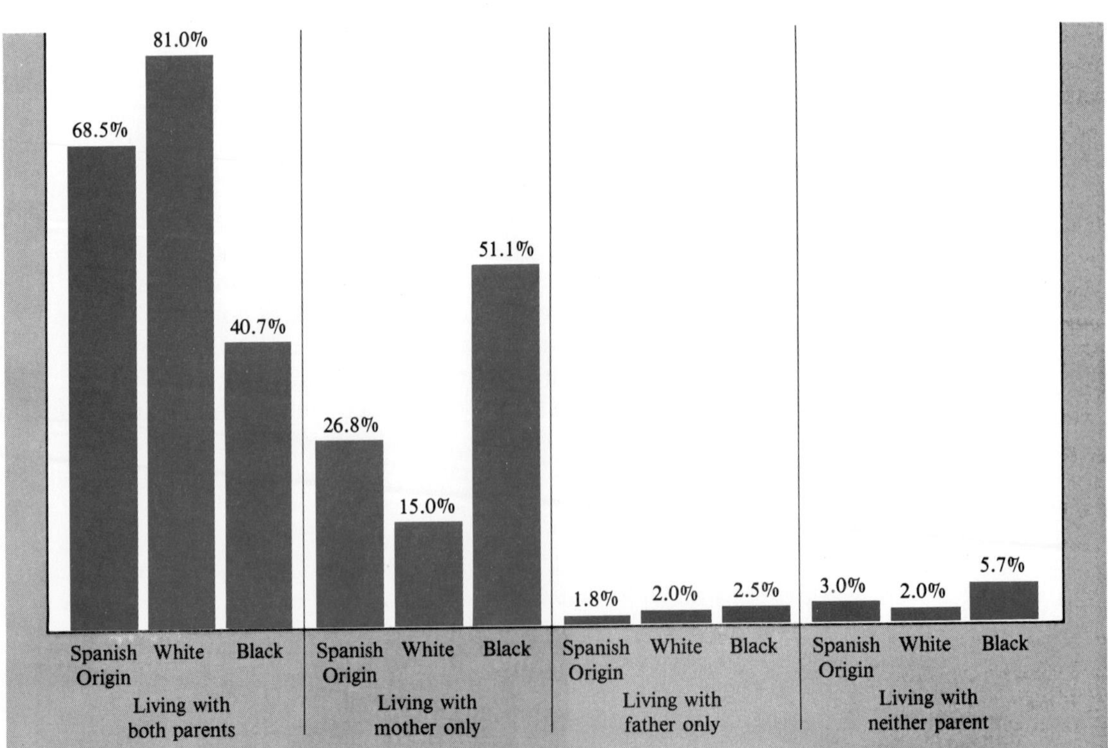

Source: Based on U.S. Bureau of the Census, Current Population Reports, Series P-20, No. 389, March 1983, 4.

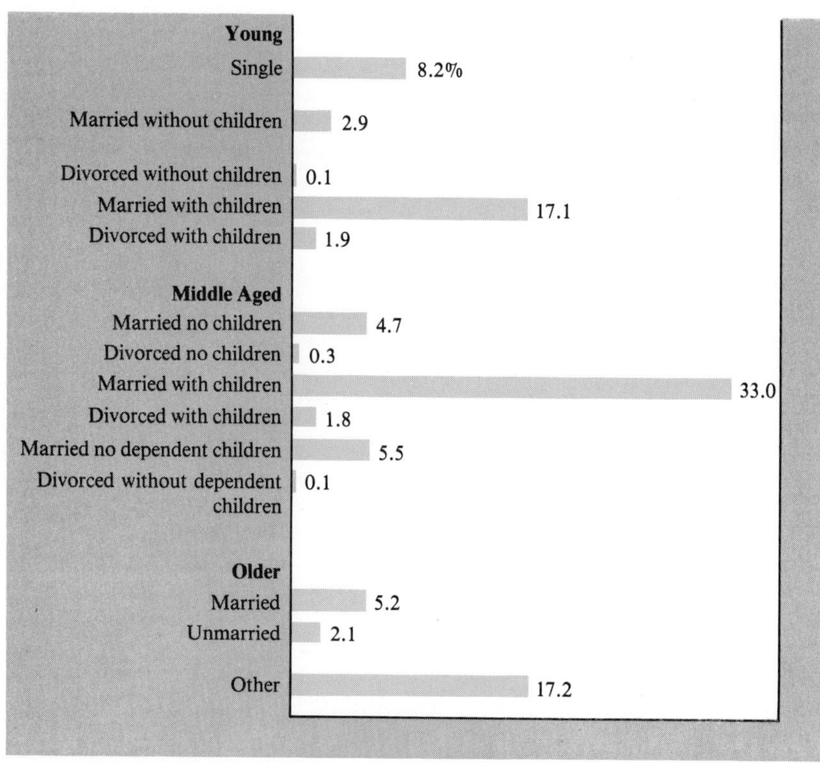

Figure 14-5
Comparison of Population Distribution across the Murphy and Staples Family Life Cycle (Percent of Population)

Source: based on Patrick E. Murphy and William A. Staples, "A Modernized Family Life Cycle," *Journal of Consumer Research* 6 (1979): 16.

and of these 79% are likely to remarry. The divorce rate, which has hit an all-time high, is continuing to rise at a gradual pace. Because divorced men tend to remarry more quickly than divorced women do, there are many more divorced women than divorced men in the population—a factor that makes it more difficult for divorced women to remarry and results in more divorced women being single heads of households than divorced men. Figure 14-7 shows the relative number of each from 1960 to 1983.

Working Women and Two-Income Families

Women are entering the work force in record numbers. About 52% of all women are employed, up from 43% in 1970. By 1990 as many as 63% of all women will be in the work force.[15] Of course, this trend has greatly increased the number of two-income families. In 1970 less than 40% of the families had two full-time workers, but by 1980 over 50% benefited from two incomes.[16] When families with one part-time worker are counted, less than 25% of all families in 1980 had only one spouse working.

There are approximately 23.7 million two-career married couples.[17]

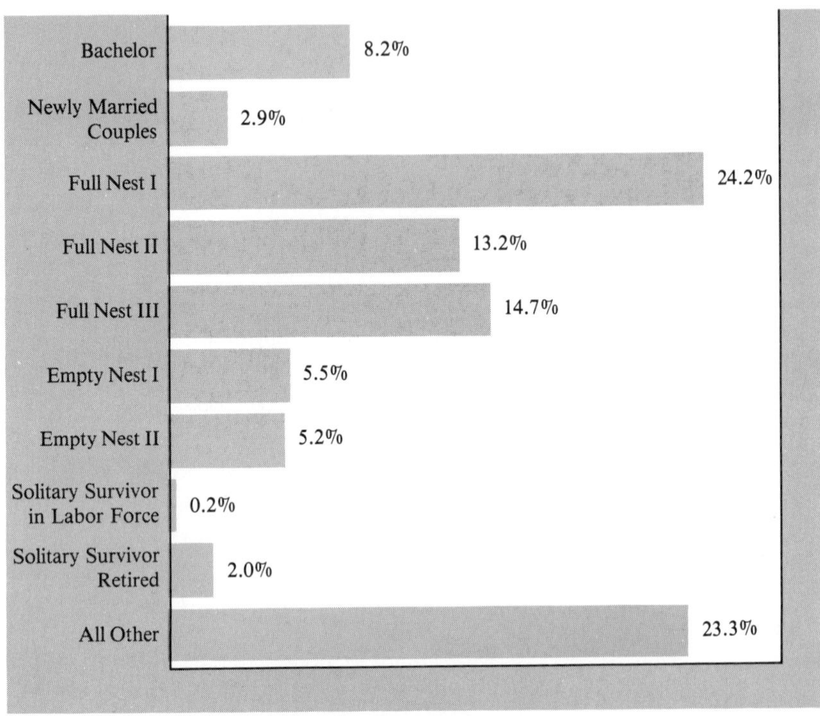

Figure 14-6
Comparison of Population Distribution across the Wells and Gubar Family Life Cycle

Source: based on Murphy and Staples, "A Modernized Family Life Cycle," 16.

Table 14-3 COMPARISON OF POPULATION DISTRIBUTIONS ACROSS THE STAGES OF TWO FAMILY LIFE CYCLES[a]

Murphy and Staples			***Wells and Gubar***		
Stage	***Number of individuals or families (000's)***	***% Total of U.S. Population***	***Stage***	***Number of individuals or families (000's)***	***% Total of U.S. Population***
1. Young single	16,626	8.2	1. Bachelor	16,626	8.2
2. Young married without children	2,958	2.9	2. Newly married couples	2,958	2.9
3. Other young					
a. Young divorced without children	277	0.1			
b. Young married with children	8,082	17.1	3. Full nest I	11,433	24.2
Infant					
Young (4–12 years old)[b]					
Adolescent[b]					
c. Young divorced with children	1,144	1.9	4. Full nest II	6,547	13.2
Infant					
Young (4–12 years old)					
Adolescent					

Table 14-3 COMPARISON OF POPULATION DISTRIBUTIONS ACROSS THE STAGES OF TWO FAMILY LIFE CYCLES[a], continued

Murphy and Staples			*Wells and Gubar*		
Stage	***Number of individuals or families (000's)***	***% Total of U.S. Population***	***Stage***	***Number of individuals or families (000's)***	***% Total of U.S. Population***
4. Middle-aged					
a. Middle-aged married without children	4,815	4.7			
b. Middle-aged divorced without children	593	0.3			
c. Middle-aged married with children Young Adolescent	15,574	33.0	5. Full nest III	6,955	14.7
d. Middle-aged divorced with children Young Adolescent	1,080	1.8			
e. Middle-aged married without dependent children	5,627	5.5	6. Empty nest I	5,627	5.5
f. Middle-aged divorced without dependent children	284	0.1			
5. Older					
a. Older married	5,318	5.2	7. Empty nest II	5,318	5.2
b. Older unmarried Divorced Widowed	3,510	2.0	8. Solitary survivor-in labor force	428	0.2
			9. Solitary survivor-retired	3,510	2.0
All other[c]	34,952	17.2	All other[c]	46,738	23.3
	203,210[d]			203,210[d]	

Source: Patrick E. Murphy and William A. Staples, "A Modernized Family Life Cycle," *Journal of Consumer Research* 6 (1979): 16. Figures were derived from U.S. Bureau of the Census data for 1973.

[a] As there are single and divorced individuals in some of the stages, the numbers were calculated as a percentage of the entire population, not just the number of families. Also, the percentages of the total for families were determined by multiplying the number of families by 2.3 (average number of children per family in 1970) and adding the parents (or parent, in divorced instances) to the number. For example, the 17.1 percent in the young married with children was computed as follows:

$$\frac{8{,}082 \text{ (2.3 children)} + 16{,}164 \text{ (parents)}}{203.210} = 17.1\%.$$

[b] As many families have children at more than one of these age levels, it is not meaningful to compute the numbers for each of these ages independently.

[c] Includes all adults and children not accounted for by the family life cycle stages.

[d] Source U.S. Bureau of the Census 1970. The numbers do not add to this total because of the calculations explained in footnote b.

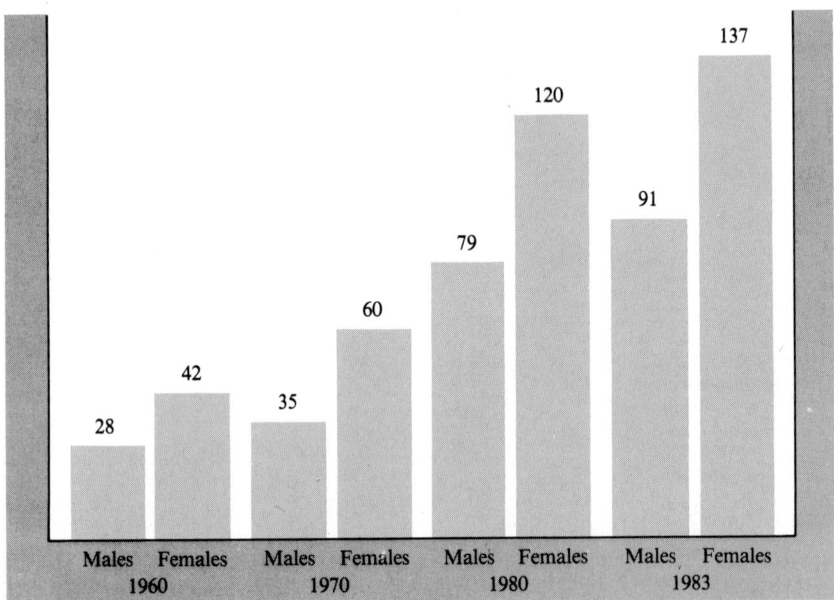

Figure 14-7
Divorce Rate per 1,000 Married Persons, 1960–1983

Source: U.S. Census Bureau, Current Population Reports, Series P-20, No. 389 (Washington, D.C.: March, 1983), 3.

They are typically younger, wealthier, and more urban-centered than other families. The vast majority of middle-income families fall into this category, whereas while the lower-income and rich categories tend to have more single-income families and families with a combination of full-time and part-time income. The proportion of one- and two-income families in three income ranges are shown in Figure 14-8.

In general, two-career families have significantly higher incomes than do one-career families. Typically the husband earns 60% of the total income, while the wife contributes about 40%. Figure 14-9 shows the differential in average income. Working couples have little discretionary

Figure 14-8
Proportion of One and Two Incomes for Married Couples According to Total Income

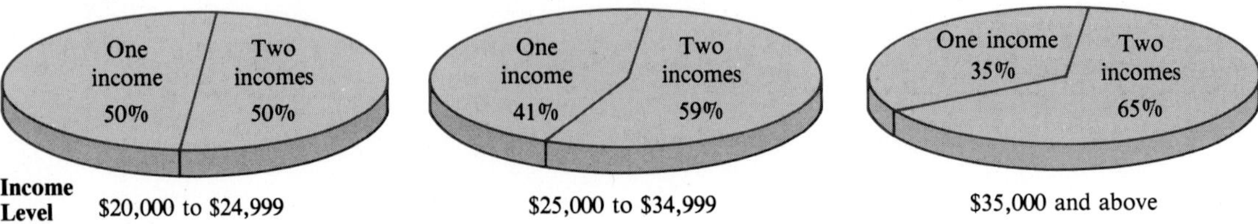

Source: U.S. Bureau of the Census, *Statistical Abstract of the United States, 1985,* 105th ed., 449.

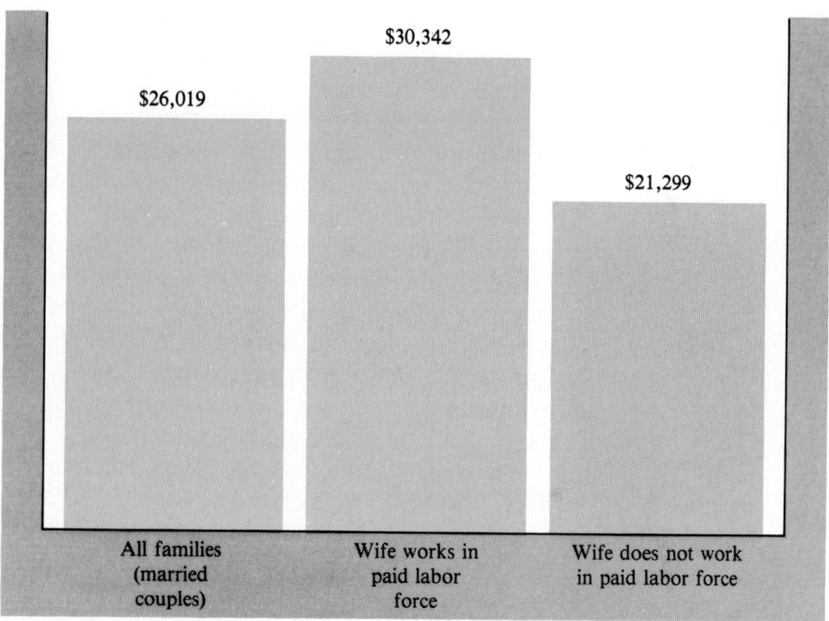

Figure 14-9
Median Family Incomes

Source: U.S. Bureau of the Census, Current Population Reports, Series P-60, No. 142. From *Statistical Abstract of the United States, 1985,* 105th ed., 449.

time; thus, these families must spend more of their incomes for convenience items, child care, clothing, and time-saving luxuries.

Women's Changing Roles

The roles of women have been changing rather markedly for about the past fifteen years. While many of these role changes have been attributed to greater numbers in the work force, the underlying cause is probably a major shift in attitudes. First, society has begun to provide women equal status with men in business, government, academia, the sciences, and the arts. Second, both men and women have begun to see that besides the traditional roles there are many others that women can enjoy. Along with the wider range of roles being filled by women are more responsibilities that influence their priorities, allocation of time, and purchasing. Whether it is a cause or an effect of their increased career opportunities, more women are seeking higher education. In 1979, 45% of all college enrollments were women; by 1980, that figure had risen to 51%.[18]

Inflation

Because both inflation and people's expectations of a better life have risen in recent years, many families that maintained a desirable standard of living on one income twenty years ago have been forced to acquire a second income in order to get ahead. Even with two incomes, however, many families cannot afford homes at today's prices and high interest rates. Therefore, families are tending to acquire homes later in life.[19] Purchase of the house itself is only part of the family's first-home investment. Many support items such as lawn and gardening equipment, interior decorations, and appliances, as well as maintenance services, may be required. To the extent that prices outdistanced income, these items are also more difficult for families to afford.

During the 1970s and early 1980s, the American public experienced "stagflation" in an economy that combined zero or even negative output and productivity growth with high inflation. Stagflation lowered family purchasing power and adversely affected the family's standard of living. Rather than helping themselves get ahead by holding down two jobs, many families required two wage earners just to be able to afford the same items one income bought before.

voluntary simplifiers

Large-scale economic problems and an increased public awareness of limited natural resources for all Americans are producing a new breed of consumer called **voluntary simplifiers.**[20] Today there are about 15 million people that can be categorized as voluntary simplifiers; and by 1987 there may be as many as 60 million. One study of their characteristics indicates that they have the following characteristics:

1. young—mostly in their 20s and 30s
2. single or young families
3. mostly Caucasian
4. of middle- or upper-class backgrounds
5. largely urban residents
6. have bimodal income (some make less than $5,000, while others make more than $15,000 annually)
7. politically independent[21]

In general, voluntary simplifiers look for material simplicity and a less cluttered life. When they shop, they select smaller, more functional, higher-quality products that promote involvement and interest and they shop in smaller, more personal stores.

Although changes in family structure produce changes in consumption practices, these changes will probably continue to be evolutionary, not revolutionary.

HOUSEHOLD CHARACTERISTICS

As mentioned earlier, the term *household* refers to any family or nonfamily unit: a single person, a married couple, or any other combination of persons inhabiting a single dwelling. Much of the descriptive information

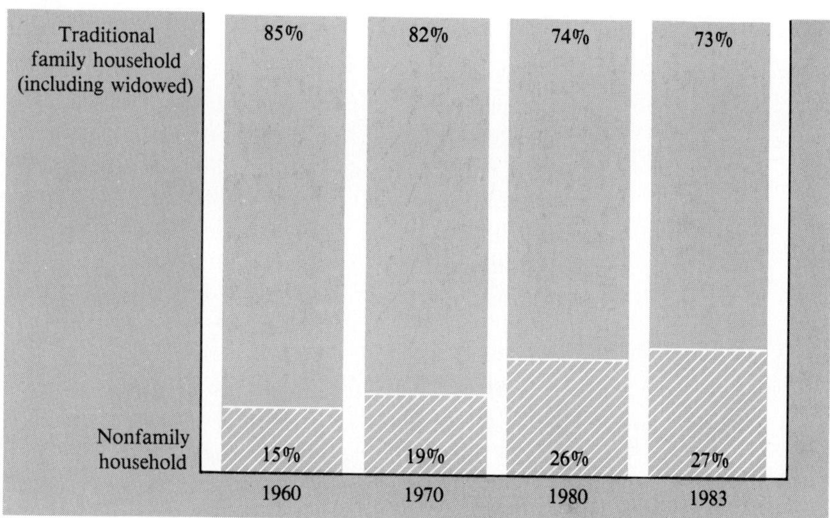

Figure 14-10
Traditional Family Households and Nonfamily Households

Source: U.S. Bureau of the Census, Current Population Reports, "Population Characteristics," Series P-20, No. 388, *Household and Family Characteristics* (March 1983): 3, 198.

available for census data and other research concerns households, rather than families, because they are important consumption units. In fact, traditional family households are declining in number, while nontraditional households are increasing. As Figure 14-10 shows, 85% of all households were traditional families in 1960, but this dropped to 73% in 1983.

Almost two-fifths of all households are made up of adults without a cohabiting spouse, as Figure 14-11 shows. This percentage is expected to increase by 1990. Already this group represents over 20 million buying units.

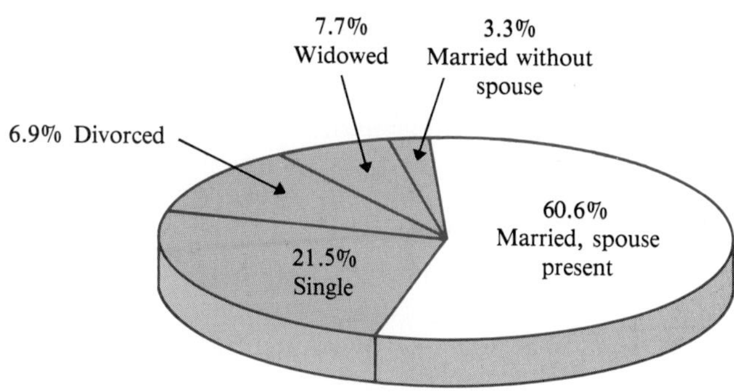

Figure 14-11
Marital Status of Householders

Source: U.S. Bureau of the Census, Current Population Reports, *Marital Status and Living Arrangements, March 1983,* Series P-28, No. 389 (June 1983): 8.

Single Adult Households

There are about 15.5 million adults living alone in the United States. In just ten years, this segment has grown from 18% to approximately 30% of all households and is likely to increase during the 1980s. While only about 15% were never married in 1980, that figure is expected to increase substantially by 1990. Single adults spend much less on food, but considerably more on alcohol, shelter, and transportation than couples do. Additionally, 39% of single adults live in central cities while only 18% of all other types of households live in central cities.

Two-Person Cohabitation and Group Households

Couples cohabiting without being married represent only about one to three million households in the United States. This is less than 2% of the total number of households according to Census Bureau data. Although this group has doubled in size during the past ten years, it remains small, notwithstanding the notoriety it has gained from articles in some popular magazines. A few years ago, estimates suggested that this group would increase at a much faster rate than actually has happened. However, it is likely that the number of unmarried couples cohabiting is larger than the census indicates, due to people's reluctance to answer these types of questions.

Another small segment is the group household made up of three or more unrelated people. This living arrangement, which was popular during the early 1970s and was portrayed on the "Three's Company" television show, has declined during the past decade. Now it is a very small, statistically almost insignificant group, mostly made up of college students and a few religious cults.

FAMILY DECISION MAKING

In light of the foregoing descriptions of the family and of household composition, we can now consider how purchase decisions are made in families. This section focuses on buying decisions in traditional families, which still constitute the largest household types.

Some purchases are conceived and carried out by one family member with little influence from other members of the family. These are called

autonomous decisions
joint decisions

autonomous decisions. Other purchases involve several family members and are called **joint decisions.** Joint decisions can be very complex; therefore they are more difficult for researchers to study than are autonomous decisions.

Marketers must remember that the sex roles within a family have an effect on how decisions are made. For example, as more and more women enter the work force, the purchasing decisions regarding food, clothing, and appliances that were previously made by the wife alone are now made more often as joint and husband-influenced decisions. This is also true of purchasing decisions that a few years ago were typically made by the husband alone, such as decisions regarding transportation and recreation. In today's family there is a trend toward more interaction between family members and, thus, more joint decision making.[22]

Joint decisions are an outgrowth of sharing, a basic family value in today's society. The polling organization Louis Harris and Associates studied one major market segment for *House and Garden* magazine and found much more joint decision making about purchases among married couples (with or without children) than among unmarried persons sharing living quarters as mates or "nonmates" (see Figure 14-12). Families of unmarried singles (nonmates) shared in only 12% of the decisions; unmarried cohabitators (mates) shared in vastly more: about 64% of the deci-

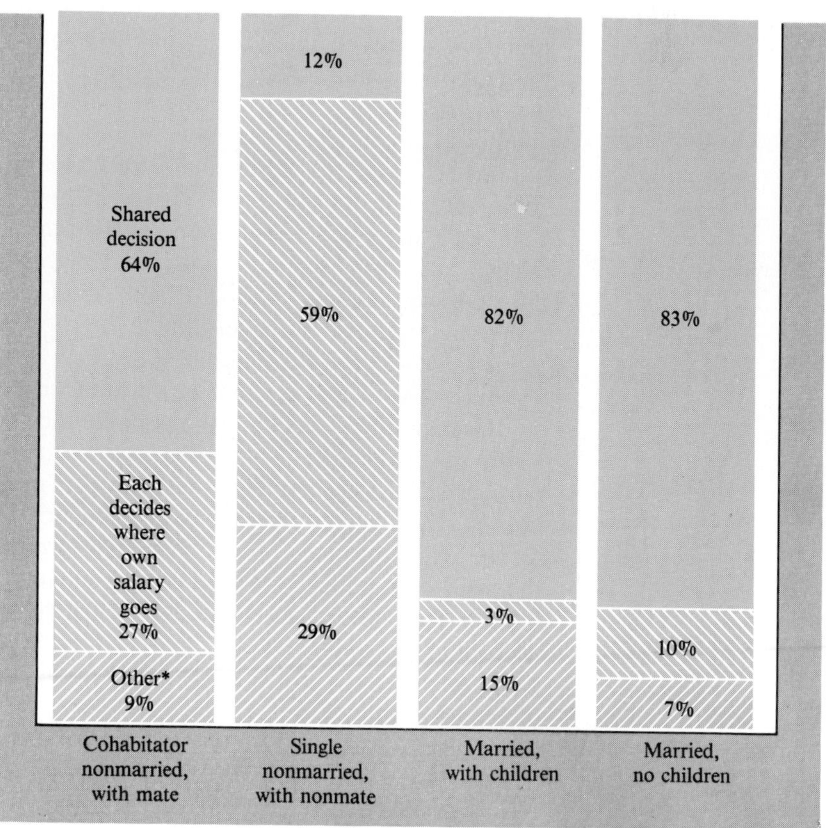

Figure 14-12 *Spending Decisions According to Living Arrangement*

Source: Louis Harris and Associates, "Togetherness among the Baby Boomers," *Sales and Marketing Management* (July 6, 1981): 41.

* Answers that did not fit the other two categories, such as "our parents decide" or "don't know."

sions. By contrast, married couples shared, to some degree, in over 80% of their purchase decisions.[23]

The Joint Decision-making Process

One study, by Harry Davis and Benny Rigaux, explored the relative influence of husbands and wives during three major phases in purchasing: problem recognition, search for information, and final decision.[24] Interestingly, there is a greater tendency for joint input during the problem recognition and final decision stages. During the problem recognition stage, spouses may need to justify a certain purchase; therefore, they openly discuss the various types of purchases which could solve the problem. This is supported by the Louis Harris study, which shows heavy joint involvement in determining which types of goods to purchase initially. Joint involvement in the final decision stage joint involvement can be caused by at least two factors. First, the importance of the actual final decision has greater implications than mere information search and, therefore, might require greater involvement by both parties. Secondly, joint involvement is a way of spreading the risk in case the decision turns out to be a poor one. Thus the responsibility for the decision is not shouldered by one partner alone.

On the other hand, the middle stage (search for information) is often the responsibility of only one partner. There are two possible explanations for this tendency. First, one or the other partner might have easier access to information or is more competent in obtaining and filtering information. Second, involving both spouses at this stage is probably redundant because no overt behavior resulting in an expenditure of money occurs until the final phase.

Harry Davis has summarized a number of published and corporate studies regarding decision making within the household. Davis noted that a *Life* magazine study shows that the frequency of joint involvement in purchase decisions is so high that selling to both the husband and wife can improve the chances of a sale by about eight to five over selling to the wife alone. While for many products, such as groceries and household goods, the wife does much of the shopping alone, she often buys items and brands that conform to the wishes of her husband or children. Further, according to Davis, a study sponsored by five magazines shows that for packaged goods, men make about 23% of the purchases but influence 32% of the brand purchases directly and 38% indirectly. Another study for *Sports Illustrated* magazine regarding pleasure travel on airplanes shows that husbands play a predominant role in initiating the idea of traveling by air, choosing a destination, and making an airline selection, while the decision to take the trip is a mutual decision in two-thirds of the cases. Studies of automobile purchases show a similar pattern: wives become more involved regarding the make and color than in initiating the purchase.[25]

syncratic decisions
autonomic decisions
husband or wife dominant decisions

Davis and Rigaux classified decisions as **syncratic** when both husband and wife are involved in decisions together; **autonomic** when decisions are usually made independently; and **husband or wife dominant** when the decision to purchase was primarily influenced by one or the other. Figure 14-13 represents the different approaches to decision making used by married couples. Various product purchase decisions are positioned in the figure according to two dimensions. The vertical axis describes the relative influence of the husband or wife in the decision. Decisions toward the top are more wife dominant, while decisions at the bottom are husband dominant. The horizontal axis describes the extent of role specialization—that is, the percentage of families reporting that a decision is jointly made. For example, decisions about kitchenware tend to be wife dominant; the wife makes most of the decision alone. Life insurance is a husband-dominant purchase; most decisions to buy insurance are made by the husband alone. Vacations, on the other hand, represent a purchase

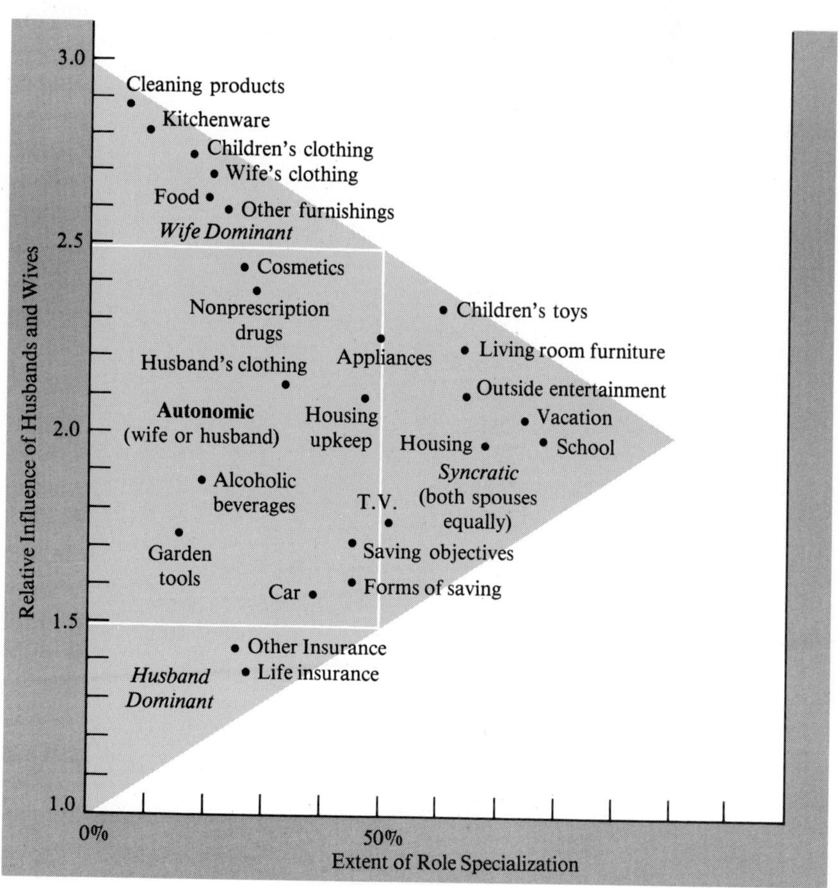

Figure 14-13
Marital Roles in 25 Decisions

Source: adapted from Harry L. Davis and Benny P. Rigaux, "Perception of Marital Roles in Decision Processes," *Journal of Consumer Research* 1 (June 1974): 57.

decision in which both spouses decide jointly and neither husband nor wife tends to dominate.

Decisions on major purchases such as housing and vacations were more often made (jointly) and after discussion, while purchases such as alcoholic beverages and garden tools involved decisions by one spouse or the other.

This approach looks at the decision in total, but it should be noted that the relative influence of husbands and wives varies not only by product class but also by decision area for each product: for example, how much to spend, where to buy, and so on.

Family Decision-making Strategies

Joint decision making is not always easy. Often husbands and wives disagree about purchasing. According to Davis, married couples use two basic strategies to make decisions: consensus and accommodation.[26] Table 14-4 summarizes the major aspects of these two main decision-making

Table 14-4 ALTERNATE DECISION-MAKING STRATEGIES

Goals	*Strategy*	*Ways of Implementing*	*Sample Situation*
Consensus (Family members agree about goals	Role structure	"The Specialist"	A woman physician selects the brand of aspirin her family will use.
	Budgets	"The Controller"	Family income limits the choice of food or clothing.
	Problem solving	"The Expert" "The better solution: the multiple purchase"	An analysis of vacation choices produces a commonly agreed to location.
Accommodation (Family members disagree about goals)	Persuasion	"The Irresponsible Critic" Intuition "Shopping together" Coercion "Coalitions"	A husband encourages his wife to accompany him in shopping for a new power boat, which she feels is extravagant.
	Bargaining	"The Next Purchase" "The Impulse Purchase" "The Procrastinator"	The new car is chosen by one spouse in exchange for the other's right to choose the next time.

Source: adapted from Harry L. Davis, "Decision Making within the Household," *Journal of Consumer Research* 2 (March 1976): 255.

consensus decisions

accommodation

strategies. **Consensus decisions** occur when family members agree about goals. For example, if both the husband and wife are seeking a vacation to relax on a sunny beach, their common goal could be attained by using a consensus approach. Conversely, when couples disagree about goals, **accommodation** decisions take place. For example, if one spouse is looking for rest and sunshine while the other wants nightlife and entertainment during the vacation, an accommodation strategy would be needed.

Consensus decisions are made using role structure, budgets, or problem solving. Accommodation decisions rely on persuasion or bargaining.

Role Structure

Using *role structure,* discussion is vastly reduced because one party assumes the role of "specialist" for certain products. For example, the wife with a degree in chemistry makes all the paint decisions, while the husband with a business background makes investment decisions.

Budgets

Budgets provide rules under which purchasing decisions are made. A certain figure is set in advance for food, clothing, and other household expenditures, thus providing an impersonal "control" over what is purchased. Family members whose purchases are constrained by the budget may wish to express dissatisfaction. Yet they tend not to blame the person or persons who set the unpopular limits. Instead, they direct their hostility at the budget itself.

Problem Solving

Problem solving is the most democratic and rational approach to making family decisions. Once goals are established, all family members give their opinions according to their knowledge and expertise. The family then analyzes the problem to find a solution. In this approach, the "expert" at solving such problems has an opportunity to provide information or obtain opinions outside the family. Sometimes during family interaction, a better solution is found that could bring about an entirely different decision. For example, rather than taking a travel vacation, the family might decide to stay at home and use the money they saved to purchase a fishing boat. Or it might lead to multiple purchases that satisfy all family members: in this case, a shorter vacation and smaller boat.

Persuasion

Persuasion is getting someone to make a decision he or she would not otherwise make. This approach can lead to ill will, but it is often used. The spouse who is not allowed to share in the decision can become the "irresponsible critic" who contributes little to initial decisions except to point out potential problems. When they go wrong, as they sometimes do, this person says, "I told you so." The use of intuition by a family member can avoid the energy required for clear communication. A "shopping together" strategy forces the decision maker to commit to look at or shop for something, thereby giving implied commitment to an unwanted item. A son or daughter might use this approach to obtain a new bicycle by telling parents that he or she simply wants them to *look* at bicycles—only to trap them at the sales area and subtly or overtly beg for the new bike. Adults do this to each other as well.

Coercion tactics exist when verbal or physical threat or abuse are used to obtain an item. Other, less apparent coercive tactics are sometimes used. For example, the person cooking might refuse to provide a decent meal until he or she is allowed to buy a home computer.

Coalitions also help to persuade dissenting family members. For example, the husband and children might form a coalition against the wife (mother) until she agrees to the vacation spot they want to visit.

For people with more traditional life-styles and attitudes, the method of persuasion is used more often to arrive at joint decisions. This seems to be particularly true where a spouse wishes to avoid conflict.[27]

Bargaining

Bargaining also has major drawbacks. Whereas one party makes concessions now in order to receive future benefits, the other party obtains current gains at the expense of losses in the future. The result is a cut-off of communication and the elimination of more satisfying compromises. For example, one spouse might agree to take whatever vacation the other one wants this year, no matter how miserable it might appear, if he or she can make the vacation decision autonomously the next year.

Another bargaining strategy involves buying something on impulse without consulting the other partner. Since the purchase has already been made, the uninvolved partner may feel the decision is over, especially if they conclude they like the purchase.

Procrastination can also be an effective means of bargaining. By delaying a purchase that has already been agreed upon, circumstances can change so that the original choice can or must be altered. An example of procrastination is delaying a purchase until the item is no longer in stock or a particular sale is over.

The strategic implications for marketers of consensus and accommodation decision making may include three general responses. First, marketers can develop products that satisfy the needs of the family as a *unit* and target communications to the family as a *group*. Second, marketers can determine to *which* family members the product is most important and orient communications to appeal to the key decision makers. Finally, marketers can allow for varying degrees of influence between spouses and appeal to both segments individually.

Children's Impact on Family Decisions

Although the discussion up to this point has centered on husbands and wives, children do have an impact on family decisions. While several studies show that children have a major influence, there are moderating factors such as the type of product and the child's age. These two variables appear in the results of a study of the number of times that mothers yield to children's purchase requests. Researchers concluded that children's influence is strongest for cereal (a category that has received heavy promotion to children) and weakest for gasoline, household cleaners, coffee, and other products they themselves do not usually consume.[28] (See Figure 14-14 and Table 14-5.) Another study revealed that while children exert relatively little influence on the overall decision process, they have potential influence by forming an alliance with either parent to produce a majority position.[29]

This information is important for marketers deciding to whom appeals will be aimed. For products about which children have significant purchase influence, the marketer may decide to target marketing efforts at the child market, and specific age groups within it, rather than to various

Figure 14-14
Frequency of Children's Attempts to Influence Purchases and Average Percentage of Mothers Yielding, Children 5–12 Years of Age

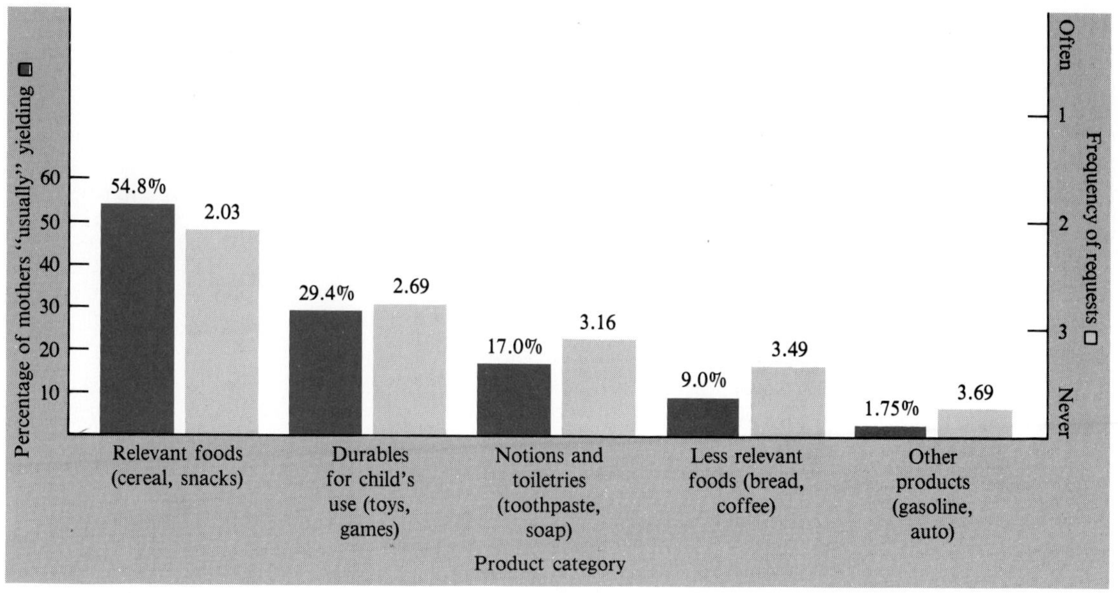

Source: based on Scott Ward and Daniel B. Wackmann, "Children's Purchase Influence Attempts and Parent Yielding," *Journal of Marketing Research* 9 (August 1972): 316–19.

Table 14-5 FREQUENCY OF CHILDREN'S ATTEMPTS TO INFLUENCE PURCHASES AND PERCENTAGE OF MOTHERS "USUALLY" YIELDING, BY AGE OF CHILD

	Frequency of Requests				*Percentage of Yielding*			
Products	***5–7 years***	***8–10 years***	***11–12 years***	***Total***	***5–7 years***	***8–10 years***	***11–12 years***	***Total***
Relevant foods								
Breakfast cereal	1.26	1.59	1.97	1.59	88	91	83	87
Snack foods	1.71	2.00	1.71	1.80	52	62	77	63
Candy	1.60	2.09	2.17	1.93	40	28	57	42
Soft drinks	2.00	2.03	2.00	2.01	38	47	54	46
Jell-O	2.54	2.94	2.97	2.80	40	41	26	36
Overall mean	1.82	2.13	2.16	2.03				
Overall percentage					51.6	53.8	59.4	54.8
Less relevant foods								
Bread	3.12	2.91	3.43	3.16	14	28	17	19
Coffee	3.93	3.91	3.97	3.94	2	0	0	1
Pet food	3.29	3.59	3.24	3.36	7	3	11	7
Overall mean	3.45	3.47	3.49	3.49				
Overall percentage					7.6	10.3	9.3	9.0
Durables for child's use								
Game, toy	1.24	1.63	2.17	1.65	57	59	46	54
Clothing	2.76	2.47	2.29	2.52	21	34	57	37
Bicycle	2.48	2.59	2.77	2.61	7	9	9	8
Hot Wheels	2.43	2.41	3.20	2.67	29	19	17	22
Record album	3.36	2.63	2.23	2.78	12	16	46	24
Camera	3.91	3.75	3.71	3.80	2	3	0	2
Overall mean	2.70	2.58	2.73	2.67				
Overall percentage					25.6	28.0	35.0	29.4
Notions, toiletries								
Toothpaste	2.29	2.31	2.60	2.39	36	44	40	39
Bath soap	3.10	2.97	3.46	3.17	9	9	9	9
Shampoo	3.48	3.31	3.03	3.28	17	6	23	16
Aspirin	3.64	3.78	3.97	3.79	5	6	0	4
Overall mean	3.13	3.09	3.26	3.16				
Overall percentage					16.8	16.3	18.0	17.0
Other products								
Automobile	3.55	3.66	3.51	3.57	2	0	0	12
Gasoline brand	3.64	3.63	3.83	3.70	2	0	3	2
Laundry soap	3.69	3.75	3.71	3.72	2	0	3	2
Household cleaner	3.71	3.84	3.74	3.76	2	3	0	2
Overall mean	3.65	3.72	3.70	3.69				
Overall percentage					2.0	.75	1.50	1.75

Source: Scott Ward and Daniel B. Wackmann, "Children's Purchase Influence Attempts and Parental Yielding," *Journal of Marketing Research* 9 (August 1972): 316–19.

Note: A total of 109 mothers were surveyed; the mothers had children 5–7 years old (n = 43), 8–10 years old (n = 32), and 11–12 years old (n = 34). The frequency of requests figure is based on a scale from 1 (often) to 4 (never).

segments of the adult market. Cereal manufacturers recognize the important role children play in selection of brands and aim their advertising accordingly.

Charles Atkin has studied parent–child interactions in purchase decisions. Figure 14-15 shows his flow diagram of interactions in the selection

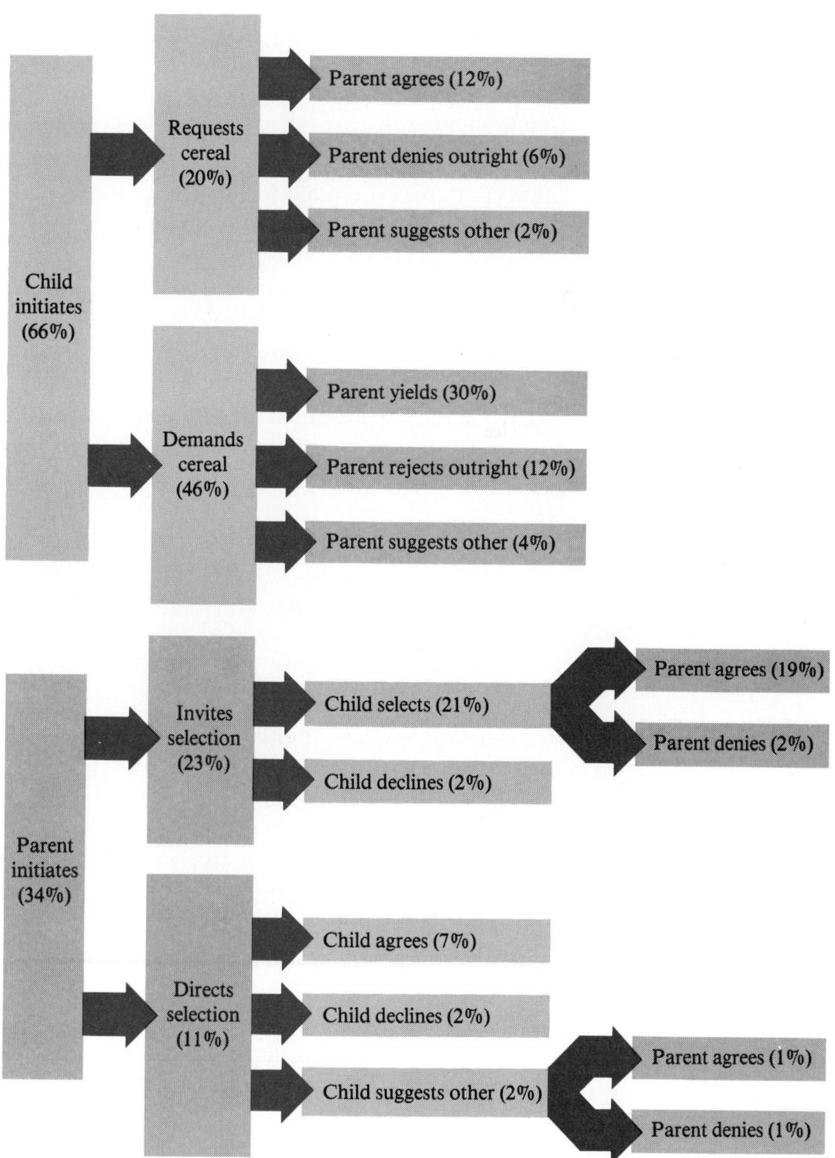

Figure 14-15
Flow of Parent–Child Interaction in Selection of Breakfast Cereal

Source: Charles K. Atkin, "Observation of Parent-Child Interaction in Supermarket Decision-Making," *Journal of Marketing* 42 (October 1978): 43.

of breakfast cereal. The child initiates the purchase two-thirds of the time. One-third of the time the parent initiates the purchase and generally invites the child's selection rather than directing the child to a particular choice. Then the child selects and the parent usually agrees. It is no wonder that children are a core target market for breakfast cereal manufacturers. For most cereals, the product design, testing, and packaging are aimed directly at this influential segment.

Clearly, the child can influence purchase decisions only when the parent lacks strong feelings about particular types or brands of products. Recently parents have become more concerned about the amount of sugar added to breakfast cereals. A new compromise product, with half the usual amount of sugar, was developed and marketed to children. This concession was intended to head off a forced retreat to the more healthy but less appealing brands the children's parents or grandparents once ate. In any case, one study has shown that the child's impact on the selection of a cereal varies indirectly with the mother's child-centeredness.[30]

In certain cases, a marketer may initiate marketing research to determine the influence various family members play in the decision to purchase its product. One candy manufacturer conducted a qualitative research study using separate focused groups for mothers and children to explore the relative importance each plays in selecting candy when shopping at the grocery store. The findings indicated that children do indeed play a major role in choice of candy brands even when they are not present in the store. It was found that when mothers shop *without* their children they typically select a bag of candy for the family that they believe will meet the approval of their children.*

Although parents can exert a powerful influence on the consumer education and awareness of their children, some parents abdicate this role. In a business feature story by National Public Radio correspondent Robert Kroelwich, a spokesman for a major shoe manufacturer explained that surveys of their store personnel indicate that children are achieving brand awareness at an increasingly early age. Whereas ten years ago the twelve-year-old might have recognized different brands of sneakers and indicated a preference, now five-year-olds—and sometimes even three-year-olds—are requesting a particular brand of sneakers. This rapid acceleration of brand awareness among children is not attributed to the influence of television or of older brothers and sisters. Rather, it is apparently the result of the variety of colors and styles now available and the prominent display of brand logos on sneakers in recent years.

This early recognition of brands combined with another recent trend has shifted the shoe manufacturer's concept of how its product is typically selected and purchased. A show sales person was asked what happens when a mother brings her child in for a new pair of sneakers. His reply indicated that increasingly mothers leave the decision up to the

* Proprietary study by a major food manufacturer.

children. Instead of buying the pair she thinks is best and telling the child, "You will wear these," now mothers ask even tiny children, "Will you wear these?" The salesperson has repeatedly attempted to explain to the mothers that their little children couldn't possibly make such decisions. However, the mothers insist that their children have a brand preference and ought to be allowed to make the decision. The salesperson concluded that children may be growing up faster these days because their parents expect them to.[31]

It is curious that although parents consider children's input in making purchasing decisions, they generally direct little information toward their children. Usually parents either purchase the items selected by their children or veto the selection altogether.[32]

active influence

A further variable in the influence of children on family decisions is the distinction between active and passive influence. **Active influence** is seen when a child insists that only Nike tennis shoes, for example, are acceptable. Passive influence comes into play when the parents decide to purchase a product with considerations for the child in mind. An example of children's passive influence would be the decision to buy a dining-room table and chairs with an easy-to-clean surface rather than in finely finished oak which the parents might prefer.

The presence of children in the family can influence the relative impact of husbands and wives on decision making. One study found that couples without children tended to make joint vacation decisions. However, husbands tended make the decision in families with children. Although children did not actively seek to influence the choice, the mere presence of children swayed the balance of decision-making power from wife to husband.[33]

Some general conclusions are possible regarding the impact children have on family purchases. First, the degree of children's influence varies across different product categories; it is relatively high for relevant products such as cereal and toys, but lower in other product areas. Children's influence also varies with age; older children have more influence on purchase decisions than younger children do.

Additionally, how much influence children have depends on how strong the parents' feelings are about particular brands or product types. Where a parent is less concerned, the child's influence is relatively high. The marketing strategies of many firms incorporate the anticipated role of children in the purchase decision. This is most apparent in the case of products such as cereal and candy, where children represent not only heavy users but also key decision influencers.

Family Expenditures

Families choose to spend their disposable income in many different ways. Traditional families (consisting of husband, wife, and children) and one-parent families have similar budgets, except that generally one-parent

Table 14-6 SPENDING FOR A FAMILY OF FOUR, 1976

	$10,041		*$23,759*	
Income (Expenditures)	*%*	*$*	*%*	*$*
Food	29.9	$ 3,002	20.4	$ 4,847
Housing	19.6	1,968	24.5	5,821
Medical care	8.9	894	4.0	950
Clothing	8.0	803	7.0	1,663
Transportation	7.6	763	7.7	1,829
Taxes	14.2	1,426	23.0	5,465
Other	11.8	1,185	13.4	3,184
Total	100.0	$10,041	100.0	$23,759

Source: David J. Ward and Robert M. Miendorf, *Consumer Finance: The Consumer Experience* (Homewood, IL: Richard D. Irwin, 1978), 13.

families have less discretionary income to work with. Single-person households vary considerably; they spend a much lower percentage on food, more on housing, and much more on alcohol and personal care. While there are always exceptions to broad generalizations, the average figures in Table 14-6 help show how funds are allocated differently for families of the same size and different incomes.

It is interesting to look at the household budgets established by recent college graduates. Table 14-7 summarizes the budgets of first-year college graduates in different family situations for comparison of expenditures. Despite relatively strong salaries, single grads and married grads without children tend to spend more than they make. Hence, many are quickly thrown into a "buy now, pay later" debt situation. However, marrieds with children who have more restricted incomes do tend to save, probably because of the feeling of responsibility for the future of the family.

Singles spend more per person for nightlife, followed by married couples without children. Couples with children spend about 15% less per adult than do single people. Married couples without children have the larger per-person travel and dining-out expenditures, while marrieds with children have heavier life and health insurance payments.

APPLICATION TO MARKETING STRATEGY

As mentioned, people are part of a basic family life cycle, although nearly one-quarter of the population now lives in single households or nontraditional living arrangements. The impact of more education and the postponement of marriage among women, as well as the need for more women

Table 14-7 FIRST-YEAR BUDGETS OF COLLEGE GRADUATES

	Singles		***For Marrieds with No Children***	***For Marrieds with Children***
	Male	***Female***		
Gross earnings:	$17,596	$17,596	$35,192	$26,394
Less taxes	3,039	3,039	7,320	4,851
Net earnings:	$14,557	$14,557	$27,872	$21,543
Less expenses:				
For apartment				
Rent	3,900	3,900	4,200	4,200
Furnishings*	1,500	1,500	2,500	2,500
Utilities	240	240	240	240
For food (at home)*	1,200	1,200	2,400	2,860
For clothing	1,300	1,500	3,000	2,700
For transportation				
Auto payments*	1,625	1,625	3,250	2,440
Insurance	900	700	1,300	1,300
Maintenance & gas	1,000	1,000	2,000	1,500
For entertainment:				
Travel	800	800	2,000	—
Dining out	1,560	1,560	3,500	500
Movies	200	100	200	100
Sporting events and equipment	400	300	600	200
Nightlife	1,560	1,560	2,000	500
For miscellaneous items:				
Life insurance	—	—	—	300
Health insurance	—	—	—	360
Student loan payments	300	300	600	600
Personal	100	100	200	200
Charity	—	—	200	—
TOTAL EXPENSES	$16,585	$16,385	$28,190	$20,500
Amount available for savings:	$(2,028)	$(1,828)	$(318)	$ 1,043

Source: developed by students at Michigan State University based on statistics from the U.S. Bureau of the Census and the U.S. Bureau of Statistics.

Singles' gross earnings are based on the average wages earned by college graduates between ages 18 and 24. The "Marrieds with No Children" category assumes two incomes; the "Married with Children" category assumes only 1½ incomes. Adjusted for 9% annual inflation. Earnings figures derived from: U.S. Bureau of the Census, Current Population Reports, Series P-60, No. 129, *Money Income for Families and Persons in the United States: 1979* (1981): 210.

Gross wages have been adjusted for taxes using a 1981 Form 1040A. Appropriate exemptions and standard deductions have been used for each category. For the sake of simplicity, state and local taxes as well as FICA payments have been ignored.

* Expenditure based on the percentage of the family budget spent on that item by family heads under age 25. U.S. Bureau of Labor Statistics, *Consumer Expenditures Survey: Diary Survey,* July 1972–June 1974 (1977): Table 3. (Other expense figures based on interviews with recent college graduates.)

to work, has altered the family life cycle. Most families now have two breadwinners.

Most married women must work for the family to maintain its standard of well being. If total productivity does not outdistance inflation, this trend will continue. Working couples are gaining more income at the expense of time with the family and for household chores. As more women work, families must spend more income for items that traditionally husbands and wives did for themselves. Thus, the demand for time-saving alternatives has increased and probably will continue to do so. Marketers are helping to fill this gap with offerings that are "time-free." For example, families eat out at fast-food restaurants, day-care centers supervise children while parents work, lawn-care services fertilize and mow grass, and condominiums, which require no external maintenance by unit owners, are becoming more popular. Many purchasers have cited quality and simplicity as reasons for buying Japanese cars; they feel that the autos are maintenance-free, thus saving on repair costs and time without transportation.

Most purchases involve family decision making. To the degree that husbands, wives, and children have different wants and perform unique roles, marketers can adjust their product lines, pricing, advertising, and distribution to target these roles. Product lines can be expanded to appeal to husbands and wives if they are likely to shop together for that product type. For example, Levi Strauss expanded its lines of jeans and other clothing to fit all ages and sexes. Designer jeans, traditionally for women, have entered the men's market. Often husbands, wives, and children are influenced differently by price. Russell Haley found that price-conscious men tend to make toothpaste decisions more often than those who are not price conscious.[34]

Advertising and promotion can be expanded to include all family members. The Johnson's Baby Shampoo ads are classics in this regard. The first ads depicted only babies as users of the product; later, appeals to the teenage daughter and mother were added. Subsequent ads appealed to fathers, a significant market segment for the product. These series of carefully targeted appeals have made Johnson's Baby Shampoo popular with entire families.

SUMMARY

Because consumers are often heavily influenced by others in their purchasing decisions, it is important to study those that may affect product or brand choice. One of the major reference groups that affects these decisions is the family.

Families are usually classified according to where the adults are in the family life cycle. Family units are defined according to age, marital status, and the presence of children in the family. By developing generalizations about the buying habits of members of each category in the family life cycle, we can more easily predict the purchase behavior of individual family units.

In recent years there have been some noticeable changes in the family life cycle. Young singles are delaying first marriages until their middle or late twenties. Consequently they are having fewer children and at an older age than has been common in the past. Also, more and more singles are choosing to forgo marriage altogether. Divorce rates have also continued to rise, creating an increase in single heads of household, who usually have less discretionary income. More women are joining the work force due to the desire for careers outside the home and the need for additional income as more women become heads of household and inflation continues to lower purchasing power.

Many changes in the family life cycle are attributed to the postwar "baby boom" which has resulted in a particularly large population of young adults in the 1980s.

Decision making within the traditional family group is a responsibility often shared by husband and wife. Each may have varying influence during the three steps of decision making: problem recognition, search for information, and final decision. The amount of influence exerted by either partner depends on the type of product being purchased, the role each partner tends to take, and the amount of expertise each partner possesses. Decisions are syncratic when both partners are involved in the purchase of a certain product type, autonomic when either one decides to buy that type of product, or husband or wife dominant when one spouse usually makes the decision on products of that type.

Joint decisions are divided into two categories: consensus decisions and accommodation decisions. Consensus decisions occur when family members agree on goals. These decisions may be made using role structure, budgets, or problem solving. Accommodation decisions result when there is a disagreement over goals and some form of concession on the part of at least one family member is required. Persuasion and bargaining are most often used to reach accommodation decisions.

Children also can have a major impact on purchasing decisions, particularly for items they use, such as breakfast cereal and their own clothing. In many cases, marketers aim their advertising for these products directly at children to capitalize on the child's influence on the purchase of these products.

It is important to note that different types of family units spend their incomes differently depending on age, marital status, and amount of income. Singles and married couples with no children spend more on entertainment and use credit more freely; married couples with children spend more on children's needs and insurance and tend to live more within their means.

By differentiating the different types of family units within the family life cycle and their respective needs, marketers can target their products to reach families more effectively. The family life cycle continues to evolve; changes that are now taking place may have an impact on what and how marketers sell in the future. Knowing how families reach decisions, and which family members are most influential in the decisions to purchase a product type, can be useful to companies that market that product. Wise marketers target their messages for maximum impact on the family's decision makers.

KEY TERMS

households
family life cycle
voluntary simplifiers
autonomous decisions
joint decisions
syncratic decisions
autonomic decisions
husband or wife dominant decisions
consensus decisions
accommodation
active influence

QUESTIONS

1. Explain the concept of the "family life cycle" as it relates to consumer behavior.

2. Where does your family fall on the life cycle? Indicate where your other relatives (brothers, sisters, cousins, grandparents) with families might be positioned. On what basis did you position them?

3. Describe some general characteristics of families at each stage of the life cycle. Use a chart to summarize your ideas and provide an example of a typical product purchased at each stage.

4. What are the potential marketing implications of current trends in family structure? How does today's "typical" family differ from a "typical" family in the 1950s?

5. Suppose a food manufacturer asked you for your recommendations about potential new products for future families. What will you tell the firm's research and development team?

6. How might the shopping behaviors of dual-career couples differ from those families in which only the husband works? Explain.

7. Distinguish between joint and autonomous decision making and provide an example of each type.

8. What is meant by *consensus* and *accommodation* in terms of family decision making? How might a marketer respond to these decision strategies?

9. Children (as well as other family members) can exert passive or active influence in purchase decisions. Explain how.

NOTES

1. "Two-Income Families: A Bittersweet Lifestyle," *U.S. News and World Report* (November 2, 1981): 85.
2. William D. Wells and George Gubar, "The Life Cycle Concept," *Journal of Marketing Research* (November 1966): 355–63.
3. Hugh Carter and Paul C. Glick, *Marriage and Divorce: A Social and Economic Study,* 2nd ed. (Cambridge, MA: Harvard University Press, 1976).
4. Patrick E. Murphy and William A. Staples, "A Modernized Family Life Cycle," *Journal of Consumer Research* 6 (June 1979): 12–22. Some material for the life-cycle stages presented in the following sections is based on Murphy and Staples, which has been updated with U.S. Census data for 1980. For an alternate view of the modern family life cycle, see Mary C. Gilly and Ben M. Enis, "Recycling the Family Life Cycle: A Proposal for Redefinition," in *Advances in Consumer Research IX,* Andrew Mitchell, ed. (St. Louis: Association for Consumer Research, 1981), 271–76.
5. U.S. Bureau of the Census, Current Population Reports, 1982, Series P-60, No. 142 (February 1984): 143.
6. James F. Engel, Roger D. Blackwell, and David T. Kollatt, *Consumer Behavior* (New York: The Dryden Press, 1978), 164.
7. "Two-Income Families," 85.
8. "Two-Income Families," 86.
9. Paul C. Glick and Arthur J. Norton, "Marrying, Divorcing, and Living Together in the U.S. Today," *Population Bulletin 32* (Washington, D.C.: Population Reference Bureau, Inc., 1977).
10. "Latest Findings on Middle-Aged Americans," *U.S. News and World Report* (August 3, 1981): 41.
11. Murphy and Staples, 16.
12. Alan C. Kerckhoff, "Patterns of Marriage and Family Formation and Dissolution," *Journal of Consumer Research* 2 (March 1976): 261–75.
13. U.S. Bureau of the Census, *U.S. Department of Housing and Urban Development Annual Housing Survey* (Washington D.C.: U.S. Govt. Printing Office, 1979).
14. "Life Begins at 55," *U.S. News and World Report* (September 1, 1980): 51.
15. T. C. Taylor, "Tomorrow's New Rich—Postwar Babies are Growing Up," *Sales and Marketing Management* 127 (October 26, 1981).
16. U.S. Bureau of the Census, Current Population Reports, "Population Characteristics," Series P-20, No. 218 (March 1970) and No. 366 (March 1980).
17. U.S. Bureau of the Census, Current Population Reports, "Household and Family Characteristics: March 1983, Series P-20, No. 388, 169.
18. Taylor, "Tomorrow's New Rich," 7–29.
19. "The Shrinking Standard of Living," *Business Week* (January 28, 1970): 74.
20. Avraham Shama, "Coping with Stagflation: Voluntary Simplicity," *Journal of Marketing* (Summer 1981): 127.
21. Shama, "Coping with Stagflation," 127.
22. Charles M. Schaninger, W. Christian Buss, and Rajiv Grover, "The Effect of Sex Roles on Family Finance Handling and Decision Influence," in *An Assessment of Marketing Thought and Practice,* Educators' Conference Proceedings, Series No. 48 (Chicago: American Marketing Association, 1982); also William J. Qualls, "Changing Sex Roles: Its Impact upon Family Decision Making," in *Advances in Consumer Research,* Andrew Mitchell, ed. (St. Louis, Association for Consumer Research, 1981), 267–70.
23. Louis Harris and Associates, "Togetherness among the Baby Boomers," *Sales and Marketing Management* (July 6, 1981): 41.
24. Harry L. Davis and Benny P. Rigaux, "Perception of Marital Roles in Decision Processes," *Journal of Consumer Research* 1 (June 1974): 51–62.
25. Harry L. Davis, "Decision Making within the Household," *Journal of Consumer Research* 2 (March 1976): 241–57.
26. Harry L. Davis, "Decision Making within the Household," 241–60.
27. Rosann L. Spiro, "Persuasion in Family Decision-Making," *Journal of Consumer Research* 9 (March 1983): 393–402.
28. Scott Ward and Daniel B. Wackman, "Children's Purchase Influence Attempts and Parent Yielding," *Journal of Marketing Research* 9 (August 1972): 316–19.
29. Pierre Filiatrault and J. R. Brent Ritchie, "Joint Purchasing Decisions: A Comparison of Influence Structure in Family and Couple Decision-Making Units," *Journal of Consumer Research* 7 (September 1980): 131–40.
30. Lewis A. Berry and Richard W. Pollay, "The Influencing Role of the Child in Family Decision Making," *Journal of Marketing Research* 5 (February 1968): 70–72.
31. Robert Kroelwich, "All Things Considered," National Public Radio, July 20, 1983.
32. Daniel B. Wackman. "Family Processes in Children's Consumption," in *Educators Conference Proceedings Series #44,* Neil Beckwith et al., eds. (Chicago: American Marketing Association, 1979), 316–19.
33. Filiatrault and Ritchie, 131–40.
34. Russell I. Haley, "Benefit Segmentation: A Decision Oriented Research Tool," *Journal of Marketing* 32 (July 1968): 30–35.

FURTHER READING

Classics

Cunningham, I. C. M., and R. T. Green, "Purchasing Roles in the U.S. Family, 1955 and 1973," *Journal of Marketing* 38 (October 1974): 61–64.

Davis, Harry L., "Dimensions of Marital Roles in Consumer Decision-Making," *Journal of Marketing Research* 7 (May 1970): 168–77.

Davis, Harry L., "Decision Making Within the Household," *Journal of Consumer Research* 2 (March 1976): 241–60.

Davis, Harry L., and Benny P. Rigaux, "Perception of Marital Roles in Decision Processes," *Journal of Consumer Research* 1 (June 1974): 51–62.

Ferber, R., and L. C. Lee, "Husband-Wife Influence in Family Purchasing Behavior," *Journal of Consumer Research* 1 (June 1974): 43–50.

Munsinger, Gary M., Jean W. Weber, and Richard W. Hansen, "Joint Home Purchasing Decisions by Husbands and Wives," *Journal of Consumer Research* 1 (March 1975): 60–66.

Sheth, Jagdish N., "A Theory of Family Buying Decisions," in *Models of Buyer Behavior,* Jagdish N. Sheth, ed. (New York: Harper and Row, 1974), 17–33.

Ward, Scott, "Consumer Socialization," *Journal of Consumer Research* (September 1980): 1–14.

Wolgast, E. H., "Do Husbands or Wives Make the Purchasing Decisions?" *Journal of Marketing* 23 (October 1958): 151–58.

Woodside, Arch G., "Dominance and Conflict in Family Purchasing Decisions," *Proceedings,* Third Annual Conference, Association for Consumer Research, M. Venkatesan, ed. (Chicago: Association for Consumer Research, 1972), 650–59.

Recent Significant Research

Belch, Michael A., George E. Belch, and Donald Sciglimpaglia, "Conflict in Family Decision Making: An Exploratory Investigation," in *Advances in Consumer Research,* Jerry C. Olson, ed. (Ann Arbor, MI: Association for Consumer Research, 1980).

Belk, Russell, Robert Mayer, and Amy Driscoll, "Children's Recognition of Consumption Symbolism in Children's Products," *Journal of Consumer Research* 10, (March 1984): 386–97.

Derrick, Frederick W., and Alane K. Lehfeld, "The Family Life Cycle: An Alternative Approach," *Journal of Consumer Research* 7 (September 1980): 214–17.

Filiatrault, Pierre, and J. R. Brent Ritchie, "Joint Purchasing Decisions: A Comparison of Influence Structure in Family and Couple Decision-Making Units," *Journal of Consumer Research* 7 (September 1980): 131–40.

Kourilsky, Marilyn, and Trudy Murray, "The Use of Economic Reasoning to Increase Satisfaction with Family Decision Making," *Journal of Consumer Research* 8 (September 1981): 183–88.

Murphy, Patrick E., and William A. Staples, "A Modernized Family Life Cycle," *Journal of Consumer Research* 6 (June 1979):12–22.

Popper, Edward T., "Mothers' Mediation of Children's Purchase Requests," in *Proceedings of the American Marketing Association Educators' Conference,* Neil Beckwith et al., eds. (Chicago: American Marketing Association, 1979), 645–48.

Qualls, William J., "Changing Sex Roles: Its Impact Upon Family Decision Making," in *Advances in Consumer Research,* Vol. 9, Andrew Mitchell, ed. (Ann Arbor, MI: Association for Consumer Research, 1982), 267–70.

Rosen, Dennis L., and Donald H. Granbois, "Determinants of Role Structure in Family Financial Management," *Journal of Consumer Research* 10 (September 1983): 253–58.

Spiro, Rosann L., "Persuasion in Family Decision-Making," *Journal of Consumer Research* 9 (March 1983): 393–402.

Wagner, Janet, and Sherman Hanna, "The Effectiveness of Family Life Cycle Variables in Consumer Expenditure Research," *Journal of Consumer Research* 10, No. 3 (December 1983): 281–91.

Weinberg, Charles B., and Russell S. Winer, "Working Wives and Major Family Expenditures: Replication and Extension," *Journal of Consumer Research* 10 (September 1983): 259–63.

Applications

Atkin, C., "Parent-Child Communication in Supermarket Breakfast Cereal Selection," in *Effects of Television Advertising on Children* Report #7, (East Lansing: Michigan State University, December 1975).

Davis, Harry L., "Measurement of Husband–Wife Influence in Consumer Purchase Decisions," *Journal of Marketing Research* 8 (August 1971): 305–12.

Nowland and Company, Inc., *Family Participation and Influence in Shopping and Brand Selection: Phase I and Phase II*. Reports prepared for *Life* Magazine.

Park, C. Whan, "Joint Decisions in Home Purchasing: A Muddling-Through Process," *Journal of Consumer Research* 9 (September 1982): 151–62.

Robertson, Thomas S., "Parental Mediation of Television Advertising Effects," *Journal of Communication* 29 (Winter 1979): 12–25.

Rosen, Dennis L., and Donald H. Granbois, "Determinants of Role Structure in Family Financial Management," *Journal of Consumer Research* 10 (September 1983): 253–58.

Scanzoni, John, "Changing Sex Roles and Emerging Directions in Family Decision Making," *Journal of Consumer Research* 4 (December 1977): 185–88.

Szybillo, George J., Arlene K. Sosanie and Aaron Tenebein, "Should Children Be Seen But Not Heard?" *Journal of Advertising Research* 17: (December 1977).

Ward, Scott, and Daniel B. Wackman, "Children's Purchase Influence Attempts and Parental Yielding," *Journal of Marketing Research* 9 (August 1972): 316–19.

15 Culture and Subculture

Objectives of This Chapter

After you have studied this chapter, you should be able to:

1. Describe three types of cultural orientation in business people.
2. Define *culture* and illustrate its role in determining current American values.
3. Show how the world's major religions influence cultural values and consumer behavior.
4. Discuss how the perception of time and other variables differs among cultures in ways that influence consumers.
5. Discuss the concept of subculture as it relates to nationality, race, religion, and ethnicity.
6. Discuss and compare two of the predominant American subcultures: blacks and Hispanics.

Culture and subculture affect consumer behavior in at least two ways. Indirectly, they provide the backdrop against which most of our day-to-day activities are cast; directly, they bear on the types of products available, purchased, and consumed within societies. This chapter begins with a discussion of culture because it is more rigorously defined and because it involves the basic elements underlying most human behavior. Then we investigate the broad categories known as *subcultures* that are embedded within each culture. Sensitivity to cultural and subcultural differences is not only important for business people operating in multinational environments but it can also help us better understand consumers within our own society.

People everywhere communicate with one another through ancient and evolutionary symbols that are part of their heritage. Many of these symbols differ from one society to the next. Even such elementary things as colors, numbers, and shapes may have significantly different interpretations across different cultures. The unique meaning that cultures attach to certain symbols and gestures can have important implications for tourists and marketers alike. For example, it has been suggested that companies should carefully avoid certain colors in packaging for export since they may be offensive in some cultures.[1] Similarly, salespeople who travel abroad may find that simple gestures taken for granted in the United States communicate an entirely different meaning to foreign buyers.[2] As the world draws closer through advancements in communication and travel technology, the influence of cultural differences on consumer behavior will become increasingly important to managers.

MULTINATIONAL BUSINESS AND THE CROSS-CULTURAL PERSPECTIVE

Despite the existence of extensive international commerce, at the turn of the century few Americans conducted business more than one hundred miles from their homes. Today, every business person is touched by multinational corporations, and it is safe to say that most business school graduates will travel abroad frequently in the course of their careers.

The extent of international trade by the United States has skyrocketed in recent years. Total exports now exceed $100 billion. Moreover, direct foreign investment in the United States recently surpassed the $100 billion mark. Many large corporations in this country transact most of their business abroad. Gillette, Coca-Cola, Dow Chemical, Uniroyal, and IBM are among the multinational firms that acquire more than half their profits from international operations.[3] Table 15-1 helps convey the immense size of multinational businesses. The total sales of several multinational firms surpass the gross national product of many nations.

Multinational corporations have experienced explosive growth in recent years. Whereas in the past much international business activity in-

Table 15-1 RANKING OF NATIONS AND MULTINATIONAL BUSINESSES ACCORDING TO GNP OR TOTAL SALES

Ranking	*Nation or firm*	*GNP or Total Sales for 1979 ($ billions)*
20	Switzerland	89.9
21	*Exxon*	84.5
22	Czechoslovakia	80.5
23	*General Motors*	66.3
24	Austria	64.6
25	Saudi Arabia	62.6
26	*Royal Dutch Shell*	62.0
27	Argentina	61.0
28	Denmark	60.8
29	Turkey	58.8
30	South Korea	55.9
31	Nigeria	55.3
32	Yugoslavia	53.8
33	Indonesia	52.2
34	South Africa	49.0
35	*Mobil Oil*	47.9
36	Venezuela	45.2
37	*American Telephone and Telegraph*	45.0
38	Norway	43.5
39	*Ford Motor Company*	43.5
40	Romania	41.8
41	Hungary	41.3
42	*British Petroleum*	40.5
43	Finland	39.4
44	*Texaco*	39.1
45	Greece	36.7
46	Bulgaria	32.7
47	*Standard Oil of California*	31.8
48	Taiwan	31.5
49	Iraq	30.4
50	Algeria	28.9
51	Philippines	28.1
52	Thailand	26.9
53	Colombia	26.4
54	*Gulf Oil*	26.1
55	Libya	23.4
56	*IBM*	22.9
57	*Unilever*	22.8
58	*General Electric*	22.5
59	Kuwait	21.9

Source: adapted from *1980 World Bank Atlas* (Washington, D. C. 1981): "Corporate Scoreboard," *Business Week* (March 17, 1980): 81; "International Corporate Scoreboard," *Business Week* (July 21, 1980): 118.

volved manufacturing, finance, and technology transfer, a great deal of the new thrust has been in marketing activities affecting consumers on a global scale. Through the introduction of new ideas and products by multinationals as well as fierce competition for traditional goods and services, consumption patterns in many nations are shifting in massive proportions. Cross-cultural business has become a fundamental part of our economic structure and plays a major role in many corporate marketing programs.

Although there has been little systematic cross-cultural research in the field of human behavior, the available information helps clarify a few of the key differences between people and nations which create such diverse consumption patterns around the globe. No book on consumer behavior would be complete without investigating the behavior of people from many nations, and this is especially fitting for one developed in the United States, a melting pot where virtually every major cultural group is represented.

Businesses and their executives can be classified into three broad categories in terms of their attitudes toward diverse cultures: ethnocentric, polycentric, and geocentric (see Figure 15-1). The **ethnocentric** view maintains that consumer needs and business operations are basically the same the world over. Although some account is taken of minor differences due to local circumstances and economic development, ethnocentrists think that their own beliefs, values, and concepts are either similar to those of other cultures or can serve as the dominant practice of business in other cultures. At the other extreme is the **polycentric** view, which sees the world as divided into many cultures, each with unique character-

ethnocentric

polycentric

Figure 15-1
Continuum of Attitudes toward Culture

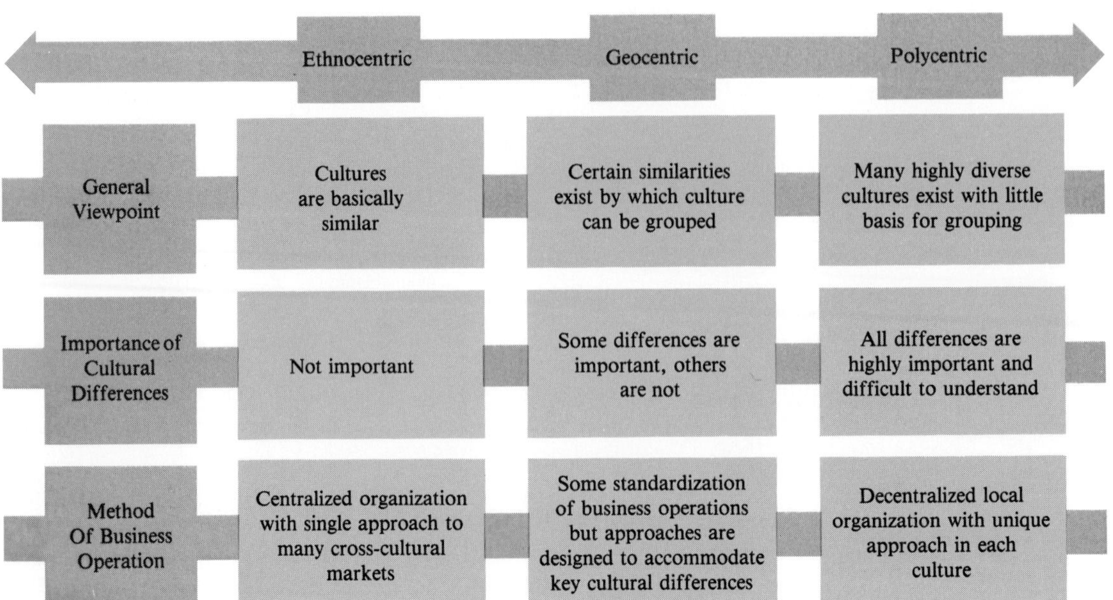
Ethnocentric
Geocentric
Polycentric
General Viewpoint
Cultures are basically similar
Certain similarities exist by which culture can be grouped
Many highly diverse cultures exist with little basis for grouping
Importance of Cultural Differences
Not important
Some differences are important, others are not
All differences are highly important and difficult to understand
Method Of Business Operation
Centralized organization with single approach to many cross-cultural markets
Some standardization of business operations but approaches are designed to accommodate key cultural differences
Decentralized local organization with unique approach in each culture

istics difficult to relate to common concepts, ideals, and patterns. Whereas the ethnocentric approach places the individual business person in the center of his or her own cultural universe, polycentrism suggests that the world is very hard to comprehend because each of its cultures must be understood in and of itself. Since for polycentrists a single unifying view of the world's cultures is impossible, polycentric businesses develop satellites that are only loosely tied to the parent organization.

geocentric The third approach can be considered a compromise between the other two. The **geocentric** perspective sees many similarities among cultures; that is, each country's unique qualities can be understood according to common dimensions that help us compare and contrast them. According to this view, in some ways business strategy should be standardized to achieve economies of scale, creativity, and excellence that have applications everywhere. At the same time, major efforts should be made to understand and account for the considerable differences among cultures—and among consumers, who are influenced by their cultures.

Primary and Secondary Consumer Demand

primary demand Consumer demand can be divided into two broad types. Product class choice, often called **primary demand,** relates to the sorts of *products* used by a particular country or culture. In the area of transportation, for example, the preference for bicycles over foot or animal travel, for motorbikes over bicycles, and for automobiles over motorcycles reflect different product class patterns in different cultures. The Philippines, India, and many other cultures contrast starkly with the United States in terms of their transportation patterns. Even such broader dimensions as a society's preference for art objects versus consumption items can yield revealing comparisons. To the degree that consumers adopt new product classes, radical social change can occur. Some of the theory regarding cross-cultural buyer behavior specifically addresses the primary demand aspect,[4] while largely ignoring brand choice.

secondary demand The other category of consumer demand, called **secondary demand,** involves *brand* choice. Clearly, culture affects the product classes selected by individuals, yet several specific variables are likely to influence particular choices. For example, the cultural value of nationalism might make some brands less appealing than others. Also, the tendency in some cultures to view the "big picture" rather than details may lead to a preference for certain brands over others. A major challenge not yet systematically addressed is to distinguish the variables affecting primary demand from those affecting secondary demand. Only a spotty and incomplete picture of how culture relates to consumer behavior can be found in the consumer literature. Most insights are derived from broad and basic knowledge about culture and are largely untested.

Culture and Consumer Behavior

Given the vast size of multinational business and the tremendous dependency of our economy and major corporations on the acceptance of our goods and services abroad, there is a surprising lack of published information about cross-cultural consumer behavior. A few studies have addressed systematically a single consumer behavior variable across a broad range of cultures. Some research has attempted to look at two or even three cultures, but little has been done on a wider scale. The problem arises partly from lack of funding for world-sized studies; but it is due mostly to the tremendous difficulty of cross-cultural research.[5] The agencies and groups that do collect data on a broad scale are primarily interested in economic conditions and flows of goods and services rather than the sociological or anthropological elements that influence fundamental decision structures. It is difficult to assemble descriptive data on consumption patterns, much less on underlying purchase decision processes, for many cultures. The very problem of observation in so many divergent cultures can make comparisons questionable. Realistically, this chapter can do no more than provide a framework for understanding elements of cross-cultural behavior and describe some key variables useful in the multinational study of consumer behavior.

It should be noted that the study of cultural aspects of buyer behavior directly involves individual consumers' choices—yet it is not focused on individuals. By definition, culture refers to the behavior of very *large* groups that are isolated from other groups over time—ranging from two or three decades to as long as thousands of years. While cultures interact for trade purposes or in times of war, the people within cultures still tend to be influenced to a great degree by traditional values they have imposed on themselves over time. Researchers have tended to describe differences in countries by using specific examples without delving into the underlying determinants; but a simple listing of differences and customs between two cultures does not begin to explain the dynamics of brand choice. Variations in customs are so vast that a listing is impractical for the cross-cultural traveling business person or a marketer.

WHAT IS CULTURE?

Culture is difficult to define because of its extreme generalness. Edward T. Hall writes:

> Culture is man's medium; there is not one aspect of human life that is not touched and altered by culture. This means personality, how people express themselves (including shows of emotion), the way they think, how they move, how problems are solved, how their cities are planned and laid out, how transportation systems function and are organized, as well as how economic and government systems are put together and function. It is fre-

> quently the most obvious and taken for granted, and therefore the least studied aspects of culture that influence behavior in the deepest and most subtle ways.[6]

culture **Culture** includes language, nonverbal communication, material objects, values, attitudes, and ways of doing things. It encompasses the social heritage of people as well as the basis for most social interaction. From the standpoint of consumer behavior, one of the more important aspects of culture is the distinctive life-style of the entire society. In addition, culture includes the religions, beliefs, laws, knowledge, food customs, art, music, technology, work habits, and institutions that distinguish one society from another. But in terms of consumer behavior, culture is the learned values, beliefs, language, symbols, and patterns of behavior shared by people in a society and passed on from generation to generation.

For most of us, culture pervades every move we make. When we think, talk, or even dream, our impressions are cast in the cultural context of our lives. Several major points arise from the definition we have chosen. First, culture is *learned,* not innate. It is passed along generations in relatively unchanged forms. Second, central to culture are its *values*—an aspect we have chosen to highlight, because values are reflected in the products and services of a consumer economy. Third, culture is transmitted by verbal and nonverbal *communication,* which often involves symbols. Certainly, much communication in marketing uses language, often ones that are foreign to us.

Culture Is Learned: Socialization

socialization
acculturation

Socialization and *acculturation* are two terms used to describe the process of absorbing or learning a culture. **Socialization** refers to learning to be a part of the culture in which one is reared. **Acculturation** is the process of taking on a new culture, for example, when a person moves from one country to another. Socialization is important to consumer behavior because many values learned in an affluent society have a commercial content.

Most psychologists agree that children learn in developmental *stages* and that socialization shapes individual characteristics and behavior through the training the social environment provides, primarily through friends, parents, teachers, and other people. As children are socialized, they learn about the specific goal objects for more generalized human wants. Culture is important to consumer behaviorists because many of these goal objects are economic in nature. Thus, during socialization (or *inculturation,* as it is often called) children learn not only the symbols and languages of a culture but also the specific types of goods and services valued by it.

The Nine Nations of North America

Although there are many theories and suggestions about ways to define and view American culture, an insightful perspective has been offered recently by Joel Garreau. His general ideas will be highlighted, and then some specific research into American consumers' values will be examined.

How many cultures are there in North America? Joel Garreau believes that there are nine, which he calls *nations*.[7] In his fascinating best-seller, Garreau asks us to forget the borders separating the United States, Canada, and Mexico as well as the provincial and state boundaries that have been erected by historical accidents or surveyors. Each of the nine nations can be considered a culture because each has a distinct way of viewing the world, according to Garreau (see Figure 15-2).

The Foundry consists of the industrial northeast. Its inhabitants see this area as the center of power in North America and do not recognize the decline in its economic dominance over the other nations. The Foundry is dotted with cities dedicated to heavy industry. This is rugged country; Garreau writes about the vicinity of Pittsburgh, where "coal-fired electrical plants split the hills with high tension lines. Steel, glass, and industrial chemical plants bring jobs—jobs that are not only dangerous and difficult, but are hit first in a slacking economy."[8] Other parts of the foundry include such cities as Ft. Wayne and Gary, Indiana; Chicago, Detroit, New York City; Trenton, New Jersey; Washington, D.C.; and the industrial cities of Canada: London, Hamilton, and Ottawa. The headquarters of hundreds of the world's major corporations are located in these cities; among them are Kodak in Rochester, New York; Westinghouse and U.S. Steel in Pittsburgh; and General Motors in Detroit.

Dixie, Garreau writes, has long been identified with stagnation: "Backward, rural, poor, and racist, a colony of the industrialized north . . . Dixie is now best described as that forever underdeveloped North American nation across which the social and economic machine of the late 20th century has more dramatically swept."[9] Dixie, consisting of a diverse culture where people refer to themselves as "Southerners," is changing with rapid economic growth.

The Islands encompass the southern tip of Florida, the Bahamas, Cuba, and other islands stretching down the coast of Latin America. Miami is an important city in this area: the drug smuggling gateway of the United States, and this traffic has become southern Florida's largest industry. Many refugees from Cuba and elsewhere settle here, become acculturated, and in turn influence the culture of people who have lived there for decades. The economy for much of The Islands is tourist-dependent. Garreau also presents a picture of danger, corruption, and intrigue: "Guns are so common on The Islands that Tony Senatore claims he

Figure 15-2 The Nine Nations of North America

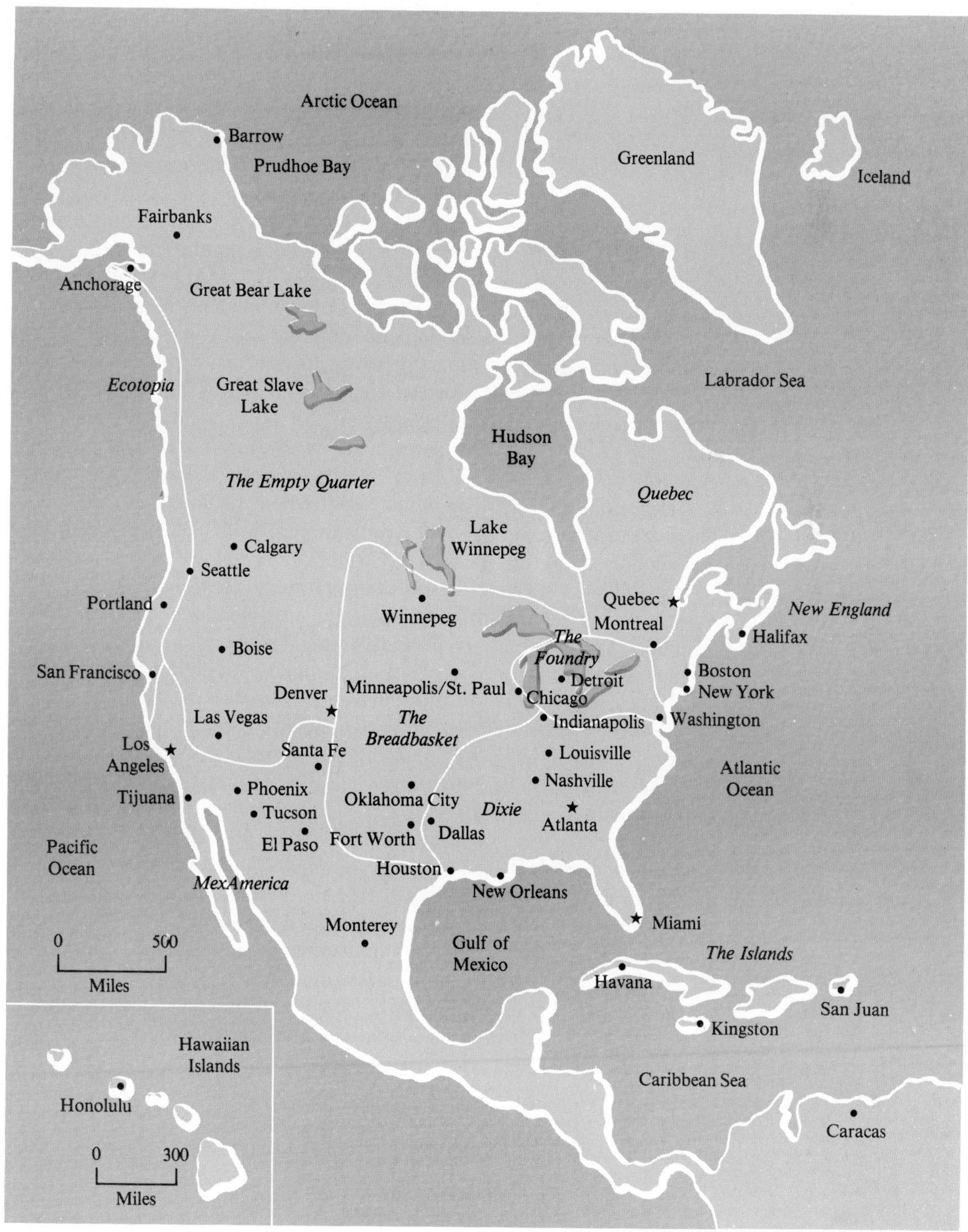

Source: Joel Garreau, *The Nine Nations of North America* (New York: Avon Books, 1981).

doesn't understand why everybody got excited when he started advertising Uzi submachine guns in the *Miami Herald*. After talking to him for a few hours I came to think that he meant that sincerely."[10]

Mexamerica comprises southern California, Texas, and Mexico. Garreau indicates that the growing Mexican influence on this area is evident in food, fashion, and music. Languages, an important element in culture, are converging here; an English-speaking person may be asked questions in Spanish first. Spanish is also becoming the second language of the airwaves. There are 37 Spanish-language radio stations in Texas, 23 in California, 6 in Arizona, and 4 in New Mexico. Los Angeles is extremely important not only because of its size but also because of its wealth. The city offers a power base for Mexamerica.

Ecotopia is a narrow area stretching north of San Francisco along the Pacific Coast. Residents like the area and do not welcome change. The tremendous natural resources provide not only beauty but also clean water and air. Seeking a utopian way of life, the inhabitants reject many of the economic and other values of North America as being materialistic, wasteful, polluting, military-industrial oriented, racist, sexist, and so on. Their attitude is reflected in the holistic philosophy of life, which gives precedence to the total-person environment. A cultural value here would be to plant trees rather than cut them, although the forests are plentiful. Since much of the trade is with Japan, the area is influenced by the values of quality and efficiency projected by Japanese goods.

New England is the poorest of all the nine nations but prides itself on being the most civilized. Garreau writes about New Englanders who abandon central heating and go out to cut firewood, which gives them a sense of smug superiority in having gone back to nature. Since New England has very poor agriculture, very few raw materials, and a diminishing population of 13 million, the scenery and surroundings have become its most important focus. Garreau indicates that New England is rapidly transforming itself into a postindustrial society with some of the finest "brain factories" in North America; Boston has 65 colleges and universities, and education is highly valued in this nation.

The Empty Quarter has vast and undeveloped natural resources, is relatively unpopulated despite a few boomtowns, and contains unexplored and unrefined deposits of oil, coal, and oil shale. It also contains nearly all of North America's uranium and has radiation-related problems. This area values wide open spaces.

The Bread Basket feeds the rest of North America and much of the world. It accounts for 18 percent of global exports of wheat and has some of the most fertile soil on the planet. A farmer needs a keen mind to untangle the web of government regulations, taxation, and agricultural risks. A sense of fairness is a primary value, as is hard work. Kansas City, Missouri, is the capital of the Bread Basket, where the economy is built on prosperity and renewable wealth. Agriculture is "heavily equipped, heavily capitalized, and based on substantial acreage."[11]

Quebec, with 6 million primarily French-speaking people and many who speak no English whatsoever, is three times the size of France and is almost entirely surrounded by English-speaking neighbors. It is economically diversified and strategically located, with a very homogeneous population. Garreau says that "the people here feel like a nation in food, music, fashion, values, education, ways of thinking, politics and many other things. They have become masters in their own houses."[12] He adds: "A people that once identified themselves as rural, Catholic, obedient, long-suffering losers have awakened to the fact that they are urban, industrialized, capable, in power of their own land—and in serious danger of having to take responsibility for their own future."[13] In addition to language, there are many deep cultural differences between Quebec and the other eight nations. The French influence has remained strong and provides this nation with a sense of unity.

Garreau's broad overview is an interesting description of North American culture and values. But most research has focused on the United States and the specific values of its consumers. Two examples, discussed next, are a study by the University of Michigan's Survey Research Center and a work by Leon Shiffman and Leslie Kanuk.

Current American Values: The Survey Research Center Study

Values are ideas reflecting a person's culture. They are broad categories of expression regarding important aspects of life. Students who value hard work, for example, have a positive attitude about spending more than the average number of hours studying.

The University of Michigan's Survey Research Center questioned 2,264 representative adults in the United States.[14] Their results indicated that the following values are predominant among Americans: self-respect; security; warm relationships with others; sense of accomplishment; self-fulfillment; being well respected; a sense of belonging; and fun, enjoyment, and excitement.

Self-Respect. Approximately 21% of those surveyed endorse self-respect as the most important value. The researcher suggests that these people want to be at peace with themselves; they want to like themselves and to be free of guilt. Members of this group tend to be Middle Americans who do not deviate drastically from the norm. Therefore, they are perhaps less willing to try new products and are likely to rely on brand names.

Security. Another 20.6% of the sample considered security their most dominant value. Most people in this group are in a low-income category, widowed, or black. They also indicated that they often have shortness of breath, trouble sleeping, dizziness, and anxiety. The researcher suggests that marketers may have stressed the security value almost to the point of saturation; it is possible to purchase home security devices, as well as "social security" through deodorants and mouthwashes.

Warm Relationships with Others. This value was selected by about 16% of the sample. Single and married women and divorced men (but not divorced women) are prominent in this category. People in the group tend to live on a very social level and have interpersonal involvements that guide their lives. Compared to others, they are more likely to give gifts. They spend more time entertaining, in community activities, and with their families. Firstborns were unlikely to select this value.

A Sense of Accomplishment. About 11.4% of the sample gave a sense of accomplishment as their most important value. They tend to be well educated, well-paid managers, and professionals with a high degree of self-direction. Many are young males and tend to be healthy, well adjusted, self-confident, and capable. Achievers who believe in the work ethic, they are conspicuous consumers of quality homes, cars, clothing, furniture, and so on. They also enjoy innovative products.

Self-Fulfillment. Self-fulfillment corresponds closely to Maslow's need for self-actualization. A little less than 10% of the respondents chose self-fulfillment as a primary value. Members of this group are demographically very similar to those who chose having a sense of accomplishment as their primary value. Both have a high degree of self-confidence. Any unhappiness expressed by this group stemmed from feeling deficient as parents or from their dislike of certain family roles. Individuality, accomplishment, and freedom are extremely important to those valuing self-fulfillment. Self-enhancing products such as sports equipment are consistent with their value system.

Being Well Respected. About 9% of the sample emphasized respect from others as a value. Unlike other groups, people in this category often feel a lack of respect from others, leading them to depression, defensiveness, and the search for approval from others. The researcher believes that these people are more likely to purchase items enhancing respect, such as costly status symbols that foster prestige, and prefer conventional clothing, furniture, and cars.

Sense of Belonging. About 8% of the respondents chose a sense of belonging as their primary value. Women, especially housewives, clerical workers, and people with a high-school education, tend to fall in to this category. Another interesting characteristic of this group is its psychosomatic symptoms, such as nervousness, dizziness, anxiousness, and frequent headaches, which may be relieved by over-the-counter drugs. Members of this group tend to be churchgoers, and those who are married generally derive a great deal of satisfaction from their marriage. Women in this category devote most of their lives to the family and act with family members in mind. They have positive attitudes toward clean laundry, clean teeth, inoffensive underarms, and so on.

Fun, Enjoyment, and Excitement. Less than 5% of the respondents selected fun or enjoyment as the primary value. Many in this group are either unemployed or have dull jobs and gain a great deal of pleasure from leisure. They tend to be childless and view parenting and housework as unfulfilling. They lack social support, and alcohol is a major part of their lives. They tend to live for the moment and, according to the researcher, want to "stop and smell the roses." People in this segment who can afford it spend money on exercise equipment, sporty cars, and vacations—on products and services that will enhance their attractiveness to the opposite sex, according to the researcher.

Ten Current American Values

Leon Shiffman and Leslie Kanuk have identified ten core values for Americans that they believe most often affect consumer behavior.[15] Table 15-2 summarizes these, provides a short description, and notes their relevance to consumer behavior.

Table 15-2 TEN AMERICAN CORE VALUES

Value	*General Features*	*Relevance to Consumer Behavior*
Achievement and success	Hard work is good; success flows from hard work	Acts as a justification for acquisition of goods ("You deserve it")
Activity	Keeping busy is healthy and natural	Stimulates interest in products that are time-savers and enhance leisure-time activities
Efficiency and practicality	Admiration of things that solve problems (e.g., save time and effort)	Stimulates purchase of products that function well and save time
Progress	People can improve themselves; tomorrow should be better	Stimulates desire for new products that fulfill unsatisfied needs; acceptance of products that claim to be "new" or "improved"
Material comfort	"The good life"	Fosters acceptance of convenience and luxury products that make life more enjoyable
Individualism	Being oneself (self-reliance, self-interest, and self-esteem)	Stimulates acceptance of customized or unique products that enable a person to "express his or her own personality"
Freedom	Freedom of choice	Fosters interest in wide product lines and differentiated products
External conformity	Uniformity of observable behavior; desire to be accepted	Stimulates interest in products that are used or owned by others in the same social group
Humanitarianism	Caring for others, particularly the underdog	Stimulates patronage of firms that compete with market leaders
Youthfulness	A state of mind that stresses being young at heart or appearing young	Stimulates acceptance of products that provide the illusion of maintaining or fostering youth

Source: adapted from Leon Shiffman and Leslie Kanuk, *Consumer Behavior,* Second Edition, (Englewood Cliffs, NJ; Prentice-Hall, Inc., 1983), 420.

The values defined by Shiffman and Kanuk pervade the advertising campaigns and commercial messages sent to our homes. For example, the slogan, "When it's time to relax, it's Miller time" suggests that Miller beer is deserved only after challenging work or sports, combining the themes and values of *achievement and success* and *activity*. Sealy Posturepedic positions its mattresses as the well-deserved "reward" for a hard day's work. Many advertisements for deodorant or hair spray also depict activity combined with success, the hustle and bustle of the professional man or woman hurrying through the day, from early morning, through important business meetings, to an evening social engagement.

Efficiency and practicality are the theme of many household products that promise to end the drudgery associated with everyday housekeeping chores, as in one ad for Congoleum flooring. The ad implies that the product resists stains, which saves the time required to get out the discoloration. Additionally, since Congoleum's protection is billed as thicker, it wears better under heavy traffic, according to the ad—a practical solution to the wear and tear children bring to a home.

The value of *progress* is communicated clearly in innumerable ads and commercials. Among them are Century 21 advertisements showing how the real estate agent can help the upwardly mobile young couple find a

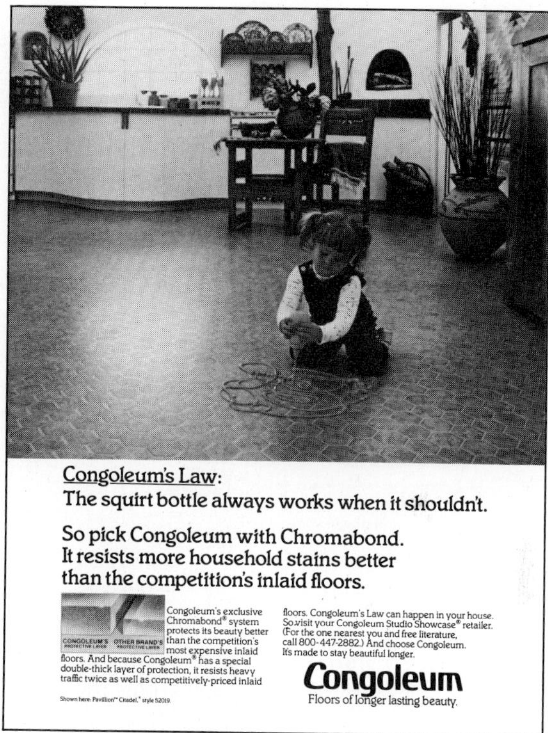

home that may appear beyond their means but is actually affordable. An ad for Better Homes and Gardens real estate emphasizes progress, depicted in general improvements in the house as the family grows. AT&T's ads for its computers stress that the system will grow with the buyer and with new computer technology as the field advances.

The value Americans place on *material comfort* increases the acceptance of convenience and luxury products that make life enjoyable. "The good life" can be seen in numerous advertisements for luxury automobiles with plus interiors, for example. Also, a sizable percentage of rental housing complexes stress the amenities; how many couples have you seen in television commercials or brochures for luxury apartments and condominiums soaking in the opulence of a hot tub? Similarly, there is a clear appeal to material comfort in ads for Jacuzzi whirlpool baths and for swimming pools.

Another core value is *individualism*. Shiffman and Kanuk remind us that Americans place a strong value on "being themselves," which means being special or exclusive in some way. Advertisements that ask people to step out from the crowd, as do some Japanese motorcycle ads, emphasize this American value. One ad pictures the motorcycle and rider leaving the crowd behind as the bike accelerates at hyper speed. The message is not

so much one of speed and power as the individuality symbolized by escaping from or leading the pack. An early Michelob Lite advertising theme asked: "Who Says You Can't Be Somebody and Still Be You?" Similarly, the Camel filter cigarettes man has always symbolized the yearning of many men to stand apart from the crowd. The desire to express one's individuality is also prominent in ads for automobiles such as Ford's Mustang, billed in one ad as "free-spirited" and "sassy."

Freedom which is similar to individualism, includes but goes beyond the political value that is at the heart of American culture and also means not having somebody else dictate what goods and services we will purchase. Further, Americans want freedom from any inconveniences nature might bestow. A feminine hygiene napkin is even named after this value to support the idea that women who use it will be free from potential embarrassments or restrictions that could be caused by the menstrual cycle.

Although freedom and individuality are important, Americans also want to behave acceptably, and another value is *external conformity*. This theme is used especially in advertisements aimed at young people going through the socialization process. They generally depict teens and preteens whose behavior is consistent with the current fad, whether it is break-dancing, skateboarding, or gymnastics.

The value of *humanitarianism* includes cheering on the underdog. More than fifteen years ago Avis challenged the market leader, Hertz, and the "We Try Harder" campaign is now famous. It stresses supporting Avis, the underdog working with fewer resources than the giant Hertz.

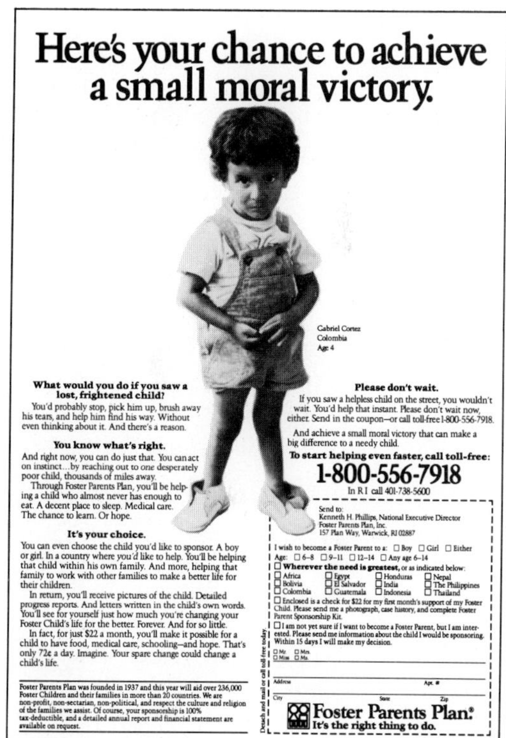

Certainly, the campaign has helped Avis build sales, but an interesting question is whether this strong emphasis on one value may be limiting, preventing Avis from appealing to other values that Americans favor, such as achievement and success. A more obvious and direct appeal to humanitarianism is reflected in ads for the Foster Parents Plan.

The last core value that Shiffman and Kanuk identify is *youthfulness,* the idea of acting young. When Charles Revson said that Revlon was not selling cosmetics but hope, he was referring to this core American value. Also, the tremendous increase in consumption of sporting goods is due partly to the desire to maintain youthfulness. Aside from the health benefits, advertisements often show older people who have kept a youthful appearance and attitude through physical activity. The National Dairy Board uses the currently popular fitness theme in it ads for milk. Ads for Grecian Formula 44 and for Oil of Olay focus on the gradual transition from older age to youth.

Three Categories of American Values

Hawkins, Best, and Coney have summarized many of the same types of values that relate to consumer behavior that we have been discussing into

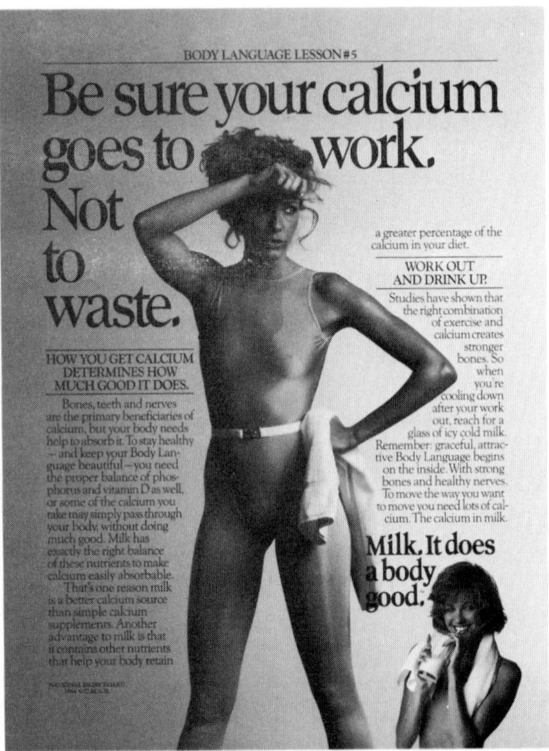

three categories: other-oriented, environment-oriented and self-oriented values.[16] Table 15-3 lists those they believe are most relevant. With three exceptions, the values are in bipolar pairs. That is, they are matched with their opposite, such as *individual* and *collective*. This indicates that values often fall along a continuum from one extreme to the other and that either extreme may predominate.

other-oriented values

Note that these values do not pertain only to the United States but may be found in all cultures. **Other-oriented values** involve the concepts of the group and the individual; but there are striking differences among cultures in the extent to which and under what circumstances individual versus group values are highly esteemed. The recent success of Japanese products on world markets has led to a considerable study of their "secret," and most research stresses the strong group orientation in Japan. In the United States, those who perform very well, even in group activities, are given rewards. The personal efforts of professional basketball stars Magic Johnson and Kareem Abdul-Jabbar are as important to fans of the Los Angeles Lakers as are their team's victories. Similarly, ads in the United States are likely to stress individualistic values and Japanese ads generally focus on groups and conformity. Another interesting dimension

Table 15-3 CURRENT AMERICAN VALUES IN THREE CATEGORIES

Other-Oriented Values

- *Individual–Collective.* Are individual activity and initiative valued more highly than collective activity and conformity?
- *Romantic orientation.* Does the culture believe that "love conquers all"?
- *Adult–Child.* Is family life organized to meet the needs of the children or the adults?
- *Masculine–Feminine.* To what extent does social power automatically go to males?
- *Competition–Cooperation.* Does one obtain success by excelling over others or by cooperating with them?
- *Youth–Age.* Are wisdom and prestige assigned to the younger or older members of a culture?

Environment-Oriented Values

- *Cleanliness.* To what extent is cleanliness pursued beyond the minimum needed for health?
- *Performance–Status.* Is the culture's reward system based on performance or on inherited factors such as family or class?
- *Tradition–Change.* Are existing patterns of behavior considered to be inherently superior to new patterns of behavior?
- *Risk-taking–Security.* Are those who risk their established positions to overcome obstacles or achieve high goals admired more than those who do not?
- *Problem-solving–Fatalistic.* Are people encouraged to overcome all problems or do they take a "what will be, will be" attitude?
- *Nature.* Is nature regarded as something to be admired or overcome?

Self-Oriented Values

- *Active–Passive.* Is a physically active approach to life valued more highly than a less active orientation?
- *Material–Nonmaterial.* How much importance is attached to the acquisition of material wealth?
- *Hard work–Leisure.* Is a person who works harder than economically necessary admired more than one who does not?
- *Postponed gratification–Immediate gratification.* Are people encouraged to "save for a rainy day" or to "live for today"?
- *Sensual gratification–Abstinence.* To what extent is it acceptable to enjoy sensual pleasures such as food, drink, and sex?
- *Humor–Serious.* Is life to be regarded as a strictly serious affair or is it to be treated lightly?

Source: Del Hawkins, Roger J. Best and Kenneth A. Coney, *Consumer Behavior* (Plano, TX: Business Publications, Inc., 1983), revised edition.

is *youth and age;* whereas the American culture values the former, many others esteem the latter. In Korea, for example, young people depicted in ads are likely to be perceived as immature, inexperienced, or in some way unwise. Because of the value of age in Korea, youth-oriented ads might backfire.

environment-oriented values

Environment-oriented values have to do with change and progress as well as the physical environment. A study conducted by Plummer suggests that Americans value cleanliness more highly than do others, as indicated by their attitude toward deodorants.[17] When asked if everyone should use a deodorant, 89% of those polled in the United States said "yes." In comparison, "yes" answers were recorded for other nationalities as follows:

French Canadians	81%	Italians	69%
English Canadians	77%	French	59%
British	71%	Australians	53%

An interesting environmental subdimension is *tradition–change*. The British have long been known for favoring the former, whereas Americans have tended to emphasize the latter. The Rolls-Royce is an excellent example of a product steeped in tradition, slow to change but clearly symbolic of this fundamental British value, which may be related to the powerful place in the world England once held as compared to today. The attitude was manifested a few years ago in the English beverage market, when many of Britain's local breweries were being taken over by national makers of pasteurized beers. Consumers wanted to preserve the traditional beers and ales. These beers were brewed locally and were naturally fermented, so that the tastes of the many local products were diverse and distinctive. In the United States, by contrast, the number of brands has been cut drastically in recent years as local breweries have been pushed out of business by larger ones, most of which offer products that at least some consumers find very hard to differentiate. Unlike British consumers, who banded together and refused to purchase the national brands in order to preserve tradition, Americans value change much more highly, and breweries in the United States that have stressed tradition have not done well. A good example is Stroh's beer, which was advertised for decades as a fire-brewed beer of German ancestry. Only after adopting a novel campaign showing Stroh's as a "party" beer did it begin to build market share. If the Stroh's approach had been used in England it would have run counter to a basic core value in that country.

The *performance–status* subdimension is also a basic cultural difference between England and the United States. On one hand, a person's ability (performance) is important in and for itself; on the other, title and background (status) surpass individual activity as valued attributes. This difference is illustrated by the reactions of tennis fans in England and in the United States to John McEnroe's sometimes vocal and demanding on-court behavior. Although some Americans have criticized his conduct on court, his tremendous skill is so widely respected that most people overlook his outbursts or even sympathize when he questions the line judges. In Great Britain, where status is an important cultural dimension, McEnroe's challenges to officials at Wimbledon are seen as major *faux pas*. Many Britons dislike his behavior, believing that even if the line judges are incorrect their status warrants respectful treatment, a status often conferred on them because of their longevity in tennis and their dedication to the sport. It is very important to consider such issues when dealing with cultures that value hierarchical status. The Queen of England and her family are honored more for the dominant values of tradition and status they embody than for any political usefulness they may serve—which, in fact, they do not.

self-oriented values

Finally, the **self-oriented values** concern behavior related to individual activities. The *active–passive* subdimension pertains to the value Americans place on a high level of physical involvement in both work and play. Americans like participation in life's adventures rather than passive observation of events and activities.

The value placed on material wealth, hard work, and immediate gratification has a powerful influence on purchasing and investment behavior in many cultures. The manner in which humor and sensual pleasures are regarded also varies by culture. In developing advertising strategies and messages, multinational firms must carefully consider the likely reaction of different cultures to humorous or sexually related ad themes to be certain they are consistent with the current values of potential customers.

Acculturation

Recall that *acculturation* is the process of learning a culture different from the one in which a person is reared.[18] Obviously, this process has important implications for multinational business, whose executives usually spend a good deal of time abroad. Several years ago, Edward T. Hall's *The Silent Language* profoundly influenced American business people operating crossculturally.[19] Hall indicated that perception of time, space, things, friends, and agreements differ among cultures and, hence, can cause many misunderstandings.[20]

Time

The way a culture conceives of time may communicate a great number of subtle points. For example, members of some cultures believe that the most important decisions should be given the greatest amount of time. Decision makers may devote long periods to the process either to enhance their own position or to communicate to the other party the importance of the issue involved. In contrast, Americans tend to operate within deadlines, viewing time as a scarce resource to be used effectively. If a business person from the United States keeps someone waiting, the visitor whose time is being wasted could correctly infer that he or she is unimportant. In a Latin culture, this is certainly not the case; schedules are not rigid, and time is seen as a resource that can be more flexibly used.

In an informal survey of American and Brazilian students, it was found that Brazilian students defined "being late" as anything over 33 minutes, while American students considered 19 minutes to be late. Moreover, the Brazilians were less likely than the Americans to attribute someone's being late to a lack of caring. Instead, they tended to blame

Table 15-4 THE PACE OF LIFE IN SIX COUNTRIES

	Accuracy of Bank Clocks	*Walking Speed*	*Post Office Speed*
Japan	1	1	1
United States	2	3	2
England	4	2	3
Italy	5	4	6
Taiwan	3	5	4
Indonesia	6	6	5

Source: Robert Levine and Ellen Wolff, "Social Time: The Heartbeat of Culture," *Psychology Today* (March 1985): 35.

unforeseen circumstances beyond the person's control. Thus, Brazilians were less apologetic for being tardy and did not blame others as harshly when they were late. In fact, some Brazilians believed that lack of punctuality implies importance and status.[21]

These findings prompted two researchers to examine time differences in various cultures quantitatively. In this study, three aspects of time were investigated to estimate the "pace of life" among different cultures: the accuracy of public clocks, the walking speed of pedestrians, and the speed of service in purchasing a stamp at the post office. The results, summarized in Table 15-4, rank the six participating countries on these dimensions. The consistency among the three measures within each country does suggest that, in fact, the "pace of life" may vary among the different cultures in the six nations.

Time has different meanings in different cultures. One reason for this is that several perceptions of time seem to be culture bound. Robert Graham has identified three different perceptions of time: linear-separable, circular-traditional, and procedural-traditional.[22] Because time is such an important dimension, how we perceive it influences most aspects of consumer behavior from interpersonal relations to economic activity.

linear-separable time

Linear-separable time is the perception of time shared by most European and North American cultures. Time is seen as linear, with a past, present, and future. Time spent in the past is valuable because of the activities then contribute to those of the present and future. In capitalist economies such as ours, placing value on the past leads to concepts such as the time value of money. Linear-separable time can be wasted, saved, and consumed. It is managed to help produce the greatest benefit. Because the future is perceived as something different from the past or present, people will invest in the future—change is valued.

circular-traditional time

Circular-traditional time differs from linear-separable time in that the future is seen *as* the past. This perception of time occurs when life follows a cycle organized around agriculture or other repeatable events (the annual flooding of the Nile, the monsoon season in Southeast Asia). Because people who perceive time this way feel they cannot alter the future, which will be similar to the past, they see no reason to better themselves or invest in the future. If they have extra money they see it as a temporary interruption in the cycle that will prevail in the long run. Thus time is not planned or particularly valued.

procedural-traditional time

Procedural-traditional time is the perception that the amount of time spent on an activity is less relevant than the activity or procedure itself. Some American Indians have had this perception; for them, once an activity begins, how long it takes is irrelevant. The next activity will start when the last one ends. Some Latin American airline personnel have this perception of time. When asked when a flight will leave, they say, "After the plane arrives and we have loaded the passengers." Planes often leave long past schedule and, from time to time, even early by a few minutes to as much as several hours. For these people, time and money are separate and people earn according to the *task* rather than the time. An important task cannot be rushed—it simply takes as much time as it takes. The concept of convenience outlets that save time would have little meaning among people with this perception.

While we might value time, and all of the shopping centers, convenience items, and products that save it, these are likely to be irrelevant in many cultures. The marketer must consider how the culture of the target market approaches time when determining whether a product's convenience is actually a benefit, or if the success and failure of a product is due to some other element. McDonald's drive-through windows may be popular in the United States, but a sit-down version of McDonald's would be more appropriate for culture with other values. Cultures placing a great premium on time as we value it are more inclined to attach a high economic value to time-saving goods and services. More leisurely cultures may prefer other values, such as long conversations with family or friends at meals; in those cultures convenience foods have much less worth and acceptance.

Space

To Americans, size equates with importance; the bigger and the higher a building is, the greater is the degree of status represented. The dean of a college of business is likely to be located in the largest office on the top floor; the university president is likely to have a larger office in a taller building. By comparison, the French try to place important executives close to the scene of action, inside the workplace where their influence can be most strongly felt. Thus a remote office location is not equated with high status.

The distance between people during conversations can also be culturally related. It is interesting to watch American and Brazilian students talking. As with many other Latins, the Brazilians expect people to stand close and even touch during conversation. To communicate friendship, a Brazilian may attempt to enter the three to five feet of empty space generally acceptable to Americans during conversation. The Brazilian may come as close as two to three inches; standing farther away could be a sign of rejection. It is not unusual to see the American backing away, trying to keep the Brazilian outside his or her personal space. Because of the different cultural perceptions of space, even internationally targeted television advertisements should consider the culture in which they are to be viewed; despite the proper language and other elements, such subtleties as the wrong interpersonal distance among the actors could create problems of acceptance.

Things

Americans are seen as materialistic. We purchase to own. American houses are adorned with objects, often expensive, that say, "We have arrived." Hall cites the Japanese, who take pride in inexpensive but tasteful things such as flowers to set a proper emotional setting.[23] They are in contrast to Americans, who are likely to prefer a status symbol based on price rather than its intrinsic value to the individual. Clearly, the extent to which a culture emphasizes material ownership as a measure of success has a profound impact on the consumption patterns of its people and the likely success of "status-oriented" marketing communications.

Friendship

Hall claims that many Americans view friends not as people to help in a disaster but as individuals who promote our movement up the social ladder.[24] In the United States, friends also may be perceived in terms of the stimulation and enjoyment they provide us. In less developed nations, however, they are important "social insurance" to offer protection in times of need. Thus in some cultures friendship is required to sustain life; in the United States it enhances life. Further, in our mobile society friends are likely to be neighbors, and when we move to a new community we usually seek new friends, maintaining one or two older friendships for some time. In nonmobile societies, where friends are made for a lifetime, the process of choosing them may be a long one, and people are less inclined to do anything to injure that strong tie. For example, when a foreign business person befriends an American, the relationship may carry more weight for him or her than it does for the American. Similarly, in commercial communications, depicting friends and friendship often connotes a more serious message in cultures other than ours, one going beyond the lighthearted aspects of friendship frequently seen in American ads.

Agreements and Negotiations

Business agreements may have different meanings in various parts of the world. In highly legalistic cultures, they must be written and signed prior to acceptance; in others, documents and legal forms are viewed as inconveniences, and the more important part of the agreement is the handshake or the meeting of minds. In the United States, agreements may be implicit or explicit; the transfer of property will require a formal document, but services often are provided according to convention. As Hall points out, when Americans consult a lawyer or doctor, or even take a taxi, they assume the charge is going to be fair, proportional to the services rendered, and very close to the going rate. This is not the case in many cultures. For example, in the Middle East it is best to settle the charge in advance, or the person providing the service is likely to set an arbitrary price.[25]

Many business persons from the United States operating in a foreign culture have believed a commitment existed when in fact it did not. Relying on our own cultural standards may create the difficulty, as when Americans negotiate with the Japanese, who consider it impolite to be disagreeable or negative toward another person's point of view. Lacking a frank "no," Americans are likely to assume agreement when just the opposite may be true.

In the course of negotiations, language often presents an obvious barrier, distorting the meaning of the participants' intentions and sometimes causing a complete breakdown in communication. Glen Fisher, a cultural anthropologist and career diplomat, points out that a word such as *compromise* has a variety of translations across cultures. Americans interpret compromise as a positive move to obtain agreement. In Spain, compromise is more likely to connote a loss of honor or relinquishment of principles.[26]

To some degree, the problem of language translation is compounded not only by a difference of interpretation but also due to a simple absence of equivalent words. For example, where Americans communicate with approximately 60,000 words, Swedes normally use less than 8,000. When this author was developing a planning system for a Swedish company, many of the concepts used in the United States dealing with competitive business strategies had no equivalent in Swedish. As a result, it was decided not to translate into Swedish; all communications took place in English, which most Swedes comprehend.

The Self-Reference Criterion

self-reference criteria

Since culture is so fundamental to all perception and yet may vary greatly, it is difficult for members of one culture to understand those of another, including their behavior as consumers. The unconscious reliance on one's own cultural values is called the **self-reference criterion,**[27] which means essentially that we are all tied to our own cultures. It is particularly difficult to understand consumers from cultures we have not learned, even if we know about certain aspects, because we are hampered by the self-reference criterion. It is often difficult for business people from the

United States to comprehend the importance of cultural elements that are not basic American values. Concepts alien to our own may go unnoticed, be misunderstood, or remain unappreciated. One illustration is intermediary buyers, who in many cultures receive some of their income through money given to them by sellers or payments "under the table." We would call these bribes. In some countries they are considered an institutionalized element of doing business, much like tips for service in restaurants and hotels. From one perspective these payments are highly unethical; from another they are culturally acceptable. Laws in the United States that prevent people from engaging in such practices are one interpretation of honesty in business dealings, a self-reference criterion. When those laws conflict with another version of that value found elsewhere in the world, they may put firms from the United States at a competitive disadvantage. Ironically, in many countries where *baksheesh* is virtually required, a tip for service in a restaurant is regarded not only as unnecessary but also as flagrant materialism, stereotypical of American behavior.

RELIGION AND CONSUMER BEHAVIOR

One of the primary aspects of culture is religion, and because it is so intimately related to values, it has major implications for consumer behavior. Religion is the core around which many cultural beliefs and habits of behavior are formed. Many anthropologists believe that a culture cannot be understood unless we also understand its religious beliefs. Since religion teaches of the ideal life, it gives rise to the norms, ideas, values, and attitudes that reflect a culture. Religion can have a *direct* bearing on an individual's behavior through the tenets or rules of conduct it lays down. It can also have an *indirect* effect because it provides the backdrop against which attitudes and values are formed, including those relating to economic life. The main religions of the world (primitive systems, Hinduism, Buddhism, Islam, and Catholic and Protestant Christianity) have deeply influenced consumer behavior because of their effect on economic development and attitudes toward consumption. These brief profiles of the world's religions suggest how religion can affect consumer behavior.

Primitive Religion

Primitive religions are frequently found in traditional societies.[28] They may be called *animism* or *ancestor* or *spirit worship, magic,* and *taboos.* Practitioners of such religions believe the souls of their ancestors leave the dead body but remain in the environment as potential influences on human life. They respect, fear, and seek to please their ancestors. Often worship is steeped in ritual and has a strong conservative orientation. Similar in many ways is the worship of spirits, whose power must be appeased so they will not wreak havoc on living people. This may be done through witchcraft, magic, and taboo, which is the prohibition against a particular activity or use of an object. Again, the purpose is to follow the wishes of entities who represent traditional values.

These beliefs are common in many countries in Asia, Latin America, and Africa. Countries in which primitive religion predominates tend to have low economic development and literacy rates. Spending power is so restricted that modern commercialization does not exist. There is a tremendous resistance to new products and ideas, and consumption beyond necessities has little appeal or relevance.

Hinduism

Almost entirely confined to India, Hinduism was brought there about 4,000 years ago by Aryans invading from the north. Its very elaborate and complex code of conduct includes a caste system based largely on skin color, designed to separate the Aryan invaders from the darker people of the south. The highest caste was the Brahmin, usually priests and teachers, followed by warriors, merchants, and craftsmen, all comprising a system with more than 3,000 castes and subcastes. One group, called *pariah* or untouchables, were outside the structure and relegated to the lowest level in society. Because membership in a caste was determined at birth, class mobility was extremely rare. Although the government of India has attempted to lessen the effect of the caste system (modified at independence from Great Britain in 1947), it is a system dating back thousands of years and thus very difficult to change.

Hinduism views family as a very extended concept, and the consumption unit is a much broader group than the nuclear family. In some cases companies and corporations are set up by families and headed by a patriarch with almost complete power. Hinduism fosters tradition through the caste system and emphasizes family. The purchase of goods and services with the intent of changing one's social class or signifying a higher status is frowned upon, as is conspicuous consumption among members of the upper class. In India, advertisements stressing class mobility are inappropriate. Many scholars of the Indian economy have concluded that Hinduism is a basically negative influence on modernization and change, and different products or ideas are very slow to develop.

Buddhism

Buddhism is essentially transplanted and revised Hinduism, analogous to the difference between Catholicism and Protestantism. While there are at least two major branches of Buddhism, in this overview we will consider it as one faith. Buddhism is found in such countries as Vietnam, Burma, Laos, Sri Lanka, Thailand, China, Japan, and Korea.

Buddha, the Enlightened One, lived about 560 B.C. in northern India as Prince Gautama, who spent the first years of his life in exquisite luxury. One day he saw an old man, a sick man, a dead man, and a begging monk, and he decided he must determine why suffering existed and how it could be overcome. His search for an answer yielded the four noble truths of Buddhism: (1) *truth of suffering*—it is part of the nature of life; (2) *truth of the cause of suffering*—the desire for possessions and selfish enjoyment; (3) *truth of cessation from suffering*—it stops when desire stops; and (4) *truth of the path leading to cessation from suffering*—eight steps a person must follow, similar to the Ten Commandments but more definitive and extensive. Notice that the religion dwells not so much on gaining something as on eliminating suffering. In general, a person must be free from lust, ill will, and cruelty; should not use harsh language or lie; should abstain from killing, stealing, and sexual abuse; should live free from luxury; should promote good and maintain an awareness of temptation. Meditation is a way to stop suffering.

From a consumer behavior standpoint, important elements in Buddhism are freedom from luxury and two other concepts, karma and Nirvana. *Karma* is similar to fate, a view of cause and effect that provides a way of moral improvement in a person's life but is also deterministic. A person's existence is tied to a previous incarnation and is predestined, a concept that implies accepting what is given rather than working for possible gain. Therefore, the quest for material goods is relatively unimportant. Related to karma is *Nirvana,* which lies at the end of the long journey of the many-times reincarnated soul. It is the peace, finally achieved, that frees a person from the cycle of being reborn. Clearly, Buddhists believe in abstention from worldly goods, which they feel cannot eliminate suffering or lead to peace of mind.

Islam

Roughly half a billion people adhere to Islam, or the Muslim religion, living in such countries as Afghanistan, Egypt, Iran, Libya, Saudi Arabia, and Turkey. Islam prescribes a detailed way of life guided by Mohammed, the Prophet of God, and the sacred book of Muslim theology, law, and practice, the Koran. The word *Islam* means to submit, and *muslim* refers to one who is submitting, who obeys the will of Allah. The law of Islam requires reciting a creed and five periods of prayer each day; daytime fasting annually during the month of Ramadan; the giving of alms or gifts; and at least once in life a pilgrimage to Mecca, Mohammed's birthplace in present-day Saudi Arabia.

An example of Islam's effect on consumer behavior is its specific prohibition against interest on loans, which is one reason Arab banks operating internationally are inclined to call payments "commissions" rather than "interest." Furthermore, many Muslims believe that actions not specifically permitted by the Koran are forbidden. Since Islamic nations are among the world's leading oil producers, per capita income tends to be high in these cultures, although that figure can be misleading because total wealth is partly redistributed through the alms the religion requires.

Christianity

In this book we consider Christianity as composed of two groups because of the marked economic difference between primarily Catholic nations and those that are mostly Protestant. Protestantism and Catholicism also have certain religious tenets that affect consumer behavior differently. The most highly developed countries of the world tend to be predominantly Christian. While some Catholic countries have high per capita income, others have incomes that are relatively low per capita. Protestant nations provide higher incomes in general and include those with the very highest per capita income.

Catholicism

Roman Catholicism emphasizes the institution of the church and its religious orders; particularly the role of priests as intermediaries between the people (laity) and God. Different practices and standards of morals are prescribed for the religious orders and the laity. The former are expected to follow the higher morality of the gospels—obedience, poverty, and chastity—which is difficult in the secular world and thus requires that they live apart. Order, hierarchy, ritual, and tradition are characteristic of Catholicism.

Protestantism

Martin Luther broke with the belief that the Church is an intermediary between God and humanity. Luther believed that "people should live the secular life religiously, to serve God within one's calling."[29] John Calvin later emphasized that because people had direct access to God, they could behave religiously in a very personal manner through belief in Jesus Christ. Salvation became an individual process, and eventually individualism grew out of Protestantism. Further, from the ideas that God accomplishes all things through people and that each person has a calling developed the importance of a person's job in life. Thus the concept evolved that a job is more than simply work; it is the way to carry out God's will and glorify him. Hard work became a tribute to God and success a mark of divine favor. Many Protestants worked to produce profit and savings, generating a store of capital, part of which was reinvested and part increasingly used to buy goods.

SUBCULTURE

What do Hispanics, hippies, yuppies, youth, and blacks have in common? In many respects perhaps very little, but each one represents an important subculture. In traditional societies there is a single underlying culture that defines values, norms, and accepted behavior. However, as society becomes more complex, groups begin to form or are added from the outside. These groups display homogeneous values and behaviors that are divergent from the basic culture. In some cases these subcultural values are transmitted intact from generation to generation, such as the Amish religious culture in certain parts of the United States. In other cases only small parts are transmitted. However, it is clear that over the long term subcultures are likely to have an effect on the total culture by introducing variations.

Seen from this perspective, our country is a patchwork quilt. Earlier we discussed Garreau's nine nations of North America and the subcultures found in various regions of the United States. Perhaps what could be called a "cowboy" subculture exists in many parts of the west, that of "rugged individualism" in the northeast, a "down-home country" subculture more than a century old in the far reaches of Kentucky and Tennessee, and the "Cajun" subculture, with its French roots, in parts of Louisiana. In some sections of the country, especially California, groups of "sun worshippers" spend their free time on the beaches and organize their economic activities to this end. In many of the ports and harbors along the coasts of New England, Florida, Texas, California, and the Great Lakes, very early in the morning one can smell the coffee and hear the clamor of thousands of people who spend a significant portion of their lives aboard sailboats or powercraft. The list could go on, identifying those groups within the broader culture, called **subgroups** or **subcultures,** who have developed a niche that in observable ways is marked by certain behaviors unique within the total culture.

subgroups
subcultures

One widely accepted definition of subculture is "a subdivision of a national culture, composed of a combination of factorable social situations such as class status, ethnic background, region and rural or urban residence, and religious affiliation but forming in their combination a functioning unity which has an integrating impact on the particular individual."[30] Notice that in this definition subculture does not necessarily combine all such elements as social class, ethnic background, and so forth, but those dimensions often are part of it. Clearly, there could be many definitions, but most important is that a subculture should have a significant effect on the individual. Numerous factors such as gender or income affect the individual, but these alone may not constitute subcultures; instead, these are generally termed *demographic* variables which affect consumers. Consequently, we would consider the women's movement not a subculture but a component of demographics, lifestyle, and family structure (single or married). Just as sex or income does not form a subculture, neither does skin color. The term *black subculture* is often used, but there is as much heterogeneity in the black population as among whites. In fact, Orientals, blacks, and whites are often found within the same subculture.

Ethnicity

ethnic background

Ethnic background refers to a distinctive origin. There are more than a hundred ethnic groups in the United States, perhaps more than in any other nation in the world. One's ethnic affiliation is usually determined by birth and is related to three elements: nationality, race, and religion. However, a person's ethnic background is not the same as a person's ethnicity. In cultural terms, **ethnicity** refers to the amount of identification an individual feels with a particular ethnic group.[31] Elizabeth Hirschman has studied research on consumer behavior in this area and writes:

ethnicity

> One black consumer may feel an especially strong commitment to black ethnicity, whereas a second may feel much less identification with this group. The degree of identification the individual feels with a given ethnic group may largely determine the level of commitment he [or] she experiences regarding the norms of the group and, thus, the degree of influence the group has on his [or] her actions and attitudes.[32]

Because marketers are interested in finding segments of the population with a great deal in common so they can be appealed to or better understood, it is useful for marketers to identify people of high ethnicity, rather than those with a certain skin color or some other attribute. Little research differentiates ethnic background from ethnicity, although the latter is likely to become more important in future studies. Much of the published work identifies ethnic difference by color, which may be confounded because it does not specifically address those people who have the greatest identification with ethnic groups. Another problem is that variables such as income correlate strongly with race, and in some cases consumer behavior characteristics attributed to racial differences may actually be related to income or where a person lives. Both of these problems will be addressed when we discuss the black subculture.

Subculture is as difficult to identify as culture. It is often used to define a range of types or classifications of people. To the degree that a relatively large group has developed a prescribed way of life for its members, whether the prescription is implied or explicit, it is possible to identify a subculture. As mentioned earlier, the most common use of the term primarily revolves around nationality, race, and religion, and some of the most familiar examples are the Jewish, American Indian, black, and Hispanic subcultures. In the United States two of the most important subcultures are blacks and Hispanics.

Black Subculture

Blacks are the largest racial minority in the United States, about 12% of the population or approximately 30 million people. Compared to the growth rate of the total population of about 4.2% between 1980 and 1984, the growth rate among blacks was approximately 6.7%, and 3.2% among whites.[33] The black population is not evenly distributed across the United States; much of it is centered in large cities and a few states. As of 1980, twelve states had more than a million blacks: New York, California, Texas, Illinois, Georgia, Florida, North Carolina, Louisiana, Michigan, Ohio, Pennsylvania, and Virginia. The greatest concentrations were in Louisiana (29%) and Georgia (27%).[34] Because two-thirds of all blacks in the United States live in these states, it is possible to focus black-oriented marketing campaigns there. However, remember that the black population is not homogeneous in terms of the variables affecting consumer behavior or with respect to that behavior itself. Table 15-5 shows differences between whites and blacks on a number of dimensions.

As the table reflects, it is clear that many of the differences between blacks and whites relate mainly to demographic factors. Also, individuals within groups have many similarities; and in each demographic category there are large numbers of blacks and whites possessing similar characteristics. Yet on the whole, blacks have substantially smaller family incomes; they tend to live in the city (as a percentage of their population, twice as many compared to whites); and they have somewhat lower education levels as a group (only about 8 percent of blacks are college graduates, compared to about 21 percent of whites). In addition, relative to whites, blacks more often are divorced and have a one-parent family. The black family is larger than its average white counterpart, and black occupations tend to be blue-collar and service-oriented rather than white-collar.

If blacks are considered as a group, we would expect to find large variations in their consumption patterns attributed to these demographic differences. This is the case with many studies of black consumers; consequently, it is hard to determine whether patterns unique to blacks should be attributed to ethnicity or to socioeconomic variables running across the black subculture in general. Donald Sexton, Jr., made an important contribution to understanding black consumers in his study of store shopping, product buying, and brand buying behaviors.[35] He found that although some studies indicate the general population thought a store's reputation for price level and quality of food was most important, a sample of black housewives believed convenient location and friendly atmosphere were more important, with low prices being least so. This difference might reflect the lack of mobility among blacks due to their relatively lower income rather than to true differences between blacks and whites. In making inferences from other studies Sexton concluded

Table 15-5 SELECTED DEMOGRAPHICS FOR BLACK AND WHITE AMERICANS

Characteristics	***Black***	***White***
Family income		
Under $10,000	38.3%	14.7%
$10,000–$24,999	38.6%	38.7%
$25,000 and over	23.1%	46.5%
Median family income	$13,267	$23,517
Area of residence		
City	48.6%	21.3%
Suburb	26.0%	43.3%
Nonmetropolitan	25.4%	35.3%
*Education**		
Less than four years of high school	43.7%	26.7%
Four years of high school	34.7%	36.6%
One to three years of college	13.8%	15.7%
Four years of college or more	7.9%	21.1%
Family structure		
Two-parent family	48.1%	82.6%
One-parent family	51.9%	17.4%
Family size		
Two persons	32.6%	41.0%
Three persons	23.8%	23.1%
Four persons	19.4%	21.3%
Five persons	12.1%	9.3%
Six persons or more	12.0%	5.3%
Occupation (among employed)		
White-collar	1,793,000	25,780,000
Blue-collar	1,976,000	17,011,000
Service and other	1,090,000	4,184,000
Farm	90,000	1,460,000
Total	4,949,000	48,435,000

Sources: U.S. Bureau of the Census, Current Population Reports, *Household and Family Characteristics, March 1983,* Series P-20, No. 388 (May 1984), 16–17; Current Population Reports, *Money Income of Households: 1981,* Series P-20, No. 137 (1984), 11, 61.

Note: Percentages may or may not total 100% due to rounding off.

* People age 25 and older.

that low income resulted in lower automobile ownership and considerably restricted mobility. He also looked at studies of department stores and discount houses and found that location was a factor; high-income blacks tended to travel more often, while lower-income blacks were confined in their shopping for new food products. Therefore, differences in the importance of store characteristics could be based on income rather than on ethnic background or ethnicity. In general, Sexton concluded, many differences among blacks and whites could be based on income rather than on ethnic background or ethnicity. For example, blacks with higher incomes who do own automobiles typically exhibit the same high mobility as whites.

In terms of product buying behavior, after summarizing a number of studies, Sexton found that, based on limited evidence, blacks are more likely to be innovators in product classes that are socially visible, such as clothing, and are likely to be leaders in these product areas. However, because of income limitations, on the whole blacks might be less innovative than whites.

As for brand-buying behavior, Sexton believes a number of studies show that higher-income blacks are more status conscious regarding brands than are lower-income blacks. Historically, blacks have thought the goods and services offered by white institutions are generally better and more trustworthy than those from establishments in black areas, or from black-owned businesses.[36] Clearly, any study of blacks will reach conclusions affected by their low levels of income. Whereas 8.9 percent of whites fall below the poverty line, 30.9 percent of the black population is in that category. This represents almost 8 million of the 28 to 30 million blacks in the United States.

Black Media Usage

Evidence suggests that blacks differ from the general population in terms of media habits as well. Marketers who intend to target the black consumer in advertising and promotion can benefit by understanding research about television, radio, and newspaper reading behavior. Table 15-6 compares the identified differences in the radio usage patterns between blacks and whites. Blacks tend to listen to the radio more hours per week, more frequently on weekends and evenings. Blacks listen to FM radio less than whites do.[37] An additional finding was that blacks are more likely than whites to listen to radio at home rather than in automobiles or other locations.

Such findings guide media buyers in their attempts to maximize the reach and frequency of ads aimed toward blacks. Certain large corporations that market many different products often retain a separate advertising agency to handle communications for products directed at specific subcultures. These firms believe that concentrated effort should be made to understand and respond to the unique language and media habits of subcultures, especially for products which show high penetration in a

Table 15-6 AVERAGE NUMBER OF HOURS OF RADIO USAGE PER WEEK FOR THE BLACK AND WHITE POPULATION

	Black	***White***
Overall	27.4 hours	23.4 hours
Hours		
6 to 10 A.M.	6.8	6.2
10 A.M. to 3 P.M.	7.2	7.1
3 to 7 P.M.	5.7	5.2
7 P.M. to midnight	5.2	3.6
midnight to 6 A.M.	2.5	1.3
Day of the Week		
Monday to Friday	19.5	17.4
Saturday	4.2	3.3
Sunday	3.7	2.7
Location		
At home	21.0	15.2
In auto	2.9	4.0
Other	3.5	4.2
Type of Station		
AM	20.9	16.0
FM	6.5	7.4

Source: adapted from Gerald J. Glasser and Gale D. Metzger, "Radio Usage by Blacks," *Journal of Advertising Research* (October 1975): 39–45.

particular subculture. For example, Kraft, Inc., employed the Proctor and Gardner ad agency to develop specialized promotional campaigns and media plans for its brand of barbecue sauce in light of the high popularity of this product among black consumers. Many major advertising agencies are opening special divisions to analyze subcultural market opportunities and design appropriate appeals. Some marketers offer products specifically designed for black consumers. At the same time, large corporate marketers such as Proctor and Gamble (Crest), United Airlines, and Heublein (Smirnoff) are gearing larger portions of their advertising to appeal to blacks.

It would be a mistake to assume that the black subculture is any more homogeneous than white. Black consumers as well as white consumers have diverse life-styles and attitudes. In many cases blacks and whites share the same life-style and attitude categories. Still, it is useful to look at the life-styles within subcultures. The findings of one study suggest that there are five separate life-style segments among black women. (See Table 15-7.)

The implication is clear. While subculture provides a useful way of understanding some fundamental differences among consumers, to be successful, marketers must often look beyond subculture to identify more specific distinctions for strategy development.

Table 15-7 LIFE-STYLE DIFFERENCES AMONG BLACK FEMALES, AGE 18–49

Segment	*Size*	*Age*	*Income*	*Basic Life-style Attitude*
Conservative traditionalist	32%	Older	Higher	Views sex, drugs, and liquor as steps along the path to degeneration.
Fashion conscious	31%	Younger	Lower	Liberated in ideas about sex, liquor, and drugs; likes to try new hairstyles; would rather dress for fashion than comfort.
Independent	16%	Middle	Significantly higher	Outgoing and on the way up. Financially secure and independent. Prefers living in suburbs to city.
Girl next door	12%	Younger	Significantly lower	Strong moral values; likes trying new hairstyles as much as she likes to bake, which she often does.
Conservative thinker	9%	Older	Significantly lower	Shops for sales, disapproves of installment purchases and belives that men should rule the household while women take care of it.

Source: adapted from "New Survey Reveals Five Lifestyle Segments of Age 18–49 Black Women," *Marketing News* (August 21, 1981): 6.

Hispanic Subculture

According to the 1980 U.S. Census, there are about 4.6 million Hispanics, representing 6.4 percent of the population. From 1970 to 1980 the Hispanic population increased by approximately 60 percent compared to the 17% increase in the black population and a less than 6% increase among whites. Today the United States has the fourth largest Hispanic population in the world. Most Hispanics (an estimated 85.3%) live in major metropolitan areas such as New York, Los Angeles, Miami, and San Antonio. Table 15-8 shows the top 30 Hispanic-populated urban areas in the United States.

Hispanics are also younger on average than blacks and Anglos, with an average age of 23 years as opposed to 25 for blacks and 31 for whites. The average number of years of education for Hispanics is low: 11.3 compared with 12.1 for blacks and 12.5 for whites. Their average family income is $14,711, comparable to that of blacks, but still considerably less than the $20,840 for whites. Much of the Hispanic population in the United States has roots in Mexico, Puerto Rico, or Cuba—all Latin cultures.

Interestingly, Hispanics are maintaining many of their cultural traditions. In addition to the fact that most are Catholic and preserve that tie, they are retaining other characteristics of their culture, such as language and the extended family structures often found in Latin America. Danny Bellenger and Humberta Valencia have given a good description of the

Table 15-8 TOP 30 HISPANIC AREAS OF DOMINANT INFLUENCE

Rank	*ADI*	*Hispanic Population (thousands)*	*Rank*	*ADI*	*Hispanic Population (thousands)*
1	New York	2,329.8	16	Dallas–Fort Worth	257.0
2	Los Angeles	2,256.8	17	Denver	232.0
3	San Antonio	849.6	18	Philadelphia	183.0
4	Miami	767.4	19	Tucson, AZ	182.1
5	San Francisco	705.8	20	Austin, TX	139.8
6	Chicago	660.1	21	Tampa–St. Petersburg, FL	133.2
7	McAllen–Brownsville, TX	533.8	22	Lubbock, TX	128.7
8	El Paso, TX	474.3	23	Salinas–Monterey, CA	108.6
9	Albuquerque, NM	465.6	24	Laredo, TX	106.9
10	Houston	459.4	25	Odessa–Midland, TX	104.2
11	Phoenix	311.6	26	Colorado Springs–Pueblo, CO	102.5
12	Fresno, CA	298.6	27	Washington[, DC]	100.0
13	Corpus Christi, TX	293.8	28	El Centro–Yuma, CA–AZ	79.5
14	San Diego	274.4	29	Detroit	70.8
15	Sacramento–Stockton, CA	274.4	30	Waco–Temple, TX	67.7
			Total of 30 markets:		12,955.6

Source: "Strategy Research Corp./National Association of Spanish Broadcasters," *Advertising Age* (April 6, 1981).

Table 15-9 SOME CHARACTERISTICS OF THE HISPANIC SUBCULTURE

Consumer Behavior

Hispanics were more likely to:

- prefer shopping at smaller stores
- dislike impersonal stores
- be ecology-minded: they agreed that products that pollute should be banned
- be cautious: they do not buy unknown brands to save money

Hispanics were less likely to be:

- skeptical of ads: they believe that advertising represents a true picture of products
- venturesome: they do not like trying new products before others do
- impulse buyers
- apathetic about shopping: they do not consider it a terrible waste of time
- credit-card holders

Media Preference

Compared to the population in general, Hispanics:

- report spending more time than other groups watching television
- exhibit a slightly more positive attitude than others do toward television
- tend to watch more variety shows and feature films
- read few weekly, biweekly, and monthly magazines (exception: *TV Guide*)
- read fewer newspapers and spend less time listening to the radio. However, Spanish magazines (*Vandidades, Selecciones,* and *Buenhogar*) have a strong readership.

Source: adapted from Danny N. Bellenger and Humberto Valencia, "Understanding the Hispanic Market," *Business Horizons* (May–June, 1982): 49.

Hispanic subculture in America; using Census Bureau data and 220 mall intercept interviews among Hispanics and non-Hispanics, the investigators were able to isolate some interesting characteristics in the Hispanic subculture (see Table 15-9).

By 1990, the Hispanic population in the United States is expected to reach 25 million. Many companies such as Pepsi-Cola are beginning to recognize the importance of Hispanics as a major opportunity worthy of special marketing efforts.[38] As more data become available about the attitudes and purchasing behaviors of Hispanics, an increasing number of firms will be exploring how to appeal to the specific interests of this subculture. Procter and Gamble (Crest toothpaste) and Anheuser-Busch (Budweiser beer) have received awards from Hispanic groups for their Hispanic-targeted advertising campaigns.[39] These ads along with those of other companies (Canadian Club, Pepsi-Cola, Winston, Pontiac) demonstrate that manufacturers can design specific appeals to reach Hispanic consumers in this country.

Ethnicity and the Jewish Subculture

Since race and subculture are not synonymous, it may be useful to examine a subculture defined by ethnicity: the American Jews. Elizabeth Hirschman investigated several hypotheses involving the relationship be-

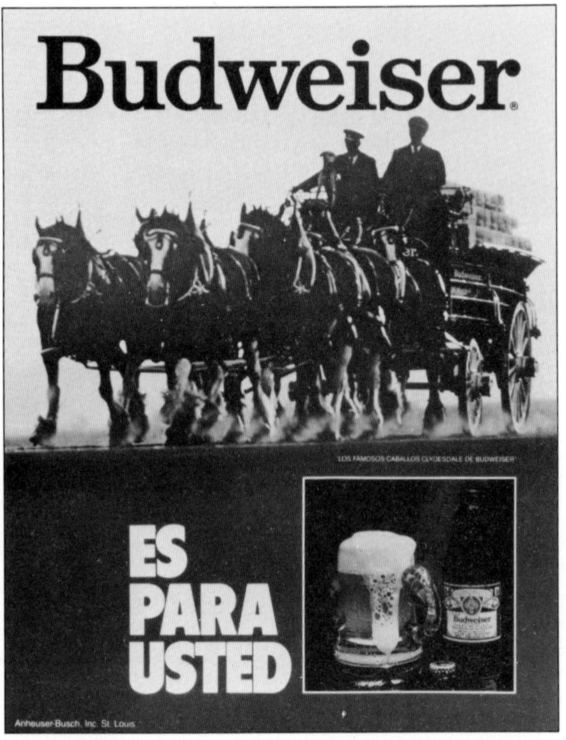

tween Jewish ethnicity and consumer behavior. The study involved a sample of Jewish and non-Jewish students from several major universities. The results suggest that Jewish consumers differ from non-Jewish consumers in terms of information processing and consumption behavior. Jewish consumers tend to receive more exposure to information as children, tend to expose themselves to more information as adults, and are more willing to adopt new products. In addition, Jewish consumers tend to share consumption information with others more often than non-Jewish consumers.

The findings imply that predominantly Jewish communities may display a higher level of innovativeness and more rapid product diffusion. Thus, Hirshman suggested that marketers might choose to target Jewish consumers in new-product introductions to speed adoption and extend favorable word of mouth regarding their products.[40]

SUMMARY

Culture is comprised of the learned values, beliefs, languages, symbols, and patterns of behavior shared by people in a society and passed on from generation to generation. Cross-cultural differences are an essential part of understanding consumer behavior. As international commerce continues to grow, the ability to understand and respond to cultural differences will become even more important for marketing managers who operate overseas. Three types of orientations that describe attitudes toward cultures are ethnocentric, geocentric, and polycentric.

An important element is that culture is learned. Socialization and acculturation are terms used to describe the process of learning a culture. A second important point is that culture is reflected in values which play a fundamental role in guiding consumer behavior within a society.

There are several approaches to viewing American culture and values. Cultural differences transcend geographic boundaries. Within the United States, predominant values include self-respect, security, warm relationships with others, and a sense of accomplishment. Outside the United States, Americans often find significant differences in the way people from other cultures perceive time, space, things, friendships, and agreements. The self-reference criterion (the fact that we are all tied to our own cultural values) explains why it is often difficult to understand other cultures.

Religion is a primary aspect of culture because it is intimately related to values. Primitive religion, Hinduism, Buddhism, Islam, and Catholic and Protestant Christianity have profoundly influenced consumer behavior and help explain differences in the economic development of some nations.

Subculture is a subdivision of national culture that often is determined by such elements as ethnic background and race. Ethnicity refers to the amount of identification an individual has with a particular ethnic group and, in many ways, is a more useful measure of subculture than is race or national origin. Two predominant American subcultures are blacks and Hispanics. These two subcultures display different consumption habits from the general population and are receiving increasing attention as marketers look for new market opportunities.

KEY TERMS

ethnocentric
polycentric
geocentric
primary demand
secondary demand
culture
socialization
acculturation
other-oriented values
environment-oriented values
self-oriented values
linear-separable time
circular-traditional time
procedural-traditional time
self-reference criterion
subgroups
subcultures
ethnic background
ethnicity

QUESTIONS

1. How do culture and subculture affect consumer behavior? Give two examples in which multinational marketers should consider these constructs when launching a product in a foreign country.

2. Ethnocentric, polycentric, and geocentric attitudes toward business abroad are likely to influence companies marketing plans and programs. How would advertising campaigns be developed for companies with each type of attitude?

3. Why has little cross-cultural research about consumer behavior been completed by academic researchers? What could be done to improve the situation?

4. Socialization is the process in which children learn the culture into which they are born. List some of the more important elements of socialization that have influenced your values toward education?

5. Thinking of Garreau's Nine Nations of North America, list how this knowledge could effect the way a marketing manager might introduce a new product.

6. In general, how do you perceive time? If you did perceive time in the other ways listed in the text, how would it be likely to effect the way you study consumer behavior? Would it influence your outlook on saving and consumption? How?

7. Could the self-reference criteria be applied equally to culture and subculture? Why or why not?

8. Why would it be important to consider religion when marketing internationally?

9. How many subcultures can you name? For each, give a value that tends to separate the subculture from the dominant culture.

10. How does ethnicity differ from ethnic background? What relevance does this have for subcultural marketing research?

11. Blacks and Hispanics are two major subcultures in the United States. Develop a plan to market computers to each group. What aspects of your plan would be adjusted to target specific aspects of each subculture?

NOTES

1. Office of Country Marketing, Bureau of Export Development Industry and Trade, "Adapting Export Packaging to Cultural Differences," *Business America* (December 3, 1979): 3–7.
2. Lennie Copeland, "The Art of International Selling," *Business America* (June 25, 1984): 306.
3. Donald Ball and Wendell H. McCulloch, Jr., *International Business* (Plano, TX: Business Publications, Inc., 1982). From *Business and International Education* (Washington, DC: American Council on Education, 1977), 9–10.
4. Jagdish N. Sheth and S. Prakash Sethi, "A Theory of Cross-Cultural Buyer Behavior," in *Consumer and Industrial Buying Behavior* (New York: North-Holland, Inc., 1977).
5. For a brief review of the inherent problems in cross-cultural research see Robert T. Green and Philip D. White, "Methodological Considerations in Cross-National Consumer Research," *Journal of International Business Studies* (Fall, 1976): 81–85.
6. Edward T. Hall, *Beyond Culture* (Garden City, NY: Anchor Books, 1981), 16.
7. Joel Garreau, *The Nine Nations of North America*, New York, Avon Books, 1981.

8. Garreau, 68.
9. Garreau, 130.
10. Garreau, 204.
11. Garreau, 333.
12. Garreau, 366.
13. Garreau, 377.
14. Lynn R. Kahle, "The Values of Americans: Implications for Consumer Adaptation," in *Personal Values and Consumer Psychology,* Robert E. Pitts and Arch G. Woodside, eds. (Lexington, KY: Lexington Books 1983), 77–86.
15. Leon Shiffman and Leslie Kanuk, *Consumer Behavior,* 2nd edition, (Englewood Cliffs, NJ: Prentice-Hall Inc., 1983), 420.
16. Del Hawkins, Roger J. Best, and Kenneth A. Coney, *Consumer Behavior,* revised edition (Plano, TX; Business Publications, Inc., 1983).
17. J. T. Plummer, "Consumer Focus in Cross Natural Research," *Journal of Advertising* (Spring 1977): 10.
18. Joseph F. Hair, Jr., and Ralph E. Anderson, "Culture, Acculturation and Consumer Behavior: An Empirical Study," in *Combined Proceedings of the American Marketing Association,* Boris W. Becker and Helmut Becker, eds. (Chicago: American Marketing Association, 1972), 423–28.
19. Edward T. Hall, *The Silent Language* (New York, Doubleday & Co., Inc., 1959).
20. Edward T. Hall, "The Silent Language in Overseas Business," *Harvard Business Review* (May/June 1960): 87–96.
21. Robert Levine and Ellen Wolff, "Social Time: The Heartbeat of Culture," *Psychology Today* (March 1985): 28–35.
22. Robert J. Graham, "The Role of Perception of Time in Consumer Research," *Journal of Consumer Research* 7 (March 1981): 335–42.
23. Hall, "The Silent Language in Overseas Business," 91.
24. Hall, "The Silent Language in Overseas Business," 92.
25. Hall, "The Silent Language in Overseas Business," 93.
26. Glen Fisher, "International Negotiation: Cross-Cultural Perception," *The Humanist* (November/December 1983): 14–18.
27. James A. Lee, "Culture Analysis in Overseas Operations," *Harvard Business Review* (March–April 1966): 106–44.
28. Material for this section is substantially based on Vern Terpstra, *The Cultural Environment of International Business,* (Cincinnati, OH: Southwestern Publishing Co., 1978), 29–63.
29. Kemper Fullerton, "Calvinism and Capitalism," *The Harvard Theological Review* 21 (1928): 163–91.
30. Milton M. Gordon, "The Concept of the Subculture and Its Applications," *Social Forces* 26 (October 1947): 40–42.
31. Elizabeth C. Hirschman, "American Jewish Ethnicity: Its Relationship to Some Selected Aspects of Consumer Behavior," *Journal of Marketing* 45 (Summer 1981): 102–10.
32. Hirschman, "American Jewish Ethnicity," 103.
33. U.S. Bureau of the Census, Current Population Reports, Series P-25, *Estimate of Population 1980–1984* (March 1985), 1. For an excellent review of the differences between whites and blacks regarding selected demographic and socioeconomic variables, see the Bureau of the Census report, *The Social and Economic Status of the Black Population in the United States: An Historical View, 1790–1978.*
34. U.S. Bureau of the Census, *Final Population and Housing Unit Count,* Series PHC-80-V (1980).
35. Donald E. Sexton, Jr., "Black Buyer Behavior," *Journal of Marketing* 36 (October 1972): 36–39.
36. Henry A. Bullock, "Consumer Motivation in Black and White," *Harvard Business Review* 39 (May–June 1961): 89–104, and 40 (July–August, 1961): 110–24.
37. Gerald J. Glasser and Gale D. Metzger, "Radio Usage by Blacks," *Journal of Advertising Research* (October 1975): 39–45.
38. "Hispanic Marketing: A Profile Grows to New Heights," *Advertising Age* (April 6, 1981).
39. "Marketing to Hispanics—Special Report," *Advertising Age* (March 19, 1984): 11–12.
40. Hirschman, "American Jewish Ethnicity," 102–10.

FURTHER READING

Classics

Douglas, Susan, and Bernard Dubois, "Looking at the Cultural Environment for International Marketing Opportunities," *Columbia Journal of World Business* 12 (Winter 1977): 102–19.

Hall, Edward T., "The Silent Language in Overseas Business," *Harvard Business Review* (May/June 1960): 87–96.

Henry, Walter A., "Cultural Values Do Correlate

With Consumer Behavior," *Journal of Marketing Research* 13 (May 1976): 121–27.

Kassarjian, Harold H., "Social Character and Differential Preference for Mass Communication," *Journal of Marketing Research* 2 (May 1965), 146–53.

Linton, Ralph, "The Concept of Culture," from *The Cultural Background of Personality,* Ralph Linton, ed. (Englewood Cliffs, NJ: Prentice-Hall, 1973), 30–36.

Robertson, Thomas S., Douglas J. Dalrymple, and Michael Y. Yoshino, "Cultural Compatibility in New Product Adoption," in *Proceedings of the American Marketing Association Educators' Conference,* Philip R. McDonald, ed. (Chicago: American Marketing Association, 1969).

Sexton, Donald E., Jr., "Black Buyer Behavior," *Journal of Marketing* 36 (October 1972).

Sheth, Jagdish N., and S. Prakash Sethi, "A Theory of Cross-Cultural Buyer Behavior," in *Consumer and Industrial Buying Behavior,* Woodside, Sheth, and Bennett, eds., (New York: North-Holland, 1977), 369–86.

Sturdivant, Frederick D., "Minority Markets and Subculture Analysis," in *Perspectives in Consumer Behavior,* Kassarjian and Robertson, eds. (Glenview, IL: Scott, Foresman and Company, 1981), 429–43.

Recent Significant Research

Bellenger, Danny N., and Humberto Valencia, "Understanding the Hispanic Market," *Business Horizons* (May–June 1982): 47–50.

Boote, Alfred S., "Psychographic Segmentation in Europe," *Journal of Advertising Research* 22, No. 6 (December/January 1982/1983): 19–25.

Green, Robert T., Jean-Paul Leonardi, Jean-Louis Chandon, Isabella C. M. Cunningham, Bronis Verhage, and Alain Strazzeri, "Societal Development and Family Purchasing Roles: A Cross-National Study," *Journal of Consumer Research* 9, No. 4 (March 1983) 436–42.

Hirschman, Elizabeth C., "American Jewish Ethnicity: Its Relationship to Some Selected Aspects of Consumer Behavior," *Journal of Marketing* 45 (Summer 1981): 102–10.

Reilly, Michael D., and Melanie Wallendorf, "A Longitudinal Study of Mexican-American Assimilation," in *Advances in Consumer Research,* Thomas C. Kinnear, ed. (Provo, UT: Association for Consumer Research, 1984) 735–40.

Villarreal-Camacho, Angelina, "Consumer Complaining Behavior: A Cross-Cultural Comparison," in *AMA Educator's Proceedings,* Patrick E. Murphy, et al., eds. (Chicago: American Marketing Association, 1983), 68–73.

Wallendorf, Melanie, and Michael D. Reilly, 'Ethnic Migration, Assimilation and Consumption," *Journal of Consumer Research* 10, No. 3 (December 1983) 292–302.

Wilkes, Robert E., and Humberto Valencia, "Shopping Orientations of Mexican-Americans," in *1984 AMA Educators' Proceedings,* Russell W. Belk, et al., eds. (Chicago: American Marketing Association, 1984), 26–31.

Applications

Arnold, Stephen J., and James G. Barnes, "Canadian and American National Character as a Basis for Market Segmentation," in *Research in Marketing,* Vol. 2, Jagdish N. Sheth, ed., (Greenwich, CT: JAI Press, 1979), 1–35.

Berger, Karen A., Barbara A. Stern, and J. K. Johansson, "Strategic Implications of a Cross-Cultural Comparison of Attribute Importance: Automobiles in Japan and the United States," in *AMA Educators' Proceedings,* Murphy, et al., eds. (1983), 327–32.

Douglas, Susan P., "Cross-National Comparisons and Consumer Stereotypes: A Case Study of Working and Non-Working Wives in the U.S. and France," *Journal of Consumer Research* 3 (June 1976): 12–20.

Douglas, Susan, and Bernard Dubois, "Looking at the Cultural Environment for International Marketing Opportunities," *Columbia Journal of World Business* 12 (Winter 1977): 102–09.

Green, Robert T., and Eric Langeard, "A Cross-National Comparison of Consumer Habits and Innovator Characteristics," *Journal of Marketing* 39 (July 1975); 34–41.

Hair, Joseph F., Jr., and Rolph E. Anderson, "Culture, Acculturation and Consumer Behavior: An Empirical Study," in *Combined Proceedings of the American Marketing Association,* Boris W. Becker and Helmut Becker, eds., (Chicago: American Marketing Association, 1972), 423–28.

Hall, Edward T., "The Silent Language in Overseas Business," *Harvard Business Review* (May/June 1960), 87–96.

Hansen, Flemming, "Managerial Implications of Cross-Cultural Studies of Buyer Behavior," in *Consumer and Industrial Buying Behavior,* Woodside, Sheth, and Bennett, eds., 387–95.

Hempel, Donald J., "Family Buying Decisions: A Cross-Cultural Perspective," *Journal of Marketing Research* 11 (August 1974): 295–302.

Solomon, Paul J., Ronald F. Busch, and Joseph Hair, Jr., "White and Black Consumer Sales Response to Black Models," *Journal of Marketing Research* 13 (November 1976): 431–34.

16 Shopping Environments and Situations

Objectives of This Chapter

After you have studied this chapter, you should be able to:

1. Explain the importance of environments and situations on purchasing.
2. Outline the effects of environmental variables on shopping-center and storage images.
3. Describe the attributes of shopping environments that influence consumers' images of them.
4. Discuss how atmospherics such as color, music, and shapes influence consumers' moods, which in turn affect purchasing.
5. Explain how other shoppers influence consumers' feelings of crowding.
6. Explain how situational factors (such as time constraints and when, where, and how products will be consumed) determine where purchases are made.

The relationship between environments and human behavior has been studied increasingly in recent years, encompassing perspectives from sociology, geography, and an emerging field called *environmental psychology*. In addition, ergonomics, or human engineering, has examined the effect of background music and other variables on human behavior.[1]

Consumers shop in many diversified environments, among them malls, shopping centers, downtown areas, outlying stores, drive-throughs, and even their own homes by way of the telephone. The choice of store types is wide as well: lavish specialty shops, supermarkets, discount stores, merchandise marts, hyperstores, and so on. Each type of shopping area and store provides a unique shopping environment. Dimensions of the shopping area, shapes, colors, sounds, aisle layouts, merchandise displays—all influence consumer responses. This chapter will look at the environmental factors and situational variables that tend to have the greatest effect on shopping choices and behavior.

Environmental factors and situational variables are distinct from one another. Neither includes intellect, personality, or psychological processes; they are not attributes or characteristics of a particular brand or product. **Environmental factors** refer to characteristics in the space that surrounds shoppers; **situational variables** are temporary and often unexpected occurrences during a shopping trip or aspects specific to product use that influence purchasing. Sometimes it is difficult to differentiate between the two, however. For example, crowding, which is discussed later in the chapter, is so prevalent that it is classified as an environmental factor here, although it could just as easily be examined as a situational variable.

environmental factors
situational variables

Rather than focus on the retailer's numerous decisions that may influence consumer choice, this chapter addresses the basic environmental and situational elements likely to affect consumer reactions. First we examine the concept of shopping center and store image; it is this image that represents shoppers' impressions of those specific environments. Then a discussion of atmosphere highlights environmental elements that can affect shoppers' moods: factors such as the colors used in various areas, the type of music played, and environmental crowding. How consumers react to these elements affect in turn the amount of energy directed to shopping. Next we will look at consumer responses to store design. Finally, we assess situational effects on shopping behavior: elements such as time that influence when and where shopping is likely to occur.

WHY PEOPLE SHOP: THE STORE ENVIRONMENT

Why do people shop? Clearly shopping centers and malls are much more than places to buy things; their environments stimulate numerous activi-

Table 16-1 WHY PEOPLE SHOP

Role playing	Expectations are based on roles such as mother, housewife, husband, or student.
Diversion	Shopping as recreation, a diversion from routine daily life.
Self-gratification	Shopping provides utility through the buying process itself; for some people, depression is alleviated by simply spending money ("When the going gets tough, the tough go shopping").
Learning about new trends	Shoppers learn about trends and new life-styles.
Physical activity	Shopping provides exercise.
Sensory stimulation	It can be interesting to browse through a store, looking at merchandise and other shoppers, or hearing background music, and enjoying scents of various sorts.
Social experiences outside the home	Shopping can be the center of social activities, including direct encounters with friends or other social contacts.
Communication with others having a similar interest	Stores provide outlets for people with hobbies and other interests in common.
Peer group attraction	Stores provide places for peers to meet (record stores for younger people).
Status and authority	Shopping provides opportunities for individuals to command attention and respect while being waited on.
Pleasure of bargains	People pride themselves on making wise purchases.

Source: adapted from Edward M. Tauber, "Why Do People Shop?" *Journal of Marketing* 36 (October 1972): 46–59.

ties and motives in shoppers. Edward Tauber used individual depth interviews to discover reasons for shopping; they are shown in Table 16-1.

It would be easier to assess the impact of shopping environments if consumers only shopped to purchase. However, they shop for many other reasons as well. These reasons should be kept in mind as we assess shopping center and store images that influence shoppers. Also when store atmosphere is discussed, it will be looked at with total shopping behavior in mind.

Shopping Center Image

A shopping center has an image that represents the complex perceptions consumers have about it. The image encompasses more than simply the sum of the stores comprising the center. One study examined image as a composite of the beliefs consumers have about a number of attributes of shopping centers. When the results of this study were analyzed statistically, it was found that sixteen attributes could be condensed into three underlying dimensions: assortment, facilities, and market posture. These are shown in Table 16-2.

Table 16-2 MAJOR DIMENSIONS OF RETAIL SHOPPING CENTER IMAGE

Attributes	*Assortment*	*Facilities*	*Market Posture*
Quality of store	X		
Variety of store	X		
Merchandise quality	X		
Product selection	X		
Special sales promotions	X		
Special events and exhibits	X		
A great place to spend a few hours	X		
Layout of area		X	
Parking facilities		X	
Availability of lunch and refreshments		X	
Comfort areas		X	
General price level			X
Store personnel			X
Conservative center			X

Source: adapted from John R. Nevin and Michael J. Houston, "Image as a Component of Attraction to Intraurban Shopping Centers," *Journal of Retailing* 56, No. 1 (Spring 1980): 85.

assortment
facilities
market posture

The researchers found that the most important aspects of stores is their **assortment** (merchandise, product quality, events), **facilities** (parking, comfort areas, and so forth), and **market posture** (store personnel, general price levels, and so forth).

Another study identified seventeen variables to help explain why shoppers went to three alternative malls:[2]

- Value for price
- Prices
- Variety of products
- Quality of stores
- Cleanliness in stores
- Variety of stores
- Friendly sales personnel
- Store hours
- Comparative shopping
- Availability of parking
- Reputation of stores
- Proximity to home

- Free parking available
- Traffic congestion
- Advertising
- Type of customer
- Buildings and landscaping

The researchers sampled consumers at the three shopping centers. A statistical technique was used to determine whether consumers at the different locations expressed a different pattern of reasons for mall preferences. Shoppers were asked to rate the center they patronized according to each of the seventeen criteria, and responses were examined to establish which criteria were most associated with shopping behavior. For each shopping area, proximity was the overriding factor and parking availability was also important. Beyond that, some criteria were more predictive for the shoppers at some centers than at the others. This indicates that shoppers select malls for varying reasons; that some like malls with certain characteristics while others prefer different ones. Therefore, shopping centers are likely to attract different types of customers based on the image they project. This is not surprising when we consider all the reasons why people shop mentioned in Table 16-1.

Store Image

Individual stores also have an image. Jay Lindquist has studied most definitions of store image and concludes that it "consists of a combination of tangible or functional factors and intangible or psychological factors that the consumer perceives to be present."[3] Lindquist reviewed past research and identified nine attributes ordinarily used to describe image. They are presented in Table 16-3.

Store image is based on a number of important factors. It is possible to measure how well a store rates in terms of a particular attribute similar to the approach we used in the attitude measurement chapter (Chapter 6). This is often a good way to determine store image, but other images along more subjective lines are sometimes sought. For example, Dale Lewison and M. Wayne DeLozier indicate that retailers may want to project the following concepts:[4]

- prestigious or economical
- contemporary or traditional
- swinging or subdued
- family or singles
- formal or informal
- friendly or reserved
- restful or active

Table 16-3 ATTRIBUTES DETERMINING STORE IMAGE

Attribute	*Description*
Merchandise	Merchandise means goods and services offered by the retail outlet; considerations are quality, selection or assortment, styling or fashion, guarantees, and pricing.
Service	This includes general service, sales clerk service, presence of self-service, ease of merchandise return, delivery, and the store's credit policies.
Clientele	Social class appeal, self-image congruency, and store personnel comprise this factor.
Physical facilities	Such items as elevators, lighting, air conditioning, and washrooms are included, along with store layout, aisle placement and width, carpeting, and architecture.
Convenience	The general convenience of the store's location and parking are factors here.
Promotion	This involves sales promotions, advertising, displays, trading stamps, symbols, and colors.
Store atmosphere	This factor concerns congeniality, which refers to a customer's feelings of warmth, acceptance, or ease.
Institutional factors	The conservative or modern projection of the store and the attributes of reputation and reliability are included in this attribute.
Post-transaction satisfaction	In essence, was the customer satisfied with the purchase and with the store if a return or adjustment was necessary?

Source: adapted from Jay D. Lindquist, "Meaning of Image," *Journal of Retailing* 50, No. 4 (Winter 1974–75): 31.

Do you perceive K-Mart as prestigious or economical? Clearly, economy is its most important characteristic; both the interior and exterior of the store reflect that. The low overhead involved in fixtures, window displays, checkout lanes, and floor covering all help to communicate the image K-Mart tries to project. Harrods, the world-famous department store in London, projects a very complex image. Its full line of items ranges from expensive mink coats to inexpensive sweatshirts, and requires very careful orchestration on the part of management. In some parts of the store clerks pay strict attention to enhancing the prestigious image, whereas elsewhere merchandise is lined up on tables to create the bargain flavor of a sale.

By way of interesting comparison to K-Mart are several successful regional chains. Many of their stores are located near K-Mart but appeal to a different segment of buyers. Their clearly upscale merchandise, liberal return policies, and prices are designed to present a more complex image than K-Mart; and the result is a very broad range of clientele.

Store image and store atmosphere are intimately related. Retailers are careful to present atmospheres that enhance their image and help shoppers want to do business with them.

Store Atmosphere

atmospherics

Philip Kotler coined the term **atmospherics** to describe the marketing tool of organizing space to create certain impacts on consumers: "Atmospherics is the effort to design buying environments to produce specific emotional effects in the buyer that enhance purchase probability."[5] Atmosphere is the quality of the space or environment perceived by the shopper. Essentially, according to Kotler it involves these sensory mechanisms: *visual*—color, brightness, size, shapes; *aural*—volume, pitch; *olfactory*—scent, freshness; and *tactile*—softness, smoothness, temperature. Thus, an atmosphere is seen, heard, smelled, and felt. All of these elements are communicated to shoppers by the store and its design, contents, merchandising philosophy, and personnel as reflected, by the objects and lighting in the store. In addition, the amount of space will affect perception, as will the density and the distribution of people within it. For example, some space is **sociofugal,** that is, it tends to separate or disperse people. Other space is **sociopetal,** which means that it draws or attracts people to central focal points.[6]

sociofugal space
sociopetal space

Atmospherics influences the consumer's initial choice of a shopping environment and then affects his or her moods once within it. Some stores are nondescript, cold, and impersonal; others are warm, friendly, excit-

ing, and dynamic. Generally, people seek the environments they perceive as providing the most potential rewards. We all learn to approach positive environments and avoid negative ones. Interestingly, when it comes to retail environments, shoppers make implied rather than explicit decisions. Elements such as color, smell, or crowding are not consciously evaluated; but they can have an amazingly strong effect on behavior. For example, shoppers who find a mall overcrowded one weekend are likely to avoid it the next time they shop, without realizing that their avoidance is due to the poor environment; they simply do not feel like going there.

Consumers may not even notice atmosphere yet still be influenced by it in terms of where they shop and for how long. In Chapter 4, on learning, we saw that stimulation is an important reinforcer. Markin and colleagues use this concept to describe how retail space may influence behavior:

> Retail space creates expectations through stimulation. For example, if a retailer wants to capitalize on high turnover, he will probably use high

> illumination and not worry too much about using sound-deadening materials. On the other hand, if he wants customers to linger or browse he uses dim lighting and soundproofing surfaces such as carpets, drapes, and padded or acoustical ceilings. The physical environment of a retail store, like other buildings, creates certain expectations about how one should act—people lower their voices and stop smiling when they enter banks and churches. Customers in retail stores often feel a sense of belonging or they sometimes feel like aliens in a strange adverse environment.[7]

Shopping malls and stores present tremendous arenas of stimulation. The lighting, layout, and traffic patterns all form cues that influence how consumers are likely to react.

Elements such as color, music, aisle and merchandise layout, and so forth, are all part of the atmosphere. Although these characteristics have physical dimensions, store atmosphere refers more to the emotional states created in consumers. The atmosphere may have an effect on store choice, but it is likely to influence behavior within the store. Donovan and Rossiter used a model developed by environmental psychologists to demonstrate the effects of store atmosphere on shopping behavior.[8] They found that responses to an environment, such as the inside of a store, involved approach or avoidance. Other researchers have identified four basic aspects: (1) a desire to stay in or leave the environment; (2) a desire to look around and explore the environment, or avoid doing so; (3) a willingness to communicate with others in the environment or to ignore them; and (4) the degree of enhancement or hindrance of satisfaction with the shopping task.[9]

Considerable data support the idea that people experience emotional states that influence their approach–avoidance behaviors in situations such as shopping. Three dimensions of emotional response to environments have been identified: pleasure–displeasure, arousal–nonarousal, and dominance–submissiveness. Using the first two dimensions as most relevant to consumer behavior, it is possible to diagram the dimensions of emotional states related to shopping environments (see Figure 16-1). Notice that arousing environments can be either distressing or exciting; sleepy environments can be gloomy or relaxing. If at the same time the arousing environment is pleasant it can be exciting. In a negative sense, an unpleasant yet arousing environment is distressing, and an unpleasant yet sleepy environment is gloomy.

According to Russell and Pratt, who devised the diagram, these elements can have much to do with shopping behavior. For example, a consumer's emotional state can influence (1) the enjoyment of shopping in the store, (2) the time spent browsing and exploring store offerings, (3) willingness to talk to sales personnel, (4) tendency to spend more money than originally planned, and (5) likelihood of returning to the store in the future. Clearly, the emotional state of shoppers deserves consideration because it influences their in-store behavior.

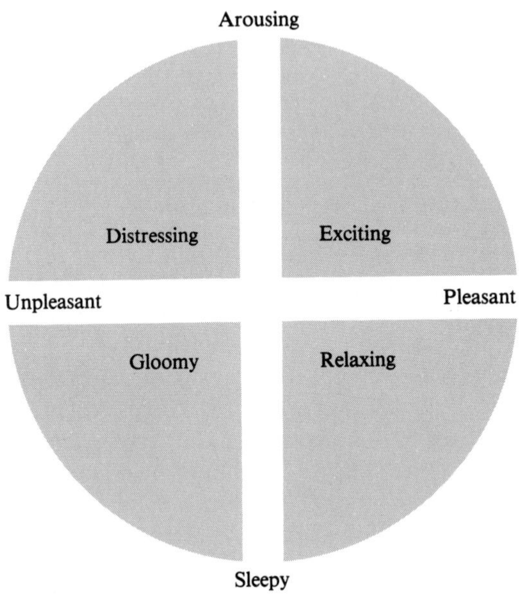

Figure 16-1
Dimensions of Emotional States

Source: Russell, J. A., and G. Pratt, "A Description of the Affective Quality Attributed to Environments," *Journal of Personality and Social Psychology* 38 (August 1980): 311–22, as reported in Robert J. Donovan and J. Rossiter, "Store Atmosphere: An Environmental Psychological Approach," *Journal of Retailing* 58, No. 1 (Spring 1982): 39.

The Influence of Color

Color has physiological and well as psychological effects on people and has often been used to create a desired atmosphere. Color can draw attention, make people feel relaxed, or create confusion. It has been shown to influence blood pressure, respiration, heart rate, and brain waves. Studies have shown that warm colors (red and yellow) are physiologically stimulating and that cool colors (blue and green) promote relaxation. Red, orange, and yellow are long-wavelength colors that increase or elevate mood states.

Color has further dramatic effects on behavior.[10] Joseph Bellizzi and colleagues found that the color red is usually described as active, adventurous, stimulating, energetic, and vital. Yellow is thought to stimulate the intellect and is associated with cheer, gaiety, and fun. The short-wavelength colors (green and blue) evoke more sedate moods. They have lower arousal value, tend to sooth or relax, and induce calm and restfulness. Green helps provide a sense of security, conformity, calm, and peacefulness. Blue indicates very controlled emotions. Bellizzi and colleagues conducted an experiment which revealed that while subjects tend to be physically drawn to very warm colors, they often feel that warm-color environments are unpleasant. Subjects sat closer to red and yellow

Table 16-4 PERCEPTIONS OF COLORS

Warm Colors					
Red:	love	sinful	*Blue:*	coolness	piety
	romance	warmth		aloofness	masculinity
	sex	excitement		fidelity	assurance
	courage	vigor		calmness	sadness
	danger	cheerfulness			
	fire	enthusiasm			
Yellow:	sunlight	gaiety	*Green:*	coolness	growth
	warmth	glory		restfulness	softness
	cowardliness	brightness		peace	richness
	openness	caution		freshness	go
	friendliness				
Orange:	sunlight	friendliness	*Violet:*	coolness	dignity
	warmth	gaiety		retiring	richness
	openness	glory			

Source: Dale M. Lewison and M. Wayne DeLozier, *Retailing Principles and Practices* (Columbus, OH: Charles E. Merrill Publishing Co., 1982), 154.

walls than to blue and green walls, yet they perceived warm environments as negative. The researchers concluded that warm colors were rated higher on an activity scale but more unfavorable on an evaluative scale. Thus, warm colors may attract people to settings that are not all that pleasant. Cooler colors may not provide as much attraction but may give a better atmosphere once the shopper is in the area. Blues tend to be rated as positive, relaxed, and more favorable. Table 16-4 summarizes the many typical perceptions of color.

Because some colors are effective for gaining attention while others provide a better background, marketers must use colors widely in designing atmosphere into store settings. For example, it might be best to use red sparingly, as an accent color to highlight certain areas; as a dominant color it may create a negative aura. Clearly, blues would not be good for specific highlighting due to their lack of intensity and attention-getting power. But they are associated with calm and would provide a very relaxing atmosphere, perhaps in an area where shoppers could browse slowly and feel at ease. Because green is often perceived as a very spacious, pleasant color, it can make small areas appear large.

Music

Music is all around us; many of us wake to its sound from an alarm radio or timer-set stereo system. Does it influence shopping behavior? In general, retail shoppers find shopping more pleasant when background music is playing. In one study, 77% of the respondents preferred music playing in the background while they shopped.[11] In another survey, major differences in sales resulted when two types of music were played in a supermarket environment.[12] Average receipts increased from about $12,000 per day (when fast-tempo music was used) to approximately $16,700 per day for slow tempo music. This represented a 38.2% increase in sales volume for the slower tempo (72 beats per minute or less) compared to the higher tempo (94 beats per minute). While it is difficult to generalize this study to

Table 16-5 MUSIC AND CONSUMER RESPONSE

Music Design Components	***Consumer Response***
Mode: major Tempo: slow Pitch: high Rhythm: flowing Harmony: simple Melody: ascending Intensity: *piano* (soft)	Serene, gentle
Tempo: fast (over 120 quarter notes per minute)	Pleasant, happy, loving, reverie, joyous, triumphant
Articulation: *staccato* (firm) Intensity: *forte* (loud)	active, energetic, lively, agitated
Articulation: *legato* (flowing) Intensity: *piano* (soft)	soft, peaceful
Articulation: *legato* (flowing) Intensity: *piano* (soft) Harmony: dissonant (complex)	Melancholy, yearning
Harmony: consonant (simple) Rhythm: fluent Tempo: fast Mode: major Pitch: high	Glad, playful, light, gay, exuberant
Harmony: dissonant Rhythm: firm Tempo: slow Mode: minor	Dramatic, ominous, fateful, dark
Mode: major Tempo: slow Pitch: low Rhythm: firm Harmony: simple Melody: ascending Intensity: *forte* (loud)	Dignified, solemn
Mode: minor Tempo: slow Pitch: high Rhythm: flowing Harmony: simple Intensity: *piano* (soft)	Dreamy, sentimental

Source: adapted from Glenn S. Omura, *Strategic Design of Store Interiors* (Greenvale, NY: Academy of Marketing Science, 1982), 76–83.

all populations, it suggests that music does affect shopping behavior. Glenn Omura investigated several types of music and consumer reactions, the results of which are given in Table 16-5. Notice the broad range of consumer responses that can result from variations in music.

Crowding

Up to this point we have talked about physical aspects of the shopping environments that are controlled by the retailer. But another important feature is the presence of other consumers. Are feelings and behavior influenced by the number of people in a shopping area? Most of us respond in some degree to the level of shopper density; some prefer to be around many other people, while others feel closed in and try to avoid crowds.

When do consumers feel crowded? Is it possible for many people to be in a store without shoppers having this feeling? When customers perceive crowding, they are likely to develop moods not conducive to shopping and to have negative feelings about the store. Retail managers are faced with an interesting dilemma because they must attract many customers in order to make a profit. Yet attracting too many shoppers can have adverse consequences. A key task is to increase the number of shoppers without allowing them to feel that they are in a dense or crowded environment.

Many consumers do most of their shopping in supermarkets, discount department stores, and shopping centers or malls that are often densely populated. In addition, heavy burdens are often placed on stores during peak shopping times because of work schedules, population shifts, and the increasing number of shoppers seeking experimentation and recreation.[13]

crowding

Crowding can be viewed both as a physical state—a large number of people in a given space—and as a psychological feeling.[14] Psychologists have attributed negative feelings about crowding to two causes. First, it contributes to mental overload, leading to a sense of inability to handle all the stimuli from the people around us. This feeling can occur from inappropriate or unfamiliar social contacts,[15] or it may simply result from too much stimulation coming from all social sources.[16] When overstimulation exists shoppers want less involvement with store employees and others; they are likely to spend less time talking to people. The crowding creates discomfort and the desire to flee the area.

A second source of negative feelings about crowding can be due to the difficulties shoppers perceive in being able to shop. They see their task as being restricted by others, who are intruding into their personal environment. Behavioral constraint theory suggests that when people feel unable to operate in the environment they may attempt to improve coordination and relations with others, which can result in conformity to traffic patterns. It is interesting to watch people in a crowded supermarket as they move at a consistent pace and carefully follow patterns; shoppers moving

against the flow are looked at with irritation, as though they have violated some social rule.

Research shows that crowding in retail establishments can have predictable effects on buyers' behavior. Some consumers tend to deviate from their shopping plan in a crowded environment. The result is that they feel generally dissatisfied with the trip and the store. If shoppers are not forced to deviate from that plan, however, crowding generally does not affect their feelings about the store or the environment. Figure 16-2 depicts consumer behavior in a crowded situation. When the number of shoppers in a store is high, physical density is high; often shoppers have to wait in aisles, and they are likely to perceive crowding. Their perception may be related to the spaciousness of the store, to too many shoppers, to a "closed-in" feeling, to restricted movement, or simply to a

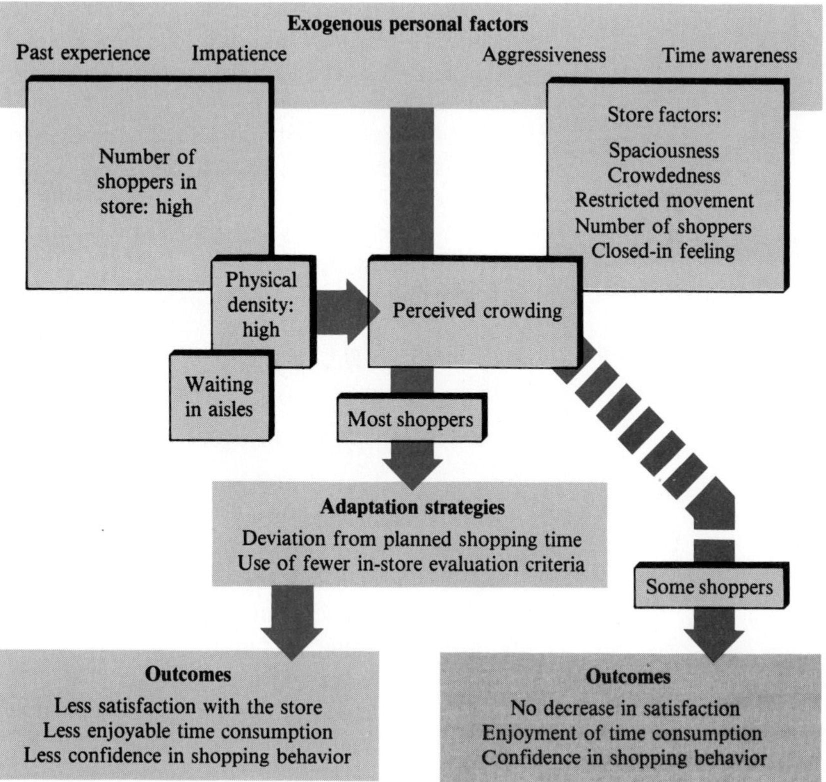

Figure 16-2
Behavior of Shoppers under Crowded Conditions

Source: adapted from Gilbert D. Harrell, Michael D. Hutt, and James C. Anderson, "Path Analysis of Buyer Behavior Under Conditions of Crowding," *Journal of Marketing Research* (February 1980): 47.

general feeling of being crowded. Personal factors, such as past experience or personality traits like aggressiveness and impatience, are likely to influence people. Those who are more aggressive or impatient are likely to feel crowded more quickly than do those who are not. Also, shoppers operating under a time constraint or who are intently aware of time perceive crowding more quickly than others do.

Once shoppers perceive crowding, they use adaptation strategies: that is, behavior which helps reduce their negative feelings about the situation. The adaptation may be a deviation from planned shopping time; they stay in the area for a shorter period of time and consequently are not likely to fulfill their purchase plans. They may use fewer in-store evaluation criteria such as unit pricing, advertisements, or comparative shopping information in making decisions. When shoppers do use adaptation strategies and deviate from their normal shopping activities, there may be several outcomes. Satisfaction with the store may decrease and shoppers may be less confident that they have made the best choices. Yet some shoppers who feel crowded do not use adaptation strategies, but shop in the same way they would in a low-density environment. For them, feelings such as store satisfaction and enjoyment of time consumption remain unchanged. Nevertheless, for a significant number of people being crowded does produce a close feeling and restricts their movement, forcing them to deviate from their plans and causing dissatisfaction.

High density can also be a positive factor for shopping behavior. Shoppers intent on buying specific products are more likely to be negatively influenced by high density. Yet under other circumstances they might like high density. Recreational shoppers and information seekers like to spend time shopping and tend not to see crowding as a major inconvenience. They enjoy watching other shoppers.

Consumer Response to Store Designs

Clearly a broad range of factors can influence consumer response to environments. Such elements as merchandising, graphics, music, store layout, fixtures, and other people help determine the mood of a shopper. Glenn Omura has conducted extensive research to identify consumer reactions to store design components. Table 16-6 highlights the more important components and the expected responses to them by consumers. Separately as well as in combination, these factors of store design comprise the physical aspects of space that influence consumer responses. For example, the way merchandise is presented can highlight feelings of fashionability, particular life-styles, drama, excitement, and so on. When consumers enter a store and find colors grouped together they think of fashion. Sports clothing displayed along with bicycles and skis is likely to evoke an image that the store promotes very active lifestyles. If merchandise is presented at a range of heights, from low tables to elevated display racks and even to hanging from the ceilings, excitement is conveyed. Graphics also have much to do with consumer responses. The use of fabric conveys warmth and softness. Large-scale or repeated graphics throughout the store space tend to create more excitement. Orderliness is communicated by a coordinated color and style of graphics, while diagonal signing provides the illusion of motion. Store layout is likely to affect consumer reactions. Activity is communicated when traffic is directed to the periphery of the retail arena. At the same time this traffic flow may cause crowding and a more businesslike feeling in the shoppers. A radial or circular design tends to elicit a very pleasant response from consumers. Even the location of display cases may communicate a great deal. For example, as Omura points out, placing display cases very close to the front of the store in a mall (close to the lease line) may eliminate the impression that the store is expensive.

The ceiling, fixtures, floor covering, lighting, walls, and partitions are more permanent parts of a retail environment. Yet designers often under-

Table 16-6 CONSUMER RESPONSE AND DESIGN COMPONENTS

Design Components	***Consumer Perception***
Merchandise Presentation	
Organize merchandise by color, trend	Fashionable
Organize merchandise by life-style (create boutiques)	Life-style
Vertical presentation	Drama
Diversity of heights	Excitement
Show all merchandise (none in storeroom)	"Full" look
Point of Purchase Graphics	
Fabric signs	Warmth, softness
Large-size, large-scale graphics	Excitement
Repetition of graphics	
Coordination of color, style of all graphics	Orderliness
Diagonal signing	Illusion of motivation
Store Layout	
Direct traffic into periphery	Activity, crowding, businesslike quality
Radial/circular layout	Pleasant
Locate display cases up to lease line (of mall store)	Eliminate fear of expensiveness
Ceiling	
Dark grey ceiling	Intimacy
Height dropped to ten feet	Quality
Made of sheet rock rather than acoustical tile	
Fixture System	
Remodel according to fashion rather than function	Fashionableness
Smoked, plexiglass L-fixtures suspended from ceiling for men's shirts	
Two-level racks	Drama
Coordinates together	
Full-face presentation	
Different from those used elsewhere in store	
Diversity of fixture heights, shapes, weights	Excitement
Two-level racks	
Narrow shelves	Full look
Small gondolas	
Short peg hooks	
Narrow end caps	
Shallow, free-standing racks	
Wood: ash, wormy chestnut, oak, natural pine	Warmth
Wooden rack	Quality
Leather	
Brass	Gentlemanly look
Bronze	
Velour	
Wood	
Wooden rack	Masculine
Barn wood, raw oak shelving	Traditional
Glass shelving	Contemporary
Floor Covering	
Green, "autumn pumpkin yellow" carpeting	Fashionable
Total carpeting (no floor-marked aisles)	Intimacy

Table 16-6 CONSUMER RESPONSE AND DESIGN COMPONENTS, continued

Design Components	***Consumer Perception***
Fine parquet	Quality
Quarry tile	
Area rugs	
Grey carpet	Contemporary sleekness Sophistication
Extend carpeting to lease line (of mall store)	Eliminate fear of expensiveness
Lighting System	
Incandescent lamps (creates contrasts)	Drama
Deep, dark shadows	Solemn, suspense, power, threatening, hostile, dejection, distress
Small, light shadows	Open, lively, friendly, safety, excitement, joy
Soft shadows	Beauty, peaceful, melancholy, pensive
Uniform brightness pattern on two-dimensional object (such as a rug)	Soft
Underlight floor fixtures	Illusion of motion
Perimeter wall lighting (if wall is 50% reflectance, lighted area near wall or wall itself should be two times brightness of background)	Pleasant
Warm light in lower illuminated areas	
Cool light in higher illuminated areas	
Matte black track lighting	Intimacy
Incandescent lamps	Quality
Track lighting	
Soft, glowing lamps	Gentlemanly look
Position light source on 45° angle on either side of line drawn from object to audience	Naturalistic
Back, side lighting	Radiant glow
Walls, Partitioning	
New paint colors, wallpapers	Fashionable
Bright fabric panels	
Fabric partitions, covering for walls	Warmth
Brick facade over support post of building	
Fabric partitions, covering for walls	Softness

Source: based on Glenn S. Omura, *Strategic Design of Store Interiors* (Greenvale, NY: Academy of Marketing Science, 1982), 76–83.

take major renovations when a retailer of one type is replaced by another. A dark grey ceiling is likely to provide a feeling of intimacy; a lowered ceiling is likely to suggest quality. The type and use of fixtures is important as well. Wood promotes a sense of warmth and quality; combined with leather and bronze it suggests a gentlemen's or masculine environment. Floor coloring and covering add to the picture: Omura indicates that carpeting throughout communicates intimacy, area rugs quality and grey carpet contemporary sleekness and sophistication. Again, extending carpeting up to the front or leaseline may eliminate the fear that the store is expensive. Lighting systems are another major aspect of the environment. And the exhibit drawn from Omura's research notes the different moods created by various types. Of course, as discussed earlier, color also affects mood.

The environment in which consumers shop is likely to have a great deal of influence on mood, which in turn affects the amount of information consumers take from the setting, the brands consumers buy, and the amount of time they are willing to spend in the store. Further, their feelings about the shopping trip after the fact will be determined to a large degree by the shopping environment. These attitudes provide reinforcement and learning that prompt customers to return to or avoid particular stores and areas in future shopping trips. Merchandise and brands—what customers ultimately buy—most certainly are important, but *where* they buy is largely a function of the store environment.

SITUATIONAL VARIABLES

How many times have you asked another person a question and they answered with "it all depends"? In so much of what we do the situation makes the difference. The same is true for shopping. Unexpected contingencies may arise at the point of purchase that require a deviation from the shopper's normal choice. For example, what do you do when your favorite brand is out of stock at a supermarket? In another situation, perhaps a point-of-purchase ad with a cents-off offer or indicating a brand with some new ingredient, may get the shopper's attention and influence choice. The comments of a salesperson or someone else may alter the way a consumer is thinking about the current purchase. All of these illustrate situational variables at or about the time brand choice is being made. **Situational variables** refer to unexpected events at the point of purchase, variances due to where, how, and by whom the products will be consumed or used and the purpose for which the purchase is made.

situational variables

Russell Belk was one of the first researchers to draw attention to situational variables. He has noted that one requirement for situational research in consumer behavior is an appropriate listing of the variables comprising a situation. According to him, there are five groups of relevant characteristics:

> (1) *Physical Surroundings* are the most readily apparent features of a situation. These features include geographical and institutional location, decor, sounds, aromas, lighting, weather, and visible configurations of merchandise or other material surrounding the stimulus object; (2) *Social Surroundings* provide additional depth to a description of a situation. Other persons present, their characteristics, their apparent roles, and interpersonal interactions . . . are potentially relevant examples; (3) *Temporal Perspective* is a dimension of situations which may be specified in units ranging from time of day to season of the year. Time may also be measured relative to some

past or future event for the situational participant. This allows conceptions such as time since last purchase, time since or until meals or payday, and time constraints imposed by prior or standing commitments; (4) *Task Definition* features of a situation include an intent or requirement to select, shop for, or obtain information about a general or specific purchase. In addition, task may reflect different buyer and user roles anticipated by the individual. For instance, a person shopping for a small appliance as a wedding gift for a friend is in a different situation than he would be in shopping for a small appliance for personal use; and (5) *Antecedent States* make up a final group of features which characterize a situation. These are momentary moods (such as acute anxiety, pleasantness, hostility, and excitation) or momentary conditions (such as cash on hand, fatigue, and illness) rather than chronic individual traits. These conditions are further stipulated to be immediately antecedent to the current situation in order to distinguish states which the individual brings to the situations from states of the individual which result from the situation. For instance, a person may select a certain motion picture because he feels depressed (an antecedent state and a part of the choice situation), but the fact that the movie causes him to feel happier is a response to the consumption situation.[17]

Belk defines situation as "all those factors particular to a time and place of observation which do not follow from a knowledge of personal and stimulus attributes, and which have demonstratable and systematic effect on current behavior."[18]

We have chosen to consider the first of Belk's categories as part of the environment created by the retailer: that is, an "objective" reality which exists for all shoppers and in which the consumer reacts. The second of Belk's groups might incorporate the factor of density or crowding, which we have classified as part of store atmosphere. It remains for researchers to clarify the definition of situation, but there is little question that a particular shopper at a particular time will have certain behaviors, attitudes, or intentions based on the situation that affect the purchase decision.[19]

Another category of situational variables involves the circumstances of consumption. Consumer attitudes toward Rice-a-Roni or Chef Boyardee pizza might be considerably different depending on whether preparing dinner for themselves, the family, or guests. Whether or not a gift is being purchased for someone is a situational variable likely to influence brand choice and the amount of shopping done.

Shopping Purpose

convenience consumers
recreational consumers

One type of situational variable is how the consumer defines the shopping task. Consumers can be categorized according to the purpose of their shopping trip. Two types of consumers are **convenience** and **recreational.**[20] The first group seeks great amounts of information and prefers areas conducive to those tasks, such as shopping malls and department stores. They spend much time shopping and may even continue to shop after purchasing. The second group dislikes shopping or is at least neutral toward it. These consumers tend to approach the process from the point of view of saving time or money. People may fit in either category in terms of their own general preference; yet while the purpose for shopping is based on individual differences, for many shoppers the situation dictates whether they are shopping for recreation or for convenience.

Another way of defining these two types of shoppers is to consider them as either task-oriented or nontask-oriented. Shoppers who are interested in the time and money involved in shopping—who wish to make shopping convenient—are task oriented or are in a task-oriented situation. On the other hand, recreational shoppers are nontask-oriented or are in a recreational situation. Task-oriented shoppers are more likely to perceive high density within a store as an inhibitor to their goal achievement and are more likely to experience retail crowding. Nontask shoppers may actually like some crowding, particularly in a mall or on the street, because it provides a stimulus: they can watch other people and discuss things with them.

Time Availability and Product Use

Time availability and time allocation can have a major effect on where consumers shop. For example, work hours generally limit the time that can be devoted to lunch; an office worker may choose a fast-food establishment such as Wendy's for lunch rather than a traditional restaurant, or lunch at home with the family. If time is severely restricted or other activities take precedence, the drive-up window can be used—this is a bit like the "filling station" approach to eating, but it has become a major choice of on-the-go consumers. Similarly, when time does not seem to be the issue, lunch with friends at a shopping center might be in order. Looking at this in another way, a study showed that situational factors, such as the weather or the person's mood, in turn influenced how time was spent.[21] Thus time is a major situational factor because activities for many people are rationed on a time basis and because other situational factors influence how the rationing is done. Some research suggests that in time-pressured situations, department stores lose patronage to mass merchandisers and discount stores.[22]

Where, when, and how the product will be consumed are additional situational variables. For example, whether an item is for self-consumption or is selected as a gift can be a factor. For gifts, mass merchandisers and specialty stores lose shoppers to department stores, and stores with quality images.[23] Apparently, shoppers want to impress the recipients with the quality of the gift source as well as with the item itself.

Russell Belk's study of snack foods provides a good example of the types of situations that can affect the products and brands purchased:[24]

- You are shopping for a snack that you and your family can eat while watching television in the evenings.
- You are planning a party for a few close friends and are wondering what to have around to snack on.
- Snacks at your house have become a little dull lately and you are wondering what you might pick up that would be better.
- You are going on a long automobile trip and are thinking you should bring along some snack to eat on the way.
- You suddenly realize that you have invited a couple of friends over for the evening and have nothing for them to snack on.
- You are at the grocery store when you get an urge for a between-meal snack.
- You are at the supermarket and notice the many available snack products; you wonder if you should pick something up in case friends drop by.
- You are thinking about what type of snack to buy to keep around the house this weekend.
- You are at the store to pick up items for a picnic you are planning with friends and are trying to decide what kind of snack to buy.
- You are thinking about a snack to have with lunch at noon.

Belk found that nearly half the variations in snack preferences depended on the type of circumstance. Beverage commercials have taken advantage of the "situation concept" to position their drinks: "Weekends are made for Michelob," "When it's time to relax, it's Miller time." Bearden and Woodside have shown that beer consumption is likely to vary whether people are entertaining close friends at home, going to a restaurant or lounge on Friday or Saturday nights, taking a weekend trip, or simply relaxing at home.[25] This suggests that marketers who want to understand brand choice more fully should identify the consumption situation at the time consumers are asked about brand preference.

SUMMARY

Many of the other chapters in the book described aspects of people and their mental processes that influence purchase behavior. This chapter explored how aspects of the shopping environment and situation are important as well.

Environmental factors and situational variables affect consumer behavior in several ways. Environmental factors are those characteristics of shopping spaces that create mall, shopping center, and store images. Parking facilities, layout of the area, clientele, and product selection are examples of attributes people use to form images. Atmospherics, the subjective quality of a space where consumers are likely to shop, affect the visual, aural, olfactory, and tactile aspects of the environment that determine mood, comfort, and general feelings. These aspects of atmospherics determine which environments are sought and avoided, how long people shop, and many specific shopping behaviors such as browsing, use of store displays, and so forth. The colors chosen for walls, floor coverings, and accents, as well as the type of background music, influence shoppers moods to the point that they affect their shopping behavior. Density of other shoppers is another environmental condition that influences the atmosphere. When consumers feel crowded they often adjust their shopping patterns and have negative feelings about the crowded store and the shopping trip.

Situational variables, such as time pressure and how the product will be consumed, also influence store selection and brand choice. As is true of other behavior, consumer behavior often depends on the situation. The purpose of a shopping trip, such as for recreation, for convenience, or to purchase a gift will influence where shopping is done and how much time is allocated.

KEY TERMS

environmental factors
situational variables
assortment
facilities
market posture
atmospherics
sociofugal space
sociopetal space
crowding
convenience consumers
recreational consumers

QUESTIONS

1. Distinguish between environmental and situational effects as consumer behaviorists define them. Provide examples of each.

2. Other than to acquire goods and services, what *are* some reasons for shopping?

3. What attributes of a store help to create its image? Select two different types of stores and use several attributes to explain what creates these distinct store images.

4. What are atmospherics? Which sensory mechanisms are involved in communicating atmospherics to shoppers?

5. A company owns two restaurants in a college town. One is near campus, serves primarily lunch, and has limited seating capacity. The other is near a suburban residential area, caters to the dinner crowd, and has plenty of space. What colors would you suggest be used in each restaurant? What objectives are you trying to achieve?

6. What does current research suggest about how consumers are likely to behave under crowding conditions? Can crowding ever be a positive factor? Explain.

7. If perception is an individual phenomenon, how can rules be developed to design stores that influence consumer responses?

8. Imagine you have been asked to design an elite menswear store, a discount record store, and a doctor's office. Briefly describe the design you might suggest and the types of components you would incorporate for each location.

NOTES

1. Ron J. Markin, Charles M. Lillis, and Chem L. Narayana, "Social-Psychological Significance of Store Space," *Journal of Retailing* 52, No. 1 (Spring 1976): 45.
2. Important criteria in shopping center patronage are adapted from James W. Gentry and Alvin C. Burns, "How Important Are Evaluative Criteria in Shopping Center Patronage?" *Journal of Retailing* 53, No. 4 (Winter 1977–78): 73–86.
3. Jay D. Lindquist, "Meaning of Image," *Journal of Retailing* 50, No. 4 (Winter 1974–75): 31.
4. Dale M. Lewison and M. Wayne DeLozier, *Retailing Principles and Practices* (Columbus, OH: Charles E. Merrill Publishing Co., 1982): 151.
5. Philip Kotler, "Atmospherics as a Marketing Tool," *Journal of Marketing* 40, No. 4 (Winter 1973–74): 50.
6. Markin, et al., "Social-Psychological Significance of Store Space," 47.
7. Markin, et al., "Social-Psychological Significance of Store Space," 49.
8. Robert J. Donovan and John R. Rossiter, "Store Atmosphere: An Environmental Psychological Approach," *Journal of Retailing* 58, No. 1 (Spring 1982): 34–37.
9. M. Mehrabian, A. and J. A. Russel, *An Approach to Environmental Psychology* (Cambridge, MA: MIT Press, 1974).
10. An interesting and useful summary of much of the color research with implications for consumer behavior may be found in Joseph A. Bellizzi, and Ayn E. Crowley and Ronald W. Hasty, "The Affects of Color in Store Design," *Journal of Retailing* 59, No. 1 (Spring 1983): 21–45.
11. M. A. Lisnen, "Like Our Music Today, Ms. Shopper?" *Progressive Grocer* 56 (October 1975): 156.
12. Ronald E. Milliman, "Using Background Music to Affect the Behavior of Supermarket Shoppers," *Journal of Marketing* 46 (Summer 1982): 86–91.
13. D. Bellenger, D. H. Robertson, and B. A. Greenberg "Shopping Center Patronage Motives," *Journal of Retailing* 53 (Summer 1977): 29–38; and M. B. Holbrook and E. C. Hirschman, "The Experimental Aspects of Consumption: Consumer Fantasies, Feelings and Fun," *Journal of Consumer Research* 9 (1982): 132–39.
14. D. Stokels, "On the Distinction Between Density and Crowding: Some Implications for Future Research," *Psychological Review* 79 (1972): 275–77.
15. A. H. Esser, "A Biosocial Perspective on Crowding," in *Environment and the Social Sciences: Perspectives and Applications,* J. Wholewill and D. Carsons, eds. (Washington, D.C.: American Psychological Association, 1972), 15–28.
16. J. A. Desser, "Toward a Psychological Theory of Crowding," *Journal of Personality and Social Psychology* 21 (January 1972): 79–83.
17. Russell W. Belk, "Situational Variables and Consumer Behavior," *Journal of Consumer Research* 2 (December 1975): 159.
18. Russell W. Belk, "An Exploratory Assessment of Situational Effects in Buyer Behavior," *Journal of Marketing Research* 11 (May 1974): 157.
19. Jacob Hornik, "Situational Effects on the Consumption of Time," *Journal of Marketing* 46 (Fall 1982): 44–55.
20. D. Bellenger and P. Korganonkar, "Profiling the Recreational Shopper," *Journal of Marketing* 53 (1980); 29–38.
21. Hornik, 44–55.
22. Bruce F. Mattson, "Situational Influences on Store Choice," *Journal of Retailing* 58, No. 3 (Fall 1982).
23. A. Ryans, "Consumer Gift Buying: An Exploratory Analysis," in *Contemporary Marketing Thought,* B. A. Greenberg and D. N. Bellenger, eds. (Chicago: American Marketing Association, 1977), 99–115.
24. Situations for the purchase of snack foods, without the statistical factors, is adapted from Belk, "An Exploratory Assessment of Situational Effects in Buyer Behavior," 160.
25. William O. Bearden and Arch G. Woodside, "Consumption Occasion Influence on Consumer Brand Choice," *Decision Sciences* 9 (April 1978): 273–84.

FURTHER READING

Classics

Bearden, William O., and Arch G. Woodside, "Situational Influence on Consumer Purchase Intentions," in *Consumer and Industrial Buying Behavior,* Woodside, Sheth, and Bennett, eds. (New York: North-Holland, 1977), 167–77.

Belk, R. W., "An Exploratory Assessment of Situational Effects on Buyer Behavior," *Journal of Marketing Research* 11 (May 1974): 157–63.

Belk, R. W., "Situational Variables and Consumer Behavior," *Journal of Consumer Research* 2, (December 1975): 157–163.

Bucklin, Louis P., "Retail Strategy and the Classification of Consumer Goods," *Journal of Marketing* (January 1963): 51–56.

Carman, James M., "Some Generalizations and Problems Regarding Consumer Problem Solving in Grocery Store Channels," in *Models of Buyer Behavior,* Jagdish N. Sheth, ed. (New York: Harper and Row, 1974), 70–87.

Hisrich, Robert D., Ronald J. Dornoff, and Jerome B. Kernan, "Perceived Risk in Store Selection," *Journal of Marketing Research* 7, (1972): 364–69.

Martineau, Pierre, "The Personality of the Retail Store," *Harvard Business Review* 36 (1958): 47–55.

Rich, Stuart U., *Shopping Behavior of Department Store Customers,* (Boston: Graduate School of Business Administration, Harvard University, 1963).

Rich, Stuart U., "The Imageries of Department Stores," *Journal of Marketing* 28 (April 1964): 10–15.

Russell, James A., and Albert Mehrabian, "Environmental Variables in Consumer Research," *Journal of Consumer Research* 3 (June 1976): 62–63.

Spencer, Hover E., James F. Engel, and Roger D. Blackwell, "Perceived Risk in Mail-Order and Retail Store Buying," *Journal of Marketing Research* 7, (August 1970): 364–69.

Tauber, Edward M., "Why Do People Shop?" *Journal of Marketing* 36 (October 1972): 46–59.

Recent Significant Research

Goldstucker, Jac L., Thomas J. Stanley, and George P. Moschis, "How Consumer Acceptance of Videotex Services Might Affect Marketing," in *1984 AMA Educators' Proceedings,* Russell W. Belk, et al., eds. (Chicago: American Marketing Association, 1984), 200–04.

Kakkar, Pradeep, and Richard J. Lutz, "Situational Influence on Consumer Behavior: A Review," in *Perspectives in Consumer Behavior,* Harold H. Kassarjian and Thomas S. Robertson, eds. (Dallas: Scott, Foresman and Company, 1981), 204–14.

Lesser, Jack A., and Susan S. Marine, "An Exploratory Investigation of the Relationship Between Consumer Arousal and Shopping Behavior," in *1984 AMA Educators' Proceedings,* Russell W. Belk, et al., eds. (Chicago: American Marketing Association, 1984), 17–21.

Miller, Kenneth E., and James L. Ginter, "An Investigation of Situational Variation in Brand Choice Behavior and Attitude," *Journal of Marketing Research* 16, No. 1 (February 1979): 111–23.

Milliman, Ronald E., "Using Background Music to Affect the Behavior of Supermarket Shoppers," *Journal of Marketing* 46, No. 3 (Summer 1982): 86–91.

Mittelstaedt, Robert A., Sanford L. Grossbart, and William W. Curtis, "Consumer Perceptions and Retail Mapping: Research Findings and Preliminary Theory," in *Consumer and Industrial Buying Behavior,* Woodside, Sheth, and Bennett, eds. (New York: North-Holland 1977), 95–110.

"Only 10% of Consumers Interested in Shopping at Home via 2-Way TV," *Marketing News* (May 29, 1981): 1.

Sinkula, James M., "A Look at Some Shopping Orientations in Single Parent Households," in *1984 AMA Educators' Proceedings,* Russell W. Belk, et al., eds., 22–25.

Stanley, Thomas J., and Pradeep Korgaonkar, "Explaining Retail Trade in the Urban Environment," in *1984 AMA Educators' Proceedings,* Russell W. Belk, et al., eds. (Chicago: American Marketing Association, 1984), 381–84.

Applications

Atkin, K., "Advertising and Store Patronage," *Journal of Advertising Research* 2, No. 4 (1962): 18–23.

Bellenger, Danny N., Dan H. Robertson, and Barnett A. Greenberg, "Shopping Center Patronage Motives," *Journal of Retailing* 53, no. 2 (Summer 1977) 29–38.

Bither, Steward W., and Ira J. Dolich, "Personality as a Determinant Factor in Store Choice," *Proceedings,* Third Annual Conference, Association for Consumer Research, M. Venkatesar, ed. (Chicago: Association for Consumer Research, 1972), 9–19.

Dash, Joseph F., Leon G. Schiffman, and Conrad Berenson, "Risk- and Personality-Related Dimensions of Store Choice," *Journal of Marketing* 40 (January 1976): 32–39.

Goldman, Arieh, "The Shopping Style Explanation for Store Loyalty," *Journal of Retailing* 53 (Winter 1977–78); 33–46.

Langeard, E., and R. Peterson, "Diffusion of Large Scale Food Retailing in France: *Supermarche et Hypermarche,*" *Journal of Retailing* (Fall 1975): 43–63.

Miller, Kenneth E., and James L. Ginter, "An Investigation of Situational Variation in Brand Choice Behavior and Attitude," *Journal of Marketing Research* 16 (February 1979): 111–23.

Monroe, Kent B., "Objective and Subjective Contextual Influences on Price Perception," in *Consumer and Industrial Buying Behavior,* Woodside, Sheth, and Bennett, eds. (New York: North-Holland, 1977), 287–97.

Monroe, Kent B., and Joseph B. Guiltinan, "A Path-Analytic Exploration of Retail Patronage Influences," *Journal of Consumer Research* 2 (June 1975): 19–28.

Nisbett, Richard E., and David E. Kanouse, "Obesity, Hunger and Supermarket Shopping Behavior," Proceedings of the American Psychological Association, *Journal of Personality and Social Psychology* (August 1969): 290.

Prassad, V. K., "Socioeconomic Product Risk and Patronage Preferences of Retail Shoppers," *Journal of Marketing* 39 (1975): 42–47.

17 Organizational Buying Behavior

Objectives of This Chapter

After you have studied this chapter, you should be able to:

1. Describe the elements in analyzing organizational purchasing.
2. Provide an understanding of the interaction between sellers and buyers of organizational goods and services.
3. Identify the stages in organizational purchasing.
4. Suggest ways in which marketers can analyze organizations, and then influence their purchase decisions.

The chain of purchases made by organizations to move products or services from their origin to the final user of the product usually involves several transactions of substantial volume. For example, the purchase of a nuclear power generation plant can easily cost billions of dollars; the purchase of airplanes, hundreds of millions. At the same time, some industrial purchases, such as office equipment or pharmaceutical products for a hospital, are more comparable to major consumer purchases in total dollar cost. Thus while consumers purchase a larger *number* of goods and services than industry does, the *dollar amount spent* for goods and services purchased by business firms far exceeds that for consumer purchases.

Many of the principles of consumer behavior are applicable to organizational buying situations. This chapter will apply many of the ideas already discussed to the organizational buying process. First we describe the types of organizations that purchase. Next we see the stages in the organizational buying process. Several buying situations are described to show how many organizational purchases occur. Next we examine buying organizations, particularly the types and roles of those involved in organizational purchasing and the motives behind their actions. An overview of the buying process itself shows how an organization moves from discovering the need for a particular product or service to its purchase and evaluation. Factors that influence the organizational buying process are then described to highlight how organizational purchases may be similar to or completely different from one another.

TYPES OF BUYING SITUATIONS

Hundreds of types of buying organizations make purchases in countless categories of goods and services. Fortunately, there are more similarities than differences among the ways these organizations evaluate suppliers and make purchase decisions. This section will describe a few of the kinds of organizations involved in purchasing and explore some of the relationships that exist between buyers and sellers.

Classes of Trade

industrial firms

Organizations belong to either the public sector or the private sector. Figure 17-1 shows the various classes of trade in the United States. In the private sector, the most important category is **industrial firms.** They purchase raw materials, processed materials, heavy and light equipment, and components or subassemblies that go into finished consumer goods. Additionally, many construction and maintenance services are sold to these organizations. Industries also purchase a great many business management services, such as financial transactions, consulting, and data processing. For example, Bethlehem Steel directs its industrial ads to firms

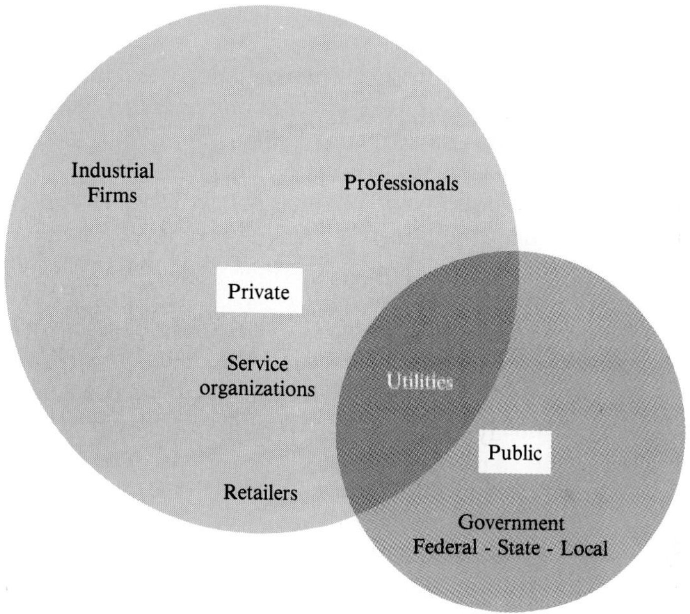

Figure 17-1
Classes of Trade in the United States

At Bethlehem, we're changing our style of managing and operating our businesses.

And the business unit concept is a key element.

More authority and responsibility for their results. More control over their destiny.

That's what we've given most of Bethlehem's operating activities by reorganizing them into business units.

Our new Steel Group is a good example. This business unit is now accountable for the production of Bethlehem's basic steel products, for the sale of those products, and for related services. Its goal is to make Bethlehem the best steel producer in this country, in terms of productivity, quality, service and profitability.

In addition to the Steel Group, we've organized a Manufactured Products Group, responsible for the manufacture and sale of wire rope, industrial fasteners, welded steel-plate products, oil country goods, corrugated culvert pipe and highway drainage products...

...a Natural Resources Group, responsible for the production and sale of products such as coal and stone...

...and a Marine Construction Group, responsible for the construction and servicing of naval and merchant vessels and offshore drilling and production equipment, and the manufacture of industrial products.

All are expected to provide their customers with products that are competitive in quality and price. And all are expected to produce a reasonable return on investment.

Bethlehem 
Bethlehem Steel Corporation
Bethlehem, PA 18016

that might use their product groups for raw materials, component parts, or construction.

service organizations

Service organizations, such as hospitals and other health-care agencies, constitute a second component of the private sector. These organizations make many large purchases, such as medical equipment, computer systems, furnishings for hotels and hospital rooms, and a wide variety of other supplies necessary to maintain their operations. One ad for Dundee Mills addresses the hotel and motel industry's need for towels as a basic supply for the operation of this type of service organization.

The third category of private-sector organizations has increased substantially in recent years. It includes professionals such as doctors, lawyers, business consultants, maintenance and repair people, architects, and accountants who work in small businesses. All of these professionals are part of a complex network of small businesses that each purchase relatively little but as a whole represent a substantial market. Retailers make up a fourth category of private-sector trade. The growth of retail establishments such as fast-food restaurants and chain stores has brought with it substantial opportunities for marketers who can benefit from retailers' increased organizational buying. The whole topic of buying at the retail level is an important subject which deserves additional study.

Dundee
for a host
of reasons.
As a good host, you give your guests what they want. And that includes soft, thick, thirsty towels. With luxury that lasts through hard wear and constant launderings. Today, as for over 92 years, that means Dundee Towels. Performance that pleases you, as well as your guests.
Dundee
Supplying America with Fine Towels
for Almost A Century
Dundee Mills • 111 West 40th Street, New York, N.Y. 10018 • Mills: Griffin, Ga.

Utilities fall within both the public and private sectors, since they are regulated by government but may be privately owned. They make huge

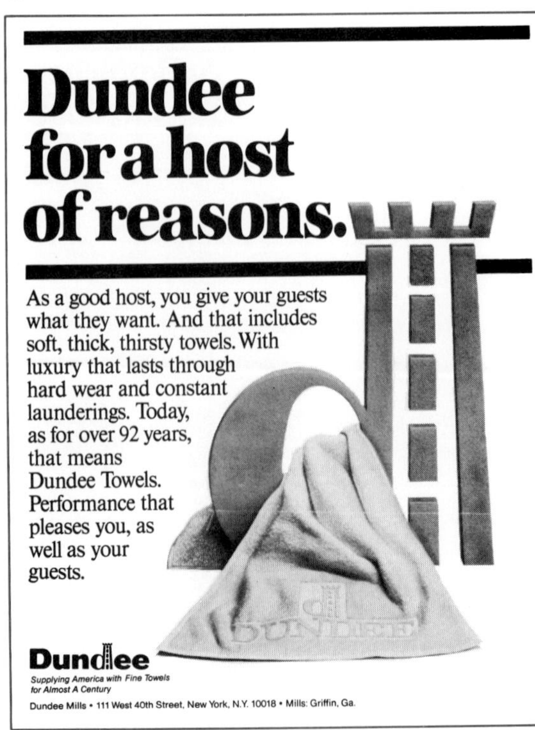

purchases of such commodities as fuels. For example, telephone companies and electric and gas utilities purchase coal, natural gas, and nuclear energy amounting to billions of dollars each year. The purchasing costs of utility companies affect the rates charged to consumers who use their services.

In the public sector, the volume of federal, state, and local government purchases is reaching proportions formerly achieved only by industry. Government purchases of administrative equipment and materials alone are staggering. Such expenditures are necessary to keep these public-sector organizations operating; without them, vital services could not be provided by the government. For example, spending for road construction is administered through government organizations. Military spending for defense systems is also a major category.

Each of these categories of purchasers has been and continues to be studied in depth. Still, many of the same concepts and principles can be used to explain the behavior of all of them. For example, all organizations have at least one person who is responsible to some degree for making decisions regarding products and services that are to be purchased. In most cases, a group of people within the organization are involved in the purchasing effort, which includes interacting with the representatives of the selling organization. Furthermore, the responsibilities for purchasing and consumption are often separated in these firms. That is, the people who purchase and service products for organizations are seldom the people who ultimately consume the products or services. Nevertheless, in the process of purchasing, the decision maker maintains open channels of communication with the end user of the products and services.

This distinction between the purchaser and user, and the formality of purchasing procedures, are the major ways organizational buying behavior differs from consumer buying. Researchers have tried to prove that organizational buying and consumer buying are very different. At first they believed that organizational buying tended to be completely rational, in keeping with the economic business model, while consumer buying tended to be primarily emotional. Later research did not support this theory, so it was revised to suggest that organizational buying was primarily rational with some emotional adjustments, while consumer buying was primarily emotional with some rational adjustments.

Today, both consumer buying behavior and organizational buying behavior are viewed as *problem solving in a social context,* where rationality and emotions affect the decisions of both types of buyers. Table 17-1 summarizes the various stages of beliefs about consumer and industrial buying.

Organizational buyer behavior may appear more rational because to a large degree it is formalized through the policies and practices of business. Yet organizational buying still involves *people selling to people;* therefore, all of the dynamics of interpersonal relations are present in organizational buying situations.

Table 17-1 STAGES IN CONSUMER AND ORGANIZATIONAL BUYING BEHAVIOR THEORY

Era	***Consumer Buying Behavior***	***Organizational Buying Behavior***
Pre-1950s	Emotional	Rational (the economic model)
Transitional period	Emotional and rational	Rational, with adjustments for emotionality
Modern concept	Problem solving in a social context	Problem solving in a social context

The Buyer–Seller Relationship

When people come together to solve problems, relationships develop. Any framework for understanding organizational buyer behavior must be based on the assumption that buyer–seller relations are very likely to grow stronger over time.[1] Due to the complexity and technical nature of most organizational buying situations, buyers and sellers must learn to work together in order to achieve the most equitable exchanges. It generally takes time for each party to understand the other. During the "courtship" period representatives of the purchasing organization express their desires to sellers. In turn, the sellers make suggestions and develop proposals to satisfy the purchasing organization's needs and to provide sufficient profit for the selling organization. Once the relationship between the buying and selling organizations is created, there may be a resistance to change. During the *relationship-building phase,* the purchasing organization does not always have the upper hand. In fact, the relationship is often said to be **symmetrical**—that is, the buying organization and the selling organization have comparable levels of power.[2] Both buyers and sellers frequently feel a very strong need to interact in order to explore all options before signing a contract. Sellers generally offer buyers information to help the buyers formulate ideas about the purchase decision. Buyers also provide sellers with information that helps the sellers do a better job of matching their products and services to the needs of the prospective buyers.

symmetrical (buyer–seller) relationship

Unlike most consumer purchasing, organizational buying involves tailoring the product to the unique needs of individual buyers. This is possible because a single buying organization often represents substantial portions of the selling organization's sales volume. Consequently, buyers and sellers learn to adjust their thoughts and ideas, as well as their actions, to each other. Social interdependencies are formed during this mutual learning process. The resulting situation is often one in which each party holds some form of power over the other. This is why elements such as trust, loyalty, and compromise become so important in organizational buying activities. Interpersonal dynamics may strongly influence any formalized "rules of the game" that result from the relationship.

From the time the buying firm recognizes an unmet need and seeks a supplier, there is a high degree of interaction between various departments within the buying firm. When the selling organization is selected, the numbers and types of interpersonal communications multiply. Therefore, the seller must have a well-organized sales and marketing team to deal with the complexity of these various buying decision makers' influencers.

David Ford studied buyer–seller relationships in industrial markets and identified five periods in the long-term development of purchasing relationships between buyers and sellers.[3]

1. *The pre-relationship period.* Most buying organizations have had extensive experience in purchasing. Thus, evaluation of a potential new supplier might arise when a new purchasing situation is encountered or when a particular episode in an existing relationship stimulates a change. This might be the negative evaluation of an existing supplier's performance or the positive efforts of a nonsupplier. Also, other information (for example, from professional publications, another buying organization, or journals) might stimulate the buying organization to investigate the possibility of a new supplier. The initial evaluation of the new supplier is largely conditioned by experience with previous suppliers, and much uncertainty regarding the new relationship may exist.

2. *The early period.* The early period is marked by discussions regarding elements such as specifications, design, and order routines. Often these items can only be resolved through commitment of a good deal of executive time and energy. During this stage, the distance between the firms begins to narrow in terms of their concept of the product or service. Nevertheless, there is still a great deal of uncertainty about the potential benefit to be derived from the time and money invested in exploring the interest and capabilities of the other party. Generally, both buyer and seller must agree to continue the relationship or it will break off. At any rate, enough energy is generally expended in this stage to assess the probable benefits of a long-term relationship. During this period, the buyer may try using the seller on a small project or for a small volume purchase.

3. *The development period.* The development period usually involves much larger-scale purchases and longer-term contracts. During this period, both parties must make extensive adaptations in order to satisfy each other's needs. Commitment increases on both sides, and any problems that occur are ironed out to create a smooth working relationship.

4. *The long-term period.* This period occurs after many major, long-term purchases have been completed satisfactorily. Because the two parties have extensive experience with each other, they now spend less time and energy exploring aspects of the relationship itself and more on directly productive elements, thereby lowering the price of the transaction. At this point, institutionalization occurs—that is, the buying process becomes routine, and the buyer–seller relationship is solidified.

5. *The final period.* Generally, the final stage occurs when very stable, established markets exist within an industry. There is extensive institutionalization, and the buyer–seller relationship is based on industry codes of practice. The final stage is more likely to occur when life cycles of the seller's products are reaching maturity.

A typical purchasing relationship might follow the above five steps in this manner:

1. Because of poor quality control from a previous supplier, Stoll Motor Company evaluates Johnson and Sons Tool Company as a possible supplier of drill bits for its assembly lines.
2. Stoll discusses specifications and other details in depth with Johnson and Sons as well as with other possible suppliers. Stoll then grants Johnson and Sons a contract for a small-volume purchase.
3. Over a period of several years, Stoll buys larger volumes from Johnson and Sons and the two firms move from single-year contracts to a five-year contract. Some discussion is necessary about acceptable allowances on the bits.
4. Year after year, Johnson and Sons consistently supplies 40% of the bits used in assembly-line operations at Stoll. The purchasing process has become routine.
5. The buyer–seller relationship is now such that Johnson & Sons' biggest customer is Stoll, which formalizes its commitment to buy a certain number of bits per year for an extended period.

A number of factors could interrupt the progression from stage 1 to stage 5 of the buyer–seller relationship. However, it is usually advantageous to both the buying and selling organizations to build a long-term relationship. By doing so, they can do a better job of penetrating the buying organization's markets. Long-term relationships with suppliers allows the buying organization to do a better, more competitive job of marketing to consumers.

Executives at Ford Motor Company have recognized the benefits of increased cooperation with their major suppliers. Recently Ford's top management has instituted policies designed to ensure longer-term cooperation with major suppliers by requiring longer-term contracts with a smaller number of supplying firms. In this way, Ford Motor Company expects to be able to work more closely with those few companies that are selected. The anticipated results include improved cooperation, efficiency, and tighter quality control. This program is a major part of Ford's intensive campaign to improve its quality and competitive position in the United States and in world automotive markets.

TYPES OF BUYING DECISIONS

Potential buyers make four different types of choices:[4] (1) *product* choices involving factors such as type, design, size, and product specifications;

(2) *supplier* choices, which include the selection of particular manufacturers and brands; (3) choices as to the *number of suppliers* to purchase from; and (4) the *decision to buy, rent or lease,* or simply to make the product internally rather than obtain it from an outside source. This book concerns primarily the buyer's decision regarding which supplier or brand to use (2). However, choices of the other three types can be made using processes similar to those described here.

new task
straight rebuy
modified rebuy

Buying decisions can be described according to their newness to the buying organization. One classification scheme divides buying decisions into new task, modified rebuy, and straight rebuy situations.[5] A **new task** situation involves a first-time purchase for the organization. A **straight rebuy** situation involves a routine purchase with which the organization has had a great deal of experience. A **modified rebuy** situation falls somewhere between these two extremes. It occurs when an organization seeks a new supplier for a product it has purchased before. The amount of problem solving is greatest in the new-task situation and least in the straight-rebuy situation. Thus these three purchasing situations are parallel to the categories of extensive problem solving, limited problem solving, and routinized response behavior used by consumers (see Figure 17-2).

Some industrial buying research has shown that new tasks and modified rebuys are fairly similar, while straight rebuys are considerably different.[6] Other researchers have described the three buying situations independently in order to more clearly delineate their differences. Furthermore, most companies are likely to have different formal purchasing procedures for these three situations. Therefore, it is important to differentiate between the two types of rebuy situations as well as between a modified rebuy and a new task situation.

Straight rebuys can be differentiated based on a number of factors. A straight rebuy often takes less than one week and seldom more than seven months, whereas new purchases and modified rebuys require from seven months to five years to complete. Second, a straight rebuy is likely to involve only two or three people; new tasks and modified rebuys often have as many as six members of the organization involved. In fact, it is

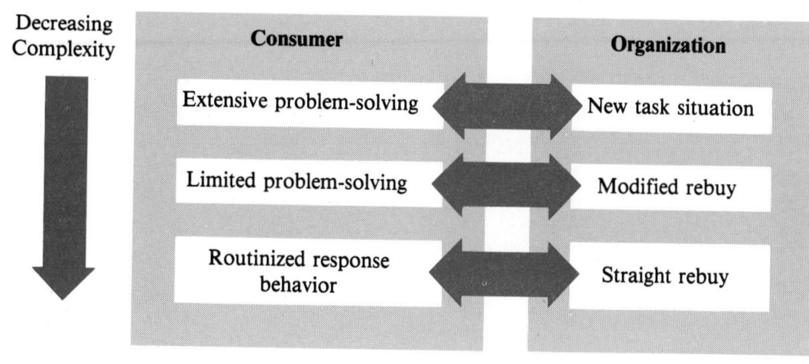

Figure 17-2
Equivalent Buying Decisions of Consumers and Organizations

normal for the purchasing agent to be part of all stages of a straight rebuy situation yet have only limited involvement in new-task and modified-rebuy purchases. Consequently, purchasing agents are much more likely to initiate the purchasing activities in straight rebuy situations. By contrast, new purchases and modified rebuys are more often initiated by people in the operations departments than by those in purchasing.

There are usually fewer distinct differences between modified rebuys and new purchases. Modified rebuys often require less time to evaluate and negotiate than new tasks, since frequently some form of standardization is in place. Fewer people are involved in a modified rebuy than in a new purchase, especially when the modification is not extensive.

Richard Cardozo has suggested that for management purposes it is useful to consider the three types of buying tasks as separate from one another.[7] In this way, managers can group buyers in a modified rebuy situation either with buyers in new-task situations or with those in straight-rebuy situations, depending on the circumstances. They can also treat modified rebuys independently. Table 17-2 illustrates many of the differences between the three types of purchasers from the earliest stage of problem recognition through the final performance evaluation of the supplier. Note, for example, that the table shows the initiator of a purchase in a new-task situation as senior management, marketing, engineer-

Table 17-2 DIFFERENCES AMONG BUYCLASSES

Activity in Purchase Process	***New Task***	***Modified Rebuy***	***Straight Rebuy***
Source of problem/opportunity recognition	New-product development Analysis of operations Expansion of capacity	Change in specifications or process for existing product Expansion of operations New offer from nonsupplier; dissatisfaction with current supplier (Resembles straight rebuy except for seeking bids from nonsuppliers)	Inventory control system Production schedule Sales forecast
Initiator of purchase	Senior management; marketing, engineering, or research	Engineering; purchasing	Purchasing, or department using the product
Source of contact with supplier	Line managers, technical specialists	Manufacturing, engineering and/or purchasing	Purchasing
Membership in decision-making unit	Senior management; functional managers; technical specialists from marketing, engineering manufacturing; purchasing specialist	Line managers, technical specialists, purchasing	Purchasing; engineering; manufacturing

Table 17-2 DIFFERENCES AMONG BUYCLASSES, continued

Activity in Purchase Process	*New Task*	*Modified Rebuy*	*Straight Rebuy*
Determination and description of characteristics and quantity of items to be purchased	Extensive requests for information and samples from vendors, informally and through formal requests for quotation to determine specifications; forecasts to determine quantity for new product	New specification from engineering; quantities from sales and production forecasts	Specifications available from prior purchases; quantities from sales and production forecasts; negligible information sought from suppliers
Search for and qualification of sources	Intensive working sessions (perhaps including site visit) with suppliers who appear interested and capable. Technical specialists interested in reducing number of prospective vendors; buyers interested in increasing number	Respond to nonsupplier initiative; contact current vendors and perhaps other nonsuppliers	Contact current vendors and perhaps others considered capable
Acquisition and analysis of proposals	Obtain and analyze formal quotations, samples, results of tests; refine specifications	In some cases, seek new quotations from established suppliers; in others, seek new information only from nonsupplier involved	For annual or continuing supply agreement, seek quotations from vendors who have qualified; for individual purchases, draw against supply agreement
Evaluation of offers, suppliers	Evaluation by technical personnel; senior management may add other considerations not directly related to value analysis	Technical evaluation of nonsupplier's offering	Evaluate against preset criteria, price and delivery offered; some organizations maintain multiple sources
Negotiation	Much negotiation on specifications, performance, and guarantee; some on delivery; little on price	Negotiation with emphasis on price and delivery	Minimum negotiation; emphasis on price, delivery and terms of sale
Selection of order routine and performance evaluation	Routine for new task varies by organization; new vendors monitored closely at first	Similar to new task for new vendor; similar to straight rebuy for established supplier	Order routine specified in supply agreement; in addition to regular informal contact, evaluation through formal vendor rating system; exception reports from using department
Length of process	7–60 months	7–60 months	1 week to 7 months

Source: adapted from Richard N. Cardozo, "Situational Segmentation In Industrial Markets," *European Journal of Marketing* 14 (May–June 1980): 266–67.

ing, or research. By contrast, the initiator in a straight rebuy is likely to be the purchasing department. Note also the complexity of the search for and qualification of sources in a new task situation as contrasted to the procedure in a straight-rebuy situation. The three types of buying situation—new task, modified rebuy, straight rebuy—are referred to as **buyclasses.**

buyclasses

The type of purchase is likely to have an impact on how the buying organization handles each stage of the purchase process. In a later section we will look more closely at each stage in the purchase process. At this time it is enough to note that whether a purchase is a new task, a modified rebuy, or a straight rebuy has a significant impact on how the buying and selling organizations carry out the purchasing process.

KEY POSITIONS IN THE BUYING ORGANIZATION

Other employees in a buying organization besides professional purchasing agents are important to the purchasing process. Because these people have different backgrounds and functions in the company, they have different motives for purchasing. Consequently, they use different criteria to evaluate organizational purchases. This section highlights the position titles of people who are most often involved in organizational purchasing and how their roles and criteria vary from situation to situation.

lateral involvement

As was mentioned before, purchasing can involve people from several areas in the company. **Lateral involvement** describes the interaction of people with different functions at approximately the same level of management within an organization. Lateral involvement in purchasing can come from areas such as purchasing, engineering, production, and sales and marketing.[8] Generally, these individuals hold positions at approximately the same level within the organization. Thus, these people have about the same status due to their positions in the company. However, their influence on purchasing can vary considerably based on their needs and backgrounds.

vertical involvement

On the other hand, decisions can involve communication up or down the chain of command within a single functional area. **Vertical involvement** refers to the interaction of different levels of management within a particular functional area involved in the purchasing decision. In many cases vertical involvement in purchasing can be as shallow as one level or as deep as five or six.[9] For example, the need to purchase new equipment may arise on the production floor and be relayed to a foreman. He might approach the production engineer, who seeks approval from the production manager or plant manager. If the purchase is quite extensive and costly, there may be a need to involve the vice president of manufacturing and even the company president. Alternatively, if the cost is relatively low, the production engineer may have authority to approve the purchase.

The Purchasing Agent

purchasing agents

Purchasing agents are hired to help their organizations buy a broad range of products and services most effectively. To contribute to the smooth running of the organization as a whole, they establish and enforce purchasing policies that help maintain consistent purchase arrangements with all of the organization's vendors. Thus, many of the purchasing agents' activities involve the *administration* of purchasing. At the same time, they are exposed to many sellers and gain a good deal of experience in negotiations. Through training programs, purchasing agents can learn how to obtain the best delivery, price, and financing possible, while meeting product specifications.

Some purchasing agents are extremely important executives in some major corporations. Others are simple order takers for procurement in other companies. Recently, because of restricted supply conditions and a greater recognition of the savings which can be achieved from cost-effective purchasing, purchasing agents have received more attention. The professional training of veteran purchasing agents varies considerably; many have backgrounds in manufacturing, engineering, business, accounting, and other fields. However, in recent years college programs emphasizing the purchasing functions have been developed. More and more students are taking these programs and are obtaining specialized education before they are hired. When they enter the work force, they may be better equipped than were their predecessors to deal with the interchange between sellers and their own buying organizations.

The Functional Managers

At one time or another in their careers, most functional managers will be involved in negotiations to buy equipment or supplies for their company. The people typically called on to play a role in purchasing decisions tend to come from the following areas:

Administration, including accounting and finance, who help evaluate the cost effectiveness of projects;
Design engineering, who buy equipment and material to be applied to products the company is marketing;
Research and development, who look at basic materials and supplies rather than specific applications;
Manufacturing, who are often responsible for production equipment and processing approaches;
Technical specialists, who advise others regarding the best brands and suppliers for a particular product type.

Additionally, a broad range of users can have immense impact on the types and brands of products selected. For example, secretaries often play a major role in determining the types of transcription and dictation equipment, and the typewriters selected for their use. Maintenance engineers provide critical input regarding products that require many replacement parts. A classic study, *How Industry Buys/1970,* showed that the relative influence of people from different areas of the organization varied according to the criteria or motives for the purchase. The study also showed that the motives themselves depended on the type of industrial products being purchased.[10] In Table 17-3, equipment purchases are examined in terms of the frequency with which different functional areas joined in the decision to initiate the purchase, make the product choice, and choose the supplier. Technical and engineering personnel participate more frequently in product selection decisions, while the purchasing department tends to have its greatest involvement in supplier selection.

ROLES IN THE BUYING ORGANIZATION

There are a number of roles played by people in the buying organization that have an impact on product and supplier choice. Among the most important are the gatekeeper, the information seeker, the advocate, the linking pin, and the decision maker. To some extent, these can be compared to roles played by family members making consumer decisions, and to member roles in all formal groups, discussed in chapters 12, 13 and 14.

Gatekeepers

gatekeepers

Gatekeepers control the flow of commercial sources of information into the buying organization. Purchasing agents have often been referred to as gatekeepers because they are usually the first people sales representatives must deal with in the buying organization. They are responsible for screening all of the potential sellers and then allowing only a few outsiders to reach key decision makers in the buying company. In the absence of a strong purchasing organization, or in cases where unusual or complicated products are being purchased, such as high-technology parts, the gatekeeper could be someone outside the purchasing area. This type of gatekeeper has special knowledge about the products or services being purchased. For example, the head of the engineering department might recommend that in all areas of the company where engineering consulting services are required, a few suppliers with whom they have working relationships should be contacted. General Motors has taken similar action to control purchases of computer hardware. Because of the size and complexity of GM, it has been approached by hundreds of selling organizations attempting to market mini- and personal computers. To facilitate internal communications and to obtain the best pricing and delivery on these products, GM has asked its computer experts to screen out vendors that are least desirable in terms of the needs of the entire organization. When other departments are planning to buy computer hardware and need information, they typically call the gatekeeper in the computer

Table 17-3 HOW INDUSTRY BUYS EQUIPMENT

		Area of the organization most likely to initiate a project leading to the purchase of new equipment									
		Overall corporate policy and planning	Operations and administration	Design and development engineering	Production engineering	Research	Finance	Sales	Purchasing	Others in company	Others outside of company
Reason for Purchase	Replace existing equipment	15.6	**43.8**	**27.8**	**51.2**	12.1	3.1	1.5	5.9	11.5	1.8
	Expand capacity	**39.4**	**45.9**	16.5	**38.8**	6.0	3.3	5.3	2.5	7.8	1.5
	Change production processes	11.1	**28.9**	**27.6**	**70.2**	14.0	.8	.9	1.6	7.4	1.6
	Take advantage of new materials	5.6	19.1	**53.4**	**46.6**	**29.5**	.7	1.7	5.6	7.7	1.8
	Manufacture new products	**35.9**	**33.4**	**34.4**	32.7	22.0	2.2	10.0	3.1	7.9	2.4
Product Choice	Who surveys alternatives and determines kind (not make) of equipment?	5.6	**22.9**	**47.6**	**52.5**	17.8	.6	1.1	16.2	10.2	1.6
	Who determines specifications and characteristics to be met by the equipment?	3.6	17.2	**54.0**	**53.8**	**18.2**	.2	.9	5.7	10.9	2.2
Supplier Choice	Who surveys available makes of the specified equipment and chooses suppliers from whom to invite bids?	3.9	17.0	**36.3**	**41.4**	10.3	1.0	1.1	**60.4**	12.1	1.3
	Who evaluates offered equipment for accord with specifications?	2.5	16.1	**45.4**	**52.4**	13.4	.4	.6	**17.7**	15.3	1.4
	Who decides which supplier gets the order?	10.2	25.3	**28.8**	**32.9**	8.4	1.9	1.3	**61.7**	11.3	1.1

Source: adapted from *How Industry Buys/1970* (New York: Scientific American, 1969), 45.

Percentages indicate the frequency with which the various management functions were reported to participate in the successive steps of the purchasing process. Boldface highlights the three most-mentioned functions for each purchasing step.

When industry as a whole buys equipment, the choice of make or supplier is limited by company preference or policy in setting up the required specifications and characteristics as follows:

	Percent of cases
Limited to one make	23
Limited to two makes	18

area and ask him or her which firms would be considered good suppliers and whom they should contact.

preferred provider lists

It is very common for buying organizations to use **preferred provider lists**. Only those firms that the company will consider when purchasing items appear on the list. For example, a hospital might have one or more vendors listed for each type of pharmaceutical product, each type of equipment, and each major supply product. In this case, the gatekeepers would be the people who initially screened the vendors and developed the list. In a family decision setting this gatekeeper's function can be compared to the role a spouse might play, for example, in choosing what makes of cars are acceptable to buy and then presenting those limited choices to the other spouse.

Clearly, excellent organizational salespeople are those who succeed in working around and through the gatekeepers. Strong salespeople know how to open the gate in order to see people in the organization that perform other crucial buying roles. Generally, the gatekeeper understands the roles played by other people in the organization; the cooperative gatekeeper can direct salespeople to whomever they should talk to in order to have the greatest impact. Successful salespeople are able to locate gatekeepers and work through them to reach others.

Information Seekers

information seekers

A great deal of information about products, competitors, and suppliers is required for major purchases. **Information seekers** locate data that can be used by themselves or others during the purchasing process. Often the purchasing department is responsible for obtaining lists of firms or alternative types of products that can satisfy the buyer's needs. However, the information-seeking task is performed by others with particular knowledge in the area—much as information seeking on consumer matters can be performed by either spouse (or by a child, although he or she does not actually make the purchase decision for the family).

The information-seeking role differs from the gatekeeping role. The information seeker looks for sources of information; while the gatekeeper tends to *reject* sources of information and limit the number of people and companies that are allowed access to the buying firm. Naturally, marketers can make the job of the information seeker easier by presenting relevant product data clearly and in an accessible manner.

Advocates

advocates

The advocate exercises a powerful influence over group decisions.[11] In fact, advocacy is a form of group leadership. **Advocates** are usually people who participate most in group discussions, have higher status, and assume leadership roles. There are both appointed leaders and emergent leaders. *Appointed leaders* generally ask questions and help the group synthesize opinions in order to arrive at conclusions. *Emergent leaders* assume responsibility on their own, offer opinions, and give recommendations.

A similar role is performed in families as they make decisions as consumers. Recall that we discussed the role of specialist or expert that a family member might play in decisions given his or her level of knowledge about a product area. Thus a leader may be appointed or may emerge naturally for family decisions as well as for buying organizations.

Advocates often obtain their power from the amount of interaction they have with organizations outside their own and from the amount of expertise they have about particular topics. Advocates can use their powerful positions to inhibit the communications (for example, the recommendations) of less powerful people in the organization. Thus advocates can serve to support one seller's offering as well as to restrict the impact of competitors' presentations. Consequently, selling organizations often seek high-status, knowledgeable, and articulate people within the buying organization to help promote their products and services. Obviously, if a salesperson is to succeed, one or more advocates must take the salesperson's side during the purchase deliberation.

Linking Pins

linking pins

Whereas advocates, information seekers, and gatekeepers are boundary people who determine how much contact takes place between selling firms and buying organizations, **linking pins** establish contact between areas in the buying organization.[12] Linking pins hold key positions that require them to interact with linking pins in other parts of the company. These people are particularly important to marketers of products and services that will have an impact on several parts of the buying company. For example, electronic data-processing and telecommunications equipment are likely to be used by many employees. It is much easier to sell to an organization when its linking pins cooperate.

Linking pins communicate with each other both formally and informally. In many cases, the communication from a selling firm to one linking pin reverberates throughout the entire company due to this communication. In order to benefit from more unified purchasing, linking pins pull together diverse organizational components. Again, it is critical for good salespeople to locate those linking pins that draw organizations together and provide maximum benefits for the amount of communication.

Yoram Wind and Thomas Robertson introduced the idea of linking pins to buyer behavior theory based on concepts from the study of organizational behavior.[13] They found that the specific organizational roles of linking pins tend to differ according to the nature of the firm, but people with similar functions (department heads) tended to act as linking pins within the various firms. For example, they discovered that within hospitals there are both administratively oriented and professionally oriented linking pins. The former were comprised of administrators holding management positions within various areas of the hospital. The latter (in this case, radiologists) perceived themselves as technical people.

Wind and Robertson also found that organizations in which administratively oriented linking pins predominated were more innovative than were organizations composed mostly of professionally oriented linking pins. This suggests that marketers should look for linking pins within the management structure as well as within the technical structure of organizations in order to best define what "glue" holds large or multifaceted companies together in a purchasing sense.

Decision Makers

Industrial buying is problem solving in a social context, as we have seen. From time to time, the social process makes it difficult to identify precisely who makes a purchase decision and when the decision is actually made. Often the selling organization solidifies its relationship with the buying group over a period of time. It is this **"creeping commitment"** to the selling organization that frequently determines who gets the order. On the other hand, in *fixed-bid purchase* situations (in which suppliers simply state a price for their product according to specifications set by the buyer) the decision to purchase could depend on how the specifications are drawn up in the first place. This is because the specifications and the price themselves might be developed in a way so that only one supplier's product fits the purchase request. Some salespeople of industrial products work closely with the buying organization at the time specifications are made to influence the buyer in favor of their product.

"creeping commitment"

In many cases the salesperson can identify exactly who will make the purchase decision. In some organizations the **decision maker** is the purchasing agent. However, it is more common for the actual decision to be made by a buying committee or by someone besides the purchasing agent who has some budgetary authority and long-term connection with the product or service. Buying committees are usually used for repeat purchases. For example, retail organizations use elaborate buying committee structures to help them provide the best products to their customers. Where buying committees are also involved in decision making, salespeople are usually asked to give presentations to the committee, or to supply information so that one member of the committee can make the presentation to the entire group.

decision maker

As already mentioned, it is not always possible to reach the decision maker directly. However, in many cases the selling organization selected is the one that has made contacts with each of the buying influencers and has most impressed the decision maker or decision-making group.

Users

users

Users are those who work with the product or service. In manufacturing firms they are the employees who use or service production equipment; when component parts are to be purchased, the users are the people who assemble the parts. In hospitals and other health-care facilities, users might be nurses and physicians, or the technicians who operate medical equipment. In other professional organizations they might be the computer programmers or the technical support staff that interface with computers. There are almost as many types of users as there are job descriptions. Their influence on the purchasing process varies from almost none to extreme.

Users can influence the entire buying process by providing valuable feedback to sales representatives about how well the product has performed. In some cases users, particularly those who have a high degree of expertise, have even provided input for the development of product specifications. The sophisticated sales representative penetrates the entire organization to obtain their feedback, in turn providing them with information to make the product or service operate as smoothly as possible. Because users often influence purchasing, it is important to understand their requirements and needs.

STAGES IN THE ORGANIZATIONAL BUYING PROCESS

buyphases

buygrid

An important early research project described the industrial buying process in eight stages, called **buyphases**. The study also described the newness of the purchase to the buyer in terms of *buyclasses*—new task, modified rebuy, straight rebuy—which were discussed earlier. Table 17-4 outlines these buyphases and buyclasses and combines them to form the **buygrid**, a convenient way to see the relationships between the two.

Since that study was done, researchers have formulated organizational buying processes. The most complete is the list supplied by Yoram Wind and Robert J. Thomas:[14]

1. ***Identification of need*** The buying organization identifies the need either to make a new purchase or to reorder products or services it has already been purchasing.

2. ***Establish specifications*** Specifications generally include the technical aspects of the product or service. During this stage, members of the buying organization carefully describe what is required to satisfy the need.

3. ***Search for alternatives*** The organization discovers sources to provide the product or service. This may involve a lengthy search for new products or a very limited search in automatic reorder situations.

4. ***Establish contact*** The buying organization or the selling firm establishes face-to-face contact for the in order to arrive eventually at some conclusion. This process may extend for only a few hours or for many years depending on the nature of the product.

Table 17-4 THE BUYGRID FRAMEWORK FOR INDUSTRIAL BUYING SITUATIONS

	Buyclasses		
Buyphases	***New Task***	***Modified Rebuy***	***Straight Rebuy***
1. Identification of need			
2. Establish specifications			
3. Search for alternatives			
4. Establish contact			
5. Set purchase and usage criteria			
6. Evaluate alternatives			
7. Budget availability			
8. Evaluate specific alternatives			
9. Negotiate			
10. Buy			
11. Use			
12. Post-purchase evaluation			

Source: from the Marketing Science Institute series, *Industrial Buying and Creative Marketing,* by Patrick J. Robinson, Charles W. Ferris, and Yoram Wind (Boston: Allyn and Bacon Inc., 1967). Adapted to include stages from later work by Yoram Wind and Robert J. Thomas, "Conceptual and Methodological Issues in Organizational Buying Behavior," *European Journal of Marketing* 14 (May–June 1980): 239–65.

5. *Set purchase and usage criteria* The buying organization establishes the basis for deciding what is to be purchased. Product attributes and criteria such as design features, pricing and delivery, or use characteristics and service standards are set.

6. *Evaluate alternatives* The buying organization matches products or suppliers with the criteria set forth in the previous stage in order to determine which source best meets the requirements of the purchasing organization. (Note that stages 5 and 6 reflect attitude theory as presented in Chapter 4).

7. *Budget availability* The buying organization allocates funds for the purchase, and approval of funding is gained.

8. *Evaluate specific alternatives* Where step 6 evaluated the general alternatives, such as the type of product and whether to purchase, lease, or rent, in this step the buying organization evaluates the specific alternatives by brand.

9. *Negotiate* At this stage, buyer and seller enter into active communication about the terms of the contract.

10. *Buy* The buyer selects a particular supplier, signs the contracts, and arranges for delivery of the product.

11. *Use* The buyer evaluates the product according to whether it does the job as anticipated.

12. *Post-purchase evaluation* The buyer makes a formal analysis of how well the supplier, as well as the product, meets the needs of the organization.

Table 17-5 THE INVOLVEMENT OF VARIOUS HOSPITAL BUYING CENTERS IN CERTAIN STAGES OF THE PROCUREMENT PROCESS

Buying Center	*Identification of Need*	*Establishment of Objectives*	*Evaluation*	*Selection*
Physicians	High	High	High	High
Nursing	Low	High	High	Low
Administration	Moderate	Moderate	Moderate	High
Engineering	Low	Moderate	Moderate	Low
Purchasing	Low	Low	Low	Low

Source: adapted from Gene R. Laczniak, "An Empirical Study of Hospital Buying," *Industrial Marketing Management* 8 (January 1979): 61.

One study of procurement of medical equipment in hospitals demonstrates how stages in the buying decision process are influenced by different people in the buying organization. Table 17-5 summarizes the results of this study. The high involvement of physicians contrasts sharply with the low involvement of purchasing people in all four stages of the procurement process. This indicates how important it is for salespeople to move beyond purchasing personnel to influential people in other parts of the organization. It is also interesting to note that administration (management) was most involved at the stage when a supplier was selected.

It is important to remember that not all purchases require the twelve buying stages just listed. Straight rebuys use the fewest stages, modified rebuys use more, and new-task situations may involve all stages of the buying process. Again, as the buying organization moves from initial problem identification through purchase of the product and subsequent evaluation and feedback, the process of creeping commitment takes place. As stated earlier, if the buying organization repeatedly finds satisfaction with the seller's products, the buyer will begin to build lasting relationships with the seller. These lasting relationships will shorten the buying process and make the purchase process simpler for both buyer and seller.

AN OVERVIEW OF INFLUENCING FACTORS: THE SHETH MODEL OF INDUSTRIAL BUYER BEHAVIOR

The buying process is seldom the same from one firm to the next, or even from one purchase to the next within a given firm. In each case, the decision-making process of the buying organization is affected by a number of factors.

While the work of Wind and others provides an understanding of the *stages* of the buying process, Jagdish Sheth created a model of industrial buyer behavior that focuses on the factors that affect the purchase process (Figure 17-3).[15]

The Sheth model should be looked at from the standpoint of the buying organization. The numbers of Sheth's diagram suggest the starting

Figure 17-3
An Integrative Model of Organizational Buying Behavior

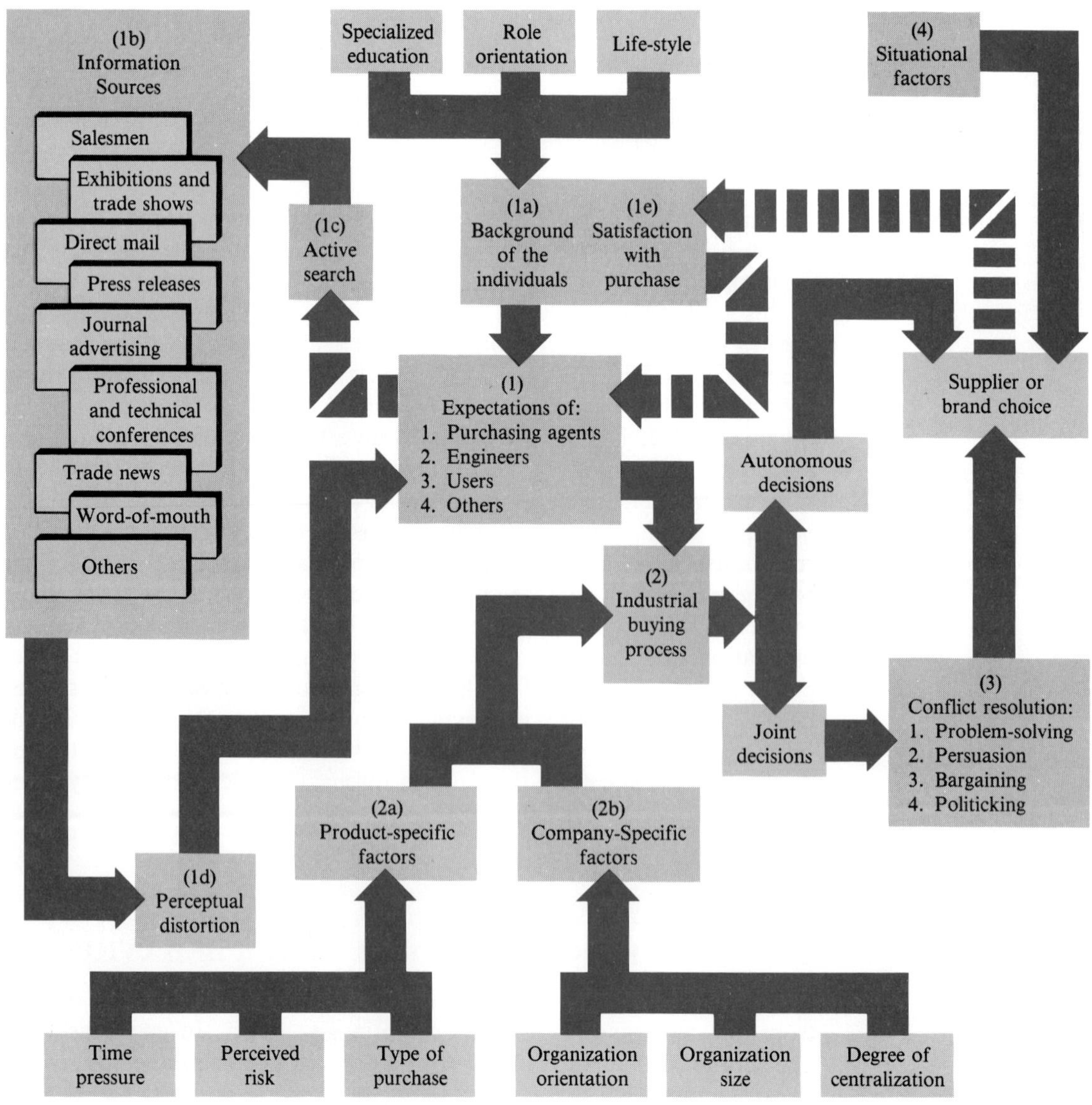

Source: Jagdish N. Sheth, "A Model of Industrial Buyer Behavior," *Journal of Marketing* 37, No. 4 (October 1973): 50–56.

point and sequence in which an industrial firm's buying behavior occurs and can be analyzed. The solid arrows indicate roughly the direction of the process that links each part of industrial buyer behavior. The dashed arrows show the feedback that occurs during and after purchase. The model includes over twenty factors that should be considered when viewing the buyer's purchase behavior from the buyer's own perspective. One factor involves the backgrounds and expectations of participants in the buying decision. Purchasing agents, engineers, users, and others in the buying organization have expectations that match their backgrounds. These expectations, in turn, influence the criteria used by the various influencers for decision making. *Specialized education* has a great deal to do with the way people look at problems. For example, engineers are likely to look at situations much differently than finance people do. Engineers are more highly trained in the technical aspects of the product and, consequently, are likely to judge the product on those aspects; financial managers may be more inclined to look at the numbers and evaluate products on the basis of profitability. Salespeople should examine and understand the specialized education of decision makers.

Role orientation refers to the way people see themselves within the organization. For example, whether they view themselves as an executive member of the buying committee or as a minor influence in the purchase process greatly affects the degree of their involvement in the decision. At the same time, the five roles of gatekeeper, advocate, linking pin, decision maker, and user clearly influence the expectations of the individuals who fill these roles. *Life-style* refers to one's mode of living, as described in Chapter 9. The life-styles of those who participate in purchase decisions affect the social processes and financial aspects of the industrial buying situation. Through these and other inputs, discussed below, the Sheth model provides a broad look at the factors that may come into play in an industrial buying decision.

The purchase criteria used by each member of the purchasing organization determine to a large degree how each perceives products and suppliers. The results of a study of the industrial purchase of solar air conditioning illustrate some of the expectations purchasers have. As Table 17-6 shows, the important decision-making criteria are somewhat different for each of the five types of purchasing influencers in this purchasing situation.

Information Sources

Expectations are also conditioned by the *sources of information,* shown on the left side of the Sheth model. Active search takes place for information from salespeople, exhibitions and trade shows, direct mail, press releases, journal advertising, professional and technical conferences, trade news, word-of-mouth, and other sources. Studies show that, in

Table 17-6 ISSUES OF IMPORTANCE IN THE FORMULATION OF INDIVIDUAL PREFERENCES FOR SOLAR AIR CONDITIONING SYSTEMS

Decision Maker	*More Important*	*Less Important*
Production engineers	Operating costs Energy savings Reliability Complexity	Cost Field proven
Corporate engineers	Cost Field proven Reliability Complexity	Energy savings Up-to-date
Plant managers	Operating costs Use of unproductive areas Up-to-date Power failure protection	Cost Complexity
Top managers	Up-to-date Energy savings Operating costs	Noise level in plant Reliability
Consultants	Noise level in plant First cost Reliability	Up-to-date Energy savings Operating costs

Source: adapted from Jean-Marie Choffray and Gary L. Lilien, "Assessing Response to Industrial Marketing Strategy," *Journal of Marketing* 42 (April 1978): 30.

general, personal sources of information are most important in the industrial buying process. However, these studies also indicate that industrial advertising is a good partner to personal selling.[16]

Sheth connects the concept of *perceptual distortion* with information sources simply to indicate that information is not seen objectively; it is distorted in a way that is unique to the receiver, whether that person is a purchasing agent, an engineer, or a user. Because each of those responsible for decision making perceives information differently, there is likely to be several opinions regarding each potential supplier.

Industrial Buying Process

Sheth expanded on prior concepts of industrial buying by indicating that product-specific factors and company-specific factors could influence various stages of the organizational buying process.

Product-Specific Factors

Product-specific factors include the product's use, specific application, and degree of standardization.[17] Product use varies widely, from products or services for maintenance, components for the organization, finished products, and materials used in the production process, to equipment of all sorts. For example, equipment could be used for replacement of existing equipment, to retrofit new equipment, to retrofit existing equipment, or for new and expanded facilities. The nature of the product has a good deal to do with who is involved in the purchase decision. For example, senior management might be interested in materials for new products, while production engineering would be interested in materials both for existing products and new products. Design engineering, on the other hand, might concentrate primarily on new products for necessary components and their specific applications. Time pressure, perceived risk, and the type of purchase affect the product-specific factors. *Time pressure* relates to the speed with which the purchase must be made. Although time pressure has received little attention from researchers, it can be a major factor. For example, when a great deal of time is required and is allotted to make a purchase, many more members of the buying organization can be involved in a purchase decision. Perceived risk was discussed at length in Chapter 3, on perception. Much of the research on perceived risk has been based on organizational buying behavior. Recall that perceived risk deals not with what can be gained, but with what can be *lost* by making the purchase. Perceived risk also involves the amount of certainty or uncertainty the buyer (in this case, the buying organization) has regarding the product. Five types of uncertainty or risks have been identified:[18]

1. Need uncertainty
2. Technical uncertainty
3. Market uncertainty
4. Acceptance uncertainty
5. Transaction uncertainty

need uncertainty **technical uncertainty** **market uncertainty** **acceptance uncertainty** **transaction uncertainty**

Need uncertainty occurs early in the purchase process when the buying organization has not yet established the specifications for the product. **Technical uncertainty** occurs when buyers are unsure about the performance of a product or service in their own particular environment. For example, they question whether a component would work in a production process specific to their organization. **Market uncertainty** occurs when buyers are unsure of the offerings from which they can select. When a wide variety of product offerings are available, buying organizations may have to maintain contact with a broad range of selling organizations. In times of extreme change, market uncertainty can be increased. **Acceptance uncertainty** is a general hesitancy which arises when people in a buying organization are not sure of their need for a product. Finally, **transaction uncertainty** involves risk associated with the terms of the sale and delivery of the product. Clearly, the newer the purchase situation, the greater the amount of perceived risk.

When uncertainty is high, buyers strive to reduce the amount of perceived risk by either decreasing the amount at stake or increasing the amount of information they have at their disposal. Decreasing the amount at stake can result in smaller purchase orders or a reluctance to pay top prices. When there is something at stake socially, others in the organization may be brought in to help make the purchase decision and, thus, spread the risk around.

The *type of purchase* refers to whether it is a new task, modified rebuy, or straight rebuy. It is interesting to see how purchases in these three categories affect the organization's use of joint decisions versus autonomous decisions in the Sheth model. New-task situations clearly involve more people, and would most likely be joint decisions rather than autonomous decisions. Modified rebuys are equally likely to be joint or autonomous decisions. Straight rebuys would most likely be autonomous decisions, handled by members of the purchasing organization or, in some cases, by people in the data processing department.

Company-Specific Factors

Three company-specific factors influence the purchasing process: the organization's orientation, its size, and its degree of centralization.

Organizations have definite *orientations*. Some companies are dominated by production; for others, marketing is most influential; in still others, finance or accounting holds sway. When marketing dominates, sales factors tend to be very important in making purchase decisions. In production-oriented organizations, production factors are most important. In finance-oriented organizations, decisions are likely to be made on the basis of cost and other financial concerns. Thus, for salespeople in the selling firm, knowing the organization's orientation is key to determining the basis for purchasing decisions and which members of the buying group are most influential in making them.

The *size of the organization* is also likely to influence the number of people involved in purchasing. For example, in very small organizations informal purchasing processes tend to dominate. Decisions are often made by key executives at the top of the organization. Very large organizations use formalized purchasing processes, and decisions are often made by members lower in the organizational structure.

The *degree of centralization* influences purchasing because highly decentralized organizations are likely to give their various departments or divisions autonomy to make their own purchases. However, such companies generally have formal buying procedures that can bog down the buyers and sellers in red tape.

Joint Decisions and Conflict Resolution

Whenever several people are involved in decision making, there is a potential for conflict. Recall the discussion, in Chapter 15, of the various strategies families use to handle conflict in the decision-making process: problem solving, persuasion, and bargaining. Similarly, Sheth has identified four ways that organizations can resolve conflicts when they occur. The first two ways, problem solving and persuasion, are considered to be "mature" methods of handling conflict because the channels of communication among the parties remain open. The second two ways, bargaining and politicking, are considered to be "immature" because each party is attempting to get "its own way" without considering the organization's goals or engaging in open communication.

Problem solving occurs when all members of the organization agree on the goals of the particular purchase. When problem solving is the basic way of resolving conflict in the buying organization, the marketers should address specific goals set forth by the organization to show how their product can, in fact, help the organization meet those goals.

Persuasion occurs when different members within the organization have different goals or criteria for the purchase. Persuasion often involves one person trying to convince another that his or her goals should take precedence over those of the second person. For example, in the case of the purchase of a computer, the purchasing agent might believe that the cost of the system is more important than software compatibility, while a user might express less concern about the system's cost and more concern about software compatibility. When the two discuss the merits of the various trade-offs, they are engaging in persuasion. In this case, marketers should align themselves with each party in addressing their differing goals.

Bargaining is used when a breakdown of communication occurs. When people in the buying organization no longer wish to continue their dialogue to arrive at a solution, they are likely to engage in bargaining behavior. One person may try to gain his or her choice of a particular product by giving another buyer in the organization the opportunity to choose the supplier of a different product. For example, one automobile manufacturer had to choose suppliers of the bumpers on certain models and the braces to hold them. Through bargaining, the bumpers were purchased from one supplier and the braces from another. In the long run, there was a problem of the incompatibility of the materials; the bumpers and the braces rusted severely and the models finally had to be recalled by the manufacturer for replacement.

Politicking occurs when members of the organization have strong ego needs. In their search for power or self-esteem, they put the goals of the organization as a whole in second place behind their own goals. Such people are looking for ego support rather than the most functional purchase choice. What usually results is a "pecking order" within the buying firm, in which an employee's influence on the purchase is proportional to his or her status in the company. When this occurs, the selling organization's claims about the superiority of its products or services go unnoticed because personalities are more important.

Bargaining and politicking are relatively immature because the open communication that should be maintained in a buying organization are cut off and the wishes of individuals, not the efforts to make the wisest choice, dominate the buying group.

Sheth's integrative model of industrial buying behavior is comprehensive. Although its scope must be adapted for each buying organization, it is a helpful representation of the major aspects of decision making in buying groups. It can also be used as a foundation for organizational marketing research and for developing sales strategies when the marketer is interested in dividing a major problem into its relevant components.

THE EFFECT OF DIFFUSION ON ORGANIZATIONAL BUYING

Just as diffusion of innovations occurs among consumers of new and innovative products, (see Chapter 13), organizations also experience diffusion in the adoption of industrial products, such as new computerized equipment, or with professional purchases, such as the adoption of new drugs by physicians. Several studies have dealt with the diffusion of different types of industrial products as well as prescriptions of new drugs by physicians.

Figure 17-4 shows the various types of firms involved in the diffusion process. Compare this figure to Figure 13-4; it is easy to see the similarity between consumers and diffusion among organizations.

Firms that tend to be *innovators* can be characterized as entrepreneurial in nature and are likely to welcome high risk as an opportunity for future success. These organizations are typically new to the field and may be staffed by aggressive young people. An example of such a firm would be Apple Computers in the early stages of its growth. The entrepreneurial approach used by its owners allowed the development of new consumer markets for personal computers.

Early adopters tend to be firms that are profitable and often are market-share leaders in their industry. While still in a risk-taking mode, these organizations are more concerned with managed growth through technical innovation. These firms are apt to watch the field carefully to identify new technologies and quickly adopt them to maintain their market superiority.

Early majority characterizes firms that tend to follow the lead set by innovators and early adopters. These companies recognize that to keep pace they must incorporate new technologies and methods; but they are unlikely to be the first to experiment with or use highly novel approaches.

Organizations in the *late majority* category are clearly not aggressive in making changes in response to innovative technology or methods. They are production oriented and tend to have lower profits that make high

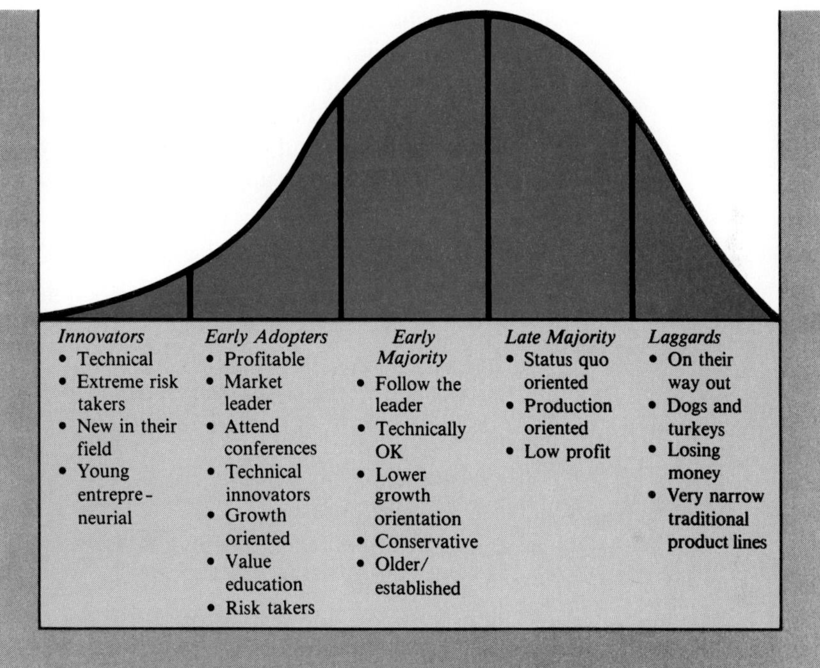

Figure 17-4
The Diffusion of Innovations among Industrial Firms (Characteristics of Companies)

investment in new technologies difficult. A primary focus of these firms is to become more efficient with existing methods.

Finally, *laggards* describe firms which are doomed to failure because they have reached a point of obsolescence in operation or market fit. They tend to have narrow, traditional product lines that are losing money.

The Flow of Communication

As in the case of new consumer products, communications about new industrial or professional products tend to flow from early adopters to the early majority and finally, to the late majority. The innovators and laggards are somewhat isolated from the communication process.

The characteristics of individuals and companies in the early adopter category place them in a key communication position. They are opinion leaders. Although they represent as little as 14% of the population, their impact is great on those who adopt new products more slowly. The amount of time required for the communication flow will depend on how easily the ideas or product can be communicated from one person to another, the complexity of the product, and the product's uses.

If marketers can predict the innovativeness of an organization, hence where it falls in the diffusion process, they can better direct their communication efforts to more effectively influence organizational buying.

Classifying buyers by their receptiveness to innovations allows sellers to assess the likelihood of an organization's purchase, and identify the organizations with highest potential to target as customers. In a recent study, Thomas Robertson and Yoram Wind examined hospitals' adoption of new medical technology and developed the following list of six dimensions of organizational psychographics that help predict the likelihood of adoption:[19]

1. *Direction:* clarity of the buying organization's objectives and priorities.
2. *Decision centrality:* level of centralization in organizational decision making.
3. *Openness of communication:* perceived desire for discussion and a flow of information by the organization's members.
4. *Achievement motivation:* degree to which organization attempts to excel.
5. *Resistance to change:* extent to which the buying organization is perceived to resist change.
6. *Conflict:* pattern of agreement or disagreement in decision making about new technology among members of the buying group.[20]

To measure these dimensions of the participating hospitals, a mail survey was given to administrators, chief radiologists, and staff radiologists at 209 participating hospitals. Statistical analyses were used to evaluate the relationship between a number of variables and innovativeness.

The results of the study indicate that to some extent it is possible to predict innovativeness based on these six dimensions. However, more research is needed to clarify the relationship and better understand how organizational innovativeness can be explained.

The diffusion process and innovation among firms has many applications for marketing strategy. Suppose, for example, that a supplier of equipment to manufacturers has the capability to develop a new technology for completely automating assembly-line operations. Since many firms employ workers assembling products on the line, the new technology offers a real savings to large manufacturers. The new system will be expensive for those who adopt it, but the supplier believes that the long-term benefits of quality and reliability of the product will be attractive to some potential buyers. Since the product could be adapted to fit a wide variety of applications, the potential market is huge. However, because nearly all firms now use some types of assembly-line operation, the supplier expects that only those who are most innovative will be likely to adopt the suppliers new technology. The marketing problem is to identify, first, which industries and firms are most likely to adopt this innovation. Second, it is anticipated that different types of people within these firms will vary in their interest and willingness to change from the current assembly-line methods. The supplier may decide to conduct qualitative and quantitative research to assess the likelihood of adoption among different industries and firms, as well as who *within* the firms will be most likely to support decisions to shift to the new technology. Based on the findings, the supplier can identify where to target marketing communications and what specific appeals will have the greatest impact among key influencers and decision makers in the buying organizations.

SUMMARY

Organizational buying involves purchases made by many types of public and private organizations. The relationship between the buyer and seller and the amount of interdependency can grow over long periods of time.

Organizational buying, like consumer buying, involves several stages, regardless of whether it is for a new task, a modified rebuy, or a straight rebuy. The exact number of stages varies according to the type of purchase situation. The buying organization is composed of many types of people assuming several roles in the purchasing process. Among the most important are the purchasing agent and people who function as gatekeepers. Purchasing agents have prime responsibility for administering the purchasing function within the organization. Gatekeepers are individuals who only allow sellers or information pertinent to the buying process into the organization. People who act as information seekers look for information regarding purchases. Advocates often bring information into the organization and also sponsor particular suppliers. Linking pins are people who facilitate communication between departments within the buying organization. Decision makers often have the responsibility of determining which supplier and product to select. Users of the product may not fall into any of the previous categories, but they are important because of their role in consuming and evaluating products that have been purchased.

Sheth's model of industrial buying behavior provides a means of investigating the many factors that affect complex buying situations. The model describes the relationship of most of the factors that influence how industrial buying decisions are made. Elements such as the expectations of people in the buying company, product-specific factors, and the organizational characteristics of the buying company influence whether the purchase decision is joint or autonomus. Sheth's model also highlights situational factors and the way conflicts are resolved in the buying firm.

The diffusion process among organizations for new and innovative products is similar to that for consumer buyers. Marketing communications generally flow from early adopters to the early majority and then to the late majority. Identifying which category an organization falls into in the diffusion process can help marketers facilitate the information flow.

KEY TERMS

industrial firms
service organizations
symmetrical (buyer–seller) relationship
new task
straight rebuy
modified rebuy
buyclasses
lateral involvement
vertical involvement
purchasing agents
gatekeepers
preferred provider lists
information seekers
advocates
linking pins
"creeping commitment"
decision maker
users
buyphases
buygrid
need uncertainty
technical uncertainty
market uncertainty
acceptance uncertainty
transaction uncertainty

QUESTIONS

1. How does the current view of organizational buying behavior compare to earlier views? What does problem solving in a "social context" mean?
2. Briefly describe Ford's five stages in buyer–seller relationships. Does this process always progress at the same rate? What factors might speed, slow, or interrupt the progression?
3. Distinguish among the three major types of buying situations: new task, straight rebuy, and modified rebuy. Provide an example with your definition of each situation.
4. What is meant by lateral involvement in organizational buying? Vertical involvement? Why would knowledge of these be important to industrial marketers?
5. Use a hypothetical buying situation to illustrate the different roles played by people within an organization. Identify the likely activities and concerns for each role with respect to the purchase.
6. Describe how product-specific factors and company-specific factors influence the organizational buying process. Include several examples of each type of factor.
7. List the five types of uncertainties (or risks) and briefly explain what is meant by each.
8. How are conflicts resolved in an organizational setting? Which of the methods would be a preferable route for each party? Why?
9. Discuss the implications of the diffusion process from an organizational buying perspective. Can you provide an example of a firm characteristic of each stage?

NOTES

1. David Ford, "The Development of Buyer–Seller Relationships in Industrial Markets," *European Journal of Marketing* 14 (May–June 1980): 339–53; Hakan Hakansson and Bjorn Wootz, "A Framework of Industrial Buying and Selling," *Industrial Marketing Management* 8 (1979): 39–49.

2. Hakansson and Wootz, 39–49.
3. The five stages of the buyer–seller relationship are based on David Ford, "The Development of Buyer–Seller Relationships."
4. Jagdish N. Sheth, "Recent Developments in Organizational Buying Behavior," in *Consumer and Industrial Buying Behavior,* Arch G. Woodside, Jagdish N. Sheth, and Peter D. Bennett, eds. (New York: North-Holland, 1977), 19.
5. For recent comprehensive coverage see Richard N. Cardozo, "Situational Segmentation of Industrial Markets," in *European Journal of Marketing* 14 (May–June 1980): 264–76.
6. Peter Doyle, Arch G. Woodside, and Paul Mitchell, "Organizations Buying in New-Task and Rebuy Situations," *Industrial Marketing Management* 8 (July 11, 1979).
7. Cardozo, 265.
8. Wesley J. Johnston and Thomas V. Bonoma, "Purchase Process for Capital Equipment and Services," *Industrial Marketing Management* 10 (1981): 253–64.
9. Johnston and Bonoma, 258.
10. *How Industry Buys/1970* (New York: Scientific American, 1969).
11. Interesting research on the advocate role has been done by Robert E. Krapfel, Jr. See "An Extended Interpersonal Influence Model of Organizational Buying Behavior," *Journal of Business Research* 10 (1982): 147–57.
12. Yoram Wind and Thomas S. Robertson, "The Linking Pin Role in Organizational Buying Centers," *Journal of Business Research* 10 (1982): 169–84.
13. Wind and Robertson, 169–70.
14. Yoram Wind and Robert J. Thomas, "Conceptual and Methodological Issues in Organizational Buying Behavior", *European Journal of Marketing* 14 (May–June 1980): 239–63.
15. Jagdish N. Sheth, "A Model of Industrial Buyer Behavior," *Journal of Marketing* 37 No. 4 (October 1973): 50–56.
16. A. D. Little, Inc., "An Evaluation of 1,100 Research Studies on the Effectiveness of Industrial Advertising," Report to American Business Press, Inc. (May 1971).
17. Cardozo, 264–76.
18. Cardozo, 273.
19. Thomas S. Robertson and Yoram Wind, "Organizational Psychographics and Innovativeness," *Journal of Consumer Research* 7 (June 1980): 24–31.
20. Robertson and Wind, 25.

FURTHER READING

Classics

Gronhaug, Kjell, "Exploring Environmental Influences in Organizational Buying," *Journal of Marketing Research* 13 (August 1976): 225–229.

Lehmann, Donald R., and John O'Shaughnessy, "Difference in Attribute Importance for Different Industrial Products," *Journal of Marketing* 38 (April 1974): 36–42.

Luffman, G., "The Processing of Information by Industrial Buyers," *Industrial Marketing Management* 3 (1974): 363–75.

Mathews, H. Lee, James Robeson, and Peter J. Bambic, "Achieving Seller Acceptability in Industrial Markets: Development of the Communication Mix," in *Consumer and Industrial Buying Behavior,* Woodside, Sheth, and Bennett, eds. (New York: North-Holland, 1977), 221–28.

McMillan, James R., "Role Differentiation in Industrial Business Decisions," in *Combined Proceedings* (Chicago: American Marketing Association, 1973), 207–11.

Sheth, Jagdish N., "A Model of Industrial Buyer Behavior," *Journal of Marketing* 37, No. 4 (October 1973): 50–56.

Sheth, Jagdish N., "Recent Developments in Organizational Buying Behavior," in *Consumer and Industrial Buying Behavior,* Woodside, Sheth, and Bennett, eds. (New York: North-Holland, 1977), 17–34.

Webster, F. E., Jr., "Informal Communication in Industrial Markets," *Journal of Marketing Research* 7 (May 1970), 186–89.

Webster, F. E., Jr., "Modeling the Industrial Buying Process," *Journal of Marketing Research* 2 (November 1965): 370–76.

Webster, Jr., Frederick E., and Yoram Wind, "A General Model for Understanding Organizational Buying Behavior," *Journal of Marketing* 36 (April 1972): 12–19.

Recent Significant Research

Crow, L. E., R. W. Olshavsky, and J. O. Summers, "Industrial Buyers' Choice Strategies: A Protocol Analysis," *Journal of Marketing Research* 15 (February 1980): 43–44.

Evans, Richard H., "Choice Criteria Revisited," *Journal of Marketing* 44 (Winter 1980): 55–56.

Hanson, J. W., "Organizational Buying Behavior: A Conceptual View of the Buying Center," in *Advances in Consumer Research* Vol. VI, W. Wilkie, ed. (Chicago: Association for Consumer Research, 1979), 622–27.

LeBlanc, Ronald P., "Organizational Buyers' Use of Information Processing Strategies: Buying Tasks Influence in Evoked Set Selection," in *The Changing Marketing Environment: New Theories and Applications,* Educators' Conference Proceedings, K. Bernhart, et al., eds. (Chicago: American Marketing Association, 1981), 182–84.

LeBlanc, Ronald P., "An Investigation of the Relationship Between Decision Strategies Used in Evoked Set Selection and Final Purchase Choice—Insights Into Organizational Buying," in *1984 AMA Educators' Proceedings,* Russell W. Belk, et al., eds. (Chicago: American Marketing Association, 1984), 37–39.

Morris, Michael H., "A Model of Coalition Formation in the Industrial Buying Center," in *1984 AMA Educators' Proceedings,* Belk, et al., eds., (Chicago: American Marketing Association, 1984), 40–44.

Robertson, Thomas S., and Yoram Wind, "Organizational Psychographics and Innovativeness," *Journal of Consumer Research,* 7 (June 1980), 24–31.

Ryan, Michael J., and Morris B. Holbrook, "Decision-Specific Conflict in Organizational Buyer Behavior," *Journal of Marketing* 46, No. 3 (Summer 1982): 62–68.

Spekman, Robert E., and Louis W. Stern, "Environmental Uncertainty and Buying Group Structure: An Empirical Investigation," *Journal of Marketing* 43 (Spring 1979): 54–64.

Thomas, Robert J., "Correlates of Interpersonal Purchase Influence in Organizations," *The Journal of Consumer Research* 9 (September 1982): 171–182.

Wilson, David T., "Developing Applied Organizational Buying Theory: A Programmatic Approach," in *Proceedings of the Division of Consumer Psychology,* James C. Anderson, ed., San Antonio, TX: American Psychological Association, 1983), 73–76.

Woodside, Arch G., and Niren Vyas, "Buying Behavior for an Industrial Commodity: A Descriptive Model of One Firm's Decision Process," in *AMA Educators' Proceedings,* Patrick E. Murphy, et al., eds. (Chicago: American Marketing Association, 1983), 51–57.

Applications

Calder, Bobby J., "Structural Role Analysis of Organizational Buying: A Preliminary Investigation," in *Consumer and Industrial Buying Behavior,* Woodside, Sheth, and Bennett, eds., (New York: North-Holland, 1977), 193–200.

Cardozo, Richard N., and James W. Cagley, "Experimental Study of Industrial Buyer Behavior," *Journal of Marketing Research* 8 (August 1971): 329–34.

Eveland, J. D., and Everett M. Rogers, "Applying a Process Model of Innovation in Organizations to Marketing Situations," in *Readings in Consumer Behavior: Individuals, Groups, and Organizations,* M. Wallendorf and G. Zaltman, eds. (New York: John Wiley & Sons, 1979), 374–79.

Martilla, John A., "Word-of-Mouth Communication in the Industrial Adoption Process," *Journal of Marketing Research* 8 (May 1971): 173–78.

Ozanne, Urban B., and Gilbert A. Churchill, Jr., "Five Dimensions of the Industrial Adoption Process," *Journal of Marketing Research* 8 (August 1971): 322–28.

Wilson, David T., "Industrial Buyers' Decision-Making Styles," *Journal of Marketing Research* 8 (November 1971): 433–36.

Wilson, Elizabeth J., and Arch G. Woodside, "Streams of Behavior in Industrial Purchasing Decisions," in *Proceedings of the Division of Consumer Psychology,* James C. Anderson, ed. (San Antonio, TX: American Psychological Association, 1983), 82–85.

18 Consumer Behavior Models

Objectives of This Chapter

After you have studied this chapter, you should be able to:

1. Explain how buyer behavior models are useful in formulating and solving marketing problems.

2. Describe the structure of models in order to evaluate properly developed models of buyer behavior.

3. Understand the basic components of the three most popular models and describe the similarities and differences.

4. Discuss how the models may be applied in marketing practice.

Models are miniature representations of reality. Like theories, they help us understand and explain complex situations by presenting the key features and ignoring unnecessary details. Models are useful in the study of consumer behavior, which by now may seem complex. By discussing such models here, rather than earlier, we are able to integrate the major concepts introduced throughout the book. In fact, without the groundwork laid in preceding chapters, the reader would not be prepared to understand how the many elements of these comprehensive models interrelate. Among the most widely accepted consumer behavior models we will consider are the Howard-Sheth Model of Buyer Behavior and the Engle, Kollat, and Blackwell (EKB) Decision Process Model. In addition to these important and popular models, a newer and somewhat different model will be presented: the Bettman Information Processing Theory of Consumer Choice.

COMPONENTS OF MODELS

Models are made up of theoretical constructs that have a logical structure. They can be thought of as formal statements of theories; and theories are made up of basic building blocks called units. A **unit** is a real or hypothetical construct that has a distinct meaning. A unit is considered hypothetical if it cannot be examined in a physical sense. For example, a motive can be described, discussed, and even analyzed, but we cannot physically touch one. Nevertheless, we *can* discuss the interrelationships of units, whether real or hypothetical. For example, in the theory that attitude is related to behavioral intentions, attitude is a unit and behavioral intention is another unit.

unit

Units are classified in two ways.[1] First, they are classified by whether or not they can be measured. In consumer behavior, units are called *nominal* if there are no known ways to measure consumers' regarding them. For example, basic motives are usually classified as nominal units because there are no standard ways to measure them, even though as hypothetical constructs they are important. On the other hand, units are called *real* if a means exists to obtain scores representing consumers' regarding the unit. Attitude is considered a real unit because it can be measured with several types of scales.[2]

Measures themselves are real, not hypothetical, because we can easily see and record them. The models described in this chapter contain hypothetical units. Some of the units are nominal and others have many measures.

A major concern of researchers is to insure that the construct they are measuring is *valid*. When researchers choose to investigate attitudes, for example, they may be using those constructs to explain consumer behavior. Obviously, we cannot directly observe an attitude. However, we can observe actions and relate them to the construct *attitude*. Thus, often researchers agree to identify attitudes (or any other construct) in observable terms. To determine the validity of a construct, investigators must ask two questions. First, Does the instrument accurately measure the construct? Second, Is the data gathered and interpreted properly? The validity of a construct is crucial to proper and accurate research.[3]

Units can be classified as endogenous (internal) or exogenous (external) to the subject of the theory. In marketing theories, **endogenous units** represent aspects of the process of buying within the individual or the firm. In terms of consumer behavior in particular, endogenous units usually relate to how specific brand choice decisions are made. For example, motive is an endogenous unit because it helps describe a major part of the buyer's purchase process. On the other hand, in marketing theories generally, **exogenous units** do not describe how purchasing occurs; rather, they are relatively permanent characteristics of the consumers or firms being studied. For example, personality and social class are exogenous units because although they help us describe types of buyers, they do not help describe the purchase process itself. For our purposes, while exogenous units do not represent part of the purchase process, they often have an influence on it. We have also seen in Chapters 9 and 11 that endogenous and exogenous units influence the *types* of products and brands selected.

endogenous units

exogenous units

WHY WE NEED MODELS

You have probably heard people say, "I don't like that course (or that book or that teaching method); it's too theoretical." They probably mean that the theories do not address situations with which they are familiar; perhaps they are too abstract, or are irrelevant. In fact, the very word *theoretical* is often used as the antonym of *practical*. Yet theories that are designed well are extremely practicable because one good theory can be used to attack a multitude of problems. In fact, the whole purpose of models or formal statements of theory is to help us solve problems.[4] Models are useful for prediction, understanding, and simplification.

Prediction and Understanding

Models are sometimes used to predict what is likely to happen at some future time if specific conditions are met. For example, if a new product is designed by the research and development department of a company, management might like to be able to assess how many of these products it will be able to sell.

Models are also used to help us understand why certain things occur. Using the same example, it might help the company to know that favorable attitudes about the new product are based on buyer beliefs about the material used to build the product.

On the surface it would appear that prediction and understanding go hand in hand. Unfortunately, this is not always the case. One of the most confusing aspects of model building is the fact that a model may be a good predictor but poor for understanding, and vice versa. For example, when the telephone company is interested in the probability that a family will make over $30 per month in long-distance phone calls, they simply look at the amount the family spent on long distance calls in previous months. They are able to accurately predict the volume of future long distance calls by projecting from the past. Although the predictive accuracy of this method is high, it does not address *why* the calls will be made.

On the other hand, the telephone company may conduct studies of perception and attitudes toward long-distance calling that help the company understand why calls are made. But such studies would fail to accurately predict actual billing amounts. The reason for the inaccuracy is that, in the second case, the set of studies would involve the use of variables that have complex meanings and are more difficult to measure. Each variable would only approximate the consumer's true perceptions and attitudes. Moreover, there is measurement error associated with each variable; and while each variable would further help explain calling behavior, the greater the number of variables that are measured in a study the more error can result in the predictions based on them.

While some marketing problems concern only prediction, and some are only aimed at understanding, most involve a certain amount of each. In general, comprehensive models, such as those presented in this chapter, involve both prediction and understanding.

Simplification

Marketers need models for the same reasons architects need blueprints. With the latter, the architect can visualize various aspects of a building prior to construction and help make any necessary adjustments in the design of the structure before committing it to steel and concrete. Additionally, blueprints may be drawn with various degrees of detail according to the architect's needs.

Similarly, consumer behavior models are made up of units or variables that represent key aspects of the consumer choice process. Consumer behavior models help analysts spot areas for improvement in their companies' dealings with consumers. How much detail should the model contain? (Should it include all aspects of consumer behavior, or just a few?) Here the *law of parsimony* can be borrowed from the natural sciences. It suggests that models or theories should achieve their objectives of adequately predicting and explaining consumer behavior in the simplest and most direct way possible. Models should not have overlapping or redundant components. Therefore, the units contained in the theories should be defined or arranged generally enough so that they do not need to be redefined through the model. For example, *attitude* and *confidence* should have separate meanings and each should be used only when necessary in a particular model. The models presented later in this chapter are parsimonious. Therefore, they help to simplify a very complex topic.

HOW CONSUMERS SOLVE PROBLEMS: THREE BRAND-CHOICE SCENARIOS

It is fall term on the university campus. Nancy Carter, Susie Adams, and Bobb Smith are all freshmen. Their only form of transportation to classes is walking. Nancy, Susie, and Bobb have all recognized the difficulty of getting to classes on time on foot. Now each of them is in the market for a ten-speed bicycle.

1. *Nancy Buys a Schwinn* When Nancy was 5 years old her grandparents bought her a bicycle. It was her first Schwinn. Her parents bought her another Schwinn at age 9, and she bought herself a new ten-speed Schwinn from her savings when she was 13. She was always satisfied with her Schwinns; she liked their durability and ease of operation.

After looking in the yellow pages of the telephone book to find the nearest Schwinn dealer, Nancy walked to the dealer and bought a woman's Schwinn very similar to her old ten-speed. On her way to the dorm, she noticed how smoothly the gears functioned and a friend commented on the quality of her new purchase.

2. *Susie Buys a Trek* Although Susie has owned several bicycles, she has never had a good ten- or fifteen-speed touring bike. After arriving on campus, Susie noticed that many female students ride ten-speeds with support bars across the top. This surprised Susie because only men and boys in her home town rode bicycles built like that.

This morning Susie noticed Nancy's new bicycle and briefly engaged her in a conversation about Schwinns. Then Susie decided that after her classes she would visit the three major bicycle dealers near campus: the Schwinn dealer, a new Fuji dealer, and the Trek dealer.

After class Susie began shopping for a bicycle. During several conversations with sales people, she began to learn about the features, benefits, and prices of various types of bikes. The Schwinn dealer showed her a copy of *Consumer Reports* magazine about bicycles, and later she carefully read the library copy of the report. Susie also had several conversations about brands throughout the week with Bobb Smith, a friend who lived in the same dormitory complex.

After considerable thought Susie decided that service, durability, light weight, reputation for touring, and cost were most important. She narrowed her choices to a Schwinn Super Le Tour, a Cannondale 400 (handled by the Schwinn dealer), a Fuji Espree, and a Trek 400. She felt the Schwinn Super Le Tour would be the most durable and service at the dealership would be excellent, but friends and salespeople at other dealerships told her it was not used by many serious bicyclists in that area. Additionally, the salesperson at the Schwinn store tended to steer her toward the Cannondale 500, with a new aluminum frame design, that was becoming popular locally.

Susie liked the looks of the Fuji Espree and felt it would meet all of her criteria. However, she was somewhat unsure about the bike's qualities. There were very few Fujis on campus and the salespeople at the Fuji dealership did not sound as experienced or knowledgeable as the others.

At one point during her bicycle shopping, Susie was approached by somebody who offered to find a used bike similar to the brand of her choice but at half the price. Fearing a "rip-off" and suspecting that the bikes sold this way were probably stolen, she answered rather forcefully, "I'm *not* interested."

Finally, Susie narrowed her choice to the Trek 400 and the Cannondale 500, both of which she considered durable, light in weight, and good for touring. Price was the only factor. Her preferred model, the Cannondale 500 was $595, about $200 over her budget. After some thought, she settled for the $400 Trek, thinking that perhaps in a couple of years she would trade it in on the more expensive model.

3. *Bobb Almost Buys a Moped* Bobb Smith decided he needed transportation very quickly. He had already been late to a math class that morning because his writing class on the other side of campus let out ten minutes late. Bobb had purchased a Raleigh ten-speed in high school but had left it at home for his brother to ride. Although Bobb liked the Raleigh, he was open to buying a new brand.

Bobb's criteria were type of gear mechanism, tires, weight, and price. After looking at the various bikes he saw around campus he decided to purchase a Fuji. That afternoon he went to the Fuji dealer. While waiting for a salesperson he noticed a display featuring a moped, (a motorized bicycle). He had not considered a moped, but he liked the way it looked. When the salesperson approached him, they began to discuss it. After asking some questions, Bobb left the dealership thinking about the reasons for buying the moped.

At dinner that evening, Bobb excitedly described the moped to Susie and Nancy. After dinner Susie suggested that the three of them ride their bikes to the intramural field to watch football. Bobb thought to himself, "Tomorrow I've got to buy a ten-speed bike."

The Basic Problem-Solving Sequence

In the three bicycle purchase scenarios, Nancy, Susie, and Bobb followed problem-solving sequences to some degree. Nancy's purchase was less complex and Bobb never made the purchase, but they all were attempting to solve a problem. Each used information from their surroundings to stimulate the identification of a problem or motive for purchasing. Each felt they wanted a bicycle for campus transportation. Each person was attentive to the problem, using information from previous purchases and obtaining new information from various sources. That is, each made an information search. The choices made by Susie and Nancy to purchase particular brands, and Bobb's choice to delay his purchase, were made using decision processes. Each of them then evaluated the choices they made.

The following sections present three consumer-behavior models to explain the scenarios. The models are in the order in which they were first developed. Therefore, each model contains more units and is more complex than the previous one. All have two things in common: they focus on purchase choice as a problem-solving process and, consistent with the theme of this book, they stress that consumer behavior is goal directed.

THE HOWARD-SHETH MODEL OF BUYER BEHAVIOR

In 1963 John Howard made a major contribution when he applied learning principles to the study of consumer behavior. In 1969 Howard collaborated with Jagdish Sheth to publish a comprehensive model of consumer behavior that went beyond Howard's original concept: The Howard-Sheth Model of Buyer Behavior. This later model represents a fundamental tool for researchers and users of consumer-behavior studies because it is a relatively advanced and widely applicable theory that incorporates accepted psychological findings in ways that are meaningful for the study of consumer behavior.

Howard and Sheth deal with three types of purchasing: extensive problem solving (first-time purchases); limited problem solving (switching to new brands); and routinized response behavior (repurchase of a familiar brand).

In the bicycle purchasing scenarios, Nancy was in routinized response behavior. Susie was in limited problem solving for a ten-speed, although she had purchased other types of bicycles before. Bobb was in a limited problem-solving phase for bicycles with an interlude of extensive problem solving regarding a moped. The concept of *simplification* inherent in this model says that consumers are assumed to move from extensive problem solving to routinized response behavior over time. In this way consumers attempt to reduce the complexity of purchasing a particular product. The psychology of *complication* occurs when buyers move from routinized response behavior back to other problem-solving stages, as Bobb did when he looked at the moped.

The Howard-Sheth model (Figure 18-1) has hypothetical units (constructs) of input and output variables that are endogenous, as well as several exogenous variables.[5] The hypothetical units or constructs are by far the most important.

Learning Constructs

Motives

nonspecific motives

There are two types of motives in the Howard-Sheth model: specific and nonspecific. **Nonspecific motives** are basic needs such as those included in Maslow's hierarchy (physiological, safety, love, esteem, and self-actualization). They are difficult to investigate in the context of buying. Susie's nonspecific motives probably revolved around social motives such as

Figure 18-1 *The Howard-Sheth Model*

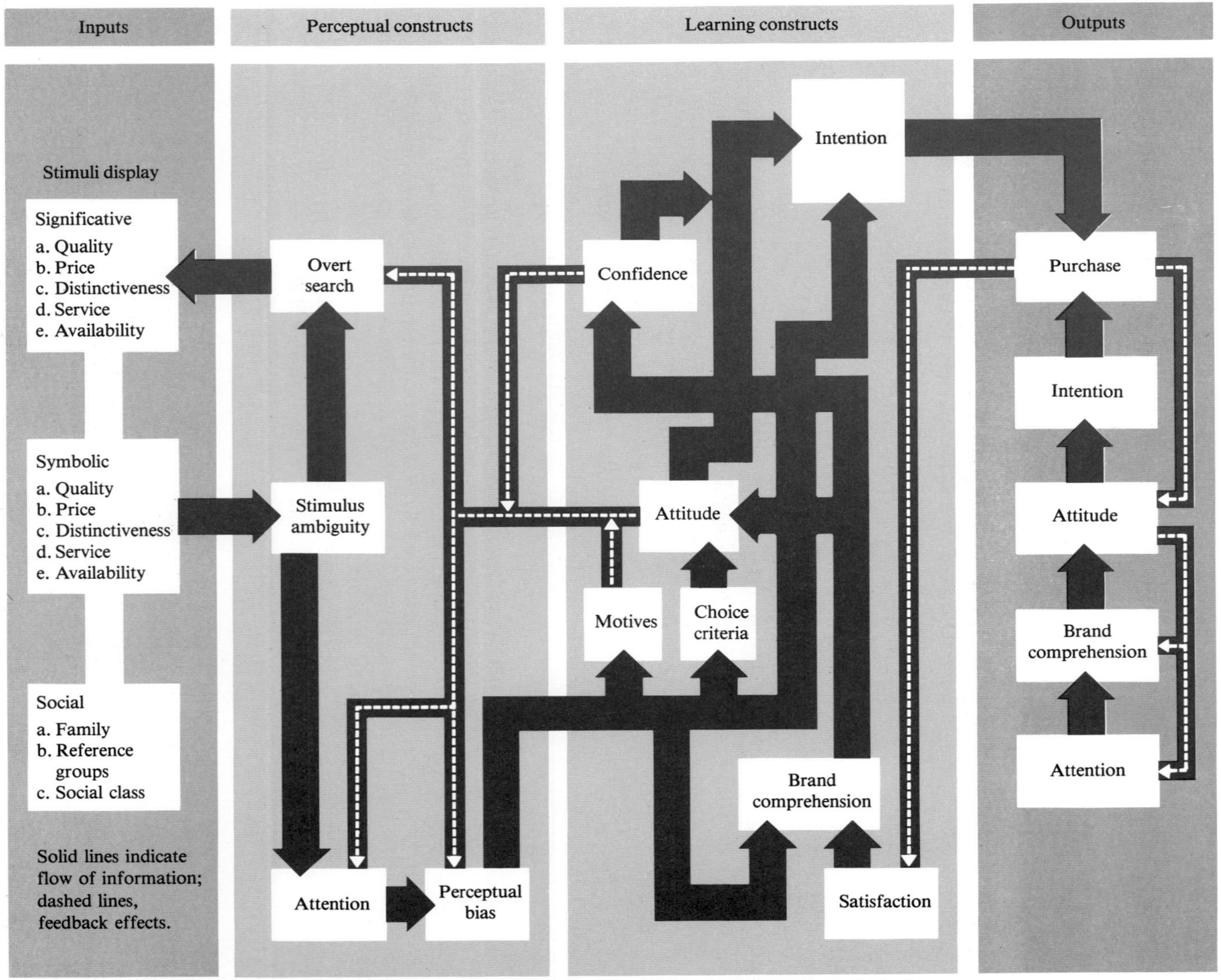

Source: John A. Howard and Jagdish N. Sheth, *The Theory of Buyer Behavior* (New York: John Wiley & Sons, 1969), 31.

power, status, or prestige, but it is difficult to make that assessment without more information. **Specific motives** are motives that are closely related to the product class being considered. For Nancy, brand name (Schwinn), durability, and ease of operation were specific motives. Susie's specific motives were service, durability, light weight, touring reputation, and cost. For Bobb, the specific motives were type of gear mechanism, tires, weight, and price.

specific motives

Brand Comprehension

brand comprehension

Brand comprehension is the extent to which the consumer can describe and discuss with others the characteristics of the brands in which they are interested. For this unit, *denotative* (or descriptive) characteristics are important. Nancy's brand comprehension was limited to a few aspects of Schwinn, while Susie and Bobb could discuss key aspects of at least three different brands.

Choice Criteria

choice criteria

Choice criteria are the relevant motives as they are ranked (or rated) from most important to least important by the consumer. Susie's dilemma about the price of her favorite bicycle demonstrates the way choice criteria influence purchases. Because price was higher in importance than anticipated touring performance, she decided to purchase the less expensive Trek. Clearly, Nancy's strongest choice criteria was that of brand: Schwinn.

Attitude

attitude

The **attitude** unit is the consumer's evaluation of brands according to the choice criteria. Attitude relates the choice criteria to each specific brand the buyer considers purchasing. Nancy and Susie rated their respective purchases high on the criteria that were important to them.

Confidence

confidence

Confidence is the amount of certainty about the brand the prospective buyer has while evaluating the brand. Recall that Nancy had a good deal of confidence in Schwinn due to her previous experience of owning that brand. Susie had relatively little confidence in her evaluations of Fuji bicycles and, therefore, did not purchase that brand.

Intention

intention

Intention refers to the buyer's estimate of whether he or she will actually purchase the brand, and when, where, and how the purchase might take place. Bobb fully intended to purchase the Fuji when he went to the bicycle shop. However, he was sidetracked by the moped.

Howard and Sheth account for differences between intention and actual purchase by identifying several inhibitory factors, such as (1) unexpectedly high price; (2) lack of availability (item is out of stock); (3) time pressure on the buyer; (4) the buyer's financial condition; and (5) social influences such as salespeople and friends.

Satisfaction

satisfaction The last learning unit is the amount of **satisfaction** derived from the purchase and consumption of the brand. Whether the brand exceeds, equals, or falls short of the expectations the buyer had prior to purchase determines his or her satisfaction level. In the scenarios, little was said about overall satisfaction resulting from the various decisions; however, Nancy did notice how smoothly the gears ran on her new purchase and a friend commented on the quality of the bike, both of which could have contributed to satisfaction.

Perceptual Constructs

The perceptual units of the Howard-Sheth model focus on information. They involve both procurement and processing of information.

Attention

attention **Attention** governs the amount of information taken in through the sensory receptors. It controls the flow of information entering the buyer's mind. In the scenarios, all three students were interested in bicycles and were trying to take in a great deal of information from several sources. For example, while walking around the campus, Susie noticed the high crossbar on many of the bikes ridden by other female students.

Stimulus Ambiguity

stimulus ambiguity **Stimulus ambiguity** describes the confusion over information currently available and the doubtfulness that new information about the brand will be available to the buyer. Buyers pay attention to novel messages—as long as they are not so novel that they are meaningless or confusing. Recall that Bobb paid attention to the moped, probably because for him it was new and unique.

Perceptual Bias

All people do not interpret information in the same way; nor do they see **perceptual bias** things exactly as they are. **Perceptual bias** helps us account for differences in interpretations of information. This is a very complex theoretical unit. None of the scenarios explicitly dealt with perceptual bias; however, Nancy, Susie, and Bobb each had his or her own interpretation of the bicycle brands and the information they gathered about them.

Overt Search

overt search **Overt search** does not refer to a passive intake of information but rather to an active seeking out of information. A good example of overt search was when Susie went to the library to use *Consumer Reports*.

Outputs

outputs The **outputs** of the Howard-Sheth model represent measurements of variables in the model. They include measures of the consumer's attention, brand comprehension, attitudes, intention, and purchase.

The Howard-Sheth model addresses many of the aspects of buying illustrated in the three bicycle purchasing scenarios. It does a good job of isolating key aspects and labeling the various stages these consumers were experiencing while making their brand choices.

THE ENGEL, KOLLAT, BLACKWELL (EKB) DECISION PROCESS MODEL[6]

The second comprehensive model has evolved through four revisions by its authors, and is likely to be revised further as more knowledge is added to this field. The Engel, Kollat, Blackwell (EKB) model was first devised in 1968, primarily to organize the subjects of a textbook on consumer behavior. In the second edition of the book, the model was revised to more closely approximate an actual consumer decision process. The third and the latest versions of the model described here, are more comprehensive and easily usable (see Figure 18-2). Essentially, the EKB model explains in more detail many of the same elements the Howard-Sheth model covers. Additionally, because of its explicit focus on the decision-making process, the EKB model tends to examine the *process* of purchasing more than it does the components of the purchasing decision. The five decision process stages in the EKB are problem recognition, search, alternative evaluation, choice, and outcomes.

Problem Recognition

Problem recognition occurs when the consumer perceives a discrepancy or difference between their actual situation and a desired situation. *Motives* and stimuli are important here. Susie's desire for self-esteem motivated her to want a good bicycle designed for touring. Remember that motives are influenced by personality, life-style, cultural norms, and values. (These units are exogenous variables in the Howard-Sheth model.)

Based on their methods of problem solving, we might conclude that Nancy's personality was more introverted while Susie's was more extroverted. Nancy reflected on her own experiences in deciding what type of bike to consider. On the other hand, Susie seemed more concerned with the opinions of others and the types of bicycles ridden by other students. This may be due to the fact that bicycles are a major feature of the campus life-style.

The second major influence on problem recognition is *stimuli,* which activate motives. For example, when the three students saw other students save travel time by riding bikes, they recognized their own problem,

Figure 18-2 *The Engel, Kollat, Blackwell High Involvement Decision Process Model of Consumer Behavior*

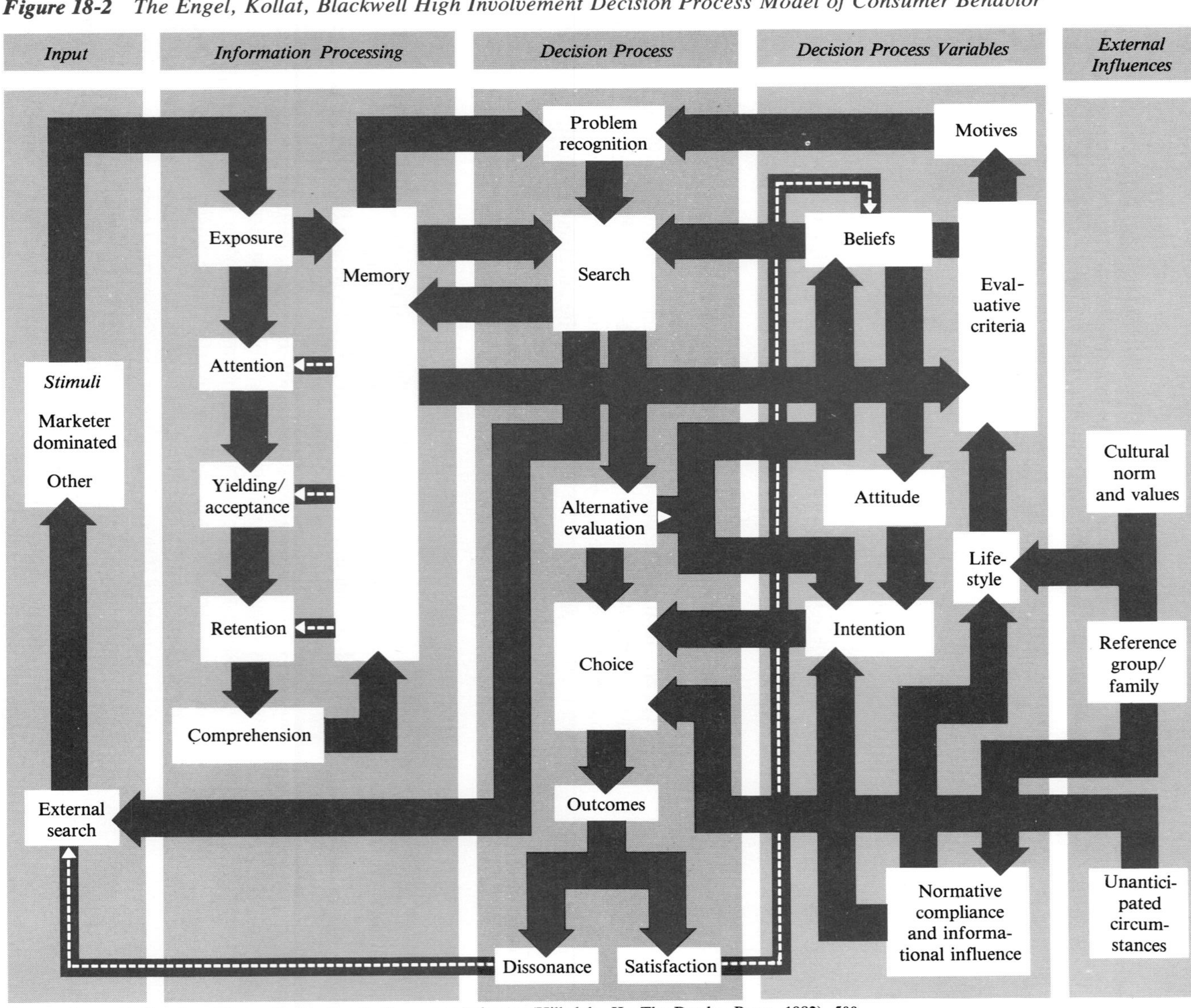

Source: James F. Engel and Roger D. Blackwell, *Consumer Behavior* (Hillsdale, IL: The Dryden Press, 1982), 500.

which visits to dealers and conversations with others helped clarify. These stimuli triggered in each of them a desire to buy a certain type of bicycle.

The influences of *cultural norms and values* on motives were discussed in Chapter 2 on motivation. The effects of these units is not explicit in the three bicycle-buying scenarios. However, to the degree that bicycles are used for convenience, culture does play a part. In the sense that college life is a culture in and of itself, bicycles as a major mode of transportation can be considered a cultural norm and thus influence the motivation to own one. Similarly, values can play a part. For instance, many people—college students in particular—have values concerned with maintaining a clean environment. Some students may be motivated to buy bicycles over other modes of transportation because they do not contribute to air pollution.

Information Processing

Between stimuli and problem recognition, the EKB model identifies four information-processing units: exposure, attention, reception, and active memory. Information processing is also relevant in the search stage, as the arrows in the model depict. Thus consumers engage in information processing to guide the search for alternatives after a problem is recognized. The four units of information processing relate to how people make sense of information.

Exposure

exposure

Nancy, Susie, and Bobb were not exposed to exactly the same information. **Exposure** describes the extent to which consumers come in contact with information. Because Nancy did not visit the Raleigh dealer, she was not exposed to any of that dealer's comments, literature, displays, or bicycles.

Attention

attention

As in the Howard-Sheth model, **attention** in the EKB model is the selective intake of information. Again, Susie selectively noticed the crossbar on the bicycles. Yet there was no assurance that the information had been received and understood in ways *intended by the marketer*.

Comprehension

comprehension

Comprehension is the outcome of information processing that indicates the objective understanding the consumer has regarding a brand or other stimulus. This is very similar to the brand-comprehension construct in the Howard-Sheth model. However, it has a broader meaning here because it includes the comprehension not only of brands but of other stimuli, such as advertisements, as well.

Yielding/acceptance

yielding/acceptance

Yielding/acceptance represents the consumer's integration of the information into memory. When yielding/acceptance occurs, additional information is likely to be accompanied by reinforcements of or changes in beliefs, attitudes, or intentions. In the scenario, Bobb's attitudes toward purchasing the Fuji were altered when he began to think about the moped.

Retention

retention

Retention is the placement of the stimulus in long-term memory. Retention occurs after the preceding steps and reflects any changes in cognitive structure that occur from yielding/acceptance.

Memory

memory

Memory relates incoming information to information already stored in the person's memory. That is, after the prospective buyer makes sense of new information he or she relates it to previous experiences. If the new information has meaning to the buyer, there is a good chance that it will be rehearsed in the mind and put into long-term memory. If it is not rehearsed, it will rapidly decay and be completely forgotten. Nancy tuned out much of the conversation related to the Trek and Fuji bicycles because, for her, it lacked significance. On the other hand, for Susie and Bobb it was significant and they stored it in long-term memory.

Search and Alternative Evaluation

search

Search, the second stage of problem solving, ties together many of the learning and attitude constructs discussed earlier in this book. Once a problem is recognized, the first step is to search in memory to see if enough information already exists to solve the problem. When buying is routinized, sufficient information has already been received and stored to make the choice. For example, Nancy's purchase of a Schwinn was routinized response behavior because it was based on experiences with past purchases of Schwinns.

alternative evaluation

Alternative evaluation becomes important when the purchase is not routinized. When both search and alternative evaluation are part of the purchase, the units of *evaluative criteria, beliefs, attitudes,* and *intention* find their way into the cognitive structure, usually in this same sequence. These units are similar to those found in the Howard-Sheth model, although the labels are somewhat different. For example, *attitude* in the Howard-Sheth model is the same as *beliefs* in the EKB model.

evaluative criteria

Evaluative criteria are the characteristics buyers use to assess brands (for example, durability and price). The Howard-Sheth model calls these characteristics *choice criteria.*

beliefs

Beliefs are the consumer's evaluation of particular brands according to the evaluative criteria. Nancy believed the Schwinn would be durable and easy to operate. Susie "believed" the Raleigh she purchased would be serviced well, have durability, light weight, and a strong reputation for racing, all at an affordable price. Bobb evaluated the Fuji as being acceptable in terms of the type of gear mechanism, its tires, weight, and price.

At the same time that consumers are learning about evaluative criteria and formulating beliefs about brands they are developing attitudes. Perhaps the easiest way of thinking about a buyer's attitude is simply how much he or she likes or prefers the brand. **Attitudes** are the positive or negative evaluations regarding the outcome of using a brand or product.

attitudes

The attitudes that develop are related to intention, although not perfectly. **Intention** is the buyer's stated expectation of actually purchasing the brand at a specific time. In general, the more positive the attitude toward purchasing a brand is, the more likely there will be a high score regarding the buyer's intention to purchase the brand.

intention

Choice

Bobb's actions illustrate the sequence of attitude, intention, and product choice. He had a favorable attitude toward a Fuji bicycle and the intention to purchase it. **Anticipated circumstances** refer to factors such as the consumer's income and ability to use the product. These did not change for Bobb. However, he was sidetracked by the moped, an **unanticipated circumstance,** and did not make the purchase. After postponing his purchase of the moped, however, his intention to buy the Fuji resurfaced.

anticipated circumstances

unanticipated circumstances

Outcomes

Outcomes, the last of the five decision process stages, refers to the amount of reinforcement or punishment associated with purchasing and using the product. Satisfaction is reinforcement. Susie's choice of a Trek was reinforced by its touring qualities, which she detected while riding the bicycle. Bobb, on the other hand, felt some degree of punishment for not purchasing a bicycle, since he could not ride to the intramural game with Nancy and Susie.

outcomes

Dissonance is a feeling that some consumers have after making a purchase.[7] At this stage shoppers often question whether they made the correct choice. When doubts about a purchase emerge, consumers typically search for information about the brand they purchased to confirm that they made the correct choice.

dissonance

The major aspects of the three bicycle scenarios were highlighted by the EKB model. In these cases we did not question the extent to which Nancy, Susie, or Bobb made good or bad decisions. Also, we did not question how much information was received and evaluation took place in their decision making. We assumed that the evaluation and analysis of information gathered was adequate for their purposes. But what if we wanted to investigate their ability to effectively use and process information? The Bettman model, which follows, addresses this aspect of the buying process.

THE BETTMAN INFORMATION-PROCESSING THEORY OF CONSUMER CHOICE[8]

Ours is an information-oriented society. A large portion of many firms' marketing expenditures are devoted to information communication. Likewise, consumers and industrial buyers invest vast amounts of time and energy to acquiring and applying information to choice situations. James Bettman has assembled theories about consumer information processing into a single model that helps to assess the consumer's ability in this area. The basic structure of Bettman's model is given in Figure 18-3.

While the Howard-Sheth and EKB models are useful to describe most problem areas in consumer behavior, they do not directly address issues of how much information consumers can effectively use. This is particularly important for advertisers, who must design messages that are effective and efficient. Also, a major public-policy issue is the amount of information consumers are able to understand and use, particularly labeling for pricing and nutritional content.

Overview of the Bettman Model

A critical factor in consumer behavior is processing capacity, a concept similar to intelligence. Processing capacity affects motivation, attention, information acquisition and evaluation, decision making and consumption.

Two elements of Bettman's model not found in the other consumer behavior models are (1) the scanner and interrupt mechanisms, and (2) interrupt interpretation and response. Since these units appear in several parts of Bettman's model, they will be described first.

scanner mechanisms
interrupt mechanisms

Consumers are continually monitoring their environment for clues and insights that might help them make purchasing decisions. This is the **scanner mechanism** at work. At the same time, there are **interrupt mechanisms** ready to stop the buyers' progress on current activities when they notice something of interest. As we have seen, *new and novel information* is likely to attract buyer's attention. This activation of their interrupt mechanism is part of learning. For example, Bobb's interrupt mechanism was triggered when he saw the moped while scanning his environment for information on a bicycle. He then began to focus on and learn about the moped instead.

A second type of interruption occurs when the consumer has *conflict*. Conflict can come in several forms—including conflicting information, goals, and analyses of information. When a conflict occurs the buyer is likely to be diverted until the conflict is resolved. For Bobb, seeing the moped created a conflict as to which type of transportation would best meet his needs. His purchase was delayed until he could resolve the conflict.

Figure 18-3
The Bettman Information-Processing Model of Consumer Choice

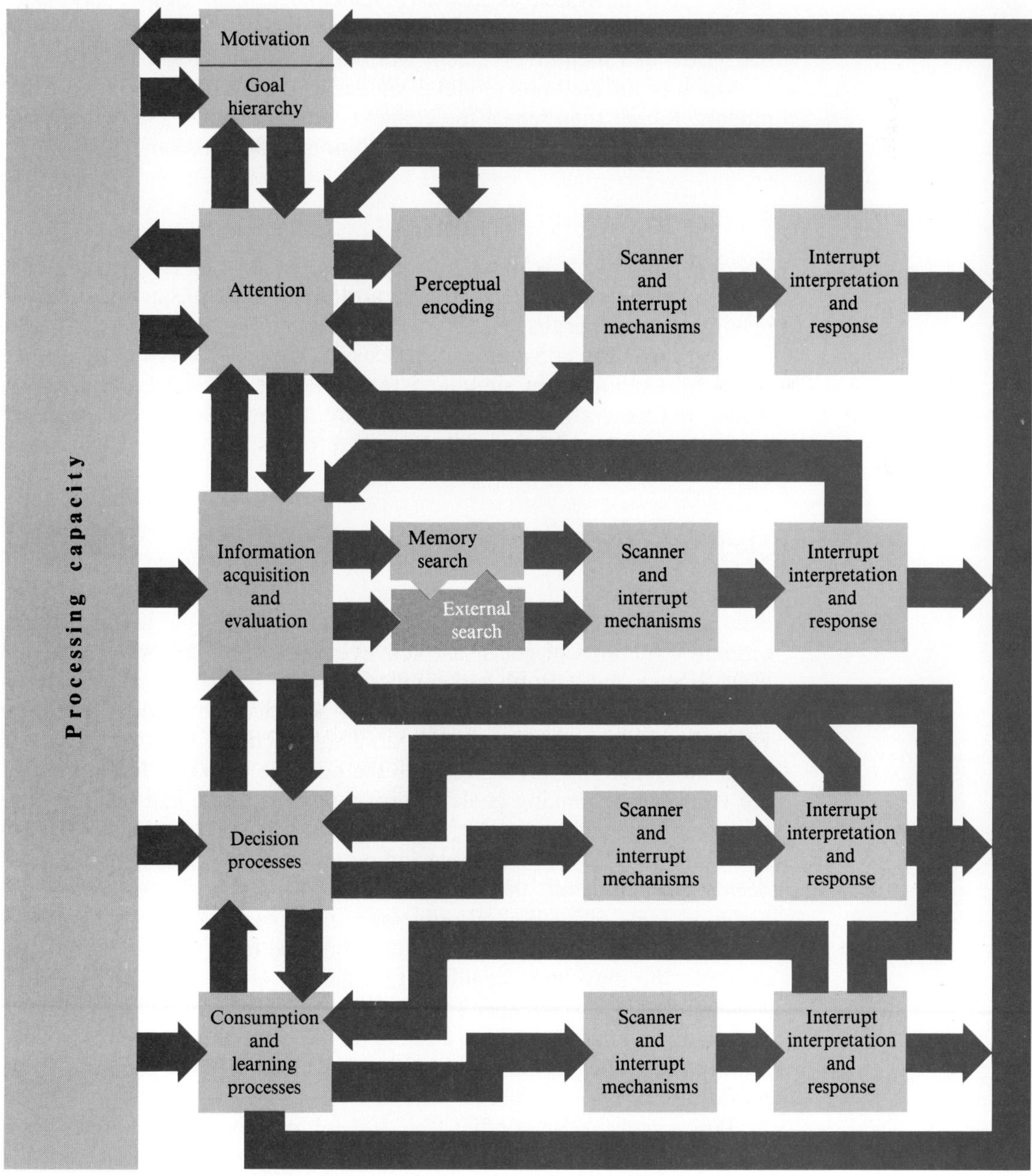

Source: James R. Bettman, *An Information-Processing Theory of Consumer Choice* (Reading, MA: Addison-Wesley, 1979), 17.

interrupt interpretation and response

Interrupt interpretation and response refers to how the new information is used. If it is used relatively passively to build a general "knowledge bank," it is classified as low-involvement learning. Conversely, high-involvement learning is acted upon or stored in the memory for future use. (Low and high involvement were discussed in Chapter 5.)

Much of the Bettman model is similar to the EKB and Howard-Sheth models. Rather than repeat the elements that are similar, we will discuss the areas in which Bettman makes additional contributions.

Processing Capacity

There is a limit to how much information a person can absorb and use to make a purchase decision. If several activities are occurring, such as making several purchases, this limited capacity must be partially allocated to each. The constraints of processing capacity can be better understood by examining in simplified form the five remaining units of the model: (1) motivation and goal hierarchy, (2) attention, (3) information acquisition and evaluation, (4) decision processes, and (5) consumption and learning processes.

Motivation and Goal Hierarchy

Consumers have goals. Some goals are more important than others; some even lead to other goals. Thus, consumers develop goal hierarchies, or ordered structures of goals, as their everyday needs and wants become clear. For example, Bobb had conflicting goals he wanted transportation and he needed to maintain his financial security. The moped purchase would have strained the second goal. Thus, a choice between goals was required. When the trade-offs of all the possible uses of a limited budget are considered, ranking goals in order of importance can become very complex. Like any consumer, Bobb was working on two types of activities simultaneously: (1) scanning and monitoring the environment, and (2) deciding on the Fuji, the moped, or neither. Each of these tasks was assigned some of his limited processing capacity. In the first case, Bobb was taking in general knowledge that could be used at a later time. For example, he may have acquired information about the store's service organization, a new backpack for bikers which he might buy in the future, and an upcoming bike race to be held on the campus. In the second case, he was using relevant information to solve his immediate problem: transportation.

When goals are in conflict, the decision process is temporarily interrupted. For example, Bobb had an approach-avoidance conflict because the moped was desirable for transportation but undesirable due to cost. An approach-approach conflict occurs when two goals are present but not simultaneously reachable. For example, an interruption also occurred when both the Fuji bicycle and the moped were desired but both could not be selected. An avoidance-avoidance conflict existed when Bobb did not want to miss his class in the morning in order to buy the bike and also did not want to walk to class the next day. Each interruption further taxes Bobb's limited decision capacity.

Attention

attention

Attention is the allocation of limited processing capacity to a particular message. Attention can occur voluntarily or involuntarily, depending on circumstances. When a person is seeking information about current goals, attention is voluntary. However, surprising, novel, or potentially threatening events lead to involuntary attention. Voluntary attention occurred when Susie read *Consumer Reports,* and involuntary attention occurred when Bobb saw the moped display.

Attention is influenced by perceptual encoding, which relates to the perceptual constructs and information processes in the previous models. However, any of the three types of conflict can again result in interruptions which help buyers gain information and improve their ability to buy other products instead of the one initially sought. An interruption is likely to create increased attention to several messages and will often influence the goal hierarchy.

Information Acquisition and Evaluation

information acquisition and evaluation

Information acquisition and evaluation involves the use of information from memory as well as from external sources. These theoretical units are particularly interesting because they relate to the memory component. Buyers first use internal information and second external information. Nancy had a lot of internal information about Schwinn that provided important data. But even with her limited search, the dealer offered some external information. The internal memory system is composed of the short- and long-term memory components similar to those postulated by the EKB model.

People use control processes to manage the flow of information in and out of memory. There are six important control processes: (1) rehearsal, (2) coding, (3) transfer, (4) placement, (5) retrieval, and (6) response generation.

rehearsal

Rehearsal is the review of material in short-term memory so that it will stay there for a time. Rehearsal also helps material enter long-term memory. For example, the placement and amount of price information can affect rehearsal. Consumers in a grocery store may see a shelf price label, review the price on the item when they put it in the shopping cart, and review it again at the check-out counter. If the price is not given on the package, consumers will be less likely to retain the price in memory.[9]

encoding

Encoding refers to the way information is entered into long-term memory. Some information is entered in pictorial form; other information is entered in symbolic form. Or information may enter memory in both forms at once. Encoding involves the association of messages about products with consumers' past experiences.

transfer

Transfer, the third control process, governs what is to be stored in memory and in what form. One buyer may tend to recall price, while another remembers nutritional or package size information.

placement

Placement deals with where the information is stored in long-term memory. Is it stored in several areas? For example, are all food items stored together while information on automobiles is stored in a separate area? Little is known about placement, but an ever-increasing amount of research is being conducted in this area.

retrieval

Retrieval refers to how easily and in what way buying information can be brought out for use. Researchers are studying ways to stimulate retrieval through message content and structure.

response generation

Response generation is the last control process in the information acquisition and retrieval unit. Items are not stored in memory the same way they were first entered. Therefore, the form information takes when it is used is somewhat altered. Additionally, consumers are likely to have to analyze many subjects and pieces of information to find the right information. For example, the consumer is likely to be required to construct a new idea from several bits and pieces of information stored in various places. This, too, is a new area of research.

Decision Processes

Consumers do not use all the information to which they are exposed. In fact, they cannot; their decision capabilities are limited. Thus, buyers use *heuristics,* or "rules of thumb," to arrive at brand choices. These guidelines save them the time and effort of making complex calculations to arrive at a decision. For example, in her purchase of a bicycle, Nancy's rule of thumb might have been: "For large purchases, buy known brands" (in her case, Schwinn).

The consumers' use of heuristics, as these decision rules are called, has implications for marketing.[11] Marketers can influence consumers by providing information in forms that conform to the rules of thumb used by their targeted markets. (Chapters 6 and 8 discussed heuristics in detail, including the conjunctive, disjunctive, and lexicographic methods of decision making.)

Consumption and Learning Processes

consumption and learning processes

Consumers continue to learn about goods and services as they use them. Bettman's last unit is **consumption and learning processes,** during which the decision rules are modified. If the product meets or exceeds customers' expectations, their rules of thumb are then simplified: "From now on, buy brand Y even if it costs more than $2.00," for example. If the product was disappointing, the rules of thumb become more complex: "Buy brand Y only if you can't find brands A and B, and then only if Y costs under $2.00." In addition to learning new heuristics, consumers learn about the brands themselves. (Learning is discussed in Chapter 4.)

Both Nancy and Susie were satisfied with their bicycle choices. Thus the next bicycle purchase for each of them is likely to be easier. Bobb did not make a purchase; but like the others, he will have learned from his experience. For example, he may have learned not to be so easily distracted when shopping. If he is still interested in the moped, he may inquire as to whether any bicycle he may purchase can be traded in on a moped later.

Bettman's information-processing model focuses more on process than the other models do, and it deals extensively with internal processes. This helps make it relatively cumbersome to use for some marketing problems. The methods for measuring the model's units and for tracing information processing have not yet been fully refined, and those that are

Table 18-1 BASIC COMPONENTS OF THREE MODELS OF CONSUMER BEHAVIOR

*Howard-Sheth**	*Engel, Kollat, Blackwell*	*Bettman*
Stimulus ambiguity–Attention–Perceptual bias (Perceptual constructs)	—	—
Motives	Problem recognition†	Motivation Goal hierarchy
Stimulus ambiguity–Attention–Perceptual bias (Perceptual constructs)	(Information processing)‡	Attention
Overt search (Perceptual subsystem)	Search	Information acquisition and evaluation
Choice criteria–Attitudes–Brand comprehension–Confidence (Learning subsystem)	Alternative evaluation	Decision processes
Intention–Purchase (Learning subsystem)	Choice	Consumption and learning
Satisfaction (Learning subsystem)	Outcomes	—

* The units in the Howard-Sheth model are ordered to correspond to the Engel, Kollat, and Blackwell, and Bettman models. They are only roughly in this order in the original model.

† Problem recognition is not completely synonymous with the motive factors in the other two models, but the EKB model provides motives as an input to problem recognition.

‡ Information processing is an input into problem recognition and is not specified as one of the decision-process stages in the original model.

Table 18-2 SUMMARY COMPARISON OF THREE MODELS OF CONSUMER BEHAVIOR

Model	*Unique Focus*	*Distinguishing Elements*
Howard-Sheth	The components (or units) of brand-choice stages	Clearly isolates components Separates learning and perceptual constructs
Engel, Kollat, Blackwell	The purchasing process used in problem solving	Has a more detailed examination of components used in the Howard-Sheth model Gives special attention to the sequence of problem solving
Bettman	The ability of the consumer to effectively use and process information	Uses concepts of scanner and interrupt mechanisms to explain information acquisition and processing

available are expensive and require extreme care in application. Nevertheless, for issues that center on the consumer's ability to make informed choices, such as legislation of price and nutritional labeling or restrictions in communication and advertising, the approach used in this model seems particularly warranted. Since it deals with the consumer's capacity for using information, the Bettman model offers insights into the preferable amounts and structure of the information marketers transmit.

In the next few years research should provide more specific insights into information processing, and we will begin to see standard ways of using the Bettman model and perhaps other information-processing models.

Table 18-1 summarizes the problem-solving sequence that is at the core of each model. The Engel, Kollat, Blackwell model and the Bettman model clearly describe this sequence. It can be discovered within the Howard-Sheth model after some searching and a few interpretations are made. Table 18-2 is a summary of the primary distinguishing features of each model.

HOW MARKETERS USE MODELS

Marketers use models in research project design, market planning, account analysis, and employee training, to name a few. The problems faced by marketing executives in various types of companies can be used to illustrate the many ways in which marketers use models.

Research Project Design

When foreign automakers made major inroads into the automobile market in the United States, it radically altered the way domestic automakers marketed their products. Unfortunately, domestic firms had done relatively little in-depth marketing research prior to the surge in foreign competition. Suddenly, important questions had to be raised about their advertising campaigns, pricing policies, dealership programs, and product designs. In particular, why did consumers want to purchase certain makes and why did they often reject domestic cars for foreign cars?

The first step in designing a research project is a problem definition. All of the major aspects of the problem are described and defined. Good models offer rather concise definitions of the major aspects. Planners for the Buick Division of General Motors began using a model to help them decide what they want to know about buyers of Buicks. Using the model, questions are raised about all major aspects of the consumer's car purchase and evaluation. Because Buick's own model provides a good overview of the variables that are likely to influence purchases, its research is more likely to provide comprehensive results tailored to Buick's needs.

Models can also suggest what must be known about prospective buyers and can offer insights into how the measurements can and should be taken. For example, models help marketers determine whether it would be most useful to look at perceptions, attitudes, or memory, or at all three, for a particular marketing problem. Additionally, researchers select the measures to coincide with the components of the model being used. Thus attitude scales might be used in a questionnaire, and data could be collected from a sample of consumers to estimate their attitudes. The marketer might decide that memory is more important to study, and that measuring memory requires an experimental design for which specific data should be collected.

After the data-collection phase of a study is completed, models offer invaluable insights into the analysis and interpretation of the results. Some domestic firms found that although auto buyers had generally favorable attitudes toward their products, prospective buyers were actually purchasing foreign makes. Further analysis showed that a lack of confidence in the domestic product was a major problem. Subsequently, a number of actions were taken to improve buyers' confidence in domestic brands. Warranties were improved and internal quality control programs were instituted. (Both confidence and attitude are found in the Howard-Sheth models.)

Marketing Planning

Marketing plans are designed to move prospective purchasers toward a company's products and services. The planning sequence generally in-situation analysis

volves a **situation analysis** in which consumer behavior toward the company's and competitors' products and services are examined. Based on this analysis the marketer first isolates the problems, opportunities, and constraints for the selling firm. For example, Coca-Cola recently changed its formulation for taste. Such a decision would be made only after extensive analysis of the situation. Although the facts are not public, the change most likely came as a result of the "Pepsi Challenge" comparative taste tests conducted by Pepsi-Cola. For years Coca-Cola has kept track of the criteria consumers use to judge colas. The objective for a mass-market product like Coke is to have a taste that appeals to a very broad range of consumers and that fits the choice criteria of a maximum number of cola drinkers. Any taste-related problem of choice among consumers would represent a constraint in direct promotions targeted against a formidable competition like Pepsi-Cola.

In the second step in a situation analysis, the marketing organization established objectives or goals that specify the types of customer responses they expect. For example, such objectives describe the number of customers the firm expects to sell to and the types of attitudes and perceptions customers should have regarding the firm's brands.

strategies

Strategies are the actions that will be taken to meet the objectives. In a military context strategy involves exercising the science and art of military command to meet the enemy in battle under advantageous conditions. To the degree that competing marketers are enemies in the world of business, strategy has a similar meaning to them. However, the real goal of marketing activities is to develop customer satisfaction (at a profit, of course). In contrast to strategies that are qualitative statements about the general activities that will accomplish objectives, **tactics** are very specific descriptions of the activities the company will take. A typical planning sequence would be: (1) conducting a situation analysis; (2) identifying problems, constraints, and opportunities; (3) establishing objectives; (4) developing strategies; and (5) deciding on tactics. All of these preliminary steps provide inputs into the forecast of sales and profit.

tactics

Account Analysis

The efforts of SCM Corporation's Glidden division to sell paint and resin to major boat manufacturers demonstrates the use of models to analyze specific potential customers. This corporation applies the Howard-Sheth Model of Industrial Buying to major potential customers. Glidden sales executives ask several key questions about each account in an effort to fully understand how each purchasing organization decides where to purchase these supplies. By using models to specify the probable behavioral aspects of each account, sales executives are able to specify sales strategies for large groups of customers.

Employee Training

Another important use of models is in training programs for marketing and salespeople. Companies invest millions of dollars in educating their employees about their products, markets, and consumers. Models help organize knowledge into easily presentable, relevant modules. General insights about why purchases are made, as well as specific material about the company's own products and services, are included in these training sessions. For example, Westinghouse makes widespread use of industrial buying models in its employee marketing-education programs attended by hundreds of sales and marketing executives annually.

CONSUMER BEHAVIOR RESEARCH: AN ONGOING PROCESS

Models can provide a common base of understanding the buyer behavior discipline. Models help us organize the field of study so a more comprehensive picture can evolve. Studies of consumer behavior have been diverse and somewhat unrelated, as we have pointed out elsewhere. Models help bring these broad-ranging inquiries together under a simple structure. When existing research is viewed as part of a broader picture, researchers can spot any inconsistencies or aspects of consumer behavior lacking sufficient research that might be overlooked otherwise. Researchers who are curious about inconsistencies in the models and who engage in studies to resolve them may contribute to the base of knowledge in this field. This new knowledge is communicated to students, who may in turn make contributions of their own. Several researchers have recently called attention to the need for further investigation in group behavior and the sociological aspects of consumer behavior.[10] Jagdish Sheth goes as far as to say that the consumer-behavior field needs to generate its own constructs rather than rely solely on those of other disciplines, such as psychology and sociology.[11] There are still many areas of consumer behavior that warrant further exploration.

SUMMARY

This chapter provided an overview of models used in consumer behavior. The components of models, their many uses, and the three most popular consumer behavior models were all discussed.

Models help us do two things: (1) understand why buyers select specific brands and (2) predict brand choice. Good models have both predictive accuracy and explanatory value, two characteristics that do not always go hand in hand in behavioral theories. By focusing attention on a few important aspects of behavior, models can simplify this very complex subject.

Models have a structure. They are made up of components or building blocks called units, and these units interrelate. Endogenous units describe the buyer's thought processes. Exogenous units deal with descriptions of buyers, such as social class; they make good segmentation variables. Units are hypothetical constructs. Although they are never seen or touched, we can discuss them in detail.

The models discussed in this chapter were the Howard-Sheth Model of Buyer Behavior; the Engel, Kollat, and Blackwell (EKB) Decision Process Model; and the Bettman Information Processing Theory of Consumer Choice. Since 1969 the Howard-Sheth model has been a useful representation of key aspects of buyer behavior. The EKB model is similar to it. However, by focusing on additional variables and the consumer's problem-solving process, the EKB model has integrated some newer material. The Bettman model focuses heavily on internal decision processes. While this is useful for public-policy issues and extensive research studies, it is currently less applicable to routine consumer-behavior situations.

Today businesses are using models more and more. The students of business who understand the theories and elements that make up the three models will be in a better position to converse with executives who use these models.

Models are important in the design of research projects. First, they tell us what to research and the variables that are likely to be useful. Second, they suggest how to measure aspects of buying. Finally, they suggest how data should be integrated for use in marketing and public-policy decision making.

Another use of models is in the marketing planning function. They help firms uncover problems and discover opportunities. Additionally, models can be selected to help identify and monitor customer responses to the firm's marketing programs. Models often provide insights to help design strategies, or statements of how the firm will respond to and influence consumers' purchases. Also, specific tactics can be stated that have an impact on customers and potential customers. Whether for strategic plans or tactical programs, models help analyze marketing situations.

Models are also useful in training and teaching. In fact, some early models were developed primarily for this purpose. When models are used in employee training programs, they help organize material and accentuate the relevant components. Specific insights into types of buying and industries can be aligned with a model's units to present a realistic and useful picture for sales and marketing personnel who are likely to influence customers and potential customers.

A major benefit of models is that they contribute to the scientific growth of the discipline. Models organize what we know into a meaningful whole, pointing out inconsistencies in research findings and suggesting new avenues of research that may prove to be fruitful.

KEY TERMS

unit
endogenous units
exogenous units
nonspecific motives
specific motives
brand comprehension
choice criteria
attitude
confidence
intention
satisfaction
attention
stimulus ambiguity
perceptual bias
overt search
outputs
exposure
attention
comprehension
yielding/acceptance
retention
memory
search
alternative evaluation
evaluative criteria
beliefs
attitudes
intention
anticipated circumstances
unanticipated circumstances
outcomes
dissonance
scanner mechanisms
interrupt mechanisms
interrupt interpretation and response
attention
information acquisition and evaluation
rehearsal
encoding
transfer
placement
retrieval
response generation
consumption and learning processes
situation analyses
strategies
tactics

QUESTIONS

1. Why are models useful for marketing managers? for marketing researchers?
2. Models are useful for both prediction purposes and to improve our understanding of consumer behavior. Give an example of how models could help the marketing manager of an auto firm in each of these purposes.
3. What parts of the Howard-Sheth model and the Engel, Kollat, Blackwell model are similar? What are the differences?
4. Using the Howard-Sheth model and the Engel, Kollat, Blackwell model, evaluate your own preference for local restaurants. Which model do you prefer? Why? Compare and contrast your answer with those of other students who have done the same thing.
5. Review Chapter 3 on perception and show how the major aspects of perception are included in the Engel, Blackwell, Kollat model.

6. What differentiates the Bettman model from the other models covered in the chapter?

7. Develop your own model to explain some aspects of consumer behavior. You may wish to use parts of the models included in the chapter. How many of your units are endogenous and how many exogenous?

8. The models in the chapter are developed, to a large extent, from the constructs covered in more depth in the previous chapters. How have the models helped relate the many different constructs previously discussed?

NOTES

1. For a detailed explanation of the types of units used in theories, see Robert Dubin, *Theory Building* (New York: Free Press, 1978), 57–87.
2. See Chapter 6, on attitude measurements and models.
3. For a detailed discussion of construct validity and attitude measurement, see Gilbert A. Churchill, Jr., *Marketing Research* (Hinsdale, IL: The Dryden Press, 1979), 251–59.
4. For the purposes of this chapter, the terms *model* and *theory* are used interchangeably.
5. Definitions for the section on the Howard-Sheth model are adapted from John A. Howard and Jagdish N. Sheth, *The Theory of Buyer Behavior* (New York: John Wiley & Sons, 1969), 32–38 and 415–20.
6. Material for this section is summarized from James F. Engel and Roger D. Blackwell, *Consumer Behavior* (Hillsdale, IL: The Dryden Press, 1982), 688–90.
7. For a further discussion of dissonance, see Chapter 4 on learning.
8. Information for this section is summarized from James R. Bettman, *An Information-Processing Theory of Consumer Choice* (Reading, MA: Addison-Wesley, 1979).
9. G. D. Harrell, M. Hutt, and J. Allen, "Universal Product Code," *MSU Business Studies* (East Lansing, MI: Graduate School of Business Administration, 1976).
10. John Zielinski and Thomas S. Robertson, "Consumer Behavior Theory: Excesses and Limitations," in *Advances in Consumer Research IX*, Andrew Mitchell, ed. (St. Louis, MO: Association for Consumer Research, 1981), 8–12.
11. Jagdish N. Sheth, "Consumer Behavior: Surpluses and Shortages," in *Advances in Consumer Research, IX*, Mitchell, ed., 13–16.

FURTHER READING

Classics

Bettman, James R., and J. Morgan Jones, "Formal Models of Consumer Behavior: A Conceptual Overview," *Journal of Business* (1972): 544–62.

Ferber, Robert, "What Do We Know About Consumer Behavior," *Selected Aspects of Consumer Behavior* (Washington, DC: National Science Foundation, 1975), 521–29.

Howard, John A., and Jagdish N. Sheth, "A Theory of Buyer Behavior," in *Changing Marketing Systems,* Reed Moyer, ed. (Chicago: American Marketing Association, 1967), 253–62.

Katona, George, "Rational Behavior and Economic Behavior," *Psychological Review* (September 1953): 307–18.

Kotler, Philip, "Behavioral Models for Analyzing Buyers," *Journal of Marketing* (October 1965): 37–45.

Lunn, J. A., "Consumer Decision-Process Models," in *Models of Buyer Behavior,* Jagdish N. Sheth, ed. (New York: Harper and Row, 1974), 34–69.

Nicosia, Francesco, *Consumer Decision Processes: Marketing And Advertising Implications* (Englewood Cliffs, NJ: Prentice-Hall, 1967).

Sheth, Jagdish N., "The Future of Buyer Behavior Theory," *Proceedings,* 3rd Annual Conference. (Urbana, IL: Association for Consumer Research, 1972), 562–75.

Recent Significant Research

Olshavsky, Richard W., and Donald H. Granbois, "Consumer Decision Making—Fact or Fiction?" *Journal of Consumer Research* 6 (September 1979): 93–100.

Grether, David, and Louis Wilde, "An Analysis of Conjunctive Choice: Theory and Experiments," *Journal of Consumer Research* 6 (March 1980): 377–88.

Laroche, Michael, and John A. Howard, "Nonlinear Relations in a Complex Model of Buyer Behavior," *Journal of Consumer Research* 6 (March 1980): 377–88.

McAlister, Leigh, "A Dynamic Attribute Satiation Model of Variety-Seeking Behavior," *Journal of Consumer Research* 9 (September 1982): 141–50.

Park, C. Whan, Robert W. Hughes, Vinod Thrkral, and Roberto Friedmann, "Consumers' Decision Plans and Subsequent Choice Behavior," *Journal of Marketing* 45 (Spring 1981): 33–47.

Rau, Pradeep, and Saeed Samiee, "Models of Consumer Behavior: The State of the Art," *Journal of the Academy of Marketing Science* 9, No. 3 (Summer 1981): 300–16.

Shugan, Steven M., "The Cost of Thinking," *Journal of Consumer Research* 7 (September 1980): 99–111.

Ursic, Michael, "Consumer Decision Making: Fact or Fiction? Comment," *Journal of Consumer Research* 7, No. 3 (December 1980): 331–33.

Yager, Ronald R., "On A Programming Model of Consumer Choice Among Multiattributed Brands," *Journal of Consumer Research* 6 (December 1979): 317–19.

Applications

Farley, John U., and Donald R. Lehman, "An Overview of Empirical Applications of Buyer Behavior System Models," in *Advances in Consumer Research,* Vol. 4, William D. Perreault, ed. (Atlanta: Association for Consumer Research, 1977).

Farley, J. U., and L. W. Ring, "An Empirical Test of the Howard-Sheth Model of Buyer Behavior," *Journal of Marketing Research* (November 1970): 427–38.

Holbrook, Morris B., "A Synthesis of the Empirical Studies," in *Consumer Behavior Theory and Application,* J. U. Farley, J. A. Howard, and L. W. Ring, eds. (Boston, MA: Allyn and Bacon, Inc., 1970).

Howard, John A., and Lyman E. Ostlund, "Applying Buyer Behavior Theory to Public Policy," in *Buyer Behavior: Theoretical and Empirical Foundations,* John A. Howard and Lyman E. Ostlund, eds. (New York: Alfred A. Knopf, 1973), 569–80.

Lehman, Donald R., Terrence V. O'Brien, John U. Farley, and John A. Howard, "Some Empirical Contributions to Buyer Behavior Theory," *Journal of Consumer Research* 1 (December 1974): 43–55.

Lussier, Denis A., and Richard W. Olshavsky, "Task Complexity and Contingent Processing in Brand Choice," *Journal of Consumer Research* 6 (September 1979): 154–65.

Park, C. Whan, "A Conflict Resolution Choice Model," *Journal of Consumer Research* 5 (September 1978): 124–35.

Taylor, James, and Jonathan Gutman, "A Reinterpretation of Farley and Ring's Test of the Howard-Sheth Model of Buyer Behavior," in *Advances in Consumer Research,* Vol. 1, Scott Ward and Peter Wright, eds. (Urbana, IL: Association for Consumer Research, 1974), 436–46.

Credits

Figures

Chapter 2: **2-2** From David Krech, Richard S. Crutchfield, and Egerton L. Ballachey, *Individual in Society,* McGraw-Hill, 1962. Used by permission.
2-4 From M. Venkatesan, "Cognitive Consistency and Novelty Seeking," in *Consumer Behavior: Theoretical Sources,* Scott Ward and Thomas S. Robertson, eds., © 1973, p. 378. Adapted by permission of Prentice-Hall, Englewood Cliffs, N.J.

Chapter 3: **3-6** From Richard M. Johnson, "Marketing Segmentation: A Strategic Management Tool," *Journal of Marketing Research,* American Marketing Association, 1971. Used by permission.
3-7 From Richard M. Johnson, "Marketing Segmentation: A Strategic Management Tool," *Journal of Marketing Research,* American Marketing Association, 1971. Used by permission.

Chapter 4: **4-1** From J. T. Cacioppo & R. E. Petty, "Effects of message repetition and position on cognitive responses, recall, and persuasion," *Journal of Personality and Social Psychology,* Vol. 37, 1979. Copyright 1979 by the American Psychological Association. Adapted by permission of the authors.
4-3, 4-4 From J. Morgan Jones, "A Dual-Effects Model of Brand Choice," *Journal of Marketing Research,* American Marketing Association, 1970. Used by permission.
4-6 From John A. Howard, *Consumer Behavior: Applications of Theory,* McGraw-Hill, 1977. Used by permission.
4-9 From Michael L. Rothschild and William C. Gaidis, "Behavioral Learning Theory: Its Relevance to Marketing and Promotions," *Journal of Marketing,* American Marketing Association, 1981. Used by permission.

Chapter 6: **6-1** From Milton J. Rosenberg, Carl J. Havland, et al., *Attitude Organization and Change,* Yale University Press, 1960. Used by permission.
6-2 From Thomas C. Kinnear and James R. Taylor, *Marketing Research: An Applied Approach,* McGraw-Hill, 1979. Used by permission.

Chapter 7: **7-1** From Richard E. Petty and John T. Cacioppo, *Attitudes and Persuasion: Classic and Contemporary Approaches.* © 1981 Wm. C. Brown Publishers, Dubuque, Iowa. All rights reserved. Reprinted by permission.
7-2 From Michael L. Ray and William L. Wilkie, "Fear: The Potential of an Appeal Neglected by Marketing," *Journal of Marketing,* American Marketing Association, 1970. Used by permission.

Chapter 8: **8-2** From S. W. Bither and G. Ungson, *Consumer Information Processing Research: An Evaluative Review,* Working Paper, Pennsylvania State University, 1975. Used by permission.
8-3 From James R. Bettmann, *An Information Processing Theory of Consumer Choice,* © Addison-Wesley, Reading, MA. Page 17, Fig. 2.1. Reprinted with permission.
8-4 From John A. Howard, *Consumer Behavior: Application of Theory,* McGraw-Hill, 1977. Used by permission.
8-8 From Julie A. Edell and Richard Staelin, "The Information Processing of Pictures in Print Advertisements," *Journal of Consumer Research,* June 1983. Permission to adapt granted by the *Journal of Consumer Research.*
8-9 From Howard Beales et al., "Consumer Research and Public Policy," *Journal of Consumer Research,* June 1981. Permission to adapt granted by the *Journal of Consumer Research.*

Chapter 10: **10-2** Reprinted from *U.S. News & World Report* issue of Sept. 19, 1983. Copyright 1983 by U.S. News & World Report, Inc.

Chapter 13: **13-1** Adapted from Everett M. Rogers and E. Floyd Shoemaker, *Communications in Innovations,* Free Press, 1971.
13-2 From John A. Czepiel, "Word-of-mouth Processes in the Diffusion of a Major Technological Innovation," *Journal of Marketing Research,* American Marketing Association, 1974. Used by permission.
13-4 Adapted with permission of The Free Press, a division of Macmillan, Inc. from *Diffusion of Innovations* by Everett M. Rogers. Copyright © 1962 by The Free Press.
13-5 From *Innovative Behavior and Communication* by Thomas S. Robertson. Copyright © 1971 by Holt, Rine-

hart and Winston. Reprinted by permission of CBS College Publishing.
13-6 From *Innovative Behavior and Communication* by Thomas S. Robertson. Copyright © 1971 by Holt, Rinehart and Winston. Reprinted by permission of CBS College Publishing.
13-7 Adapted with permission of The Free Press, a division of Macmillan, Inc. from *Communication of Innovations,* 2nd ed., by Everett M. Rogers with F. Floyd Shoemaker. Copyright © 1971 by The Free Press.
13-9 From Richard W. Olshavsky, "Time and Rate of Adoption of Innovations," *Journal of Consumer Research,* March 1980. Permission to adapt granted by the *Journal of Consumer Research.*

Chapter 14: **14-2, 14-5, 14-6** From Patrick E. Murphy and William A. Staples, "A Modernized Family Life Cycle," *Journal of Consumer Research,* June 1979. Permission to adapt granted by the Journal of Consumer Research.
14-12 From Louis Harris and Associates, "Togetherness Among the Baby Boomers," *Sales and Marketing Management,* July 1984. Used by permission.
14-13 From Harry L. Davis and Benny P. Rigaux, "Perception of Marital Roles in Decision Processes," *Journal of Consumer Research,* June 1974. Permission to adapt granted by the *Journal of Consumer Research.*
14-14 From Scott Ward and Daniel B. Wackmann, "Children's Purchase Influence Attempts and Parental Yielding," *Journal of Marketing Research,* American Marketing Association, 1972. Used by permission.
14-15 From Charles K. Atkin, "Observation of Parent-Child Interaction in Supermarket Decision-Making," *Journal of Marketing,* American Marketing Association, 1978. Used by permission.

Chapter 15: **15-2** From Joel Garreau, *The Nine Nations of North America.* Copyright © 1981 by Joel Garreau. Reprinted by permission of Houghton Mifflin Company.

Chapter 16: **16-1** From G. A. Russell and G. Pratt, "A Description of the Affective Quality Attributed to Environments," *Journal of Personality and Social Psychology,* Vol. 38, August 1980. Copyright 1980 by the American Psychological Association. Adapted by permission of the authors.
16-2 From Gilbert D. Harrell, Michael D. Hutt, and James C. Anderson, "Paths Analysis of Buyer Behavior Under Conditions of Crowding," *Journal of Marketing Research,* 1980, American Marketing Association. Used by permission.

Chapter 17: **17-3** From Jagdish N. Sheth, "A Model of Industrial Buying Behavior," *Journal of Marketing,* 1973, American Marketing Association. Used by permission.

Chapter 18: **18-1** From John A. Howard and Jagdish N. Sheth, *The Theory of Buyer Behavior,* John Wiley & Sons, 1969. Used by permission.
18-2 From *Consumer Behavior,* 4th edition, by James F. Engel and Roger D. Blackwell. Copyright © 1982 by CBS College Publishing. Reprinted by permission.
18-3 From James R. Bettmann, *An Information Processing Theory of Consumer Behavior,* © 1978, Addison-Wesley, Reading, MA. Page 17, Fig. 2.1. Reprinted with permission.

Tables

Chapter 2: **2-2** From Henry Murray, *An Exploration in Personality: A Clinical Experimental Study of Fifty Men of College Age,* Oxford University Press, 1938.
2-3 W. J. McGuire, "Psychological Motives and Communications Gratification," pp. 167–96, in *The Uses of Mass Communications: Current Perspectives on Gratification Research,* J. G. Blumber and C. Katz, eds. Copyright © 1974 by Sage Publications. Reprinted by permission.

Chapter 3: **3-1** Yoram J. Wind, *Product Policy,* © 1982, Addison-Wesley, Reading, MA. Reprinted with permission.

Chapter 4: **4-3** Walter Nord and J. Paul Peter, "A Behavior Modification Perspective on Marketing," *Journal of Marketing* (Spring 1980). Used by permission.

Chapter 5: **5-3** Richard J. Lutz, "A Functional Theory Framework for Designing and Pretesting Themes," from *Attitude Research Plays for High Stakes,* John C. Maloney and Bernard Silverman, eds. © 1979 American Marketing Association. Used by permission.

Chapter 6: **6-3** Donald R. Lehman and John O'Shaughnessy, "Differences in Attribute Importance for Different Industrial Products," *Journal of Marketing* 38 (1974). Used by permission.
6-5 Reprinted by permission of the publisher from "Monetizing Utilities for Product and Service Benefits," by G. David Hughes, in *Consumer and Industrial Buying Behavior,* Woodside et al., eds. Copyright 1977 by Elsevier Science Publishing Co., Inc.

Chapter 8: **8-2** Peter Wright and Fredric Barbour, "The Relevance of Decision Process Modes in Structuring Persuasive Messages," pp. 246–59, in *Communications Research,* vol. 2. Copyright © 1975 by Sage Publications. Reprinted by permission.

Chapter 9: **9-3** William B. Wells, "Psychographics: A Critical Review," *Journal of Marketing Research* 12 (1975). Copyright © 1975 American Marketing Association. Used by permission.
9-4 From *The Nine American Lifestyles* by Arnold Mitchell. Copyright © 1983 by Arnold Mitchell. Used by permission of Macmillan Publishing Company.
9-5 Reprinted from "Advertising Research at Anheuser-Busch (1968–1974)" by R. L. Acoff and J. R. Emshoff, *Sloan Management Review,* Winter 1975, pp. 1–15, by permission of the publisher. Copyright © 1975 by the Sloan Management Review Association. All rights reserved.
9-6 Joseph T. Plumber, "Lifestyles and Advertising: Case Studies," from *Combined Proceedings,* 1971 Spring

and Fall Conferences, Fred C. Allvine, ed. © 1972 American Marketing Association. Used by permission.

Chapter 10: **10-1** From "Sales & Marketing Management's 1983 Survey of Buying Power, Part 2," *Sales and Marketing Management* 131 (October 31, 1983).

Chapter 11: **11-1** From Donald Treiman, "Occupational Prestige," *Human Behavior* 6, No. 11 (November 1977).
11-2 From *Social Standing in America: New Dimensions of Class* by Richard P. Coleman and Lee Rainwater with Kent A. McClelland. © 1978 by Basic Books, Inc., Publishers. Reprinted by permission of the publisher.
11-3 Reprinted from *U.S. News & World Report* issue of February 14, 1977. © 1977 U.S. News & World Report, Inc.
11-5 Pierre Martineau, "Social Classes and Spending Behavior," *Journal of Marketing* 23 (1958). Used by permission.

Chapter 12: **12-2** Donald W. Hendon, "A New and Empirical Look at the Influence of Reference Groups on Generic Product Category and Brand Choice: Evidence from Two Nations," in *Proceedings of the Academy of International Business: Asia-Pacific Dimensions of International Business* (1979). Used with the permission of the Academy of International Business.
12-3 William O. Bearden and Michael J. Etzel, "Reference Group Influence on Product Brand and Purchase Decisions," *Journal of Consumer Research* (1982). Reprinted with permission from the Journal of Consumer Research.
12-4 C. Whan Park and V. Parker Lessig, "Students and Housewives: Differences in Susceptibility to Reference Group Influence," *Journal of Consumer Research* (1977). Adapted with permission from the Journal of Consumer Research.

Chapter 13: **13-1** Fred D. Reynolds and William R. Darden, "Mutually Adaptive Effects of Interpersonal Communication," *Journal of Marketing Research* 8 (November 1971). © 1971 American Marketing Association. Used by permission.

Chapter 14: **14-5** Scott Ward and Daniel B. Wackman, "Children's Purchase Influence Attempts and Parental Yielding," *Journal of Marketing Research* 9 (August 1972). © 1972 American Marketing Association. Used by permission.

Chapter 15: **15-2** Leon G. Schiffman, Leslie Lazar Kanuk, *Consumer Behavior,* © 1983, p. 420. Reprinted by permission of Prentice-Hall, Inc., Englewood Cliffs, N.J.
15-3 Del Hawkins, Roger G. Best, and Kenneth A. Coney, *Consumer Behavior* (rev. ed., 1983). © 1983 Business Publications Inc. Used by permission.
15-4 Robert Levine and Ellen Wolff, "Social Time—the Heartbeat of Culture," reprinted with permission from *Psychology Today Magazine*. Copyright © 1985 by the American Psychological Association.
15-6 Reprinted from the *Journal of Advertising Research*. Copyright © 1981 by the Advertising Research Foundation.
15-8 Reprinted with permission from the April 6, 1981, issue of *Advertising Age*. Copyright 1981 by Crain Communications, Inc.
15-9 Danny N. Bellenger and Humberto Valencia, "Understanding the Hispanic Market," *Business Horizons* (May–June 1982). © Indiana University Graduate School of Business. Used by permission.

Chapter 16: **16-2** John R. Nevin and Michael J. Houston, "Image as a Component of Attraction to Intraurban Shopping Centers," *Journal of Retailing* 57 (Spring 1980), p. 85. Used by permission.
16-3 Jay D. Lindquist, "Meaning of Image," *Journal of Retailing* 50 (Winter 1974), p. 31. Used by permission.
16-4 Dale M. Lewison and M. Wayne DeLozier, *Retailing: Principles and Practices*. 1982. Adapted with permission of Charles E. Merrill Publishing Company.

Chapter 17: **17-2** Adapted from Richard N. Cardozo, "Situational Segmentation in Industrial Markets," *European Journal of Marketing* 14 (May–June 1980).
17-3 Adapted from *How Industry Buys/1970*. Copyright © 1969 by Scientific American, Inc. All rights reserved. Used by permission.
17-5 Reprinted by permission of the publisher from "An Empirical Study of Hospital Buying," by Gene R. Laczniak, *Industrial Marketing Management* (January 1979). Copyright 1979 by Elsevier Science Publishing Co., Inc.
17-6 Jean-Marie Choffray and Gary L. Lilien, "Assessing Response to Industrial Marketing Strategy," *Journal of Marketing* 42 (April 1978). Used by permission.
Excerpt from "Situation Variables and Consumer Behavior" by Richard W. Belk reprinted with permission from the *Journal of Consumer Research* (December 1975).
Excerpt from *The Universe Within* by Morton Hunt, © 1982 by Morton Hunt, reprinted by permission of Simon & Schuster, Inc.
Excerpt from William B. Wells, "Activities, Interests, and Opinions," reprinted with permission from the *Journal of Advertising Research* 11 (1971). Copyright © 1981 by the Advertising Research Foundation.

Photos

Chapter 2: **40** Reproduced courtesy of American Express Travel Related Services Company, Inc.
42 left © 1986, PLAYBOY
42 right Courtesy N. W. Ayer
43 left Reprinted by permission of Scientific American, Inc.
43 right Courtesy of Somerset Importers and Smith/Greenland Inc.
49 Jordache Enterprises, Inc.
54 New Balance Athletic Shoe, Inc.
61 American Dental Association

Chapter 3: **69** Jockey International, Inc.
73 left top Courtesy Tree Top, Inc.
73 right top Courtesy of The Coca-Cola Company

73 left bottom Oneida Ltd.
73 right bottom © Lowe's, Inc.
82 left Reprinted courtesy of General Motors Corporation
82 right Courtesy of The Coca-Cola Company and The Marschalk Company
83 Fisher-Price, Division of The Quaker Oats Company
84 Cadillac Motor Car Division of General Motors Corporation

Chapter 4: **125** left Casablanca Industries, Inc.
125 right Revlon, Inc.
126 Johnson Camping Inc./Baxter Advertising

Chapter 6: **171** left Courtesy of Bali Company
171 right Beecham Products
184 left © J. Walter Thompson USA
184 right © 1983 Wolverine Boots & Shoes, Division of Wolverine World Wide, Inc., Rockford, Michigan 49351

Chapter 7: **196** top McNeil Consumer Products Company
196 bottom Courtesy of Nestlé Foods Corporation
201 International Playtex, Inc.
202 Reproduced by permission of American Home Products Corporation, owner of trademarks Anacin-3® © 1985 Whitehall Laboratories
203 left Chesebro-Pond's Inc.
203 right Courtesy Silver Reed America Inc.
210 left Courtesy of Shulton, Inc.
210 right Courtesy Vivitar
211 Photography courtesy of Pioneer Electronics (USA) Inc.
213 Beacon Advertising for CU Insurance. Ad produced 1979
214 Traffic Safety Association of Michigan

Chapter 8: **231** © Sears, Roebuck and Co. 1985
232 Courtesy of Budweiser
239 Prepared by Seven-Up Co. and N. W. Ayer
246 Sanyo Electric Inc.

Chapter 9: **274** Philip Morris, U.S.A.
281 Soloflex, Inc.
282 Reproduced courtesy of American Express Travel Related Services Company, Inc. Copyright 1983

Chapter 10: **301** Copyright rights to the illustrated ads and rights to the registered trademark therein are the property of Kimberly-Clark Corporation and used with their permission. Agency: Ogilvy & Mather
304 left JOHNSON'S Baby Shampoo, a product of JOHNSON & JOHNSON Baby Products Company
304 right Prepared by Sachs & Rosen Inc.

Chapter 11: **318** Courtesy Jean Patou Inc./Al Paul Lefton Co., Inc.
321 © Nissan Motor Corporation in U.S.A.
332 left McIlhenny Company
332 right International Playtex, Inc.

Chapter 12: **352** Courtesy of PLAYBOY Magazine: Copyright © 1982 by PLAYBOY
355 Reproduced courtesy of American Express Travel Related Services Co., Inc. Copyright 1983
356 Photograph: Bill Connors
366 Copywriter: Steve Jeffery. Art Director: Tom Wamback. Copyright Lever Brothers Company

Chapter 13: **385** left Black & Decker
385 right Norelco
390 Courtesy of Whirlpool Corporation

Chapter 14: **403** left Jacuzzi Whirlpool Bath
403 right Ethan Allen Inc.
404 Pinellas Suncoast, Florida
406 Missouri Division of Tourism

Chapter 15: **452** Courtesy of Sealy Inc./Bozell & Jacobs
453 Courtesy of Congoleum, © 1984
454 left Reprinted courtesy of Better Homes and Gardens® Real Estate Service
454 right Jacuzzi Whirlpool Bath
455 left Reprinted by permission of Burrell Advertising and Ford Motor Company, 1985
455 right Reproduced by permission of Foster Parents Plan, Inc.
456 National Dairy Board
472 Ron Walker/Lustrasilk Advertising Department
474 left Courtesy of The Procter & Gamble Company
474 right United Airlines
475 Courtesy of Heublein Inc. Manufacturers of Smirnoff® Vodka
478 Courtesy of Budweiser beer and D'Arcy MacManus Masius

Chapter 16: **491** HBJ Photo
492 HBJ Photo
498 top © Griffith/Veronneau
498 bottom © Griffith/Veronneau

Chapter 17: **513** Courtesy of Bethlehem Steel Corporation
514 Courtesy of Dundee Mills, Inc.

Index

N

O

W

A 6
B 7
C 8
D 9
E 0
F 1
G 2
H 3
I 4
J 5